Asking Questions about Your Data

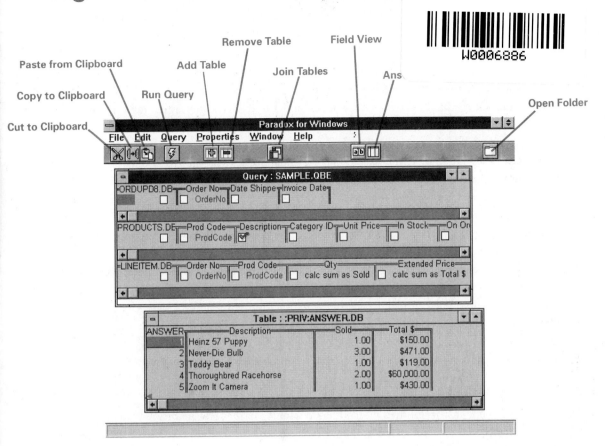

W0006886

To Do This...	See Chapter
Select fields to view in the Answer table	2, 8
Perform a query	2, 8
Select specific records to include in the Answer table	2, 8
Save and open a query	2, 8
Sort the Answer table and control its name and appearance	8
Change or delete records globally	8, 18
Use mini queries to select and work with live data in an open table or form	8
Select and sort data in custom forms and reports	2, 9, 10, 11
Combine data from multiple tables	16
Display non-matching records	16
Perform calculations on fields	16
Perform statistical summaries and frequency distributions	16
Ask questions about sets of records	16
Copy fields and records from one table to another	18
Change values in one table based on values in another table	18

Computer users are not all alike.
Neither are SYBEX books.

We know our customers have a variety of needs. They've told us so. And because we've listened, we've developed several distinct types of books to meet the needs of each of our customers. What are you looking for in computer help?

If you're looking for the basics, try the **ABC's** series. You'll find short, unintimidating tutorials and helpful illustrations. For a more visual approach, select **Teach Yourself**, featuring screen-by-screen illustrations of how to use your latest software purchase.

Running Start books are really two books in one—a tutorial to get you off to a fast start and a reference to answer your questions when you're ready to tackle advanced tasks.

Mastering and **Understanding** titles offer you a step-by-step introduction, plus an in-depth examination of intermediate-level features, to use as you progress.

Our **Up & Running** series is designed for computer-literate consumers who want a no-nonsense overview of new programs. Just 20 basic lessons, and you're on your way.

We also publish two types of reference books. Our **Instant References** provide quick access to each of a program's commands and functions. SYBEX **Encyclopedias** and **Desktop References** provide a *comprehensive reference* and explanation of all of the commands, features, and functions of the subject software.

Our **Programming** books are specifically written for a technically sophisticated audience and provide a no-nonsense value-added approach to each topic covered, with plenty of tips, tricks, and time-saving hints.

Sometimes a subject requires a special treatment that our standard series don't provide. So you'll find we have titles like **Advanced Techniques, Handbooks, Tips & Tricks,** and others that are specifically tailored to satisfy a unique need.

We carefully select our authors for their in-depth understanding of the software they're writing about, as well as their ability to write clearly and communicate effectively. Each manuscript is thoroughly reviewed by our technical staff to ensure its complete accuracy. Our production department makes sure it's easy to use. All of this adds up to the highest quality books available, consistently appearing on best-seller charts worldwide.

You'll find SYBEX publishes a variety of books on every popular software package. Looking for computer help? Help Yourself to SYBEX.

For a brochure of our best-selling publications:

SYBEX Inc., 2021 Challenger Drive, Alameda, CA 94501
Tel: (510) 523-8233/(800) 227-2346 Telex: 336311
Fax: (510) 523-2373

SYBEX

SYBEX is committed to using natural resources wisely to preserve and improve our environment. As a leader in the computer book publishing industry, we are aware that over 40% of America's solid waste is paper. This is why we have been printing the text of books like this one on recycled paper since 1982.

This year our use of recycled paper will result in the saving of more than 15,300 trees. We will lower air pollution effluents by 54,000 pounds, save 6,300,000 gallons of water, and reduce landfill by 2,700 cubic yards.

In choosing a SYBEX book you are not only making a choice for the best in skills and information, you are also choosing to enhance the quality of life for all of us.

Mastering Paradox
for Windows
Special Edition

Mastering Paradox® for Windows™
Special Edition

ALAN SIMPSON

SYBEX®

San Francisco • Paris • Düsseldorf • Soest

ACQUISITIONS EDITOR: David Clark
DEVELOPMENTAL EDITOR: David Peal
EDITOR: Sarah Wadsworth
TECHNICAL EDITOR: Chris Campagna
BOOK DESIGNER: Suzanne Albertson
SCREEN GRAPHICS: John Corrigan and Cuong Le
CHAPTER ART: Charlotte Carter
ELECTRONIC PAGE LAYOUT: Stephanie Hollier
PROOFREADER/PRODUCTION ASSISTANT: David Silva
INDEXER: Nancy Anderman Guenther
COVER DESIGNER: Archer Design
COVER PHOTOGRAPHER: Michael Lamotte
COVER PHOTO ART DIRECTION: Ingalls + Associates
Screen reproductions produced with Collage Plus.

Collage Plus is a trademark of Inner Media Inc.

SYBEX is a registered trademark of SYBEX Inc.

TRADEMARKS: SYBEX has attempted throughout this book to distinguish proprietary trademarks from descriptive terms by following the capitalization style used by the manufacturer.

SYBEX is not affiliated with any manufacturer.

Every effort has been made to supply complete and accurate information. However, SYBEX assumes no responsibility for its use, nor for any infringement of the intellectual property rights of third parties which would result from such use.

Copyright ©1993 SYBEX Inc., 2021 Challenger Drive, Alameda, CA 94501. World rights reserved. No part of this publication may be stored in a retrieval system, transmitted, or reproduced in any way, including but not limited to photocopy, photograph, magnetic or other record, without the prior agreement and written permission of the publisher.

Library of Congress Card Number: 92-83710

ISBN: 0-7821-1050-9

Manufactured in the United States of America

10 9 8 7 6 5 4 3 2 1

To Susan, Ashley, and Alec Simpson

ACKNOWLEDGMENTS

LIKE ALL books, this one was a team effort, and much credit and my sincere appreciation go to the many people on the team.

First and foremost, credit goes to Elizabeth Olson, who almost single-handedly researched, wrote, and developed the initial manuscript for most of this book. Even the great-looking sample forms and reports are Elizabeth's creations! Other writers contributing their time and talents were Virginia Andersen, David Rhodes, and Patricia Hartman. My thanks to Martha Mellor, whose superb coordination skills and good humor kept the entire team moving smoothly toward the finish line.

The efforts and suggestions of many people at SYBEX helped shape the original manuscript into its final form—especially Editor Sarah Wadsworth, Developmental Editor David Peal, and Technical Editor Chris Campagna. I'm also grateful to the full production team for their hard work over the course of an ever-shortening schedule, given the extent of the changes made to Paradox for Windows itself.

The technical support staff at Borland International deserves kudos for fielding our many questions and passing our suggestions along to program developers. Special thanks are due to Robert Ramirez for his patience and technical expertise.

Many thanks to the gang at Waterside Productions, my literary agents, for managing the "business and opportunity" aspects of my writing career.

And, as always, I thank my family—Susan, Ashley, and Alec—who once again were patient and supportive while Daddy was locked away in his office during many long hours.

Contents

CONTENTS

PART FOUR   MANAGING YOUR PROJECTS

APPENDICES

INTRODUCTION

SIMPLY STATED, Paradox for Windows is a powerful database management system that anyone can use. Historically, database management systems have been programming language-oriented, and thus best used as tools by programmers and advanced computer users. The need to remember numerous commands, functions, data types, syntax rules, file structures, and so on made the older database management systems unwieldy for the neophyte and casual user.

Then came Paradox for DOS—a new approach to database management that freed the user from having to memorize complex commands. With Paradox, even the casual computer user could effectively store, retrieve, sort, print, change, and ask questions about data by selecting options from the menus and "filling in the blanks" on standardized questionnaires.

Now we have Paradox for Windows, a dazzling, graphical database management system for the Windows 3.1 environment. Incorporating all the best ideas from Paradox for DOS, Paradox for Windows defines a new standard for database managers that places even more capabilities at the user's fingertips.

So what's paradoxical about Paradox for Windows? The paradox is that even though it's so easy to use, Paradox for Windows does not compromise on power or flexibility. You can still ask complex questions about many interrelated tables of data, and you can develop sophisticated forms and reports that only programmers dreamed about in the past—and all without writing a single program or memorizing a bunch of complex commands.

Is This Book Right for You?

This book is designed for people familiar with Windows and new to the pathbreaking database from Borland, Paradox for Windows. If you're not exactly sure what a database management system *is*, or what it is used for, you're in good hands. The first chapter of this book will show you what database management with Paradox for Windows is all about.

If you're already familiar with database management and earlier versions of Paradox, there's still plenty to interest you here. The lessons in Chapter 2 will help make your transition to Paradox for Windows a smooth one, providing the basic skills necessary to proceed with the more advanced topics presented in later chapters.

Like all books in the SYBEX *Mastering* series, this one is designed to stick to the topic at hand, namely Paradox for Windows. So we won't be spending lots of time teaching you how to use Windows, the mouse, or the keyboard. In fact, we've geared this book toward people with *some* Windows and computer experience. In particular,

* You should already be familiar with how information is organized on your hard disk in *files*, *directories*, and *drives*.

* Any prior experience with a Windows-based word processing, spreadsheet, drawing, or painting package (or any other program that's made you comfortable with the Windows environment) will be helpful. You should already have your basic Windows skills down pat.

If you're not yet up-to-speed in these areas, you can get a quick introduction from any small book on DOS, such as my own *Up and Running with DOS 5* or *The ABC's of DOS 5*, or my *Windows 3.1 Running Start*, also published by SYBEX.

Which Version of Paradox?

This book is specifically written for Version 1.0 of *Paradox for Windows*. If you're using a DOS version of Paradox, such as Version 4.0 or 3.5, this book won't help you much because the Windows version of Paradox is really a whole new animal. If you'd like to upgrade your DOS version of Paradox to Paradox for Windows, you can do so. (The upgrade cost is subject to change, so I won't give a dollar amount here.)

For minimum hardware and memory requirements, please refer to Appendix A, "Installing Paradox for Windows." For details on using Paradox for Windows on a network, please see Appendix E, "Using Paradox for Windows on a Network."

Special Features of the Book

This book is designed as both a tutorial and a reference to the many features of Paradox for Windows. Special features of the book, designed to simplify and speed your mastery of Paradox for Windows, include the following:

Endpapers Inside the front and back covers you'll find a quick reference to the Table, Query, Form, and Report windows, where you perform common tasks in Paradox for Windows.

Paradox for Windows in an Evening The lessons in Chapter 2 provide you with a quick way to get some hands-on experience with Paradox for Windows. In just a few hours, you can survey the key features of the program and develop a useful address table, data-entry form, and report of your own.

Notes and Tips   Special notes throughout each chapter provide cross-references to sections of the book that cover related features, tips with insights on creative ways to use the application's features, and warnings about problems that can occur.

Fast Tracks   The FastTracks at the beginning of each chapter provide a quick summary of specific features and techniques. Turn to the Fast Tracks when you need a quick reminder, rather than a lengthy explanation.

Optional Companion Disk   You can purchase a disk containing sample tables, reports, forms, and the order processing and purchasing application presented in this book in ready-to-use form. Although you can use this book without the companion disk, it may come in handy if you want to use some of the examples as a starting point for your own work (with the companion disk, you won't have to type in everything from scratch)! Look for the coupon near the back of the book if you're interested.

Structure of the Book

This book is designed to supplement the densely packed and somewhat technical manuals that came with your Paradox for Windows package. The purpose of the Paradox manuals is to document every available feature in great detail. The purpose of this book is to show you how to use Paradox for Windows and put it to work for your own purposes.

To make things easier for you, and to help you focus on information that's relevant to your own use of Paradox, we've divided the book into five parts:

Part One: Getting Started   Provides an overview of what Paradox is all about, and includes five hands-on lessons that will help you get up-to-speed quickly.

Part Two: Managing Data with Paradox Shows you how to create tables, enter data, customize the appearance of tables, print simple reports, and sort and query (ask questions about) your data. The focus here is on managing a single table, since this is the easiest way to learn to use these features.

Part Three: Viewing and Printing Data Paradox for Windows includes powerful drawing and design features that allow you to create truly spectacular custom forms, reports, and graphs for viewing and printing your data. In this part, we first present general procedures that are common to designing both forms and reports. Then we zero in on techniques that pertain specifically to designing a custom form, report, or graph.

Part Four: Managing Your Projects This part of the book deals with more general aspects of Paradox for Windows, such as customizing Paradox and managing your files. You may use only a small portion of the many features presented in this part of the book, so feel free to refer to it on an "as-needed" basis.

Part Five: Managing Related Tables One of the real advantages that a relational database management system like Paradox for Windows offers over word processors and spreadsheets is the ability to store information efficiently in multiple related tables of information, and then "mix and match" that information as necessary. Though not everyone will need to use multiple tables to manage information, they are useful for many business functions, such as managing orders, inventory, accounts, and so forth. In addition to discussing ways to manage multiple related tables, Part Five also shows you how to develop *applications*, which automate and simplify all aspects of managing data stored in Paradox tables. You'll learn special querying techniques that update data automatically, and you'll learn how to design "smart" automated forms using *ObjectPAL*, the object-oriented Paradox for Windows Application Language. This book presents the basics of ObjectPAL and provides several practical examples that you can adapt for your own needs. If you're interested in becoming an ObjectPAL programmer, you might want to "graduate" to a more advanced book on the topic.

Appendices   The appendices at the back of the book present more specialized information on Paradox for installers and network administrators, and for people who want to use dBASE and Paradox for DOS tables with Paradox for Windows or who want to share Paradox data with other applications. There's also a list of properties used when designing custom forms and reports.

Conventions Used in This Book

As with most Windows programs, Paradox for Windows allows you to use a mouse or the keyboard to interact with it. This book uses the following conventions to present keys, combination keys, and menu selection sequences:

↑, ↓, →, ←, **PgUp, PgDn**   Arrow and other special keys such as Ins (Insert), Del (Delete), and ↵ (Enter) are shown with the symbol commonly displayed on the key. If your keyboard is designed so that these keys are only on the numeric keypad, remember that the Num Lock key must be turned off for these keys to work properly.

Combination Keys   Combination keys, starting with Ctrl, Alt, or Shift, are separated with a plus sign (+). To press these keystrokes, hold down the first key while pressing the second key. For instance, to press Ctrl+Ins, you hold down the Ctrl key, press Ins, then release both keys.

Menu Sequences   A series of selections that you make from the menus are displayed in an abbreviated sequence with a ➤ symbol separating each selection. For example, File ➤ New ➤ Table means "Choose File from the menu bar, then choose New from the pull-down menu that appears, then choose Table from the submenu that appears." You can use either the mouse or the keyboard to choose menu options, as described in Chapter 2.

A Tip for Tyros

One of the more troublesome aspects of learning to use any new program is inadvertently choosing the wrong set of menu options and ending up in totally unfamiliar territory.

In most cases, you can simply "back out" by pressing the Escape key (labeled Esc on some keyboards, Cancel on others) until you get to more familiar territory. Clicking on any "neutral" area on the screen or clicking the Cancel button (if it's available) also serves the purpose.

PART ONE

Getting Started

CHAPTERS

CHAPTER

1

Paradox for Windows:
The Elements

fast TRACK

PARADOX for Windows is a relational database management system for Windows. A *database* is simply a collection of information or data, like a Rolodex file, file cabinet, or phone book filled with names and addresses. Whenever you access one of these paper databases, whether it be to add new information, retrieve information, change information, or sort information into some meaningful order, you are *managing* that database.

A computer *database management system* (DBMS) like Paradox for Windows lets you manage a database that's stored on a computer disk. The advantage to using a computer rather than a paper database is perhaps obvious: Tasks that may take several minutes, hours, or even days to perform with paper usually take only a few seconds or minutes to complete with Paradox.

What Can I Do with Paradox?

Paradox for Windows is an extremely flexible application that gives you virtually unlimited options for storing and managing information. The type of information you can store is limited only by your needs and your imagination. Following are a few of the many common uses of database management systems:

- Managing mailing lists and telephone directories
- Managing customer, sales lead, and membership information files

- Handling bookkeeping and accounting tasks, such as general ledger, accounts payable, and accounts receivable
- Managing orders and controlling inventory
- Managing a personal or professional library that includes pictures, photos, and sounds
- Managing and printing catalogs of photos, descriptions, and prices of your company's products
- Storing and updating employee information, including salary and sound data initially created in Windows applications *outside of* Paradox
- Analyzing and graphing sales performance and customer buying trends over time

Regardless of the type of information you want to manage with Paradox and how you want to manage that information, there's one requirement that must be met right off the bat: The information must be organized in one or more *tables*.

What Is a Table?

A table is a single body of information that's organized in rows and columns. In database terminology, we refer to each column of information in the table as a *field* and each row of information as a *record*. For example, Figure 1.1 shows a list of names and telephone numbers organized into a table, illustrating the terms *field* and *record*.

Of course, the information you plan to store might not be arranged in a table yet, so you need to think about how you might reorganize the information into a tabular format.

For instance, suppose you have a Rolodex file, with each card in the Rolodex containing the name and address of an individual, as in Figure 1.2. Each card has four lines of information on it: (1) name, (2) address, (3) city, state, zip code, and (4) phone number.

To put this information into a table, think of each Rolodex card as representing one record (row) of information. Each discrete item of information on a card (name, address, city, state, zip code) represents roughly one

FIGURE 1.1

A sample table of names and telephone numbers, illustrating the terms *field* and *record*. The entire collection of information is the *table*.

```
   Last Name    First Name    Phone        ← Field Names
   Adams        Anthony       555-1234     ←
   Baker        Barbara       555-2345     ←
   Carlson      Cassandra     555-3212     ← Rows (records)
   Duvall       Muriel·       555-6789     ←
   Edwards      Elizabeth     555-0101     ←


         ↑            ↑            ↑
            Columns (Fields)
```

FIGURE 1.2

Information on a Rolodex card

Sandy Smith
123 A St.
San Diego, CA 92122

(619)555-0987

field (column). Figure 1.3 shows how information from the Rolodex file might look when stored in a Paradox table. As you can see, we've gone one better than the simple Rolodex cards by adding a picture of each person.

Notice in Figure 1.3 that the table consists of three records (rows): one for Smith (the information shown on the sample Rolodex card), along with records for Jones and Zeepers (possibly from scraps of paper that haven't made it onto Rolodex cards). Each record contains seven fields: Last Name, First Name, Address, City, State, Zip Code, and Phone.

FIGURE 1.3

A sample table
containing three
records

Last Name	First Name	Address	City	State	Zip Code	Phone	Photo
Smith	Sandy	123 A St.	San Diego	CA	92122	(619)555-0987	
Jones	Albert	P.O. Box 12	Berkeley	CA	94710	(510)555-3232	
Zeepers	Zeke	241 Oak Ln.	Ashland	OR	89765	(123)555-9878	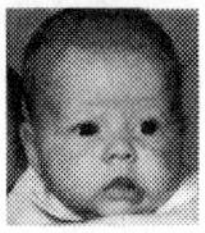

Do keep in mind that this is only a simple example. A table can store any kind of information—inventory, bookkeeping, accounts payable, receivables. . . just about anything that comes to mind. Furthermore, you're not limited to storing just text and numbers. With Paradox for Windows you can store pictures, graphs, even sounds.

Again, regardless of the *type* of information you plan to manage, that information must be stored in a tabular format. As you will see a little later, some data might be organized in several tables.

How Do I Manage a Database?

Database management is simply the job of managing the information you've stored in tables. Common management tasks include

- *Adding* new data to a table
- *Editing* data in a table
- *Deleting* data from a table
- *Sorting* a table into some meaningful order
- *Searching* (querying) a table for particular types of information
- *Printing* data from the table into formatted reports and graphs

Consider once more our Rolodex example. Occasionally it may be necessary to *add* some new cards to the Rolodex. We may want to *sort* the cards (say, alphabetically or by zip code) for easy access. We might want to *search* through them and find all the people who live in Los Angeles, for example, or all the people in the 92123 zip code area. Perhaps we just want to find out where Clark Kenney lives. If Clark Kenney moves, we may want to change (*edit*) his card to reflect his new address and phone number. (Then again, if Clark Kenney stops paying his dues, we may want to *delete* him from the Rolodex altogether.) We might want to use the data in the Rolodex to *print* various documents, such as mailing labels, form letters, or a directory.

Paradox offers many tools to help you perform these database management tasks. In fact, to simplify your work, these tools let you create *objects* that you can use over and over again to perform repetitive tasks with minimal effort. We'll talk about the various objects that you can create and use with Paradox for Windows in the sections that follow.

About Paradox Objects

Basically, an *object* is anything you can create in Paradox, such as. . .

- A table
- A data entry form or report
- Any visible (or invisible) part of a form or report
- A graphic image or sound
- A graph
- Data created by another Windows applications, such as Excel or Paintbrush
- A query or question about your data
- A folder of objects
- A piece of Paradox application language code that performs some automatic operation
- Any file on the computer

Some of the more common objects are described below.

Tables

Tables are the most fundamental Paradox object because they contain the information you want to manage. Figure 1.4 shows a table with some sample data in it on the Paradox Desktop.

NOTE   You'll get some practice creating a Paradox table in Chapter 2 and learn more of the details in Chapter 3.

Forms

Adding new data to a table and editing and deleting existing data are common database management tasks. You can add, edit, and delete data directly in a table such as the one shown in Figure 1.4.

You can also create fancy custom *forms* to enter table data on a record-by-record basis. You can even design forms that look like the paper forms that hold the information before it is entered into the table. For example, Figure 1.5 shows a customized form for entering and editing customer information.

NOTE   You'll learn to create custom forms in Chapters 9 and 10.

Reports

Another common Paradox object is the *report*. Whereas the term "forms" generally refers to information that's displayed on-screen, the term "report" generally refers to printed information.

FIGURE 1.4

A sample table on the screen. Though there may be more rows and columns in the table than can fit on the screen, you can use the scroll bars to bring other information into view.

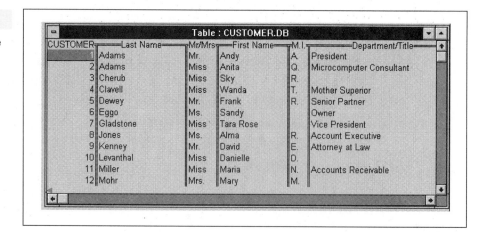

CUSTOMER	Last Name	Mr/Mrs	First Name	M.I.	Department/Title
1	Adams	Mr.	Andy	A.	President
2	Adams	Miss	Anita	Q.	Microcomputer Consultant
3	Cherub	Miss	Sky	R.	
4	Clavell	Miss	Wanda	T.	Mother Superior
5	Dewey	Mr.	Frank	R.	Senior Partner
6	Eggo	Ms.	Sandy		Owner
7	Gladstone	Miss	Tara Rose		Vice President
8	Jones	Ms.	Alma	R.	Account Executive
9	Kenney	Mr.	David	E.	Attorney at Law
10	Levanthal	Miss	Danielle	D.	
11	Miller	Miss	Maria	N.	Accounts Receivable
12	Mohr	Mrs.	Mary	M.	

Table : CUSTOMER.DB

FIGURE 1.5

A custom form for
entering and editing
data one record at
a time

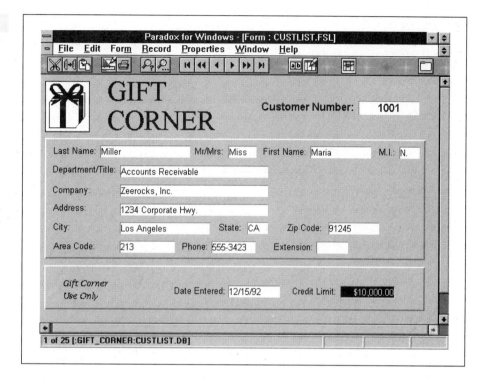

There is virtually no limit to the number of ways in which you can organize
information in a report. You can print lists, invoices, reports with totals and
subtotals, and so forth. You can even use Paradox to print form letters and
mailing labels. Figure 1.6 shows some mailing labels created from the sample
customer information table. Figure 1.7 shows a sample form letter printed
for a customer in the table.

NOTE

You'll learn how to design and create reports, form
letters, and mailing labels in Chapters 9 and 11.

FIGURE 1.6

A report is any
information printed
from one or more
tables. This sample
report contains
information organized
as mailing labels.

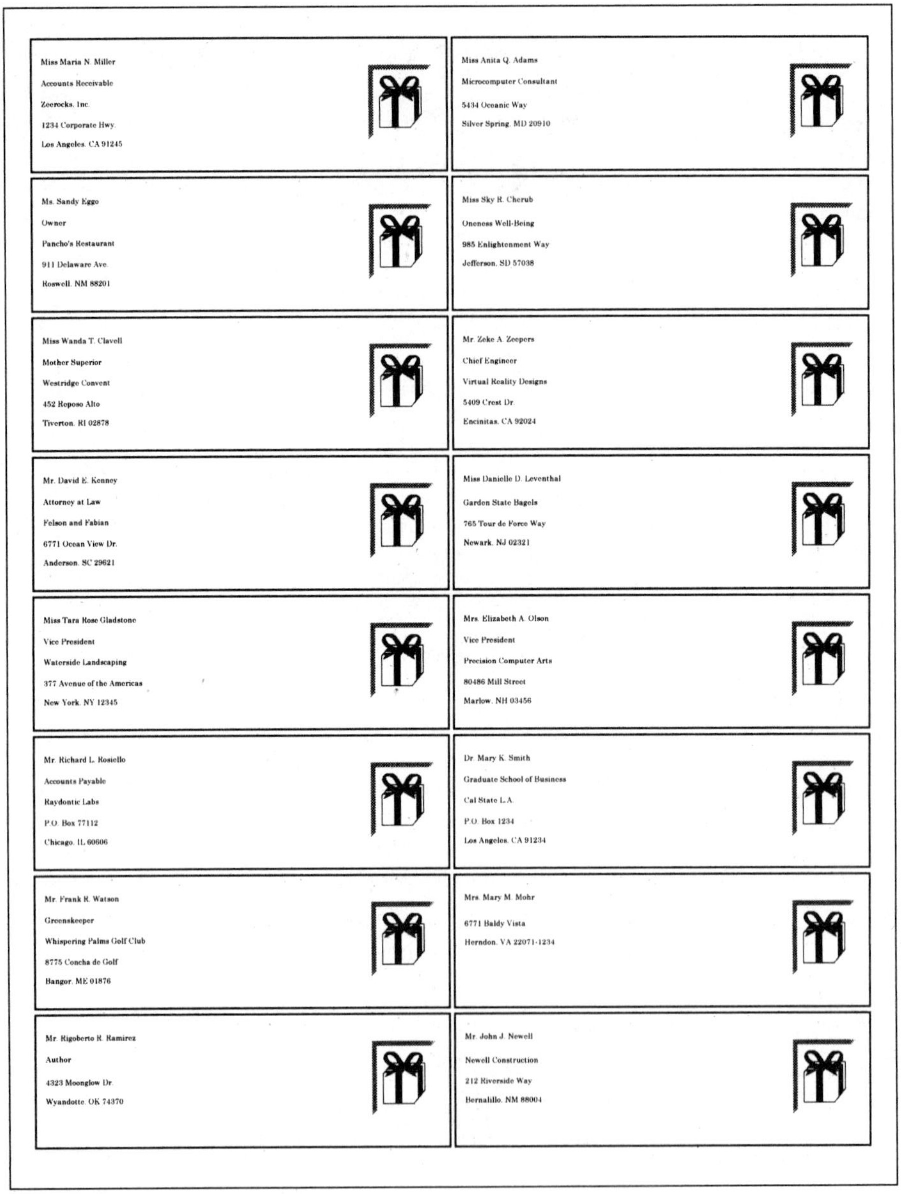

Miss Maria N. Miller Accounts Receivable Zeerocks, Inc. 1234 Corporate Hwy. Los Angeles, CA 91245	Miss Anita Q. Adams Microcomputer Consultant 5434 Oceanic Way Silver Spring, MD 20910
Ms. Sandy Eggo Owner Pancho's Restaurant 911 Delaware Ave. Roswell, NM 88201	Miss Sky R. Cherub Oneness Well-Being 985 Enlightenment Way Jefferson, SD 57038
Miss Wanda T. Clavell Mother Superior Westridge Convent 452 Reposo Alto Tiverton, RI 02878	Mr. Zeke A. Zeepers Chief Engineer Virtual Reality Designs 5409 Crest Dr. Encinitas, CA 92024
Mr. David E. Kenney Attorney at Law Felson and Fabian 6771 Ocean View Dr. Anderson, SC 29621	Miss Danielle D. Leventhal Garden State Bagels 765 Tour de Force Way Newark, NJ 02321
Miss Tara Rose Gladstone Vice President Waterside Landscaping 377 Avenue of the Americas New York, NY 12345	Mrs. Elizabeth A. Olson Vice President Precision Computer Arts 80486 Mill Street Marlow, NH 03456
Mr. Richard L. Rossello Accounts Payable Raydontic Labs P.O. Box 77112 Chicago, IL 60606	Dr. Mary K. Smith Graduate School of Business Cal State L.A. P.O. Box 1234 Los Angeles, CA 91234
Mr. Frank R. Watson Greenskeeper Whispering Palms Golf Club 8775 Concha de Golf Bangor, ME 01876	Mrs. Mary M. Mohr 6771 Baldy Vista Herndon, VA 22071-1234
Mr. Rigoberto R. Ramirez Author 4323 Moonglow Dr. Wyandotte, OK 74370	Mr. John J. Newell Newell Construction 212 Riverside Way Bernalillo, NM 88004

FIGURE 1.7

A sample form letter for a single record in the customer information table

Gift Corner

8891 Gaudy Ave * West Fantasee, CA 92222
1-800-555-GIFT

Miss Maria N. Miller
Accounts Receivable
Zeerocks, Inc.
1234 Corporate Hwy.
Los Angeles, CA 91245

Dear Miss Miller

*N*ow that the traditional gift giving season is rolling around once again, all of us at *The Gift Corner* would like to remind you that we offer a unique selection of gifts that are sure to please everyone on your list.

*O*ur new Winter catalog is chock full of great new gift items. For example, you'll find some terrific *Toys for Boys*, including hot new race cars in price ranges that are as torrid as the engines under the hoods of these babies. If you're looking for something a bit more tame, try our *Jungle Creatures Collection* -- stuffed animals that look like the real thing! And Miss Miller, if those on your gift list are itching for a winter getaway, take a look at our *Exotic Vacation Packages*. We'll guarantee some unforgettable memories! We'll even throw in a free camera, film, and developing so those memories will never be lost.

*S*o why not call your Account Representative here at *The Gift Corner* today? We'll send you a complimentary gift, just for picking up the phone and talking to us. You can reach us 24-hours a day, toll-free at **1-800-555-GIFT**. Don't delay...Call us today!

Sincerely yours,
Gondola Claplock
Gondola Claplock
The Gift Corner Customer Relations

Graphics, Graphic Images, and OLE

Like all Windows applications, Paradox for Windows can incorporate graphical information as well as text. Paradox for Windows supports three types of graphics:

Graphs and Crosstabs You can cross-tabulate data in a table and display the results in a variety of business graph formats, or as a crosstab. Figure 1.8, for example, shows a crosstab from the sample customer table that answers the question "How many customers do we have in each state and city?"

Graphic Images You can also add graphic images to your tables, forms, and reports. These graphic images may come from a variety of sources, such as clip art, scanned images, and drawing and painting applications. The sample form letter shown in Figure 1.7 included a company logo that's a graphic image.

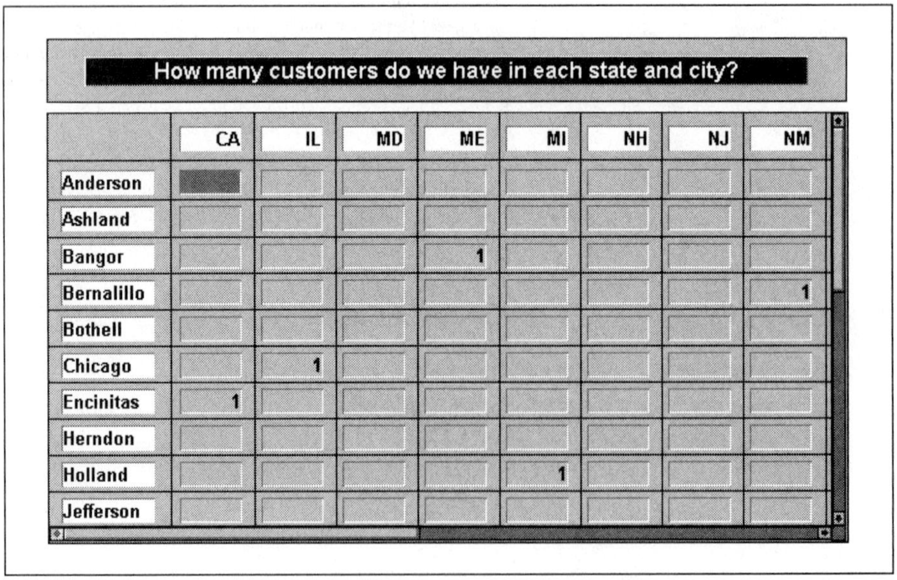

FIGURE 1.8

A sample crosstab created by Paradox for Windows. This crosstab quickly and visually answers a question that would otherwise be difficult to answer without tedious manual tabulation.

How many customers do we have in each state and city?

	CA	IL	MD	ME	MI	NH	NJ	NM
Anderson								
Ashland								
Bangor				1				
Bernalillo								1
Bothell								
Chicago		1						
Encinitas	1							
Herndon								
Holland					1			
Jefferson								

N O T E   Chapters 4, 5, 9, and 10 discuss graphics and OLE in more detail.

OLE objects   Object linking and embedding (OLE) lets you display and change graphics from other Windows products.

Queries

A *query* is basically a question—a means of finding or isolating specific records in one or more tables. For example, with a query you can

- quickly locate the name and address of a particular person in a table.
- print letters and labels for individuals in a particular city, state, or zip code region.
- print a "reorder report" for inventory items that need to be reordered.
- print a summary of all sales, subtotaled by product or date.
- print reminder letters for customers whose accounts are 30, 60, or 90 days overdue.

There's virtually no limit to the ways in which you can select data from a table in order to isolate the records you need.

N O T E   You'll learn how to query tables in Chapter 8.

Remember, you can use Paradox to manage *any* information—Paradox isn't just for business. For instance, a bird-watcher might create a table to store information about birds, including photos and sounds. Figure 1.9 shows how each "bird" record might be displayed on a custom form.

FIGURE 1.9

A custom form displaying a single record for a table of information about birds. Double-clicking the "ear" icon plays a bird song.

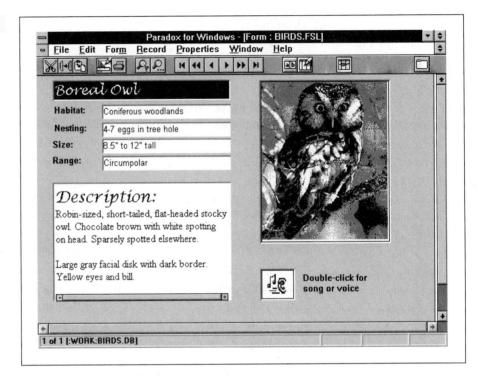

Folders

A *folder* is a collection of all the various objects that make up a particular database. For example, if you are using Paradox to manage a customer database, you could group the table, the various queries, reports, custom forms, and report formats into a single folder, as shown in Figure 1.10, for easy access. That way, once you open the folder, you can double-click any icon within the folder to access any one of its objects quickly.

NOTE   You'll learn how to create and use folders in Chapter 14.

You may hear the terms "table" and "database" used interchangeably, but a database management purist would tell you that it's incorrect to treat the terms as synonyms. A database is actually the sum total of all the

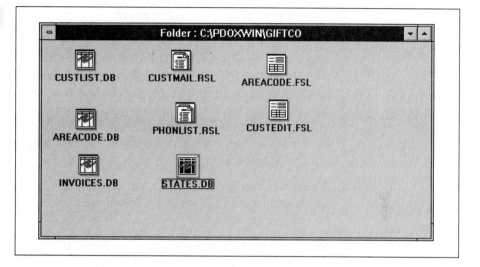

FIGURE 1.10

A sample folder containing the various objects used to manage a customer database

tables, forms, reports, and other objects that make up a single application. Therefore it would be more accurate to define the entire folder shown in Figure 1.10 as a database than to refer to any one of its objects as a database.

Managing Multiple Tables

If you've ever used a word processing or spreadsheet application, you may be thinking that you can do just about anything we've described so far with one of those programs. However, a relational database management system offers some unique capabilities that are not easily duplicated in word processors or spreadsheets.

For one thing, a relational DBMS lets you store information on separate related tables and combine that information on an as-needed basis to get answers to questions and produce complex reports.

For example, let's say you want to manage an entire mail-order business, including orders, inventory, and customer accounts. These three bodies of information represent three separate entities. Since there's no convenient way to combine all that information into a single table, you'd probably want to create three separate tables.

You'd need one table, named *Products*, to keep track of what you have in inventory. Figure 1.11 shows an example in which each item in the inventory has a product code (Prod Code), a description, and a unit price. The table also stores the quantity of each item currently in stock. You could add any other information that pertains to products (as indicated by *etc*. in the figure), such as the reorder point, manufacturer information, or whether or not the product is taxable.

A second table could contain information about customers or accounts. In the example in Figure 1.12, the name and address of each customer is stored in a table.

Finally, a third table could be used to keep track of orders. In the example shown in Figure 1.13, each record indicates who placed the order (via the customer number), what the customer ordered (via the product number), the quantity ordered, and the date that each order was placed.

Notice how compact the Orders table is. It doesn't waste a lot of disk space by repeating information that's already stored in the Customer and Products tables. Instead, it stores only the Customer Number, Product Code, Quantity, and Date of each order.

FIGURE 1.11

A sample table containing information about the current inventory

Products Table

Prod Code	Description	Unit Price	In Stock	etc...
GC-222	Heinz 57 Puppy	150.00	13	
GC-292	White Swan	1249.00	12	
GC-321	Kangaroo	2594.00	24	
GC-360	Cowardly Lion	6422.00	15	
GC-366	Tahoe Paradise Vacation	7200.00	8	
GC-510	Archery Target	500.00	6	
GC-786	Car - Hot	34430.00	56	
GC-983	Laser Printer	4270.00	24	
GC-987	Personal Computer - 486/50	3665.00	28	

FIGURE 1.12

A sample table of customers. Each customer is assigned a unique customer number (or account number).

Customer Table

Cust No	Last Name	First Name	Address	etc...
1001	Adams	Andy	123 A St.	
1002	Baker	Barbara	234 Bollinger Way	
1003	Carlson	Cara	P.O. Box 1234	
1004	Davis	Candy	17047 E. St.	
1005	Edwards	Eddie	555 Ocean Pkwy	
1006	Fabian	Francis	6565 Tumbleweed Rd.	
1007	Gomez	Lucy	564 Washington St.	
1008	Hernandez	Harry	23 NE Norfolk Blvd.	
1009	Johnson	George	P.O. Box 2212	
1010	Lawson	Linda	8808 El Camino Real	

FIGURE 1.13

A sample table containing information about orders. The Cust No and Prod Code fields indicate who placed the order and what was ordered.

Orders Table

Cust No	Prod Code	Quantity	Date Ordered	etc...
1001	GC-222	1	7/1/92	
1001	GC-292	2	7/1/92	
1001	GC-360	1	7/1/92	
1001	GC-987	1	7/1/92	
1003	GC-360	5	7/1/92	
1004	GC-983	2	7/1/92	
1010	GC-366	1	7/1/92	

Paradox, being a relational database management system, will let you combine information from these three separate tables, giving you complete flexibility in managing that information and presenting it in whatever format you wish. For example, using the information from these three tables, you could

- print invoices and packing slips for orders by combining information from the Customer, Products, and Orders tables.

- automatically subtract the quantity of each item shipped from the Products table as orders are fulfilled, so your Products table is always up to date.

- use the Orders table to verify automatically that there are enough items in stock to fulfill the order and, if not, place the order in a "backorder list" table to be fulfilled when the stock is replenished.

You could mix-and-match information from various tables however you wish in order to manage data and retrieve the information you need.

Building Applications

In addition to letting you manage information from multiple tables simultaneously, Paradox also allows you to develop custom *applications*. Applications let you automate virtually all the tasks involved in managing a database, reducing even complex tasks to simple mouse clicks.

You might think of an application as a fully automated, and much simplified, folder of objects. For instance, whereas the folder shown in Figure 1.10 includes all the objects used by a customer database, anyone who wants to work with that database needs to have some understanding of the objects in the folder and how to use them.

One of the real advantages of custom applications is that they can make it easy for someone with no knowledge of tables, forms, reports, or other objects to manage a database. To illustrate this, Figure 1.14 shows the opening screen for a custom application designed to allow staff members to manage customers, inventory, orders, and receivables with ease. Note the simple options in the pull-down menu (Add New Customers, View Customers, etc.). Other options across the menu bar (Inventory, Orders, Receivables, Vendors) could provide other easy-to-use options.

FIGURE 1.14

The opening screen
for a custom appli-
cation designed to
manage a customer
database. Users of this
application need only
choose options from
this screen; they do
not need to know
much about Paradox
or database
management.

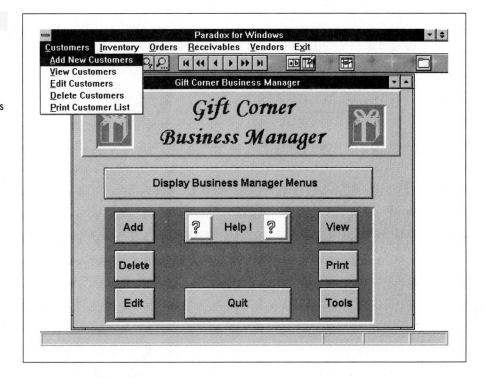

This chapter has provided an overview of database terminology and concepts, and a quick glimpse into the many features that Paradox for Windows has to offer. You've seen that Paradox can help you manage *any* kind
of information you can store on your computer—be it text, numbers, graphic
images, sound, or data created by other programs—and it can retrieve, display, and print the information in just about any format imaginable. The
only requirement is that you define the data as fields and records, which
are stored in Paradox tables.

In the next chapter, you'll take Paradox for Windows for a "hands-on" test
drive. In just five short lessons that you can easily complete in an evening,
you'll create a table, add some data to it, query and sort the table, customize a data entry form, and print an attractive report of your table's
records.

CHAPTER

2

Paradox for Windows in an Evening: Hands-On

fast ***TRACK***

To delete a record   **42**

   move the highlight to the record you want to delete, then press
   Ctrl+Del.

To insert a record   **42**

   move the highlight to where you want the new record to appear and press Ins.

To print a Quick Report of the table   **42**

   click the Quick Report button or choose <u>F</u>ile ➤ <u>P</u>rint. Choose any
   options you want in the **Print File** dialog box and choose OK.

To close a table   **43**

   choose <u>W</u>indow ➤ Close <u>A</u>ll, double-click the window's Control-menu box, or press Ctrl+F4.

To create a Quick Form   **51**

   open the table for which you want to create the form, then
   click the Quick Form button in the SpeedBar.

To switch between Form View and Table View   **58**

   press F7. If you're currently in Form View, just click the Table
   View button in the SpeedBar; if you're in Table View, click the
   Form View button.

WHEN you're learning Paradox for Windows the first step is to get a feel for the program and learn how to find your way around. It's like learning the major highways in a new neighborhood before you start exploring the side streets. In this chapter you'll explore the major highways of Paradox for Windows by creating a simple table of names and addresses and using the query, form, and report objects. Once you're familiar with these important objects, subsequent chapters will lead you through the "side streets" of Paradox for Windows.

Before You Begin the Lessons

Before you begin these lessons, you should already have installed Paradox for Windows on your computer. If you haven't done this, please follow the directions in Appendix A.

Also, you should already have your basic Windows skills down pat—including using a mouse, sizing, moving, opening, and closing windows, using dialog boxes, and so forth. If you're new to Windows, your best bet might be to spend *this* evening learning basic Windows skills. You can use the Windows *Getting Started* manual or some other tutorial, such as my own *Windows Running Start* book (also published by SYBEX) to do so. Or, for a crash course, follow the online Windows tutorial by choosing Help and then Windows Tutorial from the Windows 3.1 Program Manager menu bar.

Starting Paradox for Windows

To start Paradox for Windows, follow the steps below.

1. Go to the Windows Program Manager and double-click the Paradox for Windows group icon.

2. Within the group window, double-click the Paradox for Windows application icon (shown at left).

After a brief pause you should see the Paradox for Windows Desktop, shown in Figure 2.1.

Like most Windows applications, the Paradox Desktop contains a menu bar, a tool bar (called the SpeedBar), a status bar, and the standard Windows Control-menu box, title bar, and Minimize, Maximize, and Restore buttons.

Following Menu Sequences

Throughout this book, we'll represent a series of menu commands in the format: Choose File ➤ Working Directory.

This is a handy shortcut for "choose File from the menu bar, then choose Working Directory from the pull-down menu." You can use any of the standard Windows techniques to choose menu commands, including clicking the command you want with your mouse or holding down the Alt key and pressing the letter corresponding to the action you want (for example, Alt+F for File).

FIGURE 2.1

The Paradox for
Windows Desktop

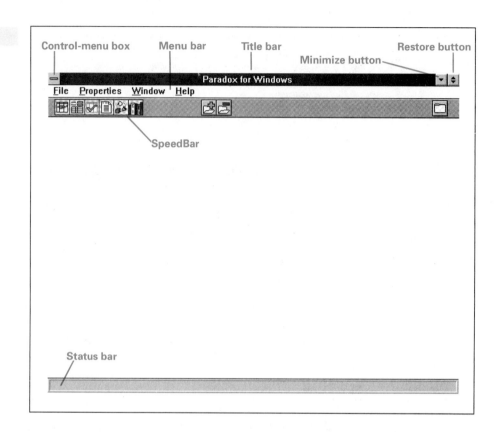

FIGURE 2.1

The Paradox for
Windows Desktop

About Clicking and Right-Clicking

As a Windows user, you're accustomed to clicking the left mouse button to choose menu and dialog box options, select text, click buttons, drag, and so forth. Paradox for Windows uses the left mouse button in all these standard ways.

Unlike most Windows applications, Paradox for Windows also takes advantage of the *right* mouse button to inspect an object's properties. To inspect a property, you simply move the mouse pointer to an object or a specific part of an object (such as a table column) and click the right mouse button (this is called "right-clicking"). Instantly, you'll see a menu of options relevant to the object you inspected. You can use property inspection to change the color, alignment, or font of a column in a table; to open a menu for a button in the SpeedBar; to customize the appearance of a field in a form or report; and much more.

NOTE If you have a three-button mouse, be sure to click the far-right button when inspecting properties.

Exiting Paradox for Windows

If you want to take a break at any time during this brief tour of Paradox, be sure to exit Paradox before turning off your computer. To exit, choose File ➤ Exit. If you've left any unsaved work on the Desktop, Paradox will ask if you want to save before returning to the Windows Program Manager. To save your work, choose Yes and provide a file name if requested.

Lesson 1: Creating a Table

Generally, the first step in using Paradox is to create a table to store your data. However, since you'll probably want to store all the tables, reports, forms, and other objects that make up the database in a single directory, your first lesson will be to create a new directory. You do that using the Windows File Manager.

Creating a New Directory

If Paradox for Windows Desktop is currently on your screen, you can follow these steps to get to the Windows File Manager:

1. Hold down the Alt key and press Tab until the small window for Program Manager appears in the center of the screen.

TIP You can use the Task List (Ctrl+Esc) to get to the Program Manager or return to Paradox.

2. Release the Alt and Tab keys to switch to Program Manager.

3. Open the Main group, then double-click the File Manager icon.

4. Click the drive button for the drive that Paradox is stored on (typically c:), then scroll to the *pdoxwin* directory. Alternatively, you can double-click the *pdoxwin* directory name to view the names of any subdirectories. If a subdirectory named *lessons* already exists beneath the *pdoxwin* directory, you cannot create another directory with that same name. Instead, you'll either have to create a directory with a different name (such as *lessons1*) when you get to Step 6, or you can skip directly to Step 7 where you'll exit the File Manager.

5. With the highlight still on the *pdoxwin* directory name, choose File ➤ Create Directory from File Manager's menu bar.

6. Type in a name, such as **lessons**, and then choose OK.

The new directory name should be listed below the *pdoxwin* directory name, as in the example shown in Figure 2.2.

7. Now close File Manager by choosing File ➤ Exit from File Manager's menu bar.

8. Hold down the Alt key and press Tab until the small window for Paradox appears in the center of the screen. Then release the Alt and Tab keys to bring the Paradox Desktop to the forefront again.

FIGURE 2.2

A new directory named *lessons,* created within the *pdoxwin* directory in File Manager

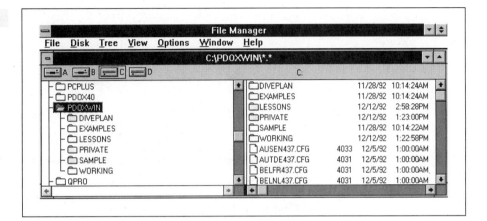

Choosing the Working Directory

Even though you've just created a new directory, you still need to tell Paradox that you want to *use* that directory to store your data. To do so, follow these steps:

1. Choose File ➤ Working Directory from the Paradox menu bar. You'll see the **Set Working Directory** dialog box.

2. Either type the complete path to your new directory (for example, *c:\pdoxwin\lessons*) or click the Browse button, double-click on the *pdoxwin* directory name, click *lessons,* and click OK. Either way, you want to make sure the text box beneath Working Directory shows the complete path to the *lessons* directory you just created, as in the example shown below.

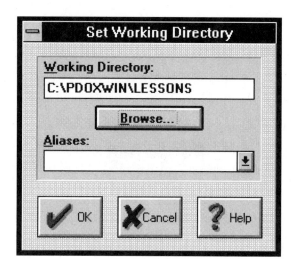

3. Choose OK.

The OK button will be dimmed and unavailable until you enter a valid path in the Working Directory text box.

Creating a New Table

Now that you've created a new directory for your table and chosen your working directory, you can create a new table. Choose File ➤ New ➤ Table, then, in the **Table Type** dialog box that appears, choose OK to accept the suggested table type, Paradox for Windows. You'll be taken to the **Create Table** dialog box shown in Figure 2.3.

Defining the Fields

Now you're ready to tell Paradox what fields you want to store in this table, the type of data each field can store, and the size of each

FIGURE 2.3

Create Table dialog
box for defining the
structure of a table

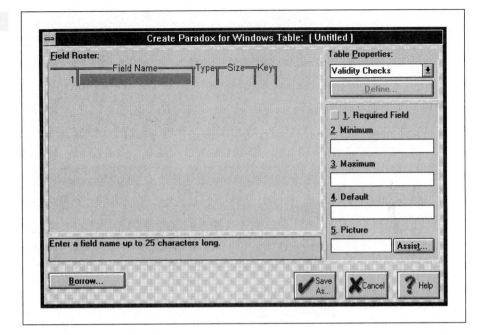

field. In this example, we'll create a small, simple table for storing names
and addresses. Simply follow these steps:

1. Type **Last Name** then press Tab to move to the next column.

2. Now you need to give the field a data type. With the highlight and
   mouse pointer in the Type column, click the right mouse button to
   view a list of available data types. Click the *Alphanumeric* field type.

3. Press Tab or ↵ to move to the Size column.

4. Type in a size (*20* will do for the Last Name field).

5. Press Tab or ↵ twice to skip the Key column and move down to
   the second row.

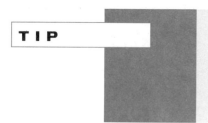

NOTE

Chapter 4 will discuss field types and the role of the key in detail. You need not concern yourself with all of that just yet.

Following the same basic steps as above, you should be able to fill in the rest of the table structure as shown in Figure 2.4. If you make a mistake, just double-click wherever you need to make a change, use the Backspace and Delete keys to erase text, then type in your correction.

TIP

Notice that we've made *all* the fields the alphanumeric (A) field type, even Zip Code and Phone. This is necessary if you want to be able to store hyphens and parentheses in the field, as in 91234-1234 and (619)555-1929.

FIGURE 2.4

Structure of the sample table we'll be using in these lessons

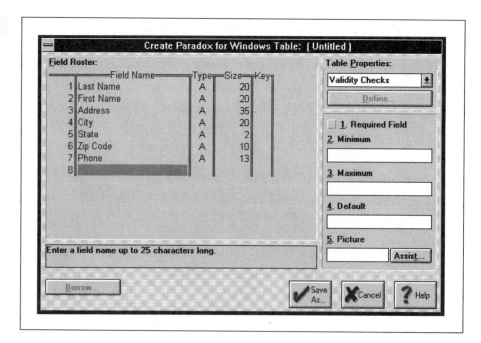

Saving the Table Structure

Once you've defined all the fields in the table, you can follow these steps to save the table structure and give it a file name:

1. Click the Save <u>A</u>s button near the bottom of the window.

2. In the **Save Table As** dialog box that appears, type in a valid DOS file name—*maillist* in this example (short for Mailing List).

3. Choose OK.

Paradox saves the table structure and returns you to the Paradox Desktop.

Taking a Break

If at any time during the course of these lessons you want to take a break, be sure to exit Paradox before turning off your computer, as described under "Exiting Paradox for Windows," earlier in this chapter.

When you resume the lessons, your working directory will be the same as it was when you exited, and any objects that were open will automatically appear on the Desktop. However, if you share a computer with other users, you may need to choose \pdoxwin\lessons again as your working directory. Use the <u>F</u>ile ➤ <u>W</u>orking Directory commands, as described earlier under "Choosing the Working Directory" to do so.

Lesson 2: Adding and Editing Data

Now that you've created a table, you can start putting some data into it. First, you need to open the table.

Opening a Table

To open the table, follow these steps:

1. Choose <u>F</u>ile ➤ <u>O</u>pen ➤ <u>T</u>able, or click the Open Table button in the SpeedBar (shown at left).

TIP To find out which button is which on the SpeedBar, move the mouse pointer to any button, then look down to the status bar to see the name of the button that the mouse pointer is on.

2. Click on *MAILLIST.DB,* then click the OK button.

The empty table appears in a Table window, with just the table name and field names across the top. Some fields will be scrolled off the right edge of the screen, as in Figure 2.5.

TIP To see as many fields as possible, click the Maximize button or double-click the title bar of the Table window.

Adding New Data

Now let's start typing in some data. If you have a Rolodex or little black book, feel free to use it for examples. Otherwise, you can just enter some fictitious names and addresses. Here's how to get started:

1. When you first open a table, it's in View mode. Before you can add or change data, you need to switch to Edit mode. To do so, click the Edit Data button in the SpeedBar (shown at left), or press the F9 key, or choose <u>T</u>able ➤ <u>E</u>dit Data from the menu bar. The word "Edit" appears down in the status bar when you're in Edit mode.

FIGURE 2.5

The new MailList table
open on the Desktop

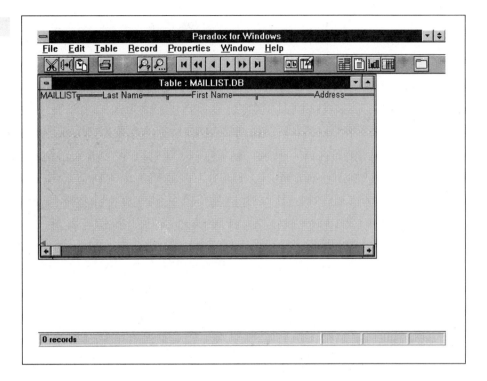

2. Type a last name, such as **Smith** or the last name of a person
   from your Rolodex or address book.

3. Press Tab or → to move to the next field, or just click the next
   field.

4. Type in a person's first name, such as **Michael**, then press Tab or
   →, or click the next field again.

5. Repeat these steps to fill in the Address, City, State, Zip Code,
   and Phone fields.

6. After you fill in a phone number, pressing Tab will automatically
   move you to the first field of the next record.

Try entering five or ten records on your own now. Figure 2.6 shows some
examples you can use. In the figure, we maximized the Table window and
used techniques discussed in Chapter 6 to narrow the table columns so
that more data is visible at once (you'll probably need to scroll across

fields for now, unless you have a 1024 × 768 monitor that can display all the data without scrolling). Again, feel free to enter any names and addresses you wish.

FIGURE 2.6

Sample records in the MailList table, shown here on a maximized window with column widths adjusted to display all the data without scrolling

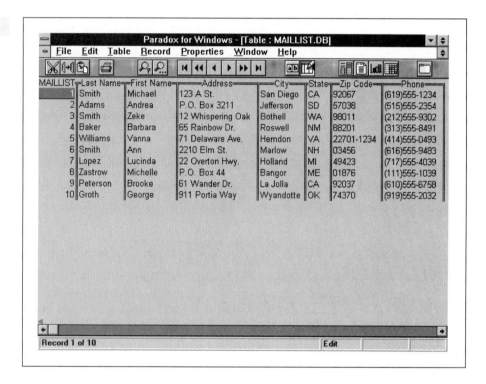

Here are some points to keep in mind as you're entering records:

• Be sure to glance at the screen to make sure the highlight is in the appropriate field before typing your entry. That way you won't inadvertently type a person's first name into the Last Name field or a zip code into the City field.

• You can make changes and corrections on the fly using the Backspace key. Or, you can use the various techniques described under "Editing Data," below, to make your changes and corrections later.

- Don't worry about entering data in alphabetical order, or any other order. As you'll see, you can sort the records into any order you want later.

- Don't worry about saving each record. Paradox saves the new data as soon as you finish filling in the fields and move to the next record.

Editing Data

Once you've filled in some records, you may find that you need to make changes or corrections. Here are some techniques you can use to do so:

- If Paradox refuses to let you make changes, you're not in Edit mode. Press F9 or click the Edit Data button to switch to Edit mode before trying to make changes.

- To change the contents of a field, first click the field or use the Tab, Shift+Tab, ↑, ↓, ←, or → keys to move to the field you want to edit.

- You can also use the buttons in the SpeedBar to move around in the table, as shown in Figure 2.7.

- When you first move the highlight to a field, the entire field becomes selected (highlighted). Anything you type will instantly *replace* whatever is already in the field. If you want to *change* rather

FIGURE 2.7

SpeedBar buttons for moving around in a table

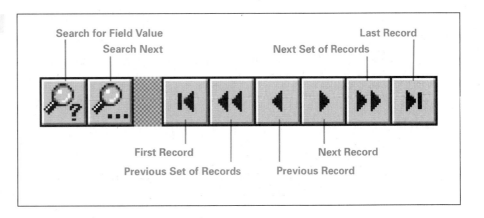

than replace the contents of the field, click the field a second time, or press the F2 key, or click the Field View button (shown at left) to switch to Field View. You can then use the mouse or the ← and → keys to move *within* the field to make changes and corrections. (Press ↵ when you've finished editing the field.)

TIP

Both the Field View button and the F2 key act as toggles, switching you into and out of Field View.

- If you make a mistake while editing and want to undo your change, choose Edit ➤ Undo or press Alt+Backspace.

- If you want to delete an entire record, move the highlight to the record you want to delete and press Ctrl+Del. (Careful, this operation cannot be undone!)

- To insert a record into the table, move the highlight to the point where you want to insert a record and press Insert (Ins). The record will be inserted above the highlight.

These pointers should be enough to get any typos or other errors out of your sample table. We'll get into still more editing techniques in Chapter 5.

Printing the Table

To print the data that's currently displayed on your screen in a tabular format, follow these steps:

1. Click the Quick Report button, shown at left, or choose File ➤ Print.

2. In the dialog box that appears, choose the Create Horizontal Overflow Page option if you want to print all the fields in the table.

3. Choose OK.

After a brief delay a copy of your table will be printed. If the page isn't wide enough to print all the fields, some fields will print on a second page.

Saving and Closing a Table

To close the table, choose <u>W</u>indow ➤ Close <u>A</u>ll, double-click the Control-menu box at the left end of the table's title bar, or press Ctrl+F4.

Lesson 3: Using a Query

Queries can play several roles in a database. Here we'll look at a few of the most common uses of queries:

- Isolating specific fields to view
- Isolating specific records to view (for example, CA residents or "Smiths")
- Determining a sort order for displaying records, such as alphabetical by name

Creating a Query

Let's create a query that prints an alphabetized list of names and phone numbers from our MailList table. Follow these steps to get started:

1. Choose <u>F</u>ile ➤ <u>N</u>ew ➤ Query. Or, right-click the Open Query button if it's available (move the mouse pointer to that button and click the right mouse button), then choose New from the menu that appears.

2. Click the *MAILLIST.DB* file name and choose OK.

NOTE   The Open Query button appears in the SpeedBar only when all windows are closed on the Desktop.

A query window containing columns for each field in the table appears, as in Figure 2.8.

Choosing Fields to View

The first step to filling in a query window is to decide which fields you want to view by marking those fields with a check mark. Follow the steps below to choose the Last Name, First Name, and Phone fields.

1. Click the empty check box under the Last Name field name. A check mark appears in the box.

2. Now click the empty check box under the First Name field name.

3. Press the End key to scroll quickly to the last column, then click the check box under the Phone field.

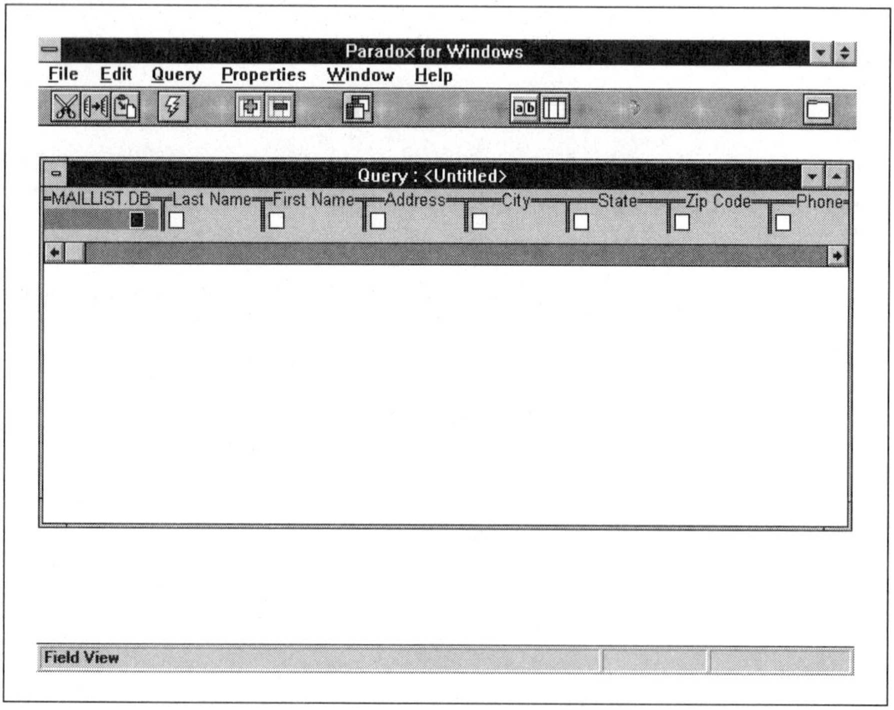

FIGURE 2.8

A new query window for our sample MailList table

Figure 2.9 shows the three fields marked with check marks. If you can't see all the fields, try widening the window by dragging the right border of the query window.

Choosing Records to View

Suppose you're particularly interested in finding the phone number for a person named Smith. To isolate records with Smith in the Last Name field, follow the steps below.

1. Press Home to move the highlight back to the first column, then press Tab to move to the Last Name column (or just click the empty area beneath the Last Name field name).

2. Type **Smith** (or some other last name that you know you've stored in your table). Be sure to use the same upper- and lower-case letters you used in the table. For example, don't type

FIGURE 2.9

Three fields, Last Name, First Name, and Phone, selected for viewing in the query window

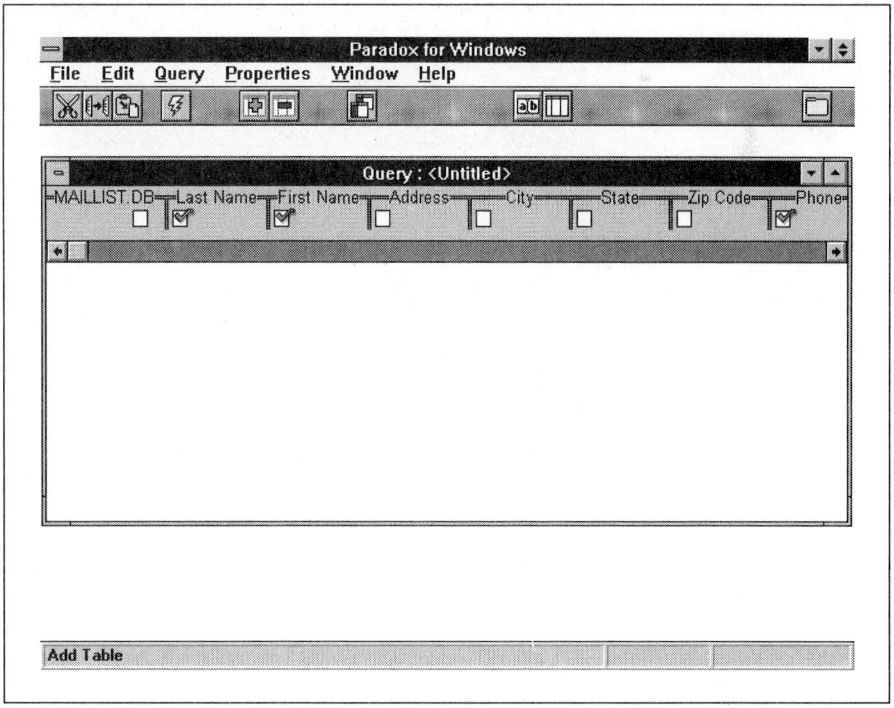

"SMITH" or "smith" if you originally entered names with an initial uppercase letter ("Smith").

Figure 2.10 shows how the query looks with Smith entered in the Last Name column.

Determining the Sort Order

Whenever you perform a query, the records are automatically sorted by the leftmost column. In this case, Last Name is the leftmost column, followed by the First Name field. Hence, if we don't do anything else to this query window, records will be sorted (alphabetized) by Last Name.

FIGURE 2.10

This query will now display the Last Name, First Name, and Phone fields of records that have Smith in the Last Name field.

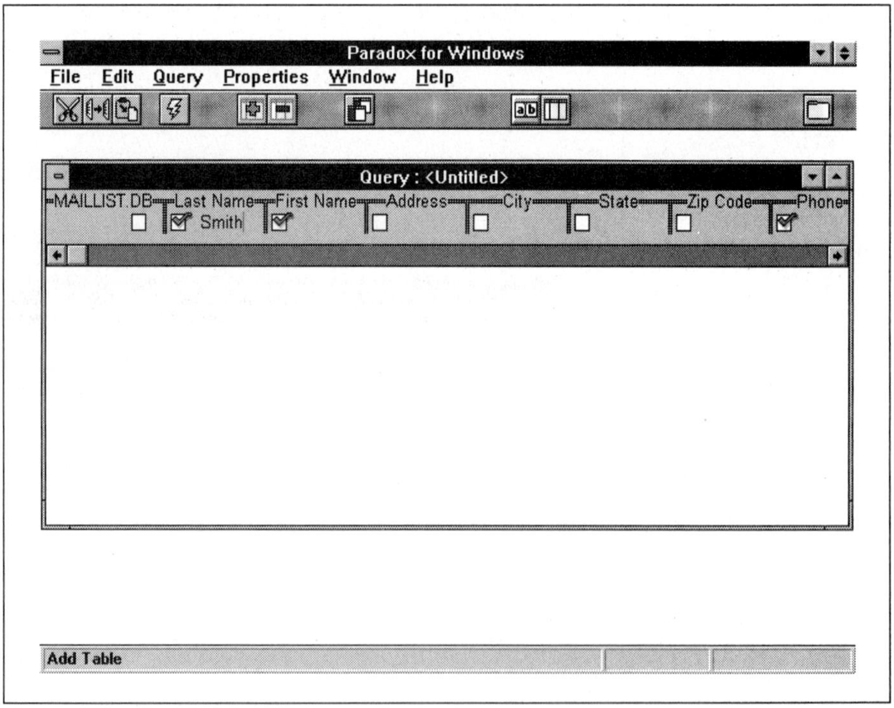

Just so you know how to control the sort order of records in a query, here's an example in which we'll sort records by Last Name and then by First Name. Follow these steps (if you're so inclined):

1. Choose <u>P</u>roperties ➤ <u>A</u>nswer Table ➤ <u>S</u>ort. You'll see the **Sort Answer** dialog box.

2. In the Available fields list, click on *Last Name,* then click the button with the → symbol on it.

3. Click the button with the → symbol on it again to move the First Name field name over to the Sort By list. At this point, the dialog box should look like this:

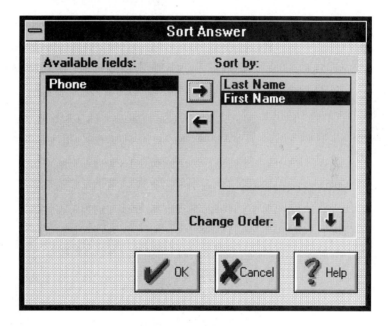

4. Because Last Name is listed first in the Sort By list, records will be alphabetized by people's last names. The First Name field will act as a tie breaker, meaning that records with identical last names will be alphabetized by first name (for example, Smith, Ann comes before Smith, Michael, which comes before Smith, Zeke).

5. Choose OK to return to the query window.

TIP There are lots of ways to control the sort order of records in a table, as you'll learn in Chapter 7.

Performing the Query

Now let's see what the query comes up with.

1. Click the Run Query button (shown at left), or choose Query ➤ Run, or press F8.

2. The results of the query appear in a new table named *Answer.db*, as shown in Figure 2.11.

As requested, the Answer table displays only the Last Name, First Name, and Phone fields, and only the Smiths, alphabetized by first name.

FIGURE 2.11

The results of a query appear in a table named *Answer.db*.

Changing the Query

Now let's modify the query so that it displays an alphabetized list of all the names and phone numbers in the table.

1. If it's visible, click on the title bar for the Query window (on Query:<Untitled), or press Ctrl+F6, or choose Window ➤ 1 Query:<Untitled> from the menu bar.

2. Scroll (if necessary) to the Last Name column, then double-click on the name Smith (or whatever name you put there).

3. Press the Backspace and Delete keys as necessary to erase Smith. Make sure that the Last Name field still contains a check mark—you just want to remove any text in that column.

4. Now perform the query again by clicking the Run Query button or by pressing F8.

This time the Answer table looks like Figure 2.12. Again, records are alphabetized by name, and only the Last Name, First Name, and Phone fields appear. However, since we removed Smith, the results of the query display all the records in the table—not just the Smiths.

Printing the Answer Table

If you'd like a quick printed copy of this phone list, just follow the same steps you used to print the MailList table. That is, click the Quick Report button, or choose File ➤ Print from the menu bar. Then choose OK from the dialog box that appears.

Saving the Query

You may want to print an updated phone list from time to time. Rather than re-creating this query in the future, you can save it so you can use it again later. To save the query, follow the steps below.

1. Choose Window ➤ Close All. A dialog box will ask if you want to save the newly created query.

2. Choose Yes.

3. Enter a valid DOS file name, such as *phonelst,* and then choose OK.

The query and the Answer table are removed from the Desktop, but your query is now stored on disk, with the file name *phonelst.qbe* in this example.

If you add, delete, or change records in the MailList table, and then perform this saved query again, the Answer table produced will reflect any changes you made to the table. Thus, you can use the query as often as you wish.

FIGURE 2.12

The Answer table after removing Smith

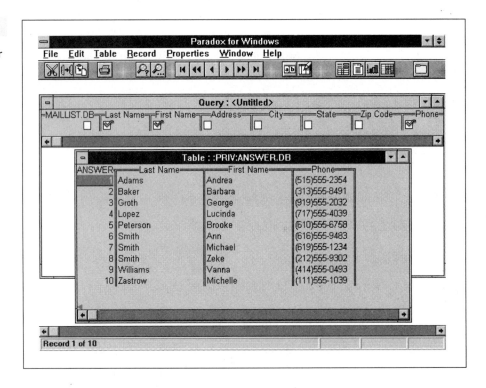

N O T E

To reuse an existing query, click the Open Query button, or choose File ➤ Open ➤ Query. Then click the name of the query you want to use and choose OK. When the query window appears on the screen, just click the Run Query button or press F8 to run the query on the latest data in your table. Choose Window ➤ Close All to tidy up the Desktop when you're done.

Though we've just experimented with some of the most frequently used features of queries, there's much, much more you can do with them. For more information on queries, please see Chapter 8.

Lesson 4: Creating and Using a Form

To get started working with forms, this lesson shows you how to create and use a Quick Form. Here's how to begin:

1. Open your MailList table by clicking the Open Table button, or by choosing File ➤ Open ➤ Table.

2. In the dialog box that appears, click on the MAILLIST.DB table name, then choose OK.

 3. To create your Quick Form, just click the Quick Form button, shown at left, in the SpeedBar.

The new form appears on the Desktop, perhaps partially overlapping the table, as in Figure 2.13.

Notice that the form displays the fields for the current record only. To scroll through records, you can press the PgUp and PgDn keys or use the scrolling arrows in the center of the SpeedBar. To scroll from field to field within the form, use the ↑, ↓, Tab, and Shift+Tab keys.

FIGURE 2.13

An instant form on the Desktop

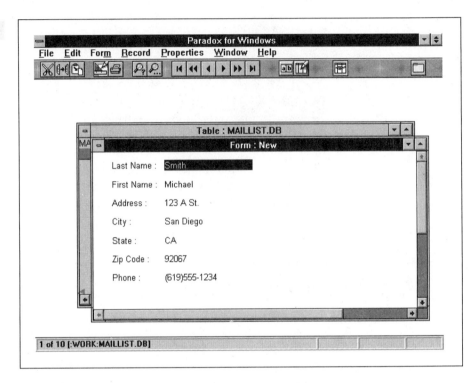

If you want to change an item of data that appears in the form, remember that you must first switch to Edit mode. You can click the Edit Data button or press F9 to do so.

Printing a Form

If you'd like to print a copy of the record that currently appears in the form, choose File ➤ Print, and choose OK in the **Print File** dialog box that appears.

Customizing the Form

Paradox for Windows' simple black and white default form may be sufficient for your needs. However, if you'd like to try customizing this form, follow these steps:

1. Click the Design button in the SpeedBar (shown at left). You'll be taken to the window used for designing forms, shown in Figure 2.14. You can maximize this window or resize it to make it larger if you wish.

2. Now let's try giving this form a real 3-D "Windows" look. First, choose Properties ➤ Designer.

3. Take a look at the Select From Inside option that appears under Design Preferences in the dialog box that appears. If that option isn't already selected (checked), click to select it. If Select From Inside is already checked, leave it as is.

4. Similarly, make sure the Frame Objects option is selected (checked). If it is not, select it now.

5. Choose OK.

FIGURE 2.14

The Form Design window maximized on the screen

Paradox for Windows - [Form Design : New *]

File   Edit   Form   Design   Properties   Window   Help

Last Name :

First Name :

Address :

City :

State :

Zip Code :

Phone :

The Select From Inside option affects how objects on the screen are selected when you click them. Notice how each field on the design form has a large frame around it and a smaller field within. The steps you followed above told Paradox to select the inner box when you first click within the frame. This is just a convenience for our current exercise, and we'll discuss it in more detail in Chapter 9. For now, let's just keep working on our customized form.

1. Move the mouse pointer anywhere within the empty box to the right of the Last Name field name, then click the mouse button. You should see sizing handles around that inner box, as shown below.

2. Now hold down the Shift key, and don't let go until we tell you to.

3. Carefully click within the inner, empty box for each of the remaining fields. You want to select all those inner boxes so your screen looks like Figure 2.15. (Keep that Shift key held down!)

4. Once all the fields are selected, release the Shift key.

5. Move the mouse pointer *inside* any selected box, then click the *right* mouse button. A menu with the title *#EditRegion* should appear on your screen.

6. Choose Frame ➤ Style from the #EditRegion menu.

7. Choose the second-to-last frame style from the options that appear, as shown below.

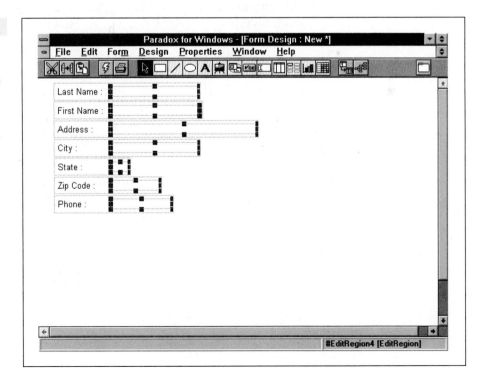

FIGURE 2.15

The inner frames of all the fields selected by clicking each while holding down the Shift key

The change might not be readily apparent on the design screen, but you'll notice a change in just a few moments. Now let's try adding a little color to this form.

1. Move the mouse pointer away from all the fields, perhaps over near the lower-right corner of the Form Design window (but not outside the window).

2. Click the right mouse button. You should see the menu shown below.

3. Choose Color, then select any color that suits your fancy from the options that appear. (The light, bright blue and the pale gray work nicely.)

The form takes on the color you selected.

TIP   If you don't like the new color of the form, simply repeat the steps above, choosing a different color in Step 3.

Now it's time to view your finished form. Here's how:

• Switch to View mode by clicking the View Data button in the SpeedBar (shown at left).

Your form should now be whatever color you selected, with the fields you selected earlier sporting that embossed Windows look, as in Figure 2.16.

FIGURE 2.16

The form after
coloring it and giving
individual fields an
embossed look

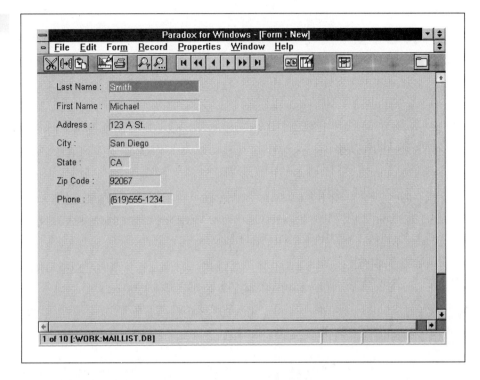

This way of doing things takes some getting used to, but trust me, once
you get a little more practice, you'll wonder how you ever got along
without Paradox for Windows! If you experienced any problems, or just
want more information, see Chapters 9 and 10.

Saving Your New Form

To save your new form, just close it and give it a name.

1. Choose Window ➤ Close All.

2. Choose Yes when asked about saving the form.

3. Type a valid file name such as *3d-form* and then choose OK.

NOTE

Paradox files follow the standard DOS naming conventions. Normally, however, you should not specify an extension when saving a Paradox file. Paradox assigns the file name extension automatically based on the type of file you're saving.

Using Your Custom Form in the Future

You can reopen your custom form at any time in the future by following these steps:

1. Click the Open Form button in the SpeedBar (if it's available), or choose File ➤ Open ➤ Form.

2. Click the form name, *3D-FORM.FSL* in this example, then choose OK.

Switching between Form View and Table View

In some cases, you may want to view an entire record on a form. However, if you want to view multiple records in your table, you might want to switch from Form View to Table View. It's easy to switch back and forth.

- If you're currently viewing data in a form (Form View), click the Table View button in the SpeedBar or press F7.

- If you're currently viewing data in Table View, click the Form View button in the SpeedBar, or press F7 again, to switch back to Form View.

T I P

You can also click any visible portion of the Table View or Form View window to switch between the two windows.

When you want to clean up the Desktop, choose <u>W</u>indow ➤ Close <u>A</u>ll.

Lesson 5: Creating a Report

The Quick Report you saw in Lesson 2 can be useful for double-checking the accuracy of data you entered into a table or printing the results of a query. But fancier jobs like displaying fields precisely where you want them in exactly the format you want, printing sorted data, and performing calculations on fields (as in an invoice) all demand custom reports.

In this lesson, you'll create a custom phone list report that's based on the query you saved in Lesson 3. When you're ready to design more sophisticated reports, you can explore Chapters 9 through 12 and Chapter 18.

Here's how to get started on the phone list:

1. If you're starting from an empty Desktop, you can right-click the Open Report button (shown at left) and choose New. Alternatively, choose <u>F</u>ile ➤ <u>N</u>ew ➤ <u>R</u>eport from the menu bar.

2. In the **Data Model** dialog box that appears, click the drop-down arrow next to the Type box, as shown in Figure 2.17. Now click <*Queries*> to base your report on a saved query instead of a table.

3. Click on the *PHONELST.QBE* query name, then click OK.

Choosing a Design Layout

The **Design Layout** dialog box appears next. As shown in Figure 2.18, this dialog box includes a sample of the basic layout of your report. You

FIGURE 2.17

The Data Model dialog box with the Type list box opened. In Paradox, you can base your reports on tables or queries.

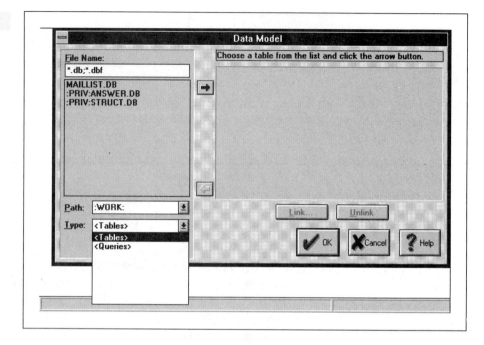

FIGURE 2.18

The Design Layout dialog box

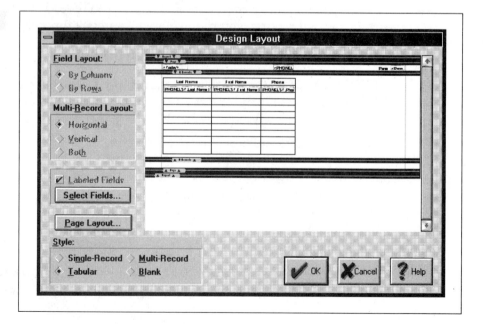

can use the options and buttons in the Design Layout dialog box to change the initial layout, or you can just stick with the default choices.

For many reports, including our sample phone list, the defaults are just fine, so click OK to accept the basic design layout. When the Report Design window appears, maximize it by clicking the Maximize button or double-clicking the title bar.

Customizing the Report

The Report Design window is almost the same as the Form Design window, with one major difference: The Report Design window includes report bands, which define the various sections of your report. Figure 2.19 shows the maximized Design Window with the report bands clearly visible.

FIGURE 2.19

The Report Design window with band labels visible

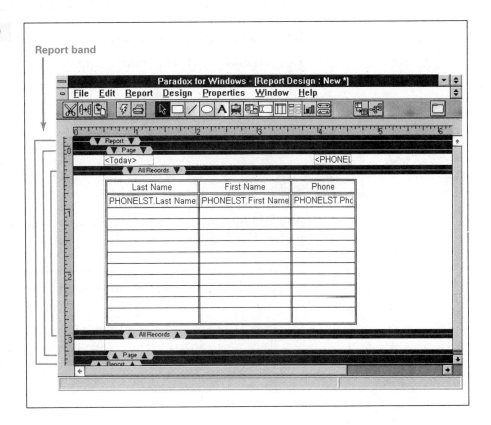

TIP If the report bands aren't obvious in the Report Design window on your screen, choose <u>P</u>roperties ➤ <u>B</u>and Labels.

Paradox for Windows automatically adds the following bands to your report:

> **Report band** Controls what prints at the beginning and end of the report.
>
> **Page band** Controls what prints at the top and bottom of each page. Initially, Paradox places a special field for the date at the top left of each page, the table name at the top center, and the page number (preceded by the word *Page*) at the top right of each page (you can use the horizontal scroll bar to see the page number information). Some blank lines appear at the bottom of each page.
>
> **Record band** Controls what prints in the body of the report.

You can place any text and objects you wish in any band of the report.

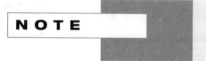

NOTE In Chapter 11 you'll learn about *group bands*, which are used to group (sort) records in a report.

Now let's add some color to the table in the record band and give it a 3-D appearance. Here's how:

1. Move the mouse pointer to an empty area in the table, below the column headers and field names but within the borders of the table.

2. Click the right mouse button to inspect the properties of the table. You'll see the property menu shown in Figure 2.20.

3. Choose *Color*.

4. If your printer can print in color, choose a pastel color from the palette. Otherwise, choose the light gray color in the second row of the second column.

5. Inspect the table again by right-clicking as in Step 2 and choose Grid ➤ Grid Style ➤ 3D from the property menu.

6. Inspect the table once more and choose Grid ➤ Record Divider from the property menu. You won't see an obvious change on the screen right now; however, choosing this option will place a horizontal line between records when you view or print the report.

FIGURE 2.20

The property list that appears when you inspect the properties of a table

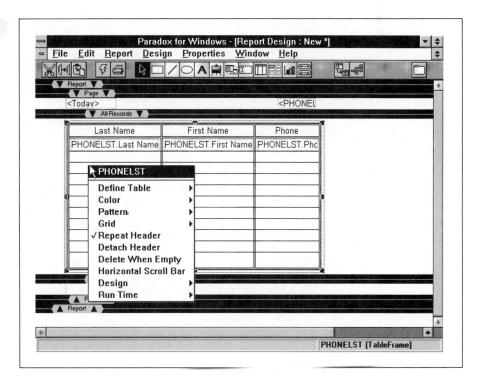

Now change the table headings to a bold font by following these steps:

1. Click the *Last Name* heading at the top of the table's first column. Selection handles will appear around the frame.

2. Now depress the Shift key while clicking the *First Name* and *Phone* headings at the top of the second and third columns of the table. Release the Shift key when you've selected all three headings.

3. Move the mouse pointer inside any of the selected areas (remember, the pointer must be *inside* the selection handles), then click the right mouse button to open the text property menu shown in Figure 2.21.

4. Choose Font ➤ Style ➤ Bold from the property menu.

FIGURE 2.21

The text property menu and selected headings

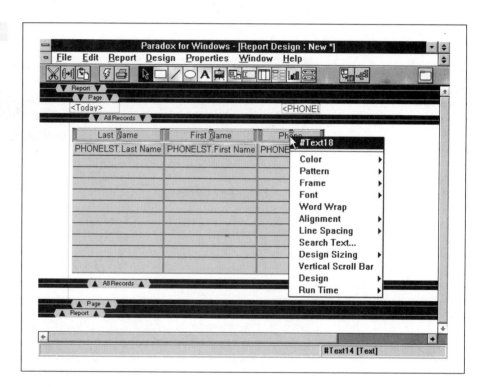

Previewing your handiwork is easy:

• Click the View Data button in the SpeedBar (shown at left), or press F8.

Your report should appear with a 3-D table and bold column headings, as in Figure 2.22. Because you based the report on a saved query, your report contains only the fields you want and is automatically sorted by last name and first name. You'll learn about other ways to sort data in Chapters 7 and 11.

NOTE If you wanted to make further changes to the report, you could click the Design button in the SpeedBar or press F8 again.

FIGURE 2.22

A preview of the phone list report

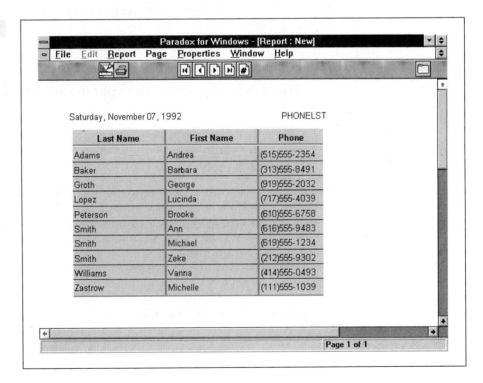

Saturday, November 07, 1992   PHONELST

Last Name	First Name	Phone
Adams	Andrea	(515)555-2354
Baker	Barbara	(313)555-8491
Groth	George	(919)555-2032
Lopez	Lucinda	(717)555-4039
Peterson	Brooke	(610)555-6758
Smith	Ann	(616)555-9483
Smith	Michael	(619)555-1234
Smith	Zeke	(212)555-9302
Williams	Vanna	(414)555-0493
Zastrow	Michelle	(111)555-1039

Printing Your Report

Now that the design for the report is complete, you're ready to print it.
Simply choose File ➤ Print ➤ Report, then choose OK to print the entire
report.

TIP   If you're currently previewing the report, you can print
the current page only by choosing File ➤ Print ➤ Page.

Saving Your New Report

To save your new report, just close it and give it a name.

1. Choose Window ➤ Close All, as usual.

2. Choose Yes when asked about saving the report.

3. Type a valid file name such as **phonerpt** and choose OK.

Using Your Custom Report in the Future

You can reopen your custom report at any time by following these steps:

1. Click the Open Report button in the SpeedBar (if it's available),
   or choose File ➤ Open ➤ Report.

2. Click the report name, *phonerpt.rsl* in this example, and choose
   OK.

As usual, just choose Window ➤ Close All when you want to clean up the
Desktop.

In this chapter you had a chance to see what it's like to work with Paradox for Windows. In just a few short lessons, you created a table, added and edited some names and addresses, performed queries to isolate a particular record and display a sorted phone list, and designed a custom form and report. You also learned how to inspect and change properties of objects by right-clicking the mouse.

Chapter 3 expands upon many points touched on during these hands-on lessons and delves into some new areas too. For example, you'll learn more about Paradox menus, the SpeedBar, creating an *alias* or "nickname" for a directory, and personalizing the Desktop. You'll also learn how to request help at any time with just the touch of a key or a few clicks of the mouse.

PART TWO

Managing Data with Paradox

CHAPTERS

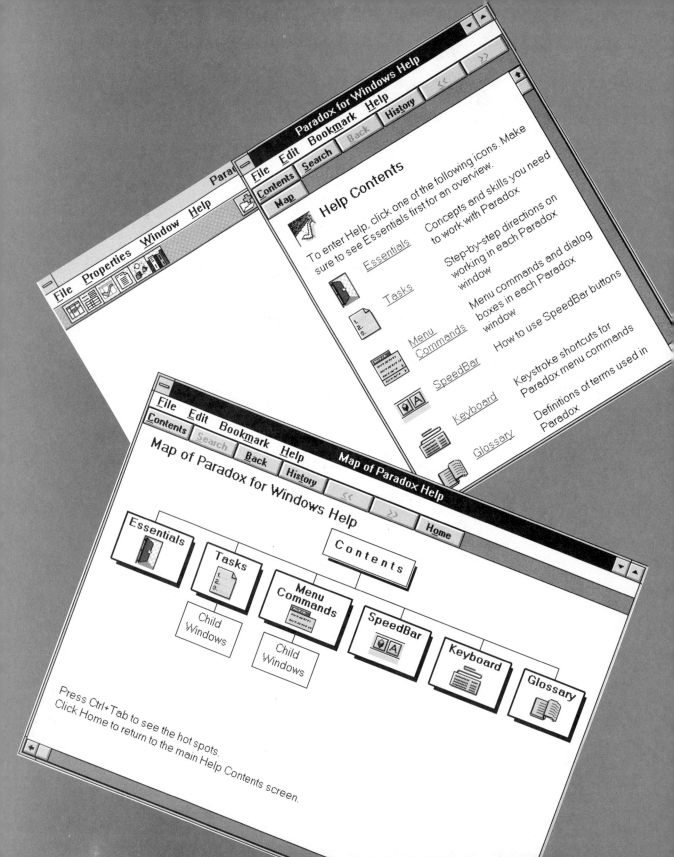

Getting Around in Paradox

f a s t **TRACK**

To get help   83

> choose the Help button if it's available, choose Help from the menu, or press the Help key (F1).

To switch to a new working directory   92

> choose File ➤ Working Directory from the Desktop. Then either type in a new working directory, or use the **Aliases** drop-down list box or the Browse button to select a directory. Choose OK.

To personalize the Paradox for Windows Desktop   97

> choose Properties ➤ Desktop, then choose appropriate options from the **Desktop Properties** dialog box that appears.

IF you worked through the lessons in Chapter 2, you probably know all that's necessary to get around in Paradox for Windows. Therefore, you may just want to browse through this chapter now, or you can refer to it for quick reminders and additional options as needed. However, if you skipped the lessons in Chapter 2, you can learn the basic skills for using the Paradox Desktop here.

Starting Paradox for Windows

The first step to using Paradox for Windows is to start the application. At this point, we'll assume that Paradox for Windows is already installed, and that its icon is available in the Windows Program Manager. (If you haven't installed Paradox yet, you will find instructions in Appendix A.) Also, as mentioned in Chapter 2, we'll assume that you already have your basic Windows skills down pat. Now, here's how you start Paradox:

1. Start Windows and go to Program Manager. You should see the Paradox for Windows icon, as shown in Figure 3.1.

TIP

If the \pdoxwin directory is in the path statement in your autoexec.bat file, you can start Windows and Paradox from the DOS prompt by typing pdoxwin and pressing ↵.

2. Double-click the Paradox for Windows icon. You'll see the group window shown below.

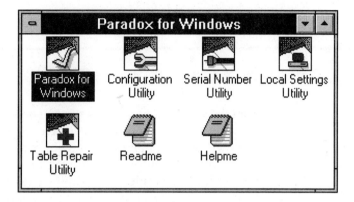

FIGURE 3.1

The Windows
Program Manager
on the screen. The
Paradox for Windows
icon is near the lower-
left corner of the
window in this
example.

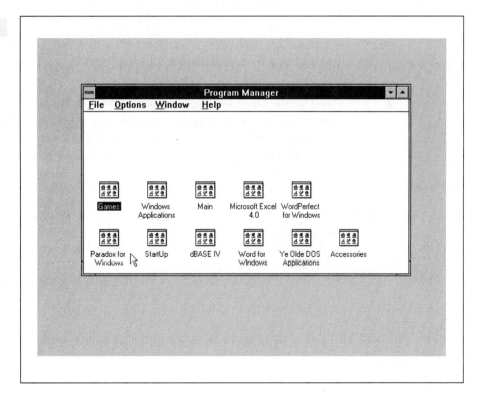

3. Double-click the Paradox for Windows icon.

You'll see the Paradox for Windows *Desktop*, described in the next section.

The Paradox Desktop

Paradox for Windows follows the *Common User Access* (CUA) guidelines that all Windows applications adhere to. Therefore, if you're a seasoned Windows user, you already know how to select menu options, get help, and work with windows and dialog boxes in Paradox for Windows. All your work with Paradox for Windows takes place at the Desktop, shown in Figure 3.2. The Paradox Desktop contains the standard buttons and features that most Windows applications offer—Control menu, title bar, Minimize and Maximize buttons, and borders. Use these features to size and position the Paradox Desktop as you would any other window.

Figure 3.2 also points out Paradox for Windows' SpeedBar, menu bar, and status bar, which are explained later in this chapter.

The Paradox Desktop is much like the Windows desktop in that it is the application window, that is, the *parent window* of all Paradox objects. All other windows in Paradox are document windows (*child windows*). Any window that you open on the Paradox Desktop can be moved and sized only within the boundaries of the Paradox Desktop.

NOTE

Within this book, the term *Desktop* always refers to the Paradox Desktop. We'll refer to other desktops by name (for example, the *Windows desktop*).

FIGURE 3.2

The Paradox for
Windows Desktop
with its standard
Windows features

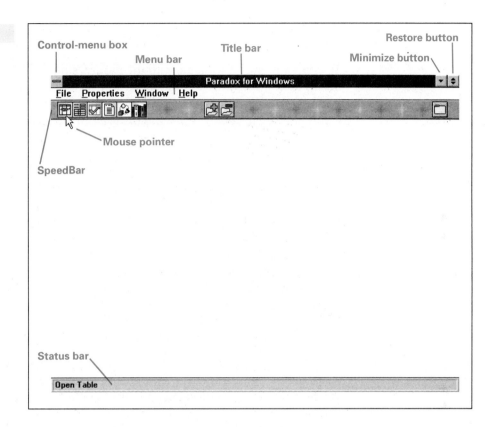

Menus and Keystrokes

As with all Windows applications, you can interact with Paradox for Windows through menus, keystrokes, and buttons.

NOTE Any menu command that's dimmed is inappropriate to the current situation, and therefore cannot be selected.

Using Menus with the Mouse

To choose menu commands with the mouse, simply click the command you want. Alternatively, you can move the mouse pointer to any command on the menu bar, hold down the mouse button, drag the highlight to the command you want, then release the mouse button.

Selecting Menu Commands with the Keyboard

As with all Windows applications, you can also select menu commands via the keyboard. For instance, you can press (and release) the Alt key or F10 key to move the highlight into the menu bar. Once the highlight is in the menu bar, you can choose commands by typing the underlined letter or by using the arrow keys to move to the command you want and then pressing ↵ to select it.

Backing Out of Menus

Occasionally, you may find that you've inadvertently chosen the wrong menu options and want to back up until you get to more familiar territory. You can use any of these techniques to back out of a menu and return to the Desktop without making a selection:

• Click in any neutral area outside the menu.

• Press Alt or Esc.

• If your menu selections have taken you to a dialog box, and you want to leave that dialog box without making a selection, click the Cancel button, shown below, or press Escape.

Conventions Used in This Book

Throughout this book, we'll display a series of menu selections in the following format: Choose File ➤ New ➤ Table. This format lets you see, at a glance, the sequence of menu options you need to choose to access a particular feature. Each menu option is separated by the ➤ symbol. The "hot key" alternative for each menu option is underscored. So, the sample menu sequence above is simply a shortcut for "Choose File, then choose New, then choose Table."

For combination keystrokes, we'll use the standard *key+key* conventions. Alt+F1 means "hold down the Alt key, press F1, then release both keys."

Understanding Paradox Menus

The menu bar lists the menus that are available at any given time. Different commands appear on the menu bar, depending on what you happen to be doing. Most windows include the File, Properties, Window, and Help menus.

The **File** menu lets you create and save Paradox objects, print reports, perform various utility functions, define network options, change settings for the Paradox environment, change the working and private directories, set up aliases (or "nicknames") for directories, and exit Paradox. We'll be discussing options on the File menu throughout this book.

The **Properties** menu contains options for controlling the appearance of the Desktop or of objects (such as tables, reports, or forms). The specific options on the Properties menu depend on what type of object you're working with. In this chapter, you'll learn how to personalize the Paradox for Windows Desktop by changing some of its properties.

The **Window** menu contains standard Windows options for controlling the appearance of windows and for switching from one Paradox child window to another.

The **Help** menu allows you to get on-screen help while you're in Paradox. See "Getting Help," later in this chapter, for more information on the Help system.

Using the SpeedBar

The SpeedBar, just below the menu bar, offers a quick alternative to the menus as a means of accessing main features. When you point to a button (move the mouse pointer to it), the status bar near the bottom of the window indicates what that button does. If you're not sure what a button is for, just move the mouse pointer to the button and glance down at the status bar. Clicking the button will then activate the feature.

Like the menu bar, the buttons that are available on the SpeedBar depend on what you happen to be doing at the moment. For example, the Paradox Desktop includes the buttons shown in Figure 3.2, but when you're designing a report or form, you'll see a different set of buttons that are relevant to reports and forms.

About Property Inspection

Though the term *property inspection* sounds like something you need to get a mortgage, it actually refers to one of the handiest of all features in Paradox for Windows.

To appreciate the value of property inspection, imagine you're looking at a screen cluttered with a table, a form, and a graph. Now, suppose you want to change a particular feature, such as the alignment, font, or color, of a column in the table. *Without* property inspection, you'd either need to search through the menus until you found the appropriate commands, or use the Help system or documentation to find information on table columns.

With property inspection, you simply move the mouse pointer to the column (or to whatever it is you want to change), then click the *right* mouse button. Instantly, you'll see options that are relevant to the object you selected.

For instance, Figure 3.3 shows how right-clicking the Category column heading in a sample table produces a menu of options that let you change the alignment, color, and font of that heading.

N O T E The extra buttons that appear in the SpeedBar in Figure 3.3 are visible only when a table is open on the Desktop, as you'll see in Chapter 4.

We'll talk about property inspection as it pertains to various objects in upcoming chapters. However, you can try it for yourself right now, if you wish, by inspecting the properties of the Open Table button.

First, move the mouse pointer to the Open Table button, then click the right mouse button. You'll see a menu of options relevant to opening a

FIGURE 3.3

To inspect (and, if you wish, change) the properties of an object, simply move the mouse pointer to the object and click the right mouse button

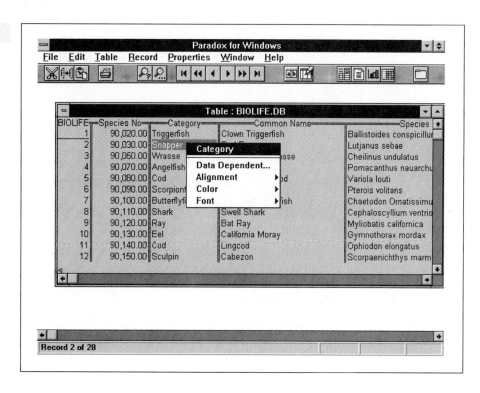

table, as shown below. You can click the left mouse button outside the menu or press Escape to leave the menu without making a selection.

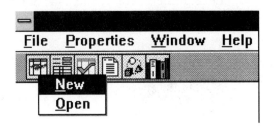

Not all SpeedBar buttons have properties. Right-clicking a button with no properties has no effect.

If you get confused about which mouse button is which, just keep the following in mind: You click the right mouse button only to inspect properties—to view or change some property of an object, or to open a menu for a SpeedBar button. For all other operations, including choosing menu and dialog box options, selecting text, clicking a SpeedBar button, dragging, and so forth, you use the *left* mouse button.

The roles of the left and right mouse buttons will be reversed if your mouse is configured for lefties. You can swap the roles of the buttons at any time using the Control Panel in the Windows Program Manager's Main group.

Throughout this book we'll use the terms "click" and "double-click" to refer to left-button mouse operations. When an action requires using the right mouse button, we'll refer to that action as *right-clicking* or *inspecting the properties*.

Getting Help

Paradox uses the standard Windows Help system to provide on-screen assistance when you need it. Two basic types of help are available to you. *Context-sensitive help* offers information specific to whatever you happen to be doing at the time. You can get more general help by using the Help contents.

Getting Context-Sensitive Help

There are two ways to get context-sensitive help:

- If a Help button is available, click it.
- If no Help button is available, move the highlight to the menu option that you need help with, then press the Help key (F1).

A Help window will open, providing information about the task or operation you're trying to perform. For example, inspecting the Open Table button on the SpeedBar and choosing New (or choosing File ➤ New ➤ Table from the Desktop menus) invokes the **Table Type** dialog box, which includes a Help button. Clicking that Help button takes you directly to the Help window for creating a table, as shown in Figure 3.4.

NOTE You'll learn how to use the Table Type dialog box in Chapter 4.

Using Jump Words and Glossary Entries

When you're in the Help system, you'll notice that some topics are underlined with a solid line and others are underlined with dots.

Solid underline (*jump word*)   Clicking a jump word in a Help window takes you to the Help page for that particular topic. (Choosing the Back button would then return you to the page you just left.)

Dotted underline (*glossary entry*)   Clicking a glossary word or topic instantly shows you the definition of that word or topic. Clicking a second time removes the definition from the screen.

FIGURE 3.4

A sample context-sensitive Help window

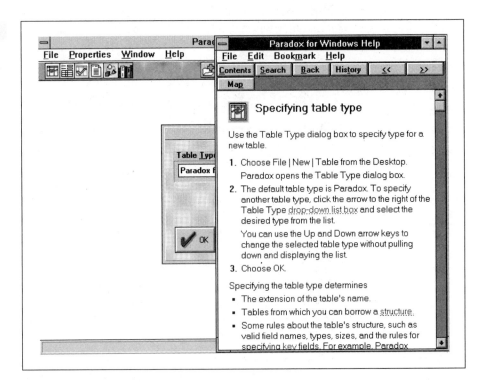

Getting More General Help

If you need more general help, you can use the Help Contents. Here's how:

- Choose Help ➤ Contents, or click the Contents button if you're already in a Help window.

The table of contents for Paradox Help will appear, as shown in Figure 3.5. You can then click on one of the icons or its underlined topic to display help

FIGURE 3.5

Paradox Help
Contents window

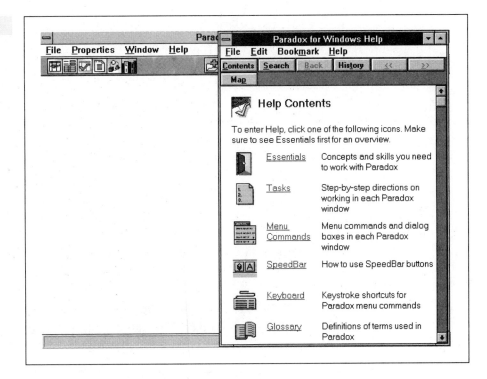

for that topic. For example, clicking the *SpeedBar* topic provides information about using the SpeedBar buttons. If you scroll to the bottom of that
Help window, you will see options for learning about specific SpeedBars.

Using the Help Buttons

The Help window includes several buttons to help you navigate the Help
system more quickly and zero in on specific topics. Table 3.1 explains each
of these buttons.

The Map button is particularly handy because it presents the Help system's
Table of Contents in a visual, hierarchical manner. When you click the Map
button, the full-screen Help map shown in Figure 3.6 appears.

TABLE 3.1: Help Buttons in the Help System

BUTTON	WHAT IT DOES
Contents	Displays the Help Contents for Paradox.
Search	Lists all the words you can use to search for topics. After choosing **Search**, type or select a word, then choose **Show Topics**. Select a topic from the list and choose **Go To**.
Back	Displays the last topic you viewed. You can back up one topic at a time, in the reverse order that you viewed the topics.
History	Displays the last 40 topics you've viewed, with the most recent topic listed first. Double-click a topic to revisit it.
<<	Displays the previous topic in a series of related topics. You can click this button repeatedly until you reach the first topic in the series.
>>	Displays the next topic in a series of related topics. You can click this button repeatedly until you reach the last topic in the series.
Map	Displays a map of the Paradox Help system. The Map window contains a Home Button, which you can use to return to the Help Contents window.

Once you're in the Help map, you can click on any topic to go immediately to that topic. Or, in the case of the Tasks and Menu Commands options, clicking once expands the icons to show more specific topics. You can then click on one of these specific topics for more detailed assistance.

If you decide to return to where you came from without choosing a topic from the Help map, click on the Home button under the Help window's menu bar. The Help window will return to its original size as soon as you leave the Help map.

FIGURE 3.6

Paradox for Windows' unique Help map provides instant visual access to major Help topics.

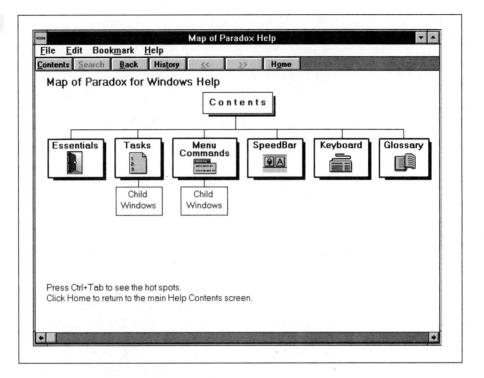

Keeping the Help Window Visible

While viewing a Help topic on the screen, you can click *outside* the Help window to return to the Desktop without closing the Help window. However, doing so may cover the Help window. If you want to be able to see the Help window while working on the Desktop, follow these steps:

1. Go back to the Help window by clicking on any visible portion of that window, by pressing Alt+Tab, or by calling up the Task List (Ctrl+Esc) and double-clicking the name of the Help window.

2. Within the Help window, choose Help ➤ Always on Top.

T I P

The Always on Top option in the Help window is a *toggle*. Choosing the option once activates the feature; choosing the option a second time deactivates it.

Now when you click on the Paradox Desktop, the Help window will remain visible. You can move and size the Help window as necessary to see whatever it is you're working on.

The Always on Top setting remains active until you exit the Help system, as described in the next section, or until you choose Help ➤ Always on Top again.

Learning More about Help

Learning to use the Help system is largely a matter of exploring. The Paradox Help system offers all the features that other Windows applications offer, such as the ability to print a Help topic (by choosing File ➤ Print Topic), copy a topic to the Windows Clipboard (Edit ➤ Copy), search for topics (by clicking the Search button in the Help window), and add bookmarks and annotations. For more information on these topics, refer to your Windows documentation or choose Help ➤ How to Use Help from the Help window's menu bar.

Exiting Help

When you've finished using the Help system, you can close it using any of the following techniques:

* Choose File ➤ Exit from the Help window's menu bar (*not* the Paradox Desktop menu bar).

* Double-click the Control-menu box in the upper-left corner of the Help window.

* Click the Help window's Control-menu box once, then choose Close.

* Press Alt+F4 when the Help window is the current window.

You'll be returned to whatever you were doing when you accessed the Help system.

Creating a Directory

One of the keys to using Paradox effectively is keeping your database objects together in a single directory. By organizing your database objects this way, you will be able to group together objects that belong together and prevent them from being mixed up with objects from unrelated databases.

NOTE   Because all the objects that make up a database are stored in a single directory, the terms *directory* and *database* are often used interchangeably in the Paradox documentation and dialog boxes.

While Paradox itself offers no particular command for creating a directory, you can easily pop out to the Windows File Manager at any time to do this job. Lesson 1 in the last chapter provided an example, detailing the steps required to create a directory.

Creating an Alias for a Directory

One of the handy little features of Paradox for Windows is its ability to give a directory name a descriptive, "user-friendly" *alias* or nickname. For instance, you can give a directory like *c:\pdoxwin\giftco* an alias such as *Gifts* or *Gift Corner*. Then, whenever you're using Paradox, you can simply designate that new name as the directory without having to use the DOS syntax or rummage through drives and directories to locate the correct path.

To assign an alias to an existing directory, follow the procedures below.

1. Choose File ➤ Aliases from the Paradox for Windows menu bar. You'll see the dialog box shown in Figure 3.7.

2. Click the New button.

3. Type the alias you want to give to the directory. You can include blank spaces (though they'll be converted to underscores), and you can use any combination of upper- and lowercase letters. For instance, *Gift Corner* is a perfectly acceptable alias name.

4. Click the text box next to *Path*, or press Tab twice.

5. Type the actual name of the directory you're assigning the alias to (e.g., *c:\pdoxwin\giftco*).

6. Click the Keep New button.

7. If you want to make this alias permanent (so that it's available in future sessions of Paradox), choose Save As.

FIGURE 3.7

The Alias Manager dialog box lets you assign "nicknames" to existing directories.

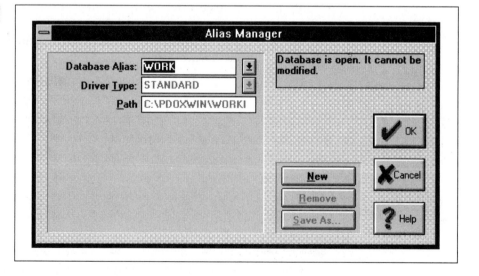

8. From the **Save File As** dialog box that appears, you can choose OK to save the current aliases in the suggested initialization file (typically *odapi.cfg*). Then choose Yes when asked for permission to overwrite.

9. Choose OK to return to the Desktop.

NOTE   See Chapter 14 for additional information on Alias Manager.

Next we'll talk about how you can choose a working directory in Paradox, using either an alias or the more standard DOS/Windows syntax.

Choosing a Working Directory

When you start Paradox, its *working directory* will be the same working directory you were using the last time you exited Paradox. If you're starting Paradox for the first time, the working directory will be a default working directory that was setup when Paradox was installed (usually *c:\pdoxwin\working*). Paradox will automatically use the working directory when it searches for tables, reports, and other objects that you've created.

Typically, one of the first things you'll want to do when starting Paradox, particularly if you share a computer with other people or have created several databases on separate directories, is to choose the working directory for your data.

Be aware that before switching to the new directory, Paradox automatically closes and saves any work in progress on the current directory. Therefore, it's particularly important to create and choose a directory before creating a new database or application. We'll be sure to remind you of this in later chapters when it's appropriate.

Whenever you're ready to switch to a new directory, just follow these steps:

1. Choose File ➤ Working Directory. You'll see the **Set Working Directory** dialog box, shown below. Notice that the entry in the Working Directory text box is automatically selected (highlighted).

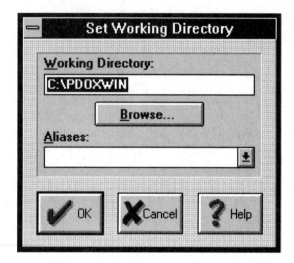

2. Select a different directory using any of these techniques:

   • If the directory you want to switch to has an alias, use the Aliases drop-down list box to select an alias, as described under "Selecting a Directory by its Alias," below.

   • Use the Browse button in the **Browser** dialog box, as described under "Using the Browser to Choose a Working Directory," below.

   • Type the complete path name of the directory you want to switch to in the Working Directory text box, as described under "Typing the Working Directory Entry."

3. Choose OK (which is only possible if you've correctly specified an existing directory).

Paradox will switch to that directory and return you to the Desktop. Any new objects you create and save will be placed in that directory. When you ask Paradox to open an object, it will search only the current working directory.

Selecting a Directory by Its Alias

If the working directory you want to switch to has an alias, you can select it from the Aliases drop-down list box. To do so, click the Aliases list box (or click the ↓ just to the right of the list box) in the Set Working Directory dialog box. A list of aliases will appear, as below.

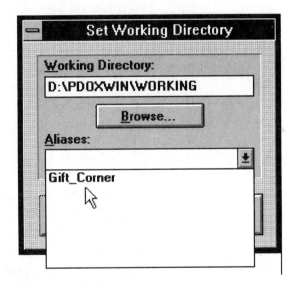

Now click the alias for the directory you want to switch to. The list box will close and the alias you chose will appear in the Aliases list box of the Set Working Directory dialog box. Click OK to have Paradox change the alias name to the path name for you, then click OK a second time to return to the Desktop with the new working directory selected.

Using the Browser to Choose a Working Directory

If the directory you want to switch to doesn't have an alias, you can use the Browse button to search through and choose a directory. When you choose the Browse button, you'll see a **Browser** dialog box like the one in Figure 3.8. Inside this dialog box, your existing directories appear as folders in a hierarchical arrangement. The darker-colored folders represent directories that have additional subdirectories within them. To choose a directory, follow the steps below.

N O T E   The Browse button that appears in other Paradox windows leads to an expanded Browser window with additional buttons and options. Please see Chapter 14 for more information on browsing.

1. If you want to switch to a different disk drive, click the drop-down list button under Aliases, then click the drive you want to switch to. The directory tree changes to reflect all the directories on the drive you specified.

2. In the directory tree, use the scroll bars, if necessary, to scroll to the directory you want to switch to.

3. If you want to switch to a subdirectory that isn't visible, first expand the parent directory by double-clicking its name or folder icon. For instance, in Figure 3.8 we scrolled down to the *pdoxwin* directory, then double-clicked it to reveal *diveplan, giftco,* and other subdirectories beneath *pdoxwin.*

4. Click on the folder or directory name you want to select.

5. Choose OK.

You'll be returned to the Set Working Directory dialog box. At this point, you can choose OK to complete the switch to a new working directory (or choose Cancel to return to the Desktop without changing the working directory).

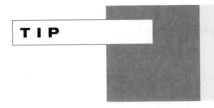

TIP

If a Browser dialog box shows you only the current directory, choosing the current drive in Step 1 will expand the directory tree to display all the directories on that drive.

FIGURE 3.8

The Browser dialog box shows the directory tree for the current drive. You can double-click the darker-colored folders to view the names of subdirectories.

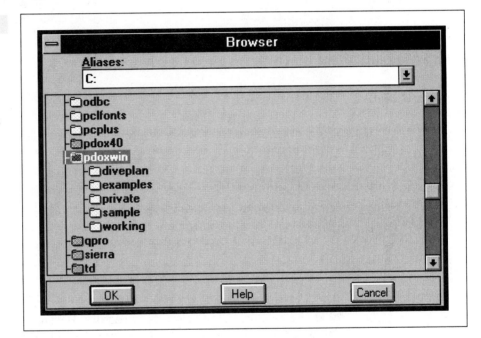

Typing the Working Directory Entry

If the directory you want to switch to has no alias and you know its exact name, you can type that name into the Working Directory text box using standard Windows techniques, as summarized below.

- To replace the current entry with a new one, simply type the new entry.

- To change the current entry, click the mouse to position the insertion point where you want to start making changes, or use positioning keys (such as Home, End, ←, or →) *before* you start typing text.

TIP

The OK button appears dim as long as the Working Directory text box contains an *invalid* (nonexistent) directory name. As soon as you fill in the name of an existing directory, the OK button is "undimmed" to indicate that the directory can be used as the new working directory.

To change to a subdirectory of the current entry (for example, to change *c:\pdoxwin* to *c:\pdoxwin\giftco*), click the mouse at the end of the text in the Working Directory text box (or press End), then type the text you want to add (*\giftco* in this example).

Choose OK after entering a valid directory name in order to return to the Desktop.

"Paradox Lost All My Data!"

Keep in mind that if you try to open a table but can't find it, chances are that you're simply in the wrong directory. Before you panic, choose File ➤ Working Directory to find out which directory you're in. Then, if necessary, choose the appropriate directory using any of the techniques just described.

About the Private Directory

You've probably noticed that the File menu lets you choose both a working directory and a *private directory*. Paradox uses the private directory from time to time to store temporary tables "behind the scenes." By default, the private directory is \pdxwin\private, nicknamed *PRIV*.

In most cases, you need not change, or even concern yourself with, the private directory. If you're on a network and have a hard disk, chances are your network administrator has already defined a private directory for your workstation. If you're using Paradox on a network and your workstation does not have a hard disk, you may need to create a private directory on the server to prevent your temporary tables from being intermingled with other users' temporary tables. See your network administrator (or Appendix E) if you need more information on this topic.

Personalizing the Desktop

There are a few simple things you can do to personalize the Paradox Desktop simply by changing its properties. These steps will get you started.

1. Choose Properties ➤ Desktop from the Paradox for Windows menu bar. You'll see the dialog box shown in Figure 3.9.

2. Make your changes (as described in the sections that follow), then choose OK.

Changing the Window Title

The title bar for the Paradox window normally contains the title *Paradox for Windows*. If you want to change that title, simply type in a new title under Title in the Desktop Properties dialog box.

FIGURE 3.9

The Desktop Properties dialog box lets you personalize the Paradox Desktop.

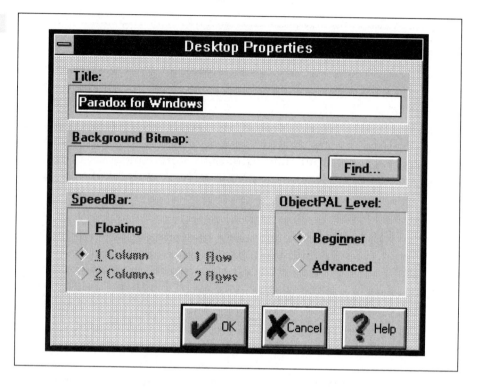

"Wallpapering" the Paradox Desktop

You can add a wallpaper image to the Paradox Desktop just as you can to the Windows desktop. The wallpaper image can be any existing graphic or any printed image that you've scanned and saved in one of the following formats:

FILE TYPE	FILE NAME EXTENSION
Bitmap (Windows)	.bmp
Compuserve Graphic	.gif
Device Independent Bit map	.dib
Encapsulated Postscript	.eps

FILE TYPE	FILE NAME EXTENSION
Paintbrush	.pcx
Run-Length Encoded	.rle
Tagged Image File Format	.tif

Paradox automatically tiles the image, so if the image is smaller than the Desktop, you'll see multiple copies of the image on the screen.

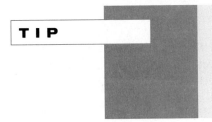

TIP

When scanning an image to use as wallpaper, you can usually scale the image to near full-screen size to fill the Desktop. Common full-screen sizes (in pixels) include 640 x 480 (VGA), 800 x 600 (Super VGA), and 1024 x 768 (XGA and others).

To choose or change wallpaper, follow the steps below.

1. If you know the exact name and location of the bitmap image you want to use, type in the path and file name, then skip to Step 6.

2. To look for images, click the Find button. You'll see a list of file names of possible .bmp, .pcx, .tif, .gif, and .eps images on the current directory.

3. To continue browsing, click the Browse button.

4. In the Browser, you can explore multiple drives and directories with the usual techniques:

   - Under Aliases, choose a drive to view all the directories on that drive.
   - Under Filters, change the file specification to list the type of files you want to search for (for example, *.bmp* to search for files with that extension).
   - In the directory tree, double-click any darkened file folder to expand or contract subdirectory names. Single-click any directory to view the files in it.

5. When you find the name of the file you want to use, click its name, then click OK at the bottom of the Browser dialog box.

6. To view the wallpaper image, choose OK from the Desktop Properties dialog box.

NOTE To remove an existing wallpaper image, delete the file name from the Background Bitmap text box in the Desktop Properties dialog box.

Figure 3.10 shows an example in which we've used a logo and business name as wallpaper. We used Bitstream's Makeup to create the text in *Gift Corner*; the gift picture is a modified WordPerfect graphic file. Notice that we've moved the SpeedBar too, as described next.

FIGURE 3.10

Sample company logo used as the Paradox for Windows wallpaper

Moving the SpeedBar

Normally, the SpeedBar stays fixed just below the menu bar on the Paradox Desktop. However, you can change it to a "floating" SpeedBar which you can move anywhere on the screen by following these steps:

1. If you haven't already done so, choose Properties ➤ Desktop to get to the Desktop Properties dialog box.

2. Under SpeedBar, click the Floating option if you want a movable SpeedBar.

3. Choose any one of the options to the right:

   - 1 Column (vertical SpeedBar, one column of buttons)
   - 2 Columns (vertical bar with two columns)
   - 1 Row (horizontal bar, one row as in Figure 3.10)
   - 2 Rows (horizontal bar with two rows)

4. Choose OK to return to the Paradox Desktop.

When you return to the Desktop, the SpeedBar appears in a separate window. You can move the SpeedBar by dragging the title bar (next to the Control-menu box) to any position on the screen. To return to a fixed SpeedBar, click the Control-menu box on the SpeedBar and choose Fix or simply double-click the Control-menu box.

Changing the Screen Colors

We'll talk about the many ways to control the color of various Paradox objects as we present those objects in upcoming chapters. For its default color scheme, Paradox uses whatever color scheme you've selected for Windows. If you want to change the colors of the Desktop, you need to go through the **Colors** dialog box in the Windows Control Panel (available in the Main group of Program Manager). See your Windows documentation for more information, if necessary.

N O T E   Changing the color scheme of the Paradox Desktop has no effect on the color of your wallpaper.

Changing the ObjectPAL Level

The ObjectPAL Level settings are used to control your access to ObjectPAL program code (known as *methods*). You can specify a Beginner level (the default setting) or an Advanced level. You'll learn more about ObjectPAL in Chapter 19.

Exiting Paradox

Before turning off your computer, and even before exiting Windows, you should *always* exit Paradox. This ensures that any new data or changes to existing data will be properly stored on disk. If you do not exit Paradox before turning off your computer, you are likely to lose data and any work you've accomplished in the current Paradox session.

You can exit Paradox in a number of different ways:

- Choose File ➤ Exit from the Desktop.
- Click the Control-menu box in the upper left-hand corner of the Paradox Desktop and choose Close from the menu that appears.
- Double-click the Paradox Desktop's Control-menu box.
- Press Alt+F4.

If you've changed any objects without saving them, Paradox will prompt you to save. You can choose Yes to save the current changes, No to abandon any current changes, or Cancel to stay in Paradox. If you choose Yes or No, you will be returned to the Windows Program Manager.

This chapter has provided a general introduction to interacting with Paradox for Windows. Paradox for Windows follows the Common User Access (CUA) guidelines that all Windows applications adhere to. If you need additional information on using Windows and Windows applications, you should read up on "Basic Skills" or "Fundamentals" in your Windows documentation. In Chapter 4, we will take a close look at designing and creating tables.

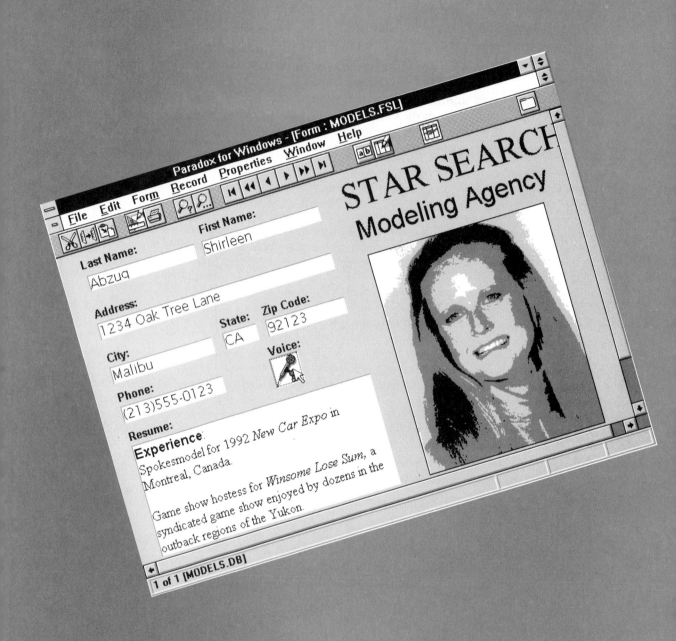

CHAPTER

4

Creating Paradox Tables

f a s t **TRACK**

To create a table   140

select File ➤ New ➤ Table, or inspect the Open Table button
in the SpeedBar and choose New from the menu that appears.
Then choose OK in the **Table Type** dialog box. Enter the
name, field type, and size of each field, and, if you wish, define
the primary key.

To specify validity checks   145

while defining the table structure on the screen, choose
Validity Checks from the drop-down list under Table Properties. Then move the highlight to the field you want to assign
validity checks to and define the checks for that field.

To save the table structure   149

click on the Save As button. Type in a valid file name for the
table structure and click OK.

To change the structure of an existing table   151

choose the File ➤Utilities ➤ Restructure options. Make the
necessary changes, then choose the Save button.

N Lesson 1 we whipped quickly through the procedure for creating a table. However, that's not to suggest that creating a table is a trivial matter. On the contrary, the table is the most fundamental object in Paradox for Windows, since tables are what you'll use to store your data. In fact, virtually everything you do in Paradox for Windows will revolve around how you've structured your tables.

As you know, you can store any kind of information in a table: names and addresses, inventory information, orders, a check register, pictures and sounds, a personal library, photographs—any information at all. The only requirement is that the data be organized in a tabular format, in other words, in columns and rows.

All but the simplest applications will require that you store data in several separate tables, rather than in a single table. In this chapter we'll examine all the factors that go into designing individual tables. The information here and in the chapters that follow will carry over to Chapter 15, where you'll learn about designing a database with multiple tables.

Planning a Table

The first step in designing a table is to plan its *structure*. That is, you've got to figure out how you're going to divide the information into separate fields, and decide how you're going to name and define each field. Your best bet might be to do this with paper and pencil, rather than online, so you can play around with your table structure before actually creating it in Paradox for Windows.

Planning the Field Names

When deciding what fields to place in a table, keep in mind the following rules for defining field names:

- The maximum width of a field name is 25 characters.

- A field name can *contain* blank spaces, but cannot *start* with a blank space.

- A field name cannot contain quotation marks ("), brackets([]), parentheses (()), braces ({}), or a hyphen followed by a greater-than sign (->). Though a field may contain the number symbol (#), the number symbol alone cannot be used as the field name.

- No two fields in the same table can have the same name. Changing the capitalization will not make field names different from one another.

Using the example of names and addresses, you might come up with the list of fields shown in Figure 4.1 for the table.

FIGURE 4.1

The field names for a table of customer names, addresses, and other information, sketched out on a scratch pad

	Field Name
1	Last Name
2	Mr/Mrs
3	First Name
4	M.I.
5	Department/Title
6	Company
7	Address
8	City
9	State
10	Zip Code
11	Area Code
12	Phone
13	Extension
14	Credit Limit
15	Start Date

Now, you might be wondering why we would bother to split people's names into four fields: Mr/Mrs, Last Name, First Name, and M.I. (middle initial). The reason is that the more fields you break the information into, the easier it will be to manage the data later on. For example, storing each person's last name in a separate field will make it easier to tell Paradox to "put the information into alphabetical order by last name" or to "find all the records for people named Smith."

Separating the fields also makes it easier to determine exactly how you might want to print them later. For example, if you wanted to print an alphabetical customer list, you could tell Paradox to list Last Name followed by a comma, followed by First Name, like this:

Adams, Andy
Baker, Barbara
Carlson, Cara

When using the same table to print formal correspondence, it would be just as easy to have Paradox put the names in a different format—Mr. or Mrs. followed by First Name, Middle Initial, and then Last Name, like this:

Mr. Andy A. Adams
Ms. Barbara B. Baker
Mrs. Cara C. Carlson

Similarly, breaking area code and telephone number into two separate fields will allow us to analyze data by area code later on. For instance, we might want to count the number of customers in the 512 area code (one of several area codes in Texas), or find out which products sell best in that part of the country. Or we might want our sales representatives to service customer accounts based on the customer's area code.

As you can see, while your first inclination might be to combine several pieces of information into a single field, in the long run you're better off dividing the information into many separate fields.

Planning the Field Types

Paradox stores different types of information in different formats. When defining your table, therefore, you need to think about what type of information will be stored in each field. Your options are described below.

N O T E

These field types are for Paradox for Windows tables only. If you use Paradox for Windows to create tables for other applications, the field types available to you may be different. (See Appendix C.)

Alphanumeric   This type of field is used for textual data containing any combination of letters, numerals, spaces, and other characters. The contents of an alphanumeric field can be anywhere from 1 to 255 characters in length. Examples of uses include names, addresses, titles, product codes—basically, any short piece of text.

An alphanumeric field can also store links to data in files created by another "DDE-capable" application such as a Windows spreadsheet (for example, Excel or Quattro Pro for Windows), word processor (for example, Microsoft Word), or other application. The links are created through a technique called *Dynamic Data Exchange* or *DDE*. Paradox for Windows can act as a DDE client or server. We'll describe DDE in more detail later in this chapter.

Memo   Like alphanumeric fields, memo fields contain textual data—letters, numerals, spaces, and other characters. However, a memo field can contain text of any length, limited only by the amount of disk space available on your hard drive. Examples of uses include résumés, job descriptions, product descriptions, journal abstracts—any text that requires more than 255 characters.

Formatted memo   This field type is the same as a memo field, but text can be embellished with attributes such as varied fonts, styles (e.g., **bold** or *italic*), and alignment options (centered, flush-right, etc.). Formatted memo fields have basically the same uses as memo fields.

Number   These fields store numbers that you might want to use to perform mathematical operations such as totals, subtotals, averages, and so forth. Number fields can accept only numeric characters (0–9), decimal points, commas, and minus signs. The range of values possible for a number field is anywhere from -10^{307} to 10^{308} with 15 significant digits. Alphabetic characters are not allowed in number fields. Examples of uses include quantities, measurements, and so on.

Short number   Like number fields, these fields contain numbers; however, short number fields are used only for whole numbers in the range of -32,767 to 32,767. No decimal point is allowed. Uses include quantities (whole number only), account numbers, and product identification numbers that do not require letters or punctuation.

$ (Currency)   These fields store numeric data representing monetary amounts. Currency data is like number data, except that all numbers are automatically rounded off to two decimal places, and negative values are enclosed in parentheses. Uses include unit prices, salaries, and hourly wages.

NOTE   Currency values are initially displayed with the currency symbol selected in the Windows Control Panel. You can change to another symbol, if you wish, using methods described in Chapter 6.

Date   These fields are used to store dates. Paradox automatically validates any entry, rejecting a date like 06/31/92 (June has only 30 days). This field type allows for date arithmetic, where you can calculate the number of days between two dates, add or subtract days from a date, and so forth. Examples of uses include hiring dates, billing dates, due dates, etc.

OLE   Object linking and embedding (OLE) fields contain objects that are placed in your table from other Windows 3.1 applications that support OLE as the server. Examples include spreadsheet cells, entire spreadsheets, written documents from a word processor, pictures, charts, animations, and sounds.

TIP   Paradox for Windows acts as an OLE *client* only. You can't use Paradox as a *server* application for OLE. We'll describe OLE in more detail in a moment.

Graphic   These fields can contain pictures that cannot be linked to another application via OLE. Examples include clip art, personal art work, scanned photos, video frames, screen captures, and charts.

Binary   This field type lets you store data that does not fit into any other field type in a Paradox for Windows table. For example, a binary field could be used to store instructions for producing a sound. The binary field type should only be used by advanced programmers, since displaying or interpreting the contents of the field requires knowledge of programming. Example of use: A sound file that can only be played using a non-Windows application or an application that does not support OLE.

Referring back to our sample CustList table, you might jot down the field types shown in Figure 4.2. (We've abbreviated "Alphanumeric" as "Alpha" to save a little space.)

You may be thinking, "Wait a minute—you just said that the number field type is for numbers. Yet you made Zip Code and Phone alphanumeric fields." The reason for making these fields alphanumeric is that neither zip codes nor phone numbers are true numbers (that is, they don't represent

FIGURE 4.2

Field types assigned to each of the fields sketched out for our sample CustList table

	Field Name	Type
1	Last Name	Alpha
2	Mr/Mrs	Alpha
3	First Name	Alpha
4	M.I.	Alpha
5	Department/Title	Alpha
6	Company	Alpha
7	Address	Alpha
8	City	Alpha
9	State	Alpha
10	Zip Code	Alpha
11	Area Code	Number
12	Phone	Alpha
13	Extension	Alpha
14	Credit Limit	$ (Currency)
15	Start Date	Date

quantities or numeric values). Defining either of these as numbers would prevent us from putting letters, leading zeros, and most punctuation into the entries.

For example, if you defined Zip Code as a number field, you would not be able to store a hyphenated zip code like 92067-3384, or a foreign post code like MJ3 OH4, or a zip code with a leading zero like 01234 in that field. Nor could you store phone numbers in a hyphenated format, as in 555-1212.

Planning Alphanumeric Field Sizes

If your table contains any alphanumeric fields, you need to decide how much space each of those fields is likely to require. You don't want to shortchange yourself when making these decisions. For example, if you allot ten characters to the Last Name field, you wouldn't be able to store a long last name like *Livingston-Gladstone* in your table, since that requires 20 characters.

On the other hand, you wouldn't want to allot 100 characters per last name, since nobody's last name is that long. You'd just be wasting disk space if you gave that much space to every last name in the table.

A reasonable length for each of the alphanumeric fields in the sample CustList table is suggested in Figure 4.3. Fields without sizes assigned to them are field types that don't require you to assign a size.

If you plan to store links to values in files created by DDE server applications, your alphanumeric field should be long enough to store the full path name of the file you're linking to, plus about 25 characters.

Planning Memo and Formatted Memo Field Sizes

If you define a memo field in your table, you will need to give that field a length within the range of 1 to 240 characters. If you define a formatted memo field, you can give it a length of anywhere from 0 to 240 characters. It's important to remember, however, that Paradox actually stores the

FIGURE 4.3

Field sizes assigned to alphanumeric fields in the sample CustList table

	Field Name	Type	Size
1	Last Name	Alpha	20
2	Mr/Mrs	Alpha	4
3	First Name	Alpha	20
4	M.I.	Alpha	2
5	Department/Title	Alpha	25
6	Company	Alpha	25
7	Address	Alpha	25
8	City	Alpha	20
9	State	Alpha	2
10	Zip Code	Alpha	10
11	Area Code	Number	
12	Phone	Alpha	8
13	Extension	Alpha	5
14	Credit Limit	Currency	
15	Start Date	Date	

contents of the memo outside the table. Therefore, your memo field can contain any amount of text, regardless of the size you assign to the field.

Assigning a size to the memo field determines how much of the field is stored in the table. For example, if you give a memo field a length of 25, the first 25 characters of the actual memo will be stored in the table. However, you can still store and display text of any length within that field.

NOTE Entering and editing memo data will be discussed in Chapter 5.

For starters, perhaps your best bet would be to assign a length of 1 to your memo and formatted memo fields. Later, after you gain some experience in using those fields, you can go back and increase the sizes if you so desire.

When to Use the OLE, Graphic, and Binary Field Types

The OLE, graphic, and binary field types can be used to store pictures and sounds in a table. OLE (object linking and embedding) is a feature of Windows 3.1 that allows multiple applications to share data. If you're not familiar with OLE, perhaps you'll want to learn more about it from your Windows documentation before making decisions about whether or not to use this field type. Some points to keep in mind when considering field types for pictures, sounds, and even lengthy bodies of text are described in the sections that follow.

What Can Go into an OLE Field?

An OLE field can contain any type of information. However, that information must come from a Windows 3.1 application that acts as an OLE server. For instance, the Windows 3.1 Paintbrush and Sound Recorder accessories are server applications, as is Microsoft Excel.

The only sure way to find out whether or not a Windows application is an OLE server is to check the documentation for that application.

Storing Pictures and Sound

If you want to store a picture in a field, your best bet might be to define the field type as OLE rather than graphic. Doing so provides an instant link to the application used to create the picture (for example, Paintbrush for a bitmap image, or Excel for a chart). OLE makes it possible to edit the picture on the fly while viewing it in Paradox for Windows. You can view and print the picture just as though it were stored in the graphic field type, so there really is no disadvantage to using the OLE field type rather than the graphic field type to store pictures.

The only reason to use a graphic field type rather than an OLE field type for storing pictures is when there's no way to bring the picture into an application that acts as an OLE server. For instance, if you want to store GIF

(Graphic Information File) images in a field, and you don't have any applications that act as an OLE server for GIF files, you'll need to store those images in a graphic field.

On the other hand, if the graphics you want to store are in bitmap (.bmp), device independent bitmap (.dib), Microsoft Paint (.msp), or early Paintbrush (.pcx) formats, or some other format that can be pasted into Paintbrush, such as Tagged Image File Format (.tif), Windows MetaFile (.wmf), or WordPerfect Graphic (.wpg), you can use the OLE data type. You may, however, need to bring the image into Paintbrush before putting it into the OLE field. We'll discuss this in more detail in the next chapter.

If you want to store sound (a .wav file) in a field, and want to be able to hear the sound simply by double-clicking the field when it's visible on the screen, define the field type as OLE.

NOTE   You can only record and play back sounds on a computer that's equipped with appropriate hardware, such as a sound card.

Our sample CustList table didn't require any of these fancy field types. But let's say you're designing a database for a modeling agency and you want to store the name and address of each model, as well as a résumé, photo, and voice sample, in a table. Figure 4.4 shows how you might structure that table.

Figure 4.5 shows a sample record from this table displayed on the screen using a custom form. The Résumé field shows only part of the résumé in this example. Double-clicking on it expands the field to show more of the résumé, which can contain any amount of text. The small microphone icon represents a sound (a recorded voice in this example). Double-clicking the microphone icon plays back the model's voice.

We'll get into the details of putting memos, pictures, and sound into these field types in the next chapter. For now, let's look at a couple of other possibilities for OLE.

FIGURE 4.4

Sample table that a modeling agency might use to store name and address, résumé, photo, and voice sample of each model

	Field Name	Type	Size
1	Last Name	Alpha	20
2	First Name	Alpha	20
3	Address	Alpha	35
4	City	Alpha	20
5	State	Alpha	2
6	Zip Code	Alpha	10
7	Phone	Alpha	13
8	Resume	Formatted Memo	1
9	Photo	OLE	1
10	Voice	OLE	1

FIGURE 4.5

A sample custom form showing data in alphanumeric, formatted memo, and OLE fields

Using OLE to Store Text and Numbers

You can also use the OLE field type to store text and numbers from external applications in a Paradox for Windows table. For instance, suppose you keep salary data in a Quattro Pro or Excel spreadsheet. If you create a field named *Salary* in a Paradox table, and then give it the OLE field type, you can paste numbers from the spreadsheet into the Paradox table.

The hefty disadvantage of storing numbers in OLE fields is that you won't have as much flexibility in formatting and querying those numbers as you would if you stored them in number or currency fields. In fact, if you need to perform any math whatsoever on the numbers in your Paradox table, you're better off defining that field as one of the numeric field types rather than as an OLE field.

You can use the OLE field type as an alternative to the memo or formatted memo field types to store lengthy bodies of text in a Paradox table. For instance, suppose you run an employment service, and you have created a table to keep track of clients' names, addresses, skills, and résumés.

If you want to be able to print and edit those résumés with a word processing program, such as Microsoft Word for Windows (Version 2.0), you can define the field for storing résumés as OLE. Then, you can paste résumés from Microsoft Word into the Paradox table as needed. If you want to edit a résumé, just double-click its field and you'll be taken to Microsoft Word with the résumé on the screen ready for editing.

NOTE   An OLE field can only store text from applications that support OLE.

The disadvantage of using an external word processor to create and edit lengthy text fields is that you cannot see or print text in that field while you're in Paradox. Instead, only an icon for the application used to create the text will be displayed. Thus, you should only use OLE to store lengthy bodies of text that you need to access only occasionally. Under most circumstances, you'll want to use the formatted memo or memo field type to store lengthy text in your Paradox tables.

In a moment, we'll take a look at how these field types might look in a Paradox table. But first, lets discuss DDE links.

When to Use DDE Links

DDE is a Windows feature that, like OLE, allows you to exchange and update data in another application. Although DDE and OLE can be used for similar purposes, there are some important differences between them. Understanding these differences will help you decide when DDE links might be appropriate.

One important difference is that DDE links always point to original, "live" data. Therefore, whether you edit the data in another application or in Paradox, your changes are made to the *original* data. When you use OLE, you're actually embedding a *copy* of the original data file; changes made in Paradox will *not* be reflected in the original file.

Another difference is that you can use DDE to pass data either from another DDE-capable application to Paradox, *or* from Paradox to another DDE-capable application. In contrast, OLE can be used to pass data in one direction only—from an OLE server application to Paradox. For example, you can use OLE or DDE to copy or link data from an Excel spreadsheet to a Paradox table. However, only DDE can be used to link data from a Paradox table field into a cell of a spreadsheet.

We mentioned earlier that OLE can be used to store just about any type of data in an *OLE field* of a Paradox table. DDE, however, is limited to linking text and numeric values from another application into an *alphanumeric field*. For this reason, DDE is most often used to exchange data stored in selected cells of a spreadsheet or fields of a table.

NOTE   As with OLE data, DDE links cannot be used to perform math calculations.

If you use both OLE and DDE, you'll quickly notice that OLE fields and alphanumeric fields containing DDE links look very different from one other (see Figure 4.6). For instance, after pasting data into an OLE field, you'll see an icon (or sometimes a picture), which represents the embedded data file. After using DDE to link data into an alphanumeric field, you'll see only a pointer, or *reference*, to the data.

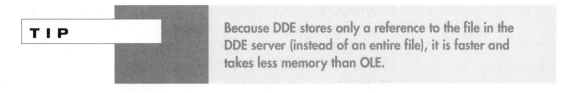

TIP

Because DDE stores only a reference to the file in the DDE server (instead of an entire file), it is faster and takes less memory than OLE.

Figure 4.6 shows a sample Paradox for Windows table with text in a memo, formatted memo, and OLE field, and with a DDE link in an alphanumeric field. Here's a description of each field:

> **Memo field**   The first column shows a sample memo field. Text can be any length, but no formatting is permitted.

FIGURE 4.6

A single record of a Paradox table with a memo field, a formatted memo field, and an OLE field containing text from a Word for Windows document. Because Paradox cannot display text from Word for Windows, only the icon for that application appears in the table. The alphanumeric field contains a DDE link to an Excel spreadsheet.

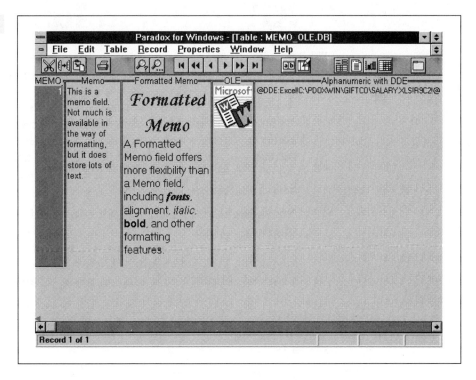

Formatted memo field   The second column shows text in a formatted memo field. Text can be any length and can use different fonts, alignment (centering, for example), and styles such as **boldface** and *italic*.

Lengthy Text in OLE field   The third column contains a Word for Windows document stored in an OLE field. Since Paradox cannot display a document created in another application, only the icon for that application appears.

Alphanumeric with DDE   The fourth column contains a DDE link to a Microsoft Excel spreadsheet. The link reference in the field specifies the name of the application (Excel), the file name (*c:\pdoxwin\giftco\salary.xls*), and the cell (row 2, column2) containing the linked data.

What NOT to Put in Tables

While you're designing your *field roster* (the names and types of fields that define the table's structure), try to follow the guidelines below.

- **Avoid creating fields to store the results of calculations.** Putting such fields in a table wastes disk space and increases the likelihood of errors since you'll have to do all the calculations yourself. Instead, you need only define fields for the raw data, then let Paradox do all the calculations. We'll talk more about calculated fields in Chapters 16 and 18.

- **Never include a field that will contain the same information in every record.** Suppose you're storing names and addresses for customers and you plan to print form letters with your company's logo at the top of each letter. There's no need to include a field for a copy of your logo with each customer's name and address. As you'll see, you can just add your company logo to the top of the form letter design (once) when it comes time to print the letters.

- **Include only fields that are directly relevant to the table you're designing.** Don't try to throw the whole kitchen sink into one table. For instance, in CustList, there's one address, city, state, zip code, and phone number for every name—a perfect one-to-one correspondence between fields. Don't put anything into the table that isn't directly relevant to customers. We'll get into this topic in more depth in Chapter 15.

- **Don't exclude fields for information you'll need.** You certainly don't want to exclude any fields that would hold information you might need later. For instance, our CustList table is sufficient for names and addresses within the United States. But if your customer list contains people outside the United States, you'll need to include a field for the country name. Also, you'll need to widen the State field to avoid limiting yourself to two-letter abbreviations.

Figure 4.7 shows an "internationalized" version of our sample CustList table that can store both U.S. and non-U.S. names and addresses.

FIGURE 4.7

A modified version of the CustList table, which can store both U.S. and foreign names and addresses

	Field Name	Type	Size
1	Last Name	Alpha	20
2	Mr/Mrs	Alpha	4
3	First Name	Alpha	20
4	M.I.	Alpha	2
5	Department/Title	Alpha	25
6	Company	Alpha	25
7	Address	Alpha	25
8	City	Alpha	20
9	State/Province	Alpha	20
10	Zip/Postal Code	Alpha	10
11	Country	Alpha	15
12	Area Code	Number	
13	Phone	Alpha	8
14	Extension	Alpha	5
15	Credit Limit	Currency	
16	Start Date	Date	

Table Structure Limitations

Paradox for Windows offers a lot of leeway in designing tables; but there are a few limitations that you need to be aware of if you're planning to design very large tables.

- A single record can contain a maximum of 255 fields.

- A single record can contain a maximum of 4000 characters, excluding memo and formatted memo fields, which can contain any number of characters. Indexed tables (described in a moment) can contain a maximum of 1350 characters per record.

- A single table can contain a maximum of 2 billion records or 262 million characters (262MB), whichever comes first.

NOTE   If you typed five characters per second for 40 hours each week, non-stop, it would take you about 7 years to reach the maximum 262 million character limit of one Paradox table!

Since you can link up to 24 tables in a single query, the real limitation of a database (that is, all the tables within a single database) is about 24 times the limitation of a single table. Joining tables will be discussed later in this book.

Once you've defined the field names, types, and sizes for your table, you *could* go online and create the table in Paradox for Windows. On the other hand, there are some optional enhancements you might want to add to your table design, as described next.

Planning Keys to Manage Data Efficiently

A primary key (usually just called a *key*) is a field or group of fields containing data that uniquely identifies each record of a table. When a primary key is defined for a table, values in the primary key fields of each record must be unique, and duplicate records are not allowed. Although primary keys are entirely optional, they can be great time savers in the long run because they help Paradox manage data more efficiently.

NOTE   Tables that have primary keys are called *keyed tables*. dBASE tables do not use keys.

In many ways, keys are analogous to street addresses. Just as no two buildings in a city can have the same street address, no two records in your table can have the same values in their key fields. And, just as unique street addresses help the mail carrier locate your home more quickly, keys provide an extremely efficient means of locating records in your table.

Keys also establish the default sort order for the table. Whenever you add a new record to the table, Paradox automatically places that record in sorted order, based on the value of the key field or fields.

Paradox for Windows stores each table's primary key in a special *index* file, called the *primary index*. The primary index contains the primary key values and corresponding record numbers. Paradox uses the index file to locate and display the records in a table.

If you've defined a primary key for a table, you can also define additional indexes called *secondary indexes*. These are used on an as-needed basis to speed queries and display data with a different sort order. Although primary index values must be unique for each record, the values in secondary indexes are not restricted in this way.

In this chapter, we'll focus on the primary index, since this is the only index that you must define while designing the structure of a table. We'll explain how to create secondary indexes in Chapter 7.

Planning the Primary Index

Keep in mind that the primary index plays three important roles in Paradox for Windows:

- Paradox ensures that no two records in a table have the same information in the primary key. This prevents you from making duplicate entries by inadvertently putting the same information into a table twice.

- Paradox uses the primary index, as appropriate, to speed up searches and other operations.

- Paradox uses the primary index to maintain an ongoing sort order based on the field or fields that define the primary key. This saves the time required to re-sort the table whenever new records are added.

N O T E   Paradox offers other ways to sort (alphabetize) records, which you'll learn about in Chapter 7.

To define a primary key for a table, you place an asterisk next to the field type in the table structure. When planning your table on paper, follow suit by jotting down an asterisk next to the field or fields that make up the primary key.

There are, of course, a few rules to keep in mind when planning the primary index:

- All the fields marked with an asterisk (*) in the table structure make up the *primary key*. (A primary key that's composed of more than one field is sometimes called a *composite key*.)

- The primary key must be the first field in the table. If you're defining a composite key, the field must be grouped together at the top of the table structure. Examples will be presented shortly.

- No two records in a table can contain the same primary key values. If you use multiple fields to define the primary key, only records that have indentical data in *all* the primary key fields are considered duplicates.

N O T E

Only one record's key can be blank. Paradox will consider all subsequent blanks to be duplicates and will not accept records that contain them.

- Paradox automatically sorts the table based on the primary key. The first field defines the main sort order, the second field defines the secondary ("tie-breaker") sort order, and so forth.

This last item is an important one because it defines the order in which records will appear in your table. For instance, let's suppose you make Last Name and First Name the first two fields in your table structure, and you mark them each with an asterisk, like this:

	FIELD NAME	TYPE	SIZE	KEY
1	Last Name	Alpha	20	★
2	First Name	Alpha	20	★
3	Mr/Mrs	Alpha	4	
4	etc.			

Because the Last Name field comes before the First Name field in the table structure, records will be alphabetized by Last Name, then by first name in the case of identical last names. Thus, regardless of the order in which you *type* the following records into the table, Paradox will always *display* those records in the order shown below.

LAST NAME	FIRST NAME
Adams	Zeke
Smith	Arlene
Smith	Bob

LAST NAME	FIRST NAME
Smith	Roger
Zeppo	Bob

Notice how the records are alphabetized by Last Name, then by First Name when the last names are identical (for example, Arlene Smith comes before Bob Smith).

Now let's suppose you put the First Name field *above* the Last Name field in the table structure, and again mark both fields with an asterisk, like this:

	FIELD NAME	TYPE	SIZE	KEY
1	First Name	Alpha	20	★
2	Last Name	Alpha	20	★
3	Mr/Mrs	Alpha	4	
4	etc.			

This tells Paradox that you want to alphabetize records by First Name, and then by Last Name in the case of identical first names. You can see the result below.

FIRST NAME	LAST NAME
Arlene	Smith
Bob	Smith
Bob	Zeppo
Roger	Smith
Zeke	Adams

Here records are alphabetized by First Name, with the Last Name field acting as the tie-breaker. That is, when the First Names are identical, names are alphabetized by Last Name (Bob Smith comes before Bob Zeppo).

Obviously, this latter sort order is not the customary way to alphabetize people's names. The example illustrates the importance of the order in which you list key fields at the top of the table structure.

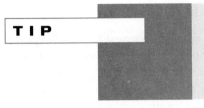

If you're still a little fuzzy on the concept of sorting or the role played by a "tie-breaker," see "Sorts within Sorts," in Chapter 7, for more information and examples.

Now let's look at some different ways that you could define a primary key in a table like our CustList example.

Using Existing Fields for the Primary Key

Always keep in mind that the primary key plays the dual role of maintaining a sort order *and* preventing duplicate entries. Thus, if you wanted to keep the records in CustList in alphabetical order by Last Name and First Name, as described above, you could simply move the Last Name and First Name fields to the top of the table structure and mark them both with an asterisk, as we did earlier.

You cannot mark a memo, formatted memo, OLE, graphic, or binary field as a primary key.

While this technique *would* keep records sorted by Last Name and by First Name within common last names, it might also present a problem. Any two records with the same entry in the Last Name and First Name fields would be considered duplicates, and Paradox would reject the newer of the two records. Thus, you could not add a record for John Smith in Omaha if the table already contained a record for John Smith in Honolulu.

Therefore, you need to think about what does, and what does not, constitute a duplicate entry. In this particular example, we might decide that any two records that have the same entries in the Last Name, First Name, Middle Initial, Zip Code, and Address fields are very likely to be duplicate entries.

If you want to keep records alphabetized by name, and only reject a new record if it has the same name, zip code, and address as some other record, you'd need to arrange and key the fields as in Figure 4.8.

There is one slight disadvantage to the primary key definition in Figure 4.8. The combined length of the keyed fields, 77 characters, makes for a fairly large key. As the table grows and the index grows in proportion, Paradox may not be able to fit the entire index into memory. Therefore, it will need to keep portions of the index on disk, which, in turn, will slow down processing somewhat as the table grows.

Using a Single Field as the Primary Key

If you're more concerned about preventing duplicate entries and getting quick access to information than you are about keeping names alphabetized, and you want to keep the primary key small, you might want to consider using a single field that uniquely identifies each record as the primary index.

Many businesses use customer phone numbers as a primary key. For instance, when I call to order a pizza, the guy on the other end of the phone always asks me for my phone number since this is the key field that uniquely identifies me in his database. If all your customers are local (within one area code), you could follow suit and define the Phone field as the primary key, like this:

	FIELD NAME	TYPE	SIZE	KEY
1	Phone	Alpha	8	★
2	Last Name	Alpha	20	

FIGURE 4.8

Defining Last Name, First Name, Middle Initial, Address, and Zip Code as the primary key keeps records sorted into alphabetical order by name.

	Field Name	Type	Size	Key
1	Last Name	Alpha	20	*
2	First Name	Alpha	20	*
3	M.I.	Alpha	2	*
4	Zip Code	Alpha	10	*
5	Address	Alpha	25	*
6	Mr/Mrs	Alpha	4	
7	Company	Alpha	25	
6	etc...			

	FIELD NAME	TYPE	SIZE	KEY
3	Mr/Mrs	Alpha	4	
4	First Name	Alpha	20	
5	etc.			

If your table includes customers from several area codes, you'd need to include the area code as part of the primary key, since any two customers might have the same phone number but different area codes. In that case, you'd need to arrange and mark the fields like this:

	FIELD NAME	TYPE	SIZE	KEY
1	Area Code	Number		★
2	Phone	Alpha	8	★
3	Last Name	Alpha	20	
4	Mr/Mrs	Alpha	4	
5	First Name	Alpha	20	
6	etc.			

Either way, the beauty of using the phone number as the primary key is that you can find all the information you need about a customer simply by typing in the customer's phone number, like my pizza guy does.

Of course, this primary key means that records will always be sorted by phone number. But, as you'll see, if you need to re-sort the records into alphabetical order by name in order to print a customer list, or into zip code order for bulk mailing, you can do so quite easily at any time.

Creating a Field for the Primary Key

A third option for defining a primary key is to create a new field that uniquely identifies each record in the table. This method is handy when there is no field, or even a combination of fields, in the table that is guaranteed to identify each record uniquely.

Many businesses do things this way, which explains why you have a social security number and umpteen different bank, credit card, and other account numbers. Those numbers uniquely identify you, or your accounts, on somebody's database.

Even the phone number, which might be a handy way for a small business to identify customers in a local community, is not a sure-fire way of identifying customers correctly. After all, people move and change their phone numbers all the time.

Going back to our CustList example, if your table is going to be large, and you plan to keep customers around for a long time, you might want to assign each customer his or her own unique identifying number by creating a new field, perhaps named *Customer Number* (or *Cust No* for short). You'd want to make sure this new Cust No field is the first one in the table structure, and then mark it as the primary key, as shown in Figure 4.9.

As you can see, there are no hard-and-fast rules for choosing the "best" fields for a primary key. It all depends on what fields are in the table and

FIGURE 4.9

A new field, named *Cust No*, added to the CustList table. Each customer will need to have a unique customer identification number in this field, since it's the primary key.

	Field Name	Type	Size	Key
1	Cust No	Number		*
2	Last Name	Alpha	20	
3	Mr/Mrs	Alpha	4	
4	First Name	Alpha	20	
5	M.I.	Alpha	2	
6	Department/Title	Alpha	25	
7	Company	Alpha	25	
8	Address	Alpha	25	
9	City	Alpha	20	
10	State	Alpha	2	
11	Zip Code	Alpha	10	
12	Area Code	Number		
13	Phone	Alpha	8	
14	Extension	Alpha	5	
15	Credit Limit	Currency		
16	Start Date	Date		

how you'll be using the table. You'll see additional examples of primary keys in upcoming chapters.

For now, let's turn our attention away from keys and look at another feature you can build into your table structure—validity checks.

Planning Validity Checks

One of the oldest acronyms in the computer world is GIGO, which stands for Garbage In, Garbage Out. In database management terms, this means that if you put meaningless information into the database, you will get meaningless information right back when printing data later.

The most common cause of entering meaningless information into a table is simply not paying attention to the screen while typing. For instance, a data-entry person might type a zip code into a Last Name field, or an account number into a credit limit field, simply because he or she is not watching the screen while typing.

Validity checks help minimize such errors by checking the data *before* it's accepted into the table. While validity checks can't prevent every imaginable error, they can certainly reduce the likelihood of errors occurring. Validity checks can also speed your data entry efforts by automatically filling in all, or part, of certain fields. Paradox for Windows offers the validity checking options summarized in Table 4.1. Each option is described in more detail in the sections that follow.

Planning a Required Field

If you want to ensure that one or more fields in the table are not left blank in any record, you can make it a *required* field. For example, you might want to make the Cust No field in the CustList table shown in Figure 4.9 a required field to ensure that each customer is assigned a customer number.

N O T E   At least one field in any table must *not* be defined as Required.

TABLE 4.1: Summary of Paradox Validity Checks

VALIDITY CHECK	PURPOSE
Required Field	The field cannot be left blank.
Minimum	The value entered into the field must be greater than or equal to the specified minimum value.
Maximum	The value entered into the field must be less than or equal to the specified maximum value.
Default	The specified value is placed into the field automatically when entering records, but can be changed if necessary.
Picture	Provides a template for the format of data entered into the field, limits entry to letters or numbers, and can also insert repetitive text automatically.

Planning Minimum and Maximum Entries

You can define a minimum or maximum value for any alphanumeric, number, short number, currency, or date field in your table. You can also specify a *range* of acceptable values by defining both a minimum and a maximum value for any of these field types. For example, you could specify that the Credit Limit field accept no value less than zero, nor greater than 10,000.

Planning a Default Value

A *default value* is a value that appears automatically in a field while you're entering data into the table. A default is only a *suggested* value which you can change whenever you want.

Suppose the sample CustList table we've been describing thus far is for a business in California, and the vast majority of customers are California residents. You might want to make CA the default value for the State field. When entering data into the table later, CA would automatically appear as the entry for the State field. You could either leave that entry as it is or change it to the abbreviation for another state.

Similarly, you could make TODAY the default value for the Start Date field, so that the current date is automatically placed in that field when you're entering new records.

N O T E   The command TODAY is a special validity check that can be used only in a date field to define the current date as the default entry for that field.

Planning a Picture Template

A picture lets you define a format, or *template,* for the contents of a field. The template limits the type of data you can enter into a field and can also type certain characters into the field for you automatically. The special characters used to define a picture are summarized in Table 4.2.

Any character other than one of the symbols listed in Table 4.2 is a *constant* (also called a *literal*). Constants are interpreted as text to be inserted into a field.

As an example picture template, you could define the picture for a field named *Social Security No* as ###-##-####. The # symbol ensures that only numeric digits will be allowed into the field. Since hyphens (-) are not one of the symbols in Table 4.2, typing 123456789 into the Social Security No field would result in 123-45-6789 because Paradox would automatically insert these constants. With this picture template, it would be impossible to omit a number or type a letter in place of a number since the picture requires nine numeric digits.

Another handy template might be #####[-####] used in a Zip Code field. The # symbols would allow only numeric characters into the field. The square brackets after the first five digits indicate that the rest of the

TABLE 4.2: Symbols Used in Picture Formats

SYMBOL	ACCEPTS
#	Numeric digits (0–9, comma, hyphen)
?	Any letter A–Z or a–z
&	Any letter, but automatically converts it to uppercase
@	Any character
!	Any character, but converts a letter to uppercase
*	The symbol that follows can be repeated any number of times
;	Interprets the symbol that follows as a literal character, not as a picture character
[]	Optional entry
{}	Specifies a group of acceptable entries
,	Separates acceptable values within a group

entry is optional. The hyphen would be inserted automatically before a sixth character was typed. Therefore, this template would accept both five-digit zip codes, like 91234, and nine-digit zip codes, like 91234-4321.

TIP

You *wouldn't* use a template like #####[-####] if you wanted your table to accept foreign zip codes with letters. The # symbol will accept only numbers.

You can do some pretty complicated things with picture templates, if you're so inclined. For instance, if you want to use a symbol as a literal character in a field, precede the symbol with a semicolon. Suppose you have an inventory system that uses the # symbol in part codes, for example, as in the part number ABC-#1234. If you tried using the picture &&&-#@@@@, then an entry such as ABC-1234 would be considered incomplete because Paradox interprets -#@@@@ as requiring five characters to the right of the hyphen. However, if you define the picture as

&&&-;#@@@@, Paradox knows that the # symbol is to be placed into the entry as a constant. So, when you typed in ABC-1234 Paradox would convert that entry to ABC-#1234.

You can also use a picture template to convert the case of letters. For example, the picture template &*? allows an entry of any length and converts the first letter to uppercase. Thus, if you define the picture template for the Last Name field as &*?, you can type *smith* as the contents of that field and Paradox will automatically convert that entry to *Smith*. The picture template !*? also allows an entry of any length and converts the first letter to uppercase. However, unlike the picture &*?, which requires the first character to be a letter, the !*? picture would let you enter a number or other symbol as the first character.

The curly brace symbols let you define a group of acceptable values for a field. When typing an entry into a field with a picture that includes curly braces, you need only type the first letter of any valid entry. Paradox will then fill in the rest of the field for you.

TIP When you go online to create your table, you can use an "Assist" button to help you create picture templates.

To illustrate, suppose your table contains an alphanumeric field named *Taxable*, which you want to fill with **Yes** for taxable items and **No** for nontaxable items. You could assign the picture template {Yes,No} to that field. Later, when entering data into that table, typing the letter **Y** would fill in the field with **Yes**; typing **N** would fill in **No**. Any other entry would be unacceptable. If you wanted the Taxable field to contain either of the single characters **Y** or **N**, you'd define the picture as {Y,N} rather than {Yes,No}.

The pictures that support alternative choices can be *nested*—that is, placed inside one another—to allow multiple choices with the same first letter. You need to nest options whenever two or more options in the list start with the same letter.

For instance, take a look at this picture:

{Mon,Tue,Wed,Thu,Fri}

When entering data into a field with this picture, typing the letter **T** would automatically fill in the field as **Tue** because **Tue** comes before **Thu** in the list of alternatives.

To provide the options **ue** and **hu** within the common **T** entry, nest these choices within the **T** entry, like this:

{Mon,T{ue,hu},Wed,Fri}

Translated into English, the above picture reads, "Accept **M**, **T**, **W**, or **F** entries. If a **T** is entered, accept either **u** or **h** before filling in the rest of the field."

TIP

To define a large list of acceptable entries, such as two-letter state abbreviations or valid part numbers from an inventory table, you can use the Table Lookup validity check described in the next chapter.

Notice that the above example has as many open curly braces as closed curly braces. When entering your own pictures, make sure that yours also have an equal number of open and closed braces.

Curly braces can also be used to force entry of a particular character instead of filling in that character automatically. For example, if you use the template ###-##-#### for a Social Security field, Paradox will automatically fill in the two hyphens when you enter the number. If you prefer to type in the hyphens yourself (but still want Paradox to reject any other character), you can enter the picture in the format ###{-}##{-}####. In a sense, {-} means, "The only option allowed here is a hyphen."

WARNING

When creating picture templates of your own, to avoid using symbols that conflict with the field type. For example, you would not want to use the ? or @ symbol in a number or currency field since these symbols require alphabetic characters and number and currency fields allow only numbers!

Figure 4.10 shows some sample validity checks jotted down on the scratchpad structure of the sample CustList table. Notice that we've decided on Cust No as the primary key that uniquely identifies each customer. We've also made Cust No a required field, so that the field is never left blank. Finally, by assigning the picture #### to the field, we've made sure that each ID number is exactly four digits long.

TIP

If you want to prevent customers from being assigned awkward customer numbers like 6 or 42, you can define a minimum validity check of 1001. Then you can assign customer numbers starting at 1001, followed by 1002, 1003, and so forth.

The #### template will limit the number of customers that can be put in the table since the largest number that fits the pattern is 9999. If we needed to allow for more customers, we could just increase the picture to #####, which can accept any number up to 99,999.

FIGURE 4.10

Sample validity checks for the CustList table jotted down on our scratchpad table design

	Field Name	Type	Size	Key	Validity Check
1	Cust No	Number		*	Required, ####
2	Last Name	Alpha	20		
3	Mr/Mrs	Alpha	4		
4	First Name	Alpha	20		
5	M.I.	Alpha	2		
6	Department/Title	Alpha	25		
7	Company	Alpha	25		
8	Address	Alpha	25		Required
9	City	Alpha	20		
10	State	Alpha	2		!!
11	Zip Code	Alpha	10		#####[-####]
12	Area Code	Number			###
13	Phone	Alpha	8		###-####
14	Extension	Alpha	5		
15	Credit Limit	Currency			$0.00 to $10,0000
16	Start Date	Date			Default=TODAY

In Figure 4.10 we've also made Address a required field and devised picture templates to help verify the area code, phone number, and zip code entries and to convert any two-letter state abbreviations to uppercase letters. We've also limited the entry in the Credit Limit field to a number between 0 and $10,000, and made the current date (TODAY) the default in the Start Date field.

The examples given here should be food for thought as you think about creating your own validity checks. Of course, you can always try working without the validity checks for a while. If you find that errors are being made consistently during data entry, you can then go back to the table structure and devise validity checks to help minimize those errors.

Creating a Table

When you're done planning your table and you have an idea of the fields the table will require, you can fire up Paradox for Windows and create the table online. Don't forget that you want to keep all the tables and other objects that belong together in a single directory. If you haven't already created the directory, you should do so first thing, using the Windows File Manager, as in the example presented in Lesson 1. Then, follow the steps below to create your table.

N O T E

If you want several network users to share data in a table, you must create the table in a shared directory. See Appendix E for more information on networks.

1. If you haven't already done so, choose File ➤ Working Directory. Then switch to the directory where you want to store the new table.

2. Choose File ➤ New ➤ Table, or inspect (right-click) the Open Table button on the SpeedBar, and choose New from the menu that appears. You'll see the **Table Type** dialog box shown below.

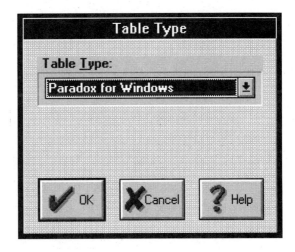

3. Assuming you want to use the standard Paradox format, choose OK to select the suggested table type, Paradox for Windows. You'll see the **Create Table** dialog box shown in Figure 4.11.

NOTE

You can define tables in a variety of formats. The format of the table you're creating (e.g., Paradox for Windows) always appears in the title bar of the Create Table dialog box. Non-Paradox formats are covered in Appendix C.

4. Type a field name, then press Tab or ↵, or click the Type column to move the highlight into the Type column.

NOTE

The Borrow button lets you use the structure of some other table as the starting point for the table you're about to create. (You can borrow a table structure only when the field roster is empty.)

FIGURE 4.11

Use the Create Table
dialog box to define
the structure of a new
table.

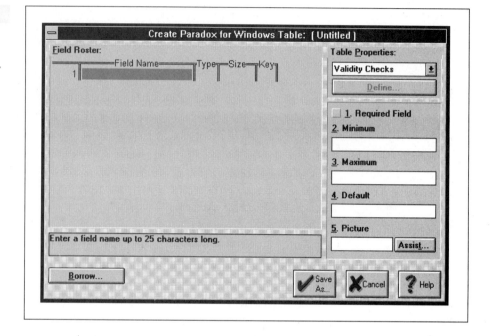

5. When the highlight is in the Type column, use any one of the following techniques to define the field type:

   • Click the right mouse button or press the spacebar to view a menu of field types (shown below). Then choose the field type you want from the menu that appears.

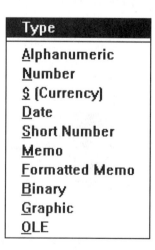

- Type the one-letter abbreviation for the field type (the underlined letter or character in the menu at left).

TIP   While defining your table structure, check the message bar below the field names for guidelines on entering information into each column.

6. If you chose a field type of number, $, date, or short number, skip directly to Step 8. If you chose another field type, press Tab or ↵ or click in the Size column.

7. If you've defined the current field as alphanumeric or memo, type in a size. If you've defined the field as formatted memo, binary, graphic, or OLE, you can either type in a size or leave the Size entry blank. If you're not sure yet what size will best suit your needs, enter 1 as the size (you can change it later, if necessary).

8. Press Tab or ↵, or click the Key Field column. If you want to make the field a primary key field, double-click or press the spacebar. An asterisk (*) appears in the column. Remember, the fields you define as the primary key must be grouped together at the top of the table structure.

9. Press ↵, Tab, or ↓ to move down to the next row.

10. Repeat Steps 4-9 until you've defined all the fields for your table. If you need to make changes or corrections along the way, use any of the techniques listed in Table 4.3.

Figure 4.12 shows how the sample CustList customer table would look after you entered the first 13 field names, types, and sizes. (If you want to duplicate that table structure exactly, refer to Figure 4.10 for field types and sizes of additional fields in the table.)

When you've finished typing the field names, types, and sizes (as appropriate), you can either save the table and start using it right away or, if you want to define validity checks, you can do so as explained in the next section.

TABLE 4.3: Techinques for Making Changes and Corrections while Defining a Table Structure

IF YOU WANT TO...	DO THIS...
Delete a column entry	Click where you want to start deleting, and use the **Backspace** or **Delete** key to delete characters. Or, select text by dragging the mouse pointer through the text, then press the Delete key. To delete all the characters in the entry, press **Ctrl+Backspace**.
Delete entire field	Move the highlight to the field you want to delete, then press **Ctrl+Delete**.
Insert new field	To insert a new field between two existing fields, move the highlight to the lower of the two existing fields and press **Insert**.
Change field name	Click wherever you want to start changing text. Type new text, or use **Backspace** or **Delete** to delete existing text. Or, select text by dragging the mouse pointer through the text, then type the replacement text. To replace all the characters in the entry, press **Ctrl+Backspace**, then type the replacement characters.
Move field	Click the row number in the leftmost column of the field you want to move. Hold down the mouse button, drag the field definition to its new location, and release the mouse button.
Start over from scratch	Choose Cancel to abandon current table structure.
Select/deselect primary key	Move the highlight to the Key column for the field and press the spacebar or double-click. An asterisk (*) appears in the Key column for the field when the key is on.

FIGURE 4.12

How the first 13 fields
from the sample
CustList table plan
look when defined in
Paradox for Windows

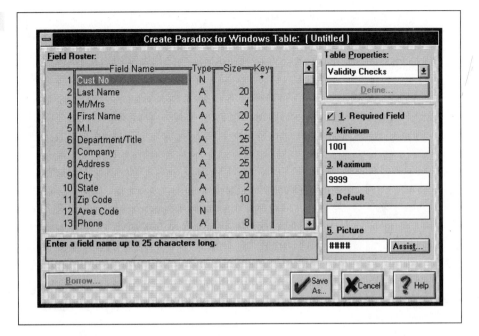

Defining Validity Checks

To define validity checks while you have the table structure on your screen, follow these steps:

1. First (and most important) move the highlight to the field that you want to define the validity checks for. You can click the field with your mouse or use the arrow keys to position the highlight.

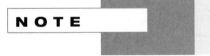

NOTE   You cannot define validity checks for memo, formatted memo, graphic, OLE, or binary fields.

2. Under Table Properties near the upper-right corner of the dialog box, make sure *Validity Checks* appears in the text box. If it does not, click the drop-down list button and choose *Validity Checks* from the list that appears.

3. If you want to make the current field a required field (one that cannot be left blank), click the Required Field check box.

4. If you want to specify a minimum acceptable value for the current field, click the text box under Minimum and type in the smallest acceptable value.

5. If you want to specify a maximum acceptable value for the field, click the text box under Maximum and type in the largest acceptable value.

TIP If you want to specify a range of acceptable values for a field, just fill in both the Minimum and Maximum validity check options.

6. If you want to specify a default value for the current field, click the text box under Default, then type in the default value.

TIP If you're defining a validity check for a date field and want to make the current date the default value, type the word TODAY in the Default text box.

7. If you want to define a picture template for the current field, click the text box under Picture. Then type in the template or click the Assist button (described below) for help.

8. Repeat Steps 1-7 as necessary for additional fields.

After defining your validity checks, you might want to take a moment to make sure you got it right before saving the table structure. Just use the ↑ and ↓ keys to move the highlight from field to field, and make sure that the validity checks that appear next to the highlighted field names are the appropriate ones for that field. For instance, in Figure 4.12, the Cust No field is highlighted. Its Required Field validity option is checked, its minimum and maximum values are defined, and the #### picture template is defined.

CREATING A TABLE 147

Using the Assist Button to Define a Picture

If you need help defining a picture validity check, follow these steps:

Assist...

1. Click the Assist button (shown at left). You'll see the **Picture Assistance** dialog box shown in Figure 4.13.
2. Click the drop-down list button under Sample Pictures to view example pictures.
3. Select an example by clicking it. A description of the picture you selected will appear in the message area near the bottom of the dialog box.
4. Click the Use button to copy the sample picture into the Picture text box.

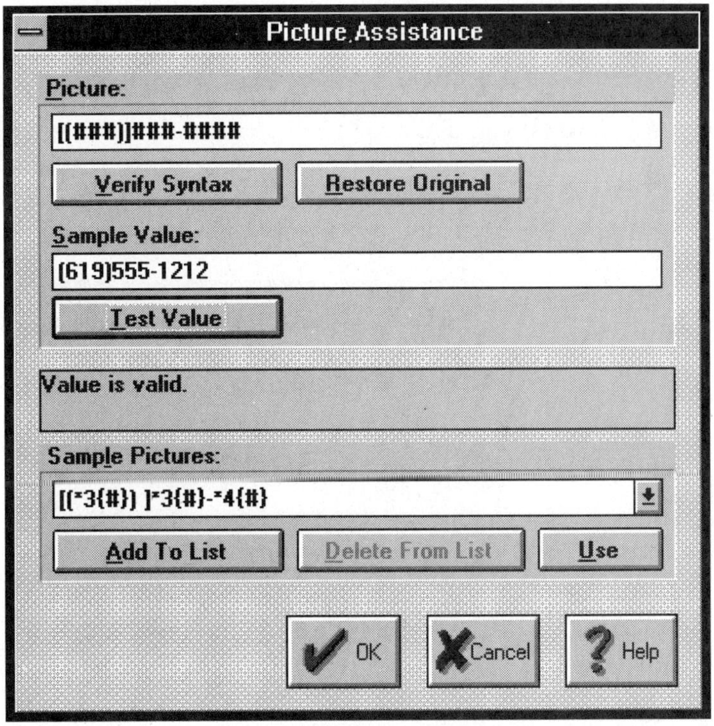

FIGURE 4.13

You can use the Picture Assistance dialog box to help define and test picture validity checks. In this example, we also typed in a sample value, which is acceptable to the currently defined picture.

5. If you wish to customize the picture further, position the insertion point in the Picture text box and make changes using the standard Windows editing techniques.

6. Use any of the techniques described below to test, change, or save the current picture. When you're satisfied with the picture template you've selected, choose OK.

When a picture appears in the Picture text box, you can check to see whether it contains any errors by clicking the Verify Syntax button. If Paradox reports errors in the message area, make any needed corrections, then click the Verify Syntax button again. If the picture has gone hopelessly awry and you can't fix it, you can erase the entire picture string or click the Restore Original button to return to the picture you had before clicking the Assist button.

You can also try out some sample values to see whether they'll be acceptable during data entry. Type a sample value into the Sample Value text box, then click the Test Value button. If the value is acceptable according to the currently defined picture, you'll see a Value is Valid message in the message area. Otherwise, you'll see an error message. If necessary, you can correct your sample value or the picture template until you're sure that the picture you've entered in the Picture text box is the one you'll want to use as a validity check during data entry.

If you'd like to save the currently displayed picture in the Sample Pictures list so that you can quickly choose it as a starting point for other picture templates, click the Add To List button. A **Save Picture** dialog box, like the one below, will appear.

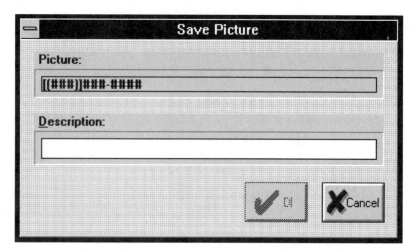

Enter a description for the picture format, then choose OK. The next time you open the Sample Pictures list box, the picture you added will appear in the list and you can select and copy it as described earlier.

To delete a picture template from the Sample Pictures list, click on the list to open it, then click on the picture template you want to delete. Then, click the Delete From List button.

NOTE   Paradox only lets you delete pictures added to the Sample Pictures list through the Add To List button.

Changing or Deleting Validity Checks

If you change your mind about a validity check you've assigned to a field, move the highlight to that field. The validity checks for that field will appear in the dialog box.

To deactivate a Required Field validity check, click the check box to remove the check mark. To deactivate a Minimum, Maximum, Default, or Picture validity check, double-click the text box for the validity check you want to clear, then press the Delete or Backspace key. To change the Minimum, Maximum, Default, or Picture assigned to the field, click the text box for the validity check and make changes and corrections using the standard text editing keys and techniques for Windows text boxes.

Saving the Table Structure

When you're satisfied with the table structure, follow the steps below to save it.

1. Click the Save As button. If you failed to complete any necessary steps or have entered invalid or conflicting field information, Paradox will prompt you to correct the problem. You'll need to make the corrections specified on the screen before proceeding.

2. When you have entered a valid table structure, you'll see the dialog box shown in Figure 4.14.

3. If you want to start entering data immediately, choose the Display Table option's check box.

4. Click the New Table Name text box, then type a valid file name without a file name extension for the table.

5. Choose OK.

You'll be returned to the Paradox Desktop. If you chose the Display Table option in Step 3 above, the open, empty table will appear on the screen. (Otherwise, the Desktop will remain empty.)

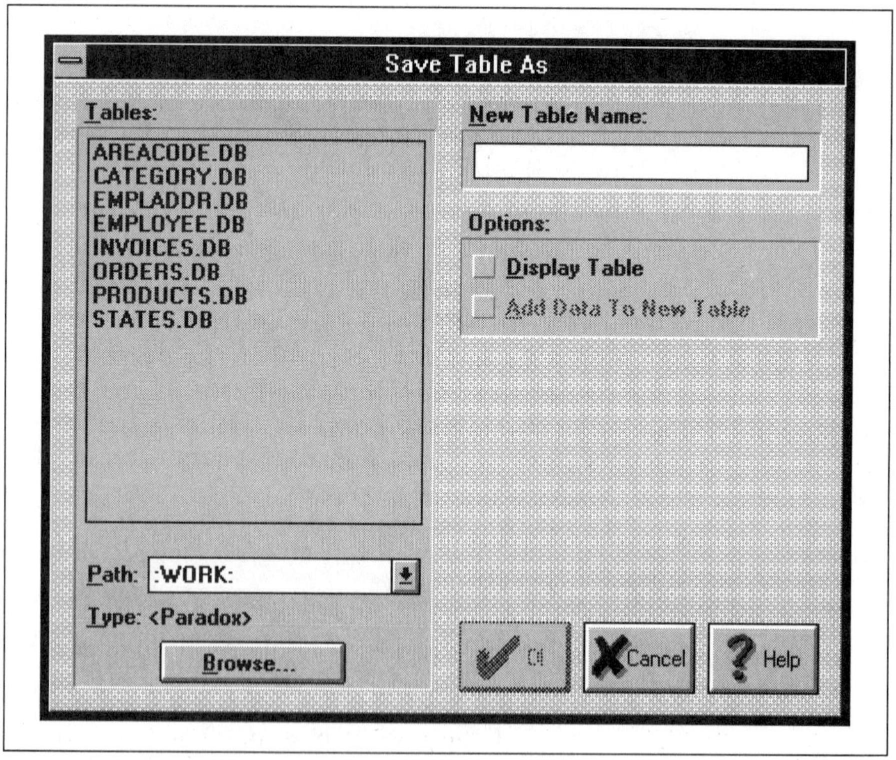

FIGURE 4.14

Use the Save Table As dialog box to save your table.

Changing a Table Structure

For future reference, be aware that you can change the structure of a table at any time by choosing File ➤ Utilities ➤ Restructure. However, if you want to change the table structure *after* you've added a lot of data to it, you'd do well to take a look at Chapter 14 before restructuring. If at all possible, plan your table carefully *before* adding data to it.

Files That Paradox Creates

When you save a table, Paradox for Windows automatically adds the extension .db to the file name you provide. Paradox might also create several auxiliary files, depending on the features used in your table design. Table 4.4 lists the file name extensions of table and auxiliary files.

WARNING

When copying a table to a floppy disk or sending it through a modem, you must include any auxiliary files for that table.

TABLE 4.4: File Name Extensions for Tables and Related Files

FILE NAME EXTENSION	CONTENTS
.db	Table
.mb	Memo, formatted memo, graphic, binary, and OLE data
.px	Primary index
.tv	Table view settings (if different from default Table View— see Chapter 6)
.val	Validity checks

Planning an Entire Database

In this chapter we've discussed all the nitty-gritty details of designing and creating a single Paradox table. But, as mentioned earlier, a database might actually require several *related* tables of information.

If you're new to database management, your best bet might be to keep working with a single table for the time being, since this is the best way to learn the basic skills. If you're experienced with database management systems, or are just curious about designing databases with multiple tables, you can peek ahead to Chapter 15 for more information on that topic. In the next chapter, you'll learn how to add data to a table and how to make changes and corrections as needed.

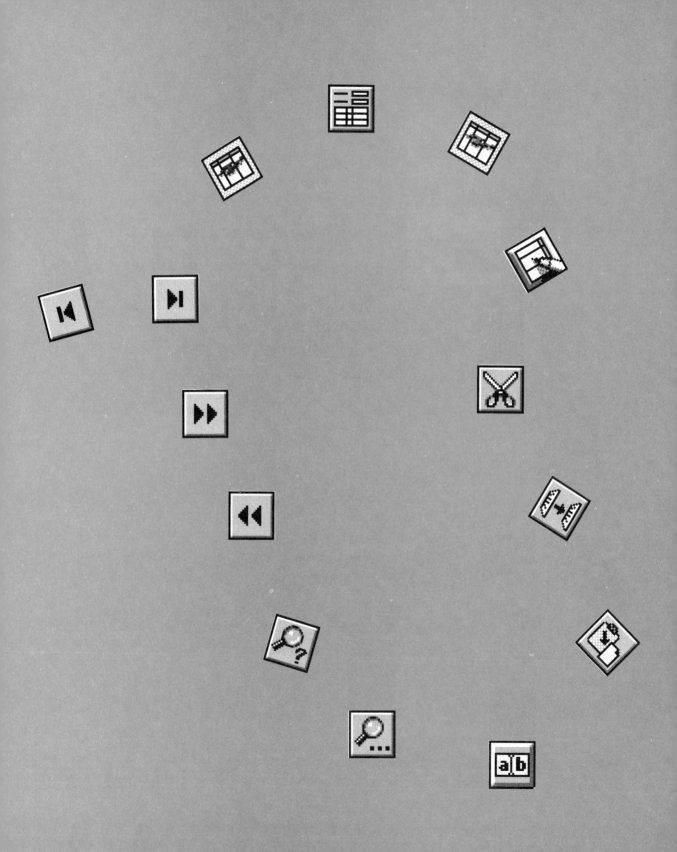

5

Entering and Editing
Table Data

f a s t TRACK

To delete the current record from the table   **177**

choose Record ➤ Delete or press Ctrl+Del.

To change the contents of a field   **178**

switch to Field View by clicking the current field again, clicking the Field View button, or pressing F2.

To enter or edit data in a special field   **192**

(memo, formatted memo, graphic, or OLE field), your first step is usually to switch to Field View by double-clicking, or clicking the Field View button, or pressing F2. Specific techniques from that point on depend on the field type.

To format text in a formatted memo field   **195**

first select the text you want to format, then click the right mouse button to access the formatting options.

To close a table   **220**

click the Control-menu box for Table or Form View and choose Close, or double-click the Control-menu box, or press Ctrl+F4.

THE first thing you'll want to do with your newly created Paradox for Windows table is to put some data in it. Of course, you'll also need to make changes and corrections to the table from time to time. This chapter explains how to open a Paradox table, add data to it, make changes and corrections, and save your work.

Opening a Table

To open a table so you can add new data to it or edit it, follow these steps:

1. If you haven't already done so, choose File ➤ Working Directory to switch to the table's directory.

 2. Click the Open Table button in the SpeedBar (if it's available), or choose File ➤ Open ➤ Table. You'll see the **Open Table** dialog box, shown in Figure 5.1.

3. If necessary, use the scroll bar to the right of the table names to scroll the name of the table you want into view.

4. Click the name of the table you want to open, then choose OK (or, just double-click the name of the table you want to open).

FIGURE 5.1

The Open Table dialog box lets you open an existing Paradox table.

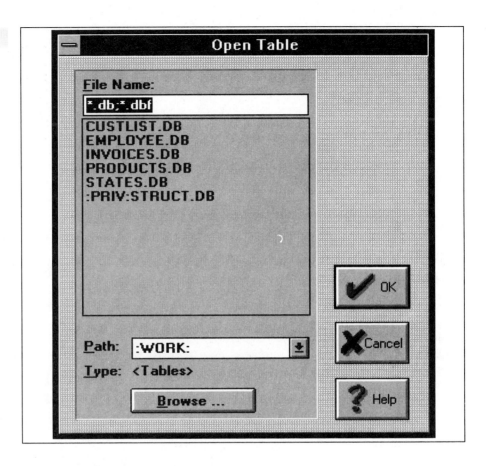

N O T E   You can also type in the name of the table you want to open or use the Path list and Browse button to locate a table that's not in the current working directory.

If the table already contains some data, you'll see whatever amount of information fits in the current window. If you have not added data to the table yet, only the field names at the top of the table structure will appear in the table, as in Figure 5.2.

The status bar near the lower-left corner of the screen indicates how many records are in the table. Notice that once you've opened a table, the -

options in the menu bar change, and a new SpeedBar, shown in Figure 5.3, appears below the menu bar. We'll describe the roles of many of those buttons as we progress through this chapter.

TIP

Remember, when you move the mouse pointer to a button, the status bar describes the function of that button. To choose a button, click it. You can also right-click some buttons to view a menu.

FIGURE 5.2

An empty table open on the Desktop. Since no data has been entered into the table yet, only the field names appear across the top of the table.

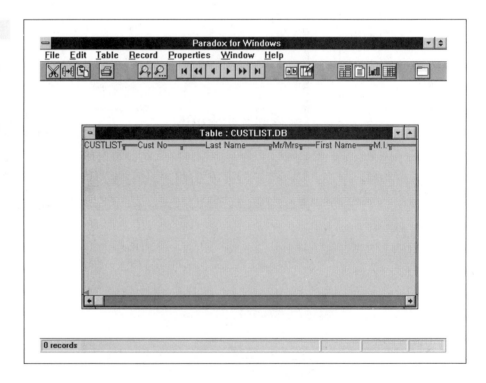

FIGURE 5.3

Once you open a table, the SpeedBar offers new buttons for working with the table.

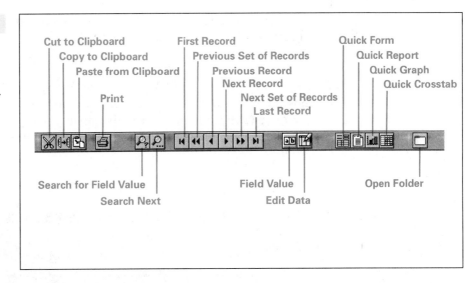

Choosing a View

Once a table is opened, you can display it in either of two views:

Table View Shows the table in tabular format, with as many rows and columns as will fit into the current window. When you're working in Table View, the window is called a *Table window*.

Form View Shows a single record at a time, as in Figure 5.4. When you're working in Form View, the window is called a *Form window*.

Here are some simple techniques for switching between Table View and Form View:

- If you're in Table View, click the Quick Form button in the Speed-Bar (shown at left), or choose Table ➤ Quick Form, or press F7 to switch to Form View.

• If you're in Form View, click the Table View button in the SpeedBar (shown at left), or choose For<u>m</u> ➤ <u>T</u>able View (or press F7) to switch to Table View.

When you switch from Table View to Form View, Paradox opens a separate Form window without closing the Table window. Therefore, in addition to using F7 to switch from one view to the other, you can also just click on any visible portion of whichever window is obscured to bring that window to the foreground.

FIGURE 5.4

A table record displayed in Form View, which lets you enter and edit data one record at a time

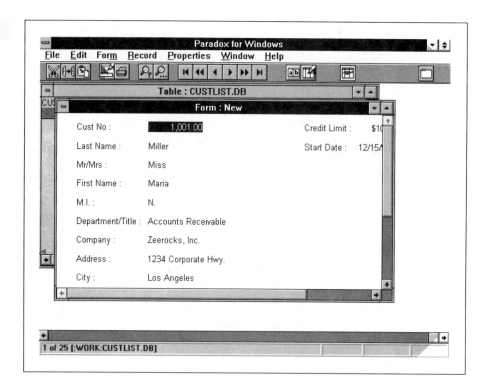

Notice that whenever you switch from Table View to Form View, the menu bar changes slightly (the Table menu is replaced by a Form menu in Form View), and the Form View SpeedBar contains two additional buttons—a Design button (for designing custom forms, as described in Chapters 9 and 10) and a Table View button (for switching back to Table View).

N O T E   Both the Form window and Table window act as standard document windows which you can move and size within the Paradox Desktop window.

Switching to Edit Mode

When you first open a table, whether in Table View or Form View, you're in *View mode,* which means you can view, but not add or change, data. If you attempt to type data into a field or make changes, Paradox will display the message "Press F9 to edit data" or "Not in Edit mode. Press F9 to edit data" and reject your keystrokes.

To add data to a table, you must first switch to Edit mode using one of the following techniques:

- Click the Edit Data button in the SpeedBar (shown at left).
- Choose <u>T</u>able ➤ <u>E</u>dit Data if you're in Table View, or choose Form ➤ <u>E</u>dit data if you're in Form View.
- Press F9.

The status bar near the bottom of the Desktop will display "Edit" indicating that you can now add data or change data in the table.

Adding Records to a Table

The steps for adding alphanumeric, numeric, and date fields are listed below. See "Entering and Editing Special Field Types," later in this chapter, for information on entering data in memo, formatted memo, graphic, and OLE fields, and for details on creating DDE links.

1. First make sure the table is open and in Edit mode, as described above (you can be in either Table View or Form View—it dosen't matter which).

2. If the table is currently empty, skip to Step 5 below.

3. Position the insertion point to the last record using any of these methods:

   * Click the Last Record button in the SpeedBar (shown at left).
   * Choose <u>R</u>ecord ➤ <u>L</u>ast from the menus.
   * Press Ctrl+F12.

4. If you're in Table View, press ↓ or F12 to create a new blank record. If you're in Form View, press PgDn or F12 to create a new blank record.

TIP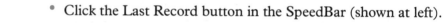

Alternatively, you can press *Insert* to insert a new blank record at the current position in the table.

5. Type the contents of the current field.

6. After filling in the current field, click the next field or press Tab or ↵ to move to the next field. (You won't be able to do this if the current field fails a validity check—more on this in a moment.)

NOTE Number fields automatically appear with commas and two decimal places of accuracy (for example, 1,001.00 for customer number 1001; 619.00 for area code 619). Dates appear in the format 12/31/92. Don't worry about that. You can easily change those formats at any time without re-entering data or changing the structure of the table, as you'll see in the next chapter.

7. Repeat Steps 5 and 6 to fill in all the fields of the current record.

8. In Table View, the highlight (cursor) will automatically move to a new blank record after you fill in the last field for the current record and press Tab or ⏎. In Form View, you must press F12 or PgDn to move to the next blank record. (Pressing Tab or ⏎ when the cursor is positioned in the last field of a record in Form View simply moves the cursor back up to the first field in the record.)

TIP If a new record that you've entered seems to disappear, it's probably just Paradox re-sorting the table on the spot.

Figure 5.5 shows some sample records added to the CustList table (though part of the table is scrolled out of view). Adding records is simply a matter of typing the contents of each field, then pressing ⏎ to move to the next field.

If you need to go back and make a correction, you can simply click on the field that you want to correct and type in a new entry. We'll discuss additional editing techniques in a moment.

How Much Data Will Fit on the Screen?

The amount of data you can see on your screen depends on the resolution of your screen. Therefore, your screen may not look like the ones shown

FIGURE 5.5

Sample data added to
the CustList table. Part
of the table is scrolled
off the screen.

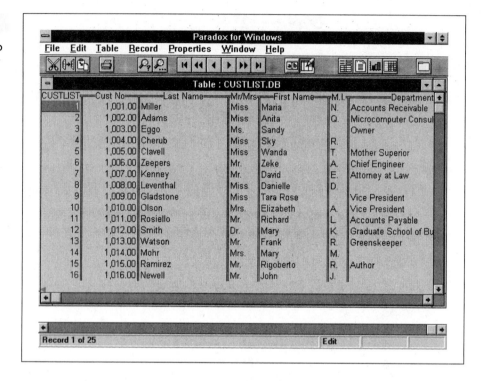

in this book. For instance, if you have a 1024 × 768 high resolution
monitor, your screen might look more like Figure 5.6.

For the most part, we'll stick with the standard VGA resolution of
640 × 480 pixels to display screens in this book, so you don't need a mag-
nifying glass to see the figures.

Typing Special Characters

When typing data in an alphanumeric field, you can type foreign and
other special characters from the IBM extended character set. The basic
technique is to turn on the Num Lock key (though this isn't required on
all keyboards), hold down the Alt key, type the three-digit number for the
character you want *using the numbers on the numeric keypad*, then release
the Alt key. Table 5.1 lists the special characters that are available to you.

FIGURE 5.6

The table shown in
Figure 5.5 displayed
on a monitor with a
resolution of 1024 x 768

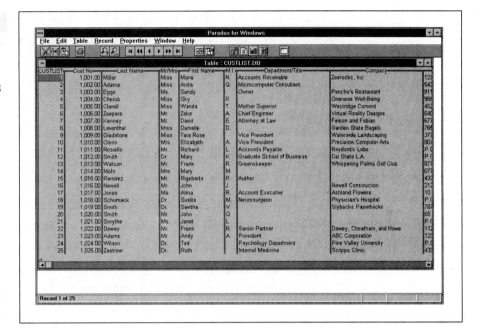

If you need to type a foreign currency sign into a currency field, you need
only change the Number Format property for that field. You'll learn how
to do that in Chapter 6.

NOTE

If the wrong special characters appear when printing
your table later, check your printer documentation for
information on switching the printer to the PC-8
symbol set.

You can also use special characters from the Windows Character Map, but
only characters within the font that the entire field is displayed in (that is,
you can change fonts for a single field, but not part of a field). We'll talk
about Character Map in more detail under "Using TrueType Special
Characters," later in this chapter.

TABLE 5.1: Special Characters from IBM Extended Character Set

CODE	CHAR	CODE	CHAR	CODE	CHAR	CODE	CHAR
128	Ç	160	á	192	└	224	α
129	ü	161	í	193	┴	225	ß
130	é	162	ó	194	┬	226	Γ
131	â	163	ú	195	├	227	π
132	ä	164	ñ	196	─	228	Σ
133	à	165	Ñ	197	┼	229	σ
134	å	166	ª	198	╞	230	μ
135	ç	167	º	199	╟	231	τ
136	ê	168	¿	200	╚	232	Φ
137	ë	169	⌐	201	╔	233	Θ
138	è	170	¬	202	╩	234	Ω
139	ï	171	½	203	╦	235	δ
140	î	172	¼	204	╠	236	⁞
141	ì	173	¡	205	═	237	∞
142	Ä	174	«	206	╬	238	ϵ
143	Å	175	»	207	╧	239	∩
144	É	176	▒	208	╨	240	≡
145	æ	177	▓	209	╤	241	±
146	Æ	178	█	210	╥	242	≥
147	ô	179	│	211	╙	243	≤
148	ö	180	┤	212	╘	244	⌠
149	ò	181	╡	213	╒	245	⌡
150	û	182	╢	214	╓	246	÷
151	ù	183	╖	215	╫	247	≈
152	ÿ	184	╕	216	╪	248	°
153	Ö	185	╣	217	┘	249	·
154	Ü	186	║	218	┌	250	·
155	¢	187	╗	219	█	251	√
156	£	188	╝	220	▄	252	ⁿ
157	¥	189	╜	221	▌	253	²
158	₧	190	╛	222	▐		
159	ƒ	191	┐	223	▀		

Entering Data in Validated Fields

If you assigned any validity checks to a field, the entry you place in that field must conform to the rules specified by the validity check. Otherwise, the cursor will seem to be "stuck" and you won't be able to move out of the field until you enter some data that satisfies the validity check. When this happens, look to the status bar for information on why your entry fails the validity check. Below are some of the possibilities.

- If you attempt to move the cursor to another record before filling in a required field, the message "Field value required" will appear in the status bar, and the cursor will remain in the record until you fill the field with some value. You'll need to move to the empty field that requires an entry, and then fill in some data.

- If you attempt to enter a value that's less than the minimum acceptable value assigned to the field or greater than the largest acceptable value for the field, the status bar will display the message "A value no less than x is expected" or "A value no more than x is expected," where x is the minimum or maximum value specified in the validity checks for that field. You cannot leave the field until you've entered a value that satisfies the validity check.

- If you've assigned a default value to a field, the default value will appear as soon as you create the new record. When you get to that field, you can retain the default entry by pressing Tab or ↵ to move to the next field. Or, you can type a new entry into the field before pressing Tab or ↵.

- If the field contains a picture template, you can only enter characters specified within the template. Paradox will beep and ignore any characters that don't fit the template, or, when you try to leave the field, you'll see the message "The field value fails picture validity check." You must re-enter the field's contents to match the picture template before you can move to the next field.

Of course, the purpose of a validity check is to prevent you from entering faulty data into a table. So, in most cases you'll simply want to fix (or complete) the entry so that it passes the validity check before moving on to the next field or record.

N O T E   If the error message in the status bar is "Key violation," see "Entering Data In Primary Key Fields," below.

Getting "Unstuck" from Validated Fields

In some cases, a value you enter into a field may fail a validity check not so much because of a problem with the data that you entered, but rather because your validity check isn't right. For example, suppose you inadvertently entered $10,000.00 as the *minimum* instead of the *maximum* acceptable value in a field. In that case, you might end up in a "Catch-22" situation where you can neither enter valid data into the field or record, nor get out of the record to change the validity check. Here's how to solve the problem:

1. First try to enter valid data into every field, and make sure all required fields contain some data. Or, delete the entry in the current field by pressing Ctrl+Backspace.

2. If you can't seem to get valid data into the record, delete the entire record by choosing Record ➤ Delete, or by pressing Ctrl+Del.

Once you get the cursor freed up, you can correct the validity check, if need be, by restructuring the table. This topic is discussed in depth in Chapter 14. Basically, all you need to do is this:

1. Starting from Table View, choose Table ➤ Restructure. You'll be taken to the **Restructure Table** dialog box.

2. Choose *Validity Checks* from the Table Properties drop-down list.

3. Move to the field that contains the problematic validity check.

4. Make whatever changes are required to correct the problem with the validity check, or delete the validity check by double-clicking it and pressing Delete.

5. Choose Save to save the structure with the new validity checks.

TIP   If you're having problems entering data into a validated field, chances are that the validity check needs to be *less* stringent, not more stringent.

Be aware that existing records must conform to the new validity checks or Paradox will not save the table. Again, if you have any problems, see Chapter 14 for more in-depth coverage of table restructuring.

After saving the new table structure, you'll be returned to the table, in View mode. If you want to add or edit data, switch to Edit mode by clicking the Edit Data button, choosing Table ➤ Edit Data, or by pressing F9.

Entering Data in Primary Key Fields

As described in the previous chapter, if you've defined a primary key for your table, Paradox will reject any new record that duplicates the data in the keyed fields of an existing record. For instance, if you've made Cust No the primary key, and assigned the customer number 1009 to a new customer, Paradox will reject the whole record if some other customer already has been assigned that customer number. Similarly, if you've defined Last Name and First Name (only) as the primary key, Paradox will reject a new record with the name Granolabar Wanda if an existing record already contains that name.

Paradox will not reject a record until you complete it. That is, you'll be able to fill in the entire record, but when you try to move the cursor to some other record, the cursor will stick in the current record and you will see the message "Key violation" in the status bar.

The easy fix in such cases is to move the cursor to the keyed field and type in a unique value. For instance, if 1009 is a duplicate entry, move to the Cust No field and type in some new number, such as 1010 or whatever the next available number is.

If the problem is the manner in which you've defined the primary key, you'll probably want to change the structure of the table to make the definition of a duplicate less stringent. You can usually do so by adding one or more fields to the primary key. For instance, suppose we defined Last Name, First Name, Address, and Zip combined as the primary key field. In that case, Paradox would only reject a new record as a duplicate if some other record had the exact same data in all four of those fields, rather than in just the Last Name and First Name fields.

If you do need to change the primary key, you'll first need to get rid of the *Key violation* error. You can do so by changing the data in one of the key fields so that it's no longer a duplicate of another record, or, if you're really stuck, by deleting the entire record with Record ➤ Delete or Ctrl+Del.

Then you can restructure the table using Table ➤ Restructure. Please refer to Chapter 4 if you need reminders on defining a primary key. Refer to Chapter 14 if you need help restructuring a table.

"My New Records Keep Disappearing!"

Don't forget that when you're using a table that you've defined a primary key for, Paradox will instantly re-sort a new record into its proper sort-order position in the table when you finish entering the record. Hence, the record may seem to disappear from the screen as soon as you've typed it!

If you're not comfortable with this disappearing act and want to make sure the new record is in the table, you can scroll to the position of the new record using any of the scrolling techniques described in the next section. For instance, if the table is keyed on the Last Name and First Name fields, and you just entered a record for someone named Bowser, you'll need to scroll to the B's to find the record in its proper sort-order position.

Data Entry Shortcuts

You can use several shortcuts when entering data into number, currency, and date fields. These are summarized below.

- You can press the spacebar instead of typing a period for the decimal point in number and currency fields.

- You can omit the leading dollar sign in a currency field. Paradox will add it automatically when you finish your entry.

- If you omit the ".00" portion of a currency amount, Paradox will automatically fill it in for you.

- When typing a date, you can press the spacebar to enter the current system month, day, or year. For example, if the current date is September 30, 1992, pressing the spacebar three times will enter the date 9/30/92.

- When entering new records into a table, you can duplicate the field entry from the same field in the previous record by pressing Ctrl+D.

- You can press Ctrl+Backspace to erase the word to the left of the insertion point.

- You can press the Home key to move to the first field in a record, or press the End key to move to the last field.

You can also use Windows' cut, copy, and paste techniques to move or copy data from one field to another (provided that any data within the record meets validity checks). There are several ways you can select data to move or copy:

- Click the field that contains the data you want to select (so the entire field is highlighted).

- Drag the mouse pointer through the portion of a field that you want to select.

- Move the mouse pointer to the place where you want to start selecting, then hold down the mouse button and drag the mouse pointer through multiple fields. You can also select multiple fields by holding down the Shift key while moving the cursor with the arrow, PgUp, PgDn, Home, End, Ctrl+Home, and Ctrl+End keys.

NOTE

If the message "In field view..." appears in the status bar while you're trying to select multiple fields, click some other field, then come back and try again. You should see the message "Selecting Fields" in the status bar, and the mouse pointer should change to a four-headed arrow when you've done it correctly.

● To select all the fields and records in the table, choose Edit ➤ Select All.

Once you've selected data to copy, you can use any of these techniques to move or copy the data to the Windows Clipboard:

 Cut To Clipboard   Deletes selected data and places it in the Windows Clipboard. Clicking this button is equivalent to choosing Edit ➤ Cut or pressing Shift+Del. Use this when you want to *move* data from the current field to another field.

 Copy To Clipboard   Copies selected data to the Windows Clipboard. Clicking this button is equivalent to choosing Edit ➤ Copy or pressing Ctrl+Ins. Use this option when you want to *copy* data to another field.

Once you've cut or copied data to the Clipboard, you can paste the data from the Clipboard into another field or, for that matter, another Windows application. If you're continuing in Paradox, you can move the cursor to the field that you want to paste the data into, provided the type of data you're moving or copying is from the same field type as the field you're moving or copying to. Do this using the third button:

 Paste From Clipboard   Pastes data from the Clipboard to the insertion point position in the current field. Clicking this button is equivalent to choosing Edit ➤ Paste or pressing Shift+Ins.

If you want to paste the selected data to another application, run that application and choose Edit ➤ Paste from that application's menu.

Moving around in a Table

You can move to any field in a table simply by moving the mouse pointer to that field and clicking the mouse button. You can also use the scroll bars to scroll through a table. In addition, you can use any of the keys, buttons, and techniques listed in Table 5.2 to get around a table.

TABLE 5.2: Techniques for Moving through a Table

TO GO TO	CLICK	OR CHOOSE	OR PRESS
First record	◄◄	Record ➤ First	Ctrl+Home or Ctrl+F11
Last record	►►	Record ➤ Last	Ctrl+End or Ctrl+F12
Next record	►	Record ➤ Next	F12 (or ↓ in Table View or PgDn in Form View)
Previous record	◄	Record ➤ Previous	F11 (or ↑ in Table View or PgUp in Form View)
Next record set	►►	Record ➤ Next Set	PgDn in Table View, Shift+F12 in Form View
Previous record set	◄◄	Record ➤ Previous Set	PgUp in Table View, Shift+F11 in Form View

TABLE 5.2: Techniques for Moving through a Table

TO GO TO	CLICK	OR CHOOSE	OR PRESS
Next field	Field		Tab, →, or ↵
Previous field	Field		Shift+Tab or ←
First field			Home
Last field			End
Left one screen	Scroll bar		Ctrl+PgUp
Right one screen	Scroll bar		Ctrl+PgDn
Locate field value	🔍?	Record ➤ Locate ➤ Value	Ctrl+Z
Locate next	🔍...	Record ➤ Locate Next	Ctrl+A

Inserting a Record

You need not be too concerned about the order in which you enter records into a table, because you can easily re-sort the records into any order you wish at any time. It's common practice to add new records to the end of the table as the need arises.

If you want to insert a new record between two existing records, move the cursor to the record that's *below* the place where you want to insert a new record, then choose Record ➤ Insert, or press the Ins (Insert) key.

Paradox inserts a new blank record above the current record. It also moves the cursor to the first field in that new record, so you can start typing immediately.

NOTE When you insert a new record into a keyed table, Paradox is still going to move the new record to its proper sort-order position!

Deleting a Record

Although you can delete an entire record from the current table you should be *very* careful about doing so because there is no way to recover a deleted record. If you're sure you want to delete an entire record, move the cursor to the record you want to delete, then choose Record ➤ Delete, or press Ctrl+Del.

The entire record is removed from the table, and Paradox instantly closes the gap between existing records.

NOTE You can delete several records in a single operation using queries (see Chapter 8).

Editing Table Data

Few of us can type a bunch of new records into a table without making a mistake. We usually need to make changes and corrections as we go along. Of course, correcting mistakes isn't the only reason you might want to edit a table. Sometimes you'll need to change information in a table just to bring it up to date (for instance, to change a customer's address after he or she moves).

You can easily change the contents of any field in any record at any time. All you have to do is open the table and switch to Edit mode (if you haven't already done so). Then move to the data you want to change by clicking on the field or by using the various cursor-positioning keys, such as ↑, ↓, →, ←, PgUp, PgDn, Tab, and Shift+Tab.

Remember that you can only edit the contents of a field while you're in Edit mode. If you're in View mode, click the Edit Data button or press F9 to switch to Edit mode.

When you get to the field you want to edit, the entire field will be *selected* (highlighted). Any new text you type will completely replace the text that's in that field. You can use any of the techniques listed in Table 5.3 to make changes to the field.

Using Field View to Make More Refined Corrections

If you want to *change* the contents of the field that the cursor is in, rather than *replace* them, you first need to switch to Field View. Here's how:

1. Move the cursor to the field that you want to change (you can be in either Table View or Form View).

2. Activate Field View using any of the following methods:

   * Move the mouse pointer to the place where you want to make a change, then click the mouse button again. (Or, you can skip Step 1 and just click twice at exactly the place you want to start making changes.)
   * Click the Field View button in the SpeedBar (shown at left).
   * Choose Table ➤ Field View (if you're in Table View) or Form ➤ Field View (if you're in Form View).
   * Press F2.

TABLE 5.3: Techniques for Changing Field Contents while in Table View or Form View

TYPING/CHOOSING...	HAS THIS EFFECT...
New text	Any new text you type completely replaces all existing text in the field.
Alt+Backspace (or Edit ➤ Undo or Escape)	Undoes the last change or deletion in a field.
Shift+Del (or Edit ➤ Cut or the Cut To Clipboard button in the SpeedBar)	Deletes the field entry and copies it to the Windows Clipboard.
Ctrl+Ins (or Edit ➤ Copy or the Copy To Clipboard button in the SpeedBar)	Copies the field entry to the Windows Clipboard.
Shift+Ins (or Edit ➤ Paste or the Paste From Clipboard button in the SpeedBar)	Pastes the previously cut or copied text from the Clipboard to the current field.
Delete (or Edit ➤ Delete)	Deletes the field entry but does not copy it to the Windows Clipboard.
↵ or Tab	Completes the change and moves to next field.
F2 (or click)	Switches to Field View

Once you've switched to Field View, the cursor, which normally highlights the entire field, is reduced to an insertion point (blinking vertical bar), and the mouse pointer changes to an I-Beam. The message "In field view, press F2 to leave field" appears at the left side of the status bar and "Field" appears at the right side of the status bar.

The roles of the arrow keys and mouse are changed to apply to the contents of the current field only, rather than the entire record. The mouse and keyboard functions are summarized in Table 5.4.

When you've finished making your changes, move to another field or press F2 again.

TABLE 5.4: Keys and Techniques Used in Field View

PRESSING/TYPING/CHOOSING...	HAS THIS EFFECT...
← and →	Moves insertion point one character left or right.
Mouse click	Moves insertion point to the I-Beam.
Home	Moves insertion point to beginning of field.
End	Moves insertion point to end of field.
Backspace	Deletes character to left of insertion point.
Delete	Deletes character to right of insertion point.
New text	Any new text you type is inserted at the insertion point.
Drag	Selects (highlights) text.
Shift+→, Shift+←	Selects character to the left or right of insertion point.
Shift+Home	Selects text from insertion point to beginning of field.
Shift+End	Selects text from insertion point to end of field.
Delete (or Edit ➤ Delete) with text selected	Deletes all selected text.
Backspace with text selected	Deletes all selected text.
New text with text selected	Replaces all selected text.
Alt+Backspace (or Edit ➤ Undo or Escape)	Undoes last change or deletion.
Shift+Del (or Edit ➤ Cut or Cut To Clipboard button in the SpeedBar)	Deletes selected text and copies it to Windows Clipboard.
Ctrl+Ins (or Edit ➤ Copy or Copy To Clipboard button in the SpeedBar)	Copies selected text to Windows Clipboard.

TABLE 5.4: Keys and Techniques Used in Field View (continued)

PRESSING/TYPING/CHOOSING...	HAS THIS EFFECT...
Shift+Ins (or Edit ➤ Paste or Paste From Clipboard button in the SpeedBar)	Pastes previously cut or copied text from Clipboard to current field.
F2 (or Field View button in the SpeedBar)	Toggles in and out of Field View.

Making Field View Stick

If you don't like the way Paradox starts replacing data as soon as you start typing in a field, you can use *Persistent Field View* to make Paradox stay in Field View. To do so, press Ctrl+F2.

You'll then need to use Tab and Shift+Tab, Alt and an arrow key, or the mouse to move from field to field. Notice that the Field View button on the SpeedBar stays depressed even as you move from field to field, the keys listed in Table 5.4 remain active within each field, and the word "Persist" appears at the right edge of the status bar.

To end Persistent Field View, just press Ctrl+F2 again.

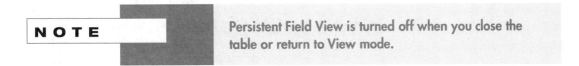

N O T E   Persistent Field View is turned off when you close the table or return to View mode.

Locking a Record

If you share data with other users on a network, and don't want others to edit a record while you're trying to edit or look at it, you can lock that record. Here's how:

1. Switch to Edit mode, then move the cursor to the record you want to lock.

2. Choose Record ➤ Lock (or press F5).

The message "Locked" appears in the status bar. Any other users on the network will be allowed to view the record, but they cannot modify it as long as you have it locked. If they try to modify the record, they will see the message "Record Locked" in the status bar.

In most cases, you don't actually need to lock records because Paradox automatically locks the current record when you begin to change any field. As soon as you move the cursor to a different record, Paradox automatically posts (saves) the change and unlocks the record.

NOTE If you're locked out of a record by another user, you can find out who has locked the record by choosing File ➤ Multiuser ➤ Display Locks, then selecting the table with the locked record.

To unlock a record that you've locked, choose Record ➤ Unlock, press Shift+F5, or move the cursor to a different record.

If you want to post (save) the record while continuing to hold the lock on it, choose Record ➤ Post/Keep Locked or press Ctrl+F5. If the table is keyed, the record will automatically move to its proper sort position. Other users will then be able to see the record, but it will remain locked so you can continue editing it. As soon as you move the cursor to a new record, Paradox will post your changes and release the lock on the record.

TIP Use Post/Keep Locked to be sure there is no key violation before you fill in the rest of the record.

Locating Records

In a small table, it's pretty easy to locate a record simply by scrolling around. But as your table grows, you will probably want to use the Locate feature to help you find a particular record or field.

TIP

You can also use queries (Chapter 8) to locate data that you want to edit. Queries are especially handy when editing very large tables.

Here's how to use Locate:

1. Move the cursor anywhere in the table (the search always begins at the top of the table).

2. Click the Locate Field Value button in the SpeedBar (shown at left), or choose <u>R</u>ecord ➤ Lo<u>c</u>ate ➤ <u>V</u>alue, or press Ctrl+Z. You'll see the **Locate Value** dialog box, shown in Figure 5.7.

3. Type the text or number you want to search for in the Value text box.

4. If the name of the field you want to search does not appear under <u>F</u>ields in the dialog box, use the drop-down list to choose a field to search. Once the drop-down list is open, you can use the ↑ and ↓, PgUp, and PgDn keys to scroll, or type the first letter of a field name until the highlight bar lands on the field you want. Then click the field name to select it.

5. If you want to match uppercase and lowercase letters exactly during the search, check the <u>C</u>ase Sensitive box (if it isn't already checked).

6. Choose the type of match you want:

- If you want to search for an exact match, click Exact Match.
- If you want to match a simple pattern, click the @ and .. option (described below).
- If you want to match a more complex pattern, click Advanced Pattern Match (described below).

7. Choose OK to perform the search.

FIGURE 5.7

The Locate Value dialog box lets you quickly move the cursor to a record containing a specific value.

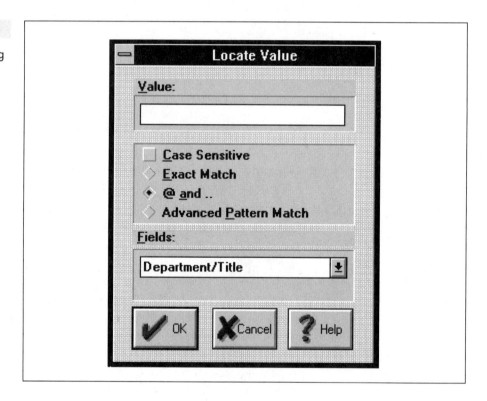

Paradox will take you to the first record below the current record that contains the value or pattern in the field you specified. If no records contain the value you're searching for, you'll see a message in the status bar indicating that the value you're searching for was not found.

If Paradox does find a record that matches the value you specified, but it's not the one you're looking for (say, Paradox finds Anita Smith, but you're looking for Wanda Smith), perform this simple step to find the next record that matches:

- Click the Locate Next button in the SpeedBar (shown at left), choose <u>R</u>ecord ➤ Locate Ne<u>x</u>t, or press Ctrl+A.

You can repeat the above step as many times as necessary until you've either located the record you're looking for or the search fails.

Using @ and .. Wildcards to Locate a Record

If you chose @ *and* .. in Step 6 above, you can use the following wildcard characters to broaden your search:

..	Matches any series of characters
@	Matches any single character

NOTE If you use wildcards and have not checked *Case Sensitive*, uppercase and lowercase letters will be treated the same.

For example, if you type *Smith* as the value to search for, your search will only find the exact word *Smith*. However, if you enter

    ..smith..

(or *..sMith..* or *..SMITH..*, assuming *Case Sensitive* is not checked), Paradox will find records that have the word *smith* embedded within the field you're searching (Smith, SMITH, sMiTh, locksmith, Smith and Wesson, and so on). Similarly, a search value of

    Sm@th

matches any text that starts with *sm*, has any single character in the third position, and ends with *th*, including Smith, smith, smyth, SMITH, and so forth.

NOTE If you don't include wildcard characters in the search value, the value is always treated as an exact match, regardless of your choice in Step 6 above. Thus, a value of *Smith* only matches "Smith" (or SMITH, smith, etc., if *Case Sensitive* is not checked).

Using Advanced Patterns to Locate a Record

When you choose *Advanced Pattern Match* in Step 6, the value you're searching for can include any of the wildcard operators listed in Table 5.5. (Note that the @ and .. wildcards are treated the same in the Advanced Pattern Match option as they are in the "@ and .." option discussed above.)

Let's suppose we're using the Advanced Pattern Match option to locate values in the Last Name field of the CustList table. The search value

S[cm]..

TABLE 5.5: Advanced Wildcard Operators for Locating Values

WILDCARD...	OPERATION
..	Matches any series of characters (same as .. in the @ and .. option).
@	Matches any single character (same as @ in the @ and .. option).
[ ]	Matches any character within the brackets.
[^]	Matches any character not contained within the brackets.
¦	Matches either the character before or after the vertical bar.
()	Groups the values within the parentheses.
^	Beginning of line.
$	End of line.
\	Treats following wildcard symbol as a regular character.

matches any last name beginning with *s*, having a second letter of *c* or *m*, and any other series of characters. Thus, this pattern matches last names of Smith, Smythe, and Schumack.

The search value

    ..s$

matches any last name ending with *s*. In our sample table, Adams, Jones, and Zeepers fit this pattern.

Finally, the search value

    ^[cow]..

matches any last name beginning with *c*, *o*, or *w* followed by any series of characters. This pattern matches Cherub, Clavell, Olson, Watson, and Wilson.

Locating a Record by Its Position

If you happen to know the record number (i.e., the sequential position) of the record you want to edit, you can move the insertion point to that record by following these steps:

1. Choose Record ➤ Locate ➤ Record Number. You'll see the dialog box below.

2. Type the number of the record that you want to search for. This can be any number in the range of 1 to whatever value is shown next to Number of Records in the dialog box.

3. Choose OK.

The cursor jumps to the record you specified, remaining in whatever column you were in before moving to the new record.

Editing Multiple Records Simultaneously

If you discover a need to make an identical change to several records in a table, you can use Locate with the "and Replace" option to make a change throughout the table. For example, let's suppose that while entering records you inadvertently typed *Los Angles* rather than *Los Angeles* into the City field for a record. Then, you used Ctrl+D to copy that entry to other records. The Locate and Replace feature would let you change all the misspelled entries in one fell swoop. (You can use queries, discussed in Chapter 8, to make more refined global changes to a table—for example, increasing a unit price in an inventory by 10%.)

Here's how to use Locate and Replace:

1. Make sure you're in Edit mode (press F9 or click the Edit Data button), and, optionally, move the cursor to the field you want to change.

2. Choose Record ➤ Locate ➤ and Replace (or press Shift+Ctrl+Z). You'll see the dialog box in Figure 5.8.

3. Choose the field that you want to search from the Fields drop-down list. (Initially, the Fields list shows whichever field the cursor is in.)

4. If you want to match uppercase and lowercase letters exactly during the search, check the Case Sensitive box.

5. Choose the type of match you want:

   • To search for an exact match, click Exact Match.
   • To match a simple pattern, click the @ and .. option.
   • To match a more complex pattern, click Advanced Pattern Match.

N O T E

Recall that the .. wildcard matches a series of characters and the @ wildcard matches any single character. Table 5.5 summarizes the Advanced Pattern Match options.

6. In the Value text box, type the text you want to locate. If you checked the Case Sensitive box in Step 4 and selected the Exact Match option in Step 5, be sure to type the *exact* value you want to locate (including the correct uppercase and lowercase letters and any punctuation or spaces). If you left the Case Sensitive

FIGURE 5.8

The Locate and Replace dialog box lets you find values and change them to new ones throughout a table.

Locate and Replace

Value:

Replace With:

☐ Case Sensitive
◇ Exact Match
◈ @ and ..
◇ Advanced Pattern Match

Fields:

Cust No ⯆

✔ OK   ✖ Cancel   ? Help

option unchecked and chose either the "@ and .." option or Advanced Pattern Match, you can broaden your search with the wildcard characters, as described earlier.

7. In the Replace With text box type the new text that you want to replace the old text with.

8. Choose OK.

TIP   Before starting the search, move the dialog box out of the way so that you can see the text highlighted as it is found.

Paradox will start its search from the beginning of the table. If, and when, Paradox locates a record that contains the text you entered in Step 6, you'll see this dialog box:

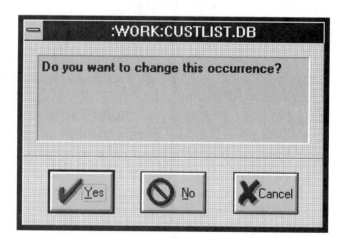

:WORK:CUSTLIST.DB

Do you want to change this occurrence?

✓ Yes   🚫 No   ✗ Cancel

You now have three choices:

• Choose Yes to replace the text in the current record and search for the next record.

- Choose No if you don't want to replace text in the current record, but want to continue searching through additional records.

- Choose Cancel to keep the current record as it is and cancel the Locate and Replace operation.

Moving to a Particular Field

Once you're in the record that contains the data you want to view or edit, you can move to a particular field using any of the following techniques:

- Move the mouse pointer to the field you want to edit and click the mouse button.

- Press Tab to move to the next field or Shift+Tab to move to the previous field.

- Use the ↑, ↓, →, and ← keys to move from field to field. (In Form View, only the ↑ and ↓ keys have any effect.)

- Press Home to move to the first field; press End to move to the last field.

- If the table has more fields than will fit into the current Table window (in Table View), or the fields are wider than will fit into the Form window (in Form View), you can use the scroll bars at the bottom edge of the window or press Ctrl+PgDn and Ctrl+PgUp to move a screen at a time. In Table View, pressing Ctrl+PgDn moves right through the fields a screen at a time, while pressing Ctrl+PgUp moves left through the fields. In Form View, pressing Ctrl+PgUp scrolls the screen to the right, and pressing Ctrl+PgDn scrolls the screen to the left.

- Choose Record ➤ Locate ➤ Field, move the highlight to the name of the field you want to move to, then choose OK.

This last method is particularly handy for moving to a specific field when each record contains lots of fields.

Entering and Editing Special Field Types

You'll need to use some special techniques to enter data in memo, formatted memo, graphic, binary, and OLE fields. Since our sample Cust-List table doesn't contain any such fields, we'll refer to a different table, named *Employee*, for the remaining examples. This table contains data on employees. Its structure is shown in Figure 5.9.

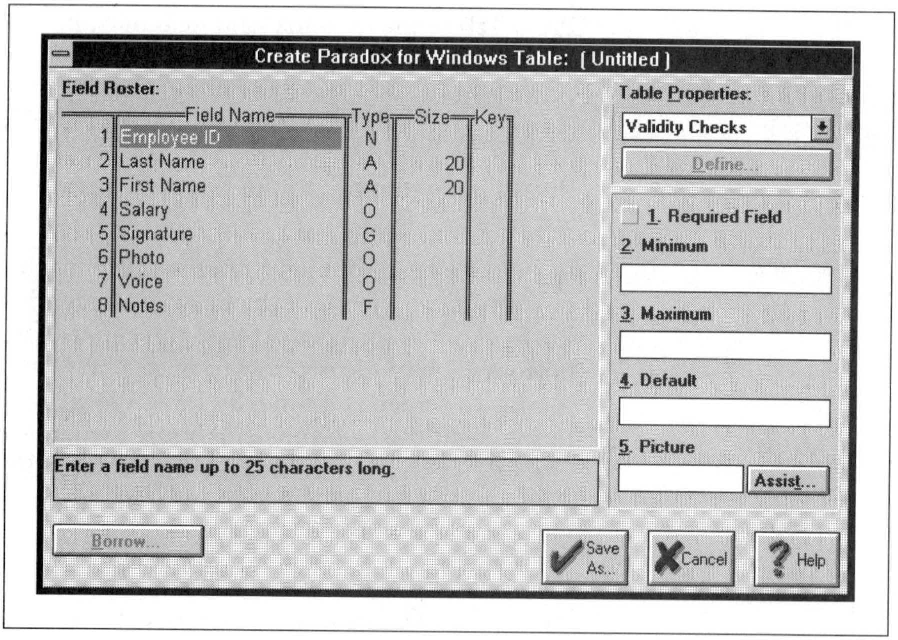

FIGURE 5.9

The Employee table structure includes graphic, OLE, and formatted memo fields.

Create Paradox for Windows Table: [Untitled]

Field Roster:

Field Name	Type	Size	Key
1 Employee ID	N		
2 Last Name	A	20	
3 First Name	A	20	
4 Salary	O		
5 Signature	G		
6 Photo	O		
7 Voice	O		
8 Notes	F		

Enter a field name up to 25 characters long.

Table Properties:

Validity Checks

Define...

1. Required Field
2. Minimum
3. Maximum
4. Default
5. Picture   Assist...

Borrow...   Save As...   Cancel   Help

Entering and Editing Memo Field Text

As you may recall, memo and formatted memo fields can contain any amount of text. In Table View and Form View, only a portion of the text appears on the screen. To add text to, view, or change the contents of a memo field, follow these steps:

1. Move the cursor to the memo or formatted memo field you want to change.

2. Make sure you're in Edit mode if you want to add text to the memo field or change its contents (press F9 or click the Edit Data button).

3. Switch to Field View (press F2, Shift+F2, click the Field View button, or double-click the memo field).

In Table View, a new *Memo View* window displays the current contents of the field, as in Figure 5.10. In addition, the status bar displays the message "In Memo View, press Shift+F2 to leave the field," and the mouse pointer changes to an I-Beam. No separate windows appears in Form View.

Regardless of whether you're using Table View or Form View, you can type and edit text using the basic techniques supported by all Windows applications. These are summarized below.

- Press ↵ *only* to end short lines of text and entire paragraphs, or when you want to insert a blank line.

- Use Backspace and Delete to make changes and corrections as you type.

- Select text by dragging the mouse pointer through that text, or by holding down the Shift key while pressing the various cursor-positioning keys (Home, End, PgUp, PgDn, and so forth).

- Delete selected text by pressing Delete or Backspace.

- Replace selected text by simply typing the new text.

- To move selected text, choose Edit ➤ Cut (or press Shift+Del or click the Cut To Clipboard button in the SpeedBar). Then move the insertion point to the new location for the text and choose Edit ➤ Paste (or press Shift+Ins or click the Paste From Clipboard button).

- To copy selected text, choose Edit ➤ Copy (or press Ctrl+Ins or click the Copy To Clipboard button). Then move the insertion point to the destination for the copied text, and choose Edit ➤ Paste (or press Shift+Ins or click the Paste From Clipboard button).

When you have finished typing or editing your text, you can save your work and return to Table or Form View using any of the techniques described under "Saving Memo Field Text," below.

Be aware that, in Edit mode, opening a memo field that already contains text instantly selects all the text in that memo. Therefore, anything you type will *replace* all the selected text.

FIGURE 5.10

Window for entering and editing text in a memo field

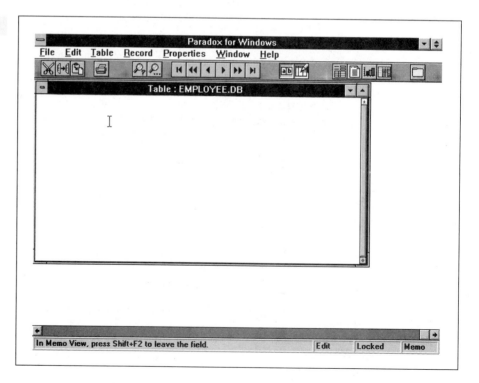

To avoid this, move the insertion point before you start typing, either by clicking where you want to make changes or by using the arrow keys or other special keys.

If it's too late for that, and you've already deleted a chunk of text, choose Edit ➤ Undo, or press Alt+Backspace or Escape to cancel your changes.

TIP   In Table View, pressing Escape cancels your changes and leaves you in the Memo View window. Choosing Edit ➤ Undo or pressing Alt+Backspace cancels your changes and returns you to the Table window.

Copying Text into a Memo Field

You can copy an external file into a memo field, as long as that external file is in text (.txt), rich text (.rtf), or Paradox text (.pxt) format. To do so, choose Edit ➤ Paste From while you're editing the memo field. Specify the directory location and complete name of the file you want to copy (for example, *c:\windows\wanda.txt*), then choose OK.

Depending on the word processor you use, you might also be able to copy text from a word processing document to the Windows Clipboard, then paste it into a memo field. However, Paradox can't read all formats from the Clipboard, so this might not work. The easiest way to find out whether or not it *will* work is to try it.

If Paradox can't read the text from the Clipboard, you'll just get an error message. In that case, you'll need to export the word processing document to rich text format or text format. Then use Edit ➤ Paste From while editing the memo field to bring in the exported file.

Formatting Memo Text

If you're working in a formatted memo field, you can apply text formatting attributes such as fonts, alignment, and line spacing. Here are the steps for formatting text in a memo field:

1. If you want to apply the formatting to all text beyond the insertion point (text you're about to type), just position the insertion point at the place where you want the change to take effect. If you want to apply the formatting to a portion of existing text, select the text that you want to format.

2. Click the right mouse button to inspect the text properties. You'll see the properties menu for a formatted memo field, as shown in Figure 5.11. The basic formatting options are summarized below.

   • To change the alignment of selected text, choose Alignment, then one of the following options: *Left* (aligns at the left edge of the window, leaving an uneven right margin), *Right* (aligns at the right edge of the window, leaving an uneven left margin), *Center* (centers the text between the left and right edges of the window), or *Justify* (text is even at both the left and right margins).

FIGURE 5.11

Text selected in a formatted memo field, with the property menu displayed

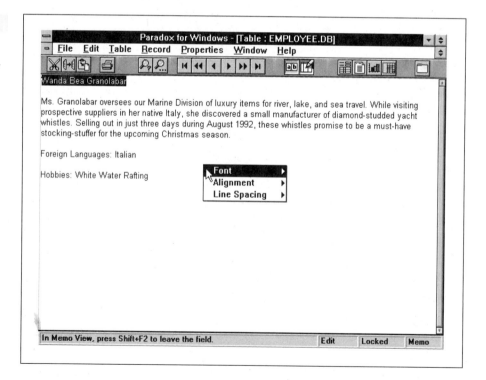

- To change the line spacing of selected text, choose Line Spacing and any one of the spacing options that appears on the submenu. Your options are 1 line, 1.5 lines, 2 lines, 2.5 lines, and 3 lines.
- To change the typeface, size, style, or color of the text, choose Font and any of the font options, which are described in the next section.

TIP

To keep the property menu from covering text you want to see, move the mouse pointer to an out-of-the-way place within the memo before you click the right mouse button.

Using Fonts and Styles

Choosing Font from the formatted memo property menu leads to the menu shown below.

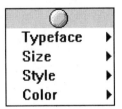

Choose the Typeface, Size, or Style option and then click on the attribute you want. If you want to assign the typeface, size, and style to the selected text all at once, click the snap button at the top of the menu. You'll see a dialog box like the one below. (The list of fonts depends on the fonts installed on your system.)

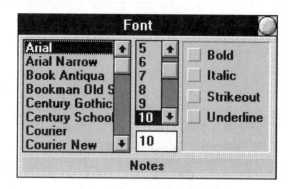

Choose whatever combination of attributes you want to apply to the text.

Changing the Color of Text

You can use the technique described above to change the color of text as well. Select the text you want to color or position the insertion point where you want the color to begin, then right-click. Choose Font ➤ Color, and you'll see a palette of colors, as shown below.

Click on the color you want, and the selected text will change to that color. (Selected text will appear in the opposite color until you deselect it by clicking the mouse button again.)

Floating Dialog Boxes

The snap button that appears at the top of certain Paradox menus, including the Font and Color dialog boxes, is particularly handy because it changes the menu or palette to a floating dialog box. You can move that dialog box if it's in the way simply by dragging the title bar.

You can click anywhere in your formatted memo to select text or reposition the insertion point without losing the floating dialog box. When you're ready to choose a new font or color, just make your selections from the floating dialog box.

To close the floating dialog box, simply click its snap button again.

A Sample Formatted Memo Field

Figure 5.12 shows an example of a formatted memo field. Following are the steps we used to type and format it.

1. First we typed the entire memo as shown in Figure 5.11.

2. Then we selected *Wanda Bea Granolabar* by dragging the mouse pointer through the text. Next we right-clicked and chose Alignment ➤ Center.

3. With the text still selected, we right-clicked and chose *Font.* Then we clicked the Snap button and chose Arial as the typeface and 18 as the size.

4. To insert the blank line, we clicked the selected text, pressed the End key to move to the end of that text, and pressed ↵.

5. We selected all remaining text below the centered title by dragging the mouse pointer through it (though pressing Shift+Ctrl+End would also do the job).

6. Then we chose Times New Roman as the typeface and 12 as the size from the floating Font dialog box. We then clicked the snap button to close the floating dialog box.

7. We dragged the mouse pointer through *must-have stocking stuffer* to select it.

8. Next we right-clicked and chose Font ➤ Style ➤ Italic.

9. Finally, we boldfaced *Foreign Languages* and *Hobbies* following the same basic procedure used earlier to italicize *must-have stocking stuffer*. (This time we chose Font ➤ Style ➤ Bold).

It's all remarkably quick and easy once you get the hang of it. What's really great is that the whole business of property inspection (right-clicking whatever it is you want to change) is used throughout Paradox for Windows, as you'll see in upcoming chapters.

FIGURE 5.12

Sample formatted memo field with fonts, centered heading, boldface, and italics

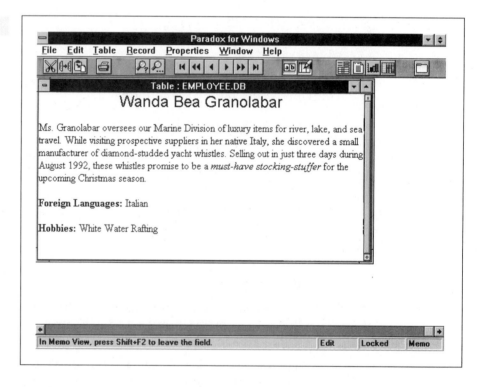

Using TrueType Special Characters

A formatted memo field can contain any of the Windows 3.1 TrueType special characters. To insert a special character, you can use the Windows 3.1 Character Map:

1. Make sure the formatted memo field is open (in Field View) and you're in Edit mode.

2. Move the insertion point to the position where you want to place the special character.

3. Go to the Windows 3.1 Character Map. (You can press Alt+Tab until Program Manager appears, then open the Accessories group and double-click the Character Map icon.)

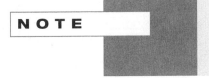

NOTE   If you're not already familiar with Character Map, see your Windows documentation for more information and other ways to insert special characters into a document.

4. In Character Map, choose any TrueType font (identified with the TT symbol) from the Font drop-down list. Figure 5.13 shows an example in which Character Map appears with Wingdings as the selected font.

5. To magnify a character, move the mouse pointer to the character and hold down the mouse button.

6. To choose a special character, click it, then click the Select but-ton. A copy of the character will appear in the Characters to Copy text box.

7. Repeat Steps 5 and 6 to select as many characters as you want.

8. Click the Copy button to copy the character(s) to the Clipboard.

9. Either minimize the Character Map window (if you think you'll need it again soon), or click its Close button to close it. You can also minimize Program Manager to get it out of the way if you want. At this point, you should be back in the memo field.

10. Choose Edit ➤ Paste, or click the Paste from Clipboard button in the SpeedBar.

If the wrong character appears, it's probably because the current font in the memo field does not match the font you selected in Character Map. To fix this, select the character or characters by dragging the mouse pointer through them or holding down the Shift key while pressing ←. Then right-click, choose *Font*, and click the snap button. Choose the same font you chose in Character Map (for instance, Wingdings), then choose a size and click the snap button to close the Font dialog box. Press → or click elsewhere in the memo to deselect the character(s).

FIGURE 5.13

The Windows 3.1 Character Map, displaying special characters in the TrueType Wingdings font

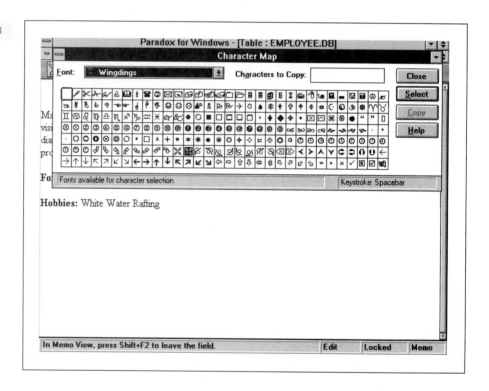

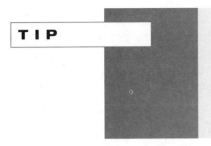

TIP

You can also use Character Map to insert a special character into an alphanumeric field. However, you can only use characters in the font that the rest of the column is displayed in. That is, you can't change the font for just a single character or record in an alphanumeric field.

Using Search and Replace in a Memo

If you're editing a particularly large memo (or formatted memo) field, you can use *Search* or *Search and Replace* within that field to locate text throughout several records, and, if you wish, change it. The procedure is basically the same as using the Record ➤ Locate ➤ Value (Ctrl+Z) and Record ➤ Locate ➤ and Replace (Shift+Ctrl+Z) options discussed earlier.

With the memo field open, move the insertion point to the place where you want to begin the search (press Ctrl+Home if you want to start the search from the top of the memo). If you want to search and replace through a portion of the memo only, select that portion of text.

Next choose Edit ➤ Search Text. Type the text you want to search for in the Search For text box. If you want to replace that text with some other text, type the replacement text into the Replace With text box. You can select or deselect the Case Sensitive option to determine whether or not you want the search to be case-sensitive. If you want to match a pattern instead of exact text, select Advanced Pattern Match and use any of the wildcards listed in Table 5.5 in your Search For text. Then click the Search button to begin the search.

TIP

If the Search and Replace dialog box is covering your text, simply drag the title bar to move it out of the way.

When Paradox finds a match, you'll see the message "Match found" in the status bar, and the text you're searching for will be selected. If you entered a replacement value and want to replace the selected text, click the Replace button. You can continue clicking the Search (or Search and Replace) button until Paradox displays the message "No match found." Choose Cancel or double-click the Control-menu box when you're finished using the Search and Replace dialog box.

Saving Memo Field Text

When you're finished entering or editing text, close the memo and save your work by pressing F2 or Shift+F2, clicking the Field View button in the SpeedBar, or choosing Table ➤ Field View (if you're in Table View) or Form ➤ Field View (if you're using a form to edit the memo field). If you're in Table View, you can close the window for the memo field by double-clicking its Control-menu box, pressing Ctrl+F4, or clicking the window's Control-menu box and choosing Close. If you're in Form View, simply click on another field.

Entering and Editing Data in a Graphic Field

You can store a graphic image in either a graphic field or an OLE field. You use the graphic field type when you can't or don't want to maintain links to the application that was used to create the graphic image.

TIP

Use a graphic field when you *don't* want to give all users access to the application used to create or edit a graphic image, or when you'll be distributing copies of the table to people.

You can store virtually any kind of graphic in a Paradox for Windows table. Figure 5.14 shows some examples. Table 5.6 lists the graphic file formats that you can place in a Paradox graphic field.

FIGURE 5.14

Examples of graphic images

Clip art

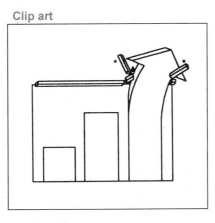

Scanned images

Business graphic

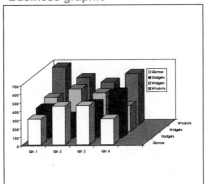

Free-form graphic

Photo/video frame

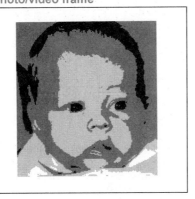

Screen Capture

TABLE 5.6: Graphic File Formats Supported by Paradox, with Typical File Name Extensions

FORMAT	FILE NAME EXTENSION
Windows Bitmap	.bmp
Computer Graphics Metafile	.cgm
Encapsulated PostScript	.eps
Compuserve "Jiff"	.gif
Paint	.pcx
Tagged Image File Format (TIFF)	.tif

Entering Pictures by File Name

You can store a graphic image in a graphic field simply by providing the location and name of the graphic, as follows:

1. Move the cursor to the graphic field and make sure you're in Edit mode.

2. If you wish, switch to Field View (double-click, press F2, or click the Field View button).

3. Choose Edit ➤ Paste From. You'll see the **Paste From Graphic File** dialog box in Figure 5.15.

4. Click the name of the graphic you want to use, or use the Path list box and Browse button to locate the graphic, then click on the name of the file you want.

5. Choose OK.

For example, suppose you have scanned several signatures and stored them in TIFF files with each person's name (*wanda.tif*, *keith.tif*, and so forth) on a directory named *c:\empsigs*. When filling in the dialog box for Wanda Granolabar's record, you'd specify *c:\empsigs\wanda.tif* as the name of the file.

FIGURE 5.15

The Paste From
Graphic File
dialog box

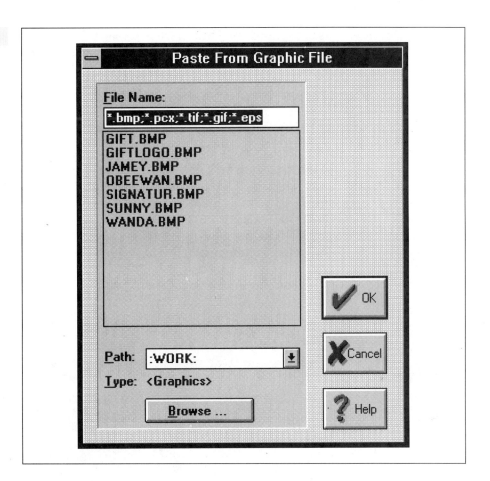

NOTE

Special fields may display <BLOB>, which stands for
Binary Large Object, followed by the type of object in
the field. We'll look at several ways to view the contents of these fields here and in the next chapter.

After choosing OK in Step 5, you're returned to Table View. Double-
clicking the Signature field (or using any of the other techniques to
switch to Field View) displays the contents of that field in a full window,

as in Figure 5.16. Double-clicking the picture, pressing F2, or closing the current window will return you to the table.

Pasting a Picture into a Graphic Field

You can also cut and paste a graphic image into a field, provided that the graphic was created, or at least can be displayed in, some other application, which we'll refer to as the *source application*. The source application must be able to display the graphic and copy it to the Windows Clipboard. That way, you can simply select the image that you want to store in your graphic field, copy (or cut) it to the Clipboard, then paste it into the graphic field. Here are the steps:

1. Run the source application, and bring the image that you want to store in your Paradox table to the screen.

FIGURE 5.16

Scanned signature placed in a graphic field

2. Select the image, or a portion of the image that you want to copy to your Paradox table.

For example, Figure 5.17 shows a photograph that we originally scanned into a bitmap (.bmp) file, sized to approximately 2.5 × 1.5 inches during the scanning process. To prepare for pasting the photo into the Paradox table, we ran the Windows 3.1 Paintbrush application, opened the bitmap image, then defined a cutout using the Pick tool.

T I P

Any time you're scanning pictures, signatures, or anything else for use in a table, it's a good idea to crop, scale, and size the image while scanning. It will be easier in the long run to manage scanned images if they're roughly equal in size before you put them into a Paradox table.

FIGURE 5.17

A photo displayed in the Windows Paintbrush accessory, selected before it's copied to the Clipboard

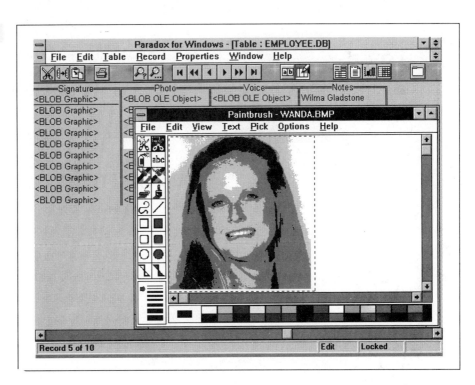

To get a copy of the cutout portion of the Paintbrush picture into a Paradox table, continue with these steps:

3. Choose <u>E</u>dit ➤ <u>C</u>opy from the source application's menu to copy the picture to the Windows Clipboard.

4. Minimize or close the source application to get it out of the way.

5. Switch to your Paradox for Windows table.

6. Move the cursor to the graphic field in the record of the table where you want to copy the image.

7. Make sure you're in Edit mode.

8. Choose <u>E</u>dit ➤ <u>P</u>aste from the Paradox menus, or press Shift+Ins, or click the Paste From Clipboard button in the SpeedBar.

Initially, you'll see only a small portion of the picture in your table. But if you move to the field and switch to Field View (or just double-click the field), the field will expand, as in Figure 5.18.

NOTE

Figure 5.18 assumes that the Photo field is the graphic field type, rather than the OLE field type. If Photo *is* the OLE field type, the photo would appear in the Paintbrush application rather than in the Paradox window—more on OLE in a moment.

After viewing the picture, double-click, press F2, or close the window to return to your table.

FIGURE 5.18

We pasted the selected image from Paintbrush into the graphic Signature field of the Employee table. Double-clicking the field displays the photo in a window.

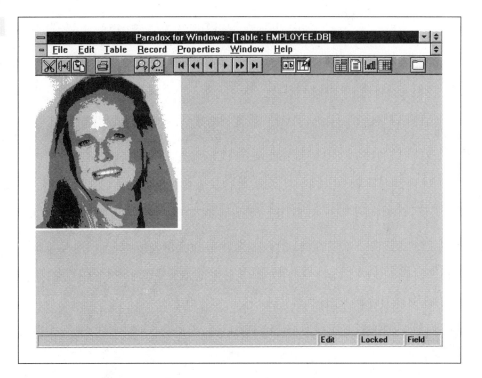

Copying Paradox Fields to Non-Paradox Files

You can copy the contents of a graphic, memo, or formatted memo field in a Paradox table to a non-Paradox file. Later, you can open that file in another application and make whatever changes you wish, without affecting the original Paradox table. To save the contents of a Paradox table field in a file, follow the steps below.

1. Move to the graphic, memo, or formatted memo field you want.

2. If you're copying a graphic field, skip to Step 5.

3. Switch to Edit mode by pressing F9 or clicking the Edit Data button.

4. Switch to Field View by double-clicking the field, clicking the Field View button, or pressing F2. This will select all the text of the memo or formatted memo field. Or, you can select a portion of text to copy by dragging the mouse pointer through it.

5. Choose Edit ➤ Copy To. If you're saving a graphic field, you'll see a dialog box like the one in Figure 5.19. If you're saving a memo or formatted memo field, the dialog box will resemble the one in Figure 5.20.

6. In the New File Name text box, type the full path and file name for the new file. You can also use the Path list box and Browse button to switch to the directory where you want to save the file, and

FIGURE 5.19

The Copy To Graphic File dialog box appears when you copy a graphic field.

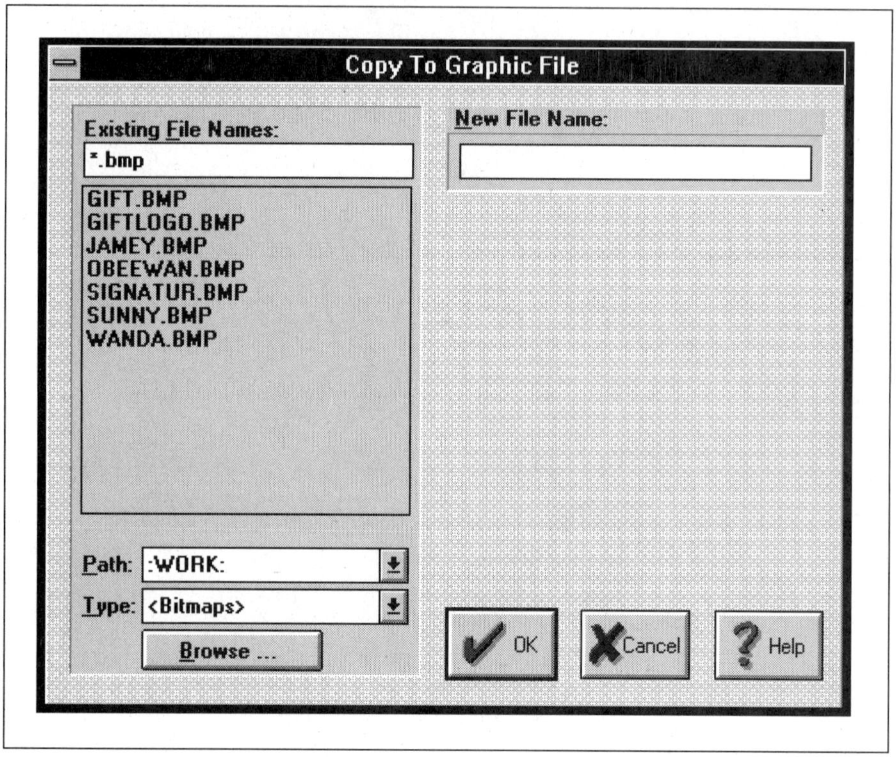

then type in the file name (see Chapter 14 for details). If you omit
the file extension, Paradox will use the default extension for the
type of data you're saving.

7. Choose OK to save the new file.

FIGURE 5.20

The Copy To File
dialog box appears
when you copy a
memo or formatted
memo field.

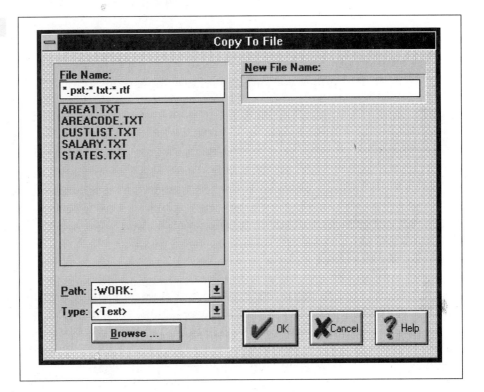

You can save memo or formatted memo fields to files with .pxt, .txt, or
.rtf extensions. The extension you specify will determine the format of the
text and the applications you can use to open and edit the file later, as
listed below:

.pxt   Paradox table format. If you save memo field
             text in this format, you can later read that text into
             another memo field by choosing Edit ➤ Paste
             From.

.txt   Standard DOS text format (no formatting) that you can read into just about any DOS or Windows application, such as DOS 5's Edit or Windows' Notepad.

.rtf   Rich Text Format that includes some formatting, and can be read by Windows applications that support RTF, such as Windows Write and Word for Windows.

When you save a graphic field, Paradox automatically assigns a .bmp (bitmap graphics) file name extension to the file. After saving the file, you can open it in any application that accepts .bmp format files, such as Windows' Paintbrush.

Using OLE Fields and DDE Links

As discussed in Chapter 3, Object Linking and Embedding (OLE) and Dynamic Data Exchange (DDE) are features of Windows 3.1 that let applications share objects. With OLE, the shared objects can be virtually anything: text from a word processing application, spreadsheet data or charts, any graphic image, or a sound (.wav file). With DDE, the shared objects can be text or numbers only (typically from a spreadsheet or word processing application).

In the OLE scheme of things, a Paradox table acts as a client. That is, you can copy an object *from* any OLE server application (the source application) *to* an OLE field in a Paradox table. In DDE, a Paradox table can act either as a client or as a server. You can copy an object *from* any DDE server application *to* an alphanumeric field in a Paradox table. Alternatively, you can copy an object *from* a field in a Paradox table *to* any DDE client application.

Here are the general steps for getting information into an OLE field or alphanumeric field of a table. We'll refer to the application that you use to create or edit the object as the *server application*; Paradox for Windows is the *client application*, and we'll assume that the table you want to put the data into is currently open on the Desktop.

1. If you haven't already done so, start the server application from the Windows Program Manager. If the application is already running, you can just switch to it using the Task List (Ctrl+Esc) or Alt+Tab.

2. In the server application, open or create the document that contains the data you want to store in your Paradox table.

3. If you intend to create a DDE link and have not already saved your file, use File ➤ Save in the server application to give it a file name.

WARNING   DDE doesn't work properly with new or "untitled" data that has not been given a file name yet.

4. If appropriate in the current server application, select the object, or a portion of the object, that you want to copy to your Paradox table, using whatever selection techniques that application offers.

5. Choose Edit ➤ Copy from the server application's menu to copy the object to the Windows Clipboard.

6. Switch back to Paradox for Windows.

7. Move the cursor to the OLE field (to embed the object) or to the alphanumeric field (to link the object) in the record of the Paradox table where you want to copy the OLE object or create the DDE link.

8. Make sure you're in Edit mode (press F9 or click Edit Data in the SpeedBar).

9. Choose Edit ➤ Paste (for OLE) or Edit ➤ Paste Link (for DDE).

You now have the original object in your server application, plus either an embedded copy of that document or a link to that document in your Paradox table.

NOTE Objects copied with Edit ➤ Paste are called *embedded* objects; those copied with Edit ➤ Paste Link are called *linked* objects. (If you choose Edit ➤ Paste in an alphanumeric field, the data will simply be copied from the Clipboard, as described earlier under "Data Entry Shortcuts.")

If you chose Edit ➤ Paste in Step 9, the object in your Paradox table will behave independently of the original object you pasted from the server application. That is, you can change the copy that appears in your Paradox table without affecting the original copy of the object. Likewise, if you change the original copy of the object outside of Paradox, that change will *not* be reflected in your Paradox table.

On the other hand, if you chose Edit ➤ Paste Link in Step 9, any changes you make to the copy in your Paradox table *will* be reflected in the original copy. Likewise, any changes you make to the original object outside of Paradox will be reflected when you edit the object from your Paradox table.

NOTE Please refer to the *client* application's manuals and online help for instructions on linking data from a Paradox table field to the client application. You can often find such information by searching for the topics *DDE* or *link*.

Editing an Embedded or Linked Object

Once you've put an OLE object in a Paradox table, changing that object is similar to changing a memo or formatted memo field. That is, you move to the OLE field you want to change, and switch to Edit mode by pressing F9 or choosing Edit Data in the SpeedBar. Then switch to Field View (double-click on the field, press F2 or Shift+F2, or click the Field View button).

Changing a DDE-linked object is almost the same. Move to the alphanumeric field you want to change, switch to Edit mode, and press Shift+F2.

Here's where the uniqueness of OLE and DDE shows itself. Rather than being taken to a Paradox window, you'll be taken to the original source application to view and edit the object. There, you can use the normal techniques within that application to edit or print the object.

WARNING

Pressing F2, double-clicking, or clicking the Field View button in an alphanumeric field that contains a DDE link *does not* open the source application. Instead, it allows you to edit the text *reference* to the object. For example, after double-clicking the text reference, you could alter the path name of the linked object, or change the data cell referenced by the link.

If you *embedded* the object in the Paradox table, using Edit ➤ Paste, the title bar of the source application will most likely indicate the type of object you're editing and the name of the Paradox field. This is a reminder that you're not editing the original object.

On the other hand, if you *linked* the object to the Paradox table, using Edit ➤ Paste Link, the title bar of the source application shows the file name of that object as a reminder that you are editing the original.

When you're done working with the object, exit the server application by choosing File ➤ Exit (or whatever command is appropriate in that application). You'll be returned to your Paradox table.

NOTE   The source application must be available in your computer if you want to access linked or embedded data. The original *document* must also remain available if you've linked it via DDE.

Some OLE Examples

Figure 5.21 shows several applications, including Paradox for Windows, on the Windows desktop. We opened, moved, and sized each one using standard Windows techniques. We also increased the height of the sample record from

FIGURE 5.21

OLE fields in a single record of the Paradox Employee table containing data from Microsoft Excel, Paintbrush, and Sound Recorder

the Employee table to display the contents of the fields better by dragging the underline at the bottom of the leftmost column downward a bit.

NOTE   You'll learn more about controlling the appearance of data in Table View in Chapter 6.

The main point of interest here is the simple technique we used to place data from the Excel, Paintbrush, and Sound Recorder applications into the Employee table, as summarized below.

- We switched to Edit mode.

- In Excel, we created and saved the Salary worksheet. Then we clicked the salary next to *Granolabar, Wanda* and chose Edit ➤ Copy from the Excel menu bar. Then we clicked the Salary field in our Paradox table, and chose Edit ➤ Paste from the Paradox menu. Paradox displays the contents of the cell and the cell's column and row coordinates (B5).

- In Paintbrush, we used File ➤ Open to open the photograph, which we'd previously scanned and saved as a bitmap file. Then we used the Pick tool in Paintbrush to define a cutout of the photograph, and chose Edit ➤ Copy from the Paintbrush menu bar. Then we clicked the Photo field in the Paradox table, and chose Edit ➤ Paste from the Paradox menu.

- In Sound Recorder, we chose File ➤ Open and opened a previously recorded sound file named *Wanda.wav*. Then we chose Edit ➤ Copy from Sound Recorder's menu bar. Next we clicked the Voice field in the Paradox table, and chose Edit ➤ Paste from the Paradox menu. (A sound always appears as an icon.)

Storing a Package in a Field

As an alternative to storing a complete picture or other object in a field, you can store an icon or *package* that represents the object. A package can contain just about anything: a picture, a sound, a spreadsheet, a word processing document—even an entire application.

To store a package in a Paradox table, you first need to create the package using the Windows 3.1 Object Packager (see your Windows documentation if you need help with that). Once you've created the package, choose Edit ➤ Copy Package in Object Packager to copy the package to the Clipboard. Then, in Paradox, move to the field you want to put the package in, and choose Edit ➤ Paste.

Once the package is in a table, you can double-click the package at any time to open it.

Closing a Table

When you're done working with a table, you'll want to close it to make sure all your data is saved to disk. You close a table simply by closing the window it's displayed in, using any of the standard Windows techniques.

Keep in mind that if you've used both Form View and Table View, you need to close both those windows in order to close the table fully. The steps you'd follow to close your table would likely be these:

1. If you have used Form View to enter or edit data, first get to the form by clicking anywhere in its window or by pressing Ctrl+F6 until the form is in full view.

2. Double-click the Control-menu box in the upper left-corner of the Form window (*not* the Control-menu box for the Paradox Desktop), or press Ctrl+F4.

3. At this point, you'll probably be taken to the Table View for the current table. If not, you can click anywhere on the Table window of the table you want to close, or press Ctrl+F6 until the table you want to close is in view.

4. Double-click the Control-menu box for the Table View's window (*not* the Control-menu box for the Paradox Desktop), or press Ctrl+F4.

TIP   The quickest way to close all the windows on the Desktop is to choose Window ➤ Close All.

When you've closed all the tables, the Desktop will be clear. You can, of course, re-open the table at any time using File ➤ Open ➤ Table, as described at the beginning of this chapter.

Using Lookup Tables to Enter Data

A lookup table is yet another way to speed and verify data entry and editing. The lookup table can contain any number of valid entries for a field. For instance, you could define a lookup table of all the valid two-letter state abbreviations in the United States, or all the valid product codes in your inventory. Once you've created a lookup table, you can use it in three ways:

- To verify entries as they're entered into a table.
- To look up a valid entry for a field.
- To copy data from the lookup table into the corresponding fields of the table you're editing.

Notice that there are two tables involved. The *lookup table* contains a list of valid entries. The other table, which we'll refer to as the *data-entry table*, is the one you're actually entering data into. For instance, if you're entering data into the CustList table and you want to ensure that no invalid two-letter state abbreviations are entered, CustList is the data-entry table and the table of valid two-letter state abbreviations is the lookup table.

Defining a Lookup Table

When creating a lookup table, you need to keep in mind the following rules and guidelines:

- The field you want to use to verify entries against must be the first field in the lookup table.

- Preferably, this first field should be the primary key for the lookup table.

- Any fields that you want to copy from the lookup table into the data-entry table must have the same field name, field type, and size in both tables.

We'll look at a couple of examples in a moment.

Defining the Relationship between Tables

After you've created your lookup table, you'll need to restructure the data-entry table and define the relationship between the data-entry table and the lookup table. During that process, you'll be given a choice of Lookup Types:

- **Just Current Field**: Data from one field in the lookup table will be copied only into the field being edited in the data-entry table.

- **All Corresponding Fields**: Data from multiple fields in the lookup table will be copied into multiple corresponding fields of the data-entry table. (Corresponding fields are those that have the same name and field type in the two tables).

You'll also be given a choice of two types of Lookup Access:

- **Fill No Help**: The lookup table verifies entries, but the person entering data in the data-entry table cannot view the lookup table.

- **Help and Fill**: The lookup table verifies entries, *and* the person entering data can pop open the lookup table to look up a valid entry.

Table 5.7 summarizes how different pairs of selections affect the relationship between the data-entry table and the lookup table.

TABLE 5.7: Lookup Table Data-Entry and Editing Validation Options

LOOKUP TYPE AND ACCESS	VALIDATE ENTRY?	VIEW LOOKUP TABLE?	COPY CURRENT FIELD?	COPY ALL MATCHING FIELDS?
Just Current Field Fill No Help	Yes	No	No	No
Just Current Field Help And Fill	Yes	Yes	Yes	No
All Corresponding Fields Fill No Help	Yes	No	No	Yes

A Simple Lookup Table Example

Creating and using a lookup table is actually much easier to do than it is to explain. So let's skip the generalities and take a look at a useful example—creating a table of valid two-letter state abbreviations as a lookup table for entering data into our sample CustList table.

WARNING

You *wouldn't* want to use a lookup table of state abbreviations if your CustList table included addresses outside the United States, since any non-U.S. state or abbreviation would be rejected as an invalid entry.

Creating the States Table

Your first step is to create a table, which we'll name *States*, on the same directory as your CustList table. A lookup table is just like any other table, so you use the standard techniques to create it.

NOTE   You can use *any* table as a lookup table. For instance, if you already have a table named *Products* that includes information about all your products, you can use *that* table as a lookup table for entering orders. Examples are presented in Chapter 15.

In this example, assuming your working directory is already the same as your CustList table, choose File ➤ New ➤ Table, then choose OK to accept Paradox for Windows as the table type. This table needs only two fields, named *State* and *State Name*, as shown below.

	FIELD NAME	TYPE	SIZE	KEY
1	State	A	2	⋆
2	State Name	A	15	

Notice that the State field has the same name, field type, and size as the State field in the CustList table (this is required). That field is also keyed for quick access. The State Name field will contain the spelled-out state name to help the person using the table find the appropriate state name. No validity checks are required in this table.

After creating the table structure, choose Save As and give the table a name—*States* in this example.

Filling in the States Table

The next step is to fill in the States table with all the valid two-letter state abbreviations and corresponding state names. Thus, if the States table isn't already open, choose File ➤ Open ➤ Table, and choose *states.db*.

Then switch to Edit mode (press F9 or click the Edit Table button) so you can enter some records.

As you fill in records, Paradox automatically alphabetizes them by the two-letter state abbreviations and rejects any duplicates, since the table is keyed on the State field. If you include Guam (GU), Puerto Rico (PR), and the Virgin Islands (VI), you'll end up with 54 records in the States table. Figure 5.22 shows how the first 16 records appear in the table.

TIP

You can find a list of all the authorized two-letter state abbreviations in the white pages of your phone book.

After filling in the States table, close it by double-clicking its Control-menu box or choosing Window ➤ Close All.

FIGURE 5.22

The first 16 records in the States table

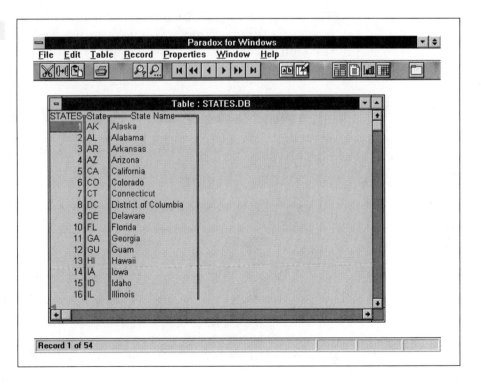

Activating the Lookup Table

The next step is to modify the structure of CustList so that it knows to use the States table as a lookup table. To get started, choose File ➤ Utilities ➤ Restructure, and choose *custlist.db* as the table to restructure.

Next, click on the State field in the **Restructure** dialog box to move the cursor to it. Then click the drop-down list button under Table Properties and choose *Table Lookup* (*not* Table Language—a common mistake). Click on Define to get to the **Table Lookup** dialog box (Figure 5.23).

The left side of this dialog box lists the names, types, and sizes of the fields in the table you're restructuring—CustList in this example. For instance, *State (A2)* indicates that the State field is an alphanumeric field with a length of two characters. Since this is the field you want to look up valid entries for, make sure it is the currently selected field. Click that field name, then click the → button next to Fields to make sure that field name appears under *Field Name* near the top of the dialog box.

The right side of the dialog box lists names of other tables in the same directory. In this example, you want to use States as the lookup table. Click on *STATES.DB*, then click the ← button next to Lookup Table.

FIGURE 5.23

The Table Lookup dialog box filled in to use *states.db* as a lookup table for the State field in the CustList table. Notice that the Just Current Field and Help and Fill options are selected.

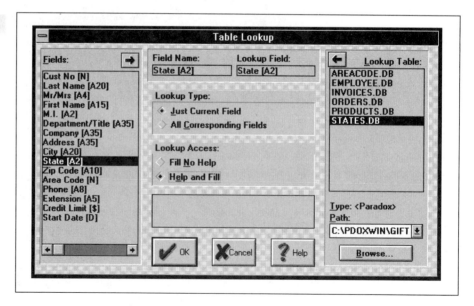

Paradox automatically places *State (A2)* under the Lookup Field option, since this is the first field in the States table.

Finally, under Lookup Type, choose *Just Current Field*, since we're verifying and copying only the State abbreviation from the lookup table to the CustList table. Under Lookup Access, choose *Help and Fill* so that the person entering data will be able to look up state abbreviations as needed. Figure 5.23 shows how the Table Lookup dialog box appears at this point, with all the correct selections made.

After finishing with the dialog box, choose OK to return to the table structure. Then choose Save to save the new table structure.

Using the Lookup Table

Now, let's say that you decide to add some new records to the CustList table or make some changes to it. Simply open that one table, CustList, and switch to Edit mode, in the usual manner. When the cursor is in the State field, the message below appears in the status bar:

Press Ctrl+spacebar for lookup help

At that point, pressing Ctrl+spacebar pops open the lookup table, as in Figure 5.24.

Now you can scroll through the table using the scroll bar at the right of the table or the ↑, ↓, PgUp, and PgDn arrow keys. When you find the two-letter state abbreviation you want, just click it and choose OK, or move to the abbreviation you want and press ↵. The abbreviation is copied into the field, and the lookup table disappears.

TIP You can also drag the lookup table by its title bar to move it, and use the Locate (Ctrl+Z) and Locate Next (Ctrl+A) shortcuts to look up a value in any field of the lookup table. You can choose Cancel or press Escape to leave the lookup table without making a selection.

Pressing Ctrl+spacebar is entirely optional. If you want, you can still type in the two-letter state abbreviation when you get to the State field.

FIGURE 5.24

The lookup table appears on the screen when you press Ctrl+spacebar with the cursor in the State field.

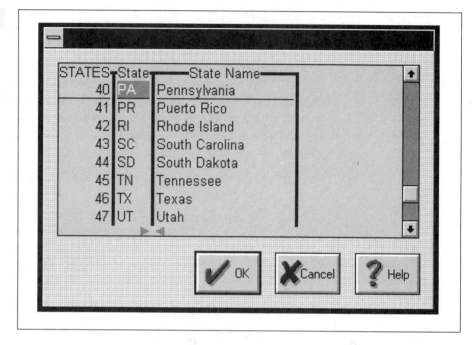

However, if you type in an invalid abbreviation (one that is not in the State field of the States table) then try to move on to the next field, Paradox will reject your entry and display this error message in the status bar:

Unable to find lookup value.

As with any validity check, you won't be able to move the cursor out of the State field until you've entered a valid two-letter state abbreviation. You can press Ctrl+spacebar at this point to choose a valid entry.

We'll look at some more advanced examples of lookup tables in Part 5 of this book.

In this chapter you've learned about the many options and techniques for entering and editing data in a table. In the next chapter, we'll take a look at techniques for controlling the appearance of data on your screen, and discuss some techniques for printing data.

CHAPTER

6

Viewing and Printing Table Data

f a s t TRACK

To change the properties of a Table View header area, data area, or grid   **243**

inspect the area you want to change by right-clicking. Alternatively, you can click on the area you want to change, then right-click, or press F6, or choose the Grid, Data, or Heading options from the Properties menu.

To inspect all the columns at once   **244**

press Ctrl+Shift+M.

To inspect all the column headings at once   **244**

press Ctrl+Shift+H.

To set up the printer before printing reports   **278**

choose File ➤ Printer Setup.

To print a Quick Report   **279**

choose File ➤ Print to print the Table window or Form window or click the Quick Report button in the SpeedBar to print the Table window. Or, click the Print button in the SpeedBar in the Table or Form window.

WHENEVER you open a table, Paradox initially displays that table in the default Table View, where field names appear across the top of the table in the same order that they're listed in the table structure. Each column is roughly the width you assigned when creating the table structure or the width of the field name, whichever is larger.

The default Table View *inherits* certain properties from settings in the Windows Control Panel. For example, the colors used in the table and the format of dates, numbers, and currency values are all determined by settings in the Windows Control Panel. You can change any of those settings to get the appearance you want for the current Table View.

TIP

You can change the default properties by creating a table named *Default* in your private directory (see Chapter 13).

Personalizing Table View

Paradox gives you two quick and easy ways to customize Table View:

- **Direct manipulation**: Click the left mouse button and drag "hot spots" to move and size objects.
- **Property inspection**: Right-click the object you want to change, and choose properties, such as fonts and colors, from menus or floating dialog boxes.

We'll look at the various direct manipulation techniques first.

Changing Table View Directly

You can use standard Windows techniques to size and move the entire Table View. You can drag the title bar to move the window or drag any border to size it. You can also use the Minimize, Maximize, and Control-menu boxes to size and move the window that contains the Table View.

You can also change Table View within the window by clicking and dragging various *hot zones,* shown in Figure 6.1.

FIGURE 6.1

Hot zones for directly manipulating Table View with the left mouse button

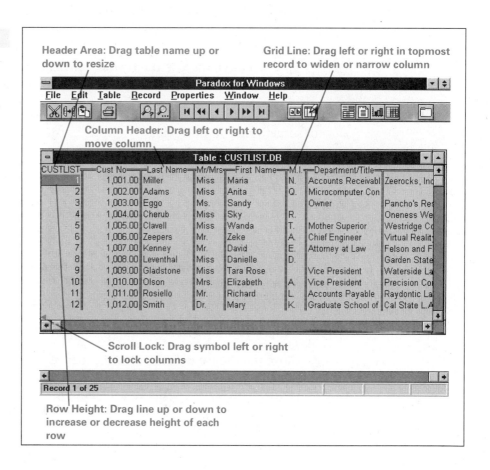

Saving and Restoring Table View Settings

Before going into detail on changing Table View, we'll tell you how to save and "undo" settings so you can experiment without committing yourself to a particular view. Here are some things to keep in mind:

- When you find a Table View that you like and you're sure you want to keep it, choose Properties ➤ View Properties ➤ Save to save those settings instantly. (You may also want to save current settings just before trying any options you're not comfortable with yet.)

- If you make a mess of things, choose Properties ➤ View Properties ➤ Restore. Any changes made since the last time you saved will be undone.

- To undo all changes and return to the default Table View, choose Properties ➤ View Properties ➤ Delete, then choose OK.

Now you can experiment to your heart's content without feeling stuck with something you don't like.

Changing the Order of Columns

It's easy to change the order of columns in Table View. This might be handy if you bunched several fields, such as Last Name, First Name, Zip Code, and Address, at the top of the table structure in order to define a primary key, but then wanted to *display* those columns in a more natural order, such as Address, City, State, then Zip Code.

You can use either of two methods to change the order of columns.

 • Move the mouse pointer to the header of the column you want to move (i.e., to the field name at the top of the column) until you see the icon shown at the left. Then hold down the left mouse button, drag the icon to the new location for the column, and release the mouse button.

- Alternatively, you can move the highlight to any column (except the column below the table name) and press Ctrl+R to rotate that column to the last column position. Each time you press Ctrl+R, the current column becomes the last column in the Table window.

Changing Column Widths

You can also widen or narrow any column in Table View. This is handy for displaying more or less text in alphanumeric and memo fields and controlling how many columns appear across the screen. For instance, in Figure 6.2 we narrowed several columns in the CustList table so we could see more information on the screen.

FIGURE 6.2

Narrowing some columns in the CustList table lets you see more data on the screen.

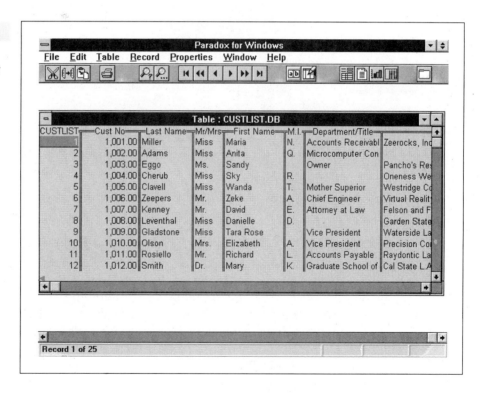

You may notice that the Department/Title field is so narrow that some of the text is clipped off in the longer fields. Not to worry—all the data is still there. Narrowing a column in Table View only changes how much you can *see*. While editing a narrowed field, you'll still be able to scroll through the entire contents of the field.

To change the width of a column, follow the steps below.

1. Move the mouse pointer to the vertical grid at the right side of the column you want to resize, in the topmost record in view (just below the field name). The mouse pointer changes to a two-headed arrow when properly placed, as in the example shown at left.

2. Hold down the mouse button and drag the icon to the right to widen the column or to the left to narrow the column.

3. Release the mouse button when the column is the desired width.

NOTE   If you make a numeric or currency column too narrow to show all the data, Paradox will display a series of asterisks (***) rather than the number. To fix this, just widen the column again. Asterisks also appear when part of a numeric or date column is scrolled off the right edge of the window. Scrolling the rest of the column into view will remove those asterisks.

Changing the Row Height

You can also change the height of each row (record) in a table. This is particularly handy if your table contains graphics or memos and you want to be able to see more of their contents as you scroll through the table. Figure 6.3 shows the sample Employee table with each row made tall enough to display the graphic in the Photo field and much of the text in the formatted memo field. (We also changed some column widths and positions.)

FIGURE 6.3

Changing the row
height in Table View is
particularly helpful if
your table contains
graphics and memos
and you want to view
more of the contents
of these fields as you
scroll through records.

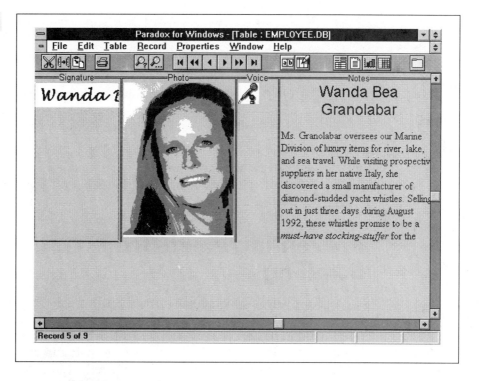

NOTE

If only the <BLOB...> message appears in a graphic,
memo, or OLE field, you can right-click the field and
check the Complete Display property. However, be
aware that scrolling through the record will be slower
if you do so.

To change the height of each row in the table, proceed as follows:

1. Move the mouse pointer to the leftmost column of the first record
   in the table. For example, if the table is currently scrolled all the way
   to the left, position the mouse pointer on the record number 1 field,
   just below the table name.

2. Now move the pointer down slightly, so that it touches the horizontal line under the first field of the leftmost column. When you've positioned it correctly, the mouse pointer will change to the vertical two-headed arrow shown at left.

3. Hold down the mouse button and drag the arrow down to make the rows taller, or drag it up to make the rows narrower. As you drag, a dotted line will appear across the window to show the height of the row.

4. Release the mouse button when the first row is the height you want. The first row and all the other rows will automatically adjust to this height.

Preventing Fields from Scrolling

Normally, as you scroll to the right through a table, columns at the left edge will scroll out of view. For example, if you scroll to the Credit Limit field in the last column of the CustList table, the customer's name scrolls off the left edge of the window, as in Figure 6.4. If you can't see the customer's name as you edit the Credit Limit field, you run the risk of changing the wrong customer's credit limit—a potentially unpleasant situation for your company and your customer.

To prevent columns from scrolling off the window, simply lock those columns into position, as follows:

1. If necessary, drag or rotate the columns you want to prevent from scrolling to the leftmost part of the table.

2. If the Table window isn't already scrolled all the way to the left, use the scroll bars (or press Home) to get to the leftmost column.

3. Move the mouse pointer to the *scroll lock*, a small triangle ◄ just above the left edge of the horizontal scroll bar on the Table window. The mouse pointer will change to a two-headed horizontal arrow, as shown at the left.

4. Hold down the mouse button and drag the scroll lock to the right or left. As you drag, the scroll lock icon will jump to just below the vertical grid line at the right of a column.

5. Release the mouse button when the column or columns you want to prevent from scrolling are to the left of the scroll lock.

FIGURE 6.4

The customer's name scrolls off the left edge of the window when you move the highlight to the rightmost column of the CustList table.

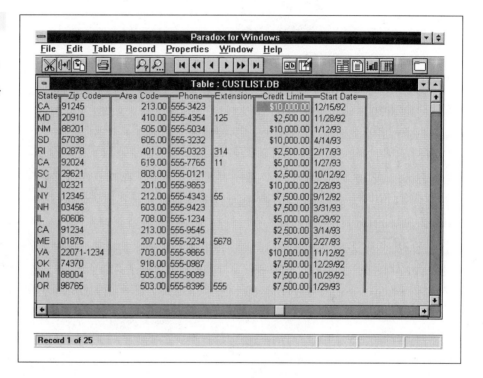

Now, whenever you scroll the Table window to the left or right, the columns you locked into place will be prevented from scrolling and will always remain visible at the left edge of the window. For example, Figure 6.5 shows the CustList table with the cursor in the Credit Limit field after moving the Last Name and First Name fields to the leftmost columns of Table View and placing a scroll lock at the First Name column.

To remove (or change) the scroll lock, first move back to the leftmost column of Table View using the horizontal scroll bar, ←, or Home key, until the symbol becomes two triangles ▶ ◀. Then drag that symbol to the far left edge of Table View or wherever you want the scroll lock.

NOTE

You cannot change the position of the scroll lock unless the Table window is scrolled all the way to the left, so that the table name and record number columns appear at the left edge of the window.

FIGURE 6.5

The Table window after moving the Last Name and First Name columns to the far left, locking those columns, and moving the highlight to the Credit Limit field at the right edge of the window

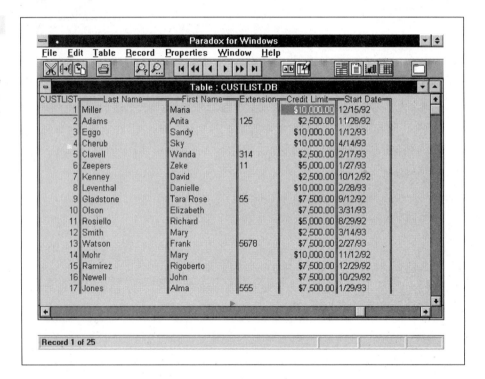

Changing the Table Header Height

To change the height of the header area at the top of a table, move the mouse pointer to the table name at the upper-left corner of the table. The mouse pointer changes to a vertical 2-headed arrow. Hold down the mouse button and drag the icon up to narrow the header area or down to widen it. As you drag, a thick horizontal bar will appear, indicating the header height. Release the mouse button when the table header is the desired height.

Changing Table View Properties

You can change the properties of a Table View header area, data area, or grid, as shown in Figure 6.6. To change the properties of any area, simply inspect (right-click) the area you want to change or click the area first, then right-click or press F6. You can also use the shortcut keys or the Properties menu, summarized in Table 6.1.

Once you've selected an area, you'll see a menu of options for changing it. The options available depend on the area you're inspecting, but will generally consist of several of the options described below.

FIGURE 6.6

You can change the properties of the header area, data area, or grid in Table View by moving the mouse pointer to the area and clicking the right mouse button.

Header area

Table : CUSTLIST.DB

CUSTLIST	Cust No	Last Name	Mr/Mrs	First Name	M.I.	Department
1	1,001.00	Miller	Miss	Maria	N.	Accounts Receivable
2	1,002.00	Adams	Miss	Anita	Q.	Microcomputer Consu
3	1,003.00	Eggo	Ms.	Sandy		Owner
4	1,004.00	Cherub	Miss	Sky	R.	
5	1,005.00	Clavell	Miss	Wanda	T.	Mother Superior
6	1,006.00	Zeepers	Mr.	Zeke	A.	Chief Engineer
7	1,007.00	Kenney	Mr.	David	E.	Attorney at Law
8	1,008.00	Leventhal	Miss	Danielle	D.	
9	1,009.00	Gladstone	Miss	Tara Rose		Vice President
10	1,010.00	Olson	Mrs.	Elizabeth	A.	Vice President
11	1,011.00	Rosiello	Mr.	Richard	L.	Accounts Payable
12	1,012.00	Smith	Dr.	Mary	K.	Graduate School of B
13	1,013.00	Watson	Mr.	Frank	R.	Greenskeeper
14	1,014.00	Mohr	Mrs.	Mary	M.	
15	1,015.00	Ramirez	Mr.	Rigoberto	R.	Author
16	1,016.00	Newell	Mr.	John	J.	
17	1,017.00	Jones	Ms.	Alma	R.	Account Executive

Data area (column)   Grid area

TABLE 6.1: Optional Keystrokes for Inspecting Data, Header, and Grid Areas in a Table View

TO INSPECT	PRESS...	OR CHOOSE...
Current column	Ctrl+M	Properties ➤ Data
All columns	Ctrl+Shift+M	
Current header	Ctrl+H	Properties ➤ Heading
All headers	Ctrl+Shift+H	
Grid	Ctrl+G	Properties ➤ Grid

Changing the Alignment

To change the alignment of data within a column or within the column header, follow these steps:

1. Inspect (right-click) the column (data area) or header you want to change, or press Ctrl+Shift+M to inspect all the columns, or Ctrl+Shift+H to inspect all the headers.

TIP

The title of the property menu tells you what you're inspecting, for example, *Last_Name* (the Last Name column), *Last_Name_Heading* (header for the Last Name column), *All* (all columns), or *All_Heading* (all column headers).

2. Choose Alignment from the property menu that appears. You'll then see this menu:

3. Choose any option:

Left   Aligns text along the left edge of the column (the default for alphanumeric and date fields).

Center   Centers text horizontally within the column (the default for field names at the top of each column).

Right   Aligns text along the right edge of the column (the default for numeric and currency values).

Top   Aligns text at the top edge of the row (the default setting).

Center   Centers text between the top and bottom edges of each row.

Bottom   Aligns text along the bottom edge of each row.

You can combine horizontal and vertical alignments. For instance, you can inspect a column and choose Alignment ➤ Left to left-align data in that column, then re-inspect the same column and choose Alignment ➤ Center (the lower Center option) to center the field contents vertically.

Changing the Colors

You can change the background color of the header area, grid, or data area by following these steps:

1. First right-click the header or column you want to color. Or, press Ctrl+Shift+M to color all the data columns, or Ctrl+Shift+H to select all column headings.

2. Choose Color from the property menu. You'll see a Color palette.

3. If you want to change just the background color, choose a color and skip the remaining steps.

4. If you click the snap button at the top of the Color palette, you'll see the dialog box below.

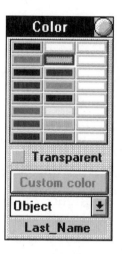

NOTE The third column of white colors is for creating your own colors, as described in Appendix D. (You cannot create custom colors in Table windows, but you can change existing custom colors.) Notice too that the bottom of the floating dialog box presents a reminder of what you're coloring.

5. Now you can use any of the following techniques to choose existing colors from the palette:

• To change the foreground color (text), choose *Font* from the drop-down list box, then choose a color.

- To choose a color for the grid, select *Grid Lines* from the drop-down list box (if the option is available), or click on the grid, then choose a color. You can also choose *Current Record* from the list box to define a color for the current record marker, described under "Customizing the Grid," later in this chapter.

- To change the background color, choose *Object* from the drop-down list box in the palette, or click in the column you want to color, then click on the color you want.

NOTE The Transparent option in the Color palette is not relevant to coloring Table View. It is useful in coloring custom forms, as you'll see in Chapter 10.

While the floating dialog box is on the screen, you can click any column or heading, or press Ctrl+Shift+M (all columns) or Ctrl+Shift+H (all headers) to choose another area to color. The message at the bottom of the dialog box changes, indicating what your next color selection will affect.

TIP You can click one of the colors on the palette and then use the arrow keys to see the effects of selecting various colors.

When you're happy with the colors you've selected, click the snap button to close the floating dialog box.

Changing the Font

It's easy to choose a screen font for the header or data area in Table View. The steps are virtually identical to changing the color or any other property.

Changing the font in Table View will have no effect on printed output. You can control printed fonts by defining a custom report format (Chapter 11).

1. Begin by inspecting (right-clicking) the column or heading you want to change the font of, or pressing Ctrl+Shift+M to change the font of all the columns or Ctrl+Shift+H to change the font of all the headings.

2. Choose *Font*. You'll see the font menu shown below.

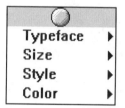

3. You can choose one of the options from the Font menu, and then select a typeface, size, style, or color and skip the remaining steps. Or, click the snap button to get the floating Font palette shown below. As usual, the bottom of the palette shows which area of Table View your choices will affect.

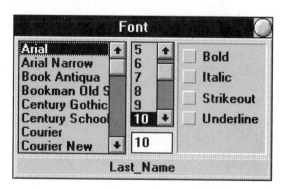

NOTE   Only fonts that you've installed for use in Windows will appear in the list of available fonts.

4. Choose any combination of typefaces, sizes, and styles.

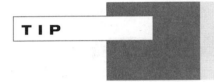

TIP   You can click in the typefaces or sizes list in the floating dialog box, then use the arrow keys to see the effects of various options.

Remember that you can move the Font dialog box out of the way by dragging its title bar. To select another area to change without losing the floating dialog box, just click outside the floating dialog box or use the shortcut keys.

When you're done changing fonts, click the snap button on the Font palette.

Customizing the Grid

The grid is the pattern of lines that appears between the columns (and, optionally, the rows) of the table. All the tables shown so far in this chapter use the following default grid settings:

- The grid background is gray.
- Horizontal grid lines appear in the heading area.
- Vertical grid lines appear between columns.
- No grid lines appear between rows.
- The horizontal and vertical lines are black.

- The grid lines are double-spaced, that is, two lines appear side by side.
- The current record marker line is hidden.

To change the grid, first inspect it by right-clicking any part of the grid or by pressing Ctrl+G. You'll see the property menu shown below. From here, you can customize many aspects of the table's grid background, grid lines, and current record marker, as described in the sections that follow.

Changing the Background Color of the Grid

To change the background color of the grid, inspect the grid and choose Color from the property menu. You'll see the familiar list of colors. Select a color as described earlier under "Changing the Colors."

TIP   To make the grid background disappear, give it the same color as the data columns and header area.

Changing the Grid Lines

To change the appearance of the grid lines, choose Grid Lines from the Grid property menu. You'll see the options shown below.

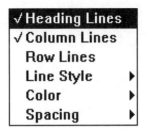

The first three items, Heading Lines, Column Lines, and Row Lines are toggles. If the item is checked, the property is activated. Choosing one of these options switches it to the opposite state ("off" if it is currently "on," "on" if it is currently "off").

To change the style of the grid lines, choose Grid Lines ➤ Line Style from the Grid property menu. Click on the line style you want from the list of line styles that appears, or click the snap button to get a floating Line Style palette. As with the floating Color and Font palettes, you can move the floating Line Style palette by dragging its title bar. When you're done changing the line style, click the snap button on the Line Style palette.

To change the color of the grid lines, choose Grid Lines ➤ Color from the Grid property menu. Click on the color you want from the list of colors that appears.

To define the number of grid lines that appear side by side, choose Grid Lines ➤ Spacing after inspecting the grid. Then choose Single, Double, or Triple to select one, two, or three lines for the grid.

Changing the Current Record Marker

Initially, your table appears without a current record marker. If you inspect the grid and choose Current Record Marker, you'll be presented with three options: Show, Line Style, and Color.

NOTE You must check the Show option if you want the Color option to have any effect. Show is also a toggle that is turned on (checked) or off (unchecked) each time you select it from the menu.

- Choose Show (if it isn't already checked) to display the current record marker. Then, if you want to change the color of the marker, inspect the grid and choose Current Record Marker again.

- To change the line style of the marker, choose Line Style, then select a line style from the Line Style palette.

- To change the color of the marker, choose Color, then select a color from the Color palette.

Once you've turned on the current record marker, you'll see that it extends all the way across Table View and moves from record to record as you scroll up and down through the table.

Example of a Customized Table View

Figure 6.7 shows an example of Table View for the sample CustList table after some color, font, and grid properties were changed. Read on to see how we got these results.

- We pressed Ctrl+Shift+M to select all data columns, chose Color, then clicked the white color.

- Next we pressed Ctrl+Shift+H to select all headers, chose Color, and clicked the white color again.

- We pressed Ctrl+G to select the grid, chose Color, and selected the white color.

- Next we pressed Ctrl+Shift+H again to select all headers, and chose Font, then the snap button. Then we chose Arial Narrow, bold, 12 pt from the Font dialog box.

The fonts used in this example are Windows TrueType fonts.

- We clicked outside the Font box and pressed Ctrl+Shift+M to select all columns. From the floating Font dialog box, we chose Lucida Fax 10 point, then clicked the snap button to close the Font dialog box.

- At this point we inspected the grid again (Ctrl+G) and chose Grid Lines ➤ Spacing ➤ Single.

- Finally, we inspected the grid one more time (Ctrl+G) and chose Current Record Marker ➤ Show. The marker appears beneath the fifth record in the figure.

FIGURE 6.7

Sample CustList table after changing color, font, and grid properties

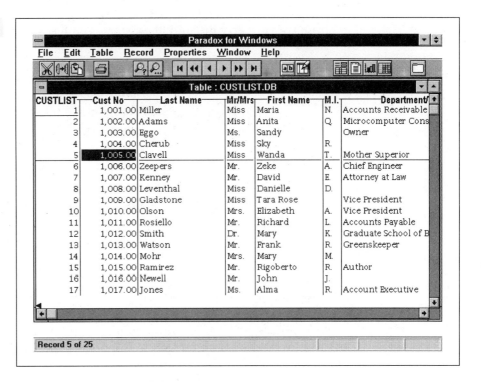

Changing the Format of Numbers

Numeric and currency values in a table are initially displayed with the format currently defined in the International settings of the Windows Control Panel.

NOTE Changing the International settings in the Windows Control Panel affects the format of numbers and dates in all Paradox for Windows tables, as well as in other Windows applications.

If you want to change the appearance of numbers or currency values in a particular column, inspect that column and then choose Number Format from the property menu that appears. You'll see this menu:

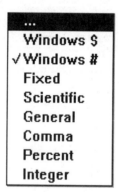

Your options are as follows:

Windows $ Uses the currency symbol and format defined in the International option of the Windows Control Panel (the default for currency fields).

Windows #   Uses the format defined for numbers in the International option of the Windows Control Panel (the default for numeric fields).

Fixed   Displays numbers with two decimal places and trailing zeros, but without thousand separators. Negative numbers are preceded by a minus sign.

Scientific   Displays numbers in exponential notation: a decimal number from 1 to 10 multiplied by an exponent of 10. Negative numbers are preceded by a minus sign.

General   Displays numbers without decimal places or thousand separators. Negative numbers are preceded by a minus sign.

Comma   Displays numbers with two decimal places, trailing zeros, and with thousands separated by a comma. Negative values are enclosed in parentheses.

Percent   Displays numbers followed by the percent sign (%), but without thousand separators. Negative numbers are preceded by a minus sign.

Integer   Displays whole numbers only, without thousand separators. Negative numbers are preceded by a minus sign. When you convert to Integer format, decimal values are rounded. However, if you later convert to another format that displays decimals, they will reappear.

WARNING
If existing numbers cannot fit into the column after you change the number format, Paradox displays asterisks instead of the numbers. You'll need to widen the column to see the numbers in their new format.

After choosing a format, you'll be returned to the Desktop and the numbers in the column you inspected will reflect the new format. Table 6.2 shows examples of how three numbers—entered as 35.75, 2500, and -2500—appear in each of the predefined formats. In the table, the Windows # and Windows $ use the United States defaults for numbers and currency.

TABLE 6.2: Sample Numbers in the Predefined Number Formats

ENTERED AS...	35.75	2500	-2500
Windows $	$35.75	$2,500.00	($2,500.00)
Windows #	35.75	2,500.00	-2,500.00
Fixed	35.75	2500.00	-2500.00
Scientific	3.5750e+1	2.5000e+3	-2.5000e+3
General	35.75	2500	-2500
Comma	35.75	2,500.00	(2500)
Percent	3575.0 %	250000.0 %	-250000.0 %
Integer	36	2500	-2500

Figure 6.8 shows the modified CustList Table View with some columns rearranged so you can see both the Cust No and Area Code columns. Notice that Cust No and Area Code are now displayed as integers. To change the format of those fields, we right-clicked the Cust No column and chose Number Format ➤ Integer. Then we right-clicked the Area Code column, and chose Number Format ➤ Integer again.

Creating Custom Number Formats

If none of the predefined number formats is to your liking, you can create your own number formats. Here's how to begin:

1. Inspect the numeric or currency column that you want to reformat, and choose Number Format, as previously described.

2. Click the header (...) at the top of the menu. If you're inspecting a currency field, the dialog box shown in Figure 6.9 will appear. If you're inspecting a number field, the dialog box in Figure 6.10 will appear.

FIGURE 6.8

The sample CustList
table after changing
the Cust No and Area
Code columns to
Integer format

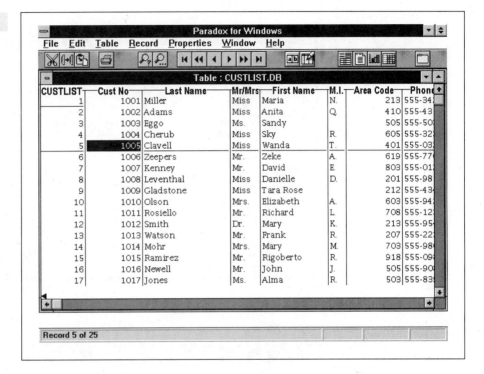

3. To create a new format, first choose the existing format (from the
   right side of the dialog box) that most closely matches the format
   you want to create. For example, if you want to define a format
   that's similar to Windows # format but encloses negative numbers
   in parentheses, choose *Windows #* from the list.

4. Click the Create button.

5. Type a name for the new format into the Name text box. For example, type **Win # with ( )** to describe a Windows # format with
   parentheses. The name you enter must be unique; that is, it cannot match any name listed under Existing Formats.

6. If you want the format you're creating to be available in future
   Paradox sessions, select the Permanent check box.

7. Now you can choose any combination of options under Format at
   the left side of the dialog box (see "Setting Number Format Options," below, for details).

FIGURE 6.9

The Select Number
Format dialog box for
currency ($) fields

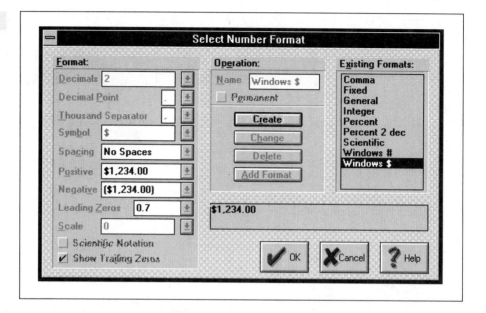

FIGURE 6.10

The Select Number
Format dialog box for
number (N) fields

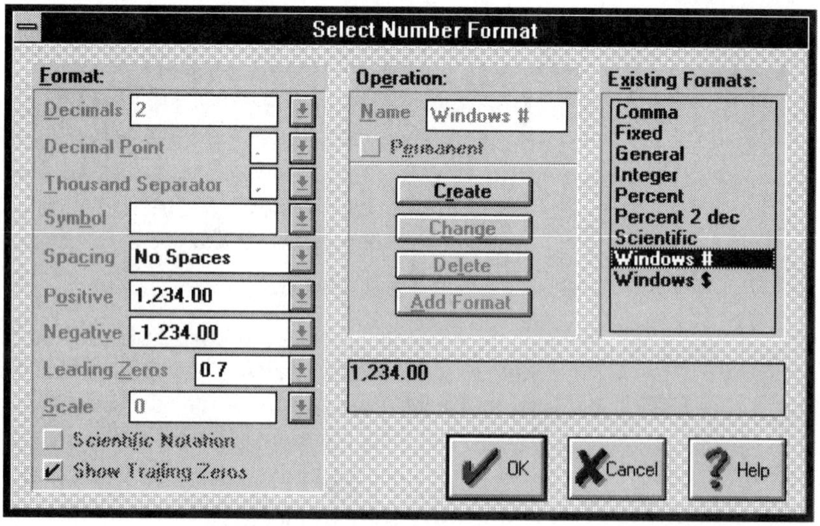

8. When the format is the way you want it, click the Add Format button. Paradox adds the new format to the list of Existing Formats and automatically highlights the new format.

9. Leave the new format highlighted in the Existing Formats list and choose OK. You'll be returned to the Desktop, and the column will be formatted according to the new specifications.

To use the new format in another column, just right-click that column and choose the format from the property menu that appears.

Setting Number Format Options

The Format options at the left side of the dialog box are summarized below.

Decimals   Defines the number of decimal places displayed to the right of the decimal point. You can type in the number of places or select the number of decimals from the list box.

Decimal Point   Defines the decimal point character. Choose a period or comma from the list box, or type in your own decimal point character.

Thousand Separator   Defines the character used as the thousand separator. Choose a space, period, or comma from the list box, or type in your own thousand separator.

Symbol   Defines the symbol or symbols displayed with the number. The predefined symbols are $, inch, lb, kg, cm, mi, and DM. You can type in any symbol or symbols you wish, or select a symbol from the list box.

T I P

To define a foreign currency symbol from the IBM PC Extended character set, turn on Num Lock, hold down the Alt key, and type one of the following three-digit numbers using the numeric keypad (*not* the numbers at the top of the keyboard): 156 (British Pound), 157 (Yen), 158 (Pesetas), or 159 (Franc).

Spacing   Defines whether a space appears between the number and the symbol preceding it. The list box options let you choose *No Spaces*, a space before *Negatives* only, a space before *Positives* only, or a space before *Both* negative and positive numbers.

Positive   Defines the position (if any) for displaying a plus sign or DB symbol for positive numbers. This option also displays a sample positive number that reflects any other settings you've made to the number format so far.

Negative   Defines whether negative numbers are enclosed in parentheses, preceded or followed by a minus sign, or followed by a CR symbol. This option also displays a sample negative number that reflects any other settings you've made to the number format so far.

Leading Zeros   Defines how many digits will appear to the left of the decimal place. The list box options are *.7* (no leading zeros), *0.7* (one leading zero), *00.7* (two leading zeros), *000.7* (three leading zeros), *0000.7* (four leading zeros), and *00000.7* (five leading zeros). If you enter fewer than the defined number of digits to the left of the decimal place, Paradox pads the number with leading zeros. For example, if you set leading zeros to *0000.7* and type in the number 47, Paradox will display the number as 0047.

Scale   Displays the number as a multiple of a power of 10. Choose an entry from the Scale list box or type in your own number. For example, choosing *3* displays numbers as a multiple of 1000 (10^3); thus, a number entered as 1000 appears as 1 million, which is 1000 x 1000. Choosing *-3* displays numbers as multiples of .001 (10^{-3}); thus a number entered as 1000 appears as 1, which is 1000 x .001.

Scientific Notation   When checked, displays numbers in exponential notation (for example, 1e+1). When unchecked, it displays numbers in decimal notation.

Show Trailing Zeros   When checked, displays numbers with as many trailing zeros as are needed to fill in the number of Decimals (decimal places) you've defined. For example, if you checked Show Trailing Zeros, defined 4 Decimals, and entered the number 47.4, the number would appear as 47.4000.

Keep in mind that when you define a number format, you're changing only the *appearance*, not the actual value, of a number. For example, if you set Decimals to 0, you won't see the "cents" in currency amounts. To display cents again, simply choose a format with two or more decimal places.

Changing or Deleting a Custom Number Format

If you need to change or delete a custom number format, first you need to return to the dialog box by right-clicking any number or currency column in Table View, choosing Number ➤ Format, and clicking ... at the top of the menu that appears. Click the name of the format you want to change or delete.

To change the format, click the Change button and choose new settings from the Format options at the left side of the dialog box. If you want to delete the format, click the Delete button. Click OK to return to the Desktop.

NOTE   You can only change or delete custom formats that you've defined. The Change and Delete buttons and Format options are dimmed when one of the pre-defined formats is selected.

Deleting a custom format usually has no effect on numbers currently displayed in that format. That is, numbers still appear as if that format existed. If you want to change the format of one of those columns, inspect the column, then choose any one of the available number formats.

WARNING   If the current column has the number format you're deleting, its format *will* change to whatever format is automatically highlighted when you click the Delete button. Before leaving the dialog box, choose the format you want.

Changing the Format of Dates

Initially, any field that you've defined as the date field type is displayed in the format defined for dates in the International settings of the Windows Control Panel. However, as with numbers, you can change the format of a date for any column within your table. As you may have guessed by now, the way to get started is to right-click any column that was assigned the date field type, then click Date Format. You'll see this menu, with the options described below.

```
      ...
√ Windows Short
  Windows Long
  mm/dd/yy
```

Windows Short   Uses the short date format defined in the International option of the Windows Control Panel (the default date format).

Windows Long   Uses the long date format defined in the International option of the Windows Control Panel.

mm/dd/yy   Displays two-digit numbers for the month, followed by the day, followed by the year, each separated by a slash (/).

Paradox assumes that two-digit year (yy) values are in the twentieth century. For dates not in the twentieth century, you must specify all digits of the year. For example, to specify June 6, 1492, you must enter it as 6/6/1492.

After choosing a date format, you'll be returned to the Desktop, and the dates in the table column you inspected will reflect the new format. Table 6.3 shows examples of how three dates—entered as 6/6/92, 11/9/1492, and 10/29/2001—will appear in each of the predefined formats. The Windows Short and Windows Long formats shown in the table use the United States default formats for dates.

If the column isn't wide enough to display dates in the Format you've selected, the dates will be truncated in the column. Just widen the column to fix that problem.

TABLE 6.3: Sample Dates in the Predefined Date Formats

ENTERED AS...	WINDOWS SHORT	WINDOWS LONG	MM/DD/YY
6/6/92	6/6/92	Saturday, June 06, 1992	06/06/92
11/9/1492	11/9/1492	Wednesday, November 09, 1492	11/09/1492
10/29/2001	10/29/2001	Monday, October 29, 2001	10/29/2001

Creating Custom Date Formats

If you don't like the predefined date formats, you can define and select your own date formats using the methods previously described for number formats. The basic steps are as follows:

1. Inspect a date column in Table View, choose Date Format from the property menu that appears, then click the header (...) at the top of the menu. You'll see the **Select Date Format** dialog box shown in Figure 6.11.

2. To create your own date format, first highlight or click on a format in the Existing Formats list that's closest to the new format you want to define.

3. Click the Create button.

4. Type a name for the new format into the Name text box. The name of the date format must be unique.

5. If you want the new date format to be available in future Paradox sessions, click the Permanent check box.

6. Choose any combination of style options listed under Format at the left side of the dialog box (see "Setting Date Format Options," below, for details on these options). Figure 6.12 shows an example, which we've named *Long, no day*, which starts with the Windows Long format, then removes the *%W* from the front of the Order option. Notice how the sample date near the lower-left corner of the dialog box displays a date in the format January 1, 1901.

7. When you're satisfied with the format, choose OK. Paradox adds the new format to the list of Existing Formats, returns you to the Desktop, and reformats the current column according to the new specifications.

FIGURE 6.11

The Select Date Format dialog box lets you choose and define custom date formats.

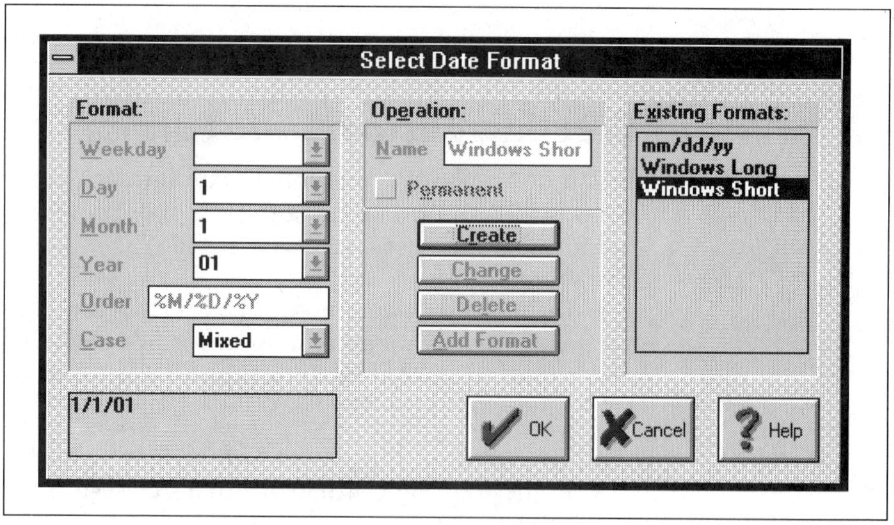

Select Date Format

Format:		Operation:		Existing Formats:
Weekday		Name	Windows Shor	mm/dd/yy
Day	1	☐ Permanent		Windows Long
Month	1			Windows Short
Year	01	Create		
Order	%M/%D/%Y	Change		
Case	Mixed	Delete		
		Add Format		

1/1/01   ✔ OK   ✖ Cancel   ? Help

FIGURE 6.12

The Select Date Format dialog box with a new format, entitled *Long, no day,* defined. The sample date at the lower-left corner of the dialog box shows how a date will look in this format.

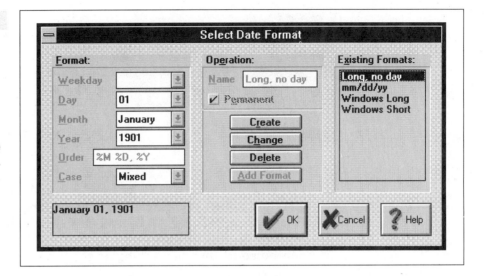

Setting Date Format Options

Here's a summary of what each of the Format options in the left side of the Select Date Format dialog box offers:

Weekday   Specifies whether the weekday is abbreviated or spelled out (for example, *Tuesday* versus *Tue*).

Day   Specifies whether the day number is displayed with or without a leading zero (for instance, *1* or *01*).

Month   Specifies whether the month appears as a number (with or without a leading zero), an abbreviated name, or a spelled-out name (*1*, *01*, *Jan*, or *January*).

Year   Specifies whether years in the twentieth century appear as two-digit numbers (with or without a leading zero) or four-digit numbers (*1*, *01*, or *1901*, for example).

NOTE The Weekday (%W), Day (%D), Month (%M), and Year (%Y) components are hidden unless you include them in the Order option text box. If you base your new or changed date format on Windows Long, the Order box will automatically include all four components of the date.

Order   Defines the order for the Weekday (%W), Month (%M), Day (%D), and Year (%Y), and any separator characters. You can edit the contents of this text box to your liking. For example, entering *%M %D, %Y (%W)* will display dates in the order *January 01, 1901 (Tuesday)*; *Jan 1, 1901 (Tue)*; and so forth, depending on the other settings in the Format area.

NOTE Changes you make to the Order text box are not reflected in the sample date at the lower-left corner of the dialog box until you click one of the other format options.

Case   Specifies the case used for weekdays and months. Your options are Mixed (as in *Tuesday January 01, 1901*), Lower (*tuesday january 01, 1901*), or Upper (*TUESDAY JANUARY 01, 1901*).

Changing or Deleting a Custom Date Format

The steps for changing a custom date format are basically the same as those described earlier for changing a custom number format. That is, go to the **Select Date Format** dialog box, click the name of the custom date format you want to change or delete, then choose the Change or Delete button as appropriate. Remember, you can only change or delete custom date formats—not the pre-defined formats.

Changing the Appearance of Memo, Graphic, and OLE Fields

When you inspect a graphic or OLE field, you'll see the five menu options shown below. Inspecting a memo or formatted memo field displays only the Complete Display, Color, and Font options. We've already described the Alignment, Color, and Font options. However, Complete Display and Magnification are new.

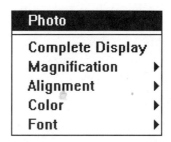

Changing the Complete Display Options

Normally, as you scroll through a table, Paradox displays the <BLOB...> message in the graphic, OLE, memo, or formatted memo field of every record except the current record. Right-clicking one of these fields and choosing the Complete Display option lets you change that. Like many properties, Complete Display is a toggle.

- When Complete Display is not checked (the default setting), Paradox displays the contents of the field in the current record only. All other records display the <BLOB...> message in that field.

- When the option is checked, Paradox displays the contents of the field in all records.

> **TIP**
>
> Scrolling through records can be unbearably slow when the Complete Display option is checked. Deselecting the Complete Display property will speed things along considerably.

Changing the Magnification

Choosing the Magnification option, available for graphic and OLE fields, takes you to this menu:

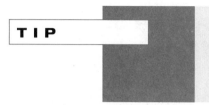

Your options are as follows:

Best Fit   Shrinks the graphic or OLE object to best fit the current width and height of the field. The proportions of the original object are retained.

25% or 50%   Shrinks the object to one quarter (25%) or one half (50%) its original size.

100%   Restores the object to its original size.

200% or 400%   Expands the object to twice (200%) or four times (400%) its original size.

Figure 6.13 shows a couple of sample records in the Employee table after rearranging the columns, changing their width and height, then checking the Complete Display option in the graphic Photo field and Notes formatted memo field, and setting the Magnification option to Best Fit in the Photo field.

FIGURE 6.13

Sample data in the Employee table after adjusting column positions, widths, and heights, then checking the Complete Display property, and setting the Magnification property to Best Fit

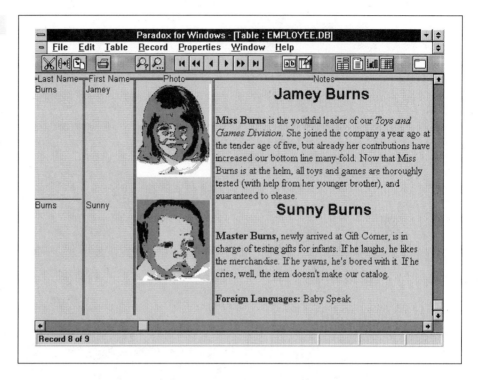

Changing Data-Dependent Properties

As you have seen, the Color and Font options in the property menu let you change the color of text or background for all records in a selected column of your table, regardless of the value in any field. In contrast, the Data Dependent property lets you use a different color or font to display fields that have a certain value or fall within a certain range of values. Changing the color or font of data based on their value makes it easy to manage information on an exception basis, since the exceptional values will stand out. In Chapter 8 you'll learn how to use queries to isolate records with specific values in one or more fields.

NOTE The Data Dependent option is available when you inspect alphanumeric, number, date, or currency fields.

Suppose you want to monitor old, unpaid invoices—for example, invoices mailed before October 1, 1992. The example in Figure 6.14 shows a sample table, named *Invoices*, in which we changed the data-dependent colors as follows:

* Invoice dates before 9/30/92 have white text on a black background.

* Invoice dates between 10/1/92 and 10/31/92 have black text on a white background.

* Any invoice with a 0 value in the Amount Paid field is displayed on a white background.

FIGURE 6.14

Data-dependent coloring draws attention to invoices with September (or earlier) and October dates, as well as invoices with 0 in the Amount Paid column.

INVOICES	Invoice Number	Order Number	Invoice Amount	Invoice Date	Amount Paid	Date Paid
1	10001	1002	$392.39	10/4/92	$0.00	
2	10002	1003	$177.90	3/5/93	$177.90	4/4/93
3	10003	1006	($84.26)	9/3/92	$0.00	
4	10004	1001	$250.73	3/5/93	$250.73	4/4/93
5	10005	1007	$460.22	9/5/92	$460.22	9/30/92
6	10006	1019	$911.44	3/5/93	$911.44	4/4/93
7	10007	1006	$276.69	3/5/93	$276.69	4/4/93
8	10008	1001	$600.26	3/6/93	$600.26	4/5/93
9	10009	1007	$962.91	9/7/92	$962.91	4/5/93
10	10010	1019	($291.88)	3/6/93	$0.00	
11	10011	1003	$972.70	3/6/93	$972.70	4/5/93
12	10012	1006	$344.25	3/6/93	$344.25	4/5/93

Table : INVOICES.DB

To create a data-dependent property, follow these steps:

1. Inspect the field you want to assign a data-dependent property to, and choose Data Dependent from the property menu. You'll see the **Data Dependent Properties** dialog box (Figure 6.15).

2. Click New Range to add a new range. For some field types, the setting is initially **> \<blank\>** (greater than a blank space), but you needn't be concerned about that.

3. In the Range Includes Values area, choose the operator that defines the type of relationship you're looking for (for example, =, >, >=, <, <=), as summarized in Table 6.4.

4. In the text box next to the operator you chose, type in the comparison value, such as a number if you're working with a numeric or currency field, a date in mm/dd/yy format if you're working with a date field, or a text value if you're looking for specific text. For example, $>=M$ highlights words beginning with the letters M through Z.

5. If you want to define a range of values to highlight, repeat Steps 3 and 4 for options above and below the **AND** operator. (We'll present some examples in a moment.)

6. Click the Set Properties button.

7. Choose Color or Font to select color or font properties for values in the range you specified.

8. Click Apply Changes to apply the range, font, and color changes to the new range and display those changes in the Ranges area of the dialog box.

9. Choose OK to apply the range to the table column you're inspecting and return to the Desktop (or choose Cancel to exit the dialog box without making any changes to either the ranges or the column).

WARNING   If you forget to click Apply Changes before exiting the dialog box, your range changes won't take effect.

As an example of defining data dependent properties, let's take a look at how we changed the sample Invoices table earlier. First, we right-clicked the Invoice Date column, chose Data Dependent, clicked New Range, and set up a data-dependent range as shown in Figure 6.16. Notice that we also colored the Sample area as white text on a black background.

FIGURE 6.15

The Data Dependent Properties dialog box lets you display certain ranges of values in a column in a different color and font.

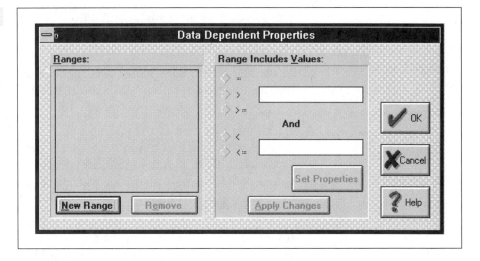

Next we clicked Apply Changes and, without leaving the dialog box, clicked New Range again to set up a second data-dependent range. This time we specified *>=10/1/92 And <=10/31/92* as the range, and colored the Sample

TABLE 6.4: Operators for Defining Data-Dependent Properties

OPERATOR	COMPARISON	EXAMPLE	MEANING
=	Equals	=12/1/92	Exactly December 1, 1992
>	Greater than	>12/1/92	Any date after December 1, 1992
>=	Greater than or equal to	>=12/1/92	December 1, 1992 or later
<	Less than	<12/1/92	Any date before December 1, 1992
<=	Less than or equal to	<=11/30/92	November 30, 1992 or earlier
AND	Combine ranges	>=11/1/92 And <= 11/30/92	All dates in November of 1992

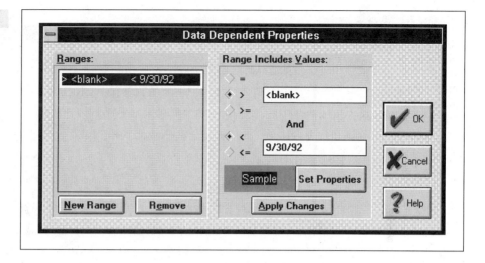

box as black text on a white background. After we clicked Apply Changes
again, both ranges were listed down the left side of the dialog box, as
shown in Figure 6.17.

After choosing OK to return to Table View, we right-clicked the Amount
Paid column, chose Data Dependent, clicked New Range, and specified
<=0 (that's a zero, not the letter *O*) as the range, as shown in Figure 6.18.
The pre-selected **> <blank>** option has no effect here. We left the Sample

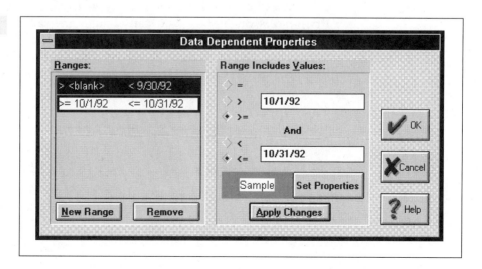

FIGURE 6.18

Data-dependent range for a number (or currency) column set up to highlight numbers that are less than or equal to zero

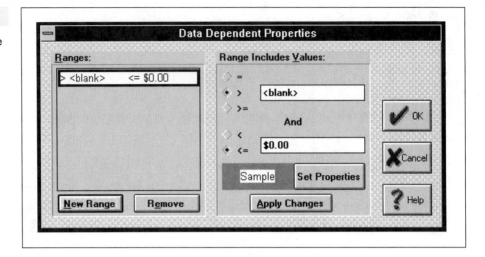

box unchanged, so that data in that range would be displayed as black text on a white background, then clicked Apply Changes, and clicked OK to return to the table.

Changing and Deleting Data-Dependent Properties

To change or delete a data-dependent range for a column, inspect the column and choose Data Dependent as usual. In the **Data Dependent Properties** dialog box, you can change any range by clicking it under Ranges and then changing the options under Range Includes Values. Alternatively, you can click the range you want to delete, then click the Remove button. Choose OK when you're ready to return to Table View.

Saving a Modified Table View

As mentioned earlier, you can save Table View settings at any time using the Properties ➤ View Properties ➤ Save options. If you don't do this, or if you make additional changes to Table View after choosing these commands, you'll see the dialog box shown in Figure 6.19 when you close the table or exit Paradox. If you choose Yes, your current view settings will be in effect the next time you open the table. If you choose No, the current view settings will not be saved.

N O T E   Table settings are saved in a file that has the same name as the table and the extension .tv.

FIGURE 6.19

This dialog box appears when you close a table or exit Paradox with unsaved Table View settings. Choosing Yes saves the current view settings. Choosing No abandons the current view.

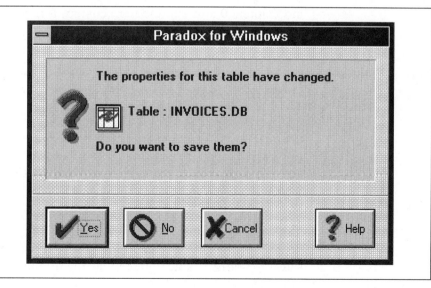

Paradox for Windows

The properties for this table have changed.

Table : INVOICES.DB

Do you want to save them?

[✔ Yes]   [🚫 No]   [✗ Cancel]   [? Help]

If you want to delete all the view settings for a table and completely restore the default view, choose <u>P</u>roperties ➤ <u>V</u>iew Properties ➤ <u>D</u>elete. Then, if you're sure you want to delete the property file, choose OK when prompted.

WARNING

You should not delete Paradox for Windows files through the File Manager or DOS prompt. Doing so can damage your data permanently because Paradox may be unable to locate all the files it needs to manage tables and other objects in your database. Please see Chapter 14 for details on managing Paradox for Windows files.

Customizing Form View

Unlike Table View, Form View does not support direct manipulation or property inspection. Instead, you use the Form Design window, discussed in Chapters 9 and 10, to design custom forms.

Quick-Printing a Table

Chapter 11, "Designing and Printing Formatted Reports," explains how to design custom reports that let you arrange printed data in just about any way imaginable. But if all you need is a quick, unformatted look at your Table View data, a Quick Report will do the job nicely.

The Quick Report will not reflect any property changes you've made to Table View. Instead, the report data will have all the "raw" Paradox default settings. Figure 6.20 shows the first page of a Quick Report of the sample CustList table. Notice that the numeric Cust No field is printed in the default Windows # format.

FIGURE 6.20

A Quick Report for the sample CustList table with overflow columns clipped off

Sunday, September 20, 1992			CUSTLIST			Page 1

Cust No	Last Name	Mr/Mrs	First Name	M.I.	Department/Title	
1,001.00	Miller	Miss	Maria	N.	Accounts Receivable	Zeerocks, Inc
1,002.00	Adams	Miss	Anita	Q.	Microcomputer Consultant	
1,003.00	Eggo	Ms.	Sandy		Owner	Pancho's Re
1,004.00	Cherub	Miss	Sky	R.		Oneness We
1,005.00	Clavell	Miss	Wanda	T.	Mother Superior	Westridge C
1,006.00	Zeepers	Mr.	Zeke	A.	Chief Engineer	Virtual Realit
1,007.00	Kenney	Mr.	David	E.	Attorney at Law	Felson and F
1,008.00	Leventhal	Miss	Danielle	D.		Garden State
1,009.00	Gladstone	Miss	Tara Rose		Vice President	Waterside La
1,010.00	Olson	Mrs.	Elizabeth	A.	Vice President	Precision Co
1,011.00	Rosiello	Mr.	Richard	L.	Accounts Payable	Raydontic La
1,012.00	Smith	Dr.	Mary	K.	Graduate School of Business	Cal State L.A
1,013.00	Watson	Mr.	Frank	R.	Greenskeeper	Whispering P
1,014.00	Mohr	Mrs.	Mary	M.		
1,015.00	Ramirez	Mr.	Rigoberto	R.	Author	
1,016.00	Newell	Mr.	John	J.		Newell Const
1,017.00	Jones	Ms.	Alma	R.	Account Executive	Ashland Flow
1,018.00	Schumack	Dr.	Susita	M.	Neurosurgeon	Physician's H
1,019.00	Smith	Dr.	Savitha	V.		Slybacks Pa
1,020.00	Smith	Mr.	John	Q.		
1,021.00	Smythe	Ms.	Janet	L.		
1,022.00	Dewey	Mr.	Frank	R.	Senior Partner	Dewey, Chea
1,023.00	Adams	Mr.	Andy	A.	President	ABC Corpora
1,024.00	Wilson	Dr.	Ted		Psychology Department	Pine Valley U
1,025.00	Zastrow	Dr.	Ruth		Internal Medicine	Scripps Clinic

To print a Quick Report of a table that's open on your screen, simply click the Quick Report button in the SpeedBar (shown at left), then choose OK in the dialog box that appears. You have quite a few options for controlling the output of your Quick Report. Let's take a look at some of those options.

Setting Up the Printer

Initially, Paradox will use the default printer and printer settings defined in the Printers option of the Windows Control Panel when you print a report. However, you might want to change the predefined printer settings for the current Paradox session if...

* You want to print to a printer other than the default printer defined in the Windows Control Panel.

• You want to change the default printer settings temporarily.

NOTE

Changes you make to the printer settings in Paradox for Windows affect the current Paradox session only. To change the settings for all future Paradox sessions, you must use the Printers option of the Windows Control Panel.

To change the printer or the printer settings, here's what you need to do:

1. Choose File ➤ Printer Setup from the Paradox Desktop menu bar. You'll see the **Printer Setup** dialog box, similar to Figure 6.21 (yours will show printers installed for use with Windows on your system).

2. If the name of the printer you want to use isn't already highlighted in the Printer Setup dialog box, click on it.

FIGURE 6.21

The Printer Setup dialog box appears when you choose File ➤ Printer Setup.

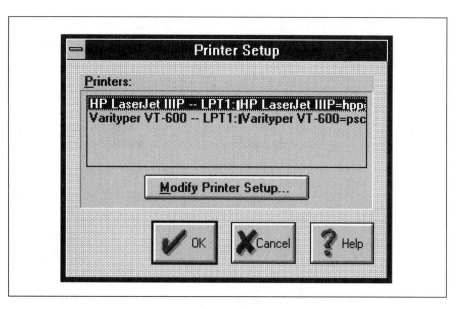

3. If you need to modify the current printer settings, choose the Modify Printer Setup button. You'll see a **Setup** dialog box similar to the one shown in Figure 6.22 (though relevant to your printer).

4. Make any necessary changes to the printer settings, then choose OK. You'll be returned to the Printer Setup dialog box.

5. Choose OK again if you want to save the current printer setup.

Be aware that any changes you make to the dialog box in Figure 6.22 affect only the current Paradox session. When you exit Paradox, the printer settings return to the defaults in the Windows Control Panel.

Printing a Quick Report

When you're ready to print a Quick Report, follow these steps:

1. Make sure the window you want to report on is opened on the Desktop. If more than one window is opened on the Desktop, activate the window you want by clicking on it.

FIGURE 6.22

The Setup dialog box appears when you choose the Modify Printer Setup button in the Printer Setup dialog box. This is the same dialog box that appears when you choose *Printers* from the Windows Control Panel and click the Setup button.

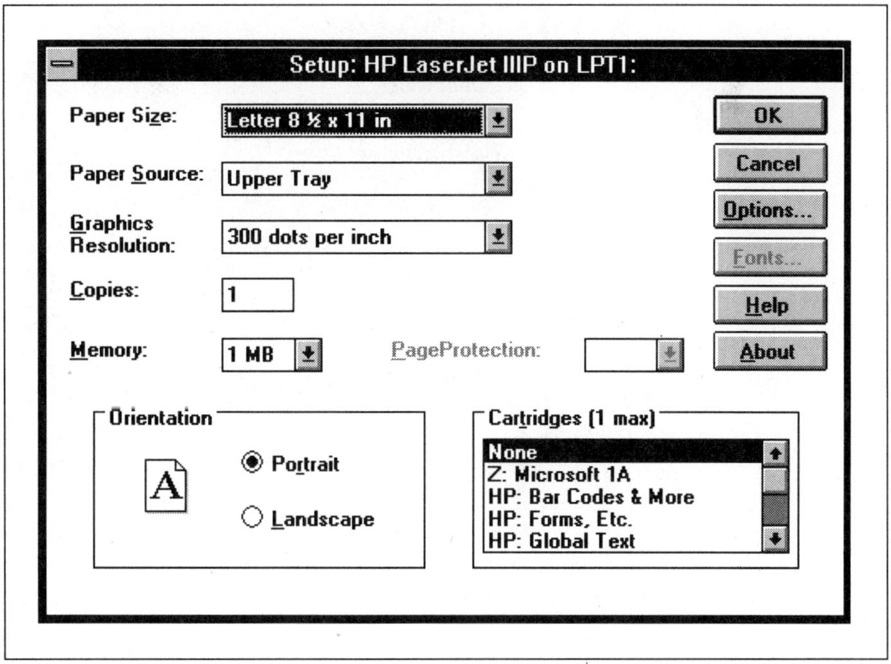

Setup: HP LaserJet IIIP on LPT1:

Paper Size: Letter 8 ½ x 11 in

Paper Source: Upper Tray

Graphics Resolution: 300 dots per inch

Copies: 1

Memory: 1 MB   PageProtection:

OK
Cancel
Options...
Fonts...
Help
About

Orientation
Portrait
Landscape

Cartridges (1 max)
None
Z: Microsoft 1A
HP: Bar Codes & More
HP: Forms, Etc.
HP: Global Text

2. If you want to print all the records in the table, make sure you're in Table View. To print data from a single record, switch to Form View and scroll to the record you want to print.

3. Choose File ➤ Print, or, if you're in Table View, just click the Quick Report button in the SpeedBar, shown at left. In either Table or Form View, you can click the Print button in the Speed-Bar (also shown at left). The dialog box in Figure 6.23 appears when you print from Table View; the one shown in Figure 6.24 appears when you print from Form View.

FIGURE 6.23

This dialog box appears when you choose File ➤ Print or click the Quick Report button in the SpeedBar from Table View.

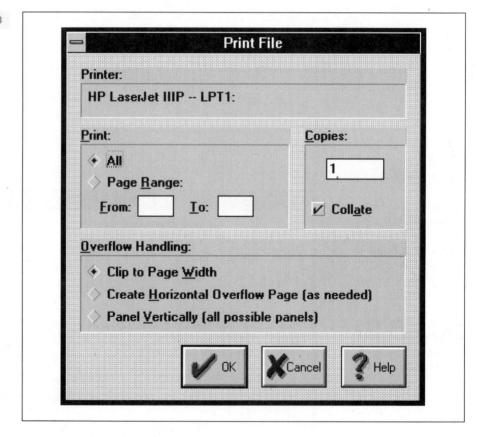

4. Choose the page range, number of copies to print, collation, and overflow handling options as described in the following sections.

5. Choose OK. After some delay (depending on how big the table is), your report will start printing.

Choosing a Page Range

You can print all the pages of data for the current table or form, or just a specified range of pages. To print all pages, select the All option in the **Print the File** dialog box.

To print a range of pages, click the Page Range option in the dialog box. Then click the From text box and type the number of the first page you want to print. Next click the To text box (or press the Tab key) and type the number of the last page you want to print.

FIGURE 6.24

This dialog box appears when you choose File ➤ Print from Form View.

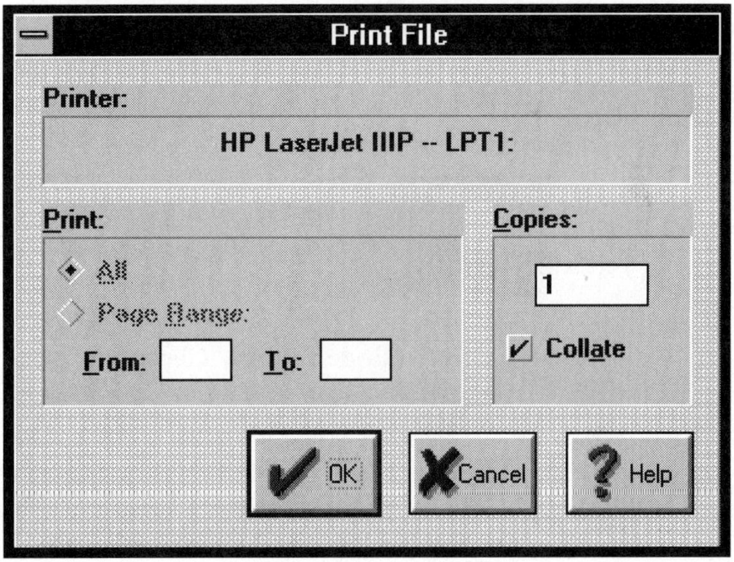

Figure 6.24 — Print File dialog box

Print File

Printer:
HP LaserJet IIIP -- LPT1:

Print:
◆ All
◇ Page Range:
From: [ ] To: [ ]

Copies:
[1]
☑ Collate

✔ OK   ✖ Cancel   ? Help

Choosing the Number of Copies and Collation

Paradox normally prints one copy of the report. If you want to print more than that, change the number in the Copies text box. By default, the Collate option in the Copies area of the dialog box is checked so that the report comes out collated. That is, when printing several copies of the report, Paradox prints them in this order: Page 1 of the first copy, Page 2 of the first copy, Page 3 of the first copy. . .; then Page 1 of the second copy, Page 2 of the second copy, Page 3 of the second copy. . .; and so forth.

If you remove the check mark from the Collated option (by clicking Collate), the report will not be collated. In that case, the report order is as follows: Page 1 of the first copy, Page 1 of the second copy. . .; then Page 2 of the first copy, Page 2 of the second copy. . .; then Page 3 of the first copy, Page 3 of the second copy. . .; and so forth.

Handling the Overflow Pages

Many tables are too wide or too long (or both) to fit on a single printed page. The Overflow Handling options in the Print the File dialog box let you control how Paradox handles the overflow pages. Your options are described below.

NOTE   Overflow handling options aren't available (or needed) when printing reports in Form View.

Clip To Page Width   Clips (cuts off) any data that doesn't fit across the page. The report in Figure 6.20 was printed with this option.

Create Horizontal Overflow Pages (As Needed)   Prints additional pages whenever necessary to fit all the data. Additional horizontal panels (columns) are printed *only* if they contain data. The pages come out in this order: Page 1, Panel 1; Page 1, Panel 2; Page 1, Panel 3; and so forth; then Page 2, Panel 1; Page 2, Panel 2; Page 2, Panel 3; and so forth. After printing, you can trim the report, then paste the pages side by side to see a complete report.

Panel Vertically (All Possible Panels)   Prints additional
panels for each page of a report that's too wide to fit on a single
page, regardless of how many pages actually contain overflow
data. Panels are printed vertically first, then horizontally. The
pages come out in this order: Page 1, Panel 1; Page 2, Panel 1;
Page 3, Panel 1; and so forth. Then Page 1, Panel 2; Page 2, Panel
2; Page 3, Panel 2; and so forth. Finally, Page 1, Panel 3; Page 2,
Panel 3; Page 3, Panel 3; and so forth. Again, you can trim and
paste the pages together to see the entire report.

Don't forget that Quick Report is simply a quick and easy way to do a
"data dump" of your table. Chapter 11 will show you how to print fancier
formatted reports.

In this chapter you've seen many ways to customize the Table View of your
data through direct manipulation and property inspection. You've also
learned how to print simple reports from your tables. When you're ready
to design fancy forms and reports, you can delve into Part III of this book.
But before plunging ahead, please take a look at the next chapter, "Sorting Your Tables."

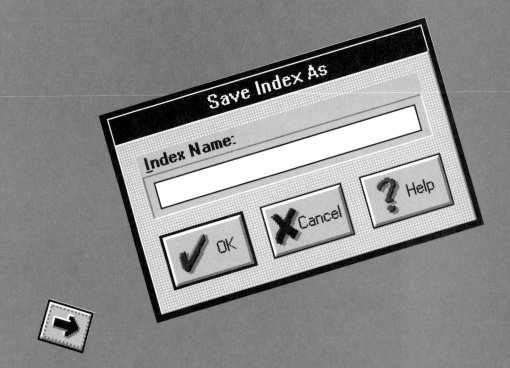

CHAPTER

7

Sorting Your Tables

fast TRACK

To arrange records in largest to smallest order   **299**

choose a descending (321...) sort direction in the Sort Order list.

When you've finished with a sorted temporary table   **304**

you may want to delete it to avoid having multiple copies of the same table on disk.

If your table has a primary key, you can speed and simplify sorting operations   **305**

by creating secondary indexes of commonly used sort orders.

To create a secondary index   **307**

change the structure of the table (File ➤ Utilities ➤ Restructure), and choose Secondary Indexes under Table Properties. Then choose the Define button, define your sort keys, and choose OK (twice) to return to the Desktop.

To use a secondary index to sort a table   **313**

choose Table ➤ Order/Range, then click the name of the secondary index you want and choose OK.

SORTING, in database management terminology, means the same thing that it does in plain English—to put things into some kind of order. For example, if your table contains names and addresses, you might want to sort records into alphabetical order by names so you can print an alphabetized list. Or, you might want to sort the records by zip code for bulk mailing.

NOTE

If a table has a primary index, its records are always ordered according to the key field or fields. Otherwise, records appear in the order in which they were entered.

Sorting leads naturally to the grouping of like information. For example, suppose you have a table that contains invoice information, including the date each invoice is due. If you sort the records by date, the bills due in January will naturally precede those due in February, which in turn precede those due in March. Similarly, if your table contains sales information, sorting that table by product code would naturally place the sales of product A-100 above the sales of product A-200, and so on.

Sorts-within-Sorts

In many cases, you'll want to sort your table on more than one field, to produce a sort-within-a-sort. For example, suppose you have a large table of names and addresses that includes about ten Smiths. If you were to sort that table by last names, all the Smiths would be grouped together like this:

LAST NAME	FIRST NAME	M.I.
Smiley	Windsor	J.
Smith	Michael	K.
Smith	Anton	A.
Smith	Zeke	A.
Smith	Jennifer	J.
Smith	Wally	P.
Smith	Anita	R.
Smith	Michael	D.
Smith	Antonio	L.
Smith	Vera	
Smith	Susan	M.
Smithsonian	Caroline	J.

Notice that the first names of all the Smiths are in random order (Michael Smith comes before Anton Smith, and so on). To sort the names alphabetically by first name within identical last names (as in a phone book), you would want to sort on Last Name *and* First Name, producing this result:

LAST NAME	FIRST NAME	M.I.
Smiley	Windsor	J.
Smith	Anita	R.
Smith	Anton	A.
Smith	Antonio	L.
Smith	Jennifer	J.
Smith	Michael	M.
Smith	Michael	D.

LAST NAME	FIRST NAME	M.I.
Smith	Susan	M.
Smith	Vera	
Smith	Wally	P.
Smith	Zeke	A.
Smithsonian	Caroline	J.

Now all the last names *and* first names are in proper alphabetical order. Notice that the second sort field acts as a "tie breaker." That is, when two individuals have the same last name, the secondary sort order (first name) is used to break the tie.

In the sort order shown above, the Last Name field is the *primary sort key* and the First Name field is the *secondary* (or second) sort key.

At this point, the only "mistake" in this sorted list is that Michael M. Smith comes before Michael D. Smith. That's easily fixed by sorting on three fields—Last Name, First Name, and M.I. (middle initial)—to produce the following result:

LAST NAME	FIRST NAME	M.I.
Smiley	Windsor	J.
Smith	Anita	R.
Smith	Anton	A.
Smith	Antonio	L.
Smith	Jennifer	J.
Smith	Michael	D.
Smith	Michael	M.
Smith	Susan	M.
Smith	Vera	
Smith	Wally	P.

LAST NAME	FIRST NAME	M.I.
Smith	Zeke	A.
Smithsonian	Caroline	J.

We achieved this sort order by making Last Name the primary sort key, First Name the secondary sort key, and Middle Initial (M.I) the third sort key.

When sorting Paradox for Windows tables, you can specify as many sort keys as you wish, so there is really no limit to the number of ways you can order and group information in a table. Since sorting is generally quick and easy, it's no big deal to sort names and addresses into zip code order to print form letters and mailing labels, then sort them into alphabetical order by name to print an alphabetical list.

Using Table ➤ Sort to Sort Tables

There are lots of different ways to go about sorting a table. Probably the simplest technique for sorting a table on-the-fly is to use the Table ➤ Sort option.

With this technique, the first steps are to open the table and get to the **Sort Table** dialog box.

1. If the table you want to sort is not currently open on the Desktop, use File ➤ Open ➤ Table (or click the Open Table button in the SpeedBar, if it's available) to open the table.

2. Choose Table ➤ Sort to get to the Sort Table dialog box. If you assigned a primary key in the table's structure (Chapter 4), the Sort Table dialog box will resemble Figure 7.1, where we've used our trusty CustList table once again. If you didn't assign a primary key, the Sort Table dialog box will resemble Figure 7.2.

SORTING YOUR TABLES

FIGURE 7.1

This Sort Table dialog box appears when you choose Table ➤ Sort for a table that has a primary index. The key icon reminds you that the table is keyed, and the Same Table option is dimmed (unavailable).

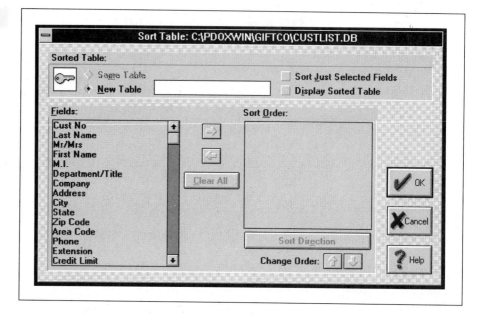

FIGURE 7.2

This Sort Table dialog box appears when you choose Table ➤ Sort for a table that doesn't have key fields defined. No key icon appears, and you can sort to either the Same Table or to a New Table.

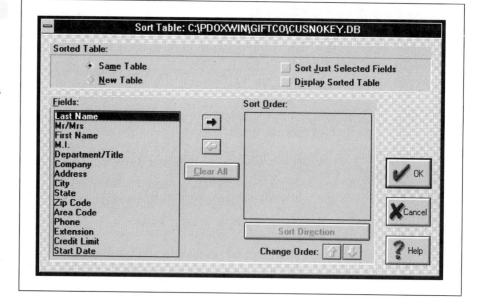

Next you need to make some decisions about how you want to handle the sort.

Sorting to the Same Table or a New Table

If the table you are about to sort has no primary key, you can sort records within the current table or place the sorted records in a new table. The disadvantage of sorting to the same table is that you cannot return the records to their original order. That's because each record will be assigned a new sequence number (record number) in the sorted table, based on its new position in the table.

If you sort to a new table, however, the original table isn't changed at all—it retains its original order. The new table will have the same field names, types, and sizes as the original table. However, this new copy of the table will have no primary key, nor will it have any of the properties you might have assigned to the original table's Table View. It will be perfect, however, for printing sorted reports, labels, form letters. . . whatever, using techniques discussed in Chapter 11.

NOTE If the table structure includes a primary key, you *must* sort to a different table, unless you use a secondary index to perform the sort, as described later in this chapter.

To sort to a separate table, name the new table by following these steps:

1. Choose the New Table option, near the top left of the Sort Table dialog box.

2. Type a name for the sorted table, such as *Tempsort* (for temporary sort table), into the New Table text box. The table you're sorting to must not be open on the Desktop.

WARNING

If you specify the name of an existing table in Step 2, Paradox will ask if you want to overwrite it when you perform the sort. Answer Yes only if you're sure you want to overwrite the existing table, or No to return to the Sort Table dialog box.

3. If you want to see the sorted table as soon as the sort is finished, choose the Display Sorted Table option to the right of the file name, as in Figure 7.3.

Choosing Fields to Sort On

As discussed earlier, sorting on multiple fields allows you to create sorts-within-sorts. You can sort on as many fields as you wish, so you need to think about which field will be the primary sort key, which field (if any) will be the secondary sort key, and so forth.

FIGURE 7.3

This Sort Table dialog box tells Paradox to send sorted output from the CustList table to a new table named *Tempsort* and to display the results on the Desktop as soon as the sort is finished.

NOTE   You cannot sort on graphic, OLE, binary, memo, or formatted memo fields.

Suppose you want to sort by Last Name, then by First Name within identical last names, then by Middle Initial within identical Last and First Names. In that case, Last Name would be the primary sort key, First Name the second sort key, and Middle Initial the third sort key.

As another example, suppose you wanted to sort alphabetically by city, then by zip code within each city. City would be the primary sort key, and Zip Code would be the secondary sort key.

To specify a field to sort on, simply copy it from the Fields list on the left side of the Sort Table dialog box to the Sort Order list on the right side of the dialog box, starting with the primary sort key. You can use any of the techniques listed below to add field names to the Sort Order list.

- Click on the name of a field you want to sort on, then click the → button (or simply double-click the field you want to sort on). You can repeat these steps to add as many field names as necessary to the list.

- As a shortcut, you can copy several adjacent field names to the Sort Order list by dragging. Just click the first field name you want to copy, hold down the mouse button, and drag the mouse pointer through the fields you want to copy. The selected fields will be highlighted in the Fields list. Release the mouse button and click the → button in the dialog box.

- If you want to copy non-adjacent field names to the Sort Order list, click on the first field, then hold down the Ctrl key while clicking the remaining fields. When you've highlighted all the fields you want to copy, click the → button.

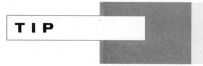

TIP   You can press Alt+A, instead of clicking the → button, to add selected fields to the list.

The fields are added to the Sort Order list in whatever order you choose them. Figure 7.4 shows an example in which Last Name is the primary sort key, First Name is the second sort key, and M.I. is the third sort key.

NOTE   If you select a range of fields that happens to extend over fields that can't be sorted on, or over fields you've already added to the Sort Order List, Paradox will ignore those fields.

FIGURE 7.4

Records will be sorted alphabetically by Last Name, by First name within identical last names, and by Middle Initial within identical last and first names.

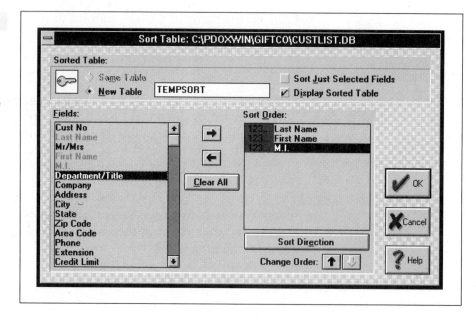

Inserting and Removing Sort Keys

Keep in mind that the order of field names in the Sort Order side of the Sort Table dialog box determines the eventual sort order. For instance, in the Sort Order list below, Start Date is the primary sort key (because it's listed first) and Last Name is the secondary sort key. Thus, the resulting sort would display records chronologically by Start Date (earliest date to latest date), with last names alphabetized for each date.

The field list below specifies a completely different sort order, even though it contains the same field names. Last Name is the primary sort key and Start Date is the secondary sort key. Thus, the sort will order records alphabetically by Last Name, then by Start Date within identical last names.

Once you've copied field names to the Sort Order list, you can use any of several techniques to rearrange the list.

- To move an existing field name in the Sort Order list to a new location, click the field name, then use the Change Order buttons ($\uparrow$ and $\downarrow$) to move the selected field name up or down.

- To move adjacent fields in the Sort Order list, drag the mouse pointer through the field names you want to move. Then use the Change Order buttons ($\uparrow$ and $\downarrow$) to move the selected field names up or down.

- To insert a new field name below an existing field name, select the field name (or names) that you want to insert from the Fields list. Then click the position in the Sort Order list that's above where you want the name(s) to appear. Click the $\rightarrow$ button or press Alt+A.

- To remove a single field name from the Sort Order list, click that field name, then click the $\leftarrow$ button or press Alt+R.

- To start over from scratch and remove all the field names from the Sort Order list, click the Clear All button or press Alt+C.

Clear All

Whenever you add a field to the Sort Order list, Paradox dims that field name in the Fields list, indicating that you can no longer add the field to the Sort Order list (because it's already there). Conversely, whenever you remove a field from the Sort Order list, Paradox returns the field name to its normal appearance in the Fields list, indicating that you can add it to the Sort Order list.

NOTE   Graphic, memo, formatted memo, OLE, and binary fields cannot be sorted and, therefore, are always dimmed and unavailable in the Fields list.

Choosing Ascending or Descending Order

Any field in your Sort Order list can be sorted in either ascending or descending order. Ascending order is smallest to largest: *A* to *Z* for text, smallest number to largest number for numeric fields, earliest date to latest date for date fields. Descending order is the opposite: *Z* to *A*, largest number to smallest, latest date to earliest.

Initially, Paradox assumes you want to sort each field in ascending order. To change the sort direction, click the field name you want to reverse in the Sort Order list, then click the Sort Direction button (shown below), or just double-click the field name in the Sort Order list. The indicator next to the field name changes to the opposite direction, that is, from *123...* (ascending order) to *321...* (descending order).

                    [**Sort Direction**]

As examples of a descending sort direction for one field and an ascending direction for another field, suppose you use the Credit Limit field from the CustList as the primary sort key, in descending order, and you make the Last Name and First Name fields the second and third sort keys, each in ascending order, as in Figure 7.5.

After you perform the sort (as described in a moment), and rearrange the columns in Table View to focus on these three fields, the resulting order would be like that shown in Figure 7.6. Notice how the credit limits are in largest to smallest order, but within each credit limit, names are alphabetized in ascending order.

N O T E

Paradox for Windows doesn't rearrange columns in Table View automatically. In Figure 7.6, we dragged the Credit Limit field over to the left edge of Table View after completing the sort.

FIGURE 7.5

Here we've opted to make Credit Limit, in descending (largest to smallest) order, the primary sort key. Within each credit limit, customer names will be alphabetized in ascending (A to Z) order.

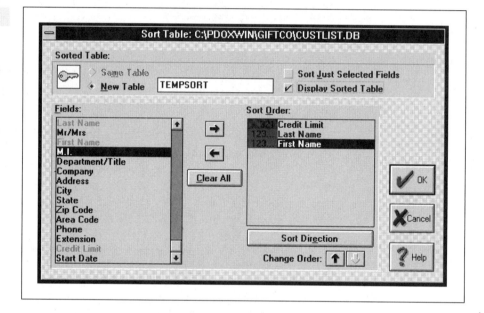

Sorting Just Selected Fields

Normally, Paradox adds any unselected fields from the table to the end of your Sort Order list just before it sorts your table (though you don't actually see that happen). This is simply a convenience, to make those fields act as additional "tie breakers" for records with identical values.

If you don't want Paradox to add unselected fields to the Sort Order list automatically, click the Sort Just Selected Fields option in the Sort Table dialog box.

FIGURE 7.6

Results of the sample sort operation shown in Figure 7.5, where Credit Limits are sorted in descending order and names are sorted in ascending order within each Credit Limit

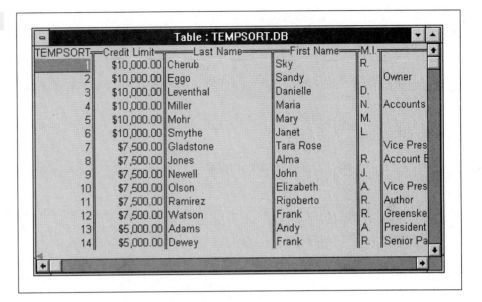

TEMPSORT	Credit Limit	Last Name	First Name	M.I.	
1	$10,000.00	Cherub	Sky	R.	
2	$10,000.00	Eggo	Sandy		Owner
3	$10,000.00	Leventhal	Danielle	D.	
4	$10,000.00	Miller	Maria	N.	Accounts
5	$10,000.00	Mohr	Mary	M.	
6	$10,000.00	Smythe	Janet	L.	
7	$7,500.00	Gladstone	Tara Rose		Vice Pres
8	$7,500.00	Jones	Alma	R.	Account E
9	$7,500.00	Newell	John	J.	
10	$7,500.00	Olson	Elizabeth	A.	Vice Pres
11	$7,500.00	Ramirez	Rigoberto	R.	Author
12	$7,500.00	Watson	Frank	R.	Greenske
13	$5,000.00	Adams	Andy	A.	President
14	$5,000.00	Dewey	Frank	R.	Senior Pa

Table : TEMPSORT.DB

Performing the Sort

When you've finished with the Sort Table dialog box and double-checked that any existing table specified in the New Table text box can safely be overwritten, click the Sort button. If you've changed your mind about the sort, choose Cancel to return to the Desktop without sorting your table.

As mentioned earlier, if you typed in the name of an existing table file when filling in the New Table text box, Paradox will display a warning before it begins the sort, asking if you want to overwrite the existing table. If you answer Yes to the prompt, Paradox will overwrite any existing information in that table with sorted data. Be absolutely certain that you want to overwrite the specified table file before performing the sort.

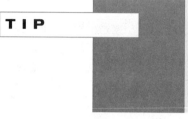

TIP

Your best bet might be to give the file name *tempsort.db* to your temporary sort order tables *always*, and use that file name only for such tables. That way, you need never worry about inadvertently overwriting an important table!

You might notice a brief delay as Paradox sorts the table. The actual time required to complete the sort, of course, depends on the size of the table being sorted and the speed of your computer.

If you chose the Display Sorted Table option in the Sort Table dialog box, the sorted table will appear over the original table, as in Figure 7.7. If you did not choose the Display Table option, you'll need to open the sorted table using File ➤ Open ➤ Table.

Keep in mind that the sort order affects only the order of *records*, not the order of fields. For example, if you sort on the Zip Code field, you would still need to scroll over to the Zip Code field to see that the records have indeed been sorted.

As mentioned previously, you can rearrange the order of fields in Table View using techniques described in Chapter 6. That can make the new sort order more apparent on your screen.

Don't forget that when you sort records to a separate table (such as *Tempsort*), the resulting table is entirely separate from the original table. If you make any changes or additions to the original table, those changes will not be reflected in the original copy of the table. Therefore, you'd just be wasting time if you scrolled through the sorted copy of the table making changes and corrections!

TIP

You can always tell exactly which table you're viewing at the moment by taking a quick glance at the table name in the title bar or the upper-left corner of Table View.

FIGURE 7.7

The sample CustList table appears in the background window in its primary key order by Cust No. The sorted version of the table, named *Tempsort*, appears in the foreground window sorted alphabetically by last name, first name, and middle initial, as shown in Figure 7.4. We dragged the Mr/Mrs field to the right a bit so you could see the alphabetized names.

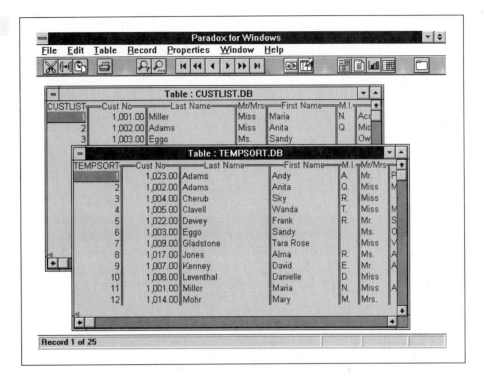

How the Sort Order Affects Form View

If you switch to Form View while viewing the sorted table, you'll only see one record at a time, of course, and the order of the fields will be as defined in the table's structure. As you scroll through records using the buttons on the SpeedBar or Record menu options, the order in which records appear will be the current sort order.

NOTE

To control the order of *fields* in a custom form, you must design the form accordingly, as explained in Chapters 9 and 10.

In practice, you'll probably want to use the sort order to print table data in some kind of formatted report. For example, you might print an alphabetized list of names and addresses, or you could print form letters and mailing labels after sorting records by zip code.

That's no problem, once you learn how to create formatted reports. We'll get to that topic in Chapter 11.

Closing the Temporary Sort Table

To avoid the confusion inherent in having multiple sorted and unsorted copies of the same table, it's a good idea to close the sorted version of the table (*Tempsort* in our example) when you're done using the sorted records. To do so, make sure the sorted table is in the currently active window. Then click that window's Control-menu box and choose Close (or press Ctrl+F4).

T I P

As an extra precaution, you can delete the temporary table when you no longer need it, using the File ➤ Utilities ➤ Delete options discussed in Chapter 14.

Using Secondary Indexes to Sort Tables

As mentioned earlier, Table ➤ Sort is just one way to sort a table. Though a quick and straightforward way to get the job done, Table ➤ Sort does have certain disadvantages:

* Sorting a huge table can be quite time-consuming.

- If the table is huge (say, 100K), and you sort to a separate table (which is required if the table has a primary key), the sorted copy of the table is going to gobble up *another* 100K.

- When you sort to a different table, you might inadvertently make changes, corrections, or additions to the sorted copy which, as noted earlier, won't be recorded in the original copy of the table.

One way around all these disadvantages is to use a secondary index file (usually called a *secondary index*). The secondary index defines an alternate order for viewing the table's records; however, unlike the sort operation discussed previously, the secondary index does not change the original location of the records.

Secondary indexes provide several advantages over sorting. They allow you to view records in sorted order with little or no time delay, require only a small amount of extra disk space to store the index file, and can speed up query operations (see Chapter 8). What's more, any changes made to the table while viewing it through the secondary index affect the *original* table, not just a copy. So you see, you really can sort your table and change it too.

There is one catch, however: You can only define a secondary index for a table after you've defined a primary index. In other words, you can only define a secondary index for a table that has one or more fields marked with an asterisk (*) in the Key column of the table's structure (as discussed in Chapter 4).

Understanding How Indexes Work

When you use either a primary or secondary index to view a table, Paradox stores a copy of the index (or as much of it as it can fit) in memory (RAM). That index is organized much like the index at the back of a book—sorted into alphabetical (or some other) order. The position of each record in the table is included in the index in much the same way that the index at the back of a book includes page numbers indicating where topics are located.

NOTE

A primary index file contains field values and record numbers for a table's primary key. A *secondary index* file contains field values and record numbers of *non-key* fields. Primary and secondary indexes are always sorted according to the values in the indexed fields.

Suppose you define an index that's based on the Last Name and First Name fields in a table. When you open the table and ask to find the record for John Smith, Paradox looks up the name John Smith in the index in memory. This takes only a fraction of a second, because Paradox doesn't need to use the disk drive to read through the index.

When Paradox finds John Smith in the index, it will determine that John Smith is in the 495th record. It can then "skip over" the first 494 records when it accesses the disk, thereby saving a considerable amount of time.

Without the aid of an index, Paradox must read through each record of the table on disk, until it happens to find the one it's looking for. For instance, if you ask Paradox to find the record for John Smith, and John Smith is the 495th record in the table, Paradox will read through the first 494 records, until it finds John Smith. This is like trying to find information in a book by flipping through all the pages until you stumble upon the topic you're looking for.

All this terminology can be confusing. It helps to remember that the term *primary key* refers *specifically* to the field or fields marked with an asterisk (*) in the Key column of the table's structure. The *primary index* is the file that stores primary key values and associated record numbers. The *secondary index* is the file containing non-key values (that is, values of fields that are not primary keys) and associated record numbers. The terms *primary sort key* and *secondary sort key* simply refer to the fields that define the main order and tie-breaker of records in a sort operation.

Preparing for Secondary Indexes

A table can have more than one secondary index. You define secondary indexes in the table's structure. Here's how to get started:

1. To avoid confusion, you might want to close all open objects on the screen by choosing <u>W</u>indow ➤ Close <u>A</u>ll.

2. Choose <u>F</u>ile ➤ <u>U</u>tilities ➤ Res<u>t</u>ructure, and choose the table that you want to define a secondary index for. You'll be taken to the **Restructure** dialog box for that table.

NOTE You can also define secondary indexes when creating a table via the Create Table dialog box (<u>F</u>ile ➤ <u>N</u>ew ➤ <u>T</u>able). However, you must define the primary index before you can define any secondary indexes.

3. Check to make sure that you've already defined a primary key for the table. That is, at least one field should have an asterisk in the Key column. (If not, choose Cancel, because you won't be able to proceed very far.)

WARNING If the table you're restructuring doesn't have a primary key, don't just randomly pick one out of a hat. Instead, make sure you understand the many important roles of the primary index (Chapter 4) as well as the ramifications of assigning a primary key to a table that already contains data (Chapter 14).

4. Click the drop-down list button under Table <u>P</u>roperties and choose *Secondary Indexes*.

Figure 7.8 shows an example in which we're ready to define secondary indexes for the sample CustList table. Notice that *Secondary Indexes* appears under Table Properties and that this table does indeed already have a primary key: the Cust No field at the top of the field roster.

FIGURE 7.8

Getting ready to define secondary indexes for the sample CustList table, which already has a primary key based on the Cust No field

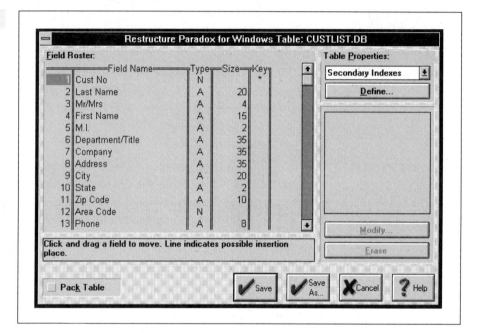

Defining the Secondary Indexes

Now you're ready to start defining your secondary indexes. Here's how:

1. Click the <u>D</u>efine button. You'll be taken to the **Define Secondary Index** dialog box.

2. Use the techniques described earlier in this chapter to copy a field (or fields) from the Fields list over to the Indexed Fields column. For example, in Figure 7.9 we copied the Last Name, First Name, and M.I. fields (in that order) to the Indexed Fields list.

As with any sort order you define, the first field in the Indexed Field list defines the primary sort key, the next field defines the secondary sort key, and so forth. As you can probably tell by now, the field order in Figure 7.9 will sort records by last name and by first name and middle initial within identical last names.

Notice that this dialog box contains the Add Field (→) and Remove Field (←) buttons, the Change Order ↑ and ↓ keys for rearranging field names, and a Clear All button. These all work exactly as they do in the Sort Table dialog box described earlier. You also have a few additional choices, under Index Options, which will be described next.

> **N O T E**
>
> A *composite* secondary index consists of two or more fields. Each table can have up to 16 composite secondary indexes and as many single-field secondary indexes as there are fields in a table.

FIGURE 7.9

Here we've copied the Last Name, First Name, and M.I. fields from the Fields list to the Indexed Fields list.

The Maintained Option

The Maintained option determines how Paradox manages the secondary index behind the scenes. If you choose this option, Paradox will update the secondary index as you add, change, and delete records in the table. This puts a little overhead on the general editing operations, which in turn can slow them down a tad. Probably, the slowdown will be imperceptible.

If you deselect the Maintained option, Paradox will update the secondary index only when it's called into play during a sort operation or query, or when linking tables via secondary indexes. (We'll be describing these operations in upcoming chapters.) This puts the slight overhead onto those operations, rather than in your general editing operations.

Chances are, you'll be less likely to notice any slowdown if you make sure the Maintained option is checked. You can always change your mind later and deselect the option to put the overhead on other operations.

The Case Sensitive Option

The Case Sensitive option determines whether Paradox distinguishes between upper- and lowercase letters. If you select this option, uppercase letters will take precedence over lowercase letters in the sort order. If you *deselect* this option, making the sort *case-insensitive*, upper- and lowercase letters will be considered the same. Figure 7.10 illustrates the difference between case-sensitive and case-insensitive sort orders.

TIP

If you happen to be familiar with such concepts, it might help to know that choosing Case Sensitive makes the secondary index perform an ASCII sort; deselecting Case Sensitive forces a standard "dictionary" sort.

If you want records to be alphabetized in the normal "dictionary" fashion, *deselect* the Case Sensitive option (this is the default setting). Notice that we've selected the Maintained option and deselected the Case Sensitive option in Figure 7.9.

FIGURE 7.10

A case-sensitive sort places words beginning with lowercase letters after words beginning with uppercase letters. A case-insensitive sort ignores upper and lowercase distinctions.

Case-Sensitive Sort Order	Case-Insensitive Sort Order
Adams	Adams
Miller	d'Elgin
Zabriski	Miller
d'Elgin	Zabriski

Saving the Secondary Index

When you've defined your sort fields and index options, follow these steps to save the secondary index:

1. Choose OK. If you've assigned more than one field to the secondary index, you'll see the **Save Index As** dialog box shown below.

2. If you've included only one field in the secondary index, the name of that field automatically becomes the name of the secondary index, and you can skip the next two steps.

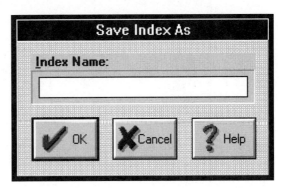

3. Type in a descriptive name for this index, such as **Alphabetical by name.** The name *cannot* be the same as a field in the table. For instance, you couldn't name this sample index *Last Name*, since *Last Name* is the name of a field in the table.

4. Choose OK.

You can repeat the steps above to create as many secondary indexes for the table as you need, up to the limits mentioned previously. For instance, Figure 7.11 shows another secondary index that can be used to sort records alphabetically into city order, and by zip code within cities.

Figure 7.12 shows yet another secondary index. This index orders records by area code and phone number—handy for telemarketing or working with customers within various area code regions.

When you've finished defining secondary indexes for a table, just choose Save from the Restructure dialog box to return to the Desktop.

FIGURE 7.11

A secondary index defined for sorting records alphabetically into city order, and by zip code within each city

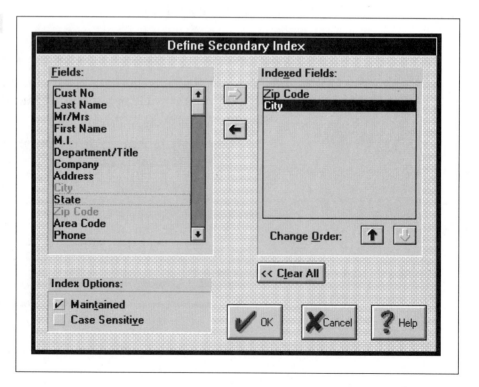

FIGURE 7.12

A secondary index
used to sort records
by area code and
phone number

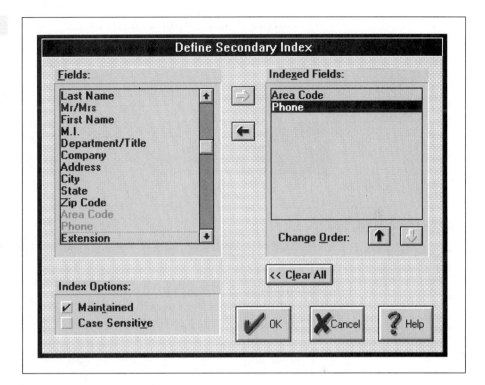

Using a Secondary Index to Sort Records

Once you've defined one or more secondary indexes, follow these steps
to sort your table:

1. If you haven't already done so, open the table you want to sort
with the File ➤ Open ➤ Table options or Open Table button.

2. Choose Table ➤ Order/Range. You'll see the **Order/Range** dialog
box, shown in Figure 7.13. The names of any secondary indexes
you've created will be listed below the primary index.

3. Notice that the primary key for the table is marked with an asterisk. Any secondary indexes you created are listed below that.

4. Choose an index by clicking its name.

5. Choose OK to return to Table View.

N O T E

Additional options in the Table Order/Range dialog box let you isolate records to display in the table. We'll talk about this aspect of Table Order/Range under "Using an Index for a Mini Query," in Chapter 8.

FIGURE 7.13

Choosing Table ➤ Order/Range lets you choose a secondary index to sort records.

Records will be displayed instantly in the sort order determined by the secondary order you chose. Again, the *fields* in Table View will be in their original order, so you may need to scroll to another field or rearrange the columns to appreciate the sort order. In Figure 7.14, for instance, we chose the sample *Alphabetical by name* secondary index as the sort order, then dragged those three columns over to the left side of Table View. As you can see, records are sorted by name.

FIGURE 7.14

Records sorted into alphabetical order by name using the secondary index defined in Figure 7.9. As you can see in the title bar, records from the original table, not a sorted copy of the table, appear in Table View.

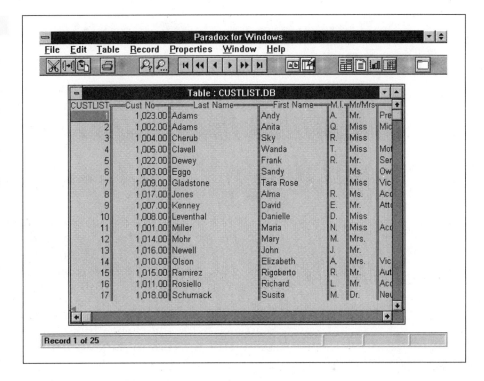

The title bar of the window indicates that we're viewing records from the original CustList table, not a sorted copy of that table. Therefore, any additions, changes, or deletions you make in this Table View will be made in the original table. Also, if you print a Quick Report, the records on the printout will be in the sort order currently on your screen.

NOTE   When you view a table using a secondary index, the physical location of the records in the table does not change. When you sort a table, the physical location of records does change.

Returning to the Original Sort Order

When you want to return to the original sort order, just repeat the steps above (that is, choose Table ➤ Order/Range). Then choose the primary index (the one marked with an asterisk) and choose OK.

Changing or Deleting a Secondary Index

To change a secondary index or delete it, follow the same basic steps you used to create the secondary index. That is, restructure the table and choose *Secondary Indexes* from the Table Properties drop-down list. Then click the name of the secondary index you want to change or delete.

If you want to change the secondary index, click the Modify button. You'll be taken to the **Define Secondary Index** dialog box, where you can add, delete, or rearrange fields and change Index Options, as described previously. Choose OK to return to the Restructure window after making your changes.

If you want to delete an index, click the name of the index you want to delete, then click the Erase button.

Finally, to save your changes and return to the Desktop, just click the Save button.

File Names for Indexes

Any secondary index that you create for a table is actually stored in two files, each with the same name as the table, but with the extensions .xg$n$ and .yg$n$ where n is a number, starting at zero, that's assigned as you create the secondary index. For instance, the first time you create a secondary index for the CustList table, that index is stored in the files *custlist.xg0* and *custlist.yg0*. The next index you create would be stored in files named *custlist.xg1* and *custlist.yg1*.

NOTE When copying a table to floppies or sending them by modem, be sure to include all index files. If you use DOS to copy the files, a simple *copy custlist.** command, followed by the destination drive and directory, will do the trick.

Still More Techniques for Sorting Tables

The T̲able ➤ S̲ort options described in this chapter are probably the easiest for sorting all the records in a table on-the-fly. However, Paradox for Windows offers a few other methods for sorting tables, as summarized below.

Queries Let you isolate specific records in a table and sort those records simultaneously into any order you wish (see Chapter 8).

File ➤ Utilities ➤ Sort This is another way to reach the **Sort Table** dialog box. Choose F̲ile ➤ U̲tilities ➤ S̲ort, and then choose the table you want to sort.

Inspecting a Table in the Browser or a Folder If the table you want to sort is in a Folder window or **Browser** dialog box, you can inspect it by moving the mouse pointer to the table icon and clicking the right mouse button. Choosing S̲ort from the menu that appears opens the Sort Table dialog box (see Chapter 14).

In this chapter we've covered a few techniques you can use to sort the records in a table. In the next chapter, we'll talk about ways to query, or search, your table.

CHAPTER

8

Querying Your Tables

f a s t TRACK

To specify an OR relationship among several criteria   350

place the criteria on different rows, or place them on the same row, separated by the OR operator.

To save a query in a file for later use   362

choose File ➤ Save or File ➤ Save As, or click the Yes button in the dialog box that appears when you close the Query window. To reuse a saved query, choose File ➤ Open ➤ Query, or click the Open Query button in the SpeedBar (if it's available), then select the file name of the query you want. Make any necessary changes, then run the query.

To change the appearance or sort order of records in the Answer table   365

click the Answer Table Properties button in the SpeedBar of the Query window.

To update a table globally   371

use the CHANGETO or DELETE operator.

To perform a simple query using an index   380

choose Table ➤ Order/Range, choose an index, and indicate the values you want to view.

TO *query* a table is to pull out all records that meet some criterion or criteria. For example, you might want to view only New York residents, or individuals in California with credit limits over $5000. Perhaps you want to send a form letter to individuals whose starting date was one year ago, or maybe you just want to look up a particular address.

You can also use queries to perform basic calculations, delete certain types of records, and much more. Paradox for Windows offers a technique known as *query by example*, or QBE, that allows you to search for information and ask questions about tables. Using query by example is a four- or five-step process in which you...

- Choose the table or tables you want to query.

- Specify the fields you want to view in the results of your query by using check marks.

- Enter *query criteria* to specify any records you want to include in the results of the query.

- Specify any calculations you want to perform.

- Perform, or *run*, the query.

The results of queries that request information are displayed in a new table named *Answer*. The Answer table will contain only the fields and records you've requested.

TIP

Secondary indexes provide a somewhat limited, though simple, technique for isolating records. See "Using an Index for a Mini Query," near the end of this chapter, for more information.

You can also perform queries that let you find records in a table, delete records from a table, change values in fields, and insert new records in a table.

Querying a Table

The first step in performing a query is to get to the Query window by following these simple steps:

1. Choose File ➤ New ➤ Query, or, if the Desktop is currently empty, inspect (right-click) the Open Query button shown at left and choose New. A **Select File** dialog box will appear, listing all the tables in the current working directory.

2. Choose the table you want to query by double-clicking its name or highlighting its name and choosing OK.

A new Query window appears on the screen, partially overlapping any other windows. The name and field names from the table you'll be querying appear across the top of the window. These make up the *query table*. You'll also notice that the menu bar includes a Query command and that the SpeedBar has changed, as shown in Figure 8.1.

NOTE

In Chapter 16 we'll discuss ways to use multiple tables in queries and advanced techniques involving complex groupings and calculations.

FIGURE 8.1

After you create a
new query and
choose a table, the
field names for that
table appear across
the top of the query
table, and a new
menu bar and
SpeedBar appear.

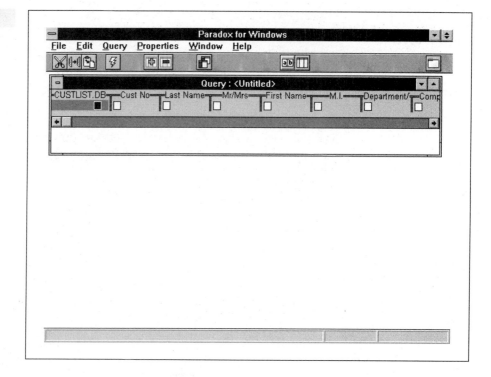

You can size and move the Query window as you would any other. For
instance, in Figure 8.1 we moved the Query window to the upper-left
corner, reduced its height, and widened it somewhat.

You can also move, rotate, widen, and narrow the columns in the query
table using the same techniques as in Table View, as discussed in Chapter 6. We'll do so in numerous figures in this chapter so you can get a better look at the query we've designed.

NOTE   The query table has the same fields in the same order
as the table it represents. However, the query table
doesn't reflect any changes to the table's properties
(such as changed column order).

Selecting Fields to View

The next step in the query procedure is to tell Paradox which fields you want to see in the results of the query. Notice the empty check boxes beneath the table name and each field name in Figure 8.1. Only fields that contain a check mark will appear in the results of the query. Initially, all the check boxes are empty, so you need to choose the fields you want to see.

Paradox provides several ways to check fields, as well as several types of check marks. If you want to use your mouse, proceed as follows:

1. Move the mouse pointer to the check box of the field you want to display in the query results. Use the horizontal scroll bar to scroll to field names outside the window.

2. Hold down the mouse button to view your options, as shown below.

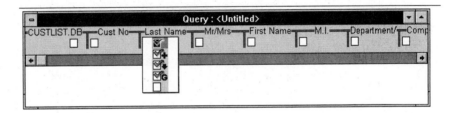

3. With the mouse button depressed, drag the highlight to the check mark you want. Release the mouse button.

TIP

As a shortcut, you can choose a plain check mark by clicking an empty check box. To "uncheck" a checked field, click the check box again or choose the empty check box from the options shown.

If you prefer to use the keyboard, follow these steps:

1. Use the Tab (or →) and Shift+Tab (or ←) keys to scroll to a field name.

2. Press F6 to insert a plain check mark, or press Shift+F6 repeatedly until the check mark you want (or the empty check box) appears in the field.

Checking All the Fields

You can check fields one at a time, or, if you want to check all the fields in the table, use the check box just below the table name. Choosing an option from that check box adds the selected check mark to all the fields in the table.

TIP To "uncheck" all the fields in the Query window, choose the blank check box under the table name.

The various types of check marks available to you are described in the sections that follow.

Using Check Plus

 The check plus displays all the records for a field, even if the records have duplicate values. For example, if you used the check plus in the State field of the CustList table, then performed the query, the results would appear as in Figure 8.2. Notice that CA appears several times in the State field of the Answer table, and that the Answer table contains 25 records (because the CustList table in this example contains 25 records).

NOTE We've rearranged windows on the Desktop in some of the figures in this chapter so you can see windows that might otherwise be covered.

FIGURE 8.2

The check plus check mark displays all the records in a field, even if the records have duplicate values. Here we used check plus to display all the states in the sample CustList table.

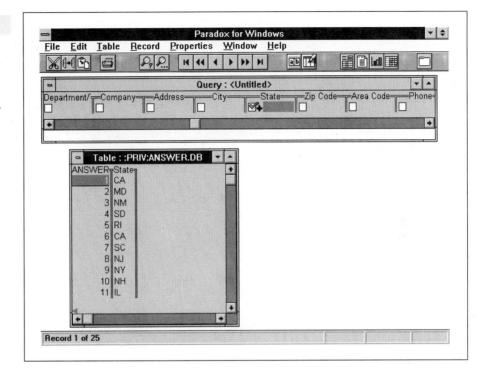

Check plus is a very common check mark to use, because in most situations you are interested in all the records that contain some value. You'll see more examples using check plus in a moment.

Using the Plain Check Mark

The plain check mark displays only unique values in a field. It displays them in ascending sorted order, so it's useful for viewing summary information.

For example, if you were to check only the State field in the query for the CustList table, the results would appear in the Answer table as in Figure 8.3. Notice that each state is listed only once; that is, no duplicate states are displayed. Also, the bottom of the screen shows that there are 17 records in the Answer table, which corresponds to the fact that there are 17 unique states in the table.

FIGURE 8.3

Placing a plain check
in the State field sorts
the states in ascending
order, listing each
state only once.
Compare this result
with Figure 8.2.

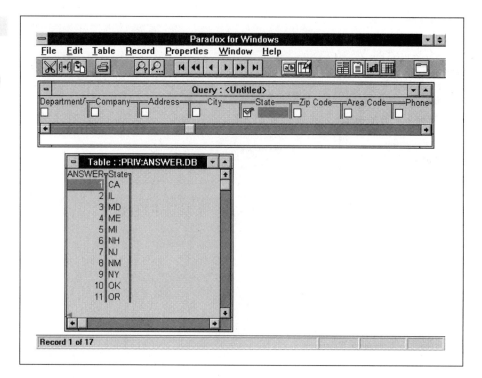

NOTE

When you check multiple fields in the query table, the
leftmost column in the Answer table (not the query
table) determines the primary sort order. We'll describe
techniques for controlling sort order under "Controlling
the Appearance of the Answer Table," later in this
chapter.

When you choose the plain check mark, you can see at a glance which
states are included in the CustList table, in alphabetical order, without
having to wade through duplicate state names.

WARNING   When you use a plain check mark in several fields, only records that have identical values in *all* the checked fields are considered duplicates.

Using Check Descending

The check descending mark functions similarly to the plain check mark, except that it displays records in descending, rather than ascending, sort order. That is, it displays only unique values, listing them in largest-to-smallest (or *Z* to *A*) order. You can see the results of a query that contains check descending in the State field in Figure 8.4.

FIGURE 8.4

Placing a check descending mark in the State field sorts the states in descending order and, like the plain check mark, lists each state only once.

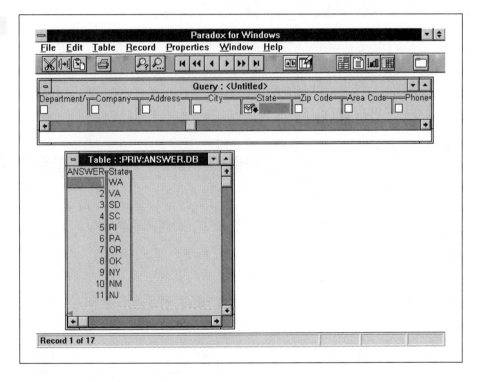

Performing the Query

 To perform a query, just click the Run Query button in the SpeedBar or choose Query ➤ Run, or press F8. After a brief delay, the requested fields appear in a table named *Answer*. Keep in mind that the Answer table contains *copies* of records from the original table.

You'll notice that as soon as the Answer table appears, the menu and SpeedBar change back to the ones used in Table View, so you can use those commands and buttons and treat the Answer table as you would any other table. As soon as you click the Query window or close the Answer table, the menu and SpeedBar switch back to the ones used to design queries.

If Your Query Fails

Before we go any further into queries, let's talk about how you can get out of a jam in the event you create a query that Paradox cannot understand. If a query fails because you didn't specify it correctly, you'll see an error message similar to the example shown in Figure 8.5.

FIGURE 8.5

If the query cannot run for some reason, an error message appears. To return to the Query window, choose OK.

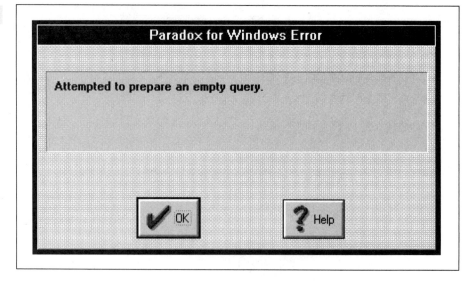

After reading the error message, choose the OK button to return to the Query window. There you can make any changes or corrections necessary to make the query run correctly.

TIP One of the most common causes of errors in a query is simply forgetting to check any fields to display before running the query!

Using the Answer Table

As mentioned earlier, the Answer table that displays the results of a query contains only a *copy* of records from the table used to perform the query. Here's a quick overview of basic techniques you can use with the Answer table should you decide to experiment with some sample queries:

- To move the Answer table so you can see the underlying query, drag the Answer table's title bar to another location.

- You can manipulate the Answer table the same way you would manipulate any Table View, as described in Chapter 6.

- If you use the plain check mark or check descending to check multiple fields to display in the query table, the Answer table will display records sorted by the leftmost field. However, Paradox does not sort records when you use check plus. You can sort the Answer table using the Table ➤ Sort options discussed in Chapter 7.

- You can "pre-design" the appearance and sort order of the Answer table using techniques described under "Controlling the Appearance of the Answer Table," later in this chapter.

- To print the Answer table, click the Quick Report button in the SpeedBar (shown at left) or choose File ➤ Print (see Chapter 6).

- To view or print a formatted report from the Answer table, choose File ➤ Open ➤ Report and the name of the report format you want to use. Then choose Change Table, specify *Answer.db* in the private directory (typically *:PRIV:Answer.db*), and click OK twice. We'll get into this in more detail in Chapter 11.

- You can move or copy records in the Answer table to another table using options discussed in Chapter 14.

- To return to the Query window, just click on the Query window, which is just behind the Answer table window. You can also choose Window from the menu bar and then click the Query option near the bottom of the menu that appears. Or, press Ctrl+F6 until you return to the Query window.

- To close the Answer table, double-click its Control-menu box, click the Control-menu box and choose Close, or click on the Answer table window and press Ctrl+F4.

- Use the same techniques to close the Query window. If you don't plan to reuse the query in the future, choose No when asked about saving it.

Although Answer has much in common with ordinary tables, it does have two features that set it apart. First, Answer is a *temporary* table that is over-written each time you run a query. If you want to prevent the results of a query from being lost the next time you run a query, you'll need to rename the Answer table after running the query (see Chapter 14).

WARNING   Never replace an existing table with the Answer table, unless you're sure you don't want the table that will be replaced.

The second thing that makes the Answer table different from other tables is the fact that it's stored in a private directory reserved for temporary objects. However, you'll still be able to open and use *Answer* as though it were in your working directory.

Be sure to type leading zeros in query criteria that include the .. operator and month or day numbers less than 10. For example, type ../05/92 (not ../5/92) to match dates on the fifth day of any month in 1992. If you prefer not to type leading zeros, you must change the LEADINGZEROM and LEADINGZEROD settings for the system date format, as described in Chapter 13.

N O T E
> When using a wildcard to find a date, the pattern you define with the wildcard operator must reflect the current International setting for dates in the Windows Control Panel, and the system date formats defined in the ODAPI Full Tree Editor (see Chapter 13).

Perhaps the most important thing to keep in mind when viewing an Answer table is that it contains only a *copy* of data from the original table. If you happen to notice a mistake that needs to be corrected while viewing the Answer table, *don't make the correction in the Answer table because the correction won't appear in the original table.* To make a correction or a change to the data, open the original table (File ➤ Open ➤ Table) and make your changes there.

Using Queries to Select Specific Records

So far, we've talked about how to start a query, select *fields* to view in the results of the query, and then perform the query. As mentioned at the beginning of this chapter, you may also want to specify certain *records* to view in a query. For example, you may want to see names and addresses of residents in a specific state or zip code area. Or, you might want to see sales transactions for a particular product or range of dates. To search for specific records, you enter a *query criterion* that defines those records.

Entering Query Criteria

To enter a query criterion into a field in the query table, move to the field you want to search using the scroll bars, mouse, arrow keys, or Tab and Shift+Tab keys, then type in your query criterion. You can type criteria into as many fields as you wish and make changes and corrections using the same techniques you use to change data stored in fields in a table. When you're ready to perform the query, just run it as described earlier in this chapter.

As you'll see in the sections that follow, there's almost no limit to the types of records you can ask for in a query.

Searching for Exact Values

If you want to search for an exact value in a field, simply type that value into the appropriate field. For example, Figure 8.6 shows the Query window with *CA* typed into the State field of the query table and several fields selected with check marks. The Answer table below the Query window, which appears after choosing Run Query, shows only records that have CA in the State field.

NOTE See "Searching for Punctuation Marks and Other Symbols," later in this chapter, for limitations on includng commas, periods, and other special symbols in your query criteria.

Even though we used plain check marks in the query table, CA appears several times in the Answer table. That's because only records that have identical values in *all* the checked fields are considered duplicates. Here you can see that no two records in the Answer table are exactly the same.

FIGURE 8.6

Defining CA as the query criterion in the State field of the query table, then choosing Run Query displays only records that have CA in the State field. In this example, we rearranged some fields in the query table so that you can see the entire query.

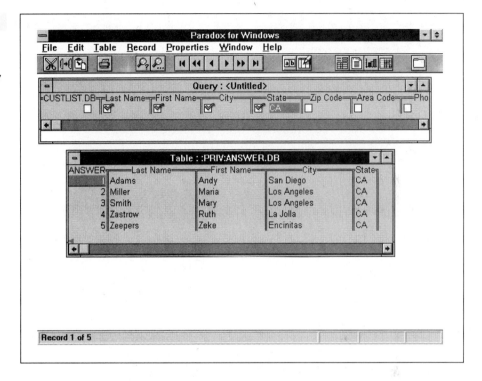

Be aware that an exact match requires a *very* exact match, including the same spacing, upper- and lowercase letters, and length. For example, had we placed *ca* rather than *CA* in the State field of the query table before performing the search, the Answer table would have ended up empty. Why? Because all the two-letter abbreviations in the State field are uppercase, not lowercase.

Similarly, a search for Smith in the Last Name field would find *only* Smith exactly—not SMITH, smith, Smithsonian, Smith & Wesson, Blacksmith, or any other name with "Smith" embedded in it. However, you *can* search for inexact matches, as we'll discuss a little later in the chapter.

Searching for a Range of Values

Often, you'll want to view records that have some value that is less than or greater than some other value. For example, you might want to view records for people who have credit limits of $5000 or more, or people with start dates on or before a specific date. You can use the comparison operators listed below to perform such queries.

OPERATOR	MEANING
=	Equal to
<	Less than
>	Greater than
<=	Less than or equal to
>=	Greater than or equal to

WARNING

Do not use commas to separate thousands in the query table. As you'll see, the comma plays a special role in queries.

Figure 8.7 shows a sample query that uses the >= operator to display records that have a value of $7500.00 or more in the Credit Limit field. The Answer table displays the appropriate records when you perform the query.

Notice that in Figure 8.7 we removed the CA query condition from the State field, since we no longer wanted to isolate records by State. When designing your own queries, make sure you erase any old query criteria that you don't want to use in the query you perform next. You can change or delete a query criterion using the same techniques used to change or delete data in a field. For instance, you can double-click a query criterion to edit it in Field View.

FIGURE 8.7

Query and resulting
Answer table to
display records with
a value of $7500.00
or more in the Credit
Limit field. We
rearranged some
fields in the query
table to make it easier
to see the entire query.

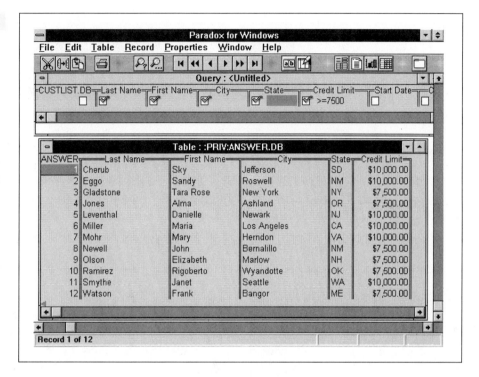

If you want a more specific range, such as values that are greater than or
equal to some value *and* less than or equal to some other value, enter two
search criteria, separated by a comma, into the field. For example, the query
criterion in the Credit Limit field of Figure 8.8 specifies that the Answer
table should include only records that contain a value that's greater than
or equal to $2500.00 and less than or equal to $5000.

You can also use the comparison operators to isolate alphanumeric fields
that fall within a range of letters. Use >= to specify the lowest acceptable
letter and < to specify one letter higher than the largest acceptable letter.
For example, the query below would display records for people whose last
names start with the letters *A* through *M*.

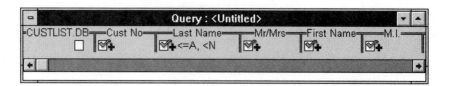

The reason you want to use <N, rather than <=M, in the second half of a search for names beginning with the letters A through M is that the letter M followed by any other letter is considered "greater than" the letter M by itself. Thus, the query criterion >=A,<N includes all names from the letter A by itself up to "Mzzzzzzzzzzzzzzz," while >A,<M would exclude MacDonald. Any name beginning with the letter N or higher is excluded from the resulting Answer table.

FIGURE 8.8

Query to display records that have a value between $2500 and $5000 (inclusive) in the Credit Limit field.

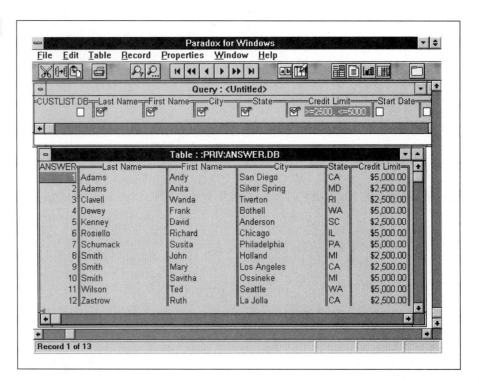

As you may recall, we originally defined the Zip Code field in the CustList table as an alphanumeric field, rather than a numeric field, to ensure that we could include leading zeros, hyphens, and letters in that field.

When you're searching the field for a range of values, however, the fact that the field is alphanumeric is of no importance. If you want to isolate records that have zip codes in the range of 92000 to 92999-9999, you would use the following query criterion:

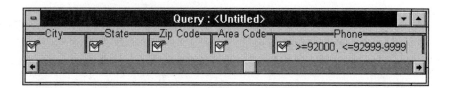

You can also search a date field for records that fall within a range of dates. For example, the query criterion *>=10/1/92,<=12/31/92,* shown in Figure 8.9, displays records that have dates in the fourth quarter of 1992 (October 1 to December 31) in the Start Date field.

Searching for Inexact Matches

Sometimes you might want to view records that match a particular pattern or contain a certain sequence of characters. In an inventory system, for example, you may want to view all records that have the characters J2 embedded in the part number. Or, if you want to look up an individual named Smith but are not sure of the spelling, you can view records that are spelled *like* Smith. The operators used for these types of searches are listed below.

OPERATOR	MEANING
..	Matches any sequence of characters, including blank spaces.

OPERATOR	MEANING
@	Matches any single character.
LIKE	Matches items similar to the criterion.
NOT	Preceding the criterion, matches items that do not match the criterion.
BLANK	Matches items that have no data in the field.
TODAY	Compares items with the current date.

FIGURE 8.9

This query displays records with dates in the fourth quarter of 1992. We rearranged fields and widened the Start Date field in the query table and the Answer table to display the example more clearly.

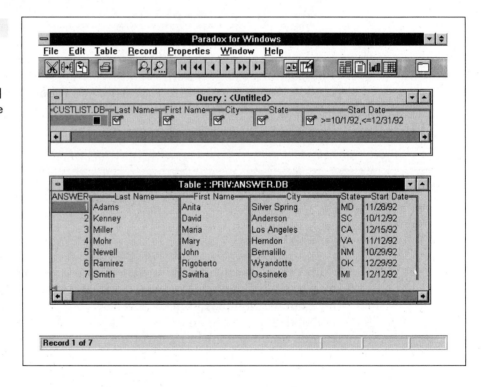

NOTE Although we've shown the operators in uppercase, you can type them in uppercase, lowercase, or mixed case. For example, *Like*, *LIKE*, and *like* are all treated the same in a query.

Finding Embedded Text

You can use the .. operator to represent any sequence of characters or numbers (including blank spaces) in a search criterion. For example, suppose you want to view records for people who live on a particular street. You can't ask for all records that contain just a street name, such as Ocean View, because the words "Ocean View" will be embedded somewhere in the middle of the address (for example, 234 Ocean View Dr.) However, you could use the .. operator to indicate the numbers preceding the street name, followed by the words Ocean View, followed by .. again to indicate any other characters. Figure 8.10 shows such a query and its results.

FIGURE 8.10

A search for records with "Ocean View" somewhere in the Address field. Again, we rearranged fields in the query table to make the query and its results easier to see.

ANSWER	Last Name	First Name	Address	City	State
1	Kenney	David	6771 Ocean View Dr.	Anderson	SC
2	Smith	Savitha	767 Ocean View Lane	Ossineke	MI

Record 1 of 2

Notice that records with the words "Ocean View" embedded in the Address field are included.

N O T E

The .. operator always makes a search case-insensitive. For instance, in Figure 8.10, even though we asked for ..ocean view.., the query found Ocean View. Likewise, a search for ..smith.. would find SMITH and smith, as well as Smithsonian, Smith & Wesson, and Blacksmith.

The more characters you include in the search criterion, the more specific the search. For example, the query below would list people who live on Crest Dr., but not Crest Ave., Crest St., Crest Blvd., etc.

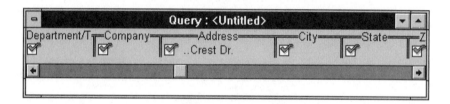

Using few characters in the search criterion tends to broaden the results. In this next example, the query criterion A.. will isolate records of all the people whose last names begin with the letter A.

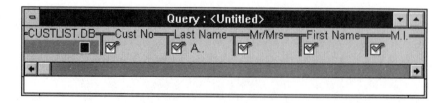

You can also use the .. operator to isolate records for a particular month in a date field. For example, the query below uses .. in place of a specific day in the Start Date field to isolate records with start days on any day of October 1992.

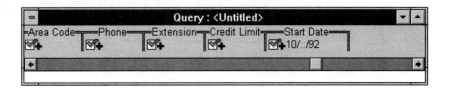

Be sure to type leading zeros in query criteria that include the .. operator and month or day numbers less than 10. For example, type ../05/92 (not ../5/92) to match dates on the fifth day of any month in 1992. If you prefer not to type leading zeros, you must change the LEADINGZEROM and LEADINGZEROD settings for the system date format, as described in Chapter 13.

NOTE When using a wildcard to find a date, the pattern you define with the wildcard operator must reflect the current International setting for dates in the Windows Control Panel, and the system date formats defined in the ODAPI Full Tree Editor (see Chapter 13).

Searching for embedded, rather than exact, text is always a good way to broaden a search if your initial search fails. For example, suppose you perform a search for the name Davis in the Last Name field, and the Answer table doesn't include all the Davises that you know are somewhere in the table. That's because searching for Davis alone didn't pick up Davis, Jr. and Davis, III, which do not exactly match Davis.

If you change your search criterion to ..Davis.. and perform the query, you might get the results you're looking for, as in the example below. Using the .. wildcard operator in ..Davis.. expands the search to Davis preceded by, or followed by, any other characters.

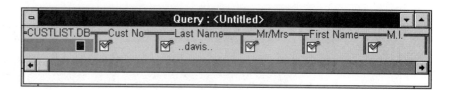

Finding Text in Memos

The .. operator is also useful for finding records with a word embedded in a memo or formatted memo field. Use the .. operator to stand for any text before and after the word you're searching for. For instance, the query in Figure 8.11 searches the Employee table for records that have the word "expert" in the formatted memo field named *Notes*.

FIGURE 8.11

This query searches for records that have the word *expert* in the Notes field of a sample Employee table. We've adjusted the row height and column width of the resulting Answer table and selected the Complete Display property so that you can see all the text of the Notes field.

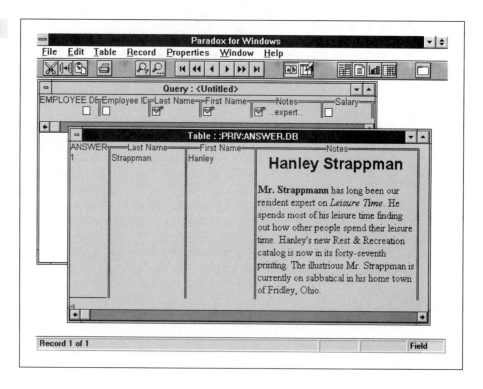

N O T E   To query a different table, just close the current Query window, then choose File ➤ New ➤ Query to start a new query.

Matching a Single Character

The @ operator is used to match a single character, as opposed to any series of characters. This is handy when you're not sure of the exact spelling of a word or phrase you're looking for. For instance, a search for Sm@th in the Last Name field would isolate records that contain *Sm*, followed by any single character, followed by *th*. Thus, names such as Smith and Smyth would be included in the Answer table.

A search for Sm@th.., as below, would find Smith, Smythe, Smithsonian, Smathers, and others that have a single letter embedded between the *m* and the *t*, with or without any characters following the *h*.

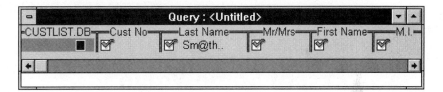

Searching for Inexact Spellings

In some cases you might want to search for a particular item of data, without knowing exactly how it's spelled. The LIKE operator comes in handy here by searching for text that's spelled like the word you provide. Just type the word **Like**, followed by a blank space, in front of the value you want to search for when specifying your search criterion. The LIKE operator is also case-insensitive and may find records that would otherwise have gone unnoticed.

The query below uses the search criterion *LIKE abzig* in the Last Name field. This will help find last names that are similar to "abzig" in spelling, including Abzug.

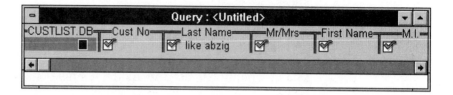

When using the LIKE operator, keep in mind the following points:

- Only records that have the same first letter as the query condition will be included in the search. For instance, the search criterion *LIKE kwik* will not find *Quick* even though they sound alike.

- If a record contains at least half of the letters in the query condition, and in the same order, it will likely be considered a match. For example, *LIKE la jla*, will find La Jolla, but *LIKE la hoya* will not.

Searching for Everything Except Some Value

The NOT operator reverses the meaning of any query criterion. For example, if you wanted to isolate non-California residents in your Answer table, you would use the query criterion *NOT CA*. Or, if you wanted to make sure that upper- and lowercase are treated equally, you could use *NOT..ca*, as shown in Figure 8.12. Notice that in the results of the query, none of the records has CA in the State field.

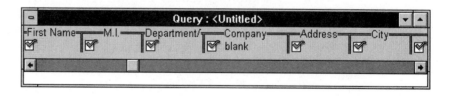

FIGURE 8.12

A search for records in the CustList table that have some value *other than* CA in the State field eliminates all CA residents from the Answer table

Searching for Blank Fields

If you want to search for records that have no entry in a particular field, use the *BLANK* operator. For example, the query below isolates records that have no entry in the Company field.

To *exclude* blank records from the results of a query, use *NOT BLANK*. For example, the following query does the exact opposite of the query shown above. Instead of displaying only records that have no entry in the Company field, it displays only records that do have an entry in the Company field.

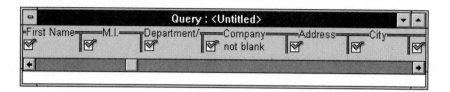

Searching for Relative Dates

The *TODAY* operator represents the current system date in your computer. Typically the system date is maintained by a clock within the computer. You can set the current date using either the Date / Time option in the Windows Control Panel, or the DATE command at the DOS command prompt.

The Windows Control Panel is accessible via the Main group in the Windows Program Manager.

You can use the TODAY operator alone to isolate records that match the current date exactly. For example, the query criterion below isolates records in the CustList table that have the same Start Date as the current system date.

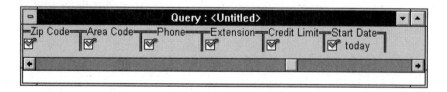

A more common use of the TODAY operator is to locate records that have dates that fall within some range of days relative to today's date. You can use the comparison operators described earlier (<, >, <=, >=) and the arithmetic operators listed below to help isolate ranges of dates.

OPERATOR	MEANS
+	Adds a number of days to the date.
−	Subtracts a number of days from the date.

Table 8.1 shows examples of query criteria used in a date field to isolate ranges of dates relative to the current system date. If your table contains accounts payable or accounts receivable data, such query criteria can help you isolate records of payables and receivables within certain ranges of dates.

Keep in mind that the TODAY operator is used only to search for records that have some day in relation to the current date. As mentioned earlier, you can use comparison operators and the .. operator to search for dates as well. For example, the query criterion *>=7/1/92,<=9/30/92* isolates records in the third quarter of 1992 (July 1, 1992 through September 30, 1992). If you're currently in the month of July 1993, and want to isolate records with dates from about a year ago, you could use the query criterion *07/../92* to find records for July of 1992.

TABLE 8.1: Examples Using the TODAY Operator to Search for Dates Relative to the Current System Date

CRITERION	DATES INCLUDED IN ANSWER TABLE
TODAY	Exactly today's date
<=TODAY	Today, and all dates prior to today
>=TODAY	Today, and all dates after today
<=TODAY, >=TODAY-30	Dates within the last 30 days, including today
>=TODAY, <=TODAY+30	Today, and all dates within the next 30 days
>=TODAY-60, <=TODAY-30	Dates between 30 and 60 days ago
<=TODAY+60, >=TODAY+30	Dates between 30 and 60 days from today

Performing AND / OR Searches

In some situations, you'll want your queries to produce only records that meet *all* the query criteria. For instance, when you are specifically trying to locate information about Andy Adams in San Diego, you would want to structure your query to find only records that contain Adams in the Last Name field *and* Andy in the First Name field *and* San Diego in the City field.

In other situations, you might want to find records that match *any* of the search criteria. For instance, if you want to isolate records for individuals residing in any of several states, you would structure your query to isolate records that have NY *or* NJ *or* PA in the State field.

The basic techniques you use in the Query window to specify AND and OR relationships among query criteria are summarized below.

- To specify an AND relationship among multiple fields, place the query criteria on the same row.

- To specify an OR relationship among multiple fields, place the query criteria in separate rows.

- To specify an AND relationship in a single field, separate the query criteria with a comma.

- To specify an OR relationship in a single field, separate the query criteria with the word OR.

TIP   To add a row to the query table, press ↓ or F12. To delete a row from the query table, move the cursor to that row and then press Ctrl+Del.

Using AND Relationships across Several Fields

When you want to isolate records that match several search criteria in different fields, place those search criteria in the same row. For example, the query shown in Figure 8.13 asks for records that have exactly "Adams" in the Last name field *and* exactly "Andy" in the First Name field. The resulting Answer table displays the only record in the CustList table that matches these criteria.

FIGURE 8.13

An AND search to isolate records that have Adams in the Last name field and Andy in the First Name field. Only one record in the sample CustList table matches these criteria.

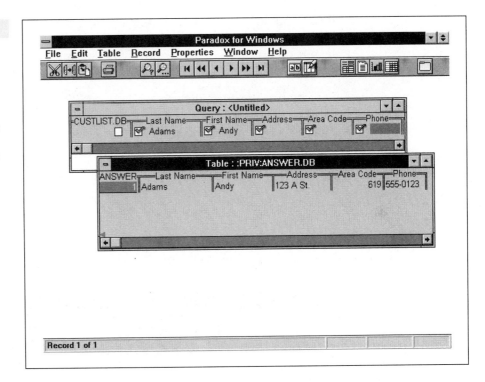

The sample query below will search for records that contain Kenney in the Last Name field, *and* Dav followed by any letters (for example, David, Dave) in the First Name field, *and* SC in the State field.

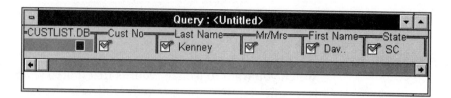

Using AND Relationships in a Single Field

If you want to specify an AND relationship among search criteria in a single field, separate the query criteria with a comma. In most cases, using multiple search criteria only makes sense when searching for ranges using comparison operators. You've already seen several examples of these.

For instance, the query criteria *>=2500,<=5000* in the Credit Limit field isolates records that contain some number that is greater than or equal to $2500 *and* less than or equal to $5000. The query criterion *>=6/1/92,<=12/31/92* in a date field isolates records containing dates that are greater than or equal to 6/1/92 *and* less than or equal to 12/31/92.

You might also want to search for records that contain a combination of words. For example, the query criterion *..spanish..,..french..* shown below would find records that contain both the words "Spanish" *and* "French" in the Notes field of the Employee table. Records that contain only "French," only "Spanish," or neither are excluded from the Answer table.

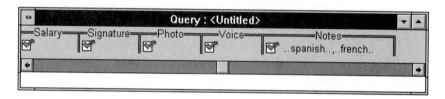

Using OR Relationships across Several Fields

If you want to search for records that contain certain values or certain other values, place the query criteria on separate lines. While working in the query table, you need only press ↓ (or F12) to create a new row. For example, the query below finds records that have *either* San Diego in the City field *or* 92 followed by any other characters in the Zip Code field. Notice how the two query criteria are on separate rows.

The query below searches for people with a last name like Smith who live in Washington *or* California. You might think of each row in the query table as representing a single question.

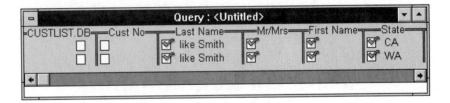

When performing this query, Paradox looks at each record in the table and asks,

- Does this record have a name like Smith in the Last Name field *and* WA in the State field?

- Does this record have a name like Smith in the Last Name field *and* CA in the State field?

If it can answer Yes to *either* of those questions, Paradox displays that record in the Answer table.

Now compare the query above to this example:

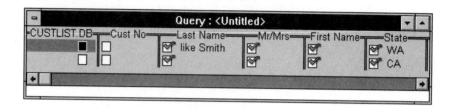

This query would produce an Answer table that contains Smiths in WA and *all* California residents, regardless of last name. Why? Because the query asks these two questions when deciding whether or not to display a record in the Answer table:

- Does this record have a name like Smith in the Last Name field *and* WA in the State field?

- Does this record have CA in the State field?

For Paradox to be able to answer Yes to the second question, and thereby display the record in the Answer table, a record need only have CA in the State field. That's because there is no query criterion in the Last Name field in the second row.

Using OR Relationships in a Field

If you want to search for any one of several given values in a field, you can either stack the values in separate rows or use the *OR* operator to separate the values you want to search for. For instance, if you want to isolate records that have NY, *or* PA, *or* NJ in the State field, you could set up the query as it appears below.

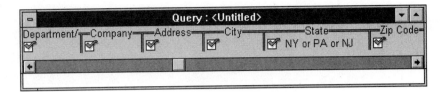

Or you could set it up like this:

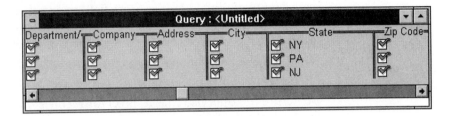

Either way, the results are the same. The Answer table displays records with NY, PA, or NJ in the State field.

Going back to an earlier example, if you wanted to locate records that have either "Spanish" *or* "French" in the Notes field, you could either stack the query conditions or separate them with the OR operator, like this:

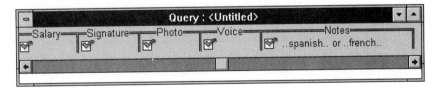

Troubleshooting Queries

When building criteria that use AND logic and OR logic at the same time, keep in mind that the way you think about the query in plain English may *not* be the way to express it in a query. For example, you might think to yourself, "I want to view CA and WA residents." Then you define the query as below.

When you run the query, however, the Answer table will be empty, regardless of how many CA and WA residents are actually in the table. Why? Because it is impossible for the State field in any single record in the table to contain both CA *and* WA. Therefore, Paradox cannot answer Yes when it asks, "Does this record have CA in the State field *and* WA in the State field?"

To isolate records for California and Washington residents, you need to structure the query so that it looks for records that have either CA or WA in the State field, like this:

Now Paradox asks two questions as it checks each record: Does this record have CA in the State field? Does this record have WA in the State field? If it can answer Yes to either question, the record is included in the Answer table.

Searching for Punctuation Marks and Other Symbols

Punctuation marks like the comma and period, and operators such as NOT, BLANK, and TODAY are always interpreted as special symbols in a query.

Suppose you want to search for a record that has *Davis, Jr.* in the Last Name field. If you simply enter the query criterion into the Last Name field of the query table as

Davis, Jr.

and perform the query, the Answer table will end up empty. Why? Because Paradox interprets the comma as the AND operator, rather than just as a comma.

If you want to include an operator or special word in a query criterion, but want to have it treated as a literal character rather than an operator, you need to enclose the query criterion in double quotation marks.

For example, if you change the query criterion to

"Davis, Jr."

Paradox will know that you are looking for Davis, Jr., not for records that contain both Davis and Jr.

N O T E   Company names often contain commas, as in *TransAmerica, Inc.* To search for that company name, you'd need to use the quotation marks: "TransAmerica, Inc."

Similarly, if you wanted to isolate records for people living in California, Oregon, or Washington, you'd have a problem. The two-letter abbreviation for Oregon is OR, which is the same as the OR operator.

The query below takes care of the problem by enclosing the two-letter abbreviation for Oregon in quotation marks. This query would then be successful in isolating records that have CA *or* OR *or* WA in the State field.

Using quotation marks in queries keeps Paradox from converting special symbols and reserved words (such as BLANK, NOT, and TODAY) into commands. This way, they will be treated as items to look up.

NOTE When typing a search criterion in double quotation marks, be sure to use the exact upper- and lowercase characters you want to match. Alternatively, you can use the .. operator to make the search case-insensitive.

Table 8.2 lists all the symbols, operators, and reserved words that you can use in queries, and tells where each is discussed. Keep in mind that if you want to search a field for any of the characters or words that appear in the first column of that table, the search criterion must be enclosed in quotation marks. Although a single period (.) is not listed as a symbol, operator, or reserved word in Table 8.2, you must enclose it in quotation marks when it precedes or follows the .. operator.

TABLE 8.2: Symbols, Query Operators, and Reserved Words

SYMBOL OR WORD	FUNCTION	CHAPTER(S)
CHECK MARK SYMBOLS		+
−	Display all values, including duplicates, in the Answer table	Chapter 8
_+	Display only unique values in the Answer table	Chapter 8
_↓	Display values in descending sorted order	Chapter 8
_G	Specify group for set operations	Chapter 16
COMPARISON OPERATORS		
=	Equal to (optional)	Chapter 8
>	Greater than	Chapter 8

TABLE 8.2: Symbols, Query Operators, and Reserved Words (continued)

SYMBOL OR WORD	FUNCTION	CHAPTER(S)
<	Less than	Chapter 8
>=	Greater than or equal to	Chapter 8
<=	Less than or equal to	Chapter 8
ARITHMETIC OPERATORS		
+	Add numbers or join alphanumeric values	Chapters 8, 16
-	Subtract	Chapters 8, 16
*	Multiply	Chapter 16
/	Divide	Chapter 16
()	Give precedence	Chapter 16
WILDCARD OPERATORS		
@	Matches any single character	Chapter 8
..	Matches any series of characters	Chapter 8
SPECIAL OPERATORS		
LIKE	Similar to	Chapter 8
NOT	Does not match	Chapter 8
BLANK	Contains no value	Chapter 8
TODAY	System date	Chapter 8
OR	One condition *or* other (or both) must be met	Chapter 8
,	Both conditions must be met	Chapter 8
AS	Field name to use in Answer table	Chapter 16

TABLE 8.2: Symbols, Query Operators, and Reserved Words (continued)

SYMBOL OR WORD	FUNCTION	CHAPTER(S)
!	Display all values, regardless of match	Chapter 16
RESERVED WORDS		
CALC	Display result in new calculated field in Answer table	Chapter 16
CHANGETO	Globally change matching values	Chapter 8
FIND	Locate matching records within table	Chapter 8
INSERT	Insert records with specified value	Chapter 16
DELETE	Delete records with specified values	Chapter 8
SET	Define set of matching values for set comparisons	Chapter 16
SUMMARY OPERATORS		
AVERAGE	Average of values on field	Chapter 16
COUNT	Number of matching items	Chapter 16
MAX	Highest value in field	Chapter 16
MIN	Lowest value in field	Chapter 16
SUM	Total of values in field	Chapter 16
ALL	Calculate summary based on all values in a group, including duplicates	Chapter 16
UNIQUE	Calculate summary based on unique values in group	Chapter 16

TABLE 8.2: Symbols, Query Operators, and Reserved Words (continued)

SYMBOL OR WORD	FUNCTION	CHAPTER(S)
SET COMPARISON OPERATORS		
ONLY	Display only those values matching values in defined set	Chapter 16
NO	Display only those values that do not match any members in defined set	Chapter 16
EVERY	Display only values that match every member of defined set	Chapter 16
EXACTLY	Displays only values that match all members of defined set and no others	Chapter 16

Querying OLE Fields

In general, OLE fields are not good candidates for a query. However, in some cases, you can search for text in OLE fields, much as you would search for text in memo fields. For example, if you pasted the contents of a résumé written in Microsoft Word into a Paradox OLE field, you could use a query to search for a specific skill you're interested in. Or, if you pasted a Microsoft Excel spreadsheet into an OLE field, you could search for a specific value or label.

Here are some points to keep in mind when using queries to search for values in OLE fields:

- You can query an OLE field that contains text or numbers.

NOTE

When you embed an object in an OLE field, a copy of that object is stored in the field (in the .mb file), so Paradox can search the contents of the field.

- When specifying the query criterion, always place the .. operator before and after the text or numbers you want to search for. Note that text and numbers are treated the same in OLE fields. For example, to search for the skill "typing 65 wpm," type **..65 wpm..** as the query criterion. Similarly, to search for a value of 100 in an OLE field that contains spreadsheet data, type **..100..** as the query criterion.

- You can use the NOT, BLANK, OR, AND, and @ operators, but cannot use LIKE or TODAY. Nor can you use comparison operators like <, <=, >, and >=.

Keep in mind that you're better off using a memo or formatted memo field if you need to store a large body of text in each record of a table and also require flexibility in querying that field. Similarly, you may want to avoid storing numbers in an OLE field.

Saving a Query

If you'll be using the same query over and over again, save the query so that you don't need to re-create it in the future. Once you've designed the query so that it accurately displays the fields and records you want to see, you can save it by following the steps below.

1. Click anywhere on the Query window to select it.
2. Choose File ➤ Save.

3. Enter a valid DOS file name in the New File Name text box. Omit the extension. (Paradox automatically adds .qbe to whatever file name you enter.)

4. Choose OK.

Reusing a Saved Query

To reuse a previously saved query, just follow these steps:

1. Choose File ➤ Open ➤ Query, or click the Open Query button on the SpeedBar (if it's available).

2. From the **Select File** dialog box that appears, choose the name of the query you want to use, either by double-clicking or by clicking and choosing OK.

3. The Query window appears on the screen. You can make any changes you wish to the query, or just run it as-is by clicking on the Run Query button.

Controlling the Appearance of the Answer Table

Normally, when you perform a query, Paradox displays the fields in the Answer table in the same order that they were defined in the original table structure—even if you rotate or drag fields in the query table. What's more, the sort order of records in the Answer table is also based on the original table structure, which can be confusing when you're trying to use check marks to control the sort order of records in your Answer table.

For instance, in Figure 8.14 notice that we've moved the Start Date field to the first column of the query table, checked it, and requested to see only records with 1993 dates in them (../../93). The resulting Answer table, however, displays records in their original column order, with Start Date at the right end of the Answer table. Records are sorted by the leftmost column—Last Name in this case.

FIGURE 8.14

Even though Start Date is in the leftmost column of the query table, Start Date is still in the last column of the Answer table. Records are sorted by Last Name—the leftmost column in the Answer table.

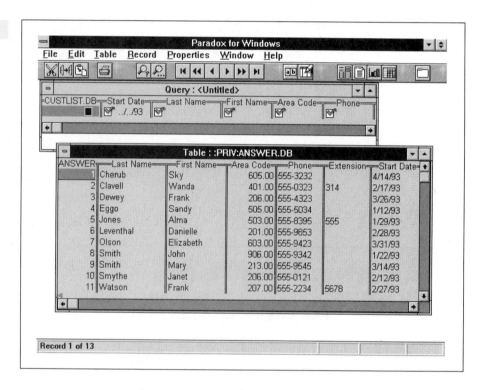

To control the exact appearance of the Answer table, you use the Properties ➤ Answer Table options on the menu bar (available only while a Query window is the active window on the Desktop).

Before you can design the Answer table, however, you need to check the fields you want to see and specify all of your query criteria. In fact, it's probably a good idea to perform the query at least once to make sure it's going to display the fields and records you want, *then* go back and fine-tune the Answer table. Here's how to get started.

1. If you've just performed the query and the Answer table is open, close the Answer table by double-clicking its Control-menu box or by pressing Ctrl+F4. The Query window should now be the currently selected window.

2. Choose Properties ➤ Answer Table ➤ Options or click the Answer Table Properties button on the SpeedBar (shown at left). You'll be taken to the dialog box shown in Figure 8.15.

We'll talk about the various options in this dialog box in the sections that follow.

FIGURE 8.15

The Answer Table Properties dialog box lets you control the proerties of the Answer table.

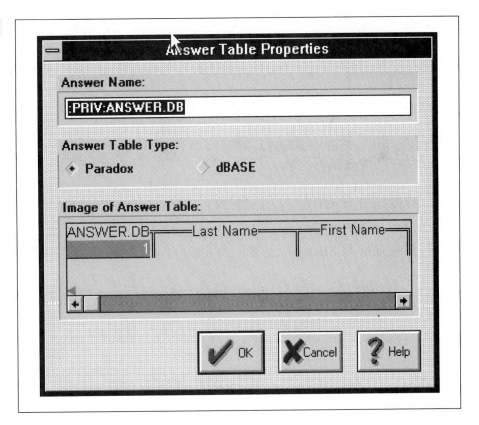

Changing the Name of the Answer Table

The first option in the **Answer Table Properties** dialog box, Answer Name, lets you use a different path or table name for storing the results of the query. You can use this option to store the results of a query to a "regular" Paradox table rather than the temporary Answer table.

For instance, if you enter *c:\pdoxwin\giftco\dateord.db* as the Answer Name, then run the query, the results of the query will be stored in a table named *dateord.db* in the *c:\pdoxwin\giftco* directory. Unlike the temporary Answer table, this new table will not be erased when you exit Paradox, so you can use its data in multiple sessions. This can also make it easier to print reports from the results of a query, as we'll explore in Chapter 11.

Be aware that when you run this query again, Paradox will automatically replace the data currently in the table with the new query results. So, make sure you don't provide the name of a table that already contains important data. For instance, you wouldn't want the results of a query to overwrite the original table, since the resulting query will usually only contain a portion of all the data in the original table.

Choosing the Answer Table Type

The Answer Table Type option lets you decide whether you want the results of the query to be stored in a Paradox table or a dBASE table. This, of course, is only relevant if you use Paradox to manage dBASE data—a topic we'll explore in Appendix C.

Controlling the Answer Table Properties

To control the width and order of columns in the Answer table, as well as the other properties (such as color, font, grid lines, and so forth), you manipulate the query table image that appears under *Image of Answer Table* in the dialog box. Using the same techniques you'd use to manipulate a regular Table View, you can...

- Move columns by dragging them, or by using the Rotate key (Ctrl+R).
- Size columns by dragging the grid line left or right.
- Change the color and font using inspection, or by using Ctrl+Shift+M (all columns), Ctrl+Shift+H (all headings), or Ctrl+G (grid).
- Drag the scroll lock marker to prevent columns from scrolling.

In Figure 8.16, for instance, we rotated the Start Date field to the leftmost column of the Answer table image and set the heading, column, and grid colors to white.

FIGURE 8.16

You can manipulate the image of the Answer table to determine the size and order of columns and other properties of the Answer table.

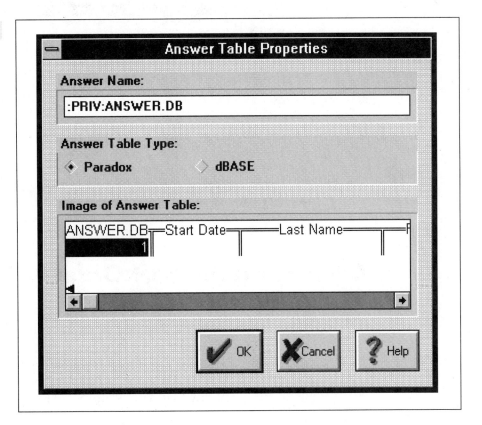

When you've finished changing the Answer Table Properties dialog box, choose OK to return to the Query window. You can then run the query in the usual manner to view your modified Answer table.

Figure 8.17 shows the Answer table after making the changes shown in Figure 8.16. Notice that Start Date is now the first column in the table, and that the Answer table has a white background.

FIGURE 8.17

After you change the image of the Answer table in Figure 8.16 and perform the query, the Answer table appears with the same properties as that image.

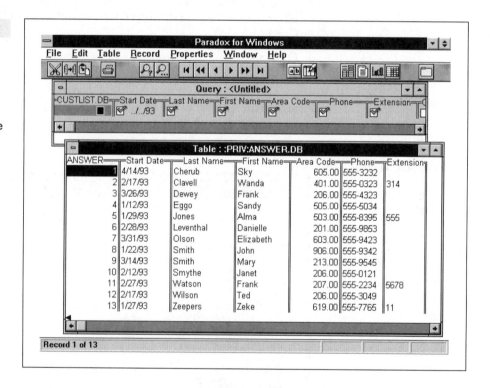

Controlling the Sort Order of the Answer Table

Suppose you want to list records in numeric order by area code, and within area code by phone number, regardless of the order in which fields appear in the Answer table or the query table. You use this dialog box in exactly the same way you'd use the Sort dialog box described in Chapter 7: Click the name of any field you want to use for a sort order, then click the → button to copy the field name to the Sort By list. You can also use the ← button to move a field name back out of the Sort By list, and use the ↑ and ↓ buttons to change the order of fields in the Sort By list. As usual, the first name in the list will be the primary sort key, the next name the secondary sort key, and so forth. In Figure 8.18 we've opted to have records sorted by area code, then by phone number within each area code.

When you've finished making changes, just click OK to return to the Query window. Then you can run the query as usual. Figure 8.19 shows the resulting Answer table after filling in the Sort Answer dialog box as illustrated in Figure 8.18. Notice that records are sorted into area code order.

FIGURE 8.18

The Sort Answer dialog box, accessed via Properties ➤ Answer Table ➤ Sort, lets you define a sort order for records in the Answer table.

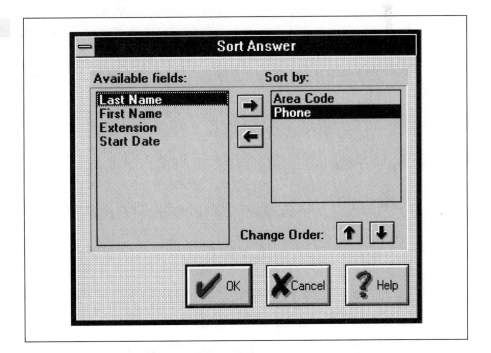

Saving the Answer Table Properties

The Answer table properties you choose affect only the query you're currently working on. In addition, they'll be "forgotten" unless you resave the query after making changes. So, when you close the query and see the dialog box asking if you want to save the current version of the query, be sure to choose Yes. Paradox saves the Answer table properties you specify when you save the query.

FIGURE 8.19

Records in the Answer table are sorted by area code, and by phone number within each area code.

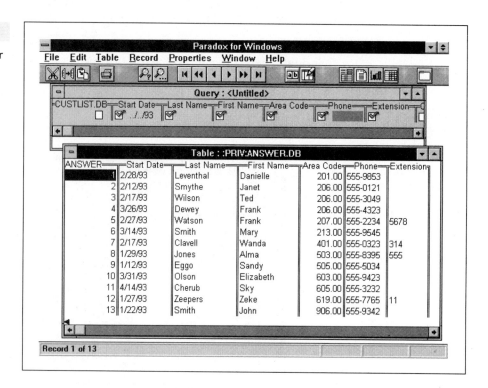

Using Queries to Manipulate Data

So far in this chapter, we've focused on using queries to *isolate* specific types of data only. That is, all our sample queries have allowed us to pull out particular fields and records from a table, and view only that information in the resulting Answer table. But you can also use queries to *update* data in a table, as we'll discuss in the next few sections.

Using Queries to Make Global Changes to a Table

Here is a technique that may someday save you many hours of tedious work. Through a process known as *global editing*, you can automatically change the contents of a field to a new value in records that meet a particular criterion.

For example, suppose you have two different people entering data into your table. One types in *Los Angeles* for all Los Angeles residents; the other types *L.A.* This creates problems, because queries that search for Los Angeles records miss those with L.A. and vice versa. Even though an OR search could take care of this, it would be better to have consistent entries.

There are countless other examples where CHANGETO queries are useful. For instance, you can increase all the unit prices of products in a particular category by 15% (or any other amount), as you'll learn in Chapter 16. You can also use CHANGETO queries to flag records that have been through some procedure, as illustrated in Chapter 18.

Playing It Safe with Queries That Change Data

When using queries that change data, keep in mind that Paradox changes a great many records quite quickly. If you're not careful, you might make the wrong change to a huge number of records. For instance, you might *intend* to change all the L.A.'s in the City field of a table to Los Angeles. But if you're not careful, you might tell Paradox to change *all* the cities to Los Angeles.

Backing Up a Table before Global Editing

To play it safe, always back up your table before you perform a query that changes (or deletes) multiple table records. If you don't, your only recourse in the event of an accident will be to retype a field or fields for each record. Not a pleasant task if there are 10,000 records in the table! Here's how to back up a table:

1. Choose File ➤ Utilities ➤ Copy.

2. In the From text box, enter the name of the table you want to back up (or just click the name of the table).

3. In the To text box, enter a name for the backup copy. For instance, in Figure 8.20 we've opted to copy the *CustList.db* table to a backup table named *CustOrig.db* (for Customer Original).

4. Click the OK button.

FIGURE 8.20

The Table Copy dialog box filled in to copy the table *CustList.db* to a table named *CustOrig.db*.

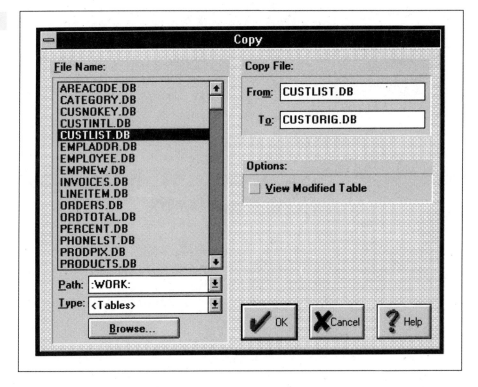

TIP

When you use Paradox for Windows' file manager rather than some other file manager to copy a table, Paradox automatically copies any auxiliary files for the table as well, such as the memo file (.mb) and the primary index (.px).

Now you can safely make any changes you want. If you inadvertently make unwanted changes, simply follow the steps above, but reverse the table names. That is, make *CustOrig.db* the source file and *CustList.db* the destination file.

TIP

For more information on copying tables and other file utilities, see Chapter 14.

Designing a CHANGETO Query

Designing a CHANGETO query is similar to designing any other query, except that you can't use check marks. Instead, first enter the query criteria required to isolate the records you want to change. For instance, in the Query window below, we've entered *L.A.* in the City field because we plan to change those records to *Los Angeles*.

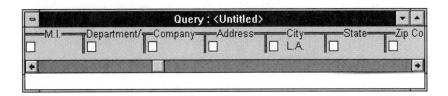

Before you do anything else, you might want to perform the query just to see which records are going to be changed in the upcoming steps. That is, check all the fields, click the Run Query button, then take a close look at the Answer table to make sure you want to change all the records that appear.

If necessary, you can refine and run the query several times until you're sure the query isolates *only* those records that you want to change.

When you're satisfied that the records that appear in the Answer table are the ones you want to change, first uncheck all the fields. Then add the command CHANGETO followed by a blank space and the new value into the field you want to change. If the field you want to change contains a search criterion, precede CHANGETO with a comma and a space. For example, in the query below, we've told Paradox to (1) isolate records that have L.A. in the City field, and (2) change the contents of the City field for those records to "Los Angeles."

Again, it's very important to specify which records you want to change. For instance, had we entered *only*

    CHANGETO Los Angeles

in the Query window, Paradox would have instantly put "Los Angeles" into the City field of every single record in the table. And, as mentioned earlier, it's not always easy to recover from a mistake like that.

NOTE If the field you're changing has any validity checks, the new values you place in that field with CHANGETO must satisfy those validity checks.

When you run a query that contains CHANGETO, Paradox does not display an Answer table. Instead, it displays a temporary table named *Changed*. This table displays all the records that have been changed (and only those records), with the original unchanged data. For instance, if our CustList table happened to contain two records with L.A. in the City field, the resulting Changed table would look like Figure 8.21.

FIGURE 8.21

The Changed table that appears as the result of a CHANGETO query contains a list of records that have been changed by the query—with the original unchanged data still in the records.

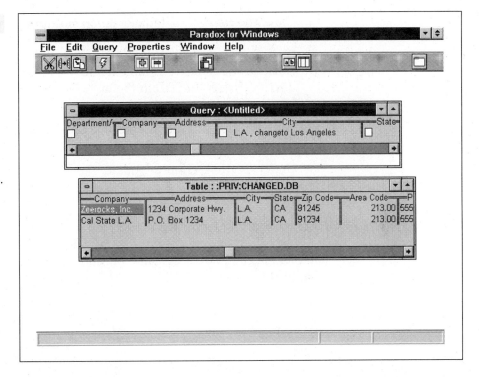

You can close the Changed table, then reopen the original table to verify the changes.

Last-Ditch Approach to Undoing a CHANGETO Query

There is one other way to recover from a bad CHANGETO query, even if you didn't make a backup of the table. Below is the basic technique, in case you get into a jam.

WARNING This method can be risky in tables that don't have a primary key, so use this recovery technique only when you don't have a recent backup.

1. Leave the *changed.db* table open on your desktop.

2. Choose File ➤ Utilities ➤ Add.

3. Click on the *changed.db* table name (most likely appearing as *:PRIV:CHANGED.DB* in the table list) to enter that table name into the From text box.

4. In the To text box, choose or type the name of the original table you changed (*CustList.db* in the previous example).

5. Under Options, choose Update.

6. Click the OK button.

After you do that, you can close all the open windows (choose Window ➤ Close All), then reopen the original table. The records should all contain their original values. (Again, for more information on file utilities, see Chapter 14.)

Using Queries to Delete Records

By placing the word DELETE in the leftmost column of the query table, you can globally delete a group of records that meet the search criteria. Once again, caution is recommended, since a single DELETE query can remove hundreds or thousands of records from a table before you've finished saying "whoops!" So make a backup copy of your table right before doing a DELETE query.

NOTE

The DELETE operator is located on the menu below the query table name. It *cannot* be used when any fields are checked.

Even after making your backup, the safest way to perform a DELETE query is as follows:

1. Start a new query as you normally would, but don't check any fields.

2. Enter the search criterion that identifies the records you want to delete. For instance, below we've created a query that will isolate records with CA in the state field.

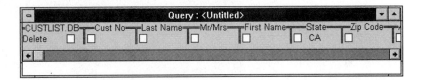

3. If you want to see which records will be deleted, check the field (or all the fields) in the query, then perform the query in the usual manner. The resulting Answer table shows which records will be deleted in later steps.

4. As necessary, repeat Steps 2 and 3 until the query correctly isolates the records you want to delete.

5. Uncheck all the fields, move to the leftmost column of the query table, then type **d** or hold down the mouse button and choose *Delete* from the menu that appears. For example, the query below will delete all records that have CA in the State field.

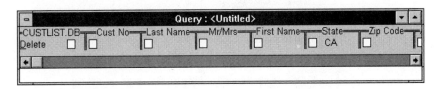

6. Perform the query as usual.

When Paradox completes the query, a new temporary table, named *Deleted*, appears on the screen, as in the example shown in Figure 8.22, where we deleted all records that have CA in the State field. This table shows you which records have been removed from the table. If you're satisfied with

FIGURE 8.22

After we ask Paradox
to delete all records
that have CA in the
State field, Paradox
displays the deleted
records in a table
named *Deleted.*

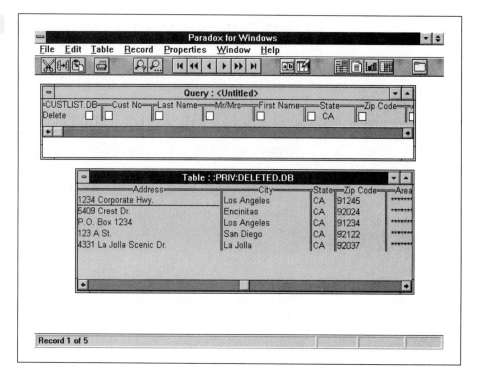

the deletion, you can close all the windows on the Desktop and open the
original table at your leisure.

NOTE   The Deleted table is removed when you exit Paradox.

Recovering from a Bad DELETE Query

If you perform a DELETE query, and upon reviewing the Deleted table
come to the conclusion that you've deleted the wrong records, or too

many records, from the original table, there is a quick and easy method for putting those records right back into the table. Here's how:

1. Choose File ➤ Utilities ➤ Add.

2. Choose *Deleted.db* (probably listed as *:PRIV:DELETED.DB*) from the Tables list to put that table name in the From text box.

3. In the To text box, enter the name of the original table that you deleted the records from.

4. Under Options, choose Append. For example, Figure 8.23 shows the **Add** dialog box filled in to copy deleted records from the Deleted table back into the CustList table.

5. Click the OK button.

If the original table is keyed, the deleted records will be back in their original sort order position within the table. If the original table has no

FIGURE 8.23

If you discover you've deleted the wrong records shortly after performing a DELETE query, you can use the Table Add dialog box to append the records from the temporary Deleted table back into the original table.

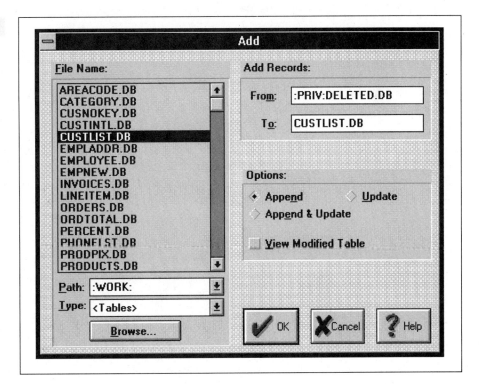

primary key, those records will be at the bottom of the original table because you "appended" them from the *Deleted.db* table to the original table.

Using an Index for a Mini Query

The query by example (QBE) technique presented so far in this chapter provides the greatest flexibility for working with groups of records. But you can also use primary and secondary indexes to isolate specific records. Though not as flexible as QBE, these queries do offer one advantage. They always display "live data" in the original table rather than in an Answer table. So, if you need to make any changes to the data you're viewing, you can do so right on the spot.

To create a mini query from a primary or secondary index, follow these steps:

1. Open the table you want to work with.

2. Choose Table ➤ Order/Range. You'll be taken to an **Order/Range** dialog box like the one shown in Figure 8.24.

3. From the Index List at the left side of the dialog box, choose the index that contains the field or fields you want to query. The Field Values list displays the field or fields that are included in the index you chose.

NOTE   If you haven't created a primary or secondary index for the current table, the Order/Range dialog box will be empty. Just choose Cancel to exit.

FIGURE 8.24

The Order/Range
dialog box lets you
choose a primary or
secondary index (if
available in the
current table) and
isolate particular
values within the
index.

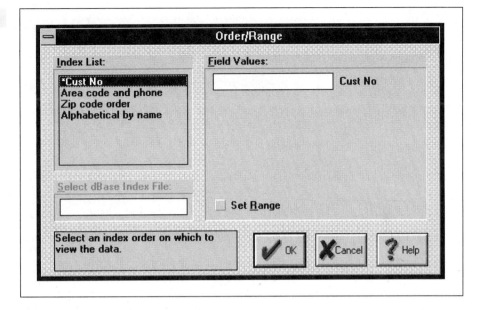

Figure 8.25 shows an example in which we chose the Area Code and
Phone Number index originally created in Chapter 7. Notice that the
fields in this table appear under Field Values.

Now you can enter specific values to isolate in the text boxes next to the
field names. There are a few rules that you need to follow:

- You can only type in an exact value—not the fancy operators
  that QBE offers. For instance "Smith" is OK, but "Sm@th",
  "..smith..", "Not Smith", and so forth are all invalid in the
  Order/Range dialog box.

- You cannot skip any fields.

- The fields in the index determine the sort order of records, and
  you cannot specify another sort order.

For instance, in Figure 8.25 you could fill in just the Area Code text box
or both the Area Code and Phone text boxes. But you cannot leave the
Area Code text box blank and fill in the Phone text box.

FIGURE 8.25

The Field Values
column lists the names
of fields included in
the currently selected
index—Area Code
and Phone in this
example.

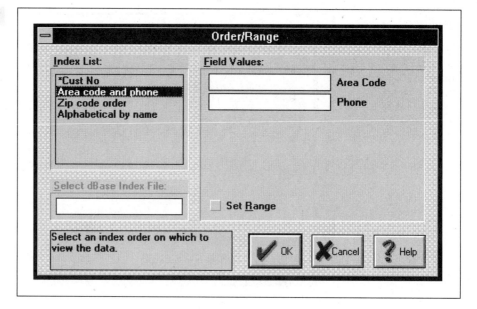

Isolating a Range of Records

With Paradox for Windows, you can isolate records that fall into some range of values. Just fill in the lowest value for the field you want to search and choose the Set Range option. A second text box for the field will appear. Put the high end of the range in this second (bottom) text box. For instance, in the Order/Range dialog box shown in Figure 8.26, we've chosen Set Range and specified records with area codes in the range of 600 to 699 as the range to view.

The rules for using ranges with composite indexes (indexes that contain multiple fields) are as follows:

- You cannot skip over any fields.

- If you are combining exact matches with ranges, the range match must be the last one in the set of fields.

For example, if the index you're using contains the three fields City, State, and Start Date, you could set an exact match on the first field (Los Angeles), an exact match on the second field (CA), and a range on the last field (1/1/93 to 3/31/93).

FIGURE 8.26

This Order/Range dialog box will isolate records that have area codes in the range of 600 to 699 (inclusive)

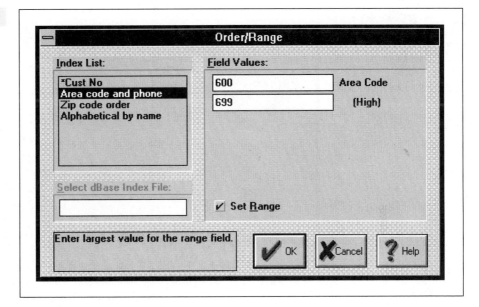

Specifying a Partial Match

If you opt to search a range, you can also specify an inexact match, where only the first character or characters of the field need to match the value you're searching for. In Figure 8.27, for example, we chose the Alphabetical by Name index and entered *A* as the field value to search for in the Last Name index. Then we chose Set Range and entered *M* into the second text box to appear. Then we chose Match Partial Strings to tell Paradox we want to view only records that start with the letters *A* through *M*.

Using the Mini Query

Once you've filled in the Order/Range dialog box, simply choose OK to activate it. Records appear in the original table, and any records that do not match the search criteria become "invisible." In fact, even the record count at the bottom of the screen acts as though the records don't exist.

FIGURE 8.27

The Order/Range dialog box set up to isolate records for customers whose last names begin with the letters A through M.

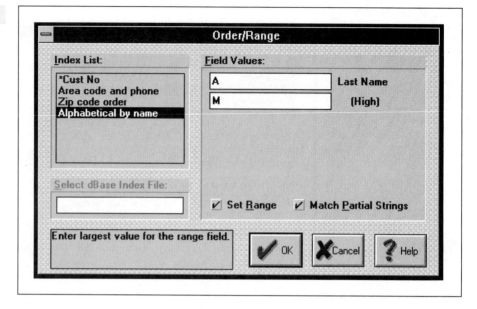

Because this is the original table and live data, you can make any changes you wish right on the spot. If you change a record so that it no longer matches the search criterion, it will seem to disappear. Any other task you perform, such as printing data, will also ignore the invisible data.

To bring the invisible records out of hiding, choose Table ➤ Order/Range again and delete the field values, or choose another index. Alternatively, you can simply close the table and reopen it.

In this chapter, you've learned the basics of using queries to search for and change data in a table. If you've been reading the chapters of this book in sequence, you now know how to use the most essential features of Paradox for Windows.

Chapter 9 begins Part 3 of this book, where you'll learn how to design fancy forms, reports, and graphs for entering and presenting data in attractive, easy to use, and easy to understand formats.

PART THREE

Viewing and Printing Data

CHAPTERS

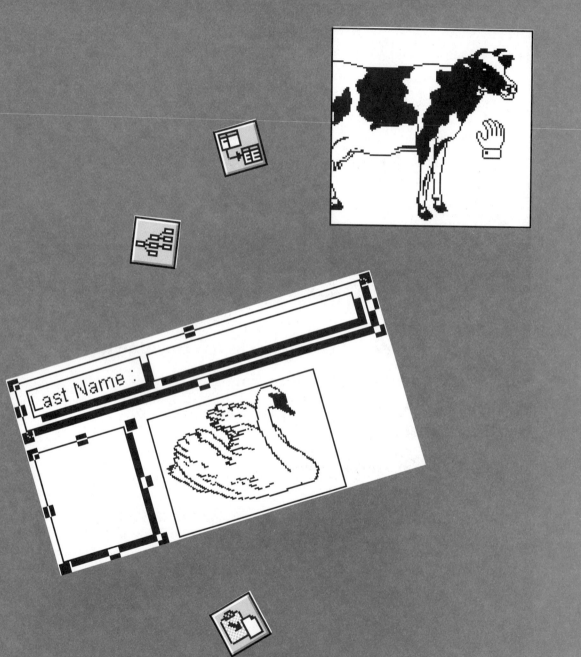

Last Name :

CHAPTER

Tools for Creating Design Documents

fast TRACK

To select design objects   **428**

> first choose the Selection Arrow in the SpeedBar. Then click
> on the object or use the Shift+click and Shift+drag techniques
> to select multiple objects. To select all objects within the cur-
> rently selected object, choose Edit ➤ Select All.

**To arrange and resize multiple objects
automatically**   **431**

> select the objects, then choose options from the Design menu.

To change the properties of objects   **436**

> select the objects, right-click, then choose options from the
> property menu that appears. To change *penetrating* properties
> of objects, hold down the Ctrl key while right-clicking the
> mouse, or press shift F6.

To create and place objects   **447**

> click the appropriate tool in the SpeedBar, then click in the
> Design window and drag the outline to define the size you
> want. You can then reposition or resize the object, or change
> its properties.

N Chapter 1 you saw several examples of jazzy forms and reports for presenting table data on-screen or in printed form. And, if you completed Lessons 4 and 5 in Chapter 2, you've already designed a simple custom form and report of your own. But what you've seen so far is just the tip of the iceberg, for the design possibilities in Paradox for Windows are limited only by your imagination.

In this chapter, we'll cover basic techniques used to design forms and reports. You'll learn how to

- Create a new design document.

- Choose a table or query to associate with your design.

- Specify an initial layout for the design.

- Customize the design by adding, removing, and rearranging design objects and changing their properties.

- Preview, print, and save a design document.

N O T E

If you haven't completed Lessons 4 and 5 in Chapter 2, please do so before reading this chapter. The concepts presented in this chapter will make a lot more sense once you've gotten your fingers wet.

In Chapters 10 and 11, we'll cover more specific techniques for designing forms and reports. Then, in Chapter 12, you'll learn how to create graphs and crosstabs of table data.

As you look through this chapter, don't be daunted by its size. Focus on the basics presented here, try some features on a new form that you use just for practice, then go back and read the details when you need them.

Be sure to experiment freely with the many design tools available—experimentation is truly your best teacher.

What Is a Design Document?

Forms and reports are called *design documents* in Paradox for Windows. *Forms* are usually designed to display table data, either for viewing or for data entry. A cleverly designed form can make data entry efficient, easy, and fun. Figure 9.1 shows a form for our Employee table, complete with three-dimensional frames, scroll bars around the note text, the Gift Corner logo and form title, and the employee's photograph and signature.

FIGURE 9.1

A data entry form for the Employee table

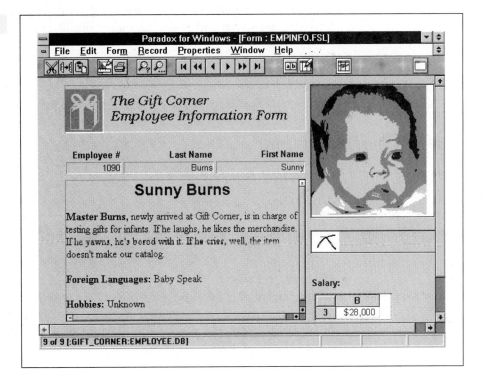

You'll see many more examples of custom forms in Chapter 10.

Reports are usually intended for printed data. You can design simple reports which display data in a "raw" form, or you can create complex summary reports that group and summarize data by various fields, and even include graphs. Figure 9.2 shows a sample customer report, sorted into alphabetical order by the customer's last name, first name, and middle initial.

What Is a Design Object?

All design documents (except completely empty ones) contain *design objects*. Certain design objects, called *data elements*, relate specifically to your data. These include tables, records, fields, graphs, and crosstabs. Other design objects, called *design elements*, are used to spruce up the design document. These include boxes, lines, ellipses, graphics, OLE objects, and text. We'll refer to both data elements and design elements simply as *objects*.

A big part of customizing a design is adding, deleting, and rearranging design objects in the document. The most exciting part of designing a document involves changing the *properties*—the appearance and behavior—of objects in the design. Each type of object has its own set of associated properties, such as color, font, alignment, and so forth. We'll be discussing object properties throughout this chapter and the three chapters that follow.

If in Doubt, Try It Out

If you've ever used a Windows drawing or painting package, you know that creating the perfect picture is largely a matter of picking a drawing tool, dragging it across the screen to define a shape or line, then adding a splash of color or some other enhancement. After a good deal of experimentation—and some creative insights—your drawing is complete.

FIGURE 9.2

A report from the
CustList table

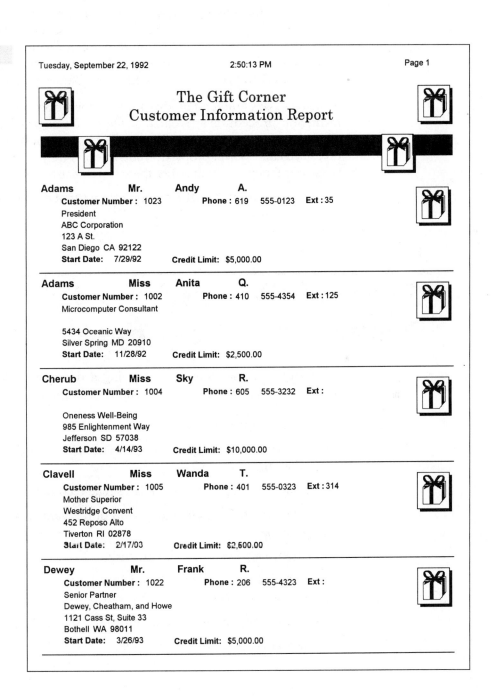

Tuesday, September 22, 1992　　　　　　2:50:13 PM　　　　　　Page 1

The Gift Corner
Customer Information Report

Adams　　　　**Mr.**　　**Andy**　　**A.**
　　Customer Number : 1023　　　　Phone : 619　　555-0123　　Ext : 35
　　President
　　ABC Corporation
　　123 A St.
　　San Diego CA 92122
　　Start Date:　7/29/92　　**Credit Limit:**　$5,000.00

Adams　　　　**Miss**　　**Anita**　　**Q.**
　　Customer Number : 1002　　　　Phone : 410　　555-4354　　Ext : 125
　　Microcomputer Consultant

　　5434 Oceanic Way
　　Silver Spring MD 20910
　　Start Date:　11/28/92　　**Credit Limit:**　$2,500.00

Cherub　　　　**Miss**　　**Sky**　　**R.**
　　Customer Number : 1004　　　　Phone : 605　　555-3232　　Ext :

　　Oneness Well-Being
　　985 Enlightenment Way
　　Jefferson SD 57038
　　Start Date:　4/14/93　　**Credit Limit:**　$10,000.00

Clavell　　　　**Miss**　　**Wanda**　　**T.**
　　Customer Number : 1005　　　　Phone : 401　　555-0323　　Ext : 314
　　Mother Superior
　　Westridge Convent
　　452 Reposo Alto
　　Tiverton RI 02878
　　Start Date:　2/17/03　　**Credit Limit:**　$2,600.00

Dewey　　　　**Mr.**　　**Frank**　　**R.**
　　Customer Number : 1022　　　　Phone : 206　　555-4323　　Ext :
　　Senior Partner
　　Dewey, Cheatham, and Howe
　　1121 Cass St, Suite 33
　　Bothell WA 98011
　　Start Date:　3/26/93　　**Credit Limit:**　$5,000.00

Designing a document in Paradox is a lot like using Paintbrush or any Windows drawing application; therefore, before tackling the tools in the Design window, you should already know something about using your mouse to draw lines and boxes, select objects, and move objects around on the screen. (You'll find Paintbrush in the Accessories window of Program Manager.)

The key to designing a Paradox for Windows document is to take a free-form, non-procedural approach. Just let your imagination run free instead of trying to do everything step by step. Try various tools, select and rearrange objects, change object properties, and so on, until you arrive at a design that suits your fancy. Just remember these watchwords as you work:

> If in doubt, try it out! And don't forget that online help is just an F1 key away.

General Steps for Designing a Document

Here are the basic steps for designing a document. We'll elaborate on these steps throughout this and following chapters.

1. Open a new design document.

2. Choose a table or query to associate with your document. This is called the *data model*.

3. Choose a design style—tabular, single record, multi-record, or blank.

4. Select the fields to include if you don't want to accept the default choices.

5. Choose a page layout, if you wish.

6. Add, delete, and rearrange design objects and change the object properties to get the look you want.

7. Preview or print the document to see the results.

8. Repeat Steps 6 and 7 as needed.

9. Save the design.

10. If you wish, assign the design to one of the Quick buttons in the SpeedBar for Table View.

Creating a New Design Document

 To begin a new form, choose File ➤ New ➤ Form from the menus. Or, right-click the Open Form button in the SpeedBar, if it's available, and choose New.

 To begin a new report, choose File ➤ New ➤ Report, or right-click the Open Report button in the SpeedBar (if it's available) and choose New.

You'll see the **Data Model** dialog box listing tables in the current working directory, as in Figure 9.3.

FIGURE 9.3

The Data Model dialog box lets you name the table or query to use as a basis for the design document.

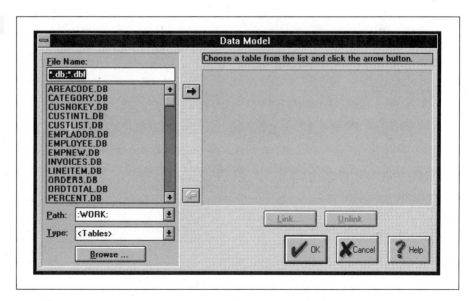

TIP You can open an existing form by choosing File ➤ Open ➤ Form or by clicking the Open Form button. To open an existing report, choose File ➤ Open ➤ Report or click the Open Report button.

Defining the Data Model

The *data model* tells Paradox which data you want to work with in your document. You can define a data model for

- a single table.
- multiple related tables.
- a query.
- no tables or queries.

NOTE We'll discuss multitable data models in Chapter 17.

Designing with a Single Table

As shown in Figure 9.3, the left side of the Data Model dialog box is just like the Open Table dialog box discussed in Chapter 5. To add a table to the data model, double-click the table name you want in the left side of the dialog box, or click once on the table name and then click the → button. The table name will move to the data model area at the right of the dialog box.

If you choose the wrong table, simply click the table in the right side of the dialog box, then click the ← button (or press Alt+D) and choose the correct table name.

You can use the Path list box and Browse buttons to choose tables that aren't in your current working directory. When you're finished defining the data model, choose OK.

NOTE You can return to the Data Model dialog box at any time by clicking the Data Model button in the Design window SpeedBar or any dialog box in which that button appears.

Designing with Saved Queries

As you know, queries provide a powerful way to select certain fields and records from your table. You can take advantage of queries by designing a document based on a saved query.

NOTE In Chapter 16 you'll learn how to perform calculations in queries, making saved queries even more useful as the basis for reports.

Suppose, for example, that you want to design a telephone directory report listing the names, area codes, and phone numbers of all your customers sorted by customer name. Using techniques discussed in Chapter 8, you could set up a query like the one in Figure 9.4. From the Query window, choose Properties ➤ Answer Table ➤ Sort options and sort the Answer table by Last Name, First Name, and M.I. Then close the Query window and save it as usual.

FIGURE 9.4

Query to select fields from the CustList table and sort the Answer table

Query : <Untitled>						
CUSTLIST.DB	Last Name	First Name	M.I.	Area Code	Phone	Exte
■	☑	☑	☑	☑	☑	☐

Now, to base your document on the saved query, go to the Data Model dialog box as described above. Then, instead of choosing a table name, click the Type drop-down list box and choose *<Query>*. Now select the query you want from the left side of the dialog box and choose OK. Complete the design (as described in this and following chapters) and save your report.

Each time you run the report in the future, Paradox will first run the query, generating a new Answer table. That way, your phone list will always be up-to-the-minute and sorted with no extra effort on your part.

WARNING Because queries do not work on "live" table data, you shouldn't use them as the basis for data entry forms. In general, it's best to use queries for reports, not forms.

Creating a Blank Design

Normally, you'll want to associate the design document with an existing table or query. However, if you wish, you can create a blank document that isn't bound to any table's data. To do so, simply choose OK in the Data Model dialog box without first choosing a table or query. If you opt to create a blank design, Paradox will skip the Design Layout dialog box described a little later in this chapter.

TIP You can always bind your design to a table or query later by clicking the Data Model button in the SpeedBar. However, you'll save time by choosing a table or query to begin with.

Inspecting Tables in the Data Model

Inspecting a table name in the right side of the Data Model dialog box leads to several useful options. The options available when designing *forms* are listed below.

Fields   Displays the field names for the table you're inspecting. This list is for reference only.

Order/Range   If your table has a secondary index, you can choose this option to sort and filter the records displayed in the form. When the Order/Range dialog box appears, select a secondary index and any values or ranges you wish to use, then choose OK to return to the Data Model dialog box. (See Chapter 7 for details on secondary indexes and the Order/Range dialog box.)

Read-Only   Prevents users from making any changes to this table.

Strict Translation   Prevents users from entering characters that aren't easily translated to other language drivers. For example, when this option is checked, typing the copyright symbol (©) into a field will cause Paradox to reject the entry and display the message "Character(s) not supported by Table Language" in the status bar.

When you inspect a table name in the data model for a *report* Paradox will list the field names for the table you're inspecting. This list is for reference only.

Choosing an Initial Design Layout

The **Design Layout** dialog box appears after you choose OK from the Data Model dialog box. There you can specify an initial layout for your design, including

- a general style for the design.
- which fields are to be displayed.
- whether fields are to be labeled or not.
- whether the page layout is for the screen or the printer.

Keep in mind that the options in the Design Layout dialog box are mainly a convenience for setting up your initial design. You don't have to change any of the settings unless you want to. However, after designing a few reports or forms, you'll appreciate the time saved by making a few choices up front.

The changes you make in the Design Layout dialog box are reflected immediately in the sample design area, so you can see what the document will look like before you get to the Design window. Note that the appearance of the Design Layout dialog box and the options available depend on the table you selected, whether you're designing a form or report, and the basic style you've chosen. For instance, Figure 9.5 shows the default Design Layout dialog box for a form, while Figure 9.6 shows the default Design Layout dialog box for a report. Both examples are based on the now-familiar Employee table.

Make any changes you want in this dialog box as described in the sections that follow. When you're satisfied with the initial layout, choose OK to get to the Design window, where you can customize the design to your heart's content.

FIGURE 9.5

The default Design Layout dialog box for a form based on the sample Employee table

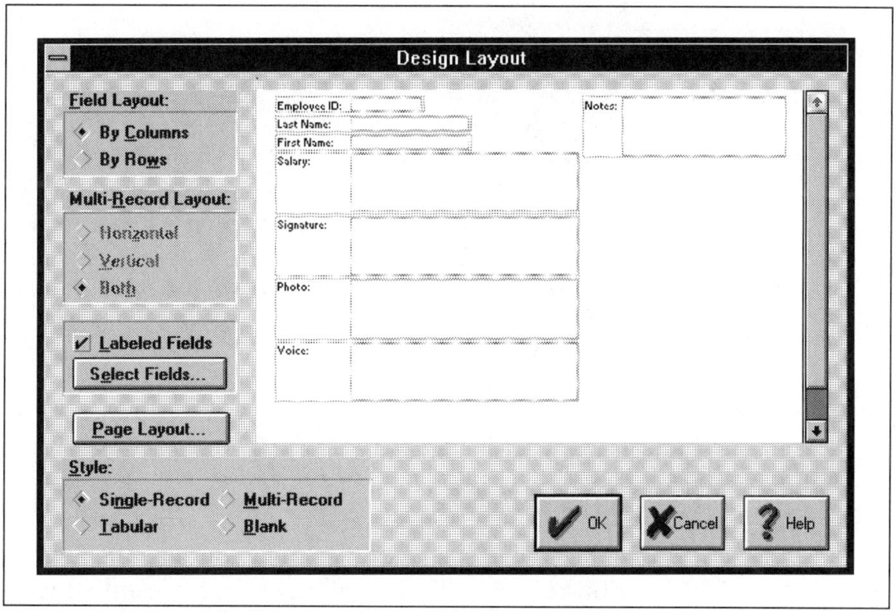

FIGURE 9.6

The default Design Layout dialog box for a report based on the sample Employee table

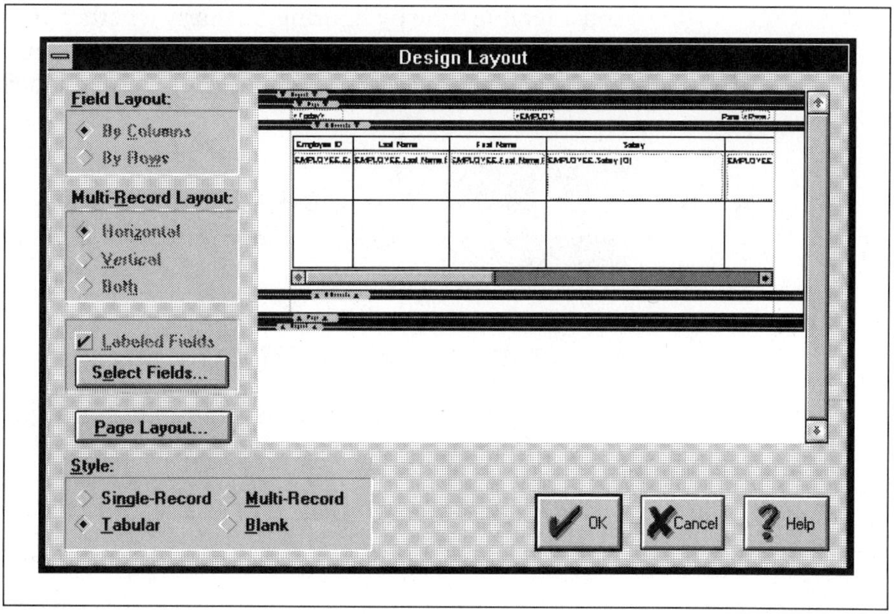

WARNING Although you'll rarely need to do so, you can return to the Design Layout dialog box later by choosing Design ➤ Design Layout from the Design window. However, be aware that if you change the design layout, your existing design will be *completely replaced*. Paradox will give you a chance to back out before taking this action. When the warning message appears, choose Yes *only* if you're sure you want to replace your design; otherwise choose No to cancel the changes.

Hiding or Showing Field Labels

A field label is a text object that contains the field name. Paradox for Windows initially displays all fields in a document with field labels.

To display field data without field labels, select the Labeled Fields option in the Design Layout dialog box to remove the check mark. You'll save considerable time by figuring out early whether you want *most* of the fields to appear with or without labels. Later, when you reach the Design window, you can inspect individual fields to turn labels on or off.

NOTE The Labeled Fields option is always checked and cannot be changed for a Tabular or Blank design style.

Choosing a Design Style

Paradox for Windows offers several styles for displaying a design, including the following:

Single-Record   Displays one record of the table at a time.

Tabular   Displays several records of the table in a table frame.

Multi-Record   Displays several records of the table in a multi-record object.

Blank   Doesn't display any records of the table.

To choose one of these styles, click the appropriate option in the Styles area of the dialog box.

N O T E   The remaining figures in this chapter show examples of form designs; the concepts illustrated are basically the same for reports.

Tabular Design Style

The simplest design style is *Tabular,* which resembles the Quick Report format discussed in Chapter 6. As shown by the sample design layout in Figure 9.7, the rows and columns look just like the table itself, with a horizontal scroll bar added. Reports initially have a tabular style.

FIGURE 9.7

A tabular design style
for the Employee table

Single-Record Design Style

The *Single-Record* design style displays one record at a time. It is the default layout for a form. You can either arrange the fields by columns (top-to-bottom) or by rows (left-to-right). To arrange fields by columns, choose *By Columns* in the Field Layout area of the Design Layout dialog box (see Figure 9.7, above). To arrange them by rows, choose *By Rows* in the Field layout area (see Figure 9.8, below).

Multi-Record Style

The *Multi-Record* design style displays several records in the table at one time and is especially handy for creating mailing labels. (Chapter 11 shows how to design multi-record mailing labels.) Notice in Figure 9.9 that the fields of a record appear in the first record region of the sample area. You can specify how you want repeated records to appear on the page by choosing options in the Multi-Record Layout area of the dialog box. Your choices are as follows:

Horizontal Records repeat across the page (this is the default multi-record layout for a report).

FIGURE 9.8

The Single-Record design style arranged in rows

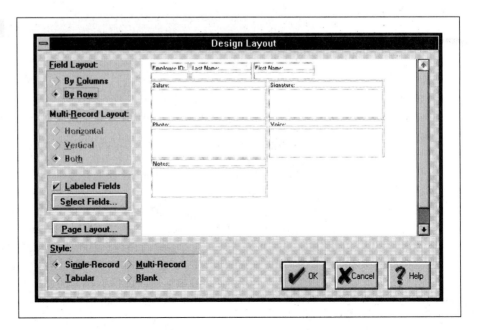

Vertical   Records repeat down the page.

Both   Records repeat both across and down the page (this is the default multi-record layout for a form).

Figure 9.9 shows the Employee design after choosing *Both* to repeat records across and down the page. (An error message will warn you if Paradox cannot fit all the fields into the multi-record layout. Choose OK to clear the message. Paradox will then place as many fields as will fit into the sample area.)

N O T E

You specify only the initial multi-record layout in the Design Layout dialog box. From the Design window you can specify the number of records across and down a page and the spacing between them. And, you can change your initial choices about the layout of repeated records.

FIGURE 9.9

A multi-record design style for an Employee table form. The Both option selected here repeats records both across and down the page.

Blank Style

The *Blank* design style erases all fields from the design. Of course, you can always use tools on the Design window's SpeedBar to add tables, records, and fields later, but with a blank design they won't be placed automatically. Note that the blank design style is *not* the same as a completely blank form, which is not associated with any table at all. The blank style is handy when you want to include very few fields in the form or report or when you're creating graphs and crosstabs.

Selecting Fields to Display

Initially, all the fields appear in the Design Layout dialog box (and in your design) in the order they are defined in the table structure. Of course, you can remove, rearrange, or add fields when you get to the Design window (as described later), but it's often easier to do this while defining the initial design layout.

To get a jump on things and save yourself many a mouse click and drag, choose the Select Fields button in the Design Layout dialog box. You'll see the **Select Fields** dialog box, as in Figure 9.10. Notice that the left side of the dialog box shows the table you've chosen for the design, while the right side shows the currently selected fields.

To place additional fields in the Selected Fields list (or remove fields), click the drop-down arrow to the right of the table name. Any fields that are already selected will appear highlighted (dark), while unselected fields won't be highlighted. Once the drop-down list is open you can use any of these techniques:

- To add a field to the Selected Fields list, hold down the Ctrl key while clicking an *unselected* field name in the drop-down list (this is called *Ctrl+clicking*). The order in which you Ctrl+click the fields determines the order they will appear in the Selected Fields list.

- To remove a field from the Selected Fields list, Ctrl+click a *selected* field name in the drop-down list.
- To add all the fields at once, simply drag the mouse through all the field names in the drop-down list.

Another way to remove a field from the design is to click the field name in the Selected Fields area of the dialog box, then click the Remove Field button.

You can reposition a field by clicking it in the Selected Fields area, then clicking the ↑ or ↓ button as needed to move the field up or down in the list.

When you're finished selecting and rearranging fields, choose OK to return to the Design Layout dialog box.

FIGURE 9.10

The Select Fields dialog box initially contains all the table fields in the order they appear in the table structure.

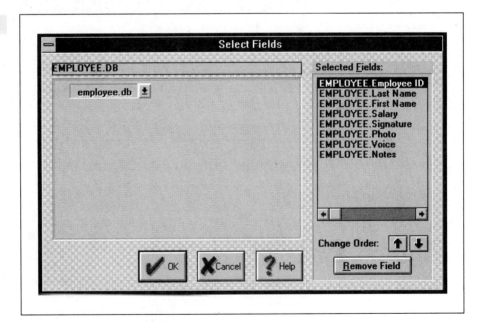

Selecting the Page Layout

Paradox chooses an initial page layout that's appropriate for the type of document you're creating. For example, reports are initially designed for the printer, while forms are designed for your computer screen. You can customize the initial page layout for a report or form by clicking the Page Layout button in the Design Layout dialog box. Figure 9.11 shows the default **Page Layout** dialog box for a form.

N O T E   You can return to the Page Layout dialog box later by choosing Form ➤ Page ➤ Layout or Report ➤ Page Layout from the Design window menus.

FIGURE 9.11

A default Page Layout dialog box for a form

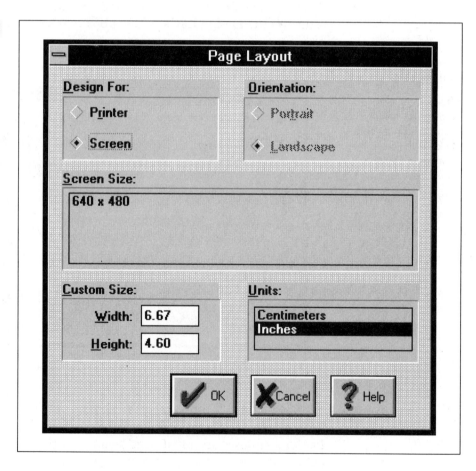

The Page Layout dialog box differs for forms and reports, so we'll wait until Chapters 10 and 11 to dig into the details. However, you should keep the following points in mind:

- You can design the document for displaying on the screen or printing on your printer. (This is true whether you're designing a report or a form.)

- If you design for the screen, you can use any screen fonts installed on your computer. However, your printer may not be able to print all those fonts or may not print them exactly as they appear on-screen. Of course, if your screen fonts match your printer fonts you should have no problem.

- When you design for the printer, Paradox restricts the screen fonts to those actually available on your printer and does its best to match the screen display to your printed output.

After making any changes you want in the Page Layout dialog box, click on OK.

N O T E If you don't choose a table or query in the Data Model dialog box, Paradox will skip the Design Layout dialog box and go immediately to the Page Layout dialog box.

Overview of the Design Window

When you choose OK in the Design Layout dialog box, the Design window appears (see Figures 9.12 and 9.13). From here you can customize every aspect of the document's appearance. You can add, remove, and rearrange objects, or you can change the appearance or behavior of any design object by inspecting it and choosing options from its property menu. You can also preview, print, and save the design.

Figures 9.12 and 9.13 show the default Paradox Design windows for an Employee form and report, respectively. As you can see, the two Design windows have much in common, though there are some differences, as indicated by labels on the figures.

The menus in the Design window provide additional options for designing, previewing, printing, and saving your document, as well as for rearranging document windows, getting help, and changing various properties. The

FIGURE 9.12

The default Form Design window for the Employee table. Notice the Form menu and the Button and Crosstab tool on the SpeedBar.

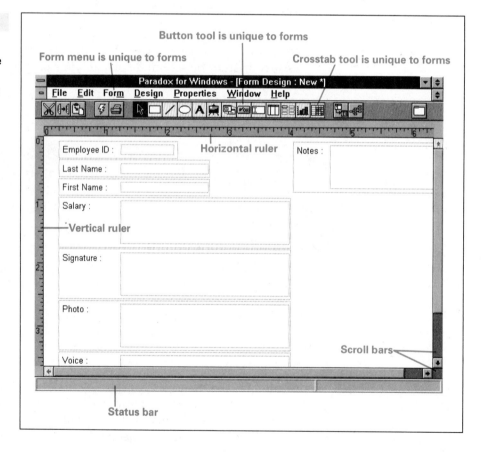

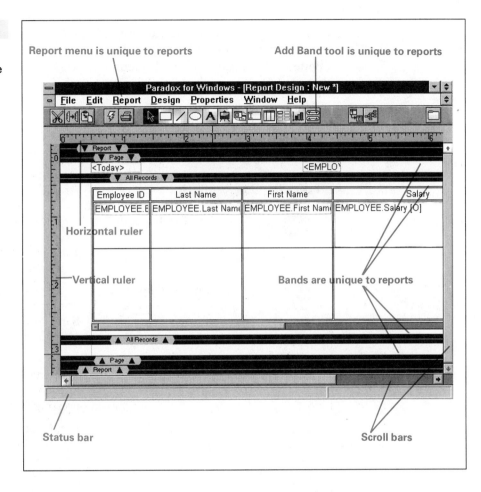

FIGURE 9.13

The default Report Design window for the Employee table. Notice the Report menu, the Add Band tool on the SpeedBar, and the report, page, and record bands in the design area

SpeedBar buttons let you add new objects to the document and offer convenient alternatives to choosing options from the menus. Table 9.1 shows each button and briefly describes its function.

TIP

The button name appears in the status bar whenever you move the mouse pointer to the button icon in the SpeedBar.

In the Design window, you can preview the form or report, print and save the document, close it, and open it again to make further changes. Before diving into the nitty-gritty of document design, let's take a quick look at these topics.

TABLE 9.1: Summary of SpeedBar Buttons in the Design Window

BUTTON	BUTTON NAME	DESCRIPTION AND MENU OR KEYBOARD EQUIVALENT (IF ANY)
	Cut To Clipboard	Cuts the currently selected text or object to the Clipboard. Same as choosing Edit ➤ Cut or pressing Shift+Del.
	Copy To Clipboard	Copies the currently selected text or object to the Clipboard. Same as choosing Edit ➤ Copy or pressing Ctrl+Ins.
	Paste From Clipboard	Pastes data from the Clipboard to the design document. Same as choosing Edit ➤ Paste or pressing Shift+Ins.
	View Data	Displays the form or report on screen with the actual data from your table. Same as choosing Form ➤ View Data, Report ➤ Preview, or pressing F8. When you're previewing a document, the View Data button is replaced by the Design button.
	Design	Returns to the Design window. Same as choosing Form ➤ Design or Report ➤ Design or pressing F8. When you're designing a document, the Design button is replaced by the View Data button.

TABLE 9.1: Summary of SpeedBar Buttons in the Design Window (continued)

BUTTON	BUTTON NAME	DESCRIPTION AND MENU OR KEYBOARD EQUIVALENT (IF ANY)
	Print	Prints the design (if you're in the Design window) or data (if you're previewing). Same as choosing File ➤ Print options (see Chapters 10 and 11).
	Selection Arrow	Selects objects in the design document.
	Box Tool	Adds boxes to the design document.
	Line Tool	Adds lines to the design document.
	Ellipse Tool	Adds ellipses to the design document.
	Text Tool	Adds text objects to the design document.
	Graphic Tool	Adds graphic objects to the design document.
	OLE Tool	Adds OLE objects to the design document.
	Button Tool	(Forms only) Adds buttons to a form. You can use ObjectPAL to assign actions that the button will perform when clicked (see Chapter 19).
	Field Tool	Adds table fields to the design document.
	Table Tool	Adds entire table frames to the design document.
	Multi-Record Tool	Adds repeating records to a design document.

TABLE 9.1: Summary of SpeedBar Buttons in the Design Window (continued)

BUTTON	BUTTON NAME	DESCRIPTION AND MENU OR KEYBOARD EQUIVALENT (IF ANY)
	Graph Tool	Adds graphs to a design document (see Chapter 12).
	Crosstab Tool	(Forms only) Adds crosstabs to a form (see Chapter 12).
	Add Band	(Reports only) Adds bands to a report (see Chapter 11).
	Data Model	Returns to the Data Model dialog box. Same as choosing Form ➤ Data Model or Report ➤ Data Model.
	Object Tree	Displays a hierarchical chart of your design. You can inspect the properties of any object in the Object Tree. Same as choosing Form ➤ Object Tree or Report ➤ Object Tree.
	Folder	Displays the objects in the current folder (see Chapter 14).

Previewing Your Document

You can preview your design at any time to see how it will look with the data filled in. To do so, simply click the View Data button in the SpeedBar (shown at left) or press the F8 key. If you're designing a form, you can also choose Form ➤ View Data, or choose Report ➤ Preview if you're designing a report. When you're previewing a document, the View Data button in the SpeedBar is replaced by the Design button.

You'll see the form or report document filled in with actual data from your table, along with any objects you added to the design. Figure 9.14, for example, shows a simple form for the Employee table previewed on the screen. Notice that we scrolled to the fifth record in the table. (To display the data in the Notes field completely, simply move the highlight to that field. To display all the data in a memo field or formatted memo field, even when the highlight isn't in the field, you must set the Run Time ➤ Complete Display property, as described in the next chapter.)

TIP

When previewing a form design, you're actually in Form View and have all the usual Form View capabilities (see Chapter 5).

FIGURE 9.14

A simple Employee form after clicking the View Data button and using the Form View SpeedBar buttons to scroll to the fifth record in the table

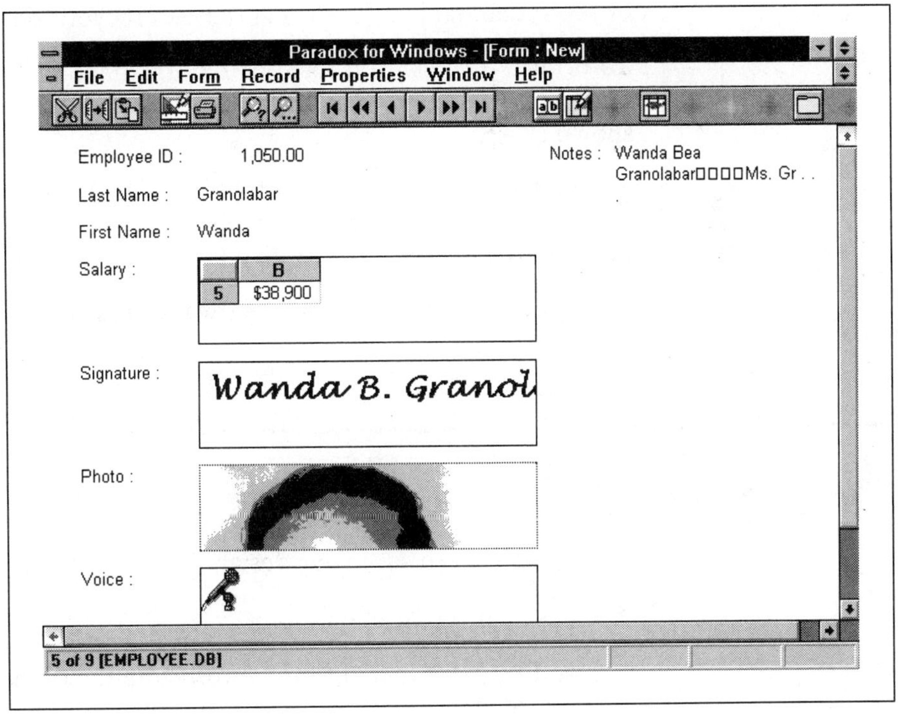

When you're ready to make additional changes to your design, return to the Design window by clicking the Design button in the SpeedBar (shown at left) or by pressing F8 again. You can also choose For**m** ➤ **D**esign (for forms) or **R**eport ➤ **D**esign (for reports).

N O T E   You can only change your design from the Design window.

Printing Your Document

Printing a report or form is quite easy. You can print either the design itself or the actual data in the format defined by your design.

 To print the *design* of a form or report, make sure you're in the Design window (click the Design button if necessary), then click the Print button shown at left.

To print the form or report with its data filled in, switch to the Form View or Report View window by clicking the View Data button, then click the Print button.

See Chapters 10 and 11 for other ways to print designs and documents.

Saving Your Document

It's a good idea to save your design document when

- you're finished designing it.
- you've spent lots of time customizing the design and want to save the changes made so far.

- you're about to try a new design technique and want to preserve your work in case the experiment is a bust.

To save changes to a new document, make sure you're in the Design window, then choose File ➤ Save. When the **Save File As** dialog box appears, enter the file name or complete path name for the document, *without an extension*, into the New File Name box and choose OK. If the file already exists, Paradox will ask if you want to overwrite it. Choose Yes if you're sure you want to overwrite the existing file, or No to return to the Save File As dialog box.

N O T E   Forms have a file name extension of .fsl, while reports have an .rsl extension.

When you use File ➤ Save to save changes to an existing document, Paradox saves your changes without further prompting. If you want to save the document under a *different* name, choose File ➤ Save As instead.

Assigning the Design to Quick Buttons

Once you've saved a design, you can assign it to a table's Quick Form, Quick Report, Quick Graph, or Quick Crosstab button in the SpeedBar.

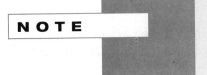

N O T E   Graphs and crosstabs (described in Chapter 12) must be saved as forms if you want to use them with Quick buttons.

To assign a preferred document to a table, follow the steps below.

1. Click the Open Table button in the SpeedBar (if it's available) or choose File ➤ Open ➤ Table and follow the usual steps to open the table you want to associate with the form, report, graph, or crosstab.

2. Choose Properties ➤ Preferred, then Form, Report, Graph, or Crosstab. Or, right-click the Quick Form, Quick Report, Quick Graph, or Quick Crosstab button in the SpeedBar.

3. Choose the file you want to assign as preferred, then choose OK.

4. Choose Properties ➤ View Properties ➤ Save.

From now on, whenever you click the Quick button in the SpeedBar, Paradox will use the preferred design to display the data. To assign a different document to the Quick button, simply repeat the steps above.

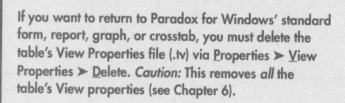

N O T E   If you want to return to Paradox for Windows' standard form, report, graph, or crosstab, you must delete the table's View Properties file (.tv) via Properties ➤ View Properties ➤ Delete. *Caution:* This removes *all* the table's View properties (see Chapter 6).

Opening an Existing Design

Of course, you needn't finish an entire design in one sitting. If you want to take a break, just save your changes and close the Design window. When you're ready to return to the design, follow these steps:

1. Click the Open Form button (to open a form) or Open Report button (to open a report), if it's available on the SpeedBar.

Or, choose File ➤ Open ➤ Form or File ➤ Open ➤ Report, as appropriate.

2. The **Open Document** dialog box appears, as shown in Figure 9.15.

3. Choose the file name you want from the File Name area. When opening forms, only files with an .fsl extension appear in the File Name list. When opening reports, you'll only see files with an .rsl extension.

4. If you wish, choose an Open mode. Your choices are as follows:

   • **View Data**   Displays the document on-screen with data filled in.

   • **Design**   Opens the document in the Design window.

FIGURE 9.15

The Open Document dialog box lets you select a document, open a report as a form (or vice versa), or change the table associated with the document.

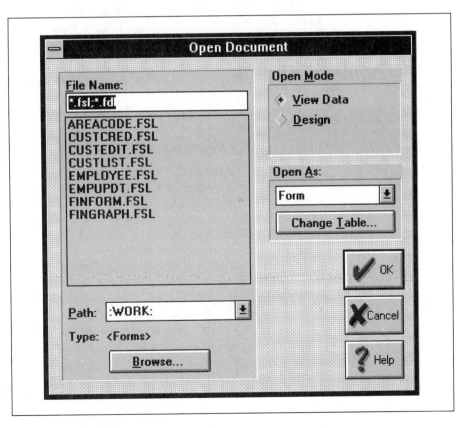

- **Print**   Prints the data instead of opening a window. This option is available for reports only and is not shown in Figure 9.15.

5. Choose additional options as described in the following sections.

6. Choose OK.

If you opened the document in View mode, which is the default choice, you can click the Design button or press F8 to return to the Design window. From there you can make any changes necessary. When you're done, save the design.

TIP

To use an existing design as the basis for a new one, open the document as described above, then choose File ➤ Save As, type a new file name, and choose OK. Make whatever changes you wish in the Design window, then choose File ➤ Save to save your changes. You can also use the Copy feature, which is discussed in Chapter 14, to copy existing designs to new files.

Choosing a Different Table

When opening a form or report, you can choose a table other than the one used to design the document. For example, suppose you design a form for the CustList table that's just perfect for a similarly structured table of inactive customers (perhaps named *OldCust*). Instead of designing the form for the OldCust table from scratch, you can simply open the original form with a different table. To do so, click the Change Table button in the Open Document dialog box and specify a different table.

When you use the Change Table button, Paradox copies the existing document's layout and properties to a new window and tries to place the corresponding fields from the table in the new form or report. You can then change and save the new design if you wish. No changes are made to the original document.

Paradox may be unable to match every field name in the design with a corresponding field in the table if the new table's structure doesn't exactly match the structure of the table used to design the document. After you choose OK to open the document, Paradox will display a dialog box like the one below for each missing field.

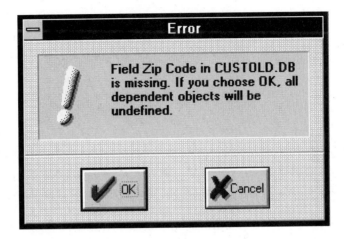

Choose OK if you don't mind having undefined fields in your form or report, or choose Cancel, then No, to back out of the operation.

NOTE Unless all the fields from the new table match fields in the existing table, you'll probably need to switch to the Design window and define or delete some field objects.

Opening Forms as Reports and Vice Versa

With Paradox for Windows, you can open a form as a report or a report as a form. This would come in handy if you designed a report that you really liked and wanted to use it as a form—or vice versa.

To change a form into a report, or vice versa, click the Open As drop-down list and choose *Report* or *Form*, as appropriate. When you use the

Open As option, Paradox copies the original document to a new one, leaving the original untouched.

When you use this feature, keep the following points in mind:

- Some objects behave differently in forms and reports. In particular, you may need to modify summary and calculated fields (see Chapter 17 for information on these types of fields).

- When converting a form to a report, the form fields appear in the *record band* of the report. Similarly, when converting a report to a form, only the fields in the record band come across to the form.

- Some form layouts aren't valid for reports.

- If the report includes a page break in the record band, Paradox creates a multipage form. Likewise, Paradox places a page break in the appropriate spot in the report's record band if you're opening a multipage form as a report.

N O T E   Chapter 10 discusses multipage forms, and Chapter 11 covers record bands and page breaks.

Tips for Using the Design Window

Now that you know the basics of creating and saving documents, let's look at some techniques for customizing documents in the Design window.

Following are a few tips to keep in mind when you begin using the Design window.

- Maximize the Design window to see more of your design (click the Maximize button or double-click the title bar).

- Use the Zoom feature to zoom in on part of the design or to reduce the design and get a better overall view. See "Zooming In and Out," below.

- Use grids and rulers to help you align, size, and separate objects. See "Using Rulers" and "Using Grids," below.

- Preview your design frequently to check your progress.

- Use the floating SpeedBar (Chapter 3) if you need more viewing room or want to move the SpeedBar tools to a more convenient spot on the Desktop. (Choose Properties ➤ Desktop.)

- If necessary, use the Undo command to back out of your most recent change. (Choose Edit ➤ Undo or press Alt+Backspace.)

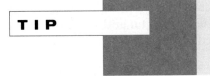

TIP   If your design is hopelessly botched, simply close the Design window and choose No when asked if you want to save your changes. Then re-open the document and begin again.

Zooming In and Out

Unless you have a big-screen monitor, you probably won't be able to see the whole design at once. The scroll bars provide one way to bring a portion of the design into view; zooming provides another. You can zoom in for a close-up view of part of your design, or zoom out for a bird's eye view of the entire design. To zoom, choose Properties ➤ Zoom, then choose any of the options listed below.

25 % or 50 %   Reduces the design to 25 or 50 percent of its normal size.

100 %   Displays the design at its normal size.

200 % or 400 %   Expands the design to 200 percent or 400 percent its normal size.

Fit Width   Sizes the design to the width of the window.

> **Fit Height**   Sizes the design to the height of the window.
>
> **Best Fit**   Sizes the design to both the width and height of the window.

Using Rulers

Whenever you move the mouse pointer around the window, the pointer position is tracked on the rulers by small, thin line markers. When you select an object in the design, segments of the rulers change color to indicate the dimensions and exact position of the object. Similarly, the ruler segments change length as you resize an object, and they move whenever you drag an object to a new position in the window. Thus, the rulers are very useful in determining the exact position or measurement of objects in the design document.

For example, in Figure 9.16 we clicked on the Salary field to select it. Notice how the shaded areas on the horizontal and vertical rulers match the width and height of the selected object.

FIGURE 9.16

The horizontal and vertical rulers in the Design window indicate the width and height of a selected object.

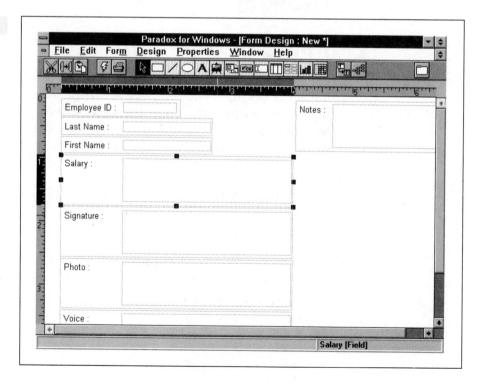

Displaying and Hiding Rulers

You can display or hide the horizontal, vertical, or expanded rulers on the Design window by choosing options from the Properties menu.

- Choose Properties ➤ Horizontal Ruler to turn the horizontal ruler on or off.

- Choose Properties ➤ Vertical Ruler to turn the vertical ruler on or off.

- Choose Properties ➤ Expanded Ruler to turn the expanded ruler on or off. (The expanded ruler lets you align text, set tabs, and choose line spacing for text, as described later.)

NOTE   Like many options in the Design window menus, the ruler options are toggles. When checked (selected), the ruler is turned on (visible). When unchecked (deselected), the ruler is turned off (hidden). Turning off the rulers gives you more workspace in the Design window.

Using Grids

Paradox for Windows can display a background of horizontal and vertical grid lines, as in Figure 9.17, to help you place and resize objects with precision. To display the grid, choose Properties ➤ Show Grid and make sure *Show Grid* is checked. Deselect the Show Grid option to hide the grid lines. Notice that lines show the grid's major divisions, while dots show the grid's minor divisions.

FIGURE 9.17

The Employee form
with grid lines visible

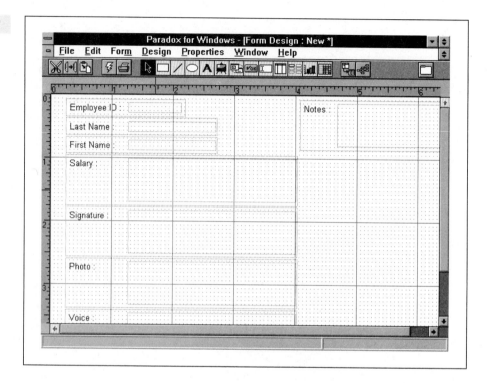

If you want all objects to align on major or minor grid lines whenever you place, resize, or move them, check the Properties ➤ Snap to Grid option. Remove the check mark to turn off the Snap-to-Grid feature. You can have objects snap to the grid whether or not the grid is visible.

Changing the Grid Settings

The grid settings control the unit of measure and divisions in both the ruler and the grid. The default unit of measure is inches, with major divisions at one-inch intervals and sixteen minor divisions per inch.

To change the settings, choose Properties ➤ Grid Settings. You'll see the **Grid Settings** dialog box, as shown below.

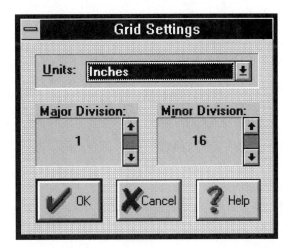

Make any of the changes listed below, then choose OK.

- To change the measurement units, open the Units drop-down list box, then choose *Inches* or *Centimeters*.

- To change the distance between the major grid lines, click the arrow buttons below the Major Division heading. Clicking ↑ increases the distance between major divisions; clicking ↓ decreases the distance.

- To change the distance between minor grid lines, click the arrow buttons below Minor Division. Clicking ↑ decreases the distance between divisions (creating more divisions); clicking ↓ increases the distance (creating fewer divisions).

Selecting Design Objects

You must select objects before you can move, resize, delete, or otherwise manipulate them in the Design window. When you select an object, "handles" appear around it. As you pass the mouse pointer over a handle, the pointer changes shape to indicate the direction you can move that handle. The example below shows a selected box and all the possible directions of movement.

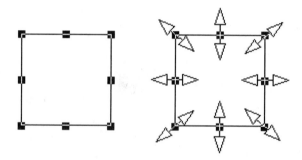

 To begin selecting an object, click the Selection Arrow tool in the Speed-Bar (shown at left), if it isn't already selected (darkened). Then, to select a single object, simply click on it.

Selecting from the Outside or Inside

When you click an object that's contained within another object, Paradox will select either the outside or the inside object first, depending on the current Designer Properties settings. For example, suppose you have a line within a box, as below.

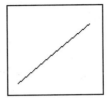

When you click on the line, Paradox's default action is to select the *outermost* object first (the box, in this example). You must click again to select the object inside it (the line). Likewise, if you had a line, within a circle, within a box, as below, the first click would select the box, the next would select the circle, and the last would select the line. Thus, the next innermost object is selected each time you click.

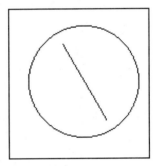

If you don't like this manner of selecting objects, choose Properties ➤ Designer, click *Select From Inside* to check the option, then choose OK. Once you've done this, you can select whatever object you click. (To restore the default setting, simply choose Properties ➤ Designer, click *Select From Inside* to remove the check mark, and choose OK.)

Whenever you select an object that's contained by another object, you can press Esc to select the next outermost object. Thus, if you've selected the line within the circle in the previous example, you can press Esc to select the circle. You can also press Tab or Shift+Tab to cycle through and select individual objects in your design.

Selecting Multiple Objects

Paradox offers several ways to select more than one object at a time. To begin, click the Selection Arrow in the SpeedBar (if the tool isn't selected already), then choose the most convenient multiselection method.

- Hold down the Shift key while clicking each object you want to select. To deselect an object, simply click it again while holding down the Shift key. This technique is called *Shift+click*.

- To select several objects that are close together, position the mouse pointer slightly outside the first object you want to select. Now hold down the Shift key, hold down the left mouse button, and drag to create a box outline around the objects. When you release the left mouse button, all the objects surrounded by the outline will be selected. This is called *Shift+drag* or *marquee selection*.

- To select all the objects inside the currently selected object, choose Edit ➤ Select All. If no object is currently selected, Paradox will select all objects on the page, if you're designing a form, or all objects in the current band, if you're designing a report.

You can deselect all the currently selected objects by pressing the Esc key repeatedly until no more objects are selected.

Moving, Resizing, and Deleting Selected Objects

After selecting an object, you can perform many operations on it, including moving it to another position in the design, resizing it, or deleting it.

To *move* selected objects, point the mouse inside the selected area (not on any handle), then drag the whole object in the desired direction. You can also use the arrow keys to move selected objects by small, precise increments up, down, left, or right. If Properties ➤ Snap To Grid is on, the object will move to the closest grid line when you press an arrow key.

You can *resize* one selected object at a time by dragging a handle in the appropriate direction. Drag a corner handle to change both the height and width of an object. Drag the top or bottom center handle to change the object's height. Drag the left or right center handle to widen or narrow the object. We'll talk about ways to resize several selected objects at once in the next section.

Deleting objects is easy: Simply select the objects and press the Del key.

T I P   If you make a mistake moving, resizing, or deleting an object, choose <u>E</u>dit ➤ <u>U</u>ndo or press Alt+Backspace right away.

Shortcuts for Managing Multiple Objects

Paradox offers some real time-savers for organizing and resizing several selected objects at once. These options are all found on the Design menu shown below.

NOTE Remember to select the objects you want before using the options described in the following sections.

Aligning Objects

Often you'll want certain objects to line up with respect to one another. So, instead of painstakingly moving each object to its proper position, just select the objects you want to line up, then choose Design ➤ Align, followed by one of these options:

Align Left   Aligns the left edges of the selected objects.

Align Right   Aligns the right edges of the selected objects.

Align Center   Aligns the selected objects along an imaginary line that passes vertically through the center of all the objects.

Align Top   Aligns the top edges of the selected objects.

Align Bottom   Aligns the bottom edges of the selected objects.

Align Middle   Aligns the selected objects along an imaginary line that passes horizontally through the center of all the objects.

Figure 9.18 shows examples of objects aligned with these options.

Resizing Several Objects at Once

The Adjust Size options let you adjust the size of multiple selected objects to achieve a symmetrical look. This is handy when your design contains several fields or other objects that you want to be exactly the same size.

FIGURE 9.18

The Design ➤ Align option lets you line up several selected objects at once.

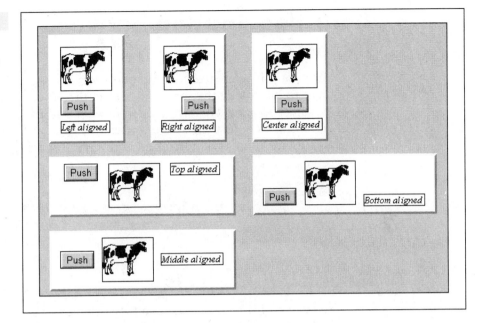

To resize several objects at once, select the objects, then choose <u>D</u>esign ➤ Adjust <u>S</u>ize followed by one of these options:

Minimum Width   Makes all objects as wide as the narrowest of the group.

Maximum Width   Makes all objects as wide as the widest of the group.

Minimum Height   Makes all objects as tall as the shortest of the group.

Maximum Height   Makes all objects as tall as the tallest of the group.

If Paradox cannot resize some of the objects you selected, those objects are ignored and the rest are resized as specified.

Adjusting Spacing between Objects

Suppose you've created a group of objects and want the spacing between them to be exactly the same. Just select the objects, then choose Design ➤ Adjust Spacing. Next choose *Horizontal* to adjust the space horizontally or *Vertical* to adjust the space vertically. Figure 9.19 shows some before and after examples of horizontal and vertical spacing.

NOTE Adjust Spacing moves objects even if you've pinned them to the design (pinning is described later).

Grouping Objects

You can group several objects so they behave as a single object. When you select the group, a single set of handles appears to surround the whole

FIGURE 9.19

Use Design ➤ Adjust Spacing to adjust the horizontal and vertical spacing between selected objects. Notice that Paradox preserves the overall width or height of the group of objects, as indicated by the arrows in the figure.

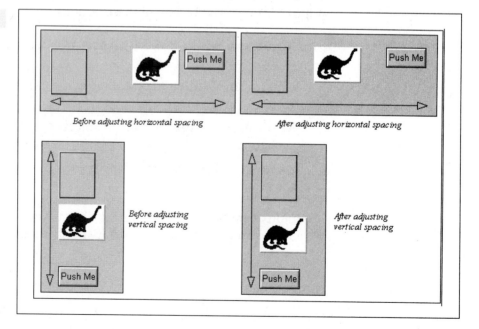

Before adjusting horizontal spacing

After adjusting horizontal spacing

Before adjusting vertical spacing

After adjusting vertical spacing

group. You can then work with the group as a whole. Note that even after you've created a group, you can still select individual objects in the group by clicking repeatedly.

To create a group, select the objects, then choose Design ➤ Group. A fine outline will appear around the selected objects. To separate a group into its individual objects, select the group by clicking on it, then choose Design ➤ Ungroup, or right-click the group and choose Ungroup from the property menu.

Stacking Objects

Objects in a design document can be in layers, on top of or underneath other objects. To change the layering of objects or groups of objects, choose Design ➤ Bring To Front or Design ➤ Send To Back.

For example, in the left side of Figure 9.20 the circle is obscuring a graphic that's behind it. To move the circle behind the graphic, we selected the circle, then chose Design ➤ Send To Back, producing the result shown in the right side of the figure.

FIGURE 9.20

In the left side of the figure, the circle covers the graphic. After selecting the circle and sending it to the back, the graphic is fully visible.

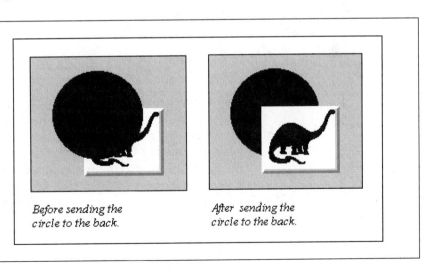

Before sending the circle to the back.

After sending the circle to the back.

Duplicating Objects

Paradox offers two ways to copy selected objects. If you want to place selected objects on the Clipboard first, follow these steps:

1. Select the object or objects you want to duplicate.

2. Choose Edit ➤ Copy (or click the Copy To Clipboard button in the SpeedBar, or press Ctrl+Ins).

3. Click in the Design window where you want the copy to appear.

4. Choose Edit ➤ Paste (or click the Paste From Clipboard button or press Shift+Ins).

If you prefer to bypass the Clipboard and perform the copy in a single step, select the object or objects you want to duplicate, then choose Design ➤ Duplicate. Paradox will put a copy of the object or objects in the document, adjacent to the original.

Inspecting Objects and Changing Properties

Every object in your document has its own set of properties, which are easily changed by inspecting the object in the Design window and selecting options from the property menu that appears. Rather than bogging you down with details of all the properties in this chapter, we'll explain basic inspection and property-changing techniques that work for *any* object in a document and discuss a few of the most important *Design* and *Run Time* properties. When you're ready for more details about individual properties, you can

* Try them out for yourself—the best approach!

- Highlight the property you're interested in on the property menu, then press F1.
- Refer to Appendix D.

Understanding Normal and Penetrating Properties

Before you can change the appearance or behavior of an object, you must inspect it. Paradox offers two ways to inspect objects: *normal inspection* and *penetrating inspection*. In the *normal* method, you right-click a single (unselected) object or right-click one or more selected objects. This leads to the property menu for the object or objects.

TIP   Instead of right-clicking, you can press F6 or choose Properties ➤ Current Object.

After right-clicking a box, we got the property menu in Figure 9.21.

Now, if we select both the box and the Last Name field and then right-click the box, we'll still get a property menu for the box. However, if we right-click the Last Name field, we'll get the field's property menu instead, as shown in Figure 9.22.

In the *penetrating* method, you first select the object or objects you want to inspect, then hold down the Ctrl key while right-clicking (this is called *Ctrl+right-clicking*) or press Shift+F6. This leads to a *penetrating property menu* composed of properties available for all the selected objects—that is, the *union* of all properties.

FIGURE 9.21

This property menu appears after right-clicking a box.

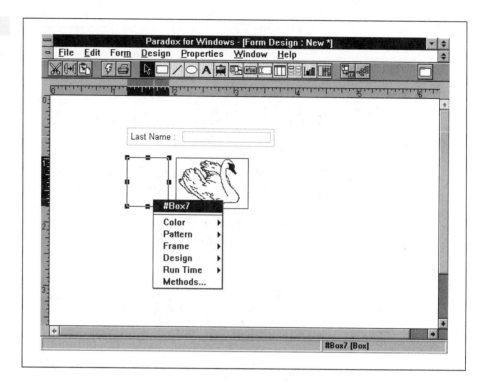

In Figure 9.23, for example, we selected the box and the Last Name field, as before, but this time we Ctrl+right-clicked the box to display a menu of properties that includes box and field properties.

TIP   Changing penetrating properties changes not only the selected objects but also any objects inside them.

Choosing Property Menu Options

To change a property, use one of the inspection methods discussed above, then choose the appropriate option from the menu (some options lead to additional menus). As usual, you can click the option you want, type the

FIGURE 9.22

The property menu for
a field appears when
we right-click the field.

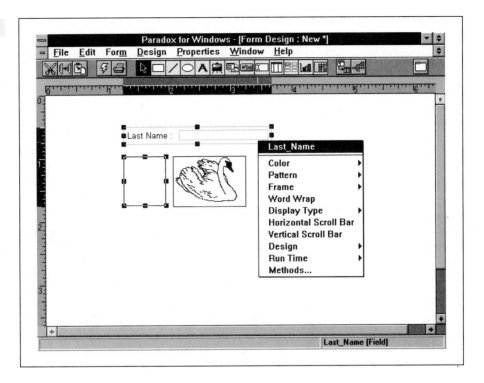

first letter of the option, or use the ↑ and ↓ keys to highlight the option
and then press ↵. (To clear the property menu without selecting an option, press the Esc key.)

TIP

To display help for a property menu option, use the
arrow key to highlight the option you're interested in
and press F1.

It's important to note that when you use the *normal* method to inspect and
choose a property, Paradox applies the property to all selected objects for
which it is valid, but not to any objects contained inside the selected objects. Thus, selecting the box and Last Name field objects, right-clicking,
and changing the Frame property produces the result below.

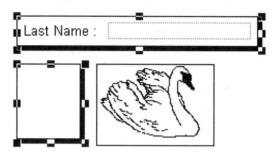

FIGURE 9.23

Ctrl+right-clicking leads to a property menu showing the union of all properties available for the selected objects. Notice the menu heading: "Objects in Selection."

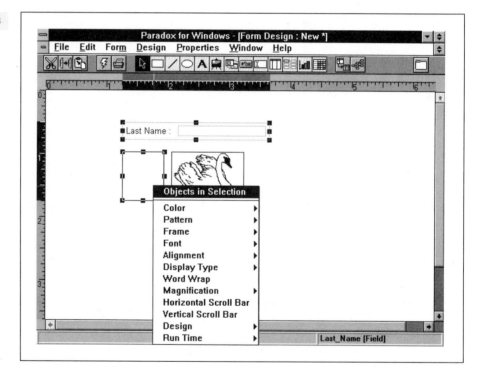

By contrast, when you use the *penetrating* method Paradox applies the chosen property to all selected objects—and to all objects contained in selected objects—for which it is valid. Therefore, if we select the same box and Last Name field objects, Ctrl+right-click, then change the Frame property, we get the result shown below.

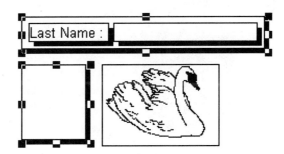

Table 9.2 summarizes the differences between normal and penetrating object properties.

TABLE 9.2: Differences between Normal and Penetrating Object Properties

Normal Object Properties	Penetrating Object Properties
To inspect: Right-click one object. Or select one or more objects, then right-click or press F6.	To inspect: Select one or more objects, then Ctrl+right-click or press Shift+F6.
Property menu header lists the type of the object you inspected (for example, #Box3).	Property menu header shows "Objects in" followed by whatever was selected when you inspected the object(s).
Properties shown apply only to the object you inspected, even if multiple objects are selected.	Properties shown are the *union* of all available properties for the selected object(s).
Changes affect the selected object(s) only, but none of the objects inside them.	Changes affect the selected object(s) *and* any objects inside them.

T I P
To change the properties of all objects on the page, press Esc until no objects (including the page) are selected. Then Ctrl+right-click to open a menu of all properties that can be used by *any* object on the form. When you change a property, Paradox will apply it to every object that can use it.

Using the Object Tree

If you create a large and complex design, you may have trouble inspecting exactly the portion you want, or you may be unable to remember what an object does or what you named it. This is where the *Object Tree* comes in handy. The Object Tree lets you step back from the design and take a look at the big picture of all the objects placed within it. You can use the Object Tree to select an object, inspect it, and even change its properties without having to scroll through the whole design.

 To view a design's Object Tree, click the Object Tree button in the Speed-Bar (shown at left). The Object Tree includes all objects in the design if no objects or multiple objects are selected. If you've selected just one object, the Object Tree includes that object only.

Figure 9.24 illustrates the Object Tree for the sample Employee form in Figure 9.1. Notice the hierarchical arrangement of objects. For example, the Employee # field consists of two parts: the text label (#Text4) and the editing area (#EditRegion5).

To select an object in the document, click its name in the Object Tree window. This highlights (darkens) the name in the Object Tree window and places selection handles around the corresponding object in the document, as in Figure 9.24. (If necessary, move the Object Tree window out of the way and scroll around the design document until you can see the selected object.)

To inspect the properties of an object, right-click (or Ctrl+ right-click) the object name in the Object Tree window. The property menu for that object will appear.

When you're finished using an Object Tree window, close it by double-clicking its Control-menu box, or click the window and press Alt+F4.

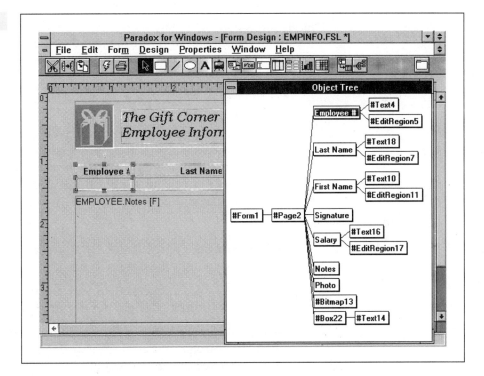

FIGURE 9.24

The Object Tree for the Employee form. In this example we clicked on the Employee # field in the Object Tree window to select it in the design.

TIP

You can select several objects by holding down the Shift key while clicking objects in the Object Tree window. To change the properties of the selected objects, right-click or Ctrl+right-click the mouse.

Using Floating Property Palettes

Paradox for Windows displays visual properties—Color, Line Style, Font, and Frame—on *palettes* instead of menus. To select an option from a palette, simply click on the option or appearance you want.

Initially, the palettes are temporary and disappear when you make a selection. However, if you want to leave a palette on the screen, just click the snap at the top of the palette. This creates a *floating palette* that you can move about on the Desktop by dragging the title bar. The floating palette remains on the Desktop until you click the snap button again.

Changing Design Properties

All object property menus include a Design choice, which affects objects in the Design window only. (Design properties have no effect when you preview or print the document.) The following options, depending on the type of object you're inspecting, appear after you choose Design from a property menu. These are toggle options, which are either checked or unchecked.

Pin Horizontal   When checked, allows the object to be moved up and down within the design, but not from side to side.

Pin Vertical   When checked, allows the object to be moved from side to side within the design, but not up and down.

Contain Objects   When checked, allows the object to contain embedded objects, so that moving or deleting the container also moves or deletes the embedded object.

Size To Fit   When checked, allows objects such as labeled fields, graphics, OLE objects, and table frames to expand or contract automatically in the Design window as needed.

NOTE   Pinning prevents you from accidentally moving an object with your mouse once you've positioned it where you want it. However, certain actions, such as aligning objects via the Design ➤ Align options, will move objects even if they are pinned.

Understanding Containers and Embedded Objects

When working with design objects, you should understand the relationship between containers and objects embedded within containers. A *container* completely surrounds and controls the behavior of all objects embedded within its frame. Thus, when you move or delete a container object, the embedded objects are automatically moved or deleted along with the container.

All objects that can use the Design ➤ Contain Objects property initially have that property turned on (checked). Thus, you only have to place an object inside another object's frame to create a contained relationship.

You can place an object inside a container in any of the following ways:

- Create the object within the frame of another object.
- Move an existing object so that it is completely contained within another object's frame.
- Move or enlarge the container to surround another object completely.
- Paste an object into another object.

If you want to break the relationship between a container and its embedded objects, inspect the container object, then deselect Design ➤ Contain Objects in the property menu. Or, select the contained object and drag it outside the frame of the container; the relationship is broken as soon as one part of the embedded object is dragged outside the container's frame.

Certain container relationships are unbreakable. For example, when working with labeled field objects, you can't move the field label (a text object) or the field edit region (where you enter data) outside the container. That's because a field object, by definition, contains all three parts: the container, the edit region, and the field label.

NOTE   The field label appears only if the Display Type ➤ Labeled property is checked.

Here are some rules about containers and embedded objects.

- Deleting or moving a container deletes or moves the objects within it.

- Deleting or moving an embedded object has no effect on the container.

- Even when an object is embedded inside a container, you can select the object by clicking it.

- You can move a pinned object's container as long as you haven't pinned the container itself.

- Moving or resizing an object to surround a pinned object *does not* cause the pinned object to be contained.

Sizing Objects to Fit their Contents

When the Design ➤ Size To Fit property is checked, a field, table, graphic, or OLE object automatically grows or shrinks to fit the size of its contents. When the property isn't checked, the object does not change size automatically, and you can resize it yourself with the mouse.

When Size To Fit is checked, the effect is slightly different for each type of object, as summarized below.

Tables   If the table doesn't have room to grow, Paradox adds a horizontal scroll bar to the table and turns off Size To Fit. When you resize a table manually with Size To Fit on, Paradox automatically resizes the table's columns.

Fields   Size To Fit remains on even if Paradox doesn't have room to resize the field object. When Size To Fit is on, Paradox resizes fields automatically when you change properties such as the font, definition, display type, and frame style—even if you've already resized the field manually.

Graphic and OLE objects   Size To Fit remains on even if Paradox doesn't have room to resize the object. You can't resize a graphic or OLE object manually when Size To Fit is on.

Changing Run Time Properties

The *Run Time properties* of an object take effect when you *run* (print or view) a document. Therefore, although you change the Run Time properties in the Design window, you won't actually see their effects until you click the View Data button in the SpeedBar or print the document. Not surprisingly, the Run Time properties available depend on the type of document you're designing and the object you're inspecting. Chapters 10 and 11 and Appendix D cover Run Time properties in more detail.

Renaming Design Objects

An object's name appears at the top of its property menu, in the Object Tree, and on the status bar when the object is selected. By default, objects are named according to their object type, with a sequential number added (for example, *#Text4* and *#EditRegion5*). You can change an object's name, if you wish, as follows:

1. Inspect the object by right-clicking.

2. Click the header at the top of the property menu.

3. Type a new name for the object in the **Object Name** dialog box, then choose OK.

NOTE   You might wish to rename an object if you'll be referring to it in calculations or in ObjectPAL methods (see Chapter 19). Otherwise, you needn't bother.

Creating New Objects

You use the tools on the Design window SpeedBar, shown in Figure 9.25, to create and place objects such as boxes, graphics, fields, tables, and so forth. See Table 9.1 for a quick summary of each tool.

FIGURE 9.25

FIGURE 9.25

The SpeedBar tools used to create objects in the Design window

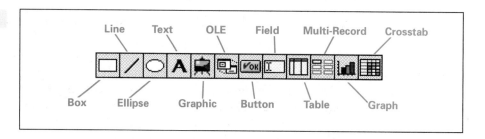

To place a new object in your design, click the tool you want, then click and drag in the Design window. When the object is the size and shape you want, release the mouse button. Normally the mouse pointer reverts to a selection arrow after you place an object. If you want to create more than one object of the same type, hold down the Shift key while clicking the tool. The tool will remain active until you select another tool.

TIP

The object is selected as soon as you release the mouse button. You can then move, delete, or resize the object, or change its properties.

Changing Properties of SpeedBar Tools

You can change the properties of any design tool in the SpeedBar, so that new objects you create already have the properties you want. For example, if you want all boxes to appear in red, you can change the Color property of the Box tool. Or, if you want to change the default text font to *Times New Roman*, you can change the Font property of the Text tool.

Paradox for Windows offers two ways to change the SpeedBar tools. The first method involves inspecting the SpeedBar tool itself; the second involves copying properties from an object to the SpeedBar.

To inspect the SpeedBar button itself, right-click the appropriate tool in the SpeedBar. Then change whatever property you want. Repeat these steps as needed.

To copy properties from an object to the corresponding SpeedBar tool, create (or select) the object you want to use. For example, if you want to change the default properties for the Box tool, create a box, then inspect the box object and change its properties to your liking. Finally, choose Design ➤ Copy To SpeedBar. Paradox will automatically copy the selected object's properties to the appropriate SpeedBar tool.

Regardless of how you change the properties of the SpeedBar, all subsequent design elements will have the new default properties. However, the change will not affect any objects already placed in the design.

TIP   To change the default properties of a page, inspect the page (by right-clicking an empty area of your design). Then change the properties and choose Design ➤ Copy To SpeedBar.

The properties you set for a tool remain in effect for all design documents until you exit Paradox. If you want to save them permanently, choose Properties ➤ Designer, then either specify a new file for the tool properties, or use the existing file and choose OK. Please see "Setting Design Window Preferences," near the end of this chapter, for more information.

Creating Boxes, Lines, and Ellipses

The simple drawing tools listed below let you add graphical elements to your design.

Box   Draws squares and rectangles in your design.

Line   Draws horizontal, vertical, and diagonal lines (with or without arrowheads). The line may be straight or curved.

Ellipse   Draws circles and ellipses.

Creating Graphics

 To place graphics in your design, you use the Graphic tool (shown at left). You can either paste a graphic from the Clipboard or from a .bmp, .pcx, .tif, .gif, or .eps file.

Begin by choosing the Graphic tool in the SpeedBar and defining the size and shape of your graphic. The words "Undefined Graphic" appear inside the frame, as illustrated below.

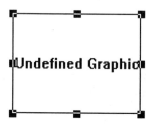

To place the graphic in the frame, inspect the object and choose Define Graphic from the property menu. Then, proceed as follows:

* To copy the graphic from the Clipboard, choose Paste.
* To copy the graphic from a file, choose Paste From and select a file.

TIP

Paradox automatically turns on (checks) the graphic's Design ➤ Size To Fit property. Before resizing the graphic, you must inspect it and turn off (uncheck) this property. To make the entire graphic fit inside the frame, inspect it and choose Magnification ➤ Best Fit.

You can crop graphics within their frames if you haven't chosen the Magnification ➤ Best Fit property. If a graphic can be cropped, you'll see a hand tool after clicking on the graphic (you may need to click more than once). When the mouse pointer changes to a hand tool, simply click and drag to move the graphic within the frame, as shown below.

Creating OLE Objects

 OLE objects can display data from other applications (graphics, sound, spreadsheets, and text) right in your design document. (You'll find a discussion of OLE in Chapter 5.) To create an OLE object, choose the OLE tool (shown at left) and drag in the Design window. Then follow these steps:

1. Switch to an OLE server and cut or copy the data you want to the Clipboard.

2. Switch back to the Paradox Design window, inspect the OLE object, and choose Define OLE from the property menu.

3. Choose Paste to place the data into the OLE object.

TIP

Paradox for Windows automatically turns on the OLE object's Design ➤ Size To Fit property. Before resizing the OLE object, you must inspect it and turn off this property. To make the entire OLE object fit inside the frame, inspect it, then choose Magnification ➤ Best Fit.

Creating Buttons

 You use the Button tool (shown at left) to create buttons on your form (buttons aren't available for reports). After defining a button, it looks like this:

From this point, you can change the label and assign a specific function to the button using ObjectPAL methods, so that clicking the button performs an action. We'll talk about buttons in Chapter 19.

Creating Graphs and Crosstabs

 The Graph tool (shown at left) is used to create charts and graphs from your Paradox table. Choose the Graph tool and drag it in the Design window to define the overall size and shape of the graph. Before Paradox can display a graph, you must tell it what information you want to use. That's the topic of Chapter 12, which covers both graphs and crosstabs.

 Crosstab objects summarize (cross-tabulate) information according to one or more columns, then display the summary in a tabular format similar to a spreadsheet. Use the Crosstab tool (shown at left) to define a crosstab by clicking and dragging. As with graphs, the crosstab starts out undefined. Note that crosstabs are available in forms only.

Working with Text Objects

Text objects are really just invisible boxes you type text into. Depending on the properties you select, the text object can either be fixed in size or grow to hold all the text you enter. If you've worked with formatted memo fields, you already know most of the techniques for editing and formatting text. But thanks to Paradox for Windows' expanded ruler, you can go beyond simple memo editing features by setting tabs and margins, text alignment, and line spacing.

Creating a Text Object

You can create a text box in either of two ways, depending on whether you want a fixed- or variable-size object initially.

A *fixed-size* text object doesn't automatically grow or shrink horizontally or vertically to fit the amount of text it contains. Therefore, you must resize the object manually if you want it to show all the text within the box.

 You create a fixed-size text object by using the click and drag technique. That is, click the Text tool in the SpeedBar (shown at the left), click in the design where you want the text to begin, and then drag the outline to define the size and shape of the object. After placing the object, type your text within the frame. Click elsewhere in the design when you're done.

Unlike fixed text objects, *variable-size* or *fit text* objects grow or shrink to fit the amount of text they contain. To create a fit text object, follow the steps below.

1. Click the Text tool in the SpeedBar.
2. Click in the design where you want the text to begin.
3. Type the text and press ↵ when you reach the desired width of the object. Then continue typing, pressing ↵ only when you want to end a paragraph or create a blank line. Paradox will automatically wrap the text at the right border and expand the box downward as you type.
4. Click elsewhere in the design when you're finished.

Regardless of how you create a text object, the Word Wrap property is on initially. Therefore, as you type in text, the text wraps automatically when it reaches the right side of the object. If you turn Word Wrap off, you can enter only a single line of text into the object.

Of course, you're not stuck with the initial settings for the behavior of a text object. To make changes, simply inspect the object and choose any of the property options listed below.

Word Wrap   When checked, this option turns on Word Wrap. If you turn off Word Wrap, you can enter only one line of text in the object.

Design Sizing ➤ Fixed Size   When this is checked, the text object stays the same size, and text wraps at the right edge and scrolls up and down within the object. You can resize fixed-size text objects manually as needed.

Design Sizing ➤ Fit Text   When this option is checked, the text object grows or shrinks to fit the text you type. With Word Wrap on, the first time you press ↵, the right margin is set and any new text automatically wraps at the right margin. If Word Wrap is off, you can enter only one line of text; the object will adjust horizontally to fit the line of text. You can resize a fit text object only if Word Wrap is on, and then only horizontally.

Design Sizing ➤ Grow Only   When this is checked, the text object grows to fit the text but does not shrink if the text does not fill the object. As with the Fit Text option, if Word Wrap is off, the object is only one line wide but will grow horizontally to fit the text you enter.

TIP

If your fixed-size text object is too small to hold all the text you've typed in, inspect the object and turn on the Vertical Scroll Bar property. You can then use the scroll bar to view all the text. Scroll bars are available only for form documents.

Formatting the Text

You can change the font, alignment, and line spacing of an entire text object or of selected text within the object.

To change the format of part of the text, select the text by dragging or using Shift+arrow, then right-click and choose options from the property menu. To change the format of an entire text object, inspect the object without first selecting any text. You can change the Typeface, Size, Style, Color, Alignment, and Line Spacing properties, as discussed in Chapter 6.

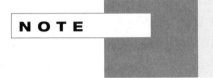

NOTE   The expanded ruler provides shortcuts for changing the alignment, tabs, and line spacing. These are discussed later in this chapter.

Editing Text

You use the standard Windows editing techniques to position the insertion point, type text, and select text in a text object. The only difference is that you may need to click more than once before the insertion point appears in the text object, depending on whether the object is currently selected. You can also cut and paste text using the options on the Edit menu or the Cut To Clipboard, Copy To Clipboard, and Paste From Clipboard buttons in the SpeedBar.

TIP   To select a word in a text object, double-click the word. To select all the text, choose Edit ➤ Select All.

Just as you can search for and replace text in a memo or formatted memo field, you can also use the Search and Replace feature in a text object. To get started, inspect the text object and choose Search Text from the property menu. Type the search text or pattern, type optional replacement text, and begin the search as described in Chapter 5.

Using the Rulers

Paradox for Windows' rulers provide some powerful word processing capabilities. For example, the expanded ruler contains useful shortcuts for aligning text, adjusting line spacing, and setting tabs. And the horizontal ruler lets you change the location of tabs, adjust the margins, and set the indent for the first line of a paragraph.

NOTE   Choose Properties ➤ Expanded Ruler or Properties ➤ Horizontal Ruler to display the expanded and horizontal rulers, respectively.

Figure 9.26 shows both rulers and some sample text. The rulers in the figure are labeled to show various buttons and markers available for changing the appearance of text. Notice how the buttons in the expanded ruler darken to show the current alignment and line spacing of text at the insertion point. Similarly, the tab well of the horizontal ruler indicates the current margins, paragraph indent, and tab settings.

Before using the rulers to change settings, indicate the amount of text you want to change, as described below.

- Select text to change settings only within that text.
- Place the insertion point at the beginning of a paragraph to change the settings in that paragraph only.
- Place the insertion point at the beginning of a blank line to change settings for new text that you type.

Changing Alignment and Line Spacing

The alignment and line spacing buttons provide a handy alternative to inspecting text. After specifying the amount of text you want to change, simply click the appropriate button in the expanded ruler. For example, click any of the first four buttons in the expanded ruler to change the

FIGURE 9.26

The expanded ruler lets you set alignment, tab stops, and line spacing. The tab well of the horizontal ruler shows current settings for text at the insertion point and includes markers for the left margin, paragraph indent, tab settings, and right margin.

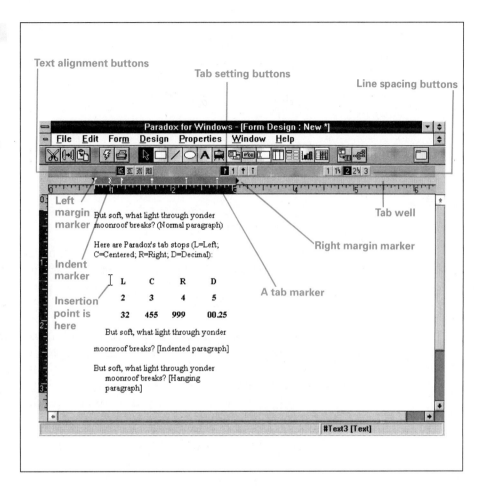

alignment to left, center, right, or justified, respectively. Click any of the last five buttons in the ruler to change the line spacing to 1, 1.5, 2, 2.5, or 3, respectively.

T I P

To change the alignment or line spacing of *all the text* in one or more text objects, select the object or objects, then click an alignment or line spacing button in the expanded ruler.

Setting Tabs

When the horizontal and expanded rulers are visible, you can set four types of tabs, as described below. These tab types are listed in their order of appearance in the expanded ruler.

Left   When you press Tab, text you type will be left-aligned at the tab stop.

Right   When you press Tab, text you type will be right-aligned at the tab stop.

Center   When you press Tab, text you type will be centered around the tab stop.

Decimal   When you press Tab, the decimal point will appear at the tab stop and text following the decimal point will appear to the right of the tab stop. If you don't type a decimal point, the Decimal tab stop will act like a Right tab.

To place a tab stop, position the insertion point or select the text as described above, then click the Left, Right, Center, or Decimal tab button in the expanded ruler (the button will darken to indicate your selection). Now click in the tab well (above the horizontal ruler) where you want the tab stop to appear. If necessary, drag the tab marker left or right to position it more precisely.

To remove a tab stop, drag it downward and out of the tab well.

Changing Margins

The default margins are the left and right borders of the selected text object. To change the margin setting, select the text or position the insertion point, then drag the left or right margin icon to its new location.

Adding Paragraph Indents

You can use the indent marker to create indented paragraphs and hanging paragraphs (see Figure 9.26 for examples). To place an indent, drag the indent marker to the desired location in the tab well. Initially, the indent and margin markers are at the same position, so you'll need to drag the indent marker by its *bottom* to move it (dragging it at the top moves the margin marker).

For an indented paragraph, place the indent marker to the *right* of the left margin marker. For a hanging paragraph, place the indent marker to the *left* of the left margin marker.

T I P

Dragging the left margin marker moves both the left margin and the indent together. Dragging the indent marker moves only the indent.

Working with Field Objects

Initially, your design will already contain fields, unless you chose a blank design style. However, you can add more fields and change field properties.

N O T E

A field is composed of the field itself, an optional text label, and the frame that surrounds them.

Paradox offers several types of fields, including the following:

- Normal table fields
- Special fields (including current date, time, page number, and total number of pages)
- Calculated fields
- Summary fields

The basic field types are discussed in this chapter, while the more advanced calculated and summary fields are covered in Chapters 12 and 17.

Creating a Field

 To place a field in the design, click the Field tool in the SpeedBar (shown at the left), then click in the design where you want to position the field, and drag to define the frame.

Defining a Field

To define the field, inspect it and choose Define Field from the property menu. You'll see a list, as in Figure 9.27, of available fields from the tables you included in the data model. Click the field name you want.

FIGURE 9.27

To define a field, inspect it and choose Define Field from the property menu, then click the name of the field you want.

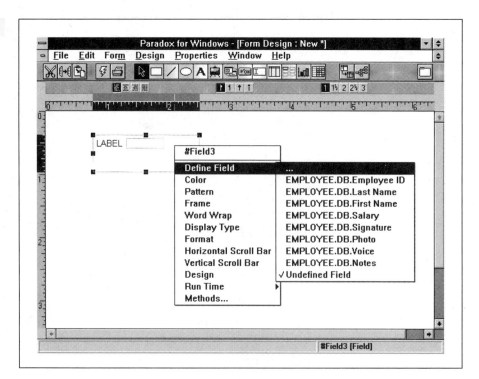

If the field you want is not on the list, click the list header (...) to display the **Define Field Object** dialog box shown in Figure 9.28. You can click the drop-down arrow next to the table name to display a list of all fields in that table and some special fields that provide information about the table. Select a field by double-clicking.

FIGURE 9.28

The list of fields for the table appears when you click the drop-down arrow next to the table name.

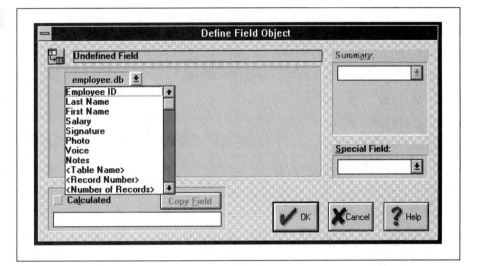

NOTE

The last four items in the drop-down list refer to the table itself: the table name (*<Table Name>*), the current record number (*<Record Number>*), the total number of records (*<Number of Records>*), and the number of fields (*<Number of Fields>*) in the table structure.

You can also select a special field that describes the design as a whole by clicking the Special Field drop-down list. These fields, shown in Figure 9.29, display the current date (*Today*), the current time (*Now*), the current page number (*Page Number*), and the total number of pages in the document (*Number of Pages*). Click to choose the item you want.

FIGURE 9.29

Fields that relate to the design as a whole appear in the Special Field list.

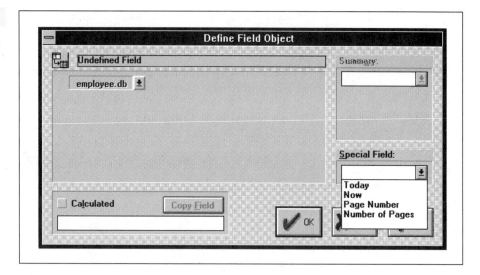

When you're finished defining the new field, click OK. At this point, you can change the field's properties, resize it, move it, and so forth.

Adding or Removing Field Labels

By default, new fields are labeled when you create them. You can edit the field label as you would any text object. To remove the field label altogether, inspect the field and choose Display Type ➤ Unlabeled from the property menu.

NOTE   Initially, the label has the Design Sizing ➤ Fit Text option turned on and Word Wrap turned off.

Formatting Field Data

You can control the field format by inspecting the field and choosing Format from the property menu. From there, you can choose predefined number, date, and other formats or create your own customized formats, as discussed in Chapter 6.

Formatting Graphic Fields

Graphic fields have two special and quite interesting properties: *Magnification* and *Raster Operation*. The Magnification property leads to the Best Fit, 25%, 50%, 100%, 200%, and 400% options described in Chapter 5.

The Raster Operation property controls interactions between a bitmap image and the background on which it is painted. These interactions are logical operations performed on the colors of the image, including Source Copy, Source Paint, Source And, Source Invert, Source Erase, Not Source Copy, Not Source Erase, and Merge Paint.

The raster operations are more easily shown than explained, so take a look at Figure 9.30, which depicts several examples of the same graphic pasted onto a light gray background. As indicated by the labels below each example, we chose a different Raster Operation property for each pasted graphic.

FIGURE 9.30

In this example we pasted several copies of the same graphic onto a light gray background, then chose different Raster Operations for each copy.

N O T E   To see a dramatic color example of the Raster Operation properties at work, open the Rasterop form in the *\pdoxwin\examples* directory that's created when you install Paradox.

Working with Table Objects

When you choose a tabular style for your form or report, or you create a table with the Table tool, you actually get a table *frame*, not a table. A table frame is composed of the following elements:

- Field objects from the source table
- Text objects, which provide labels for the fields
- A grid for the fields and labels representing the table
- Columns of fields
- Rows of records
- Headers showing the row of field labels

These components can be customized through inspection of the object properties using many of the techniques discussed in Chapter 6.

Creating a Table

 To add a table object to the design, just click the Table tool in the Speed-Bar (shown at the left), then click in the design and drag to define the size of the table. The table frame you outline will include a grid marking rows and columns, as in Figure 9.31, along with labels and undefined fields.

FIGURE 9.31

After using the Table tool to place a table in the design, you will see a table frame with undefined fields.

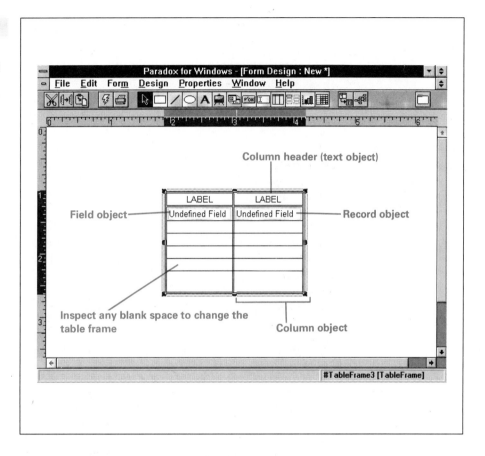

You can inspect and change properties of the table as a whole, any column (field), any row (record), the grid, any label, or any undefined field.

Defining a Table

You can use any of the following methods to define your table:

- Inspect the table frame (by right-clicking any blank space on the table) and choose *Define Table*.

- Inspect the record object (by selecting the record object, then right-clicking) and choose *Define Record*.

- Inspect each field individually (by selecting the field object, then right-clicking) and choose *Define Field*. As you might expect, this approach is more roundabout and time-consuming than the first two methods.

NOTE

The method for defining a table field is the same as for defining a field object.

After choosing Define Table or Define Record from the property menu, you'll see a list of available tables and the usual list header (...). If the table you want appears in the list, you can select it by clicking the table name. The frame expands to hold all the fields in the table, with a horizontal scroll bar added if all the fields don't fit.

Using the Define Table Object Dialog Box

You can use the **Define Table Object** dialog box to

- Add fields not already included in the table frame.

- Remove fields from the table frame.

- Rearrange fields in the table frame.

- Change the main table assigned to the data model.

- Add a table to the existing data model.

To open this dialog box, inspect the table or record, then click the header (...) of the property menu. The dialog box will resemble Figure 9.32.

The names of all tables currently in the data model appear in the table name area of the dialog box, each with a drop-down arrow next to it. You can click the drop-down arrow to see a list of all fields in the table, then select the fields you want to include in the table object (selected fields will appear in the Included Fields list). You can use the ↑ and ↓ Change Order

FIGURE 9.32

The Define Table Object dialog box. In this example, we opened the drop-down list to show the available fields for the Employee table.

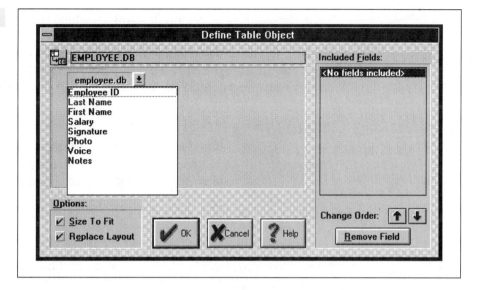

buttons to change the order of the fields, and the Remove Field button to remove fields. Or, use any of the techniques described under "Selecting Fields to Display," earlier in this chapter, to select, rearrange, or remove fields in the Define Table Object dialog box.

If you want to change the main table or add another table to the data model, click the *Data Model* button at the upper-left corner. When the Data Model dialog box appears, complete it as described earlier in this chapter, then choose OK. Adding a table to a blank design makes the table the main table for the document. Adding a table to a design that's already associated with a table creates a multitable design, and you must define the relationship between multiple tables in the Data Model dialog box (see Chapter 17).

The *Size To Fit* option in the Define Table Object dialog box controls whether the table frame expands to include all the fields you have selected. Check it to have the table expand, or uncheck it to have the table frame keep its original size and shape.

The *Replace Layout* option determines whether fields will be added to or will completely replace the contents of the existing table frame. Check the option if you want the fields in the Included Fields list of the dialog box to overwrite any currently defined fields in the table. Uncheck this option if you want new fields to be appended to the original design layout.

WARNING Checking the Replace Layout option deletes all objects currently in the record or header and rebuilds the table object. Anything in the table frame, including ObjectPAL code, will be lost.

When you're finished defining the table object, click OK. If the table contains too many fields to be viewed at once, a horizontal scroll bar will appear automatically.

Changing Table Properties and Appearance

As always, you can change properties of an entire table or parts of a table by inspection. For an especially neat three-dimensional effect, inspect the table and check the Grid ➤ 3D property. Then, add to the drama by choosing a light-colored background for the table. If you want to place horizontal dividing lines between records, inspect the table and check the Grid ➤ Record Divider property.

Scroll bars can be especially useful when your table is too wide or too deep to be viewed all at once. To add scroll bars, inspect the table frame, then choose Horizontal Scroll Bar or Vertical Scroll bar from the property menu. (Sorry, scroll bars aren't available in reports.)

If you'd like to detach the header from the rest of the table, inspect the table and choose Detach Header. Then drag the header (or the main body of the table) to create a gap between the table header and the data. If you change your mind and want to reattach the header, inspect the lower portion of the table (not the header) and choose Attach Header.

Not only can you inspect various table properties, but you can also manipulate the table with your mouse using the techniques discussed in Chapter 6.

For example, you can drag the vertical or horizontal grid lines to adjust the width of columns and rows or drag the columns to rearrange them.

Removing and adding columns takes only a few mouse clicks. The first step is to select a column by clicking at the lower edge of the column until the mouse pointer changes to a small ↑ and the column is highlighted. (To select another column, hold down the Shift key and click on the column you want.) Now, if you want to delete the selected columns, press the Del key. To insert a column, select the column that should appear to the *right* of the new column and press the Ins key. Then select the undefined field that appears, inspect it, and choose Define Field.

For some interesting effects, try stacking more than one field in a column. To do so, first resize the record area of the column by adjusting its width and height. Then, either drag existing field objects from other columns into the desired column, or create new field objects in the column. And don't forget that you can place *other* types of objects—graphics, boxes, lines, ellipses, and even other tables and graphs—within a table. Just resize the record area as needed and place the objects where you want them.

Working with Multi-Record Objects

Multi-record objects display several records at a time, using a layout that repeats horizontally and vertically on the page. These objects are especially nice for creating mailing labels (see Chapter 11 for an example).

Creating a Multi-Record Object

To create a multi-record object, choose the Multi-Record tool in the SpeedBar (shown at left), then click and drag as usual. The Design window will display a blank master record in the top left and gray repeating regions to the right and below, as shown in Figure 9.33. The entire multi-record object is surrounded by a container.

To resize the records, select the master record and drag its selection han-dles to the desired size. Paradox automatically resizes the repeating regions as well.

Defining a Multi-Record Object

When you're ready to define the fields for a multi-record object, inspect the object or the record at the upper-left corner and choose Define Record from the property menu. Then choose a table from the list, or click the header (...) to open the Define Table Object dialog box described previously.

NOTE

You can also use the Field tool in the SpeedBar to place fields individually, though this can be more time consuming.

FIGURE 9.33

A multi-record object with three fields from the Employee table. The master record is selected.

Changing a Multi-Record Layout

The **Record Layout** dialog box (shown below) appears when you inspect a multi-record object and choose Record Layout.

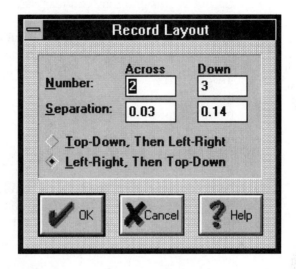

In this dialog box, you can specify the number of records across and down, the amount of space between records, and the order for printing or displaying multiple records: top to bottom, then left to right (to display by columns); or left to right, then top to bottom (to display by rows). Choose OK to return to your design.

Changing Multi-Record Properties

You can change the appearance of records within the multi-record object or the entire multi-record object. If you click on and then inspect the *master record*, your property changes will affect all the records within the object. If you click on and then inspect one of the gray *repeating records*, the property changes will affect the background and perimeter of the multi-record object.

Setting Design Window Preferences

Earlier in this chapter, you learned how to change the selection order of objects. You also learned how to copy properties to the SpeedBar and save those changes. These procedures, and a few others, are called *designer properties* because they affect the behavior of the Design window.

To get started, choose Properties ➤ Designer from the Design window menus. The **Designer Properties** dialog box shown in Figure 9.34 appears on your screen.

Using Select From Inside

As described earlier, the Select From Inside option affects how contained objects are selected. When the option is off (unchecked), outermost objects are selected before inner objects. When the option is on (checked), you'll select the object you click even if it's contained within another object.

FIGURE 9.34

The Designer Properties dialog box controls the behavior of the Design window and lets you save properties of SpeedBar tools.

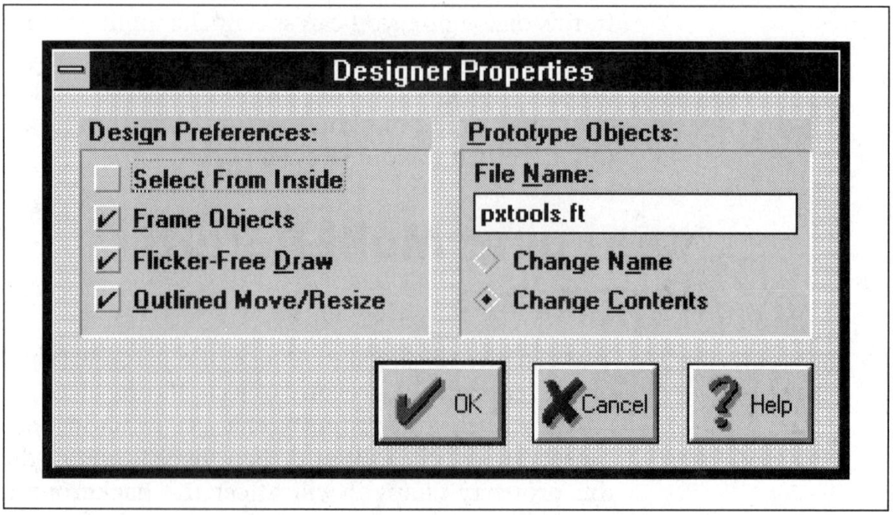

Designer Properties

Design Preferences:
☐ Select From Inside
☑ Frame Objects
☑ Flicker-Free Draw
☑ Outlined Move/Resize

Prototype Objects:
File Name:
pxtools.ft
◇ Change Name
◆ Change Contents

✔ OK   ✘ Cancel   ? Help

Using Frame Objects

Normally, objects appear with faint dotted-line frames so they're easier to locate on the screen. If you prefer to have frames appear only when you've changed an object's Frame property, turn the Frame Objects option off (uncheck it).

N O T E   The dotted-line frames never appear when you preview or print your document.

Using Flicker-Free Draw

If your screen flashes when you move or resize objects, especially in designs with a dark background, you can check the Flicker-Free Draw option to reduce the flickering. However, keep in mind that Flicker-Free Draw can slow things down when you're moving or resizing objects. Try experimenting with this option's settings to see what works best with your screen.

Using Outlined Move/Resize

The Outlined Move/Resize option determines the appearance of an object as you move or resize it. When this option is checked, only an outline of the object moves, expands, or contracts. When the option is unchecked, the object itself appears as it's moved or resized. For speedier displays, check this option.

Saving and Using SpeedBar Settings

You learned earlier how to copy properties to the SpeedBar buttons so that new objects you create will have those properties. The original properties of the SpeedBar tools are stored in a file named *pxtools.ft* in your working directory. You can change properties in this file, and you can create and use additional SpeedBar property files as needed.

TIP

Your SpeedBar property files can be stored in *any* directory on your computer. If they're not in the current working directory, be sure to specify a complete path name in the File Name text box.

Choosing a Different SpeedBar Property File

To load and use the properties of a different SpeedBar property file, choose Change Name in the Designer Properties dialog box, then type the name of an existing file into the File Name text box. When asked if you want to load the existing file, proceed as follows:

- Choose Yes to load and use the properties in the file. Any changes you've made to the SpeedBar will be discarded.

- Choose No to cancel the operation and restore the previous file name.

- Choose Cancel to cancel the operation and return to the Designer Properties dialog box, keeping the new name you typed.

Creating a New SpeedBar Property File

If you'd like to create a new file containing whatever properties are currently set for the SpeedBar tools, choose Change Name, then type a new file name (or complete path name) in the File Name text box. Your file name must be no more than eight characters, with an .ft extension (for example, *mytools.ft*). Paradox will create a new SpeedBar properties file with the name you specified. You can later load it as described above.

Updating the Current SpeedBar Property File

You can choose Change Contents, then OK, to have Paradox update the contents of the SpeedBar property file you're using with any changes you've made to the SpeedBar tools.

Restoring Default SpeedBar Property Settings

Paradox will automatically recreate the *pxtools.ft* file with default settings if that file doesn't exist in your working directory. Therefore, if you need to restore *pxtools.ft* to its original settings, specify *pxtools.ft* in the File Name text box, choose OK, then close the Design window. Now use the Windows File Manager to delete *pxtools.ft*. If you haven't done so already, exit Paradox, then start Paradox again. The next time you open the Design window, the default settings will be in effect.

This chapter has provided an overview of tools and techniques for designing custom forms and reports. In the next two chapters, we'll take a closer look at techniques for designing forms and reports, and provide many examples that you can try for yourself.

CHAPTER

10

Creating Custom Forms

fast TRACK

To add pages to a form   **514**

> choose Form ➤ Page ➤ Add if you want to add a blank page to the end of the form. To create a new page from an existing page, select the page and copy it to the Clipboard. Click on the page that should fall after the new page, then paste from the Clipboard.

To delete a page from a form   **516**

> select the page, then press the Del key. Be careful! (Immediately choose Edit ➤ Undo if you delete a page accidentally.)

To rotate the current page to the end of a multipage form   **518**

> Choose Form ➤ Page ➤ Rotate.

To display multipage forms in a tiled arrangement   **518**

> choose options from the Form ➤ Page ➤ Tile menu. The tile setting is saved along with the form.

To print the form   **530**

> switch to Form View if you want to print the current record; or switch to the Form Design window if you want to print the form design (without any data filled in). Then click the Print button in the SpeedBar or choose File ➤ Print and complete the Print File dialog box.

WHENEVER you switch from Table View to Form View by clicking the Quick Form button in the SpeedBar or pressing F7, Paradox allows you to view or edit data one record at a time. Unless you develop your own custom forms, Paradox will generate a standard form, called the Quick Form, similar to the one in Figure 10.1.

NOTE   If you define a preferred form, Paradox will use that form instead of the standard form. Chapter 9 presented steps for creating preferred forms.

In many situations, the Quick Form is just fine. But custom forms can be much better when you need to display instructions to the user during data entry, or when you want the on-screen form to resemble a paper form. For example, you can design a custom form that looks like a purchase requisition, a sales order, or even a check.

When designing a form, you can organize data in a single-record format, where one record appears on each page, or in a tabular or multi-record format, where multiple records appear on each page. You can also add graphs, crosstabs, and many other enhancements to the form. In this chapter, we'll show you how to create single-page and multipage data entry forms complete with three-dimensional effects, scroll bars, protected data fields, special fields for displaying the date and time, and more. In Chapter 12 you'll learn how to add graphs and crosstabs to your forms.

FIGURE 10.1

The Quick Form generated by Paradox for the sample CustList table

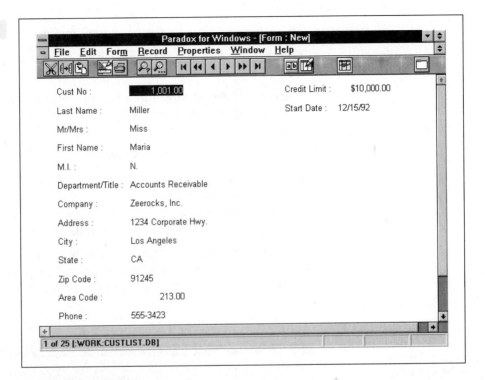

N O T E   Before continuing with this chapter, please complete Lesson 4 in Chapter 2 and at least skim through Chapter 9. Lesson 4 provides some hands-on guidance for designing a simple form, while Chapter 9 covers general techniques for designing forms and reports.

Figure 10.2 shows a custom form for editing the Credit Limit field of the CustList table. Notice that the custom form features many flourishes that make it more attractive and easier to use than the plain-vanilla Quick Form. These embellishments include the following:

- The frame styles and thicknesses give the form a three-dimensional look.

- Heading text clearly states the purpose of the form: *Credit Limit Update*.

- The company's logo, a wrapped gift, appears.

- The current date and time appear at the upper-right corner of the form.

- The records are arranged in a tabular format so the user can work with several records at once. We've also added a vertical scroll bar, a three-dimensional grid, and a record divider.

- The Cust No field title was changed to *Cust #*.

- The Credit Limit field sports a three-dimensional look and a contrasting background that identifies it clearly as the field to be edited. The user is prevented from placing the cursor in any field except Credit Limit, and all fields except Credit Limit are Read Only.

- A text object provides instructions explaining the purpose of the form and how to move the cursor through it. The vertical scroll bar makes it easy for the user to browse through the instructions.

FIGURE 10.2

A custom form for updating the Credit Limit field of existing customers in the CustList table

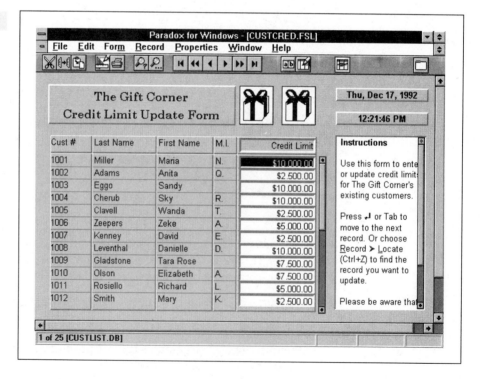

Later on in this chapter, we'll describe some of the specific techniques used to produce these effects.

Planning a Custom Form

Careful planning can help prevent data-entry errors, so it is important to give some thought to your form design before creating it with Paradox. If you are modeling the custom form on a data collection sheet or other paper form already in use, try to employ the same arrangement of fields and informational areas. This will give your custom form the look and feel the user is accustomed to.

TIP

If your existing paper forms are in need of an overhaul, make improvements now to avoid problems encountered in the past.

General Steps for Designing and Using a Custom Form

Chapter 9 covers the basic techniques for designing forms, and you should refer to that chapter for information on starting new forms, creating, selecting, and inspecting objects, and so forth. As a quick review, general procedures for developing and working with custom forms are listed below.

1. Choose File ➤ New ➤ Form from the menus or inspect the Open Form button in the SpeedBar (if it's available) and choose New.

2. In the **Data Model** dialog box, select a table or query as the basis for the design. If you wish, you can inspect the table in the right side of the Data Model dialog box, then choose the Fields, Order/Range, Read-Only, or Strict Translation options, as discussed in Chapter 9. When you're finished using the Data Model dialog box, choose OK.

3. In the **Design Layout** dialog box, specify the design layout. Initially, Paradox assigns the Single-Record layout to forms.

4. If you want to select or reorder fields, click the Select Fields button in the Design Layout dialog box, then select (or rearrange) the fields you want to include in the form. Choose OK to return to the Design Layout dialog box.

5. If you want all the fields to be labeled, leave the Labeled Fields option checked. Otherwise, remove the check mark to remove labels from all the fields.

6. If you want to change the page layout, click the Page Layout button in the Design Layout dialog box, make any necessary changes, then choose OK. (See "Choosing a Page Layout," below, for more information.)

7. Choose OK in the Design Layout dialog box to open the Form Design window.

8. Customize the design as you wish, then preview it by clicking the View Data button in the SpeedBar or pressing F8.

9. Choose File ➤ Save to save the form, then close the Form window if you wish.

10. If you want this form to be used when you click the Quick Form button in Table View, open the table to be associated with this form, then right-click the Quick Form button. Select the form name and choose OK from the dialog box that appears. Now choose Properties ➤ View Properties ➤ Save to save your changes.

11. To open an existing form, choose File ➤ Open ➤ Form or click the Open Form button in the SpeedBar (if it's available). Then choose the file name of the form, change the table if you want to

view a different table's data with this form's layout, choose an Open Mode (either View or Design), and choose OK.

TIP

If you'd like to use the currently assigned Quick Form as the basis for a new design, click the Quick Form button in the Table window, then click the Design button in the SpeedBar or press F8.

Choosing a Page Layout

Remember that the **Page Layout** dialog box is different for forms and reports. Figure 10.3 shows the default Page Layout dialog box for a form.

NOTE

You can get to the Page Layout dialog box by clicking the Page Layout button in the Design Layout dialog box or by choosing Form ➤ Page ➤ Layout when you reach the Form Design window.

When designing for the screen, you can change the width and height of the screen you're designing for as well as the units of measure. You'll also be able to choose any screen fonts that are installed on your system.

If you prefer to design for the printer, click Printer in the Design For area. The dialog box will now include a list of paper sizes for you to choose from and allow you to switch the orientation from Portrait to Landscape, as shown in Figure 10.4.

When you're finished with the Page Layout dialog box, choose OK.

NOTE   If you design for the printer, only fonts installed for the active printer will be available, Paradox will do its best to match the screen fonts displayed in the Form window to the printed output.

FIGURE 10.3

The default Page Layout dialog box for a form

Page Layout

Design For:
◇ Printer
◆ Screen

Orientation:
◇ Portrait
◆ Landscape

Screen Size:

640 x 480

Custom Size:
Width: 6.67
Height: 4.60

Units:
Centimeters
Inches

✓ OK   ✗ Cancel   ? Help

FIGURE 10.4

The Page Layout dialog box for a form, after selecting *Printer* in the Design For area and changing the orientation to Landscape. (Notice how the paper icon flipped horizontally.)

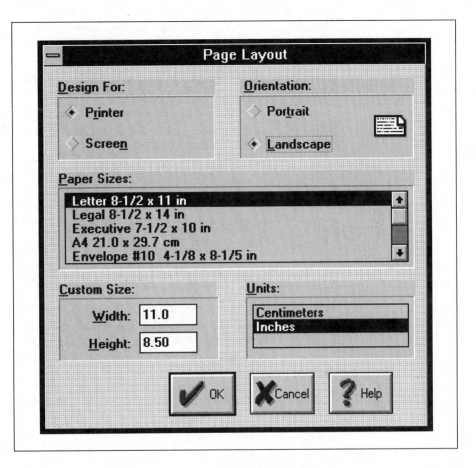

Working in the Design Window

In the Design window, you can create, position, and resize objects and change object properties, such as color, font, fill pattern, and alignment. Chapter 9 discusses general techniques for using the Design window.

Keep in mind that complex designs can be time-consuming to create. You'll need to experiment with various object arrangements and properties until you've "tweaked" the document to ultimate perfection. Therefore, it's a good idea to choose File ➤ Save as soon as you successfully complete a portion of the design. That way, if you make a series of changes you're not happy with, you can simply close the window without saving those changes. When you open the document again, it will contain the last acceptable version and you can continue from there.

Creating the Sample Credit Limit Update Form

The best way to learn form design is to go ahead and try it. So throughout this chapter, we'll show you steps for creating forms similar to those in the figures. Of course, you shouldn't feel restricted to any precise sequence of steps or to our designs for that matter. After all, you may have much better design ideas of your own.

Let's start by looking at the steps used to set up the form shown in Figure 10.2.

Placing Objects in the Sample Form

To begin the design, choose File ➤ New ➤ Form, select the CustList table in the **Data Model** dialog box, then choose OK. In the Style area of the **Design Layout** dialog box select Tabular, then click the Select Fields button to specify the fields you want to include in the design. When the **Select Fields** dialog box appears, click the drop-down arrow next to the *custlist.db* table name, click the Cust No field, then Ctrl+click the Last Name, First Name, M.I., and Credit Limit field names. Click OK to return to the Data Model dialog box, then click OK again to open the Form Design window.

Now continue with the steps listed below. When you finish, your screen will resemble Figure 10.5.

1. Maximize the Form Design window by clicking its Maximize button or double-clicking its title bar.

2. If the expanded ruler doesn't appear below the SpeedBar (see Figure 10.5), choose Properties ➤ Expanded Ruler.

3. Drag the table object to the lower-left corner of the window. Then drag the table's vertical grid lines to narrow the Cust No and Last Name fields.

4. Inspect the table object and select (check) the Vertical Scroll Bar option in the property menu.

5. Click the Cust No text object in the table header until selection handles appear around it, then use Shift+click to add the Last Name, First Name, and M.I. text objects to the selection. Inspect

FIGURE 10.5

At this point, the Design window includes the form title and the table.

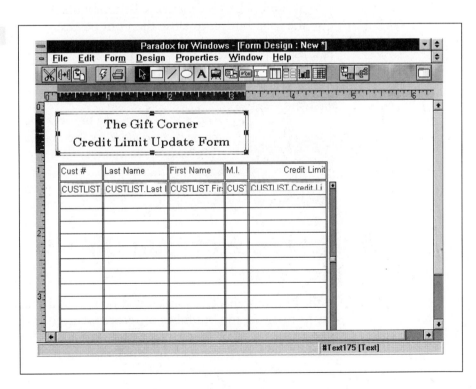

the selected objects and choose Alignment ➤ Left from the property menu. Next, click on the Credit Limit text object in the table header, inspect it, and choose Alignment ➤ Right.

6. Click on the Cust No text in the table object until the insertion point appears, then edit the text to change Cust No to *Cust #*.

7. Use the Text tool to draw the outline of the form's title above the table object (refer to Figure 10.5), then type **The Gift Corner**, press ↵, and type **Credit Limit Update Form**.

8. Press Esc to select the text box you just created, then click the $1^{1}\!/_{2}$ button in the expanded ruler to set line spacing to 1.5 lines.

9. Inspect the text box and choose Alignment ➤ Center from the property menu.

10. Inspect the text box again, choose Font, then click the snap button to open the floating Font palette. Now change the font as desired (we chose Century Schoolbook 14-point bold type). Click the snap button to close the Font palette.

The Form Design window should now resemble Figure 10.5.

TIP

Remember that you can preview your design at any time by clicking the View Data button in the SpeedBar or pressing F8. To return to the Form Design window, click the Design button in the SpeedBar or press F8 again.

Adding Special Field Objects to the Form

In the previous chapter, you learned how to add special fields, such as the record number, total number of records, current page number, date, and time, to your design. Paradox for Windows automatically updates these special fields whenever you view or edit data in the form. Notice the two special fields in the upper-right corner of Figure 10.2. The upper field is *Today* (for displaying the date); the lower field is *Now* (for the current time).

To create a special field, click the Field tool in the SpeedBar and draw a field at the appropriate location in your design. Then inspect the field and choose Display Type ➤ Unlabeled. Inspect the field again and choose Define Field from the property menu, then click the header (...) of the list. Now open the Special Field drop-down list in the **Define Field Object** dialog box and select the field you want. When you're finished, choose OK.

> **N O T E** We'll discuss the other Display Type options in the section called "Special Techniques for Displaying Fields."

Go ahead and create the Today and Now special fields, using Figure 10.6 as a guide for their placement. To format those fields for the results shown in the figure, follow the steps below.

1. Inspect the Today field, choose Format ➤ Date Format from the property menu, then click the ... header and define a custom date format as shown in Figure 10.7. Choose OK when you're finished.

2. Select the Today and Now fields, inspect them, and choose Font ➤ Style ➤ Bold.

3. With the Today and Now fields still selected, choose Design ➤ Align ➤ Align Left, then choose Design ➤ Adjust Size ➤ Maximum Width from the Design window menus.

Skipping over Fields and Preventing Changes to Fields

As mentioned in Chapter 9, Run Time properties control the behavior of an object when you view or edit data in a form. For example, you can turn off (uncheck) the Run Time ➤ Tab Stop property to prevent the cursor from landing on a field during data entry. That way, even if the user presses the Tab or ↵ key or clicks the mouse in a field where the Tab Stop property is turned off, the cursor will not stop at that field. Similarly, you can define

FIGURE 10.6

The custom form after adding the Today and Now fields

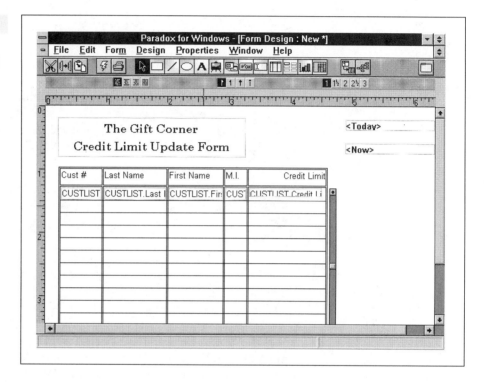

FIGURE 10.7

Our Form Date custom format is based on the Windows Long format and uses short names for Weekday and Month.

a field as Read Only, so that even if the Tab property is on (checked), the user cannot change the field.

If you're designing the sample form shown in Figure 10.2, you can try some Run Time properties now. Select the Cust No, Last Name, First Name, and M.I. *fields* in the table (*not* the header labels). Then inspect those objects and choose Run Time ➤ Tab Stop to uncheck the Tab Stop option. For extra safety, inspect those objects again and select Run Time ➤ Read Only.

NOTE   See Appendix D for a complete list of Run Time properties.

Displaying Text and Memo Fields

As you know, memo fields, formatted memo fields, and text objects can contain a lot of text. In a form design, therefore, you'll probably want to restrict the display of a memo field or text object to a prescribed area of the screen, while allowing all the text to be viewed and edited. The trick is to add vertical and horizontal scroll bars by inspecting the object and choosing Vertical Scroll Bar or Horizontal Scroll Bar from the property menu.

To create the instruction text in Figure 10.2, for example, follow the steps below. When you're finished, the Form Design window will resemble Figure 10.8.

1. Create a text object to the right of the table, inspect it, and choose Vertical Scroll Bar from the property menu.

2. Type the instruction text. (You can't see all the text in Figure 10.2, but don't worry about that—just make up your own ending.)

3. Select the Instructions heading, inspect it, and choose Font ➤ Style ➤ Bold. To underline the R in Record and the L in Locate, select the approp-riate letter, inspect it, and choose Font ➤ Style ➤ Underline.

4. Add some white space at the left and right edges of the text by moving the left margin, first-line paragraph indent, and right margin in just a touch (see Chapter 9 for instructions on doing this). The tab well in Figure 10.8 shows the settings we chose.

NOTE   We used the Character Map, described in Chapter 5, to create the special ↵ character (from the TrueType Symbol font) and the arrow character (from the Wingdings font).

Duplicating an Object

If you want more than one copy of an object or field in your design, you can either draw the object or field again, or you can copy it. Obviously,

FIGURE 10.8

The Form Design window after adding the text object and making some adjustments to the position and size of objects in the design

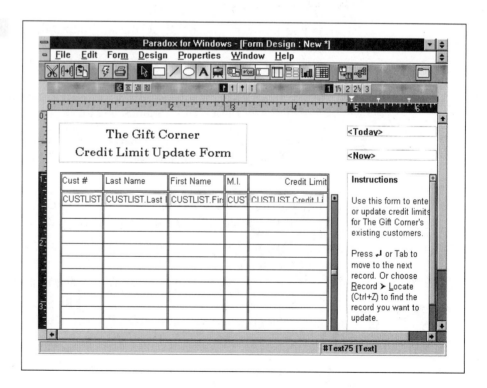

copying is the better choice because it's faster and it copies any properties assigned to the object.

WARNING

After copying or duplicating fields, be sure to change the property of any copies to Read Only and turn off the Tab Stop property as discussed earlier.

Following are the steps used to create the two gift box graphics shown in Figure 10.2. Our form at this stage appears in Figure 10.9.

1. Switch to the Program Manager, open Paintbrush in the Accessories group, and maximize the window. Then choose Edit ➤ Paste From and select the file containing the graphic (you can pick any available graphic that suits your fancy). When the graphic appears, use the Pick tool to outline the portion of the graphic you want to copy. When you're done, choose Edit ➤ Copy (or press Ctrl+Ins) and close the Paintbrush window without saving the image. (For information on using Paintbrush, refer to your Windows documentation.)

2. Return to the Paradox Form Design window, click the Graphic tool in the SpeedBar, draw the outline for the graphic, then click the Paste From Clipboard button in the SpeedBar.

3. Inspect the graphic object and choose Magnification ➤ Best Fit from the property menu. This fits the entire graphic within the graphic object box.

4. If you need to resize the graphic box, inspect it and turn off (uncheck) Design ➤ Size To Fit, then resize the box.

5. With the graphic object selected, choose Design ➤ Duplicate from the menu bar, then drag the object into position.

FIGURE 10.9

The Credit Limit Update form after creating a graphic box and duplicating it

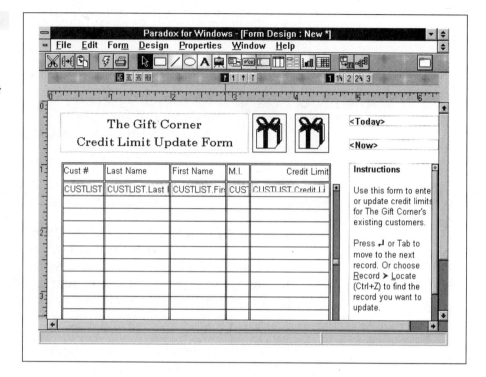

Creating Three-Dimensional Effects

At this point, the design is attractive, but not dazzling. Fortunately, with Paradox for Windows moving from drab to dazzling is easily accomplished by adding three-dimensional effects to your design.

Turning Off Size To Fit

If you're following the design steps presented in this chapter, it's time to turn off the Design ➤ Size To Fit option for all the field, table, and graphic objects. Although the effect won't be immediately obvious, this step will prevent the objects from changing size when you add the 3-D effects. To deselect the Size To Fit option, simply select the table, the graphic objects, and the <Today> and <Now> field objects, then right-click one of the selected objects and uncheck Design ➤ Size To Fit.

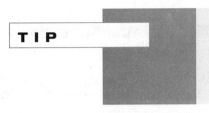

TIP

While it's not strictly necessary to turn off Size To Fit after you've sized objects, doing so eliminates the need to resize them after changing frame styles, frame thickness, fonts, field definitions, and so forth.

Selecting a Background Color

The first step to 3-D Nirvana is to select a background color for the entire page. To do so, click the page (*#Page* appears in the status bar when the page is selected), then right-click. Choose Color from the property menu and click on the color you want. In Figure 10.2 we chose a light gray background, but any pale color can be effective.

TIP

When you change the color of an object, Paradox initially assigns an opaque color. Opaque colors are best for creating three-dimensional effects. You can switch to a transparent color by selecting the Transparent option in the floating Color palette. See Appendix D for information on opaque and transparent colors and creating custom colors.

Creating 3-D Frames

After turning off the Design ➤ Size To Fit option and setting the background color to gray, you can create 3-D frames for objects in the design by following the steps below. The results appear in Figure 10.10.

1. Select the text object containing the form's title *(The Gift Corner Credit Limit Update Form)*, the Today field, and the Now field.

2. Inspect the selected objects and choose Frame ➤ Style to reveal the palette shown at left.

3. Choose the bottom frame style, which gives the framed objects a raised (convex) effect.

FIGURE 10.10

The Design window after changing the background color and frames of some objects

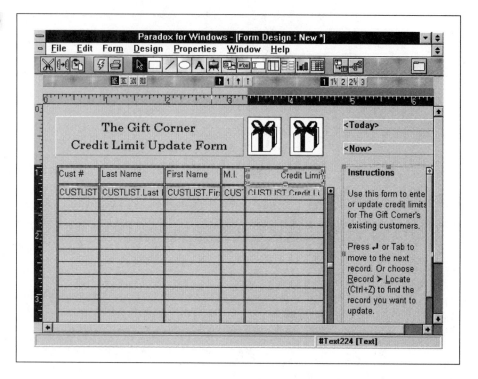

TIP

If you're having trouble locating fields after creating a gray or colored background, try returning the backgroung color to its normal transparent color or to white. You always change the background back to gray (or another color) later.

To create an indented (concave) appearance for the Credit Limit field and Instructions text objects, select the objects, inspect them, choose Frame ➤ Style, and this time, select the second-to-last frame style.

TIP

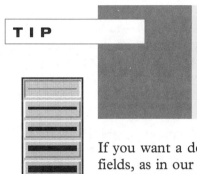

You can determine the current Color, Pattern Style, Line Style, Thickness, Frame Style, and so forth by inspecting an object and choosing the property you want to find out about. The current settings are highlighted in red on the palette.

If you want a deeper indentation for the Credit Limit and Instructions fields, as in our example, inspect those objects again and choose Frame ➤ Thickness followed by one of the line thicknesses that appear at the left. We selected the third sample from the top to produce the results shown in Figure 10.11.

FIGURE 10.11

The Design window after selecting thick frames that lend a deeply indented appearance to the Credit Limit field and Instructions text object

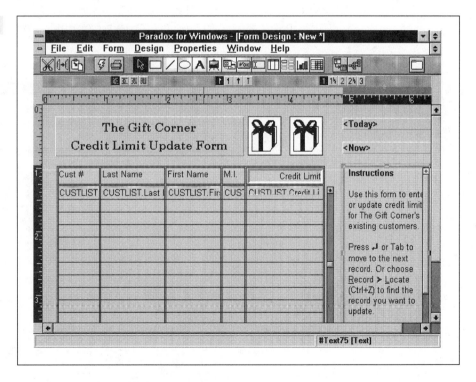

Creating 3-D Tables

Adding a three-dimensional look to tables is a snap. To begin, inspect the table, then choose Grid ➤ Grid Style ➤ 3D from the property menu. If you want a horizontal divider between each row of records (as in Figure 10.12), inspect the table again, then turn on (check) the Grid ➤ Record Divider option.

Creating Highlighted Backgrounds

Data entry will be easier if your form draws the user's eye to important information and fields. For example, the form in Figure 10.2 uses a contrasting color (white) as the background for the instructions and for the Credit Limit field—the only field you can update.

To add these finishing touches to the sample form, select the objects whose background color you want to change (the Credit Limit field and the Instructions text object in our example), inspect the objects, then

FIGURE 10.12

The sample form after adding three-dimensional effects to the table

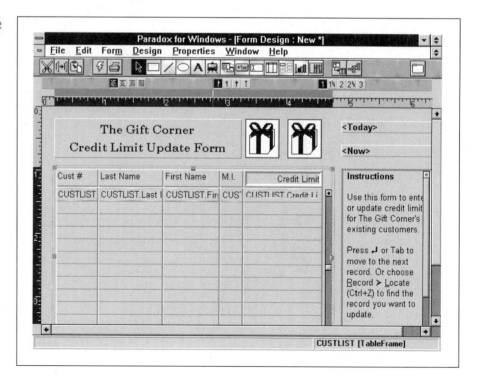

choose Color from the property menu and click on the color you want (we chose white). Figure 10.13 shows the final result in the Design window.

NOTE

Another way to make fields stand out is to choose one color for the fields and another color for field labels. You might also want to use one color for optional fields and a contrasting color for required fields.

The final step is to save the form by choosing File ➤ Save, typing a new file name, and choosing OK. To preview your handiwork, click the View Data button or press F8. If you're finished with the document, close its window by double-clicking the Control-menu box or pressing Ctrl+F4. Or, if you'd like to edit data right away, make sure you're in Form View, then press F9 to switch to Edit mode.

FIGURE 10.13

In this example, we selected the Credit Limit field in the table and the Instructions text object, inspected the properties, chose Color, then selected a color that allows the text to show through.

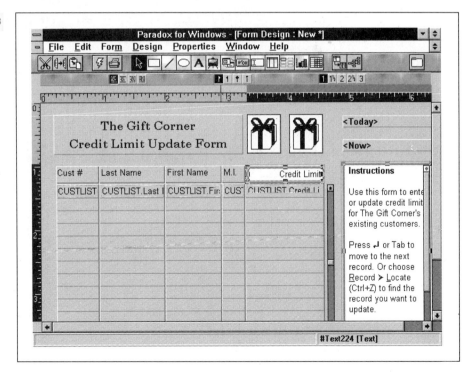

Special Techniques for Displaying Fields

Paradox for Windows offers several ways to display and enter a field's data within a form. You're already familiar with the standard labeled field, which you get automatically whenever you create a new field object. You also know how to remove labels from fields either by removing the Labeled Fields check mark in the Design Layout dialog box or by inspecting the field and choosing Display Type ➤ Unlabeled. However there's a lot more you can do, and the options available can help prevent spelling and other data entry errors and make it easy to enter values without having to type them in.

> **NOTE**   Only the Labeled and Unlabeled display types are available for graphic, OLE, memo, and formatted memo fields.

Whenever you inspect a field and choose Display Type from the property menu, the following options appear (though unavailable options will be dimmed):

```
√ Labeled
  Unlabeled
  Drop-Down Edit...
  List...
  Radio Buttons...
  Check Box...
```

Figure 10.14 shows the Form window for a sample order entry form in which we used each available display type to simplify data entry, reduce errors, and limit the number of choices the user must make. You can see a simpler example of each special field display type in Figures 10.15 and 10.16. Figure 10.15 shows the Form window, while Figure 10.16 shows the Form Design window.

NOTE

The *ordentry.fsl* form in the *\pdoxwin\sample* directory that comes with Paradox for Windows includes examples of all the field display types.

FIGURE 10.14

The Form window for an order entry form using normal fields, plus the special drop-down edit, list, radio button, and check box field types.

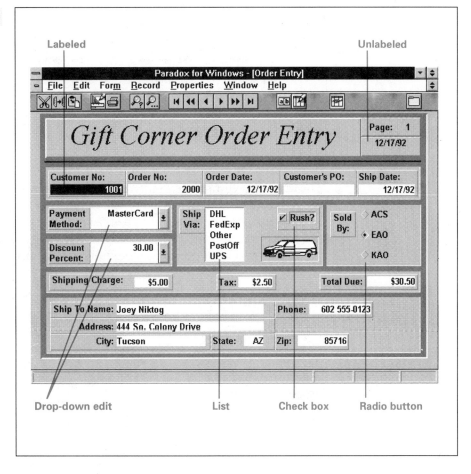

FIGURE 10.15

The Form window for a plain form that uses drop-down edit, check box, list, and radio button display types. In this example, we clicked the drop-down edit list so you can see the values in the field.

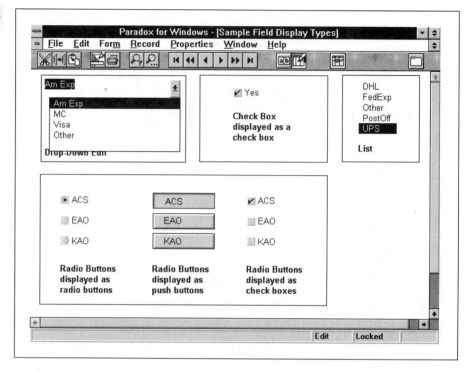

The only embellishments to the "vanilla" forms in Figures 10.15 and 10.16 are the boxes around each field and the labels describing the display type used. Notice that option button fields can appear in three different flavors: radio button (the default), push button, and check boxes. Likewise, check boxes can appear as check boxes (the default), radio buttons, or push buttons.

WARNING

The same field should never appear more than once on a real data-entry form unless you also choose the Run Time ➤ Read Only property for duplicate fields. The examples in Figures 10.15 and 10.16 are designed for illustration purposes only—not for actual data entry.

Drop-down edit, *list*, and *radio* button fields are especially handy when only a few possible values are valid for a field. You specify the valid entries for each

FIGURE 10.16

The Form Design
window for the form
shown in Figure 10.15

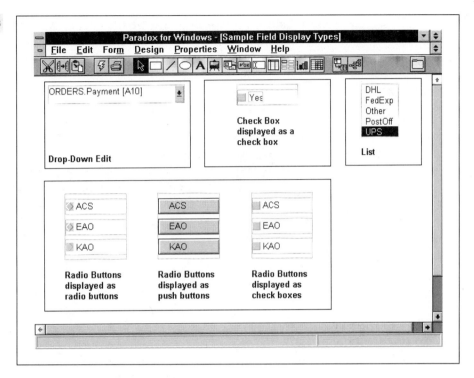

of these field types in the Design window. Then, when entering data in the
Form window, you simply pick the values you want by clicking on them.

Although each field display type has its own visual characteristics (as
you'll see in a moment), all require you to keep the following in mind:

* The field width must be wide enough to accommodate any values
  you specify.

* Values you specify when defining the field must meet requirements of any validity check for the field. For example, if your field
  requires a picture of ??? (three letters), you mustn't specify values
  like *100*, *3 blind mice*, and so forth in your list of possible values. Although you'll be able to define such field values when setting up
  the field, Paradox will reject them during data entry.

- Values you specify must be the proper type for the field. For example, you can't define a value of *20%* for a number field (because "%" is text, not a number). Again, you won't discover that the values aren't right until someone tries to choose them during data entry.

TIP

You can easily convert one field display type to another. Simply select the field object, inspect it, choose Display Type, and then select the display type you want. If a dialog box appears, complete it as described in the following sections.

Now, let's take a closer look at how to create and use the four special display types: Drop-Down Edit, List, Radio Buttons, and Check Box.

Drop-Down Edit Fields

Drop-down edit fields are especially versatile during data entry because you can type values directly into the field, or you can choose values from a drop-down list. Thus, in the sample form of Figure 10.14, we could either type in the payment method or discount percent we wanted, or we could click the drop-down arrow in the field, then click the value we want in the list. Figure 10.15 shows an opened drop-down edit field.

To create a drop-down edit field, inspect the field and choose Display Type ➤ Drop-Down Edit from the property menu. You'll see the **Define List** dialog box shown in Figure 10.17.

Follow the steps below to define values that will appear in the drop-down list when it is clicked during data entry.

1. Type in the items you wish to have the user select, one at a time, in the Item box. Press ↵ after entering each item.

2. If you want to sort the field values in alphabetical order, click the Sort List button.

3. If you need to change an item in the list, click the item in the Item List area of the dialog box, then click the Modify Item button. After making changes, press ↵.

4. If you want to move an item in the list, click on the item in the Item List area, then click the ↑ or ↓ Change Order buttons as needed.

5. If you want to delete an item, click on the item in the Item List area, then click Remove Item.

6. When you're finished entering the fields, choose OK.

N O T E Since the drop-down edit display type does not include a label, you should use the Text tool to create a label that describes the field.

FIGURE 10.17

The Define List dialog box

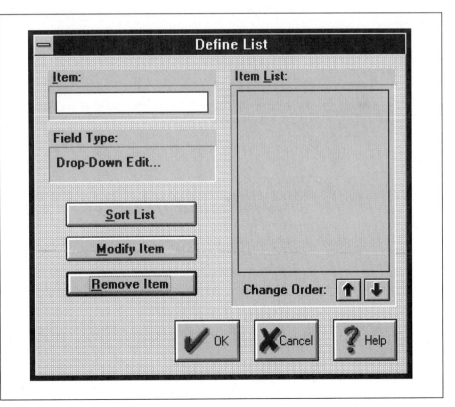

If you need to change the definition of a drop-down edit field, simply inspect the field and choose Display Type ➤ Drop-Down Edit again.

List Fields

During data entry, a list field, like the one shown in Figure 10.15, lets you choose a value from a list. However, unlike drop-down edit fields, list fields do not allow you to type a value into the field; instead you must select one of the values from the list by clicking on or highlighting the value you want. Lists can prevent typing and spelling errors, and limit the values that can appear in a field.

To create a list display type, inspect the field, then choose Display Type ➤ List. You'll see the Define List dialog box shown in Figure 10.17. Follow the steps above to define your list. If you need to change values in the list, inspect the list field and choose Display Type ➤ List again. Or, inspect the list itself—select the list field, click inside the field, then right-click—and choose *List*.

N O T E   Like the drop-down edit display type, the list display type does not include a label. You can use the Text tool to create labels for drop-down edit fields.

Radio Button Fields

Radio button fields offer the same capabilities as list fields, but are visually different. When entering data into a field displayed as radio buttons, you simply click the button you want.

To create a radio button display type, inspect the field, choose Display Type ➤ Radio Buttons, then use the techniques described under "Drop-Down Edit Fields" to fill in the Define List dialog box (Figure 10.17).

By default, Paradox creates radio buttons that look like this in the Design window:

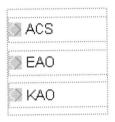

You can change the button type and style by selecting the buttons and inspecting them. When you inspect buttons, you'll see a Button property menu, as shown below.

Rad
disp..........y
radio buttons

In this menu, you can choose button Type, which leads to the Push, Radio, and Check Box options, or you can choose Style, which lets you choose either a Borland (Paradox) style button or a Windows style button. You can also inspect any of the labels within the buttons or change their text, as you would for any text object.

Check Box Fields

As mentioned earlier, a check box has two states—checked and unchecked—and is useful only for fields that can have one of two possible values, such as Yes or No.

To create a check box, inspect a field, then choose Display Type ➤ Check Box. You'll see the **Check Box Values** dialog box shown in Figure 10.18. In the top text box, enter the value the field should have when it is *checked* during data entry. In the bottom text box, enter the value the field should have when it is *unchecked* during data entry. Then choose OK.

Initially, the label in the check box contains whatever value you entered in the top text box of the Check Box Values dialog box. You can change this value as you would any text object, and it's a good idea to do so. Just keep in mind that the check box label is independent of the contents of the field. The *field* contains either the value you entered into the top text box or the value you entered into the bottom text box of the Check Box Values dialog box; however, the field *label* can display anything you want.

You can change the Button Type and Style properties of check box fields, just as you can for radio buttons. Simply select and inspect the check box button (you'll see *#Button* in the status bar) and make your choices.

Now that you know the basic methods for designing forms that contain only one page, let's turn our attention to some special techniques used for multipage forms.

FIGURE 10.18

The Check Box Values dialog box

Check Box Values

Value When **C**hecked:

Value When **B**lank:

✔ OK   ✗ Cancel   ? Help

Designing a Multipage Form

When a table contains too many fields to fit in one window, or your form design becomes too crowded, you can add pages. Figures 10.19 and 10.20 show each page of a two-page data entry form for an expanded table of information about The Gift Corner's employees. The table is named *empladdr.db*.

FIGURE 10.19

The first page of the Employee Update form, with instructions for moving to the next page, information about the current page number and total number of pages, the current date and time, and a Read Only field containing the employee's salary.

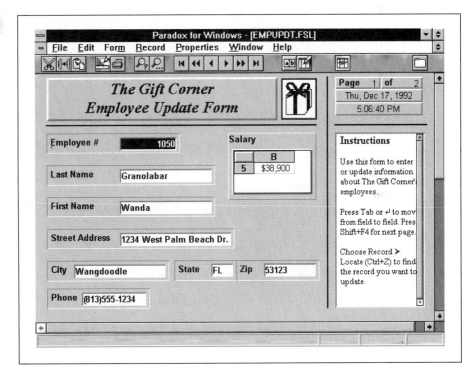

FIGURE 10.20

The second page of the Employee Update form, with a reminder about how to move to the previous page, the current page number, total number of pages, current date and time, and Read Only fields showing the current employee's first and last names.

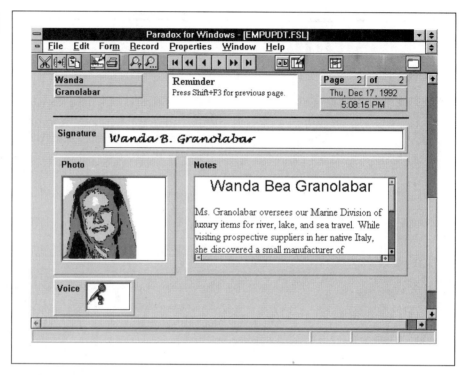

NOTE

The EmplAddr table is the same as the Employee table described earlier in this book, with the addition of Address (25), City (20), State (2), Zip (10), and Phone (13) fields. All the new fields are alphanumeric and have the sizes indicated in parentheses.

Notice in Figure 10.20 that the employee's last name and first name appear at the top left corner of the second page, so the user knows whose record is currently in view. To prevent the user from entering data into those fields accidentally, we changed their properties to Read Only and turned off the Tab Stop. At the upper-right corner, we added fields for the current page number, total number of pages in the form, and the current date and time. We also provided instructions for moving from page to page.

Finally, we checked the Run Time ➤ Complete Display property for the Notes field (a formatted memo field). This causes Paradox to display the field completely, whether or not the highlight is positioned in the field. The Run Time ➤ Complete Display property is basically the same as the Complete Display property that's available when you inspect a memo, formatted memo, graphic, or OLE field in the Table View window. (See Chapter 6.)

TIP

In multipage forms it's important to let the user know the current page number and the total number of pages in the form so that no fields are overlooked during data entry.

The initial steps for creating a multipage form are identical to those for creating a single-page form. (We chose default settings for the form in Figures 10.19 and 10.20.)

Using the Zoom Feature with Multipage Forms

Normally, each page of your form occupies the full screen and is displayed at its normal size, which is 100% magnification. However, with multipage forms, you'll often want to zoom in or out of your design by choosing Properties ➤ Zoom from the Design window menus, then selecting a magnification. The 25%, 50%, Fit Height, and Best Fit options are especially handy when working with multipage documents because they provide a bird's-eye view of several pages at once. Figure 10.21, for example, shows the Design window after we created a new form for the EmplAddr table, added a page, chose Properties ➤ Zoom ➤ Best Fit, and removed the rulers from the window.

Choosing smaller magnifications that let you see multiple pages at once can be a real time-saver. You can select multiple fields on any (or several) of the pages, then inspect and change the properties of all selected fields at once. You can also drag selected fields to other pages and easily perform cut, copy, and paste operations across pages.

FIGURE 10.21

A new two-page form shown at Best Fit magnification with all rulers turned off

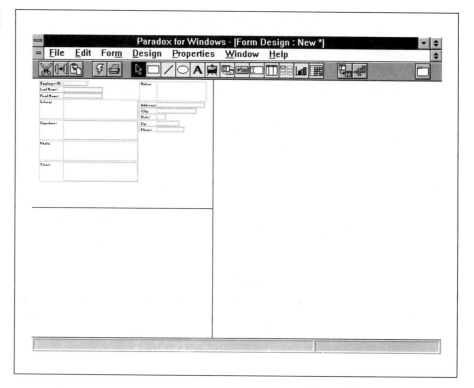

Regardless of the magnification you choose, you can use the vertical scroll bar to display additional pages. Later in this chapter, we'll describe techniques that let you navigate through multipage documents.

Adding Blank Pages to the End of a Form

Adding pages to the end of a form is very easy. Just choose Form ➤ Page ➤ Add. Paradox always adds the page after all existing pages, and the new page is selected automatically.

After adding a blank page, you can place new objects on it, or you can move to a different page, cut or copy objects from that page to the Clipboard, then return to the new page and paste the objects into the design. You can also drag objects from other pages to the blank page.

Creating New Pages from Existing Pages

Paradox for Windows lets you create a new page that's exactly the same as an existing page of a form. Here's how:

1. Select the entire page by clicking on it in the Form Design window (*#Page* will appear in the status bar).

2. Click the Copy To Clipboard button in the SpeedBar, press Ctrl+Ins, or choose <u>E</u>dit ➤ <u>C</u>opy.

3. Click on the page that should *follow* the copied page, then click the Paste From Clipboard button, press Shift+Ins, or choose <u>E</u>dit ➤ <u>P</u>aste.

A new page containing all the design objects of the original page will be added.

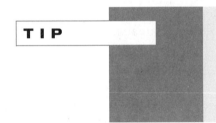

T I P   To place a blank page between existing pages, add a blank page to the end of the form by choosing Form ➤ Page ➤ Add, then cut the page to the Clipboard, click on the page that should follow the blank page, and paste the page.

Copying and Moving Fields from Page to Page

You don't have to recreate objects laboriously on each new page of a document. Instead, you can use the Clipboard to copy design objects from one page to another. To do so, select the objects you want, then click the Copy To Clipboard button in the SpeedBar (or choose <u>E</u>dit ➤ <u>C</u>opy or press Ctrl+Ins). Next, move to the page you want to copy the objects to, click the spot where you want the objects to appear (*clicking is very important!*), then click the Paste From Clipboard button (or choose <u>E</u>dit ➤ <u>P</u>aste or press Shift+Ins).

For example, when designing the form in Figures 10.19 and 10.20, we chose Form ➤ Page ➤ Add to create the second page as soon as the Design window appeared. Then we returned to the first page, selected the Last Name and First Name fields, copied them to the Clipboard, moved to the second page, clicked where we wanted the fields to appear, then pasted the fields onto the design. We also changed the Read Only and Tab Stop properties as described earlier.

You can use either of two methods to move fields from one page to another. The first method is similar to copying: Select the fields you want to move, click the Cut To Clipboard button (or choose Edit ➤ Cut or press Shift+Del). Now move to the appropriate page, click where the fields should appear, and then click the Paste From Clipboard button (or choose Edit ➤ Paste or press Shift+Ins).

The second way to move fields from page to page is much easier. First, zoom out so you can see both the source page (where you want to move fields *from*) and the target page (where you want to move fields *to*). Then simply select and drag the fields from the source to the target page. For example, to move the Signature, Notes, Photo, and Voice fields to the second page of our sample Employee Update form, we simply selected those fields, then dragged them to the blank page.

Deleting a Page

You can delete any page of a multipage form (though you need to be careful about this). Click on the page you want to delete, then press the Del key or choose Edit ➤ Delete.

NOTE   You can choose Edit ➤ Undo or press Alt+Backspace if you immediately regret deleting a page.

Navigating a Multipage Form

As mentioned earlier, you can use scroll bars in the Design window to move from page to page of your form, and you can click on the page you want if you've used the zoom feature. The Form ➤ Page menu, shown below, provides additional options for moving from page to page in a form design.

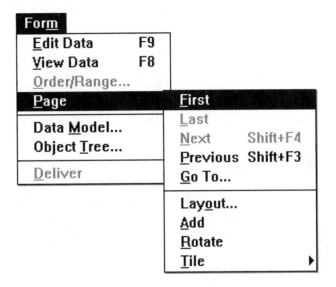

In the Form ➤ Page menu, your choices are as follows:

First   Moves to the first page of the form.

Last   Moves to the last page of the form.

Next   Moves to the next page of the form. As a shortcut, you can press Shift+F4.

Previous   Moves to the previous page of the form. As a shortcut, you can press Shift+F3.

Go To   Displays the **Go To Page** dialog box shown below. To choose a page number, either type the page you want into the Page Number text box, or click the ↑ or ↓ button to decrease or increase the page number. Then choose OK.

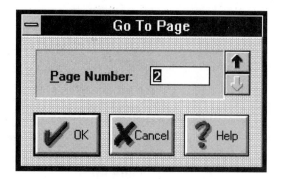

NOTE The above options are also available when you're viewing or editing data in the Form window. In the Design window, when you use these techniques to move to a page, Paradox automatically selects the page you move to.

Rotating a Page to the End of the Form

As an alternative to cutting and copying pages, you can rearrange the pages of your form by rotating pages to the end. To do so, select any page except the last, then choose For_m_ ➤ _P_age ➤ _R_otate. The currently selected page will move to the end of the form.

Tiling a Multipage Form

Normally, the pages of your form are lined up vertically in the Design window, so that you can use the vertical scroll bar to move from page to page. However, you can choose options on the For_m_ ➤ _P_age ➤ _T_ile menu to view the pages in a different arrangement, as summarized below.

Stack Pages   Stacks pages one on top of the other, with the current page on top. You cannot use scroll bars to move from page to page when this option is selected. Instead, you must choose appropriate options from the For<u>m</u> ➤ <u>P</u>age menu (or the equivalent function keys), as described earlier under "Navigating a Multipage Form."

Tile Horizontal   Tiles pages horizontally across the screen. You can use the horizontal scroll bar to move from page to page when this option is selected.

Tile Vertical   Tiles pages vertically, in the default manner. You can use the vertical scroll bar to move from page to page when this option is selected.

N O T E   The tile setting in effect when you save the form will be used when viewing or editing data.

Designing the Sample Multipage Form

You might like to try your hand at designing the sample multipage form shown in Figures 10.19 and 10.20. To begin, choose <u>F</u>ile ➤ <u>N</u>ew ➤ Form and choose all the default options. When you get to the Design window, add a second page to the form by choosing For<u>m</u> ➤ <u>P</u>age ➤ <u>A</u>dd. Now choose <u>P</u>roperties ➤ <u>Z</u>oom and reduce the magnification (or choose Best Fit or Fit Height), then use the copy and paste techniques described earlier to copy the Last Name and First Name fields to the top of the second page. Select the newly copied Last Name and First Name fields, inspect them, and change the Run Time ➤ Read Only and Run Time ➤ Tab Stop properties as described earlier.

If you can see both pages at once, drag the Signature, Photo, Notes, and Voice fields to the second page of the form; otherwise, cut and paste to move those fields to the second page. Next, rearrange the fields into the approximate configurations shown in Figures 10.19 and 10.20. If you wish, use standard editing techniques to remove the colon in the text of each field label.

Now, refer to the general guidelines presented in Chapter 9 and in this chapter, and proceed with the two sections below to complete the design. Feel free to experiment and make corrections as needed, and be sure to switch back and forth between the Design window and the Form window (by pressing F8 or using the View Data and Design buttons in the Speed-Bar) to see how the form will look with data filled in.

Designing the First Page of the Sample Multipage Form

Use the following guidelines to complete the first page of the sample form shown in Figure 10.19:

- Set the page background to gray or some other pale color.

- Create a text object for the title, then type the two centered title lines in Times New Roman 18-point bold italic type (or whatever you have available). Change the Frame ➤ Style property to the raised frame style (last selection in the palette). Change the Frame ➤ Thickness property to the third sample in the list.

- Create the two gift graphics, as for Figure 10.9.

- Add the four special fields shown in the upper-right corner (these are current page (Page Number), total number of pages (Number of Pages), current date (Today), and current time (Now)), and change the labels to bold. Change the Format ➤ Date Format property to the short month and day name used in the Today field of Figure 10.7.

- To create the 3-D effects in the special page number, date, and time fields, select and inspect the fields, then choose the raised style at the bottom of the Frame ➤ Style property palette. Choose the second sample line for the Frame ➤ Thickness property of the selected fields. Now drag the objects close together, as in Figure 10.19.

- Use the Line tool to create the vertical and horizontal lines. Change the Line ➤ Thickness property for those lines to the second thickness listed.

TIP

Before drawing lines, try zooming to a smaller magnification so you can define the full length of the lines with a single drag of the mouse.

- Create the Instructions text object as for Figure 10.8, modifying the text to describe the form you're designing.

- To create the 3-D effects for the Employee #, Last Name, First Name, Street Address, City, State, Zip, and Phone fields, select the outer frame of each field object, then change the Frame ➤ Style property to the indented (second-to-last) frame style. Next, select the edit area of each field object, change the Color property to white (or whatever color you wish), the Frame ➤ Style property to the indented frame, and the Frame ➤ Thickness property to the second thickness.

- Change the Run Time properties for the Salary field to Read Only and turn off the Tab Stop.

NOTE

Recall that Salary is an OLE field designed to contain data from a Microsoft Excel spreadsheet. We chose not to allow updates to the employee's salary.

- To create the 3-D effects in the Salary field, set the Frame ➤ Style property for the outside frame to the raised (bottom) style, then assign the same frame style to the edit region that contains the Salary data. Increase the edit region's Frame ➤ Thickness to the second sample.

- Adjust and rearrange the fields as needed.

Designing the Second Page of the Sample Multipage Form

When designing the second page of the sample form in Figure 10.20, follow these guidelines:

- Select the page number, total number of pages, current date, and current time fields in the first page of the form and copy them to the Clipboard.

- Use any of the techniques described earlier to move to the second page of the form. For example, press Shift+F4 or zoom to 50% or Best Fit and click on the second page's frame.

- Click in the upper-right corner of the page, where you want the copied fields to appear, then paste from the Clipboard.

- Create the text object containing the Reminder text, then change the Frame ➤ Style, Frame ➤ Thickness, and Color as for the Instructions text object on the previous page.

- Draw the horizontal line and change its Thickness to the second sample in the list.

- Change the Frame ➤ Style, Frame ➤ Thickness, and Color properties of the Signature, Photo, Notes, and Voice fields and edit regions as described for the previous page of the form.

- Select (check) the Run Time ➤ Complete Display property of the Notes field.

- Make any necessary adjustments, then save the form.

Changing Form Design Window Properties

As you know, the Properties menu in the Design window offers several options for controlling the appearance of the Form Design window, including

Zoom, Snap To Grid, Horizontal Ruler, Vertical Ruler, and Expanded Ruler. After setting these properties to your liking, you can save them by choosing Properties ➤ Form Options ➤ Save Defaults. If you change your mind and want to restore properties to their previous settings, you must do so *before* exiting Paradox, by choosing Properties ➤ Form Options ➤ Restore Defaults. These defaults are stored in your *pdoxwin.ini* file (see chapter 13).

Changing Form Window Properties

Paradox offers several advanced options for controlling the final appearance of your forms in the Form window. For example, you can decide whether you want your form to appear as a window or a dialog box, and you can define the title and border for the form. Here are the basic steps for controlling the appearance of the Form window:

1. Choose Properties ➤ Form ➤ Window Style, or press Esc until no objects are selected, press F6, then choose Windows Style. You'll see the **Form Window Properties** dialog box as in Figure 10.22.

2. Choose a basic style for your form (either Window or Dialog Box) in the Window Style area of the dialog box. Then choose additional options as discussed in the following sections.

3. Choose OK to save your changes and return to the Form Design window.

4. Save your form and close it.

NOTE   Table 10.1 summarizes the options available after choosing the window or dialog box style in Step 2.

FIGURE 10.22

The Form Window
Properties dialog box

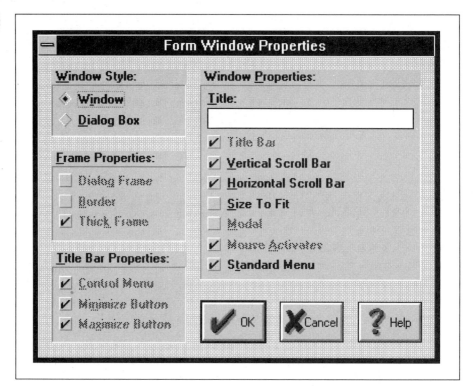

The next time you open the form in Form View, your form will have the properties you chose. Keep in mind that except for changes to the window's title, these options have *no* effect on the form's appearance in the Form Design window.

You should be very careful about the options you choose in this dialog box, because some combinations may confuse users about how to close the form. And when users don't know how to close a form, they'll be tempted to reboot the computer—an operation that's potentially hazardous to your data. Please read the following sections carefully before making changes.

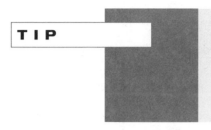

TIP When there's no obvious way to close a form in the Form window, pressing Alt+F4 will usually do the trick. (Note that pressing Alt+F4 in the *Form Design* window exits Paradox, so make sure your data appears in the form before pressing these keys.)

TABLE 10.1: Summary of Properties Available for the Window and Dialog Box Window Style

	WINDOW	DIALOG BOX
Frame Properties		
Dialog Frame		X (if Border isn't checked
Border		X (if Dialog Frame isn't checked)
Thick Frame		X
Title Bar Properties		
Control Menu		X
Minimize Button		X
Maximize Button		X
Window Properties		
Title	X	X
Title Bar		X
Vertical Scroll Bar	X	X
Horizontal Scroll Bar	X	X
Size To Fit	X	
Modal		X
Mouse Activates		X
Standard Menu	X	

Changing Window Style

When you switch to Form View, Paradox normally displays your form in a window that has the properties selected in Figure 10.22. So far, all our examples of Form windows have used the default window style.

As an alternative to the familiar window style, you can display your form in a dialog box that has these general properties:

* It opens in the center of the screen.
* It lies on top of normal windows and the Paradox menu bar.
* You *cannot* resize it, but you can move it if you include a title bar.
* You can switch to other applications by pressing Ctrl+Tab or Ctrl+Esc, or via the Control-menu box, if it's available.
* You can close the dialog box by pressing Alt+F4 or using the Control-menu box, if it's available.

The following sections explain how to customize the dialog box to your liking. Keep in mind that the most "friendly" dialog box style includes a title bar (with an informative title), the Control-menu box, a Minimize button, and a Maximize button. If your form is too large to fit on a single screen, it should also include horizontal and vertical scroll bars. The example in Figure 10.23 follows these guidelines. Figure 10.24 shows the settings used in the **Form Window Properties** dialog box to produce this form style.

Changing Frame Properties

The frame style options summarized below are available only if you've chosen a Dialog Box style.

Dialog Frame   When checked, this option displays the form in a normal Windows dialog box, where the border, colors, and other settings are determined in the Windows Control Panel.

Border   When checked, this option displays the form with a black border instead of the normal Windows style. You cannot display a title bar or choose any title bar properties if you select the Border frame property.

Thick Frame   When checked, this option displays the dialog border as a thick black line. *Thick Frame* is available only if you've selected *Border*.

T I P

To create a dialog box without a border, deselect both the Dialog Frame and Border options.

FIGURE 10.23

A sample dialog box containing a title bar, Control-menu box, Minimize and Maximize buttons, and horizontal and vertical scroll bars

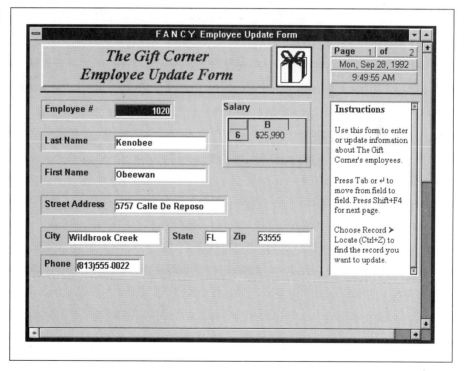

FIGURE 10.24

Form Window
Properties settings
used to produce
the form style in
Figure 10.23

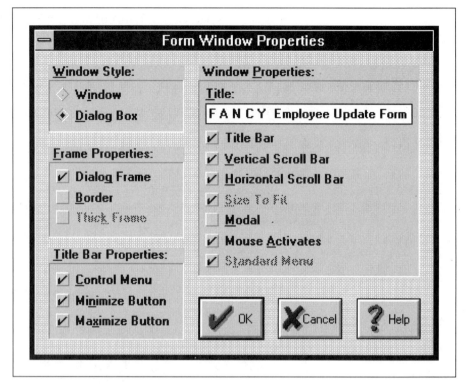

Changing Title Bar Properties

The title bar properties determine whether your dialog box will include a Control menu (Control-menu box), Minimize button, or Maximize button. When checked, the selected element appears in the dialog box; when unchecked, the element does not appear.

When you choose the Window style, all three elements are included automatically and they cannot be turned off.

Changing Window Properties

The Window Properties area of the dialog box controls a variety of attributes of the Dialog Box or Window style. Here's a summary of these options:

Title   Type whatever title you want into the Title text box. If Title Bar is also checked, this title will appear in the title bar of the window or dialog box, and under the icon if you minimize the form. To have Paradox display the file name of the form, leave the Title text box empty. To create a blank title bar, type a space in the text box.

Title Bar   When checked, this option displays the title bar in your form. In the Window style, this option is automatically selected and cannot be turned off.

Vertical Scroll Bar   When checked, this option displays a vertical scroll bar. You should include a vertical scroll bar if your form is longer than a page.

Horizontal Scroll Bar   When checked, this option displays a horizontal scroll bar. You should include a horizontal scroll bar if your form is wider than a page.

Size To Fit   When this option is checked, Paradox opens the form in a window of whatever size you chose in the Page Layout dialog box. If this option is not checked, the form opens in the Windows default size. When you select the Dialog Box style, Size To Fit is always checked and cannot be turned off.

Modal   When checked, this option prevents you from working elsewhere in Paradox until you close the form (you can, however, work in other applications). This option is available only for the Dialog Box style.

Mouse Activates   This option is used only in Dialog Box forms and is useful only if you've attached ObjectPAL methods to your form. (See Chapter 19 for an introduction to ObjectPAL.)

Standard Menu   This option is used only in Window forms and is useful only if you've written your own Form window menu in ObjectPAL and attached it to your form (see Chapter 19).

Printing a Form

Although forms are designed primarily for on-screen display, you can print a form or its design.

Printing the Form Design

Once you have designed a data entry form, you might want to print the blank form design to use as a data collection tool or for reference when designing future forms. Using the actual form for manual data collection reduces the chances of introducing errors into your table.

To print the form design, switch to the Form Design window, if you're not there already. Then click the Print button in the SpeedBar, or choose File ➤ Print. You'll see the **Print File** dialog box (discussed in Chapter 6). From this point, you can choose All to print all pages of a multipage form, or choose Page Range and define a range to print only the specified pages of a multipage form. Choose OK to begin printing.

NOTE Depending on your form design and the type of printer you have, field names in the printed design may appear garbled if Paradox cannot fit them in the space allotted. This is no cause for concern, and it will not affect the appearance of your form on the screen.

Printing Records in Your Form

You can use your form layout to print the current record (or the current set of records if your form contains a multi-record object or table frame). To do so, make sure you're in the Form window (your data should appear in the form) and choose File ➤ Print or click the Print button in the

SpeedBar. Choose a page range, or choose All to print every page of a multipage form. Specify the number of copies you want and decide whether or not you want the copies collated, as described in Chapter 6. Then choose OK to begin printing.

TIP If you want to print more than one record at a time using the form's layout, open the form as a report (see Chapter 9).

Delivering a Form

After designing and saving the perfect form, you may not want anyone else to be able to change it. To prevent other people from changing your form, open your form in the Form Design window, save your changes (if you made any), then choose Form ➤ Deliver. Paradox will create a form with the same name as your original form and an .fdl extension. For example, if your original form is named *custform.fsl*, the delivered version will be called *custform.fdl*. You can then give the .fdl file (not the .fsl) to others. They'll be able to use the form, but won't be able to switch to the Design window to change it (the Design button appears in the SpeedBar as usual, but has no effect when clicked).

WARNING Be sure to keep the original .fsl file around, or *you* won't be able to change the form.

If you need to change the form later, simply modify the original form file (with the .fsl extension), save your changes, choose Form ➤ Deliver again, then distribute the updated .fdl file.

Using the techniques presented in this chapter and your own imagination, you should now be able to create extremely sophisticated forms. But, believe it or not, Paradox for Windows offers even more features for form design, including multitable forms, calculations, and buttons that perform powerful actions when clicked. We'll delve into these topics in Chapters 17 and 19.

In the next chapter, we'll cover special techniques for designing reports, form letters, and mailing labels.

Gift Corner

Customer Phone List

Area Code	201				City	State
					Newark	NJ
Last Name	**First Name**	**Phone**	**Extension**			
Leventhal	Danielle	555-9853				

Area Code	206					State
Last Name	**First Nam**					
Dewey	Frank					
Smythe	Janet					
Wilson	Ted					

Area Code	207
Last Name	
Watson	

Area Code	212
Last Name	
Gladstone	

Area Code	21
Last Name	
Miller	
Smith	

Area Co		Free
Last N		
Clave		

Th

Gift Corner

8891 Gaudy Ave * West Fantasee, CA 92
1-800-555-(

April 21, 1993

<u>Miss Sky R. Cherub</u>
<u>985 Enlightenment Way</u>
<u>Jefferson, SD 57038</u>

Dear <u>Miss Cherub</u>:

Welcome aboard, <u>Miss Cherub</u>! *The Gift Corner* is pleased to have you as one of our new credit customers. Your credit limit of <u>$10,000.00</u> is available as of <u>Wednesday, April 14, 1993</u>.

Now that you're firmly established as one of our valued customers, you may want to peruse our exciting new catalog, which is chock full of great gift items. For example, you'll find some terrific *Toys for Boys*, including hot new race cars in price ranges that are as torrid as the engines under the hoods of these babies. If you're looking for something a bit more tame, try our *Jungle Creatures Collection* -- stuffed animals that look like the real thing! And <u>Miss Cherub</u>, if those on your gift list are itching for a holiday, take a look at our *Exotic Vacation Packages*. We'll guarantee some unforgettable memories! We'll even throw in a free camera, film, and developing so those memories will never be lost.

*S*o why not call your Account Representative here at *The Gift Corner* today? We'll send you a complimentary gift, just for picking up the phone and talking to us. You can reach us 24-hours a day, toll-free at **1-800-555-GIFT**. Don't delay...Call us today!

Sincerely yours,

Frank Lee Unctuous

Frank Lee Unctuous
Account Manager

CHAPTER

11

Designing and Printing Formatted Reports

f a s t TRACK

● **To resize a band**   548

        click the band you want to resize, move the mouse pointer until it changes into a two-headed vertical arrow, then drag the band up or down to add or remove white space above or below objects in the band.

● **To add an object to a band**   552

        resize the band to include some white space (optional), select the appropriate tool in the SpeedBar, then move the mouse pointer to the band where you want to place the object, hold down the left mouse button, and drag to define the size of the object.

● **To add a group band to a report**   555

        click the group header band that's one level higher than the band you want to add, then click the Add Band button in the SpeedBar. Choose the grouping options you want (by field value, by field range, or by number of records), then click OK. You can inspect and change properties of any group band.

● **To delete a group band**   560

        click on the group band, then press the Del key.

● **To rearrange group bands**   560

        select the group header of the band you want to move, then drag the band to its new location.

N this chapter we'll build on concepts presented in Chapters 9 and 10, focusing on techniques for designing and printing reports, form letters, mailing labels, and envelopes. If you've designed custom forms before (perhaps by reproducing the sample forms in Chapter 10 or completing Lesson 4 in Chapter 2), you should have little trouble mastering the techniques presented here. However, if you haven't yet worked through Chapters 9 and 10, please do so before tackling the more advanced topics presented in this chapter.

Typically, you'll use a *report* to print summary information about your data. For instance, you can print a telephone directory of all customers, sorted by area code, or you might want to create an employee directory complete with photos, signatures, and résumé. Perhaps you would like to produce a list of customer credit limits, sorted by state. The possibilities are limitless.

NOTE

Chapter 17 discusses advanced topics related to report design, including how to use summary and calculated fields and how to create multitable reports.

You can also design *mail merge documents*, or form letters, that are customized for each person on a mailing list. You can send new credit customers a letter of welcome that includes the customer's name and address, the amount of credit granted, and when the credit limit becomes effective—along with an appropriate sales pitch to encourage customers to spend that credit right away. You can even design personalized mailing labels or envelopes for each customer.

> **NOTE** The term *mail merge document* is frequently used to describe form letters, mailing labels, and envelopes. Although mail merge documents are really just reports in Paradox for Windows, they do involve some specialized techniques that we'll discuss later in this chapter.

Special Techniques for Designing Reports

If you've read Chapters 9 and 10 and you've designed some forms, you already know the basics of report design. However, there are a few design techniques that are unique to reports and mail merge documents, including the following:

- Using report bands to control placement of report titles, page headers and footers, and records, and to control the sort order

- Grouping related records together

- Using object properties that are unique to report design

- Using text objects to squeeze fields together in mail merge documents

Printing a Quick Report

The most basic type of report is the *Quick Report*, a simple list of data in tabular form, with labels printed at the top of each column. The Quick Report is often sufficient for checking the accuracy of data or for looking up pieces of information. However, it's not very exciting to look at.

To print a Quick Report from the Table window, click the Quick Report button in the SpeedBar, then complete the **Print File** dialog box as discussed in Chapter 6.

Figures 11.1 and 11.2 illustrate some of the most important differences between Quick Reports and customized reports. Note that a Quick Report includes all the fields in a table, regardless of whether they contain information of immediate interest. Any fields that cannot fit on a single page are either cut off (clipped) or printed on overflow pages, depending on options selected in the Print File dialog box. When printing Figure 11.1, we chose the default option (Clip to Page Width), so Figure 11.1 shows only the leftmost fields of the table.

The custom report shown in Figure 11.2 includes only the fields we want in the order we want them, and is grouped by area code and customer name. Although we didn't do so in Figure 11.2, we could have started a new page each time the area code changed. This would simplify distribution of the report if we wanted each of our sales reps to be responsible for calling customers in a specific area code.

We also added the Gift Corner logo and company name, customized the report title, used contrasting colors, placed a horizontal line, the date, and the page number at the bottom of each page, and added three-dimensional effects to tables, fields, and text objects.

General Steps for Designing and Using a Custom Report

As a quick review of concepts presented in the previous chapters, let's go over the general procedure for designing a custom report.

1. Choose File ➤ New ➤ Report from the menus or inspect the Open Report button in the SpeedBar (if it's available) and choose New.

FIGURE 11.1

The Quick Report printed from CustList's Table View after clicking the Quick Report button in the SpeedBar

Tuesday, September 29, 1992			CUSTLIST			Page 1

Cust No	Last Name	Mr/Mrs	First Name	M.I.	Department/Title	
1,001.00	Miller	Miss	Maria	N.	Accounts Receivable	Zeerocks, Inc
1,002.00	Adams	Miss	Anita	Q.	Microcomputer Consultant	
1,003.00	Eggo	Ms.	Sandy	.	Owner	Pancho's Re
1,004.00	Cherub	Miss	Sky	R.		Oneness We
1,005.00	Clavell	Miss	Wanda	T.	Mother Superior	Westridge C
1,006.00	Zeepers	Mr.	Zeke	A.	Chief Engineer	Virtual Realit
1,007.00	Kenney	Mr.	David	E.	Attorney at Law	Felson and F
1,008.00	Leventhal	Miss	Danielle	D.		Garden State
1,009.00	Gladstone	Miss	Tara Rose		Vice President	Waterside La
1,010.00	Olson	Mrs.	Elizabeth	A.	Vice President	Precision Co
1,011.00	Rosiello	Mr.	Richard	L.	Accounts Payable	Raydontic La
1,012.00	Smith	Dr.	Mary	K.	Graduate School of Business	Cal State L.A
1,013.00	Watson	Mr.	Frank	R.	Greenskeeper	Whispering P
1,014.00	Mohr	Mrs.	Mary	M.		
1,015.00	Ramirez	Mr.	Rigoberto	R.	Author	
1,016.00	Newell	Mr.	John	J.		Newell Const
1,017.00	Jones	Ms.	Alma	R.	Account Executive	Ashland Flow
1,018.00	Schumack	Dr.	Susita	M.	Neurosurgeon	Physician's H
1,019.00	Smith	Dr.	Savitha	V.		Slybacks Pa
1,020.00	Smith	Mr.	John	Q.		
1,021.00	Smythe	Ms.	Janet	L.		
1,022.00	Dewey	Mr.	Frank	R.	Senior Partner	Dewey, Chea
1,023.00	Adams	Mr.	Andy	A.	President	ABC Corpora
1,024.00	Wilson	Dr.	Ted		Psychology Department	Pine Valley U
1,025.00	Zastrow	Dr.	Ruth		Internal Medicine	Scripps Clinic

2. In the **Data Model** dialog box, choose a table or query as the basis for the design.

3. In the **Design Layout** dialog box, specify a design layout. Initially, Paradox assigns the Tabular layout to reports.

4. If you want to select or reorder fields, click the Select Fields button in the Design Layout dialog box, then select (or rearrange) the fields you want to include in the report. Choose OK to return to the Design Layout dialog box.

5. Decide whether you want labeled or unlabeled fields.

FIGURE 11.2

A custom report of the CustList table showing customer name, phone number, extension, city, and state grouped by Area Code, Last Name, and First Name

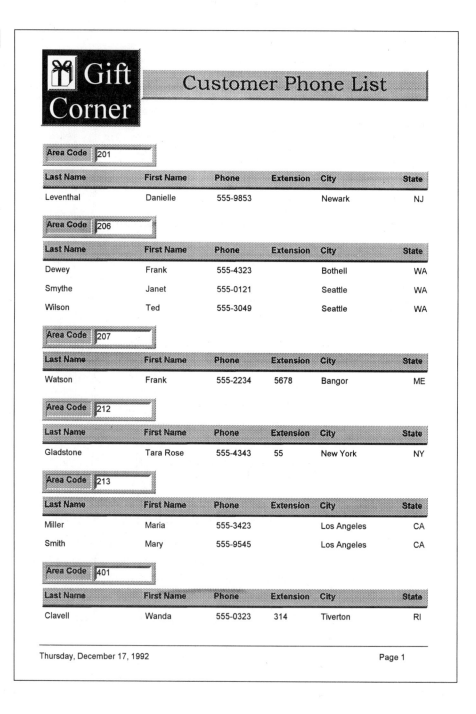

6. If you want to change the page layout, click the Page Layout button in the Design Layout dialog box, make any necessary changes, then choose OK. (See "Choosing a Page Layout," below, for more information.)

7. Choose OK in the Design Layout dialog box to open the Report Design window.

8. Use techniques discussed in Chapters 9 and 10 and in this chapter to customize your design. Preview the design by clicking the View Data button in the SpeedBar or pressing F8.

9. Choose File ➤ Save to save the report.

10. Print the report using the Print button in the SpeedBar or options on the File or Report menu as described under "Printing Report Documents," later in this chapter.

11. If you want to use this report when you click the Quick Report button in Table View, open the table you want to associate with this report, then right-click the Quick Report button. Select a report name and choose OK. Now choose Properties ➤ View Properties ➤ Save to save your changes.

12. To open an existing report, choose File ➤ Open ➤ Report or click the Open Report button in the SpeedBar (if it's available). Then choose the file name of the report, change the table if you want to use data from a different table with this report layout, choose an Open Mode (View, Design, or Print), and choose OK.

Choosing a Page Layout

The **Page Layout** dialog box appears in Figure 11.3. When you design for the printer, the dialog box includes a list of paper sizes to choose from. You can choose any of these options, or you can define a custom size by entering the Width and Height you want. You can also change the units of measure, the paper orientation (portrait or landscape), and the left, right, top, and bottom margin settings.

NOTE   To reach the Page Layout dialog box, click the Page Layout button in the Design Layout dialog box, or choose Report ➤ Page Layout when you reach the Report Design window.

If you prefer to design for the screen, click the Screen option in the Design For area. The same basic options are available, with the exception of Paper Size (this changes to Screen Size) and orientation.

When you're finished with the Page Layout dialog box, choose OK.

NOTE   When designing for the printer, only fonts installed for the currently active printer are available. Paradox will do its best to match the screen fonts displayed in the Report window to the printed output. When designing for the screen, you can use any available screen fonts.

FIGURE 11.3

The default Page Layout dialog box for a report

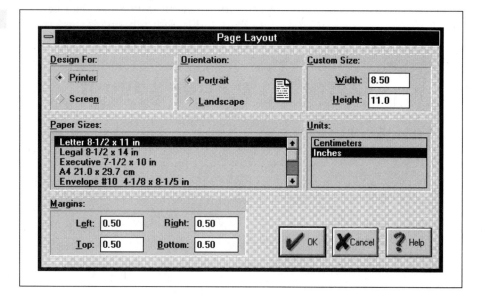

Understanding Report Bands

Not surprisingly, most of the techniques for placing design objects, changing their properties, and creating special effects in reports are exactly as described in Chapters 9 and 10. However, unlike forms, reports contain separate sections, called *bands*, which control where objects will appear in the final report. The four types of bands in reports are described below.

Report Band   Contains data to be printed at the beginning and end of the report.

Page Band   Contains data to be printed at the top and bottom of each page.

Group Band   (optional) Lets you group the records of the table. See "Grouping Your Data," later in this chapter, for more on group bands.

Record Band   Contains the table's records.

Displaying Band Labels

You can choose Properties ➤ Band Labels to display or hide the band labels. Figure 11.4 shows band labels turned on (checked), while Figure 11.5 shows band labels turned off (unchecked).

When band labels are on, each section of the report is separated by a boundary line containing a label with the name of the band and two arrows that point in the direction of the record band. (The arrows point down in headers and up in footers.) When the band labels are hidden, the labels disappear (though thin boundary lines and band names are still visible, as in Figure 11.5). Keep in mind that band labels and boundary lines never appear when you preview or print the report. They're only used in the Design window to help you define the location of information on various parts of the report.

FIGURE 11.4

The Report Design
window with the
Properties ➤ Band
labels option checked
(turned on)

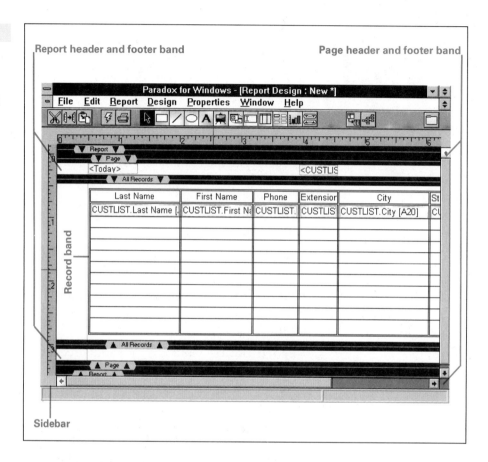

Report header and footer band

Page header and footer band

Sidebar

TIP

Turning off the band labels can give you a better idea of
what the report will look like while you're designing it.

Report Band

The report band consists of the *report header* and the *report footer*. The
report header appears at the top of the Design window. Any objects placed
in this area appear only once, at the very beginning of the report (before
any other objects). You might want to use the report header for a report

FIGURE 11.5

The Report Design window with the Properties ➤ Band labels option unchecked (turned off)

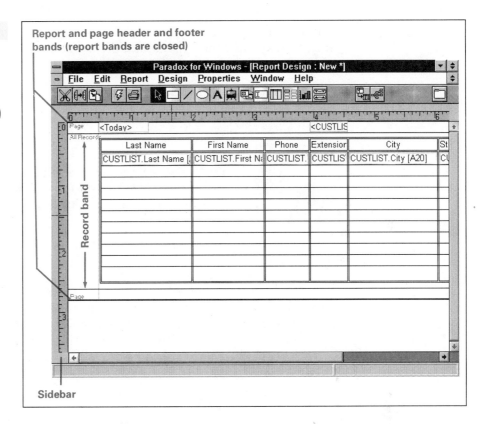

Report and page header and footer bands (report bands are closed)

Sidebar

title, an abstract, an introduction, or your company logo. Initially, the report header is empty.

The report footer appears at the bottom of the Design window, and like the report header it is initially empty. Any objects placed in the report footer appear at the end of the report, after everything else has been printed.

Page Band

The *page band* contains objects to be printed at the top and bottom of each page of the report. Like the report band, it consists of a header and a footer. The page header appears just below the report header, and any objects placed there are printed at the top of each page. Note that Paradox automatically inserts into the page header special fields for the current date <Today>, the table name, and the word "Page" followed by the current page number <Page number>.

The page footer appears just above the report footer. Objects placed in the page footer are printed at the bottom of each page.

TIP   You can select the predefined page number, table name, and page number objects and drag them from the page header to the page footer.

Record Band

The *record band* contains the records of the table you're reporting on. The data objects initially placed into the record band depend on the style of report you chose in the Design Layout dialog box. Of course, you have complete freedom to add other objects to the record band and to delete any objects placed there.

Resizing Bands

Paradox places the page, report, and record bands for you, and you cannot remove them. However, you can leave bands blank, and you can resize them with your mouse to add or remove extra space. (There is no keyboard method for resizing bands.)

TIP   Depending on your hardware, you may find it easier to resize bands when the labels are turned off. Experiment to find the best method.

Here are the basic steps for resizing a band:

1. Select the band you want to resize by clicking on it. The name of the band you selected will appear at the right edge of the status

bar. If band labels are turned on, the selected band will change color when you've selected it. (To deselect a band, press Esc.)

2. Move the mouse pointer (*without clicking*) to the top or bottom of the selected band until the pointer changes to a two-headed vertical arrow.

   - If you move the pointer to the top of the selected band, you can adjust the space above any objects in the band.
   - If you move the pointer to the bottom of the selected band, you can adjust the space below any objects in the band.

3. Now drag the band up or down. As you drag the band, the status bar at the lower-left corner of the window indicates which band you're resizing and displays the current measurements of the band. For example, the message

Resizing #Page_Footer: 8.50 by .25

means that you're resizing the page footer band, which is currently 8.50 inches wide by .25 inch high. As you drag the band up or down, the height will increase or decrease. Increasing the band height adds white space, decreasing it removes white space.

4. When the band is the height you want it, release the mouse button.

N O T E   You cannot resize a band to make it smaller than the objects it contains. To close a band completely, delete any objects it contains, then resize it (be sure to scroll to the right edge of the window when looking for objects to delete). If necessary, use Properties ➤ Zoom to zoom out so that you can see the entire design at once.

Table 11.1 contains a complete list of rules for resizing all the bands, including group bands, which are described later in this chapter.

TABLE 11.1: Rules for Resizing Bands

REPORT HEADER, PAGE HEADER, OR GROUP HEADER BANDS...	
TO CHANGE...	**SELECT THE BAND YOU WANT, THEN DRAG...**
Space above objects in the band	Upper band line (near top edge of the band) up or down. Dragging up increases the space above objects, dragging down decreases the space.
Space below objects in the band	Lower band line (near the label of the next band) up or down. Dragging up decreases the space below objects, dragging down increases the space.
RECORD BANDS...	
TO CHANGE...	**SELECT THE RECORD BAND, THEN DRAG...**
Space above objects in the band	Upper record band up or down. Dragging up increases the space above objects, dragging down decreases the space.
Space below objects in the band	Lower record band up or down. Dragging up decreases the space below objects, dragging down increases the space.
REPORT, PAGE, OR GROUP FOOTER BANDS...	
TO CHANGE...	**SELECT THE BAND YOU WANT, THEN DRAG...**
Space above objects in the band	Upper band line (near the previous band's label) up or down. Dragging up increases the space above objects, dragging down decreases the space.
Space below objects in the band	Lower band line (near the bottom of the band) up or down. Dragging up decreases the space below objects, dragging down increases the space.

At first you might find resizing bands a bit tricky, but with some practice you'll get the hang of it. Here are some secrets to accurate band resizing:

- Turn band labels on or off, depending on which method you prefer.

- Be sure to click the band you want (look at the status bar for feedback). Then wait for the mouse pointer to change to a two-headed arrow before dragging the selected band. This way you'll know exactly which band line you'll be dragging.

- Watch the left edge of the status bar as you drag to determine whether you're increasing or decreasing the band height.

- If you make a mistake and resize the wrong band, choose Edit ➤ Undo or press Alt+Backspace.

- Refer frequently to the guidelines in Table 11.1.

Placing and Using Objects in Report Bands

You create, define, inspect, and otherwise manipulate objects in reports just as you do in forms. Thus, to add an object, you select a tool in the SpeedBar, click in the band where you want the object to appear, then drag to define the object.

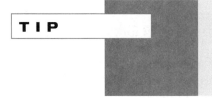

T I P

If the band is too narrow for the object, you can resize the band before placing the object. Resizing is usually optional, however, because Paradox increases the band size automatically when necessary.

Following are some useful points to remember when working with objects in a report:

- To select all the objects in a band, click in the band, then choose Edit ➤ Select All. Because each band is treated separately, you cannot select all objects in the report at once.

- To move an object from one band to another, select the object and drag it to the new location.

- To copy or cut an object from one band to another, select the object, then click the Cut To Clipboard or Copy To Clipboard button in the SpeedBar. Click in the band where you want the object to appear, then click the Paste From Clipboard button in the SpeedBar.

- Certain object properties are different in forms and reports. For example, although scroll bars are available to help you design a report, they never appear when you run reports. We'll discuss the most important properties in this chapter, then summarize the rest in Appendix D.

Grouping Your Data

Paradox lets you define optional *group bands*, which you can use to group (sort) your data. Groups can be based on the following:

- The value in a certain field (for example, by state or area code), which effectively sorts the data by that field. When you preview or print the report, the groups will be sorted in alphabetic or numeric order depending on the type of field you selected.

- A range of data. For example, you can group records based on the first four characters of the customer's last name, by $2500 increments in the customer's credit limit, or by the day, week, month, or quarter of the customer's start date.

- A specified number of records. For example, the report could print a line or leave some extra space after every ten records.

Using Nested Groups

You can define many levels of grouping, where the outermost group specifies the main (primary) sort order, the next group specifies the secondary sort order, and so forth. When one group band lies within another one, it is said to be *nested*.

In Figure 11.6 the outermost group band is based on the Credit Limit field. Nested within that group band is a group band based on the State field. This arrangement tells Paradox to print records in Credit Limit order, with records grouped by State within identical credit limits. We use additional bands to group the records further by Last Name, First Name, and M.I. (middle Initial) within each Credit Limit and State. Figure 11.7 shows a sample printout using this design.

FIGURE 11.6

The outermost group band, Credit Limit, defines the primary sort order. The next group band, State, defines the secondary sort order.

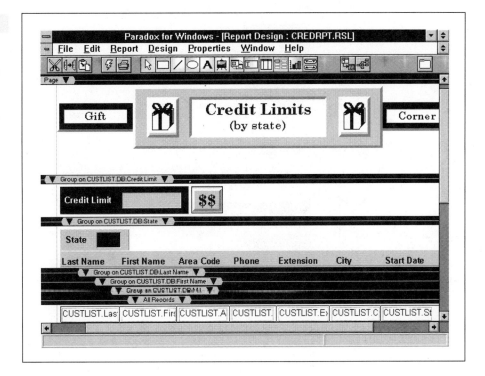

FIGURE 11.7

A sample printout from the report design shown in Figure 11.6. Notice that records are in order by credit limit, and within identical credit limits, by state. Additional group bands were used to sort records by customer name.

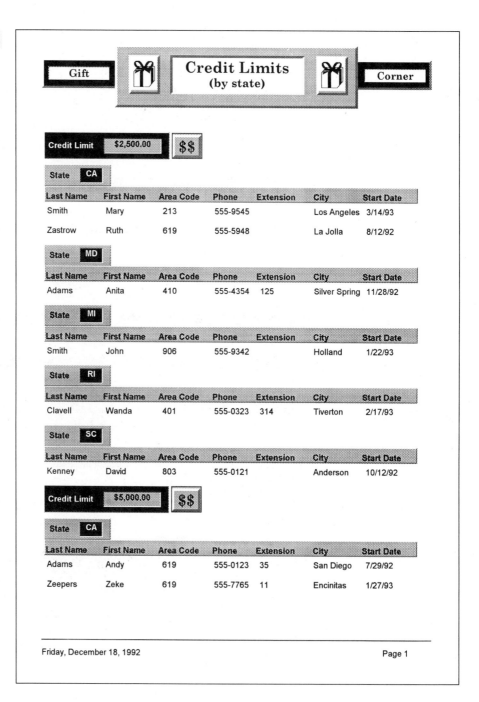

Gift		Credit Limits (by state)			Corner

Credit Limit $2,500.00 $$

State CA

Last Name	First Name	Area Code	Phone	Extension	City	Start Date
Smith	Mary	213	555-9545		Los Angeles	3/14/93
Zastrow	Ruth	619	555-5948		La Jolla	8/12/92

State MD

Last Name	First Name	Area Code	Phone	Extension	City	Start Date
Adams	Anita	410	555-4354	125	Silver Spring	11/28/92

State MI

Last Name	First Name	Area Code	Phone	Extension	City	Start Date
Smith	John	906	555-9342		Holland	1/22/93

State RI

Last Name	First Name	Area Code	Phone	Extension	City	Start Date
Clavell	Wanda	401	555-0323	314	Tiverton	2/17/93

State SC

Last Name	First Name	Area Code	Phone	Extension	City	Start Date
Kenney	David	803	555-0121		Anderson	10/12/92

Credit Limit $5,000.00 $$

State CA

Last Name	First Name	Area Code	Phone	Extension	City	Start Date
Adams	Andy	619	555-0123	35	San Diego	7/29/92
Zeepers	Zeke	619	555-7765	11	Encinitas	1/27/93

Friday, December 18, 1992 Page 1

Adding Group Bands

To add a group band to your report design, follow the steps below.

1. If you've already added one or more groups, click the group header band that's one level higher than the band you want to add. If the report doesn't have any bands yet, move on to Step 2.

2. Click the Add Band button in the SpeedBar (shown at left), or choose Report ➤ Add Band. You'll see the **Define Group** dialog box shown in Figure 11.8.

FIGURE 11.8

The Define Group
dialog box

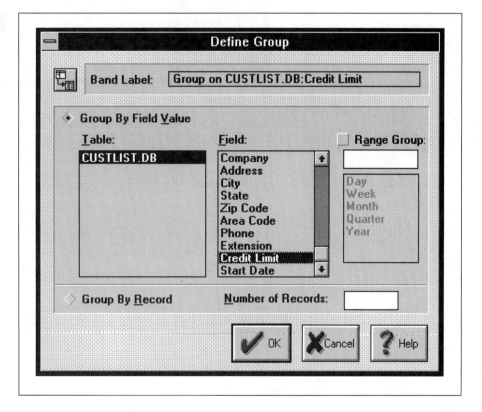

3. Choose the type of grouping you want as described in the following sections of this chapter.

4. Choose OK. The newly defined group band will appear in the Report Design window, as in Figure 11.9.

FIGURE 11.9

The Report Design window after defining a group band on the Area Code field. When printed, this report will be similar to the example in Figure 11.2, although it will not be sorted by customer name within area code.

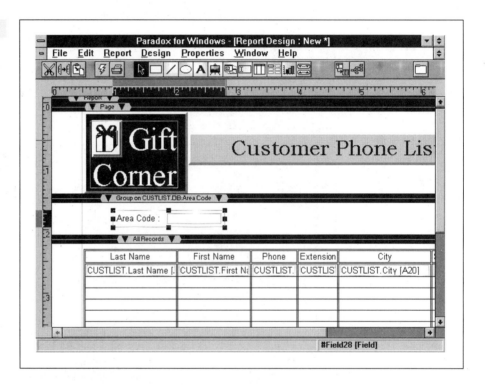

NOTE

As you make selections, the Band Label at the top of the Define Group dialog box reflects your choices.

Each group you define consists of a group header, which is identified as a ▼ **Group on** ▼ band above the record band, and a group footer, which is identified as a ▲ **Group on** ▲ band below the record band. If you choose to group by a field without specifying a range or number of records, Paradox will automatically insert a labeled field object for the field you choose into the group band header (see Figure 11.9). Otherwise, the band header and footer will just contain empty space, which creates a gap between groups of records. You can add any objects you wish to a group band, or you can remove the object and close up the group bands by resizing them.

NOTE   Group headings and footings can include basic math calculations and summaries such as subtotals. See Chapter 17 for details.

Regardless of how you group the records, Paradox performs the following steps for each group:

- Prints any blank space or objects in the group header.
- Prints the records in the group.
- Prints any blank space or objects in the group footer.

Now, let's take a moment to go over the various grouping options available.

Grouping on a Field Value

When you group on a field value, Paradox places all records having the same value for that field into the same group. When that field value changes, Paradox starts a new group. For example, in Figure 11.2 we grouped by Area Code and displayed the area code in the group header. Thus, the records appear in the order shown below.

        Area Code 201 heading
            All the records in the 201 area code

        Area Code 206 heading
            All the records in the 206 area code

        Area Code 207 heading
            All the records in the 207 area code

        and so forth...

To group by a field value, click the Group By Field Value option in the Define Group dialog box (if it isn't already selected), then double-click the field you want to group by.

Grouping on a Range

You can also group records according to a range of values. To do so, click the Group By Field Value option in the Define Group dialog box (if necessary), click the field you want to group by, then click the Range Group option in the dialog box and type or choose a value.

The way you define a group range depends on the type of field you selected. For example, if you selected an alphanumeric or memo field, you can type the number of characters to group by into the text box below *Range Group*. The default value is 1, which means that all values in the group must have the same first character, but the remaining characters can be different. If you prefer to group by the first few characters of a field, type the number of characters into the text box. For example, if you group by the first three characters of the Zip Code field (by entering 3 into the text box), you might see groups like these:

```
88201
88255
88256

91234
91245

92024
92037
```

If the field you're grouping by is numeric, you can type an interval size into the text box. For example, if you chose Credit Limit as the field to group on, and specified 2500 as the range, records would be sorted by the Credit Limit field, with credit limits between 0 and 2500 in the first group, credit limits between 2501 and 5000 in the second group, credit limits between 5001 and 7500 in the next group, and so on.

If you group by a date field, you can click a date option in the list that appears below the Range Group area. Briefly, these options are as follows:

Day   Records with identical dates are placed in groups. For example, records with a Start Date of 1/1/93 are in one group, records with 1/2/93 are in the next group, and so forth.

Week   Records are grouped by week (from Sunday to Saturday). For example, records with dates from 1/1/93 (a Friday) to 1/2/93 (a Saturday) are in one group; records with dates from 1/3/93 (a Sunday) to 1/9/93 (a Saturday) are in the next group, and so forth.

Month   Records are grouped by month. With this option, all the January 1993 dates would appear in one group, February 1993 dates in the next group, and so forth. Any records with January 1994 dates would follow records dated in December of 1993.

Quarter   Records are grouped by quarter. For example, all records in the first quarter of 1993 (January, February, and March) form one group, records in the next quarter of 1993 (April, May, and June) form the next group, records in the third quarter of 1993 (July, August, and September) form the next group, and records in the fourth quarter of 1993 (October, November, and December) form the next. Any records in the first quarter of 1994 would follow records in the last quarter of 1993.

Year   Records are grouped by year. Records with 1992 dates are in one group, records with 1993 dates are in the next group, and so on.

Figure 11.10 shows the Define Group dialog box with the Start Date range defined by Quarter.

Grouping on a Record Count

To group on a record count, click the Group By Record option in the Define Group dialog box, then type the number of records you want in each group.

The Group By Record option doesn't actually sort records. Instead, it organizes records into equal-sized groups in the printed report. For example, if you enter 5 as the number of records to group by, Paradox will place a blank space between groups of five records.

FIGURE 11.10

Define Group dialog box with the Start Date range defined by Quarter

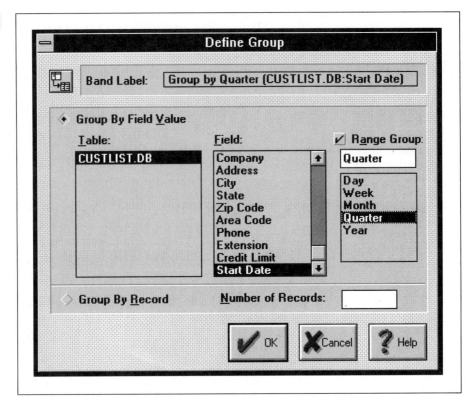

Deleting and Rearranging Group Bands

To remove a group band, simply select it and press the Del key. The band and any objects in it will disappear.

If you've defined several groups in your report and want to rearrange them, select the *group header* of the band you want to move and drag the band to its new location. Make sure any higher level sorting groups appear above the lower level groups. For example, to group the records in Figure 11.6 by state, then by credit limit within each state, drag the group header for the State group above the group header for the Credit Limit group, as shown in Figure 11.11. The first page of this printed report appears in Figure 11.12.

FIGURE 11.11

We revised the example in Figure 11.6 so that the outermost group band (primary sort order) is State. The next group band, Credit Limit, defines the secondary sort order. We also moved the table heading text from the State band to the Credit Limit band.

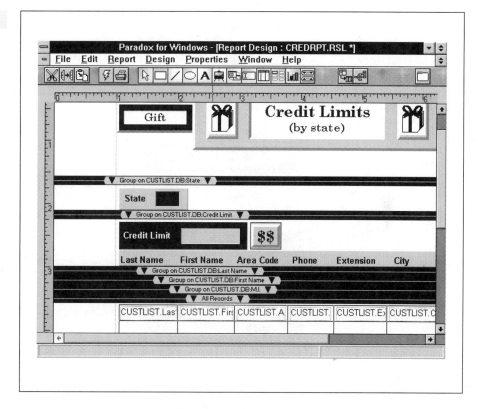

Redefining a Group

You can redefine a group at any time by inspecting the group band you want to change, then choosing Define Group. From the list of field names that appears, choose a different field for the group, or click on the header (...) to open the **Define Group** dialog box.

NOTE   Redefining a group doesn't automatically redefine the field in the group header. You'll need to do that separately.

FIGURE 11.12

Page 1 of the printed output from the report design shown in Figure 11.11. Notice that records are now in order by state, and within state, by credit limit.

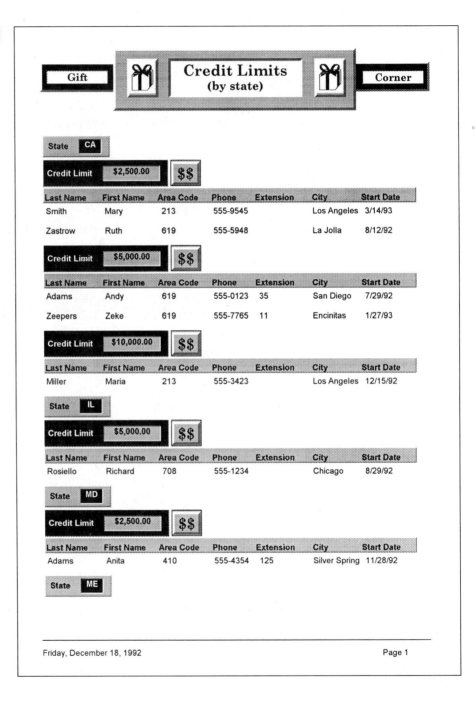

Choosing the Sort Direction for a Group

Normally, Paradox assumes you want to print grouped records in ascending sorted order. If you want Paradox to display records in descending order, inspect the header or footer of the group band you want to change, then choose Sort Order ➤ Descending. To switch the sort direction back to Ascending, inspect the header or footer again, and choose Sort Order ➤ Ascending.

Sorting without Grouping

Keep in mind that it's the blank space and any objects placed in the group header and footer bands that create the visual breaks between groups. If the group header and footer bands are empty, the records will still be sorted, but no blank lines or objects will appear between the groups. This means that you can use group bands to sort records without grouping them, simply by deleting any objects in the group header and footer bands and resizing (closing) the group header, group footer, and record bands to squeeze out any extra blank space.

When using this technique to sort records in a tabular report, your report may look better if you inspect the table, choose Detach Header, and move the table header into the page band, or into an appropriate band above the record band. For example, you could move the header into the Credit Limit band shown in Figure 11.11. After moving the table header, you may also want to move the table up within the record band. Finally, resize the record band to remove excess space below the table frame.

NOTE   Resizing or dragging the table frame also resizes or moves a detached table header. Likewise, resizing or dragging a detached table header resizes or moves the table frame.

If you want more control over the table headings than a detached table header offers, try this: Inspect the table and choose Detach Header. Select all the text fields in the header by clicking on each one, and click the Copy To Clipboard button or press Ctrl+Ins. Press Esc to select the table header, then press Del to delete it. Next, click in the band where you want the leftmost header text field to appear (widen the band if necessary), and click the Paste From Clipboard button or press Shift+Ins. If you wish, draw a box around all the text fields in the new header. You can then adjust the spacing of the text fields or the color and frame of the surrounding box as needed.

TIP Choosing a grid style of None for the table frame often gives attractive results when you're designing your own table headers.

Controlling the Sort Order for Reports

Paradox offers three ways to sort reports:

- You can use the Table ➤ Sort or File ➤ Utilities ➤ Sort options (Chapter 7), or you can use a query that produces a sorted Answer table (Chapter 8), then print the report from the sorted table.

- You can base the report directly on a saved query that produces a sorted Answer table (Chapters 8 and 9). We used this technique to sort a number of reports in this chapter that did not involve group bands.

- You can define group bands that group and sort the report, as described above.

You'll have little trouble defining the perfect sort order for your reports if you keep this important point in mind: Group band sorts override sorts performed by queries or table sort operations. Thus, there's no point in sorting your table when your report contains group bands.

Therefore, if you are using group bands in a report design and also want to sort records by other fields in the table, you must define additional group bands for each field that you want to sort by. For example, to sort the grouped reports in Figures 11.2, 11.7, and 11.12 by customer name, you would first define the higher level bands such as Area Code (Figure 11.2), Credit Limit and State (Figure 11.7), or State and Credit Limit (Figure 11.12). Next, define additional group bands for the Last Name, First Name, and M.I. (middle initial) fields. Place these bands below any higher level groups. After defining the extra bands, select and delete the field objects that appear automatically in the bands and resize the group band headers and footers to remove all the extra space from them. That's how we sorted reports in this chapter by name within some other grouping. For reports involving table objects (see Figures 11.11 and 11.12), we also detached and removed the table headers and added text objects with appropriate column headings into the group band *above* the Last Name group band.

Adding a Page Break to a Report

With Paradox for Windows, it's easy to insert page breaks in a report. For example, you might want to print a page break after the report's title page. Or, you might want to start a new page whenever the area code changes in a telephone directory report. In mail merge documents, page breaks are used to start each letter on a new page.

To add a page break to a report design, make certain the vertical ruler is visible (choose Properties ➤ Vertical Ruler if necessary), then click in the sidebar area where you want the page break to appear. A horizontal line will appear across the Report Design window and a marker will appear in the sidebar to indicate the position of the page break, as in Figure 11.13.

You can drag the page break marker in the sidebar area up or down to reposition the page break. (Do not drag the horizontal line itself, or you'll resize the band instead of moving the page break.)

FIGURE 11.13

You can insert a page
break by clicking in
the sidebar of a report
design. In this
example, Paradox will
start a new page
whenever the area
code changes.

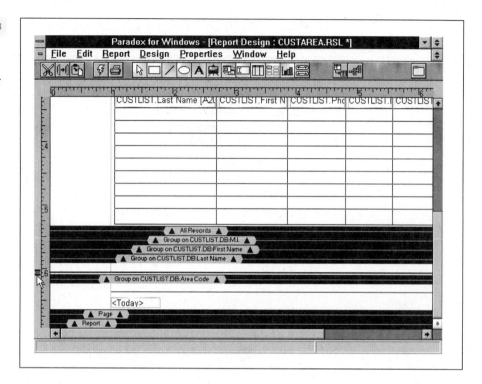

NOTE   You cannot place a page break in the page band or within an object.

To delete a page break, drag the marker to the right, out of the sidebar. When you release the mouse button, the marker and horizontal line will disappear.

Inserting Fields in Text

In general, you work with text in reports the same way you work with text in forms. In itself, that's not too remarkable—but when you insert fields

Inserting Fields in Text

In general, you work with text in reports the same way you work with text in forms. In itself, that's not too remarkable—but when you insert fields within a text object, things really start to cook. For example, suppose you perform these steps:

1. Define a report for the CustList table (or any table containing names and addresses). When you get to the **Design Layout** dialog box, choose a *Blank* style and choose OK.

2. Use the Text tool to place a text object in the record band, sizing it to about the width of your screen.

3. Now type **Dear** and press the spacebar.

4. Press F5 to place an undefined field within the text object at the cursor position. Now press the spacebar again and press F5 once more.

5. Type a colon (:), press ↵ a couple of times, then type a few sentences. (You can add more fields, if you wish, by pressing F5.)

6. Press Esc to select the text object. (This makes it easier to complete Step 7.)

7. Select and inspect the first undefined field, select Define Field, and choose the Mr/Mrs field from the property menu. Then inspect the second undefined field and choose the Last Name field. Your screen will resemble Figure 11.14.

Now preview the report by clicking the View Data button in the SpeedBar. *Voilà*! You see the beginnings of a form letter like the one in Figure 11.15. Notice how smoothly the field data integrates with the text. All it needs now is some more text, a page break to separate each letter, and perhaps a few embellishments.

FIGURE 11.14

Fields embedded in a
text object in the
Report Design window

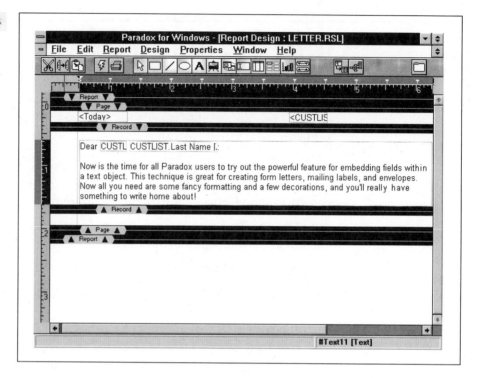

In "Designing a Mail Merge Document," later in this chapter, we'll talk
more about how you can use the basic technique of embedding fields in
a text object to create fancy form letters, mailing labels, and envelopes
that rival any you could design in a word processing package.

TIP

This technique also works in forms, though you have
less control over the spacing between text and field
objects.

FIGURE 11.15

The sample form letters produced by the design in Figure 11.14

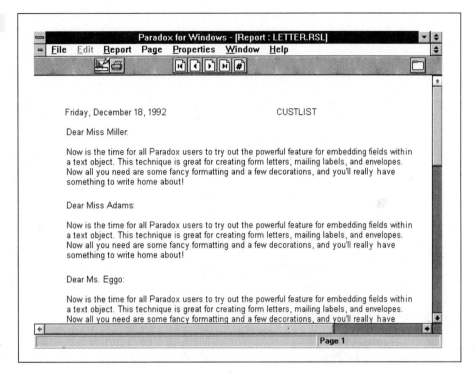

Controlling Headers, Footers, and Repeated Data

Let's turn our attention now to the many ways you can control how and when Paradox prints these sections of a report:

- Report headers
- Page headers and footers
- Group headers

- Repeated group values in the record band
- Objects in group headers
- Table headers

Printing Report Headers

Normally, the report header objects print before the page header on the first page of the report. If you prefer to have the report header appear *after* the first page header, inspect the report header band and *uncheck* the Precede Page Header property.

NOTE   Changing the Precede Page Header property has no effect in the Report Design window (since the bands don't move); however, when you preview the report, you'll see the order you've specified.

Printing Page Headers and Footers on the First Page

Paradox usually prints the page header and footer objects on the first page of the report, but you can change this. For example, you may wish to suppress the page header or footer on the first page if your report header includes graphics or other information that clashes with the page header or footer.

To prevent the page header from printing on the first page, inspect the page header band and *uncheck* Print On 1st Page. To prevent the page footer from printing on the first page, inspect the page footer band and *uncheck* Print On 1st Page.

Printing Group Headers

Recall that every group band actually consists of a group header and a group footer. When you place a field or object in the group header, Paradox prints that information at the top of each group. For instance, rather than including the credit limit and state in each record of a telephone directory that's grouped by those fields, you could omit the fields from the table and place them in their respective group bands instead, as we did in Figure 11.12.

When Paradox must split a group of records across two or more pages, it normally prints the group header again at the top of the next page. If you prefer to print the group headings only at the beginning of the group, inspect the group band and choose Headings ➤ Group Only. To return to the default setting, where headings appear both at the top of the page and at the beginning of the group, inspect the group band and choose Headings ➤ Page And Group.

Printing Repeated Group Values

When your record band contains fields that are also used to group the data, you may wish to suppress repeated values within the group. For example, if you're grouping data by state and have included the State field in the record band, you can have Paradox display the state in each record or only when the state changes.

Normally, Paradox prints repeated values in every record. To print only the *first* occurrence of repeated data, choose Report ➤ Group Repeats (this checks the Group Repeats option). For example, in Figure 11.16 we created a simple report, grouped it by the States field, Last Name, First Name, and M.I., then checked the Report ➤ Group Repeats option. Notice how the state names CA, MI, and NM appear only in the first record of each group of records for those states. Likewise, duplicate customer names are not repeated.

Conditionally Printing Objects in Group Headers

You can control when Paradox displays objects in the group's header band by inspecting objects and changing the Conditional property. The

FIGURE 11.16

In this report, which is grouped by State, Last Name, First Name, and M.I., the Report ➤ Group Repeats option is checked to prevent duplicate state and customer names from printing.

Friday, December 18, 1992   CUSTLIST   Page 1

Last Name	First Name	Phone	Extension	City	State
Adams	Andy	555-0123	35	San Diego	CA
Miller	Maria	555-3423		Los Angeles	
Smith	Mary	555-9545		Los Angeles	
Zastrow	Ruth	555-5948		La Jolla	
Zeepers	Zeke	555-7765	11	Encinitas	

Last Name	First Name	Phone	Extension	City	State
Rosiello	Richard	555-1234		Chicago	IL

Last Name	First Name	Phone	Extension	City	State
Adams	Anita	555-4354	125	Silver Spring	MD

Last Name	First Name	Phone	Extension	City	State
Watson	Frank	555-2234	5678	Bangor	ME

Last Name	First Name	Phone	Extension	City	State
Smith	John	555-9342		Holland	MI
	Savitha	555-0323	7	Ossineke	

Last Name	First Name	Phone	Extension	City	State
Olson	Elizabeth	555-9423		Marlow	NH

Last Name	First Name	Phone	Extension	City	State
Leventhal	Danielle	555-9853		Newark	NJ

Last Name	First Name	Phone	Extension	City	State
Eggo	Sandy	555-5034		Roswell	NM
Newell	John	555-9089		Bernalillo	

Last Name	First Name	Phone	Extension	City	State
Gladstone	Tara Rose	555-4343	55	New York	NY

Last Name	First Name	Phone	Extension	City	State
Ramirez	Rigoberto	555-0987		Wyandotte	OK

Last Name	First Name	Phone	Extension	City	State
Jones	Alma	555-8395	555	Ashland	OR

Conditional options are as follows:

Print At Group & Page (default setting) Paradox displays the group header object at the beginning of each group and at the top of each page, regardless of whether a group breaks across pages.

Print Only At Group Paradox displays the group header object at the beginning of each group, but not at the top of each page, unless a group begins at the top of the page.

Print Only At Page Paradox displays the group header object at the top of the page whenever a group breaks across pages, but never displays the object on the first page of the report.

Repeating a Table Header across Pages

When a table breaks across the pages of a report, you can choose whether or not to repeat the header at the top of each page. Normally, headers are repeated, but if you want to prevent this, inspect the table and uncheck the Repeat Header property.

NOTE Repeat Header will not be available if you checked the table's Detach Header property.

Using Run Time Properties

Paradox gives you considerable control over the behavior of objects and report bands when you print or preview a report. As for forms, the available properties depend on the type of object you're inspecting. To change Run Time properties, inspect an object or band, choose Run Time, then select the property you want from the submenu.

NOTE   Few Run Time properties have an obvious effect in the Report Design window.

Shrinkable and Breakable

All bands have the *Breakable* and *Shrinkable* properties. When Run Time ➤ Breakable is checked, Paradox can move some objects in the band to a new page if they don't all fit at the bottom of the current page. When this option is unchecked, Paradox keeps all objects in the band together, moving them to the next page if there isn't enough room for all of them at the bottom of the current page.

When Run Time ➤ Shrinkable is checked, Paradox will squeeze out extra white space below the last object in a band that falls at the bottom of a page. Shrinking may be necessary when all objects in the band will fit on the page, but there isn't enough room to print the white space following those objects.

NOTE   By default, both Breakable and Shrinkable are checked, and Paradox attempts to shrink the band before breaking it.

Objects also have a Breakable and Shrinkable property. If you uncheck Run Time ➤ Breakable for an object, the object will be pushed to the next page if it doesn't fit at the bottom of the current page. With the option checked, the object can be broken at the bottom of the page, with the remainder printed at the top of the next page. Similarly, checking Run Time ➤ Shrinkable allows Paradox to clip off the white space at the bottom of an object if the object would be small enough to print at the bottom of the page without the white space below it.

NOTE When both Shrinkable and Breakable are checked, Shrinkable takes precedence over Breakable. Paradox will never break a record across a page.

Pinning Objects at Run Time

Certain objects, such as tables, fields, multi-record objects, and graphs, fill with data when you run a report—growing or shrinking as necessary. As objects resize, they push or pull other objects on the page. You can prevent an object from being pushed horizontally or vertically by checking the Run Time ➤ Pin Horizontal or Run Time ➤ Pin Vertical properties (initially these properties are turned off). For example, in Figure 11.17 the Horizontal property is unchecked for the dart graphic, but checked for the gift box graphic. This means that the dart will float horizontally as the address field shrinks or grows, while the gift graphic stays put.

FIGURE 11.17

The dart graphic is not pinned horizontally, but the gift box is. Notice how the dart is pushed to the right as the address expands or shrinks, while the gift box stays at the same horizontal position. (Word wrap is turned off in the address field.)

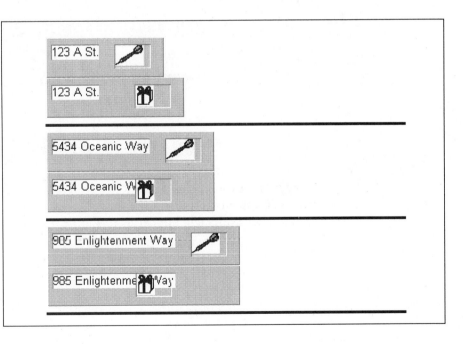

Be aware that pinning an object that might otherwise be pushed can cause an expanding object to cover up the pinned object, as in Figure 11.17. One way to solve this problem is to place the pinned object in back by selecting it and choosing Design ➤ Send To Back. You could also move the pinned object further to the right, so that it's less likely to get in the way.

Aligning Pushed Objects and Keeping Them Together

As you may recall, you can use the Design ➤ Align options in the Design window menus to align objects with respect to one another. However, some objects may be pushed out of alignment when you run the report. You can solve this problem with invisible lines or boxes.

For example, in Figure 11.18 the dinosaur graphic is pushed to the right by the address field, but the empty box is not. To keep those objects together, place a line the length of the two objects just to the left of the objects, as shown below.

Now inspect the line and check the Run Time ➤ Invisible property (the line will appear dotted on the screen). When you print or preview the report, the results will appear as in Figure 11.19.

FIGURE 11.18

Objects may not align
as expected when you
run your report

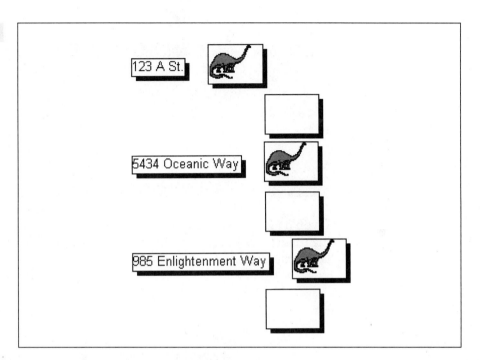

TIP

If you want to display the line, don't check Run Time ➤
Invisible for the line. The objects to the right of the line
will still be pushed together.

You can also use horizontal lines to push objects. For example, the
horizontal line in the design below will push both the dinosaur and the
empty box as the table expands. Without this line, only the dinosaur will
move down to accommodate the expanding table. (We've left the Invisible
property unchecked so that you can see the horizontal line.)

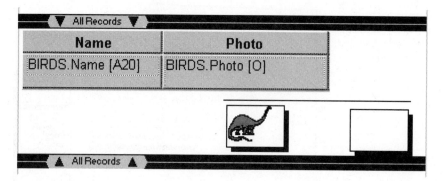

If you'd like to have Paradox push *and* pull objects together, try surrounding them with an invisible box and turn off the box's Run Time ➤ Breakable property.

FIGURE 11.19

The report in Figure 11.18, after using an invisible line to control alignment

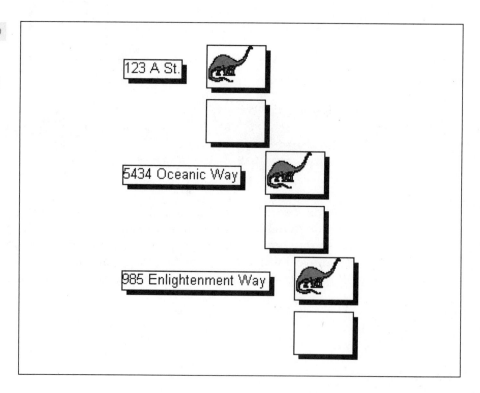

Fitting Height and Width

Paradox for Windows can grow or shrink boxes, text, ellipses, and field objects to fit their contents when you run a report, or it can keep these objects their original size.

If you turn off the Run Time ➤ Fit Height or Run Time ➤ Fit Width properties, the objects will retain their original height or width when you run the report. Turning these properties on (the default settings) allows Paradox to shrink or expand the height or width to fit their contents.

Figure 11.20 shows what happens when you preview a design in which the Run Time ➤ Fit Height property is turned off for the gray box to the right of the vertical line, and turned on for the box to the left. Notice how the boxes on the left expand to fit the word-wrapped address field. The vertical line shows the original height of the box.

FIGURE 11.20

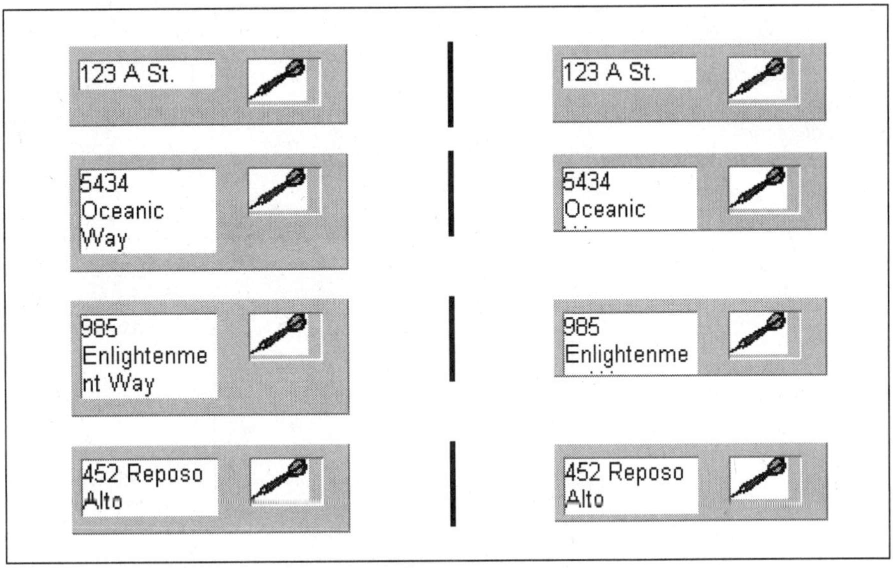

The right side of the figure shows the effects of turning Run Time ➤ Fit Height off.

Showing Records and Columns in Tables and Multitable Objects

To control how Paradox displays repeated records of a table or multi-record object, choose the Run Time ➤ Show All Records property. When Show All Records is turned on (the default setting), Paradox expands the object vertically down the page, creating as many pages as necessary to display all the records. When you turn this property off, Paradox does not expand the object; instead it repeats the object in the same size and shape until all records are displayed.

Run Time ➤ Show All Records is on for the multi-record object displayed in Figure 11.21, but off for the multi-record object in Figure 11.22.

FIGURE 11.21

A multi-record object with Run Time ➤ Show All Records turned on

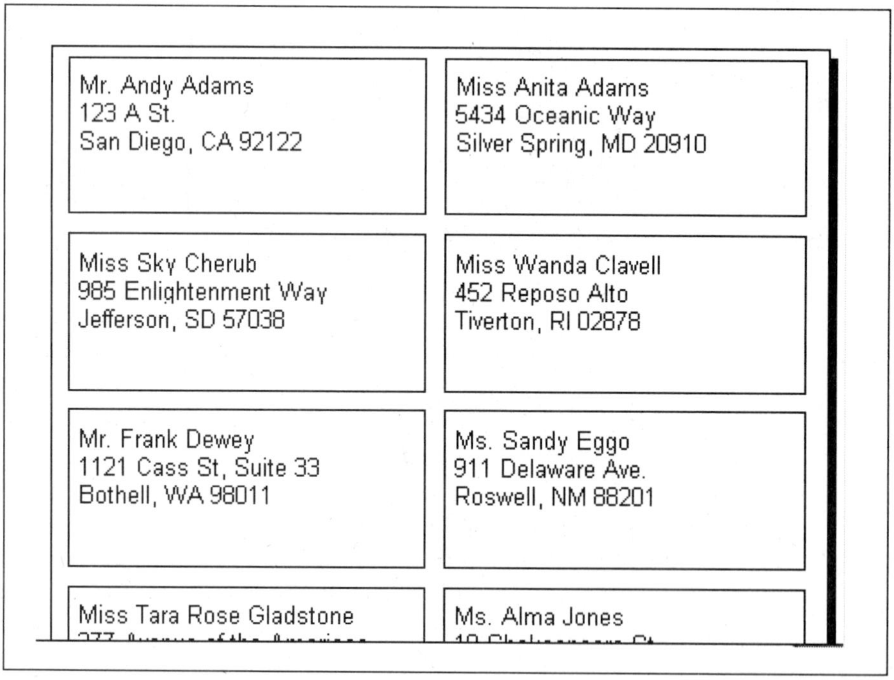

Mr. Andy Adams 123 A St. San Diego, CA 92122	Miss Anita Adams 5434 Oceanic Way Silver Spring, MD 20910
Miss Sky Cherub 985 Enlightenment Way Jefferson, SD 57038	Miss Wanda Clavell 452 Reposo Alto Tiverton, RI 02878
Mr. Frank Dewey 1121 Cass St, Suite 33 Bothell, WA 98011	Ms. Sandy Eggo 911 Delaware Ave. Roswell, NM 88201
Miss Tara Rose Gladstone	Ms. Alma Jones

FIGURE 11.22

A multi-record object
with Run Time ➤
Show All Records
turned off

You can also turn the Run Time ➤ Show All Columns property on or off for table frames. When on (checked), the table frame expands to include all the columns. When off, Paradox clips any columns that exceed the page width.

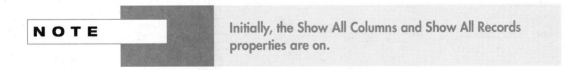

N O T E   Initially, the Show All Columns and Show All Records properties are on.

Deleting Empty Records

Normally, Paradox won't print blank records in table and multi-record objects. If you would like to have *all* records printed (even if they're blank), inspect the record object in the table frame or multi-record object and uncheck Delete When Empty. The sample report in Figure 11.23

FIGURE 11.23

Delete When Empty
removes blank records
when you preview or
print a table or
multi-record object.

shows a multi-record object with the Delete When Empty property checked.
Figure 11.24 shows what happens when this property is not checked and you
preview or print the report.

N O T E *#Record* will appear at the right edge of the status bar
when you've selected a record object.

Special Properties of Text Objects

Text objects have some special properties that are particularly useful when
you're designing form letters, mailing labels, and envelopes. The default
run-time settings are usually perfect for mail merge, so we'll just

FIGURE 11.24

When Delete When
Empty is not checked,
blank records appear
along with those
containing data.

summarize them here. You'll see more examples of these properties later in "Designing a Mail Merge Document."

Controlling Widows and Orphans

Contrary to what you might think, widow and orphan control is not a new government program to keep women and children off the streets. A *widow* is actually a single line of text at the top of the page that has been separated from the paragraph it ends. An *orphan* is a single line of text at the bottom of a page that has been separated from the paragraph it begins.

Paradox will prevent orphans and widows if you inspect a text object and check its Run Time ➤ Orphan/Widow property (this is *not* on by default). If you're designing form letters that might expand to more than one page, it's a good idea to turn this property on.

Controlling Field and Line Squeeze

Field and line squeeze properties are very useful in mail merge documents, where fields embedded within text objects may vary in length or be blank.

When Run Time ➤ Field Squeeze is checked, text to the right of a field object is pulled in or pushed automatically out to fit the width of the field. This prevents unsightly gaps within lines that contain empty fields.

When Run Time ➤ Line Squeeze is checked, blank fields that appear on a line by themselves are ignored, instead of being printed as blank lines. This option is handy when printing mailing labels and form letters with inside addresses that contain some empty fields.

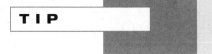

TIP   Paradox will squeeze out extra space between fields that may be blank if you enclose them in a text box.

Designing a Mail Merge Document

As mentioned earlier in this chapter, letters, mailing labels, and envelopes fall into the single category of *mail merge documents*. The only thing that's really special about mail merge documents is that they consist primarily of fields embedded within text objects. Objects placed within the text wrap along with the text and appear as part of the body of text when you print or view the document.

For example, the form letter in Figure 11.25 welcomes new credit customers to a business. Although most of the text is the same for each addressee, the inside address, salutation, credit limit, and start date near the top of the letter contain data that is specific to each individual, and the customer's name appears again in the second paragraph of the letter. (To help you locate the areas where actual field values appear, we've underlined them in Figure 11.25.) Notice how smoothly these fields are integrated into the form letter.

Figure 11.26 shows the top portion of the Report Design window for the welcome form letter. In this illustration, you can see how the field names from the CustList table are interspersed throughout the text. The completed design for this report appears in Figure 11.32.

The steps for beginning mail merge documents are nearly identical to those for creating regular reports. The only difference is that you should select a Blank or Single-Record style in the Design Layout box if you're creating a form letter or envelope, or a Multi-Record style if you're designing mailing labels.

FIGURE 11.25

The welcome letter
that is sent to new
credit customers

Gift
Corner

8891 Gaudy Ave * West Fantasee, CA 92222
1-800-555-GIFT

April 21, 1993

Miss Sky R. Cherub
985 Enlightenment Way
Jefferson, SD 57038

Dear Miss Cherub:

Welcome aboard, Miss Cherub! *The Gift Corner* is pleased to have you as one of our new credit customers. Your credit limit of $10,000.00 is available as of Wednesday, April 14, 1993.

Now that you're firmly established as one of our valued customers, you may want to peruse our exciting new catalog, which is chock full of great gift items. For example, you'll find some terrific ***Toys for Boys***, including hot new race cars in price ranges that are as torrid as the engines under the hoods of these babies. If you're looking for something a bit more tame, try our ***Jungle Creatures Collection*** -- stuffed animals that look like the real thing! And Miss Cherub, if those on your gift list are itching for a holiday, take a look at our ***Exotic Vacation Packages***. We'll guarantee some unforgettable memories! We'll even throw in a free camera, film, and developing so those memories will never be lost.

Free!

*S*o why not call your Account Representative here at *The Gift Corner* today? We'll send you a complimentary gift, just for picking up the phone and talking to us. You can reach us 24-hours a day, toll-free at **1-800-555-GIFT**. Don't delay...Call us today!

Sincerely yours,

Frank Lee Unctuous

Frank Lee Unctuous
Account Manager

FIGURE 11.26

The welcome letter in the Report Design window. We reduced the size of the screen and removed the rulers so you can see more of the document.

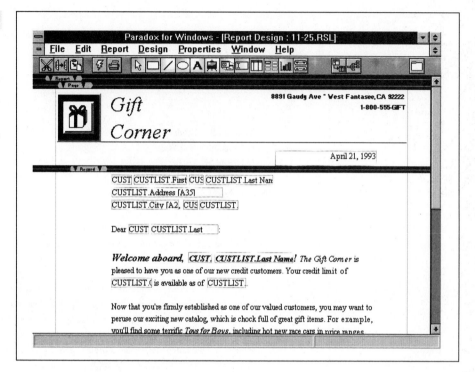

TIP

If you plan to send letters to only a few people on your list, rather than to everyone in a table, you can extract names with a query. You can also use the query to sort your letters.

In the section below, we'll focus on techniques for designing form letters. Later in this chapter, you'll learn how to create mailing labels and custom envelopes.

Getting Started with Form Letters

After reaching the Report Design window, you can set up the report headers, page headers, and groups (if needed), or you can do this after you've designed the body text of the form letter.

The next step is usually to place a text object in the record band by selecting the Text tool and dragging in the report band to define the width of your letter. You needn't worry about how tall the text object is, since Paradox will expand it automatically as you add text and fields to it. Figure 11.27 shows a new text object placed in our design.

TIP

You may want to inspect the text object and choose Vertical Scroll Bar or Design Sizing ➤ Fit Text to facilitate text entry.

Now click in the text object until you see the insertion point. If you want the letter to start with an inside address, don't type anything—just skip to the next section to find out how to place fields and objects. Otherwise, type the text you want to appear before the first field or object within the body text.

FIGURE 11.27

A text object defined in the record band of the Report Design window

Placing Fields and Objects in a Form Letter

You can place fields or other objects into the text of a form letter either before or after you've typed in text. Here are the basic steps:

1. Position the insertion point where you want the new object to appear. You can either position the mouse at the appropriate location or use the cursor positioning keys (the arrow keys, Home, End, Ctrl+Home, Ctrl+End, and so forth).

2. Select the tool you want from the SpeedBar, then click and drag the mouse to define the size of the object. If you're placing a field object, just press F5 as a shortcut.

T I P

To place a field or object on a line by itself, press ↵ at the end of the line above where the object should appear. Then place the field or object and press ↵ again.

Typically, when designing a form letter, you type some text into the document, then place a field or other object wherever you want it to appear within the text. For example, to enter the salutation in the first line of the welcome letter in Figure 11.26, we followed these steps:

• We typed **Dear**, pressed the spacebar, pressed F5, pressed the spacebar, pressed F5, typed a colon, then pressed ↵ twice.

• After creating each line of the salutation, we inspected each field individually and defined it as usual.

NOTE   We could have used the Field tool to place the fields and defined each field name as soon as we placed the field. However, the method described above is quite a bit faster.

From this point, you simply repeat the process of typing text until you need to add a field or object. Then press F5 to add a field or use the Speed-Bar to place other objects. If you discover that you forgot to add an object to the text, it's no problem. Simply move the insertion point to the appropriate position and place the object.

Working with Embedded Objects

Objects embedded in text retain their usual characteristics—that is, you can select them and inspect their properties. However, you can think of them as "super" characters. For example,

- If the insertion point is just to the left of an object, pressing the → key will move the insertion point just after the object. Similarly, pressing the ← key while the insertion point is immediately to the right of an object positions the insertion point just to the left of the object.

- You can delete an object by positioning the insertion point just after the object and pressing the Backspace key. Or, position the insertion point just before the object and press the Del key. (If you inadvertently delete an object, immediately choose Edit ➤ Undo or press Alt+Backspace.)

- Press ↵ to add blank lines after existing text and objects and before new text and objects.

- Just as when typing characters into the document, you can only add objects just before or after existing text or within existing text. Thus, if your text object contains only two short lines, you cannot place an object at the lower-right corner of the text object.

While you're working in a text object that contains embedded fields, you may need to go back and select one of the objects, perhaps to redefine it, resize it, or change its properties. When the mouse pointer is an insertion point, you can't simply click on an object since doing so merely repositions the insertion point. To get around this problem, press the Esc key, then click on the object you want. You can then Shift+click to select additional objects within the text. As usual, handles will appear around the selected object. You can then resize the object, inspect and change its properties, delete the object by pressing the Del key, or copy or cut it to the Clipboard.

Although you can drag a selected object to a new position in the text, it's difficult to do so accurately. Therefore, it's best to select the object, cut or copy it to the Clipboard, position the insertion point where you want the object to appear, then paste the object from the Clipboard. (If you'd rather, you can delete the object and create it again in its new position.)

Preventing Unwanted Blank Spaces

Certain field properties cooperate with text properties to provide smooth insertion of fields within text. For example, the Run Time ➤ Fit Width and Run Time ➤ Fit Height properties are activated for fields automatically, so that field objects shrink or expand to fit the data they contain. At the same time, the Run Time ➤ Line Squeeze and Run Time ➤ Field Squeeze text properties eliminate any undesirable white space surrounding inserted fields. (As mentioned earlier, Field Squeeze closes up the text around the field data, while Line Squeeze causes Paradox to ignore blank lines.)

These field and text Run Time properties are automatically active (checked) when you create a text object. If you have problems fitting text around field data, or your document contains unwanted blank spaces or lines, you might want to inspect the text and field Run Time properties to see if you changed them accidentally.

NOTE Although it's often easier to create a text object first, and then embed fields or other objects inside, it is possible to draw a text object around existing fields. We'll show you the steps for doing this in a later section, "Creating Mailing Labels."

Sorting Your Output

Any of the sorting techniques presented earlier will sort mail merge documents. Thus, you can sort the table first, base your mail merge design on a query, or use group bands.

WARNING Be sure to sort your letters and envelopes in the same order. Otherwise, you'll have to match each printed letter with its correct envelope manually.

Creating Mailing Labels

Many people use database packages to print mailing labels from tables, and Paradox for Windows' multi-record objects are ideal for printing on the many varieties of labels used with laser and dot matrix printers. Figure 11.28 shows a page of printed labels for the CustList table, while the design used for the labels appears in Figure 11.29.

Before beginning your mailing label design, you should figure out the following:

- Which table you need to use
- The size, layout, and margins of the label sheets
- The height and width of each label
- The number of columns of labels across the page and the amount of space separating each label

FIGURE 11.28

A sample page of
sheet labels for the
CustList table

Mr. Andy A. Adams ABC Corporation 123 A St. San Diego, CA 92122	Miss Anita Q. Adams 5434 Oceanic Way Silver Spring, MD 20910	Miss Sky R. Cherub Oneness Well-Being 985 Enlightenment Way Jefferson, SD 57038
Miss Wanda T. Clavell Westridge Convent 452 Reposo Alto Tiverton, RI 02878	Mr. Frank R. Dewey Dewey, Cheatham, and Howe 1121 Cass St, Suite 33 Bothell, WA 98011	Ms. Sandy Eggo Pancho's Restaurant 911 Delaware Ave. Roswell, NM 88201
Miss Tara Rose Gladstone Waterside Landscaping 377 Avenue of the Americas New York, NY 12345	Ms. Alma R. Jones Ashland Flowers 10 Shakespeare St. Ashland, OR 98765	Mr. David E. Kenney Felson and Fabian 6771 Ocean View Dr. Anderson, SC 29621
Miss Danielle D. Leventhal Garden State Bagels 765 Tour de Force Way Newark, NJ 02321	Miss Maria N. Miller Zeerocks, Inc. 1234 Corporate Hwy. Los Angeles, CA 91245	Mrs. Mary M. Mohr 6771 Baldy Vista Herndon, VA 22071-1234
Mr. John J. Newell Newell Construction 212 Riverside Way Bernalillo, NM 88004	Mrs. Elizabeth A. Olson Precision Computer Arts 80486 Mill Street Marlow, NH 03456	Mr. Rigoberto R. Ramirez 4323 Moonglow Dr. Wyandotte, OK 74370
Mr. Richard L. Rosiello Raydontic Labs P.O. Box 77112 Chicago, IL 60606	Dr. Susita M. Schumack Physician's Hospital P.O. Box 11221 Philadelphia, PA 23456	Mr. John Q. Smith 65 Overton Hwy, Box 112 Holland, MI 49423
Dr. Mary K. Smith Cal State L.A. P.O. Box 1234 Los Angeles, CA 91234	Dr. Savitha V. Smith Slybacks Paperbacks 767 Ocean View Lane Ossineke, MI 49766	Ms. Janet L. Smythe P.O. Box 3384 Seattle, WA 98762
Mr. Frank R. Watson Whispering Palms Golf Club 8775 Concha de Golf Bangor, ME 01876	Dr. Ted Wilson Pine Valley University P.O. Box 463 Seattle, WA 98103	Dr. Ruth Zastrow Scripps Clinic 4331 La Jolla Scenic Dr. La Jolla, CA 92037
Mr. Zeke A. Zeepers Virtual Reality Designs 5409 Crest Dr. Encinitas, CA 92024		

WARNING

Be sure to use mailing labels that are suitable for your printer. In particular, avoid using continuous forms designed for dot matrix printers with laser printers, because laser printers get very hot and can be damaged if the adhesive backing of the labels melts.

FIGURE 11.29

The multi-record report design for the CustList mailing labels shown in Figure 11.28. We based this design on a query that sorts the CustList table by the customer name field.

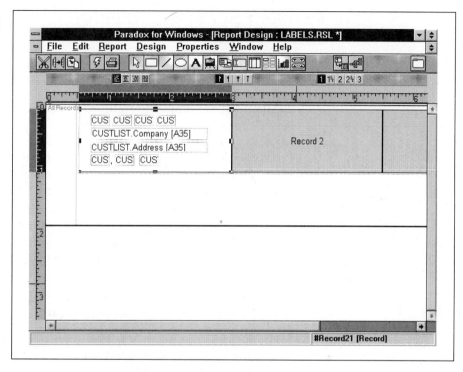

The best way to learn how to create mailing labels is to try it for yourself. So, in this example, we'll design labels based on the CustList table, using the Mr/Mrs, First Name, M.I., Last Name, Company, Address, City, State, and Zip Code fields. We'll assume the label sheet contains three columns and ten rows of labels, with half-inch margins around the edges of each page. Each label is 2.5 inches wide and one inch tall, and there is no vertical or horizontal space between labels.

WARNING   The fields you select must fit the measurements of your labels, so don't pick too many!

Defining the Initial Mailing Label Design

Listed below are the basic steps for defining an initial design for the labels.

1. Create a new query that sorts the CustList table by the customer's last name, first name, and middle initial. To do so, choose File ➤ New ➤ Query, and choose the CustList table. When the Query window appears, check every field in the query table. Next choose Properties ➤ Answer Table ➤ Sort, double-click the Last Name, First Name, and M.I. fields (in that order) in the Available Fields area of the **Sort Answer** dialog box (see Chapter 8), and choose OK. Test your query by clicking the Run Query button in the SpeedBar or by pressing F8. Now click on the Query window, choose File ➤ Save, type **CustSort**, and choose OK. Finally, close all the windows (choose Window ➤ Close All).

2. Create a new report (File ➤ New ➤ Report), click the Type drop-down list in the **Data Model** dialog box, select <Queries>, then select CUSTSORT.QBE and choose OK.

3. In the **Design Layout** dialog box, choose a Multi-Record design style, remove the check mark from the Labeled Fields options, then click the Select Fields button and choose the fields you want.

4. When you get back to the Design Layout dialog box, click Page Layout and make sure the margins are set to 0.50 all around. Choose OK twice to get to the Report Design window.

Getting Rid of the Page Bands

Now that you've reached the Design window, maximize it, choose Properties ➤ Zoom ➤ Fit Width, then delete the Date, Table Name, and Page Number field objects from the page header band. Close up the page header and footer bands, then zoom back in to 100% magnification.

NOTE You can hide the band labels by choosing <u>P</u>roperties ➤ Band L<u>a</u>bels.

Squeezing Fields and Lines

If you preview your document now, you'll see that the design doesn't look at all right because the fields aren't squeezed properly. To solve this problem, you need to surround some of the fields by a text object.

1. Select the Mr/Mrs, First Name, M.I., and Last Name fields, then choose <u>D</u>esign ➤ Adjust <u>S</u>ize ➤ Minimum <u>W</u>idth.

2. Drag the selected fields slightly to the right.

3. Now drag First Name to the right of Mr/Mrs, drag M.I. to the right of First Name, and drag Last Name to the right of M.I., as shown below. Don't worry about keeping the fields lined up perfectly. This step just gives you some extra room to draw a text object around all the fields.

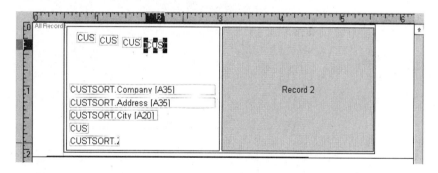

4. Choose the Text tool in the SpeedBar and drag the text object outline so that it surrounds the fields completely and is nearly as wide as the master record. When you release the mouse button, the fields will bunch up next to one another, as shown below.

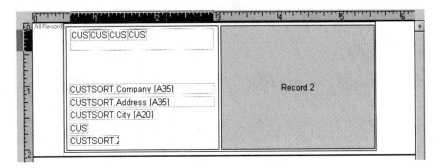

5. Inspect the text object and choose Design Sizing ➤ Fit Text.

6. Select the Company and Address fields and drag them immediately below the name fields you just placed.

7. Repeat Steps 1 through 5 for the City, State, and Zip Code fields. You should get the results shown below.

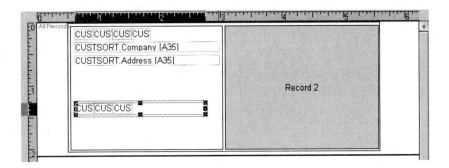

8. Drag the text object containing the City, State, and Zip Code fields just below the address.

9. Press Esc to select the Record object, then choose Edit ➤ Select All to select all four lines of the mailing label.

10. Align the objects at the left by choosing Design ➤ Align ➤ Left. Next, choose Design ➤ Adjust Spacing ➤ Vertical to even up the vertical spacing between lines.

Save your report with the name *labels*, preview the document, then return to the Report Design window.

NOTE

As a shortcut, we could have embedded all the fields in a single text object, pressed ↵ after each line of the label, and added punctuation as described below. However, the method used here takes advantage of the Run Time ➤ Fit Height property of fields, which prevents Paradox from printing blank lines when all the fields in a line are empty. For example, many of our records have a blank Company field, which is squeezed out in the mailing labels shown in Figure 11.28.

Adding Punctuation between Fields

When previewing your labels, you probably noticed that the fields in the first and last lines appeared next to one another, without any space or punctuation between them. Now it's time to remedy that problem.

To place spaces after each word in the addressee's name (the first line of the label), select the text object at the top of the mailing label and click just inside the object's right border so that you see the blinking insertion point. Press Ctrl+Home to move to the beginning of the text object. Now press → and type a space. Repeat this last step until all the name fields are properly separated in the first line.

Placing punctuation in the City, State, and Zip Code line is done almost the same way. This time, select the text object in the last line of the mailing label and click inside the right border to place the insertion point. Press Ctrl+Home, then press → to move past the City field, type a comma, and press the spacebar. Press → to move past the State field, then type one or two spaces to separate the State and Zip Code.

In Chapter 17 you'll learn how to refine the punctuation with conditional logic.

Your multi-record object should now resemble the example below.

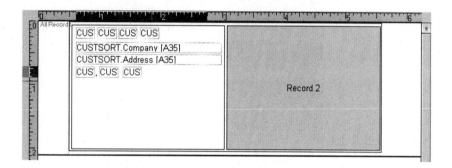

Now save your report again, preview the report to see your progress, then switch back to the Design window.

Making Your Report Fit the Labels

Now you're ready to resize the report so it fits the dimensions of your labels. This involves changing the record layout to match the spacing between labels and the number of labels across, changing the height of the multi-record region to match the height of one label, and resizing the width of the record region to fit the dimensions of the label.

If you haven't done so already, now is a good time to hide the band labels.

Your first job is to change the *record layout*—the amount of space between labels and the number of labels across. Select the Record object (you'll see *#Record* in the status bar) and make it slightly narrower by dragging its right edge to the left. Now, inspect the record and choose Record Layout.

Change the values in the dialog box to match those below (or whatever fits the labels you're using).

Choose OK when you're finished with the Record Layout dialog box. The multi-record object will be resized to include a third record.

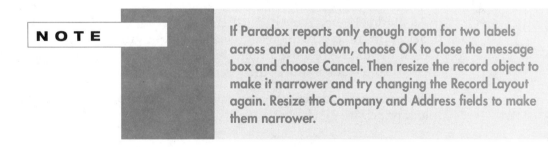

NOTE

If Paradox reports only enough room for two labels across and one down, choose OK to close the message box and choose Cancel. Then resize the record object to make it narrower and try changing the Record Layout again. Resize the Company and Address fields to make them narrower.

Next, change the *height* of your mailing labels by selecting the bottom border of the record (not the multi-record region) and resizing it to one inch. Watch the left side of the status bar as you resize. Release the mouse when you've resized to 1.00 inch. The records will readjust as shown below.

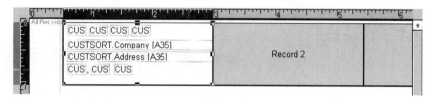

Now resize the width of the label, dragging the right border of the record until it matches the width of one label (2.5 inches in our example), as indicated in the status bar.

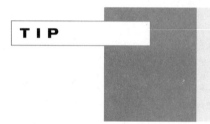

TIP

If Paradox only lets you resize the label to about 2.46 inches, try selecting the multi-record object (click in the gray record area), and press ← a few times until the record won't move any more. Then try resizing the right border of the record again.

Next, select the four mailing label lines and center them within the record frame (you may need to reduce the width of some of the lines). Preview and make any required adjustments.

As the final step, you need to remove the frames around the records: Select the multi-record object (click one of the gray records), Ctrl+right-click the mouse, choose Frame ➤ Style from the property menu, then choose the blank frame at the top of the list.

Now preview your report again, make any desired adjustments, then save and print your labels.

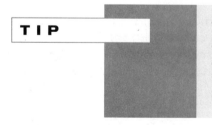

TIP

To avoid wasting expensive labels, print your test runs on plain paper. Then place the printed report in front of a page of blank labels (lining the pages up exactly) and hold the pages up to a light to see the label outlines behind the printed samples.

Creating Envelopes

If your laser printer can print envelopes, either with an envelope tray or manual feed, you can design a report to print custom envelopes. Figure 11.30 shows an envelope printed with Paradox for Windows that includes a company logo, return address, and the customer's mailing address. The design for this envelope appears in Figure 11.31.

FIGURE 11.30

A sample envelope, including company logo, return address, and the customer's mailing address

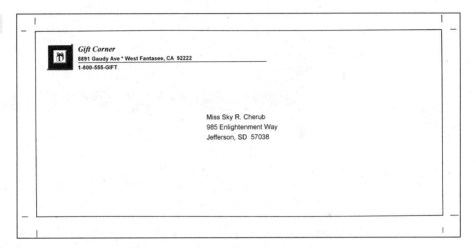

Designing for a standard number 10 envelope (9 $\frac{1}{2}$ inches by 4 1/8 inches) is easy. Just follow the steps below to get started.

1. Create a new report by choosing File ➤ New ➤ Report, then choose a table or query.

2. When you reach the **Design Layout** dialog box, follow these steps:

   • Choose a Single-Record style, turn off field labels, and select the fields you want to use.
   • Click the Page Layout button and define your page layout. Choose *Landscape* orientation and paper size *Envelope #10*.
   • Click OK twice to get to the Report Design window.

FIGURE 11.31

The design of the sample envelope shown in Figure 11.30

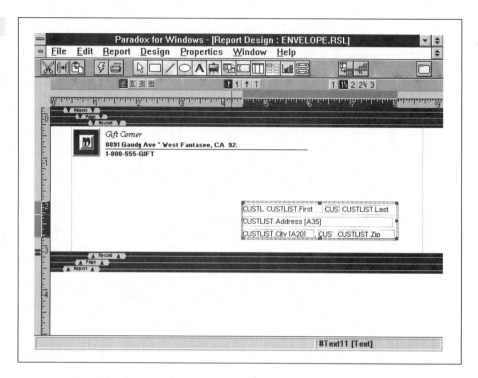

NOTE

Because many laser printers have "dead zones" where they cannot print, you may need to adjust the margins in the Page Layout dialog box (however, the default settings work for most printers). For example, if your printer has a dead zone of 0.25 inch at the left and right edges of the page, make sure your margins are at least that wide.

When you reach the Report Design window, remove the fields from the page header and close the page header and footer bands as for labels. Then use the techniques discussed above for mailing labels to design the addressee information.

Here are some additional guidelines:

• Position the addressee lines so that the first line begins about 2 inches from the top of the record band and 4.5 inches from the left edge.

• Place the inside address and any graphic logos at the upper-left corner of the record band, as in Figure 11.31.

• Place a page break at the bottom of the record band.

When you've completed your design, save it, then preview and print the envelopes.

NOTE   If printing doesn't begin right away, check to see whether your laser printer is prompting you to insert an envelope. You may need to push a "Continue" button or perform some other action to start printing. See your printer manual for details.

Changing Report Design Window Properties

As you know, the Properties menu in the Design window provides several options for controlling the appearance and behavior of the window. After setting the properties, you can save them by choosing Properties ➤ Report Options ➤ Save Defaults. If you change your mind immediately, you can choose Properties ➤ Report Options ➤ Restore Defaults to undo the most recent Save Defaults. The property settings become permanent when you exit Paradox.

N O T E   Although you can't restore properties after exiting Paradox, you can easily reset any property you wish, then choose Properties ➤ Report Options ➤ Save Defaults again.

Printing Report Documents

Paradox offers several ways to print reports and designs. These are outlined in the sections below.

Printing Your Report Design

You may find it handy to print the report design, which shows all the objects and bands in the report. To begin, make sure you're in the Report Design window, then choose File ➤ Print ➤ Design or Report ➤ Print ➤ Design.

The **Print File** dialog box appears with the page options preselected to print only the first page (and without Overflow Handling options). Click OK to begin printing the design as it appears in the Design window. Figure 11.32 shows the design for the sample form letter presented earlier in this chapter. As with forms, field names in the printed report design may appear garbled if Paradox cannot fit them in the space allotted. This appearance is normal, and it will not adversely affect the output of your report.

FIGURE 11.32

A sample design for
the form letter in
Figure 11.25

▼ Report ▼
▼ Page ▼

Gift
Corner

8891 Gaudy Ave * West Fantasee, CA 92222
1-800-555-GIFT

April 21, 1993

▼ Record ▼

CUST CUSTLIST.First CU CUSTLIST.Last Na
CUSTLIST.Address [A35]
CUSTLIST.City [A2 , CU CUSTLIST

Dear CUST CUSTLIST.Last
Name [A20]

Welcome aboard, CUST CUSTLIST.Last Na ! *The Gift Corner* is
pleased to have you as one of our new credit customers. Your credit limit of
CUSTLIST. is available as of CUSTLIST .

Now that you're firmly established as one of our valued customers, you may want to
peruse our exciting new catalog, which is chock full of great gift items. For example,
you'll find some terrific *Toys for Boys*, including hot new race cars in price ranges
that are as torrid as the engines under the hoods of these babies. If you're looking for
something a bit more tame, try our *Jungle Creatures Collection* -- stuffed animals
that look like the real thing! And CUST CUSTLIST.Last Na , if those on your gift
list are itching for a holiday, take a look at our *Exotic Vacation Packages*. We'll
 Free! guarantee some unforgettable memories! We'll even throw in a free camera, film, and
developing so those memories will never be lost.

*S*o why not call your Account Representative here at *The Gift Corner* today? We'll
send you a complimentary gift, just for picking up the phone and talking to us. You
can reach us 24-hours a day, toll-free at **1-800-555-GIFT**. Don't delay...Call us
today!

Sincerely yours,

Frank Lee Unctuous

Frank Lee Unctuous
Account Manager

▲ Record ▲
▲ Page ▲
▲ Report ▲

NOTE　The page break at the bottom of the record band does not appear in Figure 11.32, though it is present in the actual form design. Page breaks force Paradox to start each record's form letter on a new page.

Printing Your Records

Paradox for Windows offers several ways to print a report in the layout specified by its design. Your options are as follows:

* Click the Print button in the SpeedBar of either the Report Design or Report window.
* Choose File ➤ Print ➤ Report from either window.
* Choose Report ➤ Print ➤ Report from either window.

If you don't want to modify the design or view the data before printing, you can also print from the **Open Document** dialog box that appears when you choose File ➤ Open ➤ Report. After selecting the report name, simply choose the Print option in the Open Mode area of the dialog box, change the table, if you wish, then choose OK.

While previewing the report, you can also print the current page by choosing File ➤ Print ➤ Page or Report ➤ Print ➤ Current Page.

TIP　You can use the buttons in the SpeedBar or options on the Page menu of the Report window to move to and view any page in your report.

All of the methods listed above produce the **Print File** dialog box (although the dialog box won't include an Overflow Handling area if you're printing only the current page). Choose the appropriate print options, as described in Chapter 6, then choose OK to begin printing.

Restarting the Print Job

As a general rule, any report that you print and distribute should contain the latest and greatest information. However, if you operate in a multi-user (network) environment, someone else might edit the data before the report has finished printing.

Fortunately, Paradox lets you decide how to proceed if data changes while your report is printing. To select an option, choose Report ➤ Restart Options from the Report Design window. You'll see the **Restart Options** dialog box shown below.

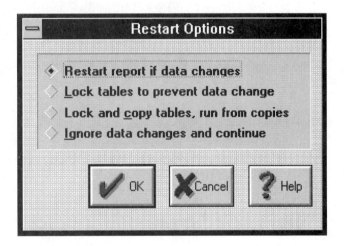

Your Restart options are described below.

> **Restart report if data changes**   Starts printing the report over again if data changes, regenerating queries if necessary. This is the default option and the best choice if you're sure no one will be editing your table data while the report is printing. (This option is not available for dBASE tables.)

> **Lock tables to prevent data change**   Prevents other users from editing the table while your report is printing. Paradox immediately releases the lock when printing is complete. If the lock fails, you should stop the report, then start it again later.

NOTE *Lock tables to prevent data change is the least polite of the restart options, and you should use it sparingly to remain in the good graces of other network users.*

Lock and copy tables, run from copies Locks everyone out just long enough to copy the tables to disk. Paradox uses the copied version of your table(s) to print the report, deleting the copies when printing is complete. This option is more considerate of other users since copying to disk is faster than printing an entire report. However, reports on large tables can require a lot of disk space, and it's still possible that someone could change the original table data while your report is printing from the copy.

Ignore data changes and continue This is the fastest option, because the report continues even if someone changes the data during printing. This option is useful for rough reports where accuracy and consistency are not a top concern. (This is the default option for dBASE tables.)

Choose the option that's best for your report (and your colleagues), then choose OK.

Tips for Faster Printing

The speed of printing reports can be influenced by many factors, especially in a multi-user environment. Here are some tips to speed up report printing:

* Turn on the Windows Print Manager whenever you're printing to a local printer, or when printing small to medium-sized reports on a network.

* Turn off the Windows Print Manager when you're printing a large document on a network. This prevents Paradox from sending the report to the Print Manager first, saving both time and memory.

Delivering a Report Document

Like forms, reports can be delivered so that users can print and preview them, but not make any changes. To prevent others from changing your report design, open it in the Report Design window, then choose Report ➤ Deliver. Paradox will create a report with the same name as the original, but with an .rdl extension. For example, if your original form is named *custrept.rsl*, the delivered version will be named *custrept.rdl*. You can then give the .rdl file to other users.

> **WARNING**   Don't discard your original .rsl file, or *you* won't be able to change the report.

If you need to change the report later, just modify the original report file (with the .rsl extension), choose Report ➤ Deliver again, then distribute the updated .rdl file once more.

In this chapter, you've learned special techniques for creating custom reports, form letters, mailing labels, and envelopes. The most important differences between report and form design involve the use of report bands to separate your data into sections and group data, the expanded Run Time properties available for report objects, and the extra field- and line-squeezing that result when you surround fields and other objects within a text object.

In the next chapter, you'll learn how graphs and crosstabs can be used to analyze, summarize, and present large amounts of data in an attractive and useful form. After mastering the skills presented in Chapters 9 through 12, you'll be well on your way to designing just about any document you can imagine. When you're ready to create advanced forms and reports, turn to Chapter 17 to learn how to set up multitable documents and use summary and calculated fields.

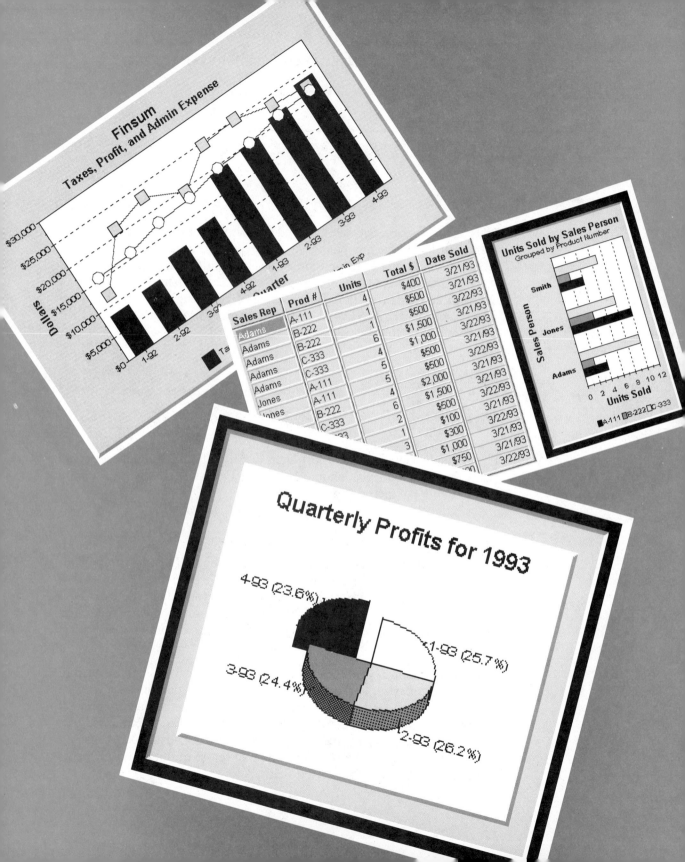

CHAPTER

12

Graphing Your Data

fast TRACK

● **To control whether titles, axes, labels, and legends
    appear**   **642**

  inspect the graph, select Options, and select one of the Show
  options on the menu.

● **To add a crosstab to a form**   **664**

  click the Crosstab tool in the Design window SpeedBar, click
  in your design, and drag to define the size of the crosstab.

● **To create a new "crosstab-only" document**   **665**

  click the Quick Crosstab button in the Table window's Speed-
  Bar. Or, create a new form and choose a Blank style in the
  Design Layout dialog box. When you reach the Design win-
  dow, use the Crosstab tool to place the crosstab.

● **To inspect an entire crosstab object**   **666**

  select the crosstab, move the mouse pointer to an empty area
  at the upper-left corner of the crosstab, then right-click.

● **To inspect a crosstab "hot zone"**   **667**

  select the crosstab, move the mouse pointer to an empty area
  inside the boundaries of the hot zone, and right-click.

● **To define the Categories, Column, and Summaries for
    a crosstab**   **668**

  inspect the crosstab, choose Define Crosstab, click the header
  (...) of the list that appears, and fill in the **Define Crosstab**
  dialog box.

PARADOX offers you a whole new way to analyze and summarize your table data, either visually in *graphs* or in spreadsheet formats called cross-tabulations (or *crosstabs* for short). Graphs and crosstabs are handy for digging out the hidden treasures of information that are so often buried under mountains of data.

The techniques used to design graphs and crosstabs are extensions of concepts presented in Chapters 9 through 11. Just remember that graphs and crosstabs are simply objects within a design document—just like boxes, tables, fields, and so forth. Once created, they can be moved, resized, copied, deleted, and customized in plain or fancy flavors.

In this chapter, you'll discover how easy it is to plot data on graphs and to refine graphs to your own specifications. You'll find a rich variety of business graphs, including bar graphs, pie charts, line graphs, and others you may never have seen before. When we get to crosstabs, you'll learn how to group, summarize, and analyze your data in a handy spreadsheet format.

NOTE   Graphs can be used in both forms and reports. Crosstabs are available only in forms.

Summarizing Data with Graphs

Graphs present information visually, in keeping with the idea that one picture is worth a thousand words. With Paradox for Windows, you can choose from 17 different types of graphs. You can choose from bar and line graphs, stacked bars, columns, pie charts, three-dimensional ribbons and surfaces, and more, depending on the data and what you want to do with it. Just be aware that not every type of graph makes sense for each set of data.

Throughout this chapter, we'll base our sample graphs and crosstabs on two tables containing financial information. The structure of the first table, *SalesReg*, is shown in Figure 12.1, and its sample data appears in Figure 12.2. The structure of the second table, *FinSum*, appears in Figure 12.3, and Figure 12.4 shows its data.

FIGURE 12.1

The structure of the SalesReg table

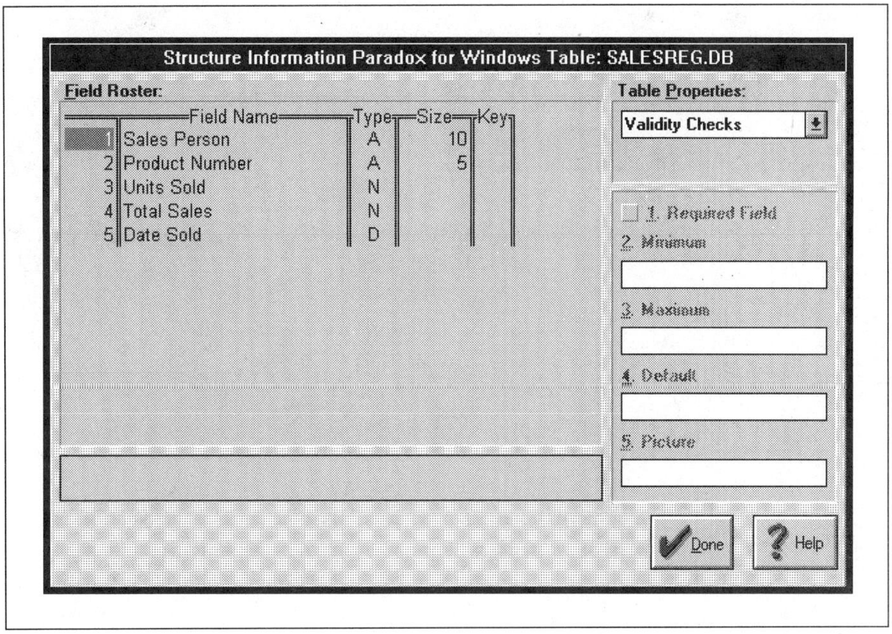

FIGURE 12.2

Sample data for the
SalesReg table

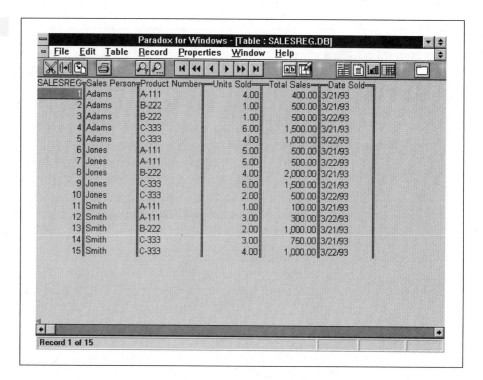

NOTE   You'll learn how to display the structure of a table in
Chapter 14.

Let's take a moment to look at some of the types of graphs that Paradox
for Windows has to offer.

Exploring Graph Types

The purpose of a graph is to display information in a form that's easy to
understand: a feat that requires creativity on your part and versatility from
the graphic tools you use. Fortunately, the tools provided by Paradox for

FIGURE 12.3

The structure of the FinSum table

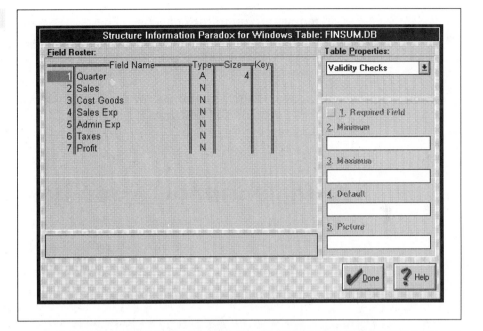

FIGURE 12.4

Sample data for the FinSum table Sum tables.

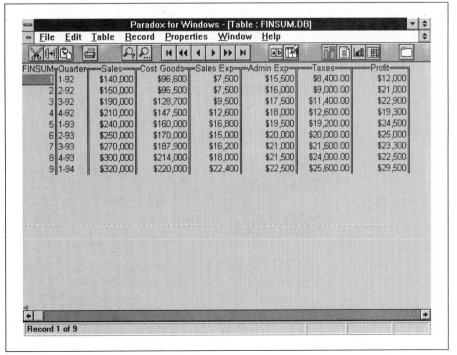

Windows are up to the challenge. These offer eight types of two-dimensional graphs and nine types of three-dimensional graphs, all that you can customize as you wish. Each type of graph is described briefly below, and several of the graph types are illustrated in Figures 12.5 and 12.6.

It's easy to switch from one type of graph to another, so you should experiment to find the best graph for your data. To change the graph type, simply inspect the graph, choose Graph Type from the property menu, and select the graph you want.

Two-Dimensional Graph Types

The following two-dimensional graph types are available in Paradox for Windows.

XY Graph   Uses the values assigned to the X (horizontal) and Y (vertical) axes to plot points with a line connecting them. XY graphs show the relationship between two or more variables. For example, an XY graph can show how sales relate to profit in the FinSum table.

2D Bar   (default graph type) Uses a single vertical bar to represent each data element (Figure 12.5A). 2D bar graphs can be useful for comparing values over a period of time.

2D Stacked Bar   Shows the value of each series of data relative to the total by stacking series elements. The stacked bar graph in Figure 12.5B illustrates the relative impact of sales, taxes, and profit for each quarter.

N O T E   A *series* is a single field from a table that is plotted on a graph.

2D Rotated Bar   Reverses the X and Y axes, with the bars laid out horizontally. Rotated bar graphs are often used to represent and compare performance over time.

FIGURE 12.5

Examples of the many types of 2-D graphs you can design in Paradox for Windows. These graphs display data from the SalesReg and Fin

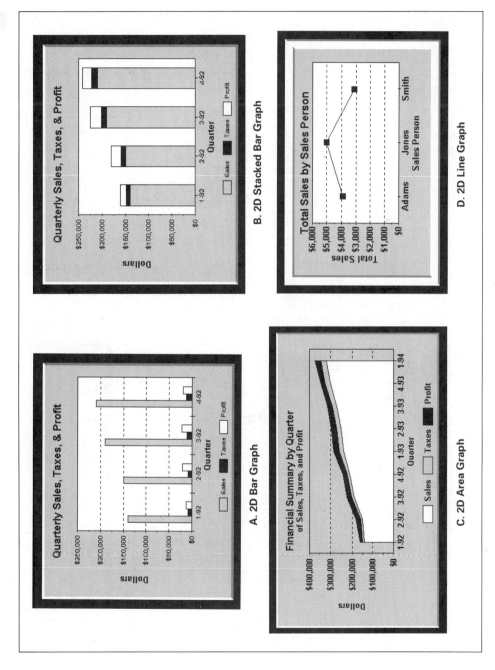

FIGURE 12.6

A few of the many types of 3-D graphs you can design in Paradox for Windows. These graphs display data from the SalesReg and FinSum tables.

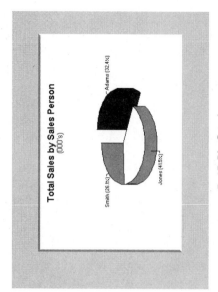

B. 3D Pie Graph

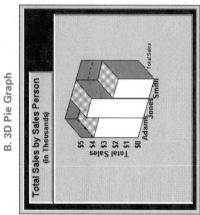

D. 3D Step Graph

A. 3D Surface Graph

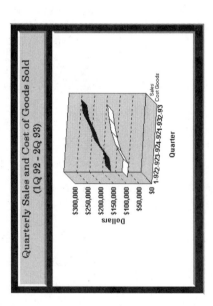

C. 3D Ribbon Graph

2D Area   Presents the information of a stacked bar graph with the smoothness of a line graph. The area graph is often used to show changes in values over time (see Figure 12.5C).

2D Line   Often used to show the changes in a value (or values) over time, so that you can easily see the dips and rises in your data. The x-axis on a line graph is often a progression of time, but can be used to plot any series of values (see Figure 12.5D).

N O T E   As discussed later in this chapter, line graphs can include a variety of marker types, no markers at all, or markers only. Furthermore, on 2D bar, 2D line, and 2D area graphs, you can change the graph type of any individual series to bar, line, or area.

2D Columns   Similar to pie charts in that they show the values in a single series as percentages of the whole. Instead of slicing up a circle, as a pie chart does, a column graph stacks slices vertically on a rectangular column.

2D Pie   Displays the values of a single series as percentages of the whole, slicing up the percentages in a circle. Each pie chart plots one series of values only (that is, a single field from the table), and each slice represents one record in the table.

Three-Dimensional Graph Types

The three-dimensional graph types all display data series on a three-dimensional grid (an x-, y-, and z-axis). The series can be bars, areas, ribbons, pies, columns, or steps, as described below.

3D Bar, 3D Stacked Bar, and 3D Rotated Bar   Resemble the corresponding 2D bar graphs except that the bars appear on a three-dimensional grid.

3D Area   Resembles the corresponding 2D area graph, except the areas appear on a three-dimensional grid.

3D Surface   A three-dimensional version of a line graph, with the lines flowing smoothly into one another (see Figure 12.6A). This format can give you a better view of the contours of your data, and is especially useful for seeing the effects of several data components at once. You must specify at least two y-axis fields to display a 3D surface graph.

3D Columns   Resemble the corresponding 2D column graph, except the column appears on a three-dimensional grid.

3D Pie   Resembles the corresponding 2D pie chart, except the slices appear on a three-dimensional grid (see Figure 12.6B).

3D Ribbon   Essentially a line graph on a 3D grid, with each line flattened out into a segmented ribbon. Like line graphs, these work well to show trends and patterns over time (see Figure 12.6C).

3D Step   Similar to a 3D bar graph, except that the bars of a series touch, as shown in Figure 12.6D. The effect of a 3D step graph can be more dramatic than a 3D bar graph, but sometimes the steps obscure data behind them.

Anatomy of a Graph

Once you understand the anatomy of a graph, you'll have a better idea of which parts can be customized through property inspection. So let's take a moment to go over the terms used to describe the elements of a graph.

Figure 12.7 shows a customized graph with the most important elements labeled. This graph began as a 2D line graph, but we changed the Taxes series to bars for variety and altered the default markers for the Admin Expense series. We also changed the color of each series, the graph, and the graph background, customized the title of the graph and each axis title, and added a subtitle.

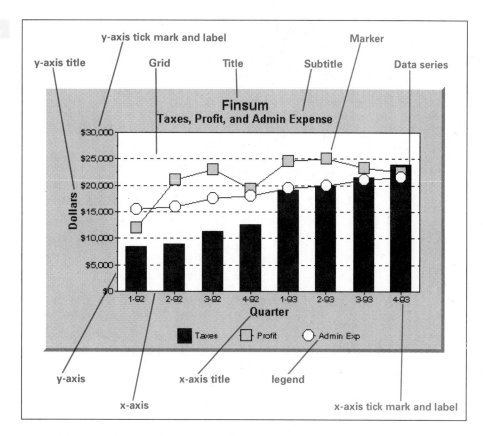

FIGURE 12.7

A sample graph with
the elements labeled

Depending on the type of graph you choose, Paradox will use any or all
of the elements described below.

Axes   The horizontal (x) and vertical (y) lines that establish the
range of values plotted on the graph. Normally, the x-axis cate-
gorizes the data and the y-axis measures the values. This is true for
all Paradox graphs except pie charts and columns (which have no
axes) and rotated bar graphs (where the x- and y-axes are reversed). Data on the x-axis appears in sorted order from smallest value to largest.

NOTE Three-dimensional graphs also have an imaginary z-axis projecting outward from the graph.

Series A single field that you plot against the y-axis. The first y-axis definition is called the *first series*, the second, the *second series*, and so forth.

Titles Text that appears at the top of the graph and along the axes. By default, Paradox uses the table name as the graph title and field names for axis titles. However, the graph title and axis titles can contain any text you want. You may also enter a subtitle, which will appear below the graph title.

Legend The visual key that identifies the series in a graph. You can change the location and appearance of the legend.

Tick marks Small marks along an axis that divide it into segments of equal length. These make the graph easier to read and indicate the scale. In some types of graphs, horizontal grid lines extend from each tick mark on the y-axis (you can remove these if you wish).

Labels Text appearing near each tick mark to identify values on the axes.

Scale Definition of the range of values on the axes and the increments used to divide the axes by tick marks.

Slice Representation of a single graphed value on a pie or column chart.

Understanding Graph Data Types

Paradox for Windows offers three ways to analyze data in a table: *tabular*, *1-D summary*, and *2-D summary*. These are called the *data type* of the graph because they refer to the way Paradox analyzes data before plotting it.

NOTE Do not confuse the graph data type with the graph type. The *data type* describes how the data is analyzed, whereas the *graph type* describes the picture used to display the results of the analysis.

Tabular Data Type

The tabular data type simply lays out the field values in a visual way, plotting each value as it is stored in the table. Thus, the height of a bar or line, or the width of a pie slice corresponds to an exact field value. For example, the tabular graph in Figure 12.8, taken from the SalesReg table, shows the number of units sold by Adams. Notice that each sales transaction is a separate bar, and the height of the bar indicates the number of units sold.

NOTE Tabular graphs are the default data type. You can define one x-axis field and as many numeric y-axis fields as you wish in a tabular graph.

FIGURE 12.8

This tabular bar graph shows the number of units sold in each of Adams' sales transactions.

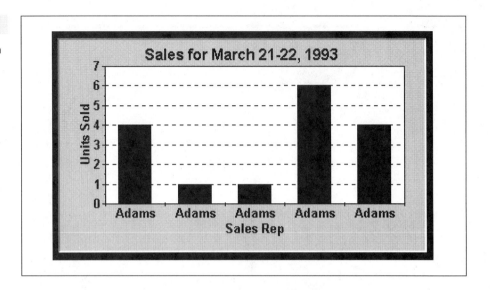

1-D Summary and 2-D Summary Data Type

While tabular graphs are useful for presenting small amounts of data, they lead to cluttered and complicated graphs with no summarized (totaled) results when used with large tables. A better way to graph data in the SalesReg table would be to group and summarize the records first. For example, you might want to graph each salesperson's total sales. Or, you might want to go one step further and graph each salesperson's total sales *for each product*. Here's where 1-D summary and 2-D summary graphs can help.

NOTE   You could also use a query to summarize your data, and then graph the results. Chapter 16 explains how to pose queries that perform calculations on numeric data.

In a *1-D summary* graph, the x-axis field contains values to be grouped together, so that all records with the same values in the x-axis field are placed in the same group. In essence, the table is sorted by the x-axis field. The y-axis field or fields in a 1-D summary graph are used to perform and display the results of some calculation within each group. For example, to calculate and graph the total number of units sold by each salesperson in the SalesReg table shown in Figure 12.2, we would create a 1-D summary graph, making Sales Person the x-axis field and Units Sold the y-axis field.

A *2-D summary* graph is the same as a 1-D summary graph, except that it lets you group data by a second field. Thus, we could graph the total units sold by each salesperson for each product in the table. To do so, we would create a 2-D summary graph, specify Sales Person as the x-axis field, Units Sold as the y-axis field, and Product Number as the field to group by.

NOTE

Only the tabular graph type is allowed in reports. However, you can print forms containing 1-D and 2-D summary graphs, so this restriction shouldn't pose a serious problem.

In most cases, you will probably use graphs to generate totals (or sums). However, 1-D and 2-D summary graphs can perform any of several operations on the field used as the summary value.

As you read the descriptions of each operation below, take a look at the sample 1-D summary graphs in Figure 12.9 and the 2-D summary graphs in Figure 12.10. Notice that the y-axis in the sample graphs is labeled to indicate the summary operator used to produce the graph. Although the 2-D summary graphs in Figure 12.10 are nearly identical to the 1-D summary graphs in Figure 12.9, they've been broken down further by product number. So, instead of displaying only one value in each group on the x-axis, the 2-D summary graphs show three values for each salesperson: one value

FIGURE 12.9

A series of 1-D summary bar graphs showing how each summary operator graphs the unit sales per salesperson. The y-axis in each graph is labeled with the type of summary operator used to produce the graph.

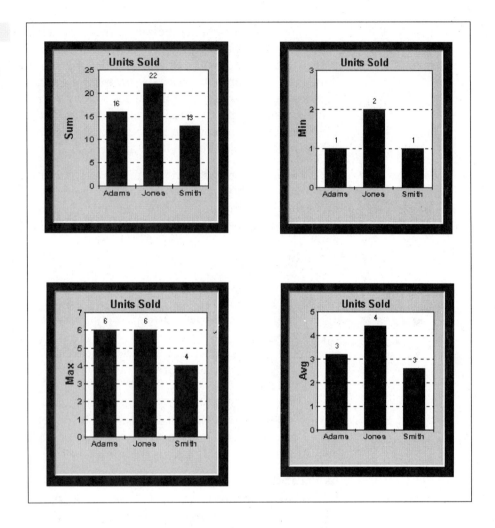

for each of the three product numbers. The legends and subtitles in Figure 12.10 identify Product Number as the field used to group the data.

SUM   For each record of each group on the x-axis, SUM totals the non-empty values in the corresponding y-axis field. For instance, the SUM example in Figure 12.9 graphs the total units sold by Adams (16 units), followed by the total units sold by Jones (22 units), followed by the total units sold by Smith (13 units).

FIGURE 12.10

A series of 2-D summary bar graphs based on the same data as in Figure 12.9, with data grouped by salesperson and product number. Again, the y-axis in each graph is labeled with the type of summary operator used to produce the graph.

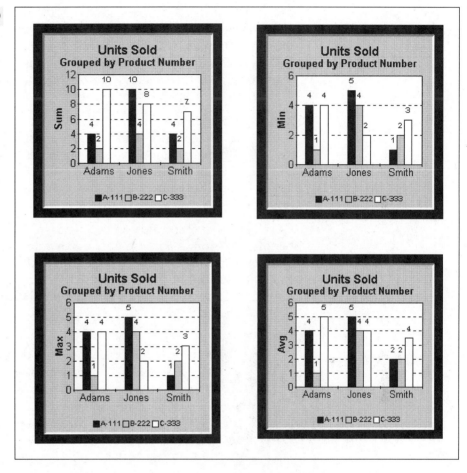

In Figure 12.10 the sums are broken down by product number. Thus the first group in the SUM example of Figure 12.10 shows the total units of product A-111 sold by Adams (4), the total units of product B-222 sold by Adams (2), and the total units of product C-333 sold by Adams (10). The next group shows the total units of each product sold by Jones, and the last group shows the total units of each product sold by Smith.

MIN   For each value on the x-axis, MIN graphs the smallest of all the individual values found in the corresponding y-axis field. In the 1-D summary example, this is the smallest number of units sold by each salesperson. In the 2-D summary example, the MIN operator graphs the smallest number of units sold by each salesperson for each product number.

MAX   For each value on the x-axis, MAX graphs the largest of all the individual values found in the corresponding y-axis field. In the 1-D summary example, this is the largest number of units sold by each salesperson. In the 2-D summary example, you'll see the largest number of units sold by each salesperson for each product number.

COUNT   For each value on the x-axis, COUNT tallies the number of corresponding non-empty y-axis values. In the 1-D summary example, this would be the count in the SalesReg table for each salesperson. In the 2-D summary example, this is the count for each salesperson for each product number.

NOTE

In the SalesReg table, all records contain values in the Units Sold field, so the counts are equal to the number of transactions for each salesperson. In the 1-D summary, each salesperson has a COUNT of 5, for a total of 15 transactions. In the 2-D summary, Adams has 1 transaction for product A-111 and 2 transactions each for B-222 and C-333; Jones and Smith have 2 transactions each for A-111 and C-333 and 1 for B-222 (for a total of 15).

AVG   For each value on the x-axis, AVG graphs the average of all the individual values found in the corresponding y-axis field. In the 1-D summary example, this is the average number of units sold by each salesperson. In the 2-D summary example, AVG graphs the average number of units sold by each salesperson for each product number. The average is the sum of the non-null values divided by the count of the non-empty values.

STD   For each value on the x-axis, STD graphs the standard deviation of all the individual values in the corresponding y-axis field. STD is meaningful only with large samples.

VAR   For each value on the x-axis, VAR graphs the statistical variance of all the individual values found in the corresponding y-axis field. Like STD, VAR is meaningful only with large samples.

Here are some rules to keep in mind about 1-D and 2-D summary graphs:

* You can define one x-axis field and multiple y-axis fields in a 1-D summary graph.

* You can define one x-axis field, one group-by field, and one y-axis field for a 2-D summary graph.

* The y-axis field must be currency, number, or short number for any operator except COUNT.

Designing a Graph

As with other aspects of document design, setting up graphs isn't a strictly sequential process. Once you've created the basic graph object, you can define its properties in just about any order. In this chapter, we'll summarize the basic procedures for creating graphs. Then, with these techniques in mind, you can take the approach that suits you best.

Regardless of how you define your graph, Paradox will make some initial choices concerning the graph title, axis titles, labels for tick marks, scaling, and so forth. For example, the default title for the graph is the table name; there is no subtitle; the axis titles are taken from field names, where appropriate; tick mark labels are derived from the data values in the x- and y-axes; and the tick mark scale and increments are calculated automatically, based on the data being plotted. You can customize any of these settings, as you will learn later in this chapter.

Creating a Graph

 To add a graph to an existing form or report document, click the Graph tool in the Design window SpeedBar (shown at left), then click in your design and drag the mouse to define the initial size of the graph. For example, the form in Figure 12.11 includes a table object showing three fields from the FinSum table and an undefined 2D bar graph whose size was outlined using the Graph tool. Keep in mind that the graph shown in the Design window is simply a replica or *template* of the actual graph, which will probably look quite a bit different when you preview or print it.

FIGURE 12.11

A newly created graph initially appears as an undefined 2D bar graph.

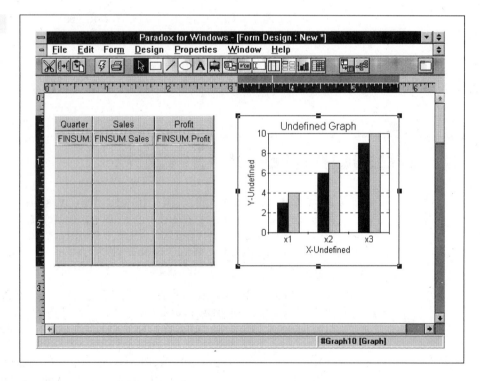

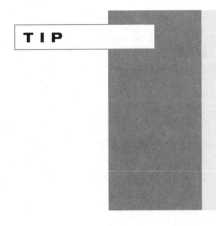

T I P

If anyone changes data that's used in a graph you're currently displaying in Form View, Paradox will update the affected data in the graph as soon as the user moves the cursor to another record in the table and you refresh the graph in Form View. The quickest way to refresh the graph is to press F8 twice (this switches between the Form Design and Form View windows). If the graph is on the same form as the table you're updating, it will be refreshed as soon as you move the cursor to another record.

You can also create a new form that includes the graph only—with no other fields from the table. To do this, simply choose File ➤ New ➤ Form, choose your table in the **Data Model** dialog box, then select a Blank style in the **Design Layout** dialog box and click OK. Next, use the Graph tool as described above to place the graph into your design.

T I P

In reports, your best bet is to place the graph in the report header or report footer band.

Creating a Quick Graph

If you're in Table View and haven't yet assigned a preferred graph to the table, there's another way to create a graph: Simply click the Quick Graph button in the SpeedBar (shown at left) to begin defining a graph for the table immediately. (This opens the **Define Graph** dialog box shown later in Figure 12.13.)

We'll explain how to use the Define Graph dialog box in a moment. For now, note that the Quick Graph button creates a new form, just as if you had chosen File ➤ New ➤ Form, specified the table that is open on the Desktop, chosen a blank design style, and defined a default graph as described in the next section.

If you've already assigned a preferred graph to the table, clicking the Quick Graph button in Table View will immediately display the graph in a new Form window. You can then click the Design button in the Speed-Bar or press F8 if you want to change the design.

TIP

To create a preferred graph, open the table, right-click the Quick Graph button in the SpeedBar, choose the form that contains your graph, and click OK. Then choose Properties ➤ View Properties ➤ Save to save your changes.

Inspecting the Entire Graph Object

Like other objects in a design, graphs can be customized in a variety of ways. It should come as no surprise that you define and customize a graph by changing *properties* of the graph object or one of its hot zones.

We'll explain how to inspect a hot zone in the next section. Now, let's look at the basic techniques for inspecting the graph object itself:

- Select the graph by clicking it. Press F6, or move the mouse pointer to an empty area just inside the selection handles of the graph and right-click.

- Or, click the Object Tree button in the SpeedBar (see Chapter 9), then right-click the graph object (labeled *#Graph*).

Figure 12.12 shows the property menu for a graph object. From this property menu, you can choose Define Graph (explained in a moment) to define your graph, or you can choose any of the other options to customize the graph. (Note that some options are not available for reports.)

FIGURE 12.12

The Graph property menu appears when you inspect the graph.

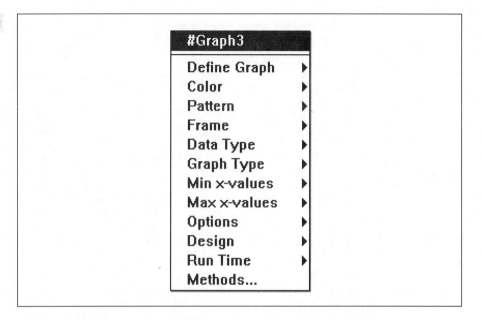

#Graph3
- Define Graph ▶
- Color ▶
- Pattern ▶
- Frame ▶
- Data Type ▶
- Graph Type ▶
- Min x-values ▶
- Max x-values ▶
- Options ▶
- Design ▶
- Run Time ▶
- Methods...

N O T E

In this chapter, we'll focus on properties that are unique to graphs. Please refer to Chapter 9 for general information on changing properties, and to Appendix D for a complete list of properties.

Inspecting the Graph Hot Zones

Graphs contain many hot zones that you can inspect and change. These include the title box, axes, data series, legend box, background, and other areas that depend on the type of picture you're using to display the graph. At first you might have trouble locating the hot zones, but with practice you'll soon become an expert.

To locate a hot zone and change its properties, select the graph by clicking it, then move the mouse pointer to the area you want to inspect. When the mouse pointer changes to a small ↑, right-click to open the property menu. In the example below, we moved the mouse pointer to the first data series hot zone (indicated by the ↑ in the first bar above the *x3* label on the x-axis).

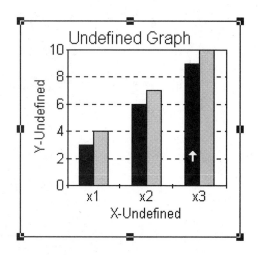

Using the Define Graph Dialog Box

You can define the table, graph data, x- and y-axis fields, and any groups in a single step, or you can inspect individual areas of the graph. It's probably easiest to start with the "all at once" approach described below. Later we'll explain how to set up the graph definition on a piece-by-piece basis.

To define a graph, inspect the entire graph object (not a hot zone) as described previously and choose Define Graph. You'll see a list of the tables defined in the **Data Model** dialog box, plus the list header (...). At this point, you have two choices: You can define a default graph, or you can define the table, fields, and graph data type more precisely.

To define a *default* graph for the table, simply click the table name in the property list. Paradox will create a 2D bar graph, in which the leftmost numeric field in the table defines the x-axis, and the remaining numeric fields, in left-to-right order, become the y-axis fields. From here, you can preview the graph or you can inspect various elements of the graph—including the graph itself—to customize further.

If you prefer not to define a default graph, click the header (...). If you're designing a form, you'll see the Define Graph dialog box shown in Figure 12.13. If you're designing a report, the Define Graph dialog box won't include a Graph Type area, since your only option is to create a tabular graph.

FIGURE 12.13

The Define Graph dialog box lets you define the table, fields, data type, and groups all at once.

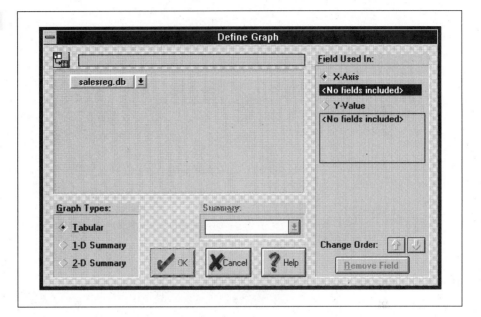

From this point, the steps are as follows:

1. If you wish to add or delete a table, click the Data Model button at the upper-left corner of the dialog box and choose the table you want, as described in Chapter 9. Click OK when you're finished. The Data Model button is handy for graphing a table *other* than the one you first specified in the Data Model dialog box.

2. If you're designing a report, skip to Step 3. When designing a form, you can click Tabular, 1-D Summary, or 2-D Summary in the Graph Types area.

- If you choose 1-D Summary, the Define Graph dialog box will change to resemble Figure 12.14.
- If you choose 2-D Summary, the dialog box will resemble Figure 12.15 instead.

3. To define the X-Axis, Y-Value, or Grouped By fields, click the appropriate option in the Field Used In area of the dialog box.

4. Click the drop-down arrow next to the table, then click the appropriate field or fields.

5. Make any of the changes listed below.

- To change the summary operator for a field (1-D and 2-D summary graphs only), click the Y-Value field you want to summarize in the Field Used In area, then click the Summary list box and select the summary operator you want.
- To rearrange the order of fields, click the field you want to move in the Field Used In area, then click the ↑ and ↓ Change Order buttons as appropriate.

FIGURE 12.14

The Define Graph dialog box for a form after choosing 1-D Summary in the Graph Type area. Notice that the Y-Value area moves down in the dialog box.

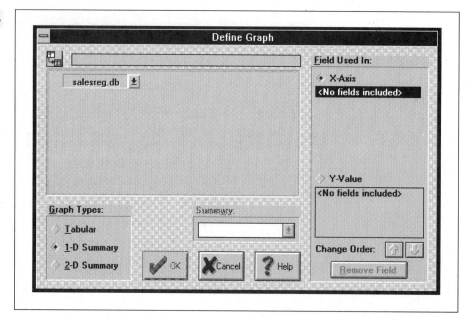

- To remove a field, click the field in the Field Used In area, then click Remove.

6. When you're finished, choose OK.

Defining the X- and Y-Axis Fields

If you'd like to define fields for the x- or y-axis individually, inspect the axis title or tick marks for the axis you want to change. The property menu for the x-axis appears below.

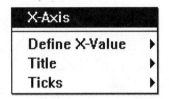

And here's the y-axis property menu:

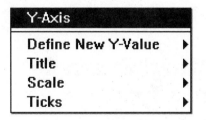

Now, choose Define X-Value or Define New Y-Value and choose a field name from the list that appears. If you want to plot more than one series on the y-axis, inspect the y-axis title or tick marks again and choose another field name.

FIGURE 12.15

The Define Graph dialog box for a form after choosing 2-D Summary in the Graph Type area. Notice that the Y-Value area moves down and a new Grouped By area appears in the dialog box.

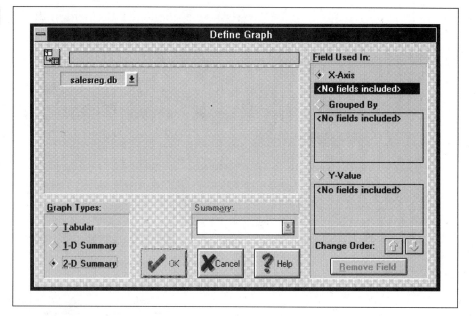

NOTE The fields available depend on the data type and graph type; unavailable fields will be dimmed.

Changing the Graph Data Type

Recall that the default graph data type is Tabular, which simply uses the selected pictorial format to display values as they appear in the table. When designing a form, you can change the data type of the graph at any time by inspecting the graph object, choosing Data Type, then selecting the data type you want (Table, 1D Summary, or 2D Summary). Graphs in Reports are always Tabular, and you cannot change the date type.

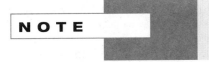

NOTE   You can also use the Define Graph dialog box, discussed earlier, to change the data type of a graph.

Changing the Graph Type

As you define your graph, you may want to experiment with different graph types to determine which format presents your data in the clearest and most attractive way. Changing the graph type is easy: Simply inspect the graph object, choose Graph Type, and select the graph type you want from the menu that appears. Later on in this chapter, we'll provide some tips to help you choose the most effective representation for your graphs.

Figure 12.16 shows the menu of graph types. The graph types available depend on the graph's data type and the fields you've selected for the

FIGURE 12.16

You can choose any of 17 different graph types to display your data.

XY Graph
√ 2D Bar
2D Stacked Bar
2D Rotated Bar
2D Area
2D Line
2D Columns
2D Pie
3D Bar
3D Stacked Bar
3D Rotated Bar
3D Area
3D Surface
3D Columns
3D Pie
3D Ribbon
3D Step

x-axis and y-axis. For example, you can't choose an XY graph type if one of the axes contains alphanumeric data.

Once you choose a graph type, the Design window immediately changes to reflect your selection.

Redefining Graph Elements

Most elements in the graph object have Define properties, which let you redefine the element. For example, the property menu for a title includes a Define Graph property. Similarly, the x-axis property menu has a Define X-Value option, while the y-axis menu includes a Define Y-Value (or Define New Y-Value) property.

When you choose Define from a property menu, a list of options appears. You can either choose one of the options or click the header area of the list (...) and make choices from a dialog box.

TIP

To save time, you can open the Define Graph dialog box and define the fields in one step.

Using the Graph Object's Options Property

You can determine whether your graph will display a title and subtitle, a legend, grid, axes, and data labels. If you find that a graph is too cluttered, consider removing one or more of these elements. If you'd like the graph to convey more information, you can display these elements. Either way, you will need to inspect the graph object, choose Options, and select one of the options below.

Show Title   When checked, this option displays the graph title and subtitle. When it is unchecked, the title and subtitle are removed from the graph.

Show Legend   When checked, this option displays a legend. When it is unchecked, no legend appears.

Show Grid   When checked, this option displays grid lines that begin at each y-axis tick mark on the graph. Unchecking the option removes the grid lines from the graph. Note that grid lines will not appear unless *Show Axes* is also checked.

Show Axes   When this option is checked, tick marks and tick labels appear on the graph. When the option is unchecked, tick marks, tick labels, and any grid lines will disappear from the graph.

Show Labels   When checked, this option displays labels showing the value of each data series. When Show Labels is unchecked, no data labels appear.

Rotation   This option controls the rotation of 3-D graphs (described later in this chapter).

Elevation   This option controls the elevation of 3-D graphs (described later in this chapter).

Note that the available options and their default settings depend on the type of graph you're defining.

NOTE   If you want to customize the titles, legend, or tick marks, be sure the corresponding Show Title, Show Legend, or Show Axes option is checked.

Customizing Graph Titles and Subtitles

If you want a special title to appear at the top of the graph, inspect the title hot zone near the top of the graph. You'll see the following property menu (2D-Summary graphs also have a Define Group option).

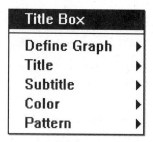

Choose *Title* if you want to customize the first title line, or *Subtitle* to customize the second title line. Then choose *Text*, *Font*, or *Use Default*, as indicated below.

- To customize the title or subtitle text, choose *Text*, type your text in the dialog box that appears, and choose OK.

- To change the font, choose *Font* followed by the Typeface, Size, Style, and Color options.

- To return customized title or subtitle text to the default, or vice versa, choose *Use Default*. When the option is checked, Paradox uses the default title or subtitle. When the option is unchecked, Paradox uses the customized text you've supplied.

TIP

If you don't need a subtitle but you do want some extra space to appear below the graph's title, inspect the title hot zone, choose Subtitle ➤ Text, press the spacebar (to create a blank subtitle), and choose OK.

The title and subtitle options don't provide a great deal of flexibility and they limit the number of characters you can type. If you need fancier titles and subtitles than the above options allow, or you want to place the titles outside the graph object, turn off the titles altogether by inspecting the graph object and unchecking Options ➤ Show Titles. Then use the Text tool in the SpeedBar to draw a text object where you can type in the text you want. You can change the properties of the text box if you want to customize the title further.

Customizing Axis Titles

Changing titles on the x-axis and y-axis is just as easy as customizing the graph titles: Inspect the appropriate x-axis or y-axis hot zones, choose *Title*, then choose *Text*, *Font*, or *Use Default*, as described above.

N O T E   To locate the axis hot zone, select the graph, then move the mouse pointer near the axis title or the tick marks. The mouse pointer changes to ↑ when it hits a hot zone.

Customizing Tick Labels

If you wish to customize the tick mark labels, inspect the appropriate axis title or tick mark area and choose *Ticks* from the property menu. The options available depend on the data type of the axis labels and the axis you're changing. These options include the following:

Font   Provides options for changing the Typeface, Size, Style, and Color of the label.

Number Format   Lets you change the number format for the tick mark labels (see Chapter 6).

Alternate   Available for the x-axis only. Checking this option staggers the x-axis labels to prevent them from overlapping. Choose this option if the x-axis labels are too long to allow space between each one.

Scaling the Axes

The Scale option on the property menu for an axis allows you to control the range of numeric values displayed. Although you can always define the scale for a y-axis that is plotting numeric values, x-axis scaling is available only for XY graphs.

NOTE Choosing the Scale property leads to the following options: Auto-Scale, Logarithmic, Low Value, High Value, and Increment.

By default, Paradox figures out how to scale the graph axes based on the data being plotted. For example, if the smallest value to be plotted is 1000 and the largest value is 5100, Paradox automatically sets up the y-axis to extend from 0 to 6000. Automatic scaling is in effect when the Scale ➤ Auto-Scale property option is checked.

If you uncheck the Scale ➤ Auto-Scale property, you can set your own minimum (Low) and maximum (High) values that display or accentuate a trend or value. When defining scaling, make sure the range you select includes all the values to be graphed; otherwise the resulting graph may show inaccurate results. For example, if you set the high end of the y-axis to 2000, data values larger than 2000 will always appear at the top of the graph. Thus, a value of 5000 would appear as 2000.

You can also customize the Increment used to separate the tick marks along the axis. For example, if you set a Low Value of 0 and a High Value of 5000, Paradox will automatically place tick marks at 2000 and 4000 on the y-axis. However, if you change the tick mark increment value for the y-axis to 1000, Paradox will place tick marks at 1000, 2000, 3000, 4000, and 5000.

To define your own scaling, first inspect the axis you want to scale, then uncheck the Scale ➤ Auto-Scale option. The Low Value, High Value, and Increment options will be available the next time you choose the Scale property. Now, for each component of the scale that you want to change, inspect the axis, choose Scale, select Low Value, High Value, or Increment, as appropriate, type the value you want into the dialog box that appears, and choose OK. (We used manual scaling to adjust the High Value for many graphs shown in this chapter.)

Logarithmic Scaling

Regardless of whether Paradox is scaling your data automatically or you are scaling it manually, you might want to use logarithmic scaling when plotting series with wide ranges of magnitude. In a logarithmically scaled axis, each major division of the axis represents ten times the value of the previous division. For example, the first tick mark is .1, the next is 1, the next is 10, the next is 100, and so forth.

To choose logarithmic scaling, inspect the axis, then check the Scale ➤ Logarithmic option. To return to normal scaling, uncheck the option.

NOTE   If you uncheck Auto-Scale and check Logarithmic, Paradox will automatically set positive values (> 0) for Scale ➤ Low Value and Scale ➤ High Value. Make sure that these values remain positive if you define low and high values of your own. Also, be aware that the Y-Values in your table must be positive if you wish to scale them logarithmically.

Controlling the Amount of Data Shown in the Graph

When viewing your graph, you may find that it's too cluttered to show the specific data points or trends you're interested in. Fortunately, you can limit data values in any of the ways described below.

- Base your graph on a saved query. A carefully constructed query can reduce confusion by eliminating unnecessary data points from the graph.

- Use 1-D summary and 2-D summary graphs which are (or cross-tabs, described later in this chapter) to summarize your data.

- You can specify the number of values to display along the x-axis of your graph and the number of groups that appear in a 2-D summary graph.

To use the last method, inspect the graph object, then choose one of the following options:

Min X-Values   Lets you specify the minimum number of x-axis values that can appear in a graph. After choosing Min X-Values, choose a number from the list (1 to 8) or click the header area, type your own value, and choose OK.

Max X-Values   Lets you specify the maximum number of x-axis values that can appear. Again, you can choose a value from 1 to 8, or click the header area to type in your own value.

Max Groups   Defines the maximum number of group-by values in 2-D summary graphs. Choosing this option limits the number of bars that appear in each group on the x-axis. Again, you can choose a value from 1 to 8, or click the list header and type in your own value. The graph in Figure 12.17 shows total sales for each salesperson in the SalesReg table, grouped by the Product Number field, with Max Group set to 2.

FIGURE 12.17

This 2-D summary graph is limited to displaying only two groups.

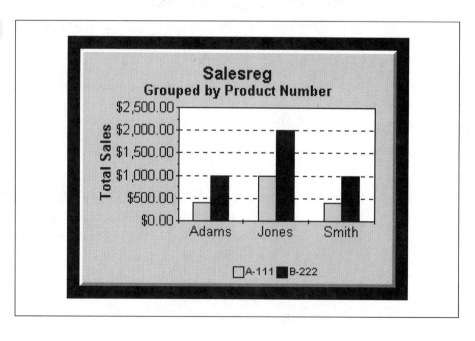

Customizing the Graph Series

In addition to customizing the overall features of a graph, you can customize individual series. To do so, inspect the hot zone for the series you want to change. For example, if you want to change the appearance of the first series in a 2D line graph, click the graph object and move the pointer near the line you want to change. Then, when the mouse pointer changes to ↑, right-click. You'll see a property menu similar to the one below.

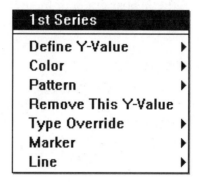

All series property menus let you redefine the field used for the series (Define Y-Value), change the series color (Color) or pattern (Pattern), and remove the series from the graph (Remove This Y-Value). The remaining options depend on the type of graph and series you're inspecting, as explained in the sections below.

NOTE   Remember that you can also use the Define Graph dialog box to delete, redefine, and reorder the fields used for Y-values in the graph.

Type Override

The series property menus for 2D bar, 2D area, and 2D line graphs include a Type Override option to change the graph type used to represent an individual series. For example, in a 2D bar graph, each series normally appears as a bar; in a 2D area graph, each series is plotted as a line with the area below it filled in; and in a 2D line graph, each series is represented by a line. By choosing the Type Override option, you can change an individual series to 2D line, 2D bar, or 2D area. To return the series to its original representation, choose Type Override ➤ None from the property menu.

The Type Override option is especially useful if you want to draw attention to one or more data series. For example, suppose we want to compare sales with the cost of goods in our FinSum table. We used Type Override in the 2D bar graph of Figure 12.18 to emphasize this comparison by displaying the Sales series as a 2D line.

Markers

Paradox for Windows offers a variety of styles for marking individual data points in line graphs. The default marker style is a filled box, but you can change this by inspecting the series whose marker style you want to change, then choosing Marker from the property menu. The marker styles are shown in Figure 12.19.

FIGURE 12.18

A combined graph based on the Sales and Cost of Goods fields from the FinSum financial summary table

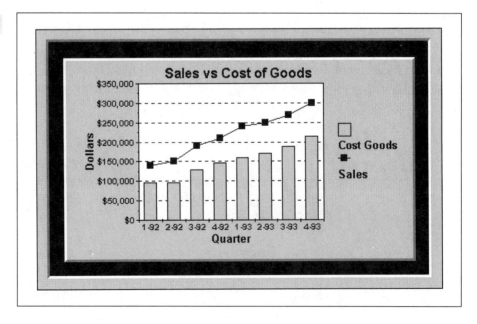

FIGURE 12.19

Marker styles for lines
in a graph

✓ Filled Box
Hollow Box
Filled Down-Triangle
Hollow Down-Triangle
Filled Circle
Hollow Circle
Filled Triangle
Hollow Triangle
+
Boxed +
x
Boxed x
Filled Triangles
Hollow Triangles
Vertical Line
Horizontal Line

Line Styles

You can change the line style, color, and thickness of a 2D line by inspecting the series you want to change, choosing Line, then choosing Line Style, Color, or Thickness.

TIP

To display a series with markers but without a line connecting them, inspect the series, choose Line ➤ Line Style, then choose the top (blank) line style from the Line palette.

Customizing the Legend

A legend provides a key to each series on the graph. Paradox for Windows automatically uses the fields in the table to identify each series plotted on the graph. For example, the legend in the 2D summary graph in Figure 12.20 identifies the first series as sales of Product A-111, the second as sales of B-222, and the third as sales of C-333. Figure 12.20 also illustrates how placing a graph and a table side-by-side on the same form can help make sense of the data.

Although you cannot change the text of the labels in the legend, you can change the appearance and position of the legend. To do so, first make sure the legend appears on the graph in the Design window (if necessary, inspect the graph object and choose Options ➤ Show Legend). Then click the graph object, move the mouse pointer to a *text label* in the legend (*not* to a legend box) and right-click. The Legend Box property menu will appear, as below.

FIGURE 12.20

The graph legend identifies each data series. In this example, we placed the graph and table side-by-side to illustrate how summarized data in a graph can help you get a quick understanding of detailed tabular data.

Sales Rep	Prod #	Units	Total $	Date Sold
Adams	A-111	4	$400	3/21/93
Adams	B-222	1	$500	3/21/93
Adams	B-222	1	$500	3/22/93
Adams	C-333	6	$1,500	3/21/93
Adams	C-333	4	$1,000	3/22/93
Jones	A-111	5	$500	3/21/93
Jones	A-111	5	$500	3/22/93
Jones	B-222	4	$2,000	3/21/93
Jones	C-333	6	$1,500	3/21/93
Jones	C-333	2	$500	3/22/93
Smith	A-111	1	$100	3/21/93
Smith	A-111	3	$300	3/22/93
Smith	B-222	2	$1,000	3/21/93
Smith	C-333	3	$750	3/21/93
Smith	C-333	4	$1,000	3/22/93

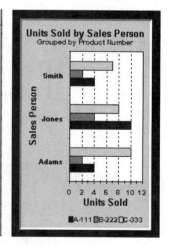

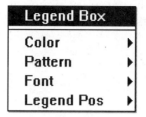

From this point, you can change the background color or pattern of the legend, or the font of the legend labels. To position the legend box at the right or bottom of the graph, choose *Legend Pos.*

TIP

If you're having trouble locating the hot zone for a series, turn on the legend, then move the mouse pointer to the legend *box* (not the legend label) for the series you want to change. As usual, you can right-click when the mouse pointer changes to ↑.

Changing Rotation and Elevation in 3-D Graphs

The rotation and elevation properties of a 3-D graph work together to create a three-dimensional effect. Rotation turns the graph around the y-axis, while elevation turns the graph around the x-axis. You can change the rotation and elevation of any 3-D graph except 3-D Columns and 3D Pie. To do so, inspect the graph object, choose Options, then choose *Elevation* or *Rotation* and select the number of degrees you want to elevate or rotate the graph. You can choose 0, 15, 30, 45, 60, 75, or 90 degrees.

NOTE

The default elevation for a 3-D graph is 60 degrees; the default rotation is 30 degrees.

Figure 12.21 shows the effect of rotation and elevation on a 3D stacked bar and a 3D ribbon graph. Some combinations will work better than others.

FIGURE 12.21

Various combinations of rotation and elevation on a 3D stacked bar and a 3D ribbon graph. We've unchecked the Options ➤ Show Axes property in these examples.

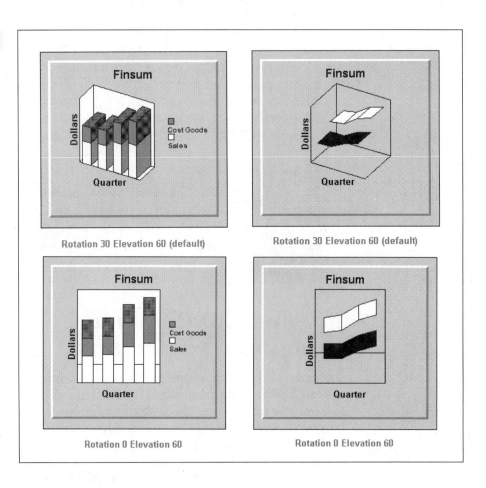

Rotation 30 Elevation 60 (default)

Rotation 30 Elevation 60 (default)

Rotation 0 Elevation 60

Rotation 0 Elevation 60

Adding Colors or Patterns to the Graph Background

We've already talked about how to customize individual data series properties, including the color and pattern. You can also change the color or pattern of background areas of a graph, including the background of the entire graph and the background area containing the data series.

To change the background color or pattern of the entire graph, inspect the *graph object*, then choose Pattern or Color. To change the color or pattern of an area containing the data series, inspect the *hot zone* for the area you want to change, then choose Color or Pattern.

Keep in mind that the areas you can change depend on the type of graph you're designing, as summarized below.

BACKGROUND AREA	TYPE OF GRAPH
Entire graph	All
Background	All 2D Bar, Area, and Line graphs except 2D Columns and 2D Pie.
Left Wall, Back Wall, or Base Floor	All 3-D graphs except 3D Columns and 3D Pie

Figure 12.22 shows three representative graph types—a 2D Bar, a 3D Area, and a 3D Pie—on the Design window and points out the areas you can inspect to change the background color or pattern.

Special Techniques for Pie Charts and Column Graphs

Many of the enhancements that can be added to graphs do not apply to pie charts and column graphs because they have no axes and can only display a single series (data from a single field). However, Paradox for Windows offers other ways to customize pie charts and column graphs.

Label Format

You can change the labels on pie slices by inspecting the graph object, choosing Label, and then selecting any of the options below.

Font   Presents Typeface, Size, Style, and Color options.

Number Format   Presents number format options (available only when you've selected Label Format ➤ y-Value).

GRAPHING YOUR DATA

FIGURE 12.22

You can change the color or pattern of various background areas in a graph. The areas you can change depend on the type of graph.

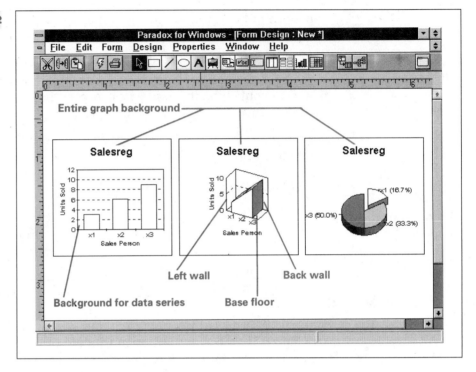

Label Format ➤ No y-Value Displays the x-axis value, but no y-axis value, for the slice.

Label Format ➤ y-Value Labels each slice with the x-axis value and the actual table value, if it fits.

Label Format ➤ y in Percent Labels each slice with the x-axis value and the percentage of the whole series the slice represents. (This is the default setting.)

Slices

You can fill or color each slice in a pie chart or column graph individually, and you can "explode" individual slices in a pie chart for emphasis. Inspect the slice you want to change, then perform any of the steps below.

- Choose *Color* to change the color of the slice.

- Choose *Pattern* to change the fill pattern of the slice.

- Choose *Explode* to separate the slice from the rest of the pie. You can explode any or all slices in a pie. To bring an exploded slice back into the pie, inspect the slice and choose *Explode* again.

Figure 12.23 shows the 1993 quarterly profit from the FinSum table as a pie chart. Note that each slice is a different color, and the pie slice for the fourth quarter of 1993 is exploded.

NOTE   We created the pie chart in Figure 12.23 from a query that selected only those records with ..-93 in the Quarter field (see Chapter 8).

FIGURE 12.23

Quarterly profit for 1993 represented as a pie chart. This example is based on a query that isolated records with ..-93 in the Quarter field of the FinSum table.

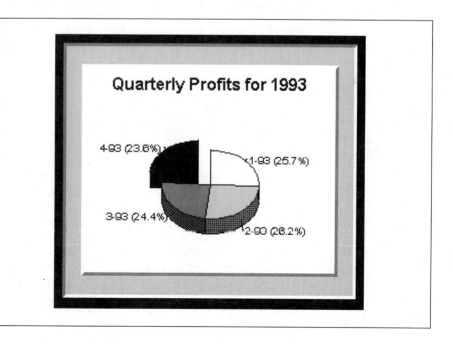

Graph Design Tips

You've now learned all the techniques necessary for designing graphs in Paradox for Windows. In this section, you'll find tips to help you develop graphs that are professional-looking and easy to understand.

The most crucial decision you'll make when designing graphs is to pick the graph type that most clearly represents your data. For example, consider using a line graph to illustrate trends. When you want to show how each element contributes to a total, an area or stacked bar graph might do the best job. If your goal is to compare values, standard bar graphs and rotated bar graphs are good choices. And finally, when you're trying to show the relative contribution of different parts to a whole, a pie chart is ideal.

If you're not sure which graph is best for a particular purpose, experiment until you find the right graph. To switch to a new graph type, just inspect the graph and choose Graph Type, specify a different graph type, and then click the View Data button in the SpeedBar to see the results.

Avoid cluttering your graphs with unnecessary data or labels, as this will obscure the message you're trying to convey. For example, if your objective is to show commissions for sales people in the Western region, there's no need to show commissions for sales people in the Eastern and Overseas regions unless you want to compare commissions by region. If necessary, use a query to reduce the amount of data, consider a 1-D or 2-D summary, use the Order/Range feature if your table has secondary indexes, or reduce the number of x-axis values displayed.

Be sure to make important information stand out in your graphs. For example, explode the most important slice or slices in a pie chart, use bright colors or more noticeable patterns for key data items, or choose a different font to highlight vital information.

The graph's title may appear highlighted (dark) when you switch to Form View, especially if the graph is the first (or only) data object in the form. To prevent this behavior, inspect the graph object in the Form Design window and choose Run Time ➤ Tab Stop to uncheck the option.

Finally, don't forget that graphs can be combined with information in forms, reports, and form letters. Figure 12.24 illustrates how an effective graph can be integrated into a form letter to emphasize a point.

Now, let's turn our attention to crosstabs, which let you analyze and summarize data using tables instead of pictures.

Summarizing Data with Crosstabs

Cross tabulations (or *crosstabs*) are very useful for reducing and arranging data from a large table into a smaller table that's easier to understand. Like 1-D and 2-D summary graphs, crosstabs can classify data by one or more categories, summarize the data within these categories, and sort the summarized information. Instead of displaying the results in a graph, the results of a crosstab appear in a spreadsheet format.

In Figures 12.25 and 12.26, you see two crosstabs for the sample Sales-Reg table. Both crosstabs summarize the total number of units sold by date, though one displays the dates vertically along the left side of the crosstab, while the other displays the dates horizontally across the top. The orientation depends on how you define the crosstab fields.

NOTE Like 1-D summary and 2-D summary graphs, crosstabs are available only in forms, not reports. However, you can print forms that contain crosstabs.

One-dimensional crosstabs, like those in Figure 12.25 and Figure 12.26, group data by only one category (for example, by date). Two-dimensional crosstabs can group by more than one category. Figure 12.27 shows a crosstab with sales broken down by salesperson (rows) for each date (columns).

FIGURE 12.24

This form letter includes a graph informing investors that sales continue to rise.

Gift Corner

8891 Gaudy Ave * West Fantasee, CA 92222
1-800-555-GIFT

August 18, 1994

Dr. Susita M. Schumack
P.O. Box 11221
Philadelphia, PA 23456

Dear Dr. Schumack,

The Gift Corner is enjoying its greatest sales performance in years. As you can see from the graph below, our sales have risen steadily over the past several quarters.

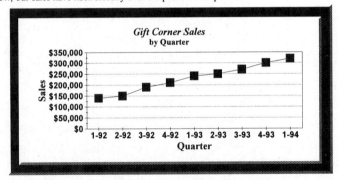

And there's more good news! We project continued growth with even greater gains, thanks to new product lines that will hit the market over the next year. Furthermore, our profitability is expected to climb dramatically due to the big tax cut on corporate profits recently enacted by Congress.

Dr. Schumack, we're proud to count you among our loyal investors and trust that you'll be as pleased by our financial results as we are. If you have any questions, please don't hesitate to call me at the toll-free number on our letterhead.

Sincerely,

Gondola Claplock

Gondola Claplock
Manager, Investor Relations

FIGURE 12.25

A one-dimensional crosstab showing the total quantity of each product sold on each date. In this example, the dates are arranged vertically down the left side of the crosstab.

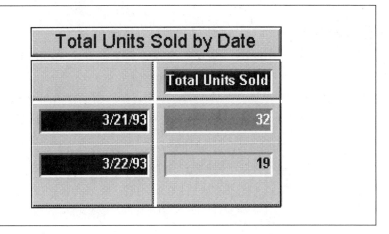

FIGURE 12.26

Another crosstab of the total number of each product sold on each date. In this example, the dates appear horizontally across the top of the crosstab.

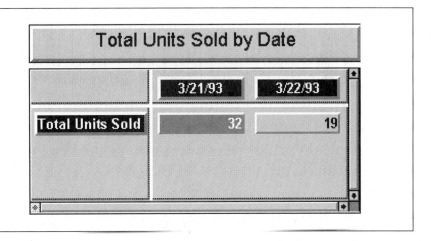

FIGURE 12.27

A two-dimensional crosstab summarizing Total Sales by Sales Person and Date Sold

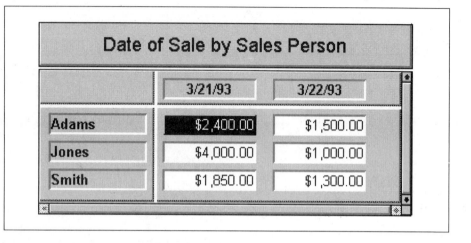

Anatomy of a Crosstab

The three main components of a crosstab are described below.

Column Specifies the field to group by. In Figure 12.27 the column field is Date Sold. This component is analogous to the x-axis in 1-D summary and 2-D summary graphs.

Categories Become the row labels in the crosstab. In Figure 12.27, the category field is Sales Person. The Categories component (which is optional) corresponds to the Grouped By field of a 2-D summary graph.

Summaries Display the results of a calculation at the intersection of each row and column in the crosstab. In Figure 12.27, the summary field is Total Sales. The Summaries component corresponds to the y-axis in a 1-D summary or 2-D summary graph.

You may define only one column field for a crosstab, but you can have as many categories and summaries as you wish.

Understanding Crosstab Summary Operators

Crosstabs can use the same summary operators as 1-D and 2-D summary graphs. These operators are described briefly below.

Sum Shows totals for each non-empty row and column pair.

Min Shows smallest of all individual values for each row and column pair.

Max Shows largest of all individual values for each row and column pair.

Count Counts the number of non-empty records for each row and column pair.

Avg Shows the average of all individual non-empty values for each row and column pair.

Std Shows the standard deviation of all individual values for each row and column pair (meaningful only with large samples).

Var Shows the statistical variance of all individual values for each row and column pair (meaningful only with large samples).

Designing a Crosstab

A crosstab, like a graph, is simply an object in your document design. The steps for designing crosstabs are a lot like those for designing graphs.

Creating a Crosstab

 To add crosstabs to existing forms, click the Crosstab tool in the Design window SpeedBar (shown at left), then click in your design and drag to define the initial size of your crosstab. A crosstab with undefined Categories, Column, and Summaries fields will appear on the Form Design window as in Figure 12.28.

The crosstab shown on the Design window is only a *template* of the actual crosstab that will appear when you preview or print the form.

After outlining the basic crosstab, you'll need to define it. The steps for defining crosstabs are described a bit later in this chapter.

FIGURE 12.28

The crosstab initially appears with undefined Categories, Column, and Summaries fields.

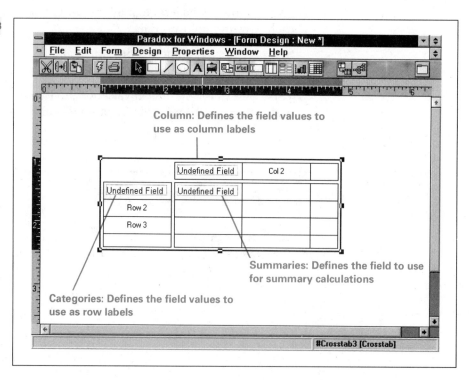

If you want to, you can create a new form that includes just the crosstab. Choose File ➤ New ➤ Form, choose your table in the **Data Model** dialog box, then select a Blank style in the **Design Layout** dialog box and click OK. Next, use the Crosstab tool as described above to place the crosstab into your design.

T I P

As with graphs, if anyone changes data that's used in a crosstab you're currently displaying in Form View, Paradox will update the affected data in the crosstab as soon as the user moves the cursor to another record in the table and you refresh the crosstab in Form View (for example, by pressing F8 twice). If the crosstab is on the same form as the table you're updating, it will be refreshed as soon as you move the cursor to another record.

Creating a Quick Crosstab

You can use the Quick Crosstab button in Table View either to create a new crosstab form or to display a form containing a crosstab.

 If you're in Table View and haven't assigned a preferred crosstab to the table, click the Quick Crosstab button in the SpeedBar (shown at left). You'll be taken to the **Define Crosstab** dialog box, which is described later in this chapter.

If you've already created a preferred crosstab for the table, clicking the Quick Crosstab button will display the crosstab in a new form. You can then click the Design button in the SpeedBar or press F8 to change the design.

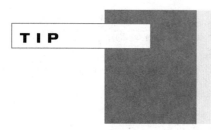

TIP To create a preferred crosstab, open the table, right-click the Quick Crosstab button in the SpeedBar, choose the form that contains your crosstab, and click OK. Then choose Properties ➤ View Properties ➤ Save to save your changes.

Inspecting the Entire Crosstab Object

When you are ready to define the fields of a crosstab or change its properties, you must inspect the crosstab object or its hot zones.

Inspecting the crosstab object leads to the property menu displayed in Figure 12.29. This menu lets you define all the fields for the crosstab and change the properties of the crosstab object.

You can use either one of the following techniques to inspect the crosstab object:

* Select the crosstab by clicking it. Then press F6 or move the mouse pointer to an empty area at the upper-left corner of the crosstab (just inside the selection handles) and right-click.

FIGURE 12.29

The Crosstab property menu

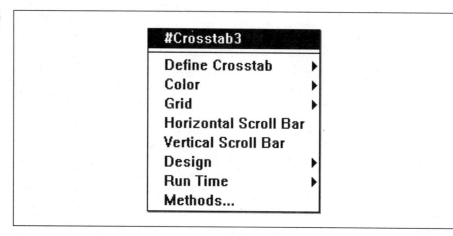

- Use the Object Tree to inspect the crosstab object, its Column, Categories, and Summaries, or any of its fields. This is often easier than insecting the crosstab hot zone.

Inspecting the Crosstab Hot Zones

You can inspect the Categories, Summaries, or Column hot zones whenever you want to add a category, summary, or column to the crosstab, or you want to change the properties of an individual category, summary, or column.

To inspect one of these hot zones, click on the crosstab, then move the mouse pointer to an empty area inside the boundaries of the hot zone you want to change and right-click. Figure 12.30 shows the hot zones for a selected crosstab object.

FIGURE 12.30

Hot zones on a selected crosstab object

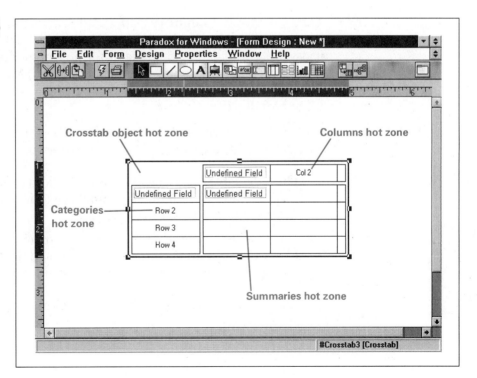

You can also inspect an individual field within the crosstab and change its properties. To do so, simply click the field, then right-click.

Defining Crosstab Fields One by One

You can define crosstab fields individually, or you can specify them all at once. The simplest crosstab uses field names from your table as the column, category, and summary fields. To define these fields, select the undefined field object you want, then right-click. Next choose Define Field from the menu and select a field name from the list.

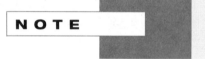

NOTE   You may not use the same field more than once in a crosstab. Unavailable fields are dimmed in the field list.

When you specify a summary field, Paradox automatically determines the default operator for that field. SUM is the initial default for all numeric fields, while COUNT is the default for non-numeric fields. If you want to use one of the other summary operators (MIN, MAX, COUNT, AVG, STD, or VAR) for a numeric field, you must open the **Define Crosstab** dialog box, described below.

If you prefer to specify all fields for the crosstab at once, inspect the crosstab object, choose Define Crosstab from the property menu, then...

- Click the table name if you want Paradox to assign the first three fields in your table to the Column, Categories, and Summaries fields of the crosstab, respectively.

- Click the list header (...) if you want to specify each field individually, you want to reorder, remove, or add fields, or you want to change the summary operators for fields in the crosstab.

Clicking the list header leads to the Define Crosstab dialog box shown in Figure 12.31.

FIGURE 12.31

The Define Crosstab
Dialog box is similar
to the Define Graph
dialog box described
earlier in this chapter.

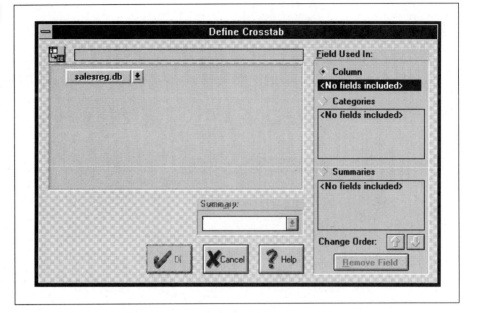

Using the Define Crosstab
Dialog Box

Here are the steps for defining all fields and summary operators of your
crosstab at once:

1. If you want to add a table to the data model, click the Data Model
   button in the upper-left corner of the dialog box, choose a table,
   and click OK. (This step is optional.)

2. For each field that you want to define, click the appropriate option
   in the Field Used In area of the dialog box. Then click the drop-
   down arrow to the right of the table name and click the field you
   want to assign. (You can click several fields when assigning
   Categories or Summaries.)

3. If you want to change the summary operator for a field, click the
   field you want to change in the Summaries list. Then click the
   Summary drop-down list and click on the operator you want.

4. If you want to remove a field, click the field in the Fields Used In area of the dialog box, then click the Remove button.

5. If you want to change the order of a field in the Categories or Summaries list, click on the appropriate field, then click the ↑ or ↓ Change Order button to move the selected field up or down in the list.

6. When you're finished, click OK.

N O T E   Remember that the Column field appears across the top of the crosstab, the Categories fields appear down the left side, and the Summaries fields are in the main part of the crosstab.

Adding a Category Field

You may want to summarize your table data by more than one category. For example, you could analyze the sales made by each salesperson, broken down by product.

To add a field (category) in the row area, inspect the Category area of the crosstab object (where the numbered rows appear) and choose Add a Category. Select the field you want, or click the list header (...), fill in the **Define Field Object** dialog box, and choose OK.

N O T E   You can also use the Define Crosstab dialog box to add a category.

When you run a crosstab with multiple categories, the category field names appear in the leftmost column of the crosstab object, and the table data is sorted first by the top category, then by subsequent categories. If you want to reposition these fields, return to the Define Crosstab dialog box, click the field you want to reorder in the Categories list, and use the ↑ and ↓ Change Order buttons.

Figure 12.32 shows a crosstab with multiple categories. Here, total sales for each date are categorized by salesperson *and* product number. Notice the separate rows for each unique combination of category values: Adams and A-111, Adams and B-222, Adams and C-333, and so forth. Figure 12.33 shows the design window used to produce this crosstab.

The crosstab in Figure 12.32 includes the following features:

- The Column is the Date Sold field of the SalesReg table.

- The Categories are the Sales Person and Product Number fields.

- The Summaries field is the Total Sales field, and the SUM operator is used.

FIGURE 12.32

This crosstab shows product sales grouped by Date Sold and categorized by Sales Person and Product Number.

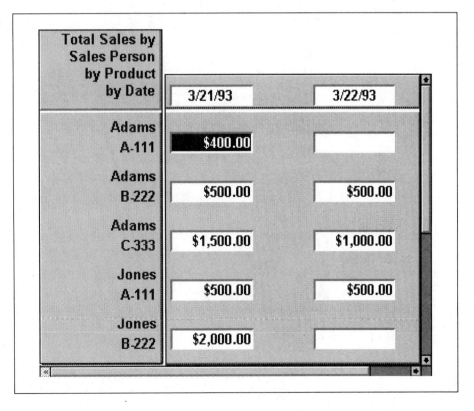

FIGURE 12.33

The Form Design window used to create the crosstab shown in Figure 12.32

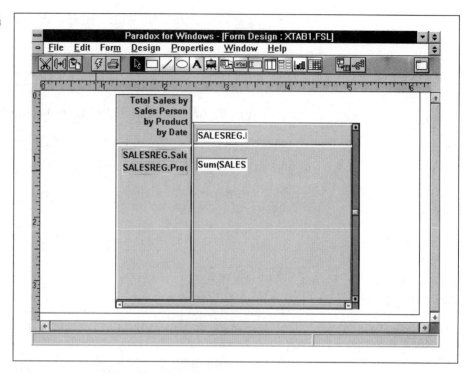

- We added vertical and horizontal scroll bars, which allow scrolling through the crosstab when it is displayed in the Form window. We changed the grid style of the crosstab to 3-D.

NOTE

The grid lines and the row and column numbering disappear from the crosstab in the Design window when the 3-D grid style is selected.

- We placed a text object at the upper-left corner of the crosstab table and typed each line of the crosstab title. We right-aligned the title text and used a bold font, then colored the text box gray and changed its frame style.

- Using the box tool, we drew boxes around the left and right columns of the crosstab to give it a more finished look.

- We changed the font and frame styles and colors of the field objects in the crosstab.

Adding a Summary Field

If you need to add a summary field to the crosstab, inspect the Summary area of the crosstab object (the empty area in the body of the crosstab), then choose Add a Summary. Select the field you want from the list, or click the list header (...) and complete the **Define Field Object** dialog box.

N O T E   You can also use the Define Crosstab dialog box to add a summary.

Suppose you want to compute total sales and sum the total units sold by each salesperson in the SalesReg table. In this case, you need two summary fields: one for the dollar value of all sales by each salesperson and one for the total number of units sold by each salesperson.

Figure 12.34 shows a crosstab that does the job. Here the Column is the Date Sold field, the Categories field is Sales Person, and the two Summaries fields are Units Sold and Total Sales. Figure 12.35 shows the Form Design window for the crosstab in Figure 12.34.

Most of the techniques used to enhance the crosstab in Figure 12.34 should be familiar to you by now, but here are some highlights:

- We placed a gray box around the entire crosstab.

- We placed a text object with the overall title for the crosstab inside the box and added two text objects containing the $$ characters in a large font. The typeface is Times New Roman.

- We added a short horizontal line below the Sales Person field to separate the units sold from the total sales figures for each salesperson.

FIGURE 12.34

A crosstab, categorized by Date Sold, and summarized by Units Sold and Total Sales for each Sales Person

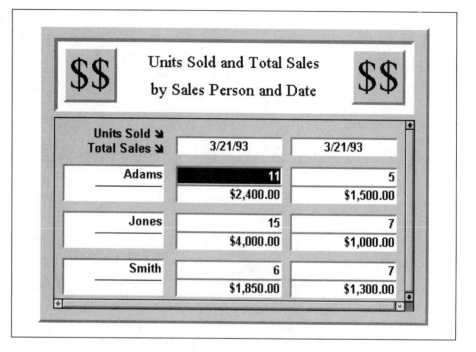

- We added a text object in the upper-left corner of the crosstab to explain the contents of the two summary fields. The arrows are available in the Wingdings TrueType font; they were placed using the Character Map (see Chapter 5).

- We added three-dimensional effects by changing the color, frame style, and frame thickness of various objects.

Redefining a Column

You can change the grouping of information in a crosstab simply by changing the field used for the crosstab columns. For example, recall that Figure 12.27 showed daily sales for each salesperson grouped by date sold. We changed the grouping to Product Number simply by redefining the column, as in Figure 12.36. (Of course, we also modified the title to reflect the data shown.)

FIGURE 12.35

The Form Design window for the crosstab in Figure 12.34

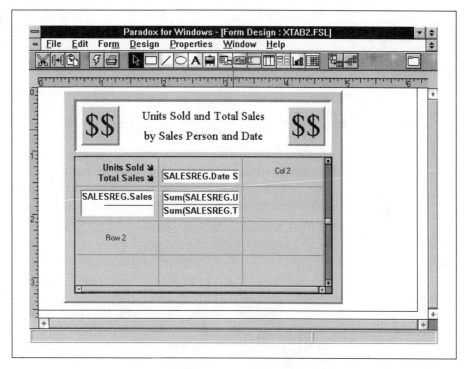

To redefine the column field, inspect the column area (any empty area in the numbered columns), choose Define Column Field from the property menu, and select an available field.

FIGURE 12.36

The crosstab from Figure 12.27 with the column changed from Date Sold to Product Number, and the title modified accordingly

Products Sold by Sales Person

	A-111	B-222	C-333
Adams	$400.00	$1,000.00	$2,500.00
Jones	$1,000.00	$2,000.00	$2,000.00
Smith	$400.00	$1,000.00	$1,750.00

NOTE As always, you can also inspect the crosstab object, click the list header (...) to open the Define Crosstab dialog box, and change the field used in the Column.

Adding Titles to Crosstabs

Unlike graphs, crosstabs do not have legends that clarify which fields are being displayed, how things are summarized, and why. Nor do they have any specific title or subtitle areas. Therefore, it's especially important to add titles and labels to your crosstabs using the Text tool in the SpeedBar. For example, the row label in Figure 12.26 is a text object, as are the titles in all the crosstab examples in this chapter. You can use any of the techniques discussed in Chapters 9 and 10 to customize the text object properties.

TIP If you place a box, line, ellipse, text, graphic, or OLE object in the same cell with the Categories or Summaries field, the object will be repeated throughout the crosstab.

Customizing Crosstab Objects

As with graphs, most areas of the crosstab object can be inspected and customized. You can use property inspection to change crosstab colors and grid style, add or remove scroll bars, change Design and Run Time properties, and redefine Column, Categories, and Summaries fields. All crosstab properties are changed in the standard way: Inspect the appropriate object or hot zone and choose from the property menu.

When changing color in a crosstab, keep in mind that the area you inspect in a crosstab determines which area is colored. For example, coloring the crosstab object itself changes the entire background color of the crosstab. However, inspecting the Categories, Summaries, or Column area and changing the color affects only the area you inspected. Thus, you can control the color of the row labels (categories), the body of the crosstab (summaries), and the column labels (columns). Similarly, inspecting a field in the crosstab and changing its color affects that field only.

Here are two other valuable facts concerning properties:

- Although the Grid, Horizontal Scroll Bar, Vertical Scroll Bar, and Methods properties appear on all the property menus, they affect the entire crosstab—not just a single area.

- Only the crosstab object includes a Design property, which you can use to pin the crosstab vertically or horizontally within your form design.

Changing the Dimensions of Crosstabs

Crosstabs are a special kind of table object, with the usual grid lines, rows, and columns normally found in tables. You can use many of the direct manipulation techniques described in Chapter 6 to change the dimensions of crosstabs.

For example, to change the width of all the crosstab table columns, move the mouse pointer to the vertical grid line at the right edge of Column 1. When the pointer changes to a two-headed horizontal arrow, drag the grid line to the left or right.

To change the height of all the rows, move the mouse pointer to the horizontal grid line at the bottom edge of Row 1, and when the pointer changes to a two-headed vertical arrow, drag the grid line up or down.

To change the width of the Categories column (which contains the row labels), move the mouse pointer to the vertical grid line between the numbered rows and the first column. When the two-headed horizontal arrow appears, drag to the left or right.

NOTE Be sure to change the height or width of fields and text objects to accommodate changes to the dimensions of the crosstab table.

You can also drag the borders or corners of the crosstab frame to show more or fewer rows and columns.

Combining Crosstabs and Graphs

Sometimes a crosstab or a summary graph alone isn't enough to provide the clearest understanding of your data. But who says you can't use both at once? Simply place a 1-D or 2-D summary graph side-by-side with a crosstab of the same data on your form, and you'll be able to spot trends easily while viewing numbers that explain those trends.

For example, the crosstab in Figure 12.37 summarizes total sales for each salesperson by date sold, while the 2-D summary graph next to the crosstab displays the same information graphically. In the graph on the right, you can quickly see that sales were stronger on 3/21/93 (thanks primarily to stellar performance by Jones on that day), and you can instantly compare the daily sales for each salesperson. The crosstab ties the visual display to exact dollar amounts of total sales by each person. Figure 12.38 shows the Form Design window for Figure 12.37.

FIGURE 12.37

A combined form with
both a crosstab and a
2-D summary graph.
The form presents total
sales for each
salesperson by date
sold.

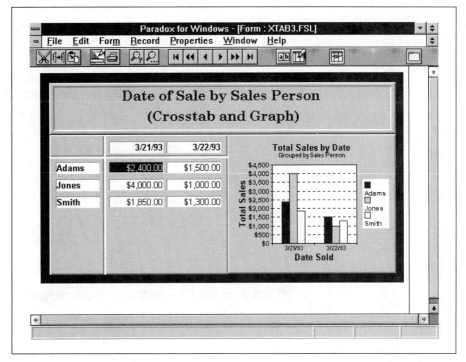

This chapter introduced you to the rich variety of graphs available for
presenting your data, and to crosstabs, which summarize your data in a
tabular format. When deciding whether to use a graph or a summary (or
both) to display your data, keep in mind that 1-D summary and 2-D summary graphs and crosstabs are closely related: Both can classify data by
categories, summarize data within categories, sort the summarized information, and display the results. The main difference is that graphs show
pictures—trends, patterns, and so forth—whereas crosstabs report hard
numbers.

You've now completed Part III of this book. In the next chapter, we'll
begin Part IV by looking at the many ways you can customize the Paradox
for Windows environment to suit your requirements and working style.

FIGURE 12.38

The Form Design
window for the form
in Figure 12.37

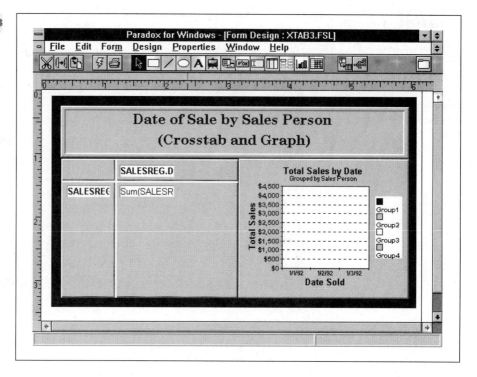

PART FOUR

Managing Your Projects

CHAPTERS

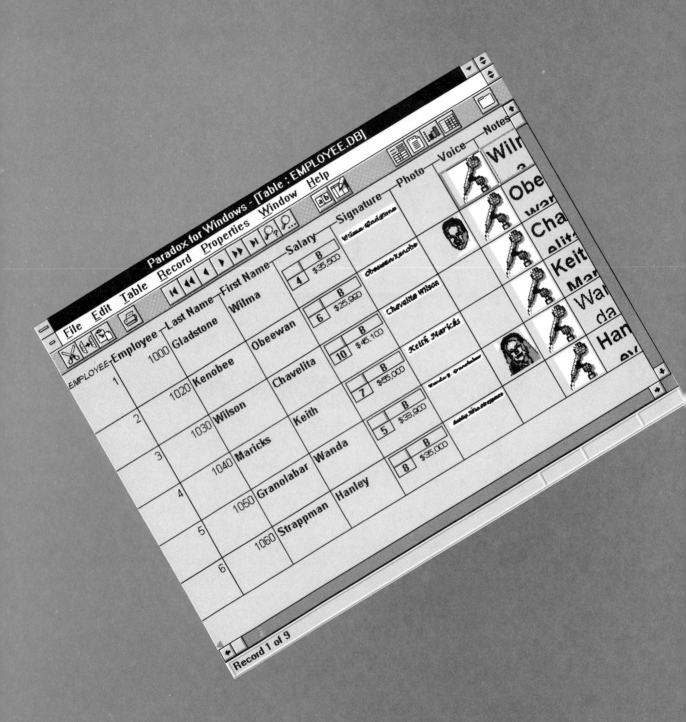

CHAPTER

13

Customizing Paradox
for Windows

fast TRACK

To change the default table properties   693

create a table named *Default* in your private directory, then define one field for each type of data you plan to store in any table. Add at least one row of data to *Default*, change its Table View properties, then choose Properties ➤ View Properties ➤ Save and close the table.

To change ODAPI configuration settings   698

double-click the Configuration Utility icon in the Paradox for Windows program group and make changes in the dialog box very carefully. Do not make changes unless you thoroughly understand their implications.

To change the serial number and signature information   704

double-click the Serial Number Utility icon in the Paradox for Windows program group. Make the necessary changes, then choose OK.

To change the location of your Paradox for Windows local directories   709

double-click the Local Settings Utility icon in the Paradox for Windows program group.

WHEN you install Paradox for Windows, many settings are determined automatically. For example, screen colors, printer, available fonts, and date and number formats are defined in the Windows Control Panel and Windows Setup applications. Other settings are controlled either from within Paradox for Windows or through stand-alone utility applications that are placed in the Paradox for Windows program group during installation.

Default settings, like certain rules, are designed to be changed. In this chapter, you'll learn how to customize Paradox for Windows. (For information about customizing Paradox for Windows on a network, refer to Appendix E.) Of course, changing default settings is entirely optional. If you are satisfied with the way Paradox runs on your computer, you can leave the default settings as they are.

As you browse through this chapter, keep in mind that some settings can be changed in more than one way. For example, Paradox for Windows takes its initial date and number formats from settings in the Windows Control Panel; however, you can also define custom formats within Paradox by changing the properties of date and number fields in tables, forms, and reports (see Chapter 6).

"When Do My Settings Take Effect?"

Some changes, such as switching to a new working directory, changing properties in the Table window, and updating Desktop properties, take effect immediately. Others are implemented when you restart Paradox. Still others, such as updates made from Windows Setup, take effect only after you restart Windows. But regardless of when the change takes effect, the new setting becomes the default for all future Paradox for Windows sessions—until you change the default again.

Getting Information about Your Settings

From time to time, you may need information about the resources of your computer system. Such information might come in handy when calling Borland's technical support hotline, or when refining default settings to maximize Paradox's performance on your computer. Windows and Paradox for Windows both provide access to system information.

Displaying Your Paradox for Windows Serial and Version Number

Like most Windows applications, Paradox for Windows can display your signature information (that is, your name and company name), serial number, and program version number. To view this information, choose Help ➤ About. You'll see the **About Paradox for Windows** dialog box.

To display an Internal version number, press Alt+I while viewing the dialog box. The number will appear in the lower left-hand corner. Choose OK to exit the dialog box. Later in this chapter, you'll learn how to change the signature information and serial number using the Serial Number Utility application.

Displaying Paradox for Windows System Settings

The File ➤ System Settings options shown below provide information about your Paradox for Windows system.

```
Auto Refresh...
Blank As Zero...
Drivers...
ODAPI...
```

Auto Refresh displays, and lets you determine, how often Paradox updates your current view of data on a network (see Appendix E for details).

Blank As Zero is a toggle option that controls how Paradox treats blank fields during calculations. Please see "Calculating with Blank Fields," later in this chapter, for details.

The remaining options are covered in the following two sections.

Displaying Database Driver Settings

Paradox for Windows can connect to various database drivers, which are installed with Paradox for Windows. (See Appendix A for installation instructions.) As long as you're connected to a driver, you can create, update, and display a table for that driver. For example, when connected to the Paradox and dBASE drivers, you can create and update Paradox for DOS, Paradox for Windows, and dBASE tables.

To view the list of available drivers, choose File ➤ System Settings ➤ Drivers. Choose OK when you're finished viewing the list.

Displaying the ODAPI Settings

ODAPI is an acronym for Open Database Application Programming Interface: the database engine that allows Paradox for Windows to share tables and files with other applications, such as dBASE for Windows and Quattro Pro for Windows. An application that uses the ODAPI engine is said to be "ODAPI-hosted."

To display the current ODAPI settings, choose File ➤ System Settings ➤ ODAPI. You'll see the **ODAPI System Information** dialog box shown in Figure 13.1. See "Using the Configuration Utility," later in this chapter, to find out what the settings mean and how to change them.

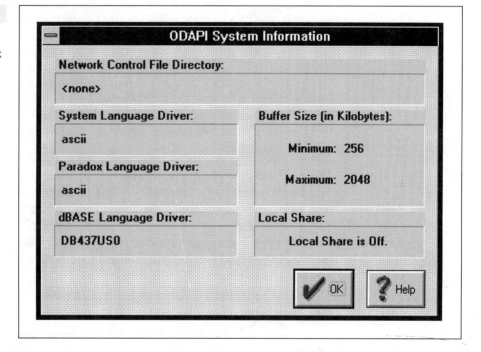

FIGURE 13.1

The ODAPI System Information dialog box

Using Windows Setup and Control Panel to Customize Your Computer

Like most Windows applications, Paradox for Windows learns about your machine configuration and preferred Windows settings by reading initialization files, which are maintained by the Setup and Control Panel applications in the Main group of the Windows Program Manager. You'll find instructions for using these applications in your Windows documentation.

You must run *Setup* when first installing your Windows system, and again whenever you change the monitor, keyboard, mouse, or network in use. Paradox cannot take advantage of newly installed hardware unless you've properly configured it through Setup or other applications supplied by the hardware vendor.

Control Panel provides many options for configuring and customizing your Windows system. The changes you make are stored in the *control.ini* and *win.ini* initialization files in the *c:\windows* directory. These files are consulted each time you start Windows or Paradox for Windows. The Control Panel options that are most important for customizing the Paradox environment are Color, Date, Time, Fonts, International, Keyboard, Mouse, Network, and Printers.

TIP
To change printer settings temporarily choose File ➤ Printer Setup from the Paradox for Windows menus.

Changing the Default Directory Settings

If you store files in many different directories, you may wish to change the default *working directory* where Paradox looks for tables, reports, forms, and other permanent files. To change your working directory, follow these steps:

1. Choose File ➤ Working Directory to open the **Set Working Directory** dialog box.

2. Type the name of the working directory. Be sure to include both the drive and directory name (for example, *c:\pdoxwin\giftco)*, and be sure that the specified directory exists. You can also use the Browse button or Aliases drop-down list to locate the directory you want.

3. Choose OK.

TIP

As an alternative to changing your working directory, you can use the Aliases or Path drop-down lists or the Browse button discussed in Chapters 3 and 14 to locate files and directories.

In addition to choosing a working directory, you can also choose a *private directory* for your network workstation. Each network workstation must have its own private directory for storing temporary tables such as *Answer* and *Changed* to avoid conflicts with other network users' temporary tables. Typically, this is the *\pdoxwin\private* directory on the local hard disk (if your computer has one) or your home directory on the network drive.

If you're running Paradox on a single-user computer, you'll still have a private directory, which you can change if necessary.

To change the private directory, follow the steps below.

1. Choose File ➤ Private Directory. You'll see the Private Directory dialog box.

2. Type the name of the private directory. Again, be sure to include both the drive and the directory name, and be sure that the directory you specify exists. If you prefer, you can use the Browse button to select a directory.

3. Choose OK.

4. If asked whether you're sure you want to close all Desktop windows and continue, choose Yes.

NOTE

Private directory file names will appear at the bottom of the file list in any Open or Save dialog box. You can also access the private directory by clicking the *:PRIV:* alias in any Path or Aliases drop-down list.

Calculating with Blank Fields

You can control how Paradox for Windows treats blank fields during calculations by using the File ➤ System Settings ➤ Blank As Zero option. Blank As Zero works on Paradox number and short number fields, and dBASE number and float number fields. (We'll explain how to perform calculations in Part 5 of this book.)

When Blank As Zero is *checked*, blank fields used in calculations are treated as if they contain a numeric value of zero. To understand how this works, imagine that you want to calculate the extended price, including sales tax, for each record in a query, report, or form. Further suppose that you've specified a Tax Rate of 7.75 (for 7.75%), a Unit Price of $35.00, and a blank value for the quantity ordered (Qty). With Blank As Zero selected, Paradox will treat the blank quantity ordered field as if it contained a zero. In the calculation below, a zero would be placed in the extended price field, which is probably *not* the result you want.

[Qty] * [Unit Price] * (1 + ([Tax Rate]/100))

When Blank As Zero is not checked (the default setting), any calculation that uses a blank field value will end up with a blank result. In the calculation above, the extended price field would therefore remain blank. The unchecked setting assumes that if a field is empty, its contents are probably either intentionally or accidentally omitted. Rather than assuming the blank field is meant to be zero, Paradox refuses to perform the calculation so you don't end up with an incorrect result.

Deciding which option to use for blank fields is a matter of personal preference. However, keep in mind that you are more likely to get incorrect results in a calculation if you treat blank fields as zeros.

TIP

To make blank or zero values stand out in the Table window, inspect the fields you're interested in, choose Data Dependent from the property menu, and select a contrasting background color or font for blank or zero values (see Chapter 6).

Changing the Default Table Properties

Paradox for Windows offers many ways to customize the properties of the Table window. You can change screen colors, column widths, column order, number and date formats, fonts, data-dependent properties, and more. After customizing the Table window, you can save the changes by choosing Properties ➤ View Properties ➤ Save.

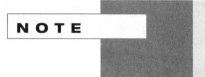

NOTE

Whenever you change a table's properties or assign a preferred form, report, graph, or crosstab in the Table window, Paradox updates the table's *.tv* or *.tvf* file.

Suppose you want to right-align all date fields, use single-lines for the grid, show table headings and text fields in a bold font, italicize the table name, and define a new row height. Changing the properties of each table in your database to meet these specifications would certainly be time consuming.

Fortunately, Paradox for Windows lets you establish and store default Table View properties. You simply create a table named *Default* in your private directory and assign the properties you want to use as your new defaults. In the future, any table that doesn't already have its own Table View property file (*.tv*) will automatically use the settings from the Default table. The tedium of inspecting and changing properties for each new table is gone forever. (Of course, you can always override the new default Table View properties for specific tables whenever you want to, as explained in Chapter 6.)

Follow these steps to establish the Default table and its properties:

1. Choose File ➤ Working Directory, type the name of your private directory (typically *c:\pdoxwin\private*), and choose OK.

2. Choose File ➤ New ➤ Table, select the table type you want (usually Paradox for Windows), and click OK. The Table Type you choose determines whether the default table is for Paradox for Windows or dBASE.

3. Define a field for each data type (see Chapter 4), then click the Save As button. The structure shown in Figure 13.2 is useful for any Paradox for Windows table.

4. When prompted for the table name, type **default**, then choose OK.

FIGURE 13.2

A sample structure for
a Default table

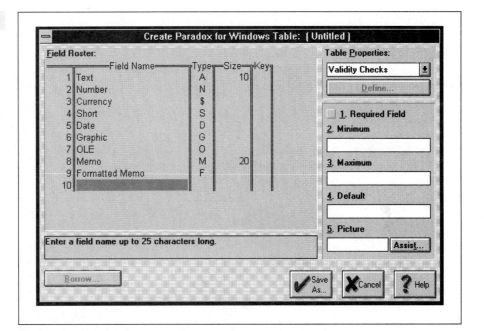

NOTE   A Paradox for Windows default table is named
default.db. A dBASE default table is named *default.dbf*.

Now open the Default table, switch to Edit mode (press F9), add one or
more rows of sample data, then customize the table however you like. Figure 13.3 shows a Default table with custom grids, row heights, data formats,
and other modified properties. When you're ready to save the properties,
choose Properties ➤ View Properties ➤ Save. If you created a Paradox for
Windows table, the default Table View properties file will be *default.tv*.
The dBASE Table View properties file is *default.tvf*.

Now close the Default table, switch to your preferred working directory,
and open your tables as usual. Any tables that don't already have a *.tv* (or
.tvf file will get their properties from the *default.tv* (or *default.tvf*) file in
your private directory. For example, notice how the Employee table
shown in Figure 13.4 has inherited the properties of the Default table in
Figure 13.3.

FIGURE 13.3

The Default table in the Table window. In this example, we modified the grid, table name, row height, and headings, and defined custom properties for various fields.

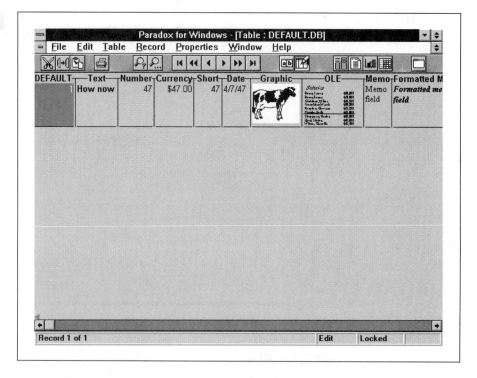

As for any Paradox table, you can change the *default.db* (or *default.dbf*) table's properties, structure, or data at any time. If you want to return to Paradox's built-in properties, simply delete the *default.tv* (or *default.tvf*) file: Open the Default table in your private directory, choose Properties ➤ View Properties ➤ Delete, and choose OK.

Changing the Default Designer Settings

In Chapter 9 you learned the basics of defining properties of objects in forms and reports. Chapter 9 also explained how to change the *default*

FIGURE 13.4

The Employee table displayed with the properties established by the Default table. We narrowed some columns to display all the fields, but made no other changes to properties that Employee inherited.

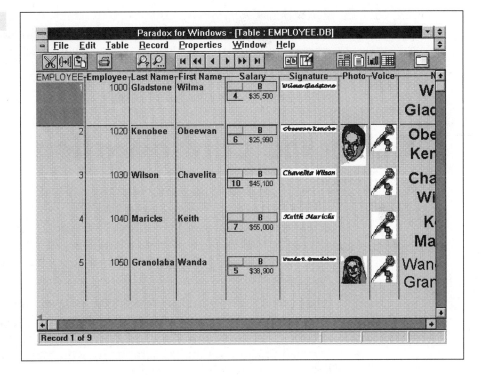

(or prototype) properties for all new objects. Recall the two basic methods for changing prototype properties:

- Inspect a tool in the SpeedBar and change its properties.
- Create an object (such as a graph), modify its properties, then select the object and choose Design ➤ Copy To SpeedBar.

The properties you set for a tool remain in effect for all design documents until you exit Paradox. If you want to keep the properties, choose Properties ➤ Designer and complete the **Designer Properties** dialog box, as explained in Chapter 9.

> **N O T E**
>
> Default object properties are usually stored in the *pxtools.ft* file in your working directory.

Using the Configuration Utility

The Paradox Configuration Utility allows you to change the initialization settings for ODAPI, the system that allows Paradox to share tables and files with other ODAPI-hosted applications such as Quattro Pro for Windows and dBASE for Windows.

The initial ODAPI settings are established when you install Paradox and, once set, they rarely need changing. In fact, most users will never need to run the Configuration Utility, as it is primarily designed for Paradox network administrators and programmers who must customize a Paradox system or "tweak" it to meet special needs. Because few people need this utility, we'll describe it only briefly.

> **N O T E**
>
> To display the current settings without changing them, choose <u>F</u>ile ➤ S<u>y</u>stem Settings ➤ <u>O</u>DAPI from the Paradox for Windows menus.

To run the Configuration Utility, switch to the Windows Program Manager, then double-click the Configuration Utility icon in the Paradox program group. You'll see the **ODAPI Configuration Utility** dialog box shown in Figure 13.5.

Make changes in the ODAPI Configuration Utility dialog box as you would in any other dialog box. That is, type values into the text boxes, choose options from the drop-down list boxes, and click option buttons, as appropriate.

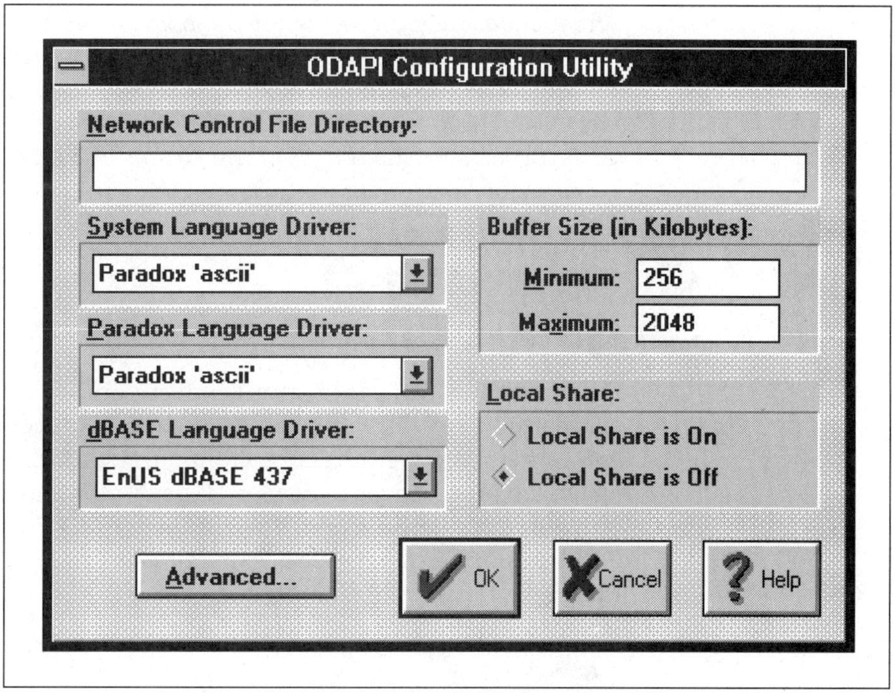

FIGURE 13.5

The ODAPI
Configuration Utility
dialog box

When you've finished making changes, click OK. Your changes will take effect after you exit all ODAPI-hosted applications and restart one. Any changes you make in the Configuration Utility are usually stored in *c:\windows\system\odapi.cfg*, which Paradox reads at startup. You can use the Local Settings Utility, described later in this chapter, to change the default location of *odapi.cfg*.

The following sections briefly describe each of the ODAPI Configuration File settings that you can change.

Changing the Network Control File Directory

The network control file directory tells ODAPI where to find *pdoxusrs.net*. You must set this directory if you want to share tables and files with other users and applications.

When choosing a directory for the *pdoxusrs.net* file, be sure to choose (or create) a directory in which users can read, write, and delete files. Also, you must use the same directory for all applications that use *pdoxusrs.net*, including Paradox 4.0, Paradox for Windows, and Quattro Pro for Windows. Please see Chapter 15 of the *Getting Started* manual that comes with Paradox for Windows for additional information.

Changing the Language Drivers

Different countries use different conventions for sorting, capitalizing, and comparing text. On your computer, these conventions are enforced by *language driver* programs. The Configuration Utility allows you to specify which language driver to use for all new system tables, for Paradox tables only, and for dBASE tables only. In the United States, the default System and Paradox Language Driver is *Paradox 'ascii'* and the default dBASE Language Driver is *EnUS dBASE 437*.

NOTE

In Figure 13.5 and in the three language driver drop-down lists in the ODAPI Configuration Utility dialog box, the numbers refer to the driver's *code page*, which defines the exact set of characters used for a particular country or region. Please see your DOS manual for more information about code pages.

When you create a Paradox table, the language driver is included in the table's definition. This driver governs the table's sorting operations and other character operations, regardless of subsequent changes to system settings. Chapter 14 explains how to determine which language driver was used to create a table and how to change the language driver of an existing table. Note that the language driver options affect your Paradox, dBASE, and ODAPI files only. They have no effect on other language or country-related settings, such as date, number, or currency formats, which are controlled through the International option of Control Panel.

Changing the Buffer Size

The buffer size controls the minimum and maximum amount of computer memory (RAM) that Paradox sets aside for table data. Both settings are in Kilobytes (KB):

Minimum   The smallest amount of RAM that Paradox reserves for table data. This can be any integer greater than 32 and less than or equal to your maximum buffer size. For best performance, set the minimum buffer size to one-third of your *available extended memory*.

Maximum   The largest amount of memory you want Paradox to use. This can be any integer up to the total amount of extended memory available on your workstation. For best performance, set the maximum buffer size to two-thirds of your *available extended memory*.

Extended memory is the amount of memory beyond 1MB. For example, a computer with 8MB of total memory has 7MB of extended memory. *Available memory* refers to the amount of memory usually available to the application. Consider again the 8MB machine: If you reserve 1MB of extended memory for a disk cache (for example, *smartdrv.exe*), you have 6MB of *available extended memory* (Total memory (8MB) – 1MB – reserved (1MB) = 6MB). With 6MB of available extended memory, the ideal minimum buffer size is 2048KB, and the ideal maximum buffer size is 4096KB.

For database-intensive operations such as running queries and utilities and navigating through very large tables, you may wish to set the maximum buffer size to eighty percent of the physical memory, or physical memory minus 2MB, whichever is greater. This will improve database performance, but may slow down other Windows tasks, including non-database operations in Paradox for Windows.

N O T E

Consider *reducing* the maximum buffer size settings if you need to run other applications while running Paradox for Windows. Be sure to leave enough memory available for your other applications. If in doubt, simply use the default settings, which should be adequate for most situations.

Changing the Local Share

Local share controls whether Paradox performs network-style file locking on your local hard drive. Choose *Local Share Is On* if you need to run a non-ODAPI application (such as Paradox 4.0 or ObjectVision) while Paradox is working with a table. If you set local share on, you must load SHARE (by typing **share** at the DOS prompt or including this command in your *autoexec.bat* file), and you must specify a directory for the network control file before starting Windows and Paradox.

You do not need to set local share on if you're using ODAPI-hosted applications like Quattro Pro for Windows, or if no other applications will use your tables at the same time. Setting local share on when you don't really need it can slow down the performance of your machine.

Advanced Options

The Configuration Utility's *Advanced* button allows you to configure ODAPI drivers and optimize database performance through the **ODAPI Full Tree Editor** dialog box.

In general, the Advanced button should be used by *advanced users only* because incorrect settings can cause problems with your system. However, you may wish to use it if you're not happy with the way Paradox handles query criteria involving dates and the ".." wildcard. Suppose, for example, that you're using a query to find records with start dates in August of 1993. Placing the criterion *08/../93* in the Start Date field of the CustList query table will select the records you want; however, the criterion *8/../93* will come up empty when you run the query. Similarly, the criterion *../04/93* will find start dates on the fourth of the month, but *../4/93* will not. Why? Because Paradox expects you to type a leading zero in the month and day portion of the query criterion.

If you prefer to omit leading zeros when typing query criteria involving dates and the ".." wildcard, follow these steps:

1. Click the Advanced button in the ODAPI Configuration Utility dialog box. The ODAPI Full Tree Editor dialog box will appear.

2. Click *SYSTEM* in the Category list, click *FORMATS* in the Group list, click *DATE* in the Section list, and click *LEADINGZEROM* in the Item list. Your screen will resemble Figure 13.6.

3. Change the contents of the Value text box from TRUE to **FALSE**.

4. Click *LEADINGZEROD* in the Item list.

5. Change the contents of the Value text box from TRUE to **FALSE**.

6. Choose OK twice.

FIGURE 13.6

The ODAPI Full Tree Editor dialog box after clicking SYSTEM, then FORMATS, then DATE, then LEADINGZEROM.

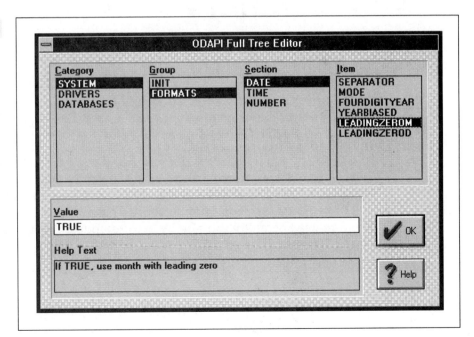

The next time you start Paradox and type query criteria like the examples above, you can (and should) omit leading zeros. To return the leading zero settings to their defaults, repeat the steps above, changing the values in Steps 3 and 5 from FALSE to **TRUE**.

N O T E   See Chapter 8 for information on queries. For details on using the advanced configuration options, click the Help button or refer to the *advodapi.txt* file in your Paradox directory (usually *c:\pdoxwin*).

Changing Serial Numbers and Signature Information

When you install Paradox for Windows, you'll be asked to provide serial number and signature information. Recall that the serial number and signature information appear when you choose Help ➤ About from the Paradox for Windows menus.

When you purchase additional Paradox packages for a network, you will receive new serial numbers to add to your network license. Once Paradox is installed, the network administrator can use the Serial Number Utility to add these serial numbers, or to change or delete existing serial numbers. The utility can also be used to update the user name and company signature information.

WARNING Adding or deleting serial numbers changes the user count, which controls the number of people who can use Paradox on a network concurrently. Therefore, the Serial Number Utility *should not* be used to update serial numbers when people are using Paradox on the network.

To start the utility, switch to the Program Manager, then double-click the Serial Number Utility icon in the Paradox for Windows group window. The Serial Number Update Program dialog box will appear, as in Figure 13.7.

FIGURE 13.7

The Serial Number
Update Program
dialog box

Serial Number Update Program

Serial Number:

Total User Count:

4

AA930A11031630
AA930A30517631

Add

Delete

User Name:
Hanley Allen Strappman

Company Name:
RNAA Inc.

OK   Cancel   Help

If you want to change the user name or company name, simply edit the appropriate text box. To add a serial number, type the serial number into the Serial Number text box, then click Add. To delete a serial number from the list, click the serial number you want to delete, then click Delete.

Understanding Paradox for Windows Initialization Files

As the name suggests, *initialization files* determine settings that take effect when you start Paradox for Windows. For example, initialization files control the appearance and settings of Paradox windows, and set the current working directory and Desktop configuration. Because Paradox updates most initialization settings automatically, most users will never need to know how they work.

In the sections that follow, we'll briefly describe each initialization file and how it is updated. If you need more information, please see the "Getting Started" documentation that comes with Paradox for Windows, or refer to the *settings.txt* file in the Paradox directory (*c:\pdoxwin*).

ODAPI Initialization File

The ODAPI initialization file (*c:\windows\system\odapi.cfg*) is a binary file that keeps track of initial settings for the ODAPI engine. This file is updated whenever you make changes through the Configuration Utility or permanently save or delete an alias via the File ➤ Aliases option in Paradox for Windows.

Keep in mind that the ODAPI settings remain in effect while any application that uses ODAPI is running. For example, if you run Quattro Pro for Windows and then start Paradox for Windows, Paradox will use the ODAPI settings that were loaded with Quattro Pro for Windows. To display the current ODAPI settings, choose File ➤ System Settings ➤ ODAPI.

Windows Initialization File

The Windows initialization file (*c:\windows\win.ini*) tracks the location of your working and private directories, default command-line options for starting Paradox, and the location of the *odapi.cfg* file. This text file also contains general Windows defaults.

The *win.ini* file is updated when you install Paradox, change the working and private directory for Paradox, or use the Local Settings Utility (described later).

NOTE   Although most updates to *win.ini* are automatic, you must add default command-line options manually. Appendix A provides information about command-line options, which temporarily override settings in the initialization files when you start Paradox from a command line.

Paradox Initialization File

The Paradox initialization file (*c:\windows\pdoxwin.ini*) contains your preferences for the Paradox for Windows Desktop, Desktop properties such as the title and SpeedBar appearance, the Form and Report window properties, and any custom date and number formats you define. This text file is updated automatically whenever you exit Paradox.

Paradox Working Directory Initialization File

The working directory initialization file, *pdoxwork.ini*, describes the contents of a working directory's folder. This text file is updated (or created) whenever you switch to a new working directory or exit Paradox. Its settings can be used to override defaults in *pdoxwin.ini*.

Control Panel Initialization File

Paradox for Windows inherits many configuration settings from Windows itself, including the default colors for windows and menus, printer information, your network type (if any), international settings for documents and tables, and the formats and values of the system Date and Time variables.

Changes to these settings are made through the Windows Control Panel and are stored in the *c:\windows\control.ini* text file.

Changing the Initialization Files

Most changes to Paradox for Windows initialization files are made automatically through Paradox for Windows menu options, the Windows Control Panel, and the standalone Paradox utility applications. These methods are always the easiest and *safest* ways to update your preferences.

On rare occasions, however, you may need to use a text editor, such as the Windows Notepad or DOS Edit command, to view or edit the *win.ini*, *pdoxwin.ini*, and *pdoxwork.ini* files. If you do use a text editor, please be *extremely* careful. An editing mistake can corrupt the file and make it unusable, not only for Paradox for Windows but also for other Windows applications that may need it. As a precaution, always back up your .ini files before changing them. The best advice is, if you're not sure how to edit the files safely, leave them alone.

> **WARNING**
>
> Paradox provides tools for updating the *odapi.cfg*, *default.db*, *default.dbf*, and *pxtools.ft* files. *Never* edit these files with a text editor because you can damage your copy of Paradox and the data in your tables.

Changing Your Paradox for Windows Local Settings

The default working directory, private directory, and location of the ODAPI configuration file are defined when you install Paradox. You can change the local and private directories from within Paradox at any time (those changes take effect immediately).

You can also use the Local Settings Utility to change all three settings at once from outside Paradox for Windows. To use this utility, switch to Program Manager, then double-click the Local Settings Utility icon in the Paradox for Windows group window. The **Paradox for Windows Local Settings** dialog box appears, as shown in Figure 13.8.

Edit the current settings as necessary, then choose OK. Your changes will update the *win.ini* file and take effect the next time you start Paradox for Windows.

NOTE   The Local Settings Utility provides the only method, other than manual editing, of updating the location of the ODAPI configuration file.

In this chapter we've discussed many ways to customize the default settings for Paradox for Windows. As mentioned at the outset, changing default settings is entirely optional. If you are happy with the way Paradox is running on your computer, you can leave the default settings alone.

FIGURE 13.8

The Paradox for
Windows Local
Settings dialog box

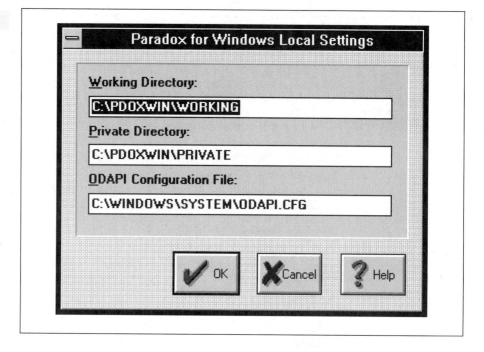

The next chapter presents tools for managing Paradox for Windows files. We'll delve into the Browser and explain how to work with folders. We'll also show you how to rename, copy, and delete files (including tables), move and copy records from one table to another, protect your data, and restructure tables.

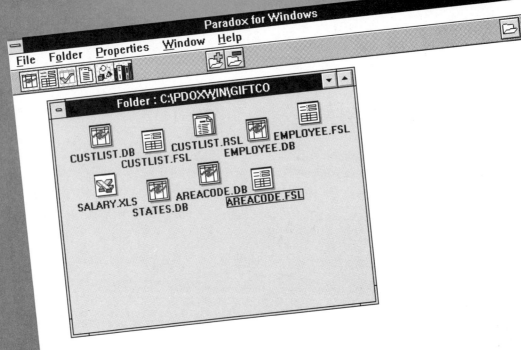

CHAPTER

14

Managing Your Files

fast TRACK

● **To use the Alias Manager to add or delete aliases**   **717**

  choose File ➤ Aliases. After defining aliases, you can use them to access a database from any directory on your computer.

● **To use the Browser**   **720**

  to locate and manage objects on your computer, simply click the Browse button in any dialog box where it is available. If necessary, use the Aliases list, the Type list, Filters, and directory tree to locate the file you want, then select the file and choose OK. While in the Browser, you can right-click any object and select file management options from the menu that appears.

● **The Folder window**   **727**

  allows you to keep related objects together. To open the Folder window, click the Open Folder button in the SpeedBar. To add objects to the folder, click the Add Folder Item button, select the objects you want to add, then choose OK. To remove objects from the folder, click the Remove Folder Item button, select the objects you want to remove, then choose OK (the objects remain on the computer's disk). You can inspect any object in the folder.

● **To manage tables and files**   **733**

  choose File ➤ Utilities, then select Rename, Copy, or Delete.

AS you develop more Paradox for Windows objects—tables, forms, reports, and so forth—you'll need to learn how to manage them. In this chapter, you'll learn how to perform some important file management tasks, including

- locating and managing tables, records, and other files
- obtaining information about Paradox tables
- restructuring existing tables
- adding password protection to tables
- repairing damaged tables.

NOTE   Please refer to Appendix B for information on importing and exporting data between Paradox and other applications.

Using Aliases

In Paradox, a database is a collection of files—tables, forms, reports, and so forth—located in a directory on your local hard disk or on a network. As mentioned in Chapter 3, an *alias* is a nickname that provides quick access to your database.

Suppose you have stored a database in the directory *c:\pdoxwin\giftco*. If you assign an alias, such as *Gift_Corner*, to that directory, that alias will appear in the Path list of any dialog box that displays a list of file names.

From then on, you can simply click the alias name instead of typing a path name. To view the names of files stored in another directory, simply click the Path drop-down arrow and click the alias name you want.

NOTE   Paradox automatically provides two aliases. The :WORK: alias stands for the current working directory. The :PRIV: alias represents your private directory (usually *c:\pdoxwin\private*).

Aliases provide several advantages:

- They offer a handy, error-free alternative to typing complete path names.

- They allow you to access a database from any directory on your computer.

- You can give aliases meaningful names that are easier to remember than path names. For example, the alias *Chap1_Figures* is easier to remember than a long path name like *d:\pdoxwin\masterng\chap01\figures*.

- You can change the path name of an alias at any time. When you do so, any forms, reports, and other Paradox objects that refer to that alias name will automatically refer to the new directory path.

- You can use aliases instead of full path names when referring to files in ObjectPAL applications. This means that you can move applications to other directories without having to recode all references to files. See Chapter 19 for more information about ObjectPAL applications.

Using the Alias Manager

The Alias Manager allows you to view or change the path names of existing aliases, delete aliases, and add new ones. To open the **Alias Manager** dialog box, choose File ➤ Aliases. You'll see the dialog box shown in Figure 14.1.

FIGURE 14.1

The Alias Manager
dialog box

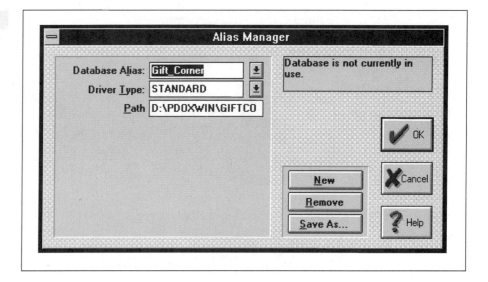

Viewing or Changing an Alias Path Name

To view or change the path name for an existing alias, open the Alias Manager dialog box and proceed as follows:

1. Click the Database Alias drop-down arrow to display the list of aliases.

2. Click the alias you want to view or change. The path name assigned to the alias will appear in the Path text box.

3. If you want the alias to point to a different directory, change the path name in the Path text box. The directory must already exist.

4. Save your changes as described below under "Saving Alias Changes."

NOTE To change a database alias *name*, you must delete the alias as described below, then create a new one with the desired name.

Adding an Alias

To add a new alias, open the Alias Manager dialog box, then follow these steps:

1. Click the New button.

2. If you want to use an existing alias as a model for the new one, click the Database Alias drop-down arrow and select the alias.

3. Type a name for the new alias in the Database Alias text box. The alias name must be unique, and can include any combination of letters, numbers, and spaces. Spaces are automatically converted to underscore (_) characters.

4. If you want to change the path name, type the complete path name in the Path text box (for example, *c:\pdoxwin\graphics*). The directory must already exist.

5. Save your changes as described below.

Deleting an Alias

To delete an alias from the Alias Manager dialog box, simply click the Database Alias drop-down arrow, click the name of the alias you want to delete, click the Remove button, then save your changes as described below. Removing an alias has no effect on the directory that the alias referenced.

Saving Alias Changes

You can save your changes in the Alias Manager dialog box either for the current Paradox session only, or for all future Paradox sessions.

If you want your changes to exist only until you exit Paradox for Windows, click the Keep New button, then click OK or Cancel to close the Alias Manager dialog box.

If you want to save the changes permanently, click the Save As button to open the **Save File As** dialog box. Choose OK, then answer Yes to overwrite the existing *odapi.cfg* file (see Chapter 13). When you return to the Alias Manager dialog box, you can either make additional changes or choose OK or Cancel to exit the dialog box.

Using the Browser

The Browser is a powerful tool for locating and managing objects (files) in any directory on your computer. To open the Browser, simply click the Browse button in any dialog box where it is available. Figure 14.2 shows a sample Browser dialog box.

TIP

If you simply want to view files in a directory that has an alias, use the Path list instead of the Browse button— it's faster. You can also use the Type drop-down list (if it's available) to restrict the type of file listed.

The left half of the dialog box shows the *directories* on the computer. The right half of the window shows an alphabetical list of *file names* in the currently selected directory. You can use the Aliases, Type, Filters, and directory areas of the dialog box to display other directories and files, as discussed below.

After locating the file you want, click it and choose OK. You'll either be returned to the dialog box you came from or Paradox will immediately take some action on the selected file.

If you wish to return to the dialog box you came from without selecting a file or changing the directory, choose Cancel.

FIGURE 14.2

The Browser is a powerful tool for locating and managing files in any directory on your computer.

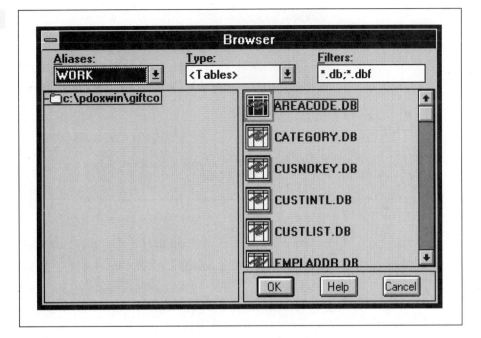

Using the Aliases List

To switch to another directory temporarily, click the Aliases drop-down arrow in the Browser, then click an alias name. To see the aliases for your disk drives (A:, B:, C:, D:), scroll to the top of the aliases list. To switch to the root directory of a disk drive, simply click the drive's alias.

Using the Type List

The Type drop-down list in the Browser allows you to restrict the file list to a specific type of file. The types available depend on which dialog box you were using when you opened the Browser. For example, after choosing File ➤ Open ➤ Table and clicking Browse, only the <Tables> type is available in the Type list. Table 14.1 describes all the available file types.

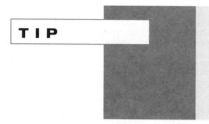

T I P

To work with *all* the file types that Paradox recognizes, open the Folder window, click the Add Folder Item button in the SpeedBar, click the Type drop-down arrow and choose *<Files>*, then click Browse. We'll discuss the Folder window later in this chapter.

TABLE 14.1: File Types Included in the Type List

FILE TYPE	DESCRIPTION
<Files>	All file types (*.*).
<Forms>	Paradox forms (*.fsl, *.fdl). See Chapter 10.
<Libraries>	ObjectPAL libraries (*.lsl, *.ldl). See Chapter 19.
<Queries>	Paradox query files (*.qbe). See Chapter 8.
<Reports>	Paradox reports (*.rsl, *.rdl). See Chapter 11.
<Scripts>	ObjectPAL script files (*.ssl, *.sdl). See Chapter 19.
<Tables>	Paradox and dBASE tables (*.db, *.dbf).

Using Filters

Filters provide another way to restrict the list of files in the Browser. To create a filter, type a file name or extension (or both) into the Filters text box, then press ↵.

You can use either of the DOS wildcard characters listed below in the file name or extension.

- The asterisk (*) represents a whole word or a group of characters. For example *.*exe* represents all files with an *.exe* extension. The wildcard *c*.** represents all files beginning with the letter *c* and having any extension.

- The question mark (?) represents a single character. For instance, *?????.** lists files with up to five letters and any extension.

Keep in mind that the filter works in conjunction with the Aliases and Type specifications. As an example, the filter $c*.*$ normally specifies all files beginning with the letter c and having any extension. However, if you've also specified *Gift_Corner* as the alias and a <Tables> file type, you'll only see file names of tables that begin with the letter c in the *c:\pdoxwin\giftco* directory.

TIP   You can also use wildcards in any text box that displays a list of file names. Press ↵ after typing the wildcard to redisplay the list.

Browsing through Directories

The computer's file system is organized into a tree structure of directories, subdirectories, and files. The highest level of the tree is called the *root* directory; all other directories branch out below the root directory. A directory within a directory is called a subdirectory.

The left side of the Browser displays the alias directory and its subdirectories. To switch to any directory shown in the left side of the window, click the desired folder icon or directory name. The file names for the selected directory will appear in the right side of the window. The results of using these techniques to switch to the *c:\pdoxwin* folder appear in Figure 14.3.

Notice that some directory folders are shaded. Shaded folders identify directories that contain subdirectories. Initially, each shaded folder icon is "closed" and subdirectory folders are not visible. To open the shaded folder icon and reveal its lower-level subdirectories, simply double-click the folder icon or name. Then click a subdirectory folder or name to display file names in that subdirectory. In Figure 14.4, we double-clicked the *pdoxwin* folder, then clicked the *giftco* folder to display the files in the *c:\pdoxwin\giftco* subdirectory.

To close an opened subdirectory, double-click its icon or directory name again. The subdirectory folders will disappear.

FIGURE 14.3

The Browser after clicking the *pdoxwin* folder

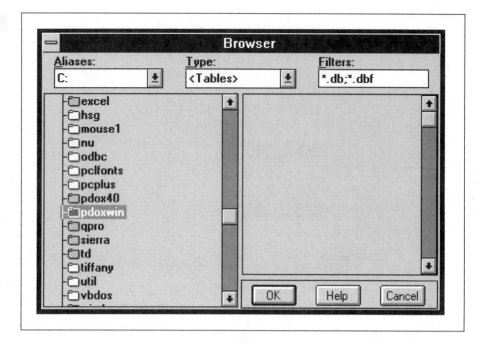

FIGURE 14.4

To display the sub-directories below a directory, double-click the shaded directory icon.

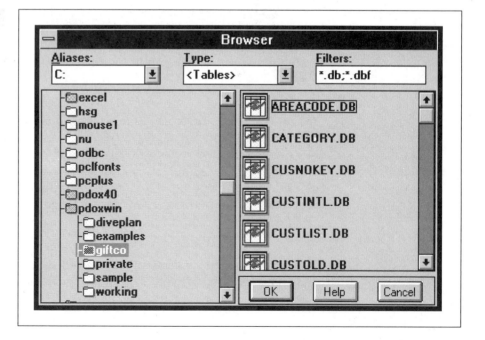

Inspecting Objects in the File Browser

Once you've located an object in the Browser, the fun begins. You can right-click any file object to "do something" with that object, depending on the type of object you're inspecting.

Notice in Figure 14.4 that each file name is preceded by an icon indicating the type of data stored in the file. For example, the icon next to the *areacode.db* table resembles the Open Table icon in the SpeedBar. Form and report icons resemble the Open Form and Open Report buttons on the SpeedBar. Data files created by other applications, such as Notepad, Lotus 1-2-3, Paintbrush, and Excel, have the icons of their parent application. Executable files (*.exe*, *.com*, and *.bat*) have "lightning bolt" icons.

Most file objects can be inspected by right-clicking or pressing F6. For example, right-clicking a table file opens the property menu shown in Figure 14.5. (This property menu is similar to the File ➤ Utilities menu.)

FIGURE 14.5

Inspecting a table object in the File Browser opens the property menu shown here.

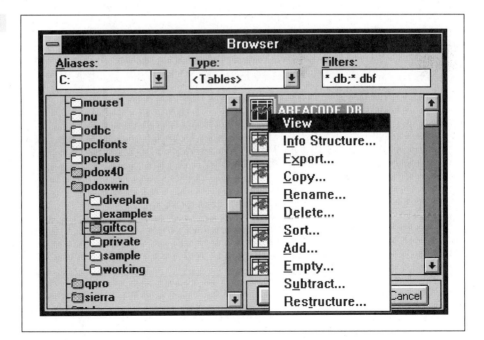

The options on the property menu are always specific to the type of object you're inspecting. Table 14.2 provides an alphabetical list of properties you'll encounter when inspecting icons in the Browser dialog box or Folder window.

TABLE 14.2: Properties You'll Encounter When Inspecting Icons in the Browser Dialog Box or Folder Window

PROPERTY	EXPLANATION
Add	Add records from this table to another table.
Copy	Copy this object to a new object.
Delete	Delete this object.
Delimited Text Import	Import this text file into a table in delimited text format. See Appendix B.
Design	Open the Design window for this object. See Chapters 9-12 and 19.
Empty	Remove all records from this table.
Export	Export this table to another application. See Appendix B.
Fixed Length Import	Import this text file into a table in fixed length text format. See Appendix B.
Import	Import this spreadsheet file into a table. See Appendix B.
Info Structure	Display information about the table's structure.
Open	Open this query. See Chapter 8.
Play	Play this ObjectPAL script. See Chapter 19.
Print	Print this report document. See Chapter 11.
Print With	Request the table to use, then print this report document. See Chapter 11.
Rename	Change the name of this object.
Restructure	Change the structure of this table.
Run	Run this query. See Chapter 8.

TABLE 14.2: Properties You'll Encounter when Inspecting Icons in the Browser Dialog Box or Folder Window (continued)

PROPERTY	EXPLANATION
application W/Params	Run this application with command-line parameters. Type the parameters (but do not type the program name), then choose OK.
Run *application*	Run this application.
Sort	Sort this table. See Chapter 7.
Subtract	Remove records from a target table if they match records in this table.
View	Open this table in Table View. See Chapter 6.
View Data	Display the data in the format defined by this document. See Chapters 9, 10 and 12.
View With	Request the name of the table to use, then display the data in the format defined by this document. See Chapters 9, 10, and 12.

Managing Folders

Paradox for Windows folders are handy for organizing and accessing related objects. A single folder can contain files from one subdirectory of your computer's hard disk or a collection of objects located in different directories or even different network servers. Once placed in a folder, an object can usually be opened by double-clicking it.

Paradox for Windows folders can contain any type of file stored on your computer or network, including Paradox objects and non-Paradox objects such as spreadsheets, text files, and executable programs. Table 14.3 lists the file extensions of all Paradox for Windows objects.

TABLE 14.3: File Extensions for Paradox for Windows Objects

EXTENSION	TYPE OF OBJECT
.db	Paradox table
.dbf	dBASE table
.dbt	Memos for a dBASE table
.fdl	Delivered form
.fsl	Saved form
.ftl	Temporary form document
.ldl	Delivered ObjectPAL library
.lsl	Saved ObjectPAL library
.ini	Initialization file
.mb	Memos for a Paradox table
.mdx	Maintained index of a dBASE table
.ndx	Non-maintained index of a dBASE table
.px	Primary index of a Paradox table
.qbe	Saved query
.rdl	Delivered report
.rsl	Saved report
.rtl	Temporary report document
.ssl	Saved ObjectPAL script
.stl	Temporary ObjectPAL script document
.tv	Table View settings for a Paradox table
.tvf	Table View settings for a dBASE table
.val	Validity checks and referential integrity for a Paradox table
.xnn	Secondary index for a Paradox table (where nn is a number)
.ynn	Secondary index for a Paradox table (where nn is a number)

When you place objects into the folder of the working directory, these objects will appear as icons whenever you open the Folder window. You can add or remove icons from the folder at any time. Figure 14.6 shows a sample Folder window for the *c:\pdoxwin\giftco* directory opened on the Desktop.

NOTE The folder's file names are stored in the [Folder] section of the *pdoxwork.ini* file that Paradox creates in each subdirectory you use. Chapter 13 provides details about the *pdoxwork.ini* file.

FIGURE 14.6

Each subdirectory can have its own folder. This example shows the Folder window for the *c:\pdoxwin\giftco* directory opened on the Desktop.

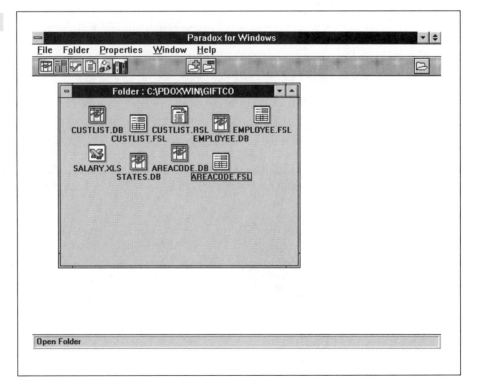

To open the Folder window, first make sure you're in the working directory that contains the folder (choose File ➤ Working Directory, if necessary). Then click the Open Folder button in the SpeedBar (shown at left), or choose File ➤ Open ➤ Folder.

After opening a folder, you can accomplish the following:

* Add icons to the folder.
* Delete icons from the folder.
* Show all files in the current working and private directory.
* Rearrange the icons.
* Inspect or double-click icons in the folder.
* Close the folder.

These operations are explained in the following sections.

Adding Icons to a Folder

Folders can contain icons of objects stored in any directory on your computer or network. If you want to add an icon to the open Folder window, follow the steps below.

 1. Click the Add Folder Item button in the SpeedBar (shown at left), or choose Folder ➤ Add Item. The **Select File** dialog box appears.

NOTE The Add Folder Item button is available whenever the Desktop is empty or the Folder window is active (that is, opened and in front). The Folder menu is available *only* when the Folder window is active.

2. Use any of the techniques below to select the files you want to add to the Folder window:

* To add one icon, double-click the file name, or click the file name and choose OK.

- To add icons for several adjacent file names, hold down the Shift key while clicking or dragging each adjacent file name in the list, then choose OK.

- To add icons for several non-adjacent file names, hold down the Ctrl key while clicking each non-adjacent file name in the list, then choose OK.

- To add an icon for a file in a directory outside your working directory or private directory, use the Path list or Browse button to switch to that directory. Then select icons as described above.

When you return to the Folder window, the selected files will appear as icons in the folder. Files added from a directory outside your working or private directory will appear in file lists of the working directory, just as if they were part of the working directory.

N O T E   Adding an icon to a folder does not move or copy the file from the original location. It merely adds a reference or pointer to that file.

Removing Icons from a Folder

When you no longer want an icon to appear in the Folder window, you can remove it. Keep in mind that removing an icon from the folder has no effect on the file saved on the computer's disk. The file still exists; it just won't appear in the Folder window.

To remove an icon from the Folder window, click the Remove Folder Item button in the SpeedBar (shown at left), or choose Folder ➤ Remove Item. Select the file or files you want to remove (double-click or use the click, Shift-click, or Ctrl-click methods discussed in the previous section and choose OK). The Remove Folder Item button is available whenever the Desktop is empty or the Folder window is active.

> **TIP** To delete a single icon from the folder, simply click on the icon, press the Del key, and choose OK.

When you return to the Folder window, the icon will no longer appear. If you removed an icon for an object in a directory outside the current working directory, that object will no longer appear in file lists of the working directory; however, you can use the Browser or change the working directory to locate it.

Showing All Files

Normally, the Folder window displays only the icons you added manually. To display icons of *all* files in your current working directory and private directory, make sure the Folder window is opened and active, then choose Folder ➤ Show All Files.

To remove the extra icons from the folder, simply choose Folder ➤ Show All Files again. The icons will disappear from the Folder window.

Rearranging Icons in a Folder

Sometimes the icons in the Folder window become jumbled, with some icons covering others. While you can rearrange the icons by dragging them from one place to another in the Folder window, it's quicker to choose Folder ➤ Tidy Icons to have Paradox offset each icon automatically so that all the file names are visible.

Inspecting Icons in the Folder

With related database objects nicely organized in the Folder window, activating an object—that is, opening a table or form, printing a report, or starting an application—is simply a matter of double-clicking the icon, or inspecting the icon and selecting a property from the menu.

Objects in folders have the same properties as objects in the Browser dialog box (see Table 14.2). Double-clicking an icon in the Folder window selects the first option on the property menu. Inspecting an icon allows you to select any property on the object's menu.

Closing the Folder Window

When you're finished using the Folder window, you can close it by double-clicking the Folder window's Control-menu box, pressing Ctrl+F4 when the Folder window is active, or clicking the Open Folder button in the SpeedBar.

Managing Tables and Files

From time to time, you may need to rename, copy, or delete tables and other files. You may also want to add and remove records from one table if they match records in another, and you may wish to empty a table of all its records. In the following sections, we'll discuss techniques for managing tables and files. Later we'll explain ways to manage records.

When performing file management, table management, and record management operations, keep the following points in mind:

- Paradox cannot normally perform management operations on objects that are locked by network users (including yourself). If objects are locked, you may see an error message indicating that Paradox cannot complete your request because someone is currently working with them.

- For best results, close forms, reports, other Paradox windows, and other applications that reference objects you want to work with.

- For utmost safety, use Paradox for Windows tools—not DOS commands or the Windows File Manager—to perform file management operations on Paradox for Windows tables and related files. Paradox file management tools handle tables and their associated files automatically; however, DOS commands and the File Manager do not. Managing files from outside Paradox could, therefore, result in incomplete or damaged tables and databases.

Renaming Paradox for Windows Files

The Rename option allows you to assign a new name to an existing Paradox for Windows file. Before renaming files, however, you should consider the potential pitfalls listed below:

- The new name cannot be the same as the original name *unless* you're renaming to a different drive or directory.

- Once renamed, a table cannot be found by associated objects such as forms, reports and queries. After renaming a table, you can use the Change Table option when opening a form or report that's expecting the old table name. (If you forget to use the Change Table option, Paradox will give you a chance to supply the table name.) See Chapter 9 for more information on opening forms and reports. Paradox does not offer any such options for finding renamed tables when you open a query that's expecting the old table name.

- You cannot use Rename to change a table's type. A Paradox table must be renamed as a Paradox table (*.db*), and a dBASE table must be renamed as a dBASE table (*.dbf*). (Use *Copy*, described later, if you need to change a table's type.)

- You cannot rename a table that is identified as the parent table in a referential integrity relationship. Referential integrity is discussed in Chapter 15.

With these points in mind, you can follow the steps below to rename a Paradox for Windows file.

1. Choose File ➤ Utilities ➤ Rename.

2. If you want to rename a file other than a table, click the Type drop-down list and choose a file type.

3. Type the name of the file you want to rename into the From text box, or select the file from the File Name list.

4. Type the new name for the file into the To text box. If you want to move the file to a drive or directory other than the working directory, you must include the complete drive and directory path.

5. If you want to view the renamed table, click the View Modified Table Option.

6. Click the OK button.

As a shortcut, you can choose Table ➤ Rename (if the table you want to rename is opened on the Desktop), or inspect the file icon in the Browser or Folder window and choose Rename from the property menu. Type the new name for the file and choose OK.

When you rename a *table*, the renamed table will include all the primary index, secondary index, validity check, and property files associated with the original table.

WARNING   Forms, reports, queries, and applications will continue to look for the table under its original name. Paradox will give you a chance to search for the table if it can't be found under the original name when you open a form or report, but it doesn't provide that option for other types of files.

Copying Paradox for Windows Files

When you copy a Paradox for Windows file, you create an exact duplicate of the original. Copying is useful for making backups of important data, creating a new table with the same structure and data as the original table, and changing the type of a table from Paradox to dBASE or dBASE to Paradox.

The steps for copying a Paradox for Windows file are as follows:

1. Choose File ➤ Utilities ➤ Copy.

2. If you want to copy a file other than a table, click the Type drop-down list and choose a file type.

3. Type the name of the file you want to copy into the From text box, or select the file from the File Name list.

4. Type the new name for the file into the To text box. Be sure to include the file extension. If you want to copy the file to a drive or directory other than the working directory, you must include the complete drive and directory path.

5. If you want to view the copied table, click the View Modified Table option.

6. Click the OK button. If the destination file already exists, Paradox will ask if you want to overwrite it. Choose No to return to the dialog box without overwriting the existing file, or Yes to replace the existing file with the one you're copying.

As a shortcut, you can inspect the file icon in the Browser or Folder window and choose Copy from the property menu. Type the new name for the file and choose OK. If the new file already exists, you'll be asked if you want to overwrite it.

When you copy a *table*, the copied table will include all the index and validity check files associated with the original table, but none of the forms, reports, or queries designed for the original table.

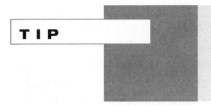

TIP To use the copy instead of the original table when opening a form or report, click the Change Table button in the Open Document dialog box. See Chapter 9 for more information.

Copying to a New Table Type

To copy a Paradox for Windows table to a dBASE table, or a dBASE table to a Paradox for Windows table, simply include the appropriate extension when specifying the new file name. Enter a .db extension to create a Paradox table or a .dbf extension to create a dBASE table.

Paradox automatically adjusts field types when you copy to a different table type. See Appendix C for more information.

Copying Tables with Referential Integrity Relationships

Referential integrity relationships are not always preserved when you use the Paradox Copy command to copy parent and child tables. Please see Chapter 15 for information on this topic.

Deleting Paradox for Windows Files

You can use the Delete option to delete Paradox for Windows files. Keep in mind that once tables and files are deleted, they can't be recovered through Paradox. Before deleting an object, you should be very sure that it isn't required by other Paradox objects—forms, reports, queries, applications, and so forth—since deleting objects needed by other files can damage your database.

NOTE If you delete an object accidentally and realize the mistake immediately, you may be able to recover the object with the DOS *Undelete* command, a utility designed to retrieve deleted files from current backups. (You should always keep current backups of every Paradox file!)

If you're certain that you want to delete a Paradox for Windows file, follow the steps below.

1. Choose File ➤ Utilities ➤ Delete.

2. If you want to delete a file other than a table, click the Type drop-down list and choose a file type.

3. Type the name of the file you want to delete in the Delete File text box, or select the file from the File Name list.

4. Click the OK button.

5. When asked if you're sure you want to delete the file, choose Yes to delete the file, or No to return to the dialog box without deleting the file.

As a shortcut, you can inspect the file icon in the Browser or Folder window and choose Delete from the property menu. When asked to confirm the deletion, choose Yes to delete the file or No to leave the file alone.

When you delete a *table*, Paradox removes the table and its associated indexes, table property files, and validity check files.

Managing Records

The Add, Subtract, and Empty options discussed below provide handy tools for copying and moving records from one table to another, and removing all records from a table without deleting the table itself.

Adding Records from One Table to Another

You can use the Add feature to copy or add records from one table to another without having to retype them. *Add* is also useful for combining information from several tables into a single table.

To add records to a table, proceed as follows:

1. Choose File ➤ Utilities ➤ Add, or inspect the icon of the table you wish to copy records from in the Browser dialog box or Folder window and choose Add from the property menu. You'll see the **Add** dialog box shown in Figure 14.7.

FIGURE 14.7

The Add dialog box

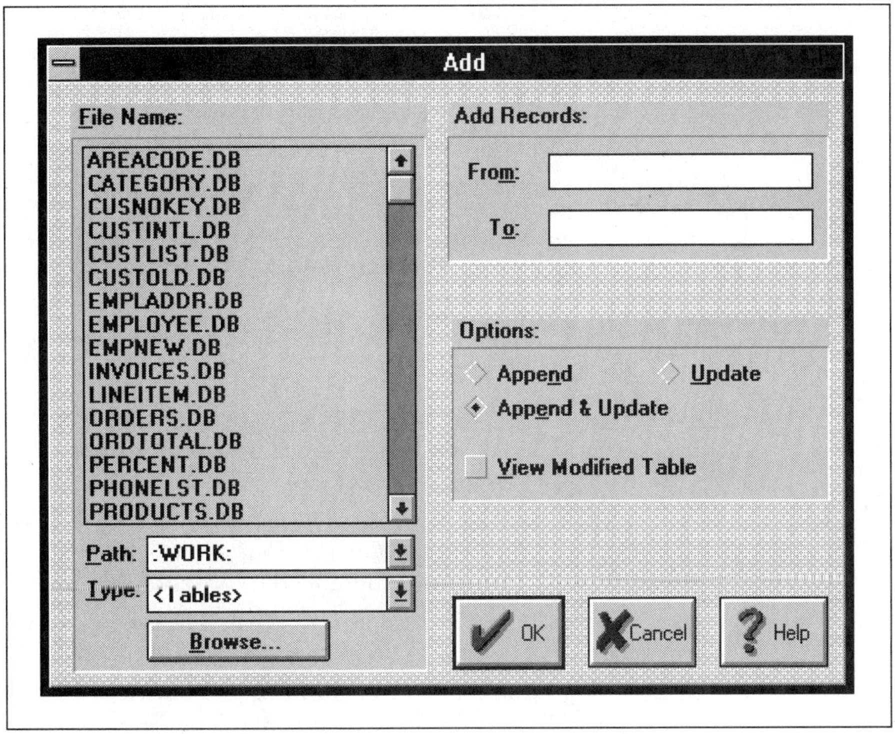

2. If necessary, type the file name and extension of the table you're copying *from* into the From text box, or click in the From text box and select the table name from the File Name list.

3. Type the file name and extension of the table you're copying *to* into the To text box, or click in the To text box and select the table name from the File Name list.

4. Choose *Append, Update,* or *Append & Update,* as described below.

5. If you want to open the target table after copying it, click View Modified Table.

6. Click the OK button.

Choosing an Update Option

When adding records from one table to another, you must tell Paradox how to perform the update to the target table. The behavior of the update options depends on whether or not the table has a primary index (see Chapter 4). You can choose one of the update options listed below from the Table Add dialog box.

Append   Records from the source table are added to the target table. *Append* is the only option allowed for tables without primary indexes (that is, non-keyed tables).

- If the target table is non-keyed, records are added after existing records.

- If the target table is keyed, records in the source table that do not violate the key conditions are inserted in their proper sort order. Records that violate the key conditions are stored in a temporary *Keyviol* table in your private directory. You can edit the records in *Keyviol* to eliminate the duplicate keys, then add them to the target table.

   If *Keyviol* already exists, Paradox creates *Keyviol1*, then *Keyviol2*, and so forth, up to *Keyvio99* to hold the newer records. You should rename or copy these temporary tables if you want to keep permanent copies.

Update   Records from the source table overwrite matching records of the target table, and the original records from the target table are saved in the temporary *Changed* table in your private directory. Records from the source table that don't match those in the target table are ignored. This option is available only if the target table is keyed.

If *Changed* already exists, Paradox creates *Changed1*, then *Changed2*, and so forth, up to *Change99* to hold the newer records. The *Changed* tables are deleted when you exit Paradox. You should rename or copy these temporary tables if you want to keep permanent copies.

Append & Update   Combines the add and update options to add new records to a table and update existing records in the target table (following the above rules). This option is only available for keyed tables and is the default choice.

Keep in mind that *Add* never changes the source table. However, you should watch out for some minor catches when using this option:

- The two tables should have compatible structures. For example, you cannot add records from a table containing Last Name, First Name, and Address fields to a table containing Amount, Qty, and Date fields. If you wish to combine tables with incompatible structures, you should use multiple-table queries (see Chapter 16) and rename the Answer table to create a new table with a new structure.

- If two compatible tables are combined, but the receiving table has a key field, records that violate the rule of uniqueness in the key field are stored in the *Keyviol* table. You can edit or delete records in the *Keyviol* table, then use the *Add* option once again to add records from the *Keyviol* table to the receiving table.

NOTE   If you do try to add tables with incompatible structures, Paradox will give you a chance to trim the incompatible data. If you choose not to trim the data, the problem records will be stored in a Problems table. The error messages and options available to you when adding data from one table to another are similar to those for restructuring a table, as described later in the section "Restructuring a Table."

Subtracting Records from a Table

You already know how to remove individual records from a table by pressing Ctrl+Del while in Edit mode or using the Delete operator in a query. However, for bigger jobs that involve keyed tables with compatible structures, you can use the Subtract command. *Subtract* removes from the target table all records with key field values that exactly match corresponding key fields of records in the source table. *Subtract* has no effect on the source table.

NOTE   *Subtract* works only when the two tables have compatible structures and both are keyed. You cannot use *Subtract* on dBASE tables.

Let's now take a look at the steps for subtracting records in one keyed table from records in another keyed table:

1. Choose File ➤ Utilities ➤ Subtract, or inspect a table icon in the Browser dialog box or Folder window and choose Subtract from the property menu. The **Subtract** dialog box shown in Figure 14.8 will appear.

FIGURE 14.8

The Subtract
dialog box

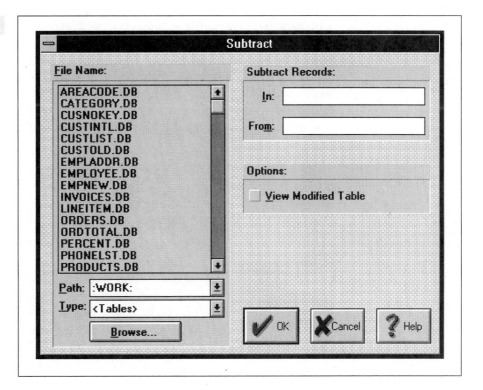

FIGURE 14.8

The Subtract
dialog box

2. If necessary, type the file name and extension of the table containing the records you want to subtract into the In text box, or click in the In text box and select the table name from the File Name list.

3. Type the file name and extension of the table you want to remove records from in the From text box, or click in the From text box and select the table name from the File Name list.

4. To open the target table after deleting records, click View Modified Table.

5. Click the OK button.

6. When asked if you're sure you want to delete records from the target table, choose Yes if you want to delete the records, or No to return to the Subtract dialog box without deleting any records.

Using Subtract to Remove Completed Transactions

To understand just how useful *Subtract* can be, suppose you have an accounts-receivable system in which you bill clients at the end of the month for purchases made during the previous month. You store these charges in the Charges table shown in Figure 14.9.

At the end of November, you could set up the query shown at the top of Figure 14.10 to pull out all records with purchase dates in October. Before running the query, choose Properties ➤ Answer Table ➤ Options and change the Answer Name to *billed.db* in the working directory. (Be sure to change the path name as well as the file name.)

NOTE   Instead of choosing Properties ➤ Answer Table ➤ Options, as suggested above, you could run the query, then use the Rename command to change the Answer table file name to *Billed* (in the working directory).

FIGURE 14.9

The Charges table

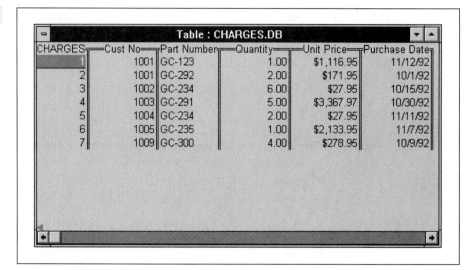

Table : CHARGES.DB

CHARGES	Cust No	Part Number	Quantity	Unit Price	Purchase Date
1	1001	GC-123	1.00	$1,116.95	11/12/92
2	1001	GC-292	2.00	$171.95	10/1/92
3	1002	GC-234	6.00	$27.95	10/15/92
4	1003	GC-291	5.00	$3,367.97	10/30/92
5	1004	GC-234	2.00	$27.95	11/11/92
6	1005	GC-235	1.00	$2,133.95	11/7/92
7	1009	GC-300	4.00	$278.95	10/9/92

FIGURE 14.10

A query for charges in
the month of October,
and the resulting
Billed table

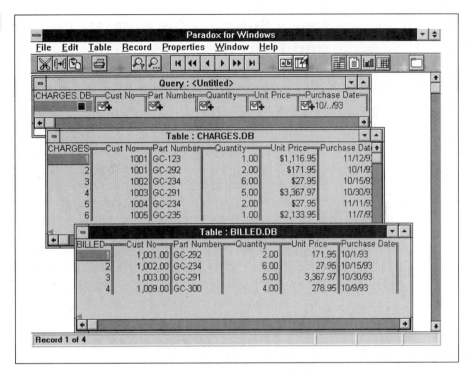

As shown in Figure 14.10, the Billed table contains only transactions for
October. You can print invoices from the Billed table using an invoice
report designed for any table that has the same structure and field names
as *Billed*. To print the report, choose File ➤ Open ➤ Report, click Print
in the Open Mode area of the **Open Document** dialog box, click the
Change Table button, select the Billed table, and choose OK.

After billing the October transactions, you can use *Subtract* to remove
them from the Charges table. The Billed table contains the transactions
to be subtracted. In the **Subtract** dialog box, specify **Billed** in the In text
box and **Charges** in the From text box. When the subtraction is complete,
the Charges table will no longer contain charges for October.

Using Subtract for Bulk Mailings and Error Recovery

Now that you've seen a complete example, it should be easy to imagine other applications for the table utility options. Here are two ideas to get you started.

Suppose you're planning a special mailing to introduce an extra-hot, low-priced item that everyone is sure to want. Assuming your list of inactive clients is stored in a table named *Inactive*, you can perform a query on that table to isolate customers who haven't ordered within the past year. Using Properties ➤ Answer Table ➤ Options in the Query window or the Rename command, rename the resulting Answer table to *PastYear*. Then use *Add* to add the names from PastYear (the source table) to a master mailing list table named *MailMast*. Next, create a form letter to introduce the new product, and print the letters. After the mailing is complete, use *Subtract* to remove the inactive customers from the master mailing list. (You can add these customers again after they purchase your new product.)

Here's a way to recover from a common—and potentially serious—mistake. Imagine that you performed a query to delete many records from a table, then suddenly realized that you didn't intend to delete those records at all. Recall that during a Delete query, Paradox moves deleted records into the *Deleted* table in your private directory. If you discover the mistake immediately (or have renamed the Deleted table), you can restore the deleted records. Choose the Add command, then specify Deleted as the source table and your original table as the target table. Paradox will retrieve the deleted records and your original table will be as good as new.

NOTE To delete records globally, place the Delete operator just below the table name in the query table. Specify selection criteria to use for deletions, then click the Run Query button in the SpeedBar. See Chapter 8 for more information on queries.

Emptying a Table

You can use the Empty command to remove all records from a table. This is particularly useful in databases in which updated transactions are copied to a history file using *Add*, then deleted from the current transactions table (see Chapter 18).

Be careful with the Empty command! Once records are emptied from a table, they cannot be retrieved. Paradox doesn't create a Deleted table when you use *Empty*, and you cannot use DOS Undelete or other utilities to recover records.

To empty a table, follow these steps:

1. Choose File ➤ Utilities ➤ Empty, or Table ➤ Empty (in Table View), or inspect a table icon in the Browser dialog box or Folder window and choose Empty from the property menu. If you see the **Empty** dialog box shown in Figure 14.11, continue with Step 2. If you see a **Warning** box instead, skip to Step 4.

2. If necessary, type the table's file name and extension into the Empty Table text box, or select the table name from the File Name list.

3. Click the OK button.

4. When asked if you're sure you want to empty the records, choose No to leave the table unchanged or choose Yes to delete the records.

FIGURE 14.11

The Empty dialog box

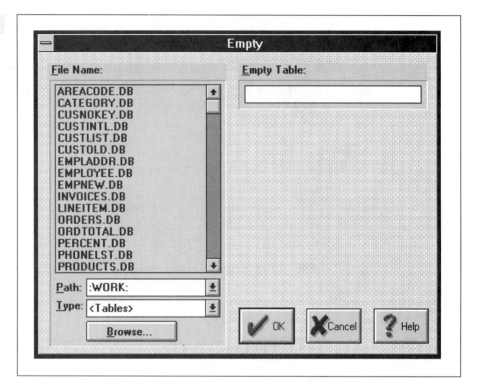

Getting Information about Your Table

You can display the structure of any table and later print the table's structure in a default or custom report format.

To display the table's structure, choose File ➤ Utilities ➤ Info Structure, or Table ➤ Info Structure (in Table View), or inspect a table icon in the Browser dialog box or Folder window and choose Info Structure from the property menu. If the **Select File** dialog box appears, select a table name, then choose OK.

Paradox will display the table structure in a **Structure Information** dialog box resembling the one in Figure 14.12. This dialog box is similar to the Create Table dialog box (see Chapter 4) and the Restructure Table dialog box (discussed later in this chapter); however you can only *view* the structure of the table, not change it.

You can use any of the following techniques to navigate the Structure Information dialog box:

- To display the properties of a field, click the field. If the property you're interested in isn't selected in the Table Properties list box, click the Table Properties drop-down arrow and choose the property you want. For example, in Figure 14.12, the mouse is positioned in the first field (Cust No), *Validity Checks* is selected in the Table Properties list, and the Required Field is checked (indicating that Cust No is a required field).

FIGURE 14.12

A sample display from the Info Structure option

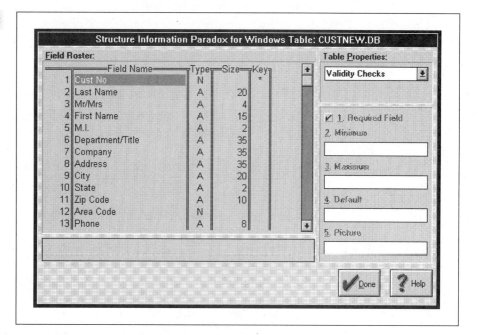

- If a Detail Info button appears, click it to open a dialog box with more detailed information about the property. When you're finished viewing the information, click Done or OK to return to the Structure Information dialog box.

- When you're finished viewing the structure information, click the Done button.

Figure 14.12 shows the structure for a Paradox table named *CustNew*, which is similar to our trusty CustList table. However, to make things more interesting, we added these features to CustNew:

- *Cust No* is a key field and is required.

- *State* has a default value of CA and a lookup table named *States*.

- *Area Code* is required and has a picture value of #{0,1}#.

- *Credit Limit* has a default value of 10,000, a minimum value of 1000, and a maximum value of 25,000.

Now, you may be thinking "The Structure Information dialog box is very nice, but how do I get a *printed copy* of the table's structure?" Unfortunately, there's no push-button answer to this question, but a solution *is* available.

Each time you use Info Structure, a copy of the table structure you're viewing is stored in the temporary *struct.db* table in your private directory. Like any table, Struct can be viewed and printed. Before looking at ways to view and print the Struct table, it's worthwhile to note the following points:

- Struct is overwritten with new data each time you request structure information and whenever you create or restructure a table.

- Struct is deleted when you exit Paradox.

- Changing Struct has no effect on the table it describes. Only the Restructure command (described later) can change the structure of the original table.

- Because Struct is overwritten each time you view a table's structure, you must copy or rename it if you want to keep a permanent copy.

Exploring the Struct Table

You can open the Struct table in your private directory as soon as you close the Structure Information dialog box. Each field of Struct describes a field in the table you just reviewed.

To open the Struct table, choose File ➤ Open ➤ Table or click the Open Table button in the SpeedBar (if it's available). Then select the file *:PRIV:STRUCT.DB* (near the bottom of the file list) and choose OK. Struct will appear in a Table window, as shown in Figure 14.13.

FIGURE 14.13

The fields in the Struct table document the structure of a table.

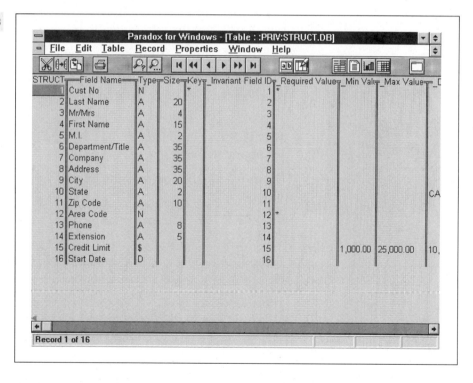

Each record in Struct describes one field in the table you requested information about. Within each Paradox for Windows Struct table record, the fields are as follows:

Field Name   Contains the name of the field being described.

Type   Contains the type of the field: A (Alphanumeric), N (Number), $ (Currency), D (Date), S (Short Number), M (Memo), F (Formatted Memo), B (Binary), G (Graphic), or O (OLE).

Size   Contains the size of the field.

Key   Contains an asterisk (*) for key fields; non-key fields are blank.

_Invariant Field ID   Contains a numeric identifier for the field. This ID remains the same (invariant) even if you change the original order of the table's fields.

_Required Value   Contains an asterisk (*) if the field is required; non-required fields are blank.

_Min Value   Contains the minimum allowable value for this field, if one was defined.

_Max Value   Contains the maximum allowable value for this field, if one was defined.

_Default Value   Contains the default value for this field, if one was defined.

_Picture Value   Contains the picture for this field, if one was defined.

_Table Lookup   Contains the name of the lookup table for this field, if one was defined.

_Table Lookup Type   Contains a number describing the type of lookup table used. The number is 0 (zero) if no lookup table is used, and non-zero if a lookup table *is* used.

You can change the appearance of Struct using direct manipulation or property inspection in the Table window (see Chapter 6). You can also define custom forms or reports for Struct.

Printing the Struct Table

If you simply need a quick report of the Struct table, you can open the table on the Desktop, then click the Print or Quick Report button in the SpeedBar. Although the quick report is the easiest way to print a table's structure, you'll probably find the report to be remarkably unattractive.

Fortunately, you can create and save a custom report (or form) for the Struct table, using techniques covered in Chapters 9 through 11. After creating the report or form, you can reuse it any time you want to print or view the Struct table.

N O T E　　The Struct tables generated for Paradox and dBASE tables are different; therefore, you'll need to design one report and form for the Paradox Struct table and another for the dBASE Struct table.

Figure 14.14 shows an example of a customized Struct table report. We used a simple query (see Figure 14.16) to limit the report to just the Cust No, Area Code, State, and Credit Limit fields from CustNew, both to conserve space and to focus on the most interesting fields.

Here are the basic steps we used to create the report in Figure 14.14:

- We chose File ➤ Utilities ➤ Info Structure, chose the CustNew table to report on (though any Paradox table will do), then clicked Done to generate a Struct table.

- Next we chose File ➤ New ➤ Report, selected *:PRIV:STRUCT.DB* in the **Data Model** dialog box, and chose a Single-Record layout in the **Design Layout** dialog box (see Chapter 9).

- We then created the report design shown in Figure 14.15 and saved it with the name *Structur*.

FIGURE 14.14

A sample report of the Struct table

Table Structure Report

Field Name: | Cust No

Type: N Size: [ ] Key: *
_Invariant Field ID : 1 _Required Value: *
_Min Value: [ ] _Max Value: [ ] _Default Value: [ ]
_Picture Value: [ ]
_Table Lookup: [ ] _Table Lookup Type: 0

Field Name: | Area Code

Type: N Size: [ ] Key: [ ]
_Invariant Field ID : 12 _Required Value: *
_Min Value: [ ] _Max Value: [ ] _Default Value: [ ]
_Picture Value: #{0,1}#
_Table Lookup: [ ] _Table Lookup Type: 0

Field Name: | State

Type: A Size: 2 Key: [ ]
_Invariant Field ID : 10 _Required Value: [ ]
_Min Value: [ ] _Max Value: [ ] _Default Value: CA
_Picture Value: [ ]
_Table Lookup: STATES.DB _Table Lookup Type: 1

Field Name: | Credit Limit

Type: $ Size: [ ] Key: [ ]
_Invariant Field ID : 15 _Required Value: [ ]
_Min Value: 1,000.00 _Max Value: 25,000.00 _Default Value: 10,000.00
_Picture Value: [ ]
_Table Lookup: [ ] _Table Lookup Type: 0

FIGURE 14.15

The design for the
sample report in
Figure 14.14

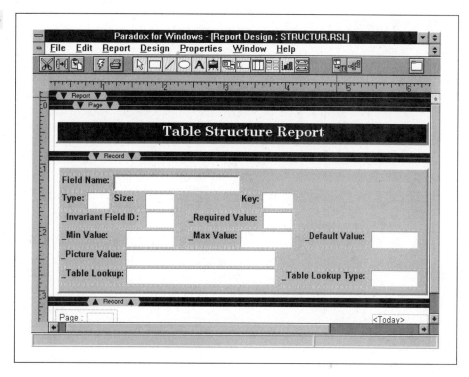

With the report design complete, we were ready to design a query to place
selected records from the Struct table into the Answer table. To begin, we
chose File ➤ New ➤ Query, placed the values we wanted in the Field
Name column, then placed a check plus in all the columns, as shown in Figure 14.16. Next, we saved the query with the name *Structur* and clicked the
Run Query button in the SpeedBar to create the Answer table.

TIP

To report on the entire Struct table, simply skip the
query steps. To place records from another table's
structure into the Answer table, generate the Struct table
for the table you're interested in, modify the query to
select the appropriate field names, then run the query.

FIGURE 14.16

A query to limit the output of the report to just the Cust No, Area Code, State, and Credit Limit fields

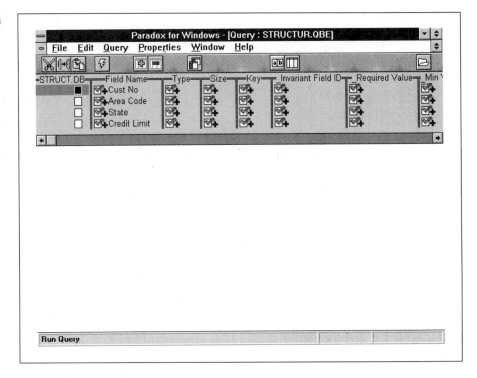

When we were ready to use the Structur report, we chose File ➤ Open ➤ Report, then clicked the report name in the File Name list of the **Open Document** dialog box. To use the query results from the Answer table (instead of the Struct table for which it was designed), we clicked the Change Table button, double-clicked *:PRIV:ANSWER.DB* in the File Name list, then clicked OK to view the report on screen. To print the report, we clicked the Print button in the SpeedBar and completed the **Print File** dialog box.

TIP

You can assign your custom report as the preferred report for Struct. To do so, open Struct in the Table window, right-click the Quick Report button, select the report name you want, then choose OK.

Restructuring a Table

Once you've created a table, added some data to it, and used it for a while, you may decide to change something about its basic structure. For example, you might want to add a field for storing the customer's Fax number to the CustList table, or you may need to lengthen a field such as Company or Address.

Restructuring a table is almost identical to creating one. However, restructuring can lead to data loss and key violations and, therefore, should not be undertaken unless you understand its potential effects.

Before restructuring a table, it's a good idea to back it up using the Copy command or another backup utility. That way, if the restructuring creates unexpected (or unsatisfactory) results, you can restore the original data with little fuss or lost time. If you prefer, you can save the original table with a new name (as described later) to leave the original table untouched.

Restructuring Pitfalls and Limitations

Before looking at the actual steps involved in restructuring a table, you should consider the following points:

- You cannot use *Restructure* to change a Paradox table to a dBASE table, or a dBASE table to a Paradox table. Use the Copy command instead.

- You cannot use *Restructure* to change the name of a table. Use the Rename command instead.

- Adding keys to a table that previously had no keys, or had different keys, may cause key violations where data already in the table violates the new key. For example, a key violation will occur if more than one record has the same value for a newly defined key field. Paradox removes records that violate the key from the original table and places them in a temporary *Keyviol* table in your private directory. The Keyviol table will appear on the Desktop after the restructuring is complete. You can change the records in Keyviol to comply with the new key requirements, then use the Add command to return the records to the original table.

- If you change a field's type and the data in that field cannot be converted to the new type, Paradox will ask you to confirm the change. If you choose not to allow the change, Paradox will move records that cannot be converted into a temporary *Problems* table in your private directory. The Problems table will appear on the Desktop after the restructuring is complete. As with key violations, problem records can be corrected, then returned to the original table.

- If you add or change a validity check, lookup table, or referential integrity rule (see Chapter 15), and existing data doesn't comply with it, Paradox will give you the option of placing the non-compliant records in the *Keyviol* table. Again, you can correct the records and return them to the original table.

- You may be prevented from restructuring parent or child tables that are related through referential integrity rules (see Chapter 15). If you're not sure whether a table is involved in a referential integrity relationship, choose the Info Structure command described earlier, select *Referential Integrity* from the Table Properties list, and use the Detail Info button. Please see Chapter 15 for more information on referential integrity.

Note that if a Problems table already exists, Paradox will create *Problem1*, then *Problem2*, and so forth, up to *Proble99*. Similarly, if Keyviol already exists, Paradox will create *Keyviol1*, *Keyviol2*, and so forth, up to *Keyvio99*. You should rename or copy these temporary tables if you want to keep permanent copies.

Don't forget to fix problems or key violations, or rename the Problems and Keyviol tables before moving on to the next task or exiting Paradox.

General Steps for Restructuring a Table

To modify the structure of a table, follow these steps:

1. Close any windows of documents that reference the table you want to restructure. This prevents error messages caused by locked tables.

2. Choose File ➤ Utilities ➤ Restructure, or Table ➤ Restructure (in Table View), or inspect a table icon in the Browser or Folder window and choose Restructure from the property menu.

3. If the **Select File** dialog box appears, choose the name of the table you want to restructure.

4. When the **Restructure Table** dialog box appears, you can revise the table's structure.

5. Save your changes as described in the next section.

Figure 14.17 shows a sample Restructure Table dialog box. As for the Create Table dialog box discussed in Chapter 4, you can use the arrow keys or mouse to move the cursor around and make changes. The Ins and Ctrl+Del keys allow you to insert and delete fields. The Table Properties list allows you to change validity checks, table lookup, secondary indexes, referential integrity, and table language, as described later in this chapter.

> **N O T E**
>
> The Restructure Table dialog box for dBASE tables is slightly different from the one shown in Figure 14.17. See Appendix C for more information on restructuring dBASE tables.

Saving the Restructured Table

When you're satisfied with the new table structure, you can click either the Save or Save As button.

The Save button overwrites the old structure with the new structure. The Save As button provides a more cautious way to save your changes because it creates a new table with the structure you've defined, leaving the old table intact. If you're not sure what potential problems and data loss might arise as a result of restructuring a table, it's best to use Save As rather than Save. After adding corrected records from the Keyviol and Problems tables to the new table (if necessary) and inspecting it carefully,

FIGURE 14.17

The Restructure Table dialog box

you can delete the old table, then use File ➤ Utilities ➤ Rename to change the name of the new table to the old table name.

When you click Save As, you'll see the **Save Table As** dialog box. Follow these steps to complete the dialog box:

1. In the New Table Name text box, type the new file name and extension for the table. The extension must be the same as for the original table.

2. To display the new table after restructuring is complete, click Display Table.

3. To add as much data from the old table as suits the structure of the new table, leave the Add Data To New Table option checked. If you prefer to create an empty table and add data later, click Add Data To New Table to deselect it.

4. Click OK.

If the new name you specified in Step 1 is the same as an existing table's name, you'll be asked to decide whether you want to overwrite the existing table. Choose Yes to overwrite the table, or No to return to the Save Table As dialog box without overwriting the table.

Understanding the Restructure Warnings

If the restructure will result in data loss or other problems, you'll see a **Restructure Warning** dialog box similar to the one shown in Figure 14.18 after choosing Save or Save As.

The top of the Restructure Warning dialog box displays a question about a specific field in the table. To take the action the question suggests, click Yes. To avoid the action, click No. Records that no longer meet the requirements for the table will move to the Problems Keyviol table.

FIGURE 14.18

The Restructure
Warning dialog box

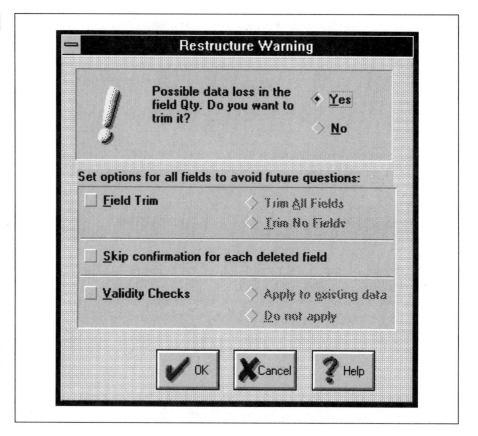

The remaining check boxes allow you to set options that guide Paradox's future handling of restructuring problems for this table. You can check any of the options discussed below to avoid further questions about fields that require special handling.

Field Trim   Check this option to specify the trimming method for all fields. Then select *Trim All Fields* to have Paradox trim characters from the end of field values that exceed the new length of the field; or select *Trim No Fields* to have Paradox move all records containing data that exceeds the new length of fields into the Problems table.

Skip Confirmation for Each Deleted Field   Check this option to delete fields without further confirmation.

Validity Checks   Check this option to specify whether or not all fields must satisfy the validity checks. Then select *Apply To Existing Data* to have Paradox move records that no longer meet the conditions of new validity checks, lookup tables, or referential integrity rules to the Keyviol table; or select *Do Not Apply* to allow existing records to violate validity checks and remain in the original table.

NOTE   The default settings shown in Figure 14.18 provide the greatest control over how Paradox handles potential data loss.

After selecting options in the Restructure Warning dialog box, choose OK to continue restructuring or choose Cancel to stop restructuring and return to the Restructure Table dialog box.

Changing Your Mind

If you make a mistake when defining a new structure for a table and want to return to the original structure, click the Cancel button in the Restructure Table dialog box. Paradox will cancel the changes you made and return to the Desktop.

Now, let's take a look at specific ways to change a table's structure.

Adding a Field

To add a field to the table, click on the field that's just below the point where you want the new field to appear, then press the Ins key. A blank line will open up above the highlighted field. Now type the new field name, field type, and size (if necessary). Remember to mark new *primary key* fields with an asterisk (*) and place them before any non-key fields.

When you add fields to an existing table, Paradox does not automatically update forms or reports associated with that table. You must open the Form or Report Design window for the document and use the Field tool to add new fields to the design.

Deleting a Field

To delete a field from the Restructure Table dialog box, simply click on that field and press Ctrl+Del. Deleting a field erases all data stored in that field, and therefore has great potential for data loss. When you save the table structure after deleting a field, Paradox will display the Restructure Warning dialog box and ask for confirmation. Choose Yes if you want to delete the field, or No to leave the field and its data in the table.

NOTE The confirmation warning won't appear if you click the Save As button and remove the check mark from the Add Data To New Table option before choosing OK.

Deleted fields lose their definitions in any form or report documents associated with the table. The next time you open the document, Paradox will warn you that missing fields will be undefined. To solve this problem, return to the Form or Report Design window for the document, redefine or delete the undefined fields, then save the revised design.

WARNING If you delete a field that's used in a query, Paradox will not be able to open that query in the future.

Renaming a Field

To change the name of a field, simply click on the appropriate field name in the structure and type in the new name.

The next time you open a form or report containing a field that you've renamed, Paradox will reconcile the name change automatically.

WARNING   If you rename a field that's used in a query, Paradox will not be able to open that query in the future.

Changing a Non-Key Field to a Key Field

You can change a non-key field to a key field by placing an asterisk (*) in the Key column of the dialog box. However, make sure that all the key fields appear at the top of the field roster in the proper sort order. If necessary, rearrange the fields as described below. (See Chapter 4 for more information on primary keys.)

Remember that converting an existing non-key field to a key field can result in key violations. Records that do not comply with the new key will be moved to the Keyviol table.

Rearranging Fields

To rearrange fields in the field roster, use your mouse to point to the leftmost column (field number) of the field you want to move, then hold down the left mouse button. The pointer will change to a vertical arrow, and horizontal lines will appear above and below the field to be moved. Drag the field to its new position and release the mouse button.

Changing the Length of a Field

Lengthening an alphanumeric field (for instance, from a size of 20 to 25) will not usually cause any problems, though you might have to change the format of a custom form or report later to accommodate the new width.

Shortening an alphanumeric field (for example, from 25 to 20) may cause data loss if the table contains data that is longer than the new width. When you shorten an alphanumeric field, Paradox will display the Restructure Warning dialog box shown in Figure 14.18.

Changing the Type of a Field

You can change field types (alphanumeric, numeric, currency, date), though you may run into the same problems as when shortening an alphanumeric field. Paradox will warn you of any potential data loss and give you the Restructure Warning options described earlier in this chapter.

Generally, you won't want to change the type of data in a field. However, if you've made an error at the outset, it's easy enough to do. If you remember to put numeric values in either numeric or currency fields, dates in date fields, and all other text and numbers in alphanumeric fields, you will probably never have to change a field type.

Remember that Paradox also offers the S field type for *short numbers*. A short number field can contain whole numbers (no decimal places) in the range of -32,767 to 32,767. Until you are an experienced Paradox user, you should avoid this field type. It has the advantage of conserving memory, but the small range of acceptable numbers makes it very restrictive. For example, the number 1.1 is unacceptable because it has a decimal place, and the zip code 40001 is unacceptable because it is too large.

Table 14.4 summarizes the possible consequences of changing field types.

Changing Table Properties

Chapter 4 discussed validity checks and other properties you can define when creating a table. The procedures for changing properties are the same as for defining them in the first place. However, you must take extra care that data already in your table will meet the revised criteria. The

TABLE 14.4: Consequences of Changing Field Types

	TO A	TO N	TO $	TO D	TO S	TO M	TO F	TO B	TO G	TO O
From A	Yes	P	P	P	P	Yes	No	No	No	No
From N	Yes	Yes	Yes	No	Yes	No	No	No	No	No
From $	Yes	Yes	Yes	No	Yes	No	No	No	No	No
From D	Yes	No	No	Yes	No	No	No	No	No	No
From S	Yes	Yes	Yes	No	Yes	No	No	No	No	No
From M	Yes	No	No	No	No	No	Yes	Yes	No	No
From F	No	No	No	No	No	Yes	Yes	Yes	No	No
From B	No	No	No	No	No	No	No	Yes	No	No
From G	No	No	No	No	No	No	No	Yes	Yes	No
From O	No	No	No	No	No	No	No	Yes	No	Yes

Yes means the conversion is allowed, but may result in some trimming.

No means the conversion is not allowed under any conditions.

P means the conversion is allowed, but will undoubtedly generate the Problems table.

EXPLANATION OF FIELD TYPE ABBREVIATIONS

FIELD TYPE ABBREVIATION	DESCRIPTION
$	Currency
A	Alphanumeric
B	Binary
D	Date
F	Formatted Memo
G	Graphics
M	Memo
N	Number
O	OLE
S	Short Number

general procedures for changing a table property in the Restructure Table dialog box are listed below.

1. If you want to add or change validity checks or a lookup table for a field, select the field you want to change.

2. Click the Table Properties drop-down arrow, then choose the property you want to change. Your options are as follows:

> **Validity Checks**   Provides constraints or checks on the values entered for this field. (See Chapter 4.)
>
> **Table Lookup**   Assures that a value entered into this field is a legitimate value for a corresponding field in another table. (See Chapters 5 and 15.)
>
> **Secondary Indexes**   Defines indexes on non-key fields in the table. These indexes are used for sorting and speeding up query operations that link multiple tables. (See Chapter 7.)
>
> **Referential Integrity**   Ensures that ties between like data in this table and other tables cannot be broken. (See Chapter 15.)
>
> **Password Security**   Assigns master and auxiliary passwords to a table (described in "Using Passwords to Protect Tables," below).
>
> **Table Language**   Assigns the language driver that controls sorting, capitalization, and text comparison operations. (See Chapter 13.)
>
> **Dependent Tables**   Displays the name of child tables that are linked to this table through referential integrity. This option is for reference only.

3. Complete the specifications for the property you chose.

Please see "Restructuring Pitfalls and Limitations," earlier in this chapter, for an explanation of how Paradox handles data that no longer complies with the table properties you set.

Borrowing a Structure from an Existing Table

When defining a new table, you can borrow the table's structure from an existing table (see Chapter 4). However, the Borrow feature is not available in the Restructure Table dialog box. Fortunately, there's an easy way around this limitation. Choose *Restructure*, select the table you want to use as the basis for a new table's structure, then click Save As when the **Restructure Table** dialog box appears. Type a new table name in the **Save Table As** dialog box, select Add Data To New table to *remove* the check mark from that option, select *Display Table* if you wish, then choose OK. The table structure and related files (but none of its data) will be copied to the new table.

Using Passwords to Protect Tables

When you password protect a table, users cannot perform any operation on that table without first supplying the correct password. You can establish a password for the table as a whole, and you can assign specific types of rights to the table or to individual fields. Passwords are especially useful for adding security to shared tables on a network.

Before jumping into the procedure for defining a password, please note the following points:

- The password can be up to 15 characters long, including spaces.
- Case matters. That is, the password *Hello* is *not* the same as *hello*. Therefore, pay attention to case as you enter your password.
- The password does not appear on the screen as you type it. Instead, you'll see a series of asterisks, one for each letter you typed. This is a safety precaution to prevent others from watching what you enter on the screen.

- You cannot view a password-protected table or change or remove the password if you do not know the password. Therefore, you should write down your password and store it in a safe place where you can find it easily.

- If your data is sensitive enough to deserve password protection, you should avoid obvious passwords like your first name, initials, nickname, the names of pets, spouses, friends, and so forth.

Adding a Password

To define a password for a table, close the table (if it's currently open), then follow the steps for creating or restructuring the table (see Chapter 4 and "Restructuring a Table," in this chapter). When you reach the **Create Table** or **Restructure Table** dialog box, follow the steps below.

1. Choose *Password Security* from the Table Properties list.

2. Click Define to open the **Password Security** dialog box.

3. Type the password you want in the Master Password text box. The master password secures all rights to the table.

4. Type the same password in the Verify Master Password text box.

5. If you want more specific security, you can click the Auxiliary Passwords button, as described later in this chapter.

6. Choose OK to return to the Create Table or Restructure Table dialog box.

7. Choose Save or Save As to save your changes.

N O T E

If the passwords entered in Steps 3 and 4 aren't identical, you'll be prompted to reenter one of them.

Keep in mind that if several tables are assigned the same master or auxiliary passwords, entering the password for one table will provide access to all tables with that password. This can be both a blessing and a curse.

On the positive side, this feature can save time because you can assign the same password to several related tables. When you open the tables, Paradox will request the password for only one table of the group.

The downside, of course, is that you risk assigning the same password to unrelated (and potentially sensitive) tables. For example, you wouldn't want a table of salaries to have the same password as a table of volunteers for the company picnic.

Changing or Removing a Password

If you've defined a password for a table, you can change or remove it at any time.

To change a password, follow the steps below.

1. Go to the **Restructure Table** dialog box and choose Password Security from the *Table Properties* drop-down list box.

2. Click the Modify button. You'll see the **Password Security** dialog box shown in Figure 14.19.

3. If you wish to change the master password, click the Change button, type the new password in the Master Password text box, then confirm the change by retyping the same pass-word in the Verify Master Password text box.

4. If you wish to change auxiliary passwords, click the Auxiliary Passwords button (described in the next section).

5. Choose OK to return to the Create Table or Restructure Table dialog box. If you change your mind and want to return to the previously saved passwords, click the Revert button and choose OK.

6. Choose Save or Save As to save your changes.

To delete the master password and its associated auxiliary passwords, repeat Steps 1 and 2 above, then click the Delete button. Choose OK to return to the Create Table or Restructure Table dialog box and choose Save or Save As.

FIGURE 14.19

The Password Security
dialog box for an
existing password

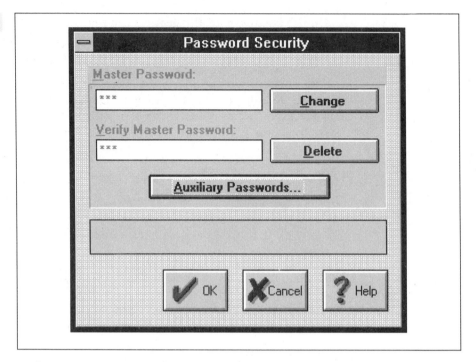

Defining Auxiliary Passwords

The master password provides all rights to the table and its fields. You can also assign auxiliary passwords that restrict the rights granted for the entire table or individual fields in the table. When the user opens the table with an auxiliary password, only the limited rights will be available. For example, you can create an auxiliary password that allows users to read a table but prevents them from changing it.

Clicking the Auxiliary Passwords button in the Password Security dialog box opens the **Auxiliary Passwords** dialog box shown in Figure 14.20. Before going into the steps for assigning auxiliary passwords, let's take a closer look at table rights and field rights.

FIGURE 14.20

The Auxiliary
Passwords dialog box

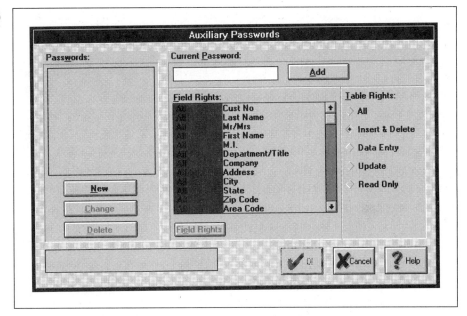

Understanding Table Rights and Field Rights

Table rights control what users can do with an entire table and all of its fields. Table 14.5 explains the table rights you can assign through auxiliary passwords.

To select a table right, specify an auxiliary password (as described below), then simply click the option in the Table Rights area of the Auxiliary Passwords dialog box.

NOTE   Each auxiliary password can confer only one of the types of table rights listed in Table 14.5.

TABLE 14.5: Table Rights You Can Assign through Auxiliary Passwords

TABLE RIGHT	WHAT IT DOES
All	Provides all rights to any function of the table, including the ability to restructure or delete it.
Insert & Delete	Allows users to insert or delete records, but not empty or delete the table. This is the default setting.
Data Entry	Allows users to enter data in the table, but not delete, restructure, or empty the table.
Update	Allows users to view fields and change non-key fields of a table, but not insert or delete records or change key fields.
Read Only	Allows users to view the table, but not change it in any way.

Field rights provide another level of protection for individual fields in the table. Available field rights are listed in Table 14.6.

To select a field right, specify an auxiliary password, click the field you want to change in the Field Rights area of the Auxiliary Passwords dialog box, then click the Field Rights button to cycle through each available right. Alternatively, you can double-click a field to cycle through the rights.

TABLE 14.6: Field Rights You Can Assign through Auxiliary Passwords

FIELD RIGHT	WHAT IT DOES
All	Provides all rights on the field, within the limits of the specified table rights.
ReadOnly	Allows users to view, but not change, the data in the field.
None	Prevents users from viewing or changing the data in that field. Paradox hides the values in the field when the table is opened. This is useful for sensitive data like salary information within an employee record.

Assigning and Changing Auxiliary Passwords

To specify auxiliary passwords for a table, go to the Auxiliary Passwords dialog box and follow these steps:

1. If the cursor is not in the Current Password text box, click the New button.

2. Type the auxiliary password into the Current Password text box.

3. Select a table right to associate with this password.

4. Assign the field rights for the password.

5. Click *Add* to add the password to the Passwords list.

N O T E   Unlike master passwords, auxiliary passwords will appear on your screen when you define them. Be sure to perform these steps in private.

6. Repeat Steps 1 through 5 to specify as many auxiliary passwords as you need.

7. Choose OK twice to save the master passwords and auxiliary passwords and return to the Create Table or Restructure Table dialog box.

8. Choose Save or Save As to save your changes.

If you want to change an existing auxiliary password in the Auxiliary Passwords dialog box, click the password in the Passwords list, click *Change*, make the changes you want, then click *Accept* to accept them or *Revert* to return the password to the list unchanged. If you wish to remove an auxiliary password, click the password in the Passwords list, click *Change*, then click *Delete*.

Using a Password-Protected Table

When you attempt to work with a password-protected table, Paradox will display the **Enter Password(s)** dialog box shown below.

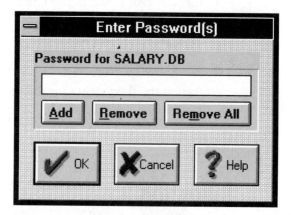

You must type in the correct password in order to proceed. Asterisks will appear on the screen as you type, so type carefully. When you've entered the correct password, choose OK or press ↵. If you do not enter the correct password, Paradox will continue displaying the Enter Passwords(s) dialog box until you either type the correct password or choose Cancel to return to the Desktop.

TIP

You can enter passwords for several tables at once by typing a password and clicking *Add* for each password you wish to add. When you're finished, choose OK.

Remember that entering the master password gives you full access to the table. Entering an auxiliary password gives you only the rights defined for that password in the Auxiliary Passwords dialog box.

Clearing Passwords from Memory

Once you access a password-protected table by entering the appropriate password, you can access that table as often as you wish during the current Paradox session without having to reenter the password. When you exit Paradox, the password is released and you'll need to enter it again before you can reopen the table.

This is convenient, since reentering the password each time you need a table becomes tedious. But there is a drawback: If you walk away from your computer during a session, anyone who sits down at your computer will be able to access all your password-protected tables without reentering the passwords. (This is even more of a problem on a network.)

If you want to release a password without exiting Paradox for Windows, choose File ➤ Utilities ➤ Passwords. When the **Enter Password(s)** dialog box appears, type the password you want to remove from memory and click *Remove*. To remove all passwords from memory at once, click *Remove All*. When you're finished with the dialog box, click OK.

After you clear passwords, Paradox will require you to reenter the passwords to access the tables again.

Repairing Damaged Tables

Paradox tables may become damaged through power failures, hardware failures, bad network cards or connections, removing a floppy disk that Paradox is accessing, or rebooting your computer while Paradox is active in memory. Although such damage is extremely rare, it can be devastating, especially if the damaged table contains huge amounts of data or data that would be difficult to reenter because you haven't backed it up or printed it yet.

Fortunately, first aid is available through a table repair program named *tutility*. This utility program can verify and rebuild Paradox tables. Although Tutility is a DOS-based program, it lets you use your mouse, and it sports a Windows-like interface that you should adjust to quite easily.

Before running Tutility, you should study the documentation in the *tutility.doc* file (usually located in *c:\pdoxwin\tutility.doc*). Once you understand the implications of using the program, you're ready to run it. First exit Paradox for Windows, then either double-click the Table Repair Utility icon in the Paradox for Windows group of Program Manager, or return to the DOS prompt and type **Tutility** and press ↵. If you need additional help, press F1.

WARNING

Tutility should *never* be considered a substitute for backing up your Paradox databases, especially since it can only be used to repair damaged Paradox 3.5, Paradox 4.0, and Paradox for Windows *tables*. Tutility cannot repair forms, reports, or other non-table objects.

This chapter has covered the many tools provided to help you manage Paradox for Windows files. So ends Part 4 of our odyssey into Paradox for Windows. In the next chapter, we'll begin our exploration of Paradox for Windows' most sophisticated features with a discussion of designing databases with multiple related tables.

PART FIVE

Managing Related Tables

CHAPTERS

Bill To Customer #: 1002

Ship To: Joe Adams

5434 Oceanic Way

Silver Spring, MD 20910

Gift Corner
Order Form

Order Date	Payment		Ship Via
12/1/92	☐ Check Enclosed ☐ Bill Me Later ☒ PO # _110-5A_ ☐ Master Card ☐ VISA		☒ US Mail ☐ UPS ☐ Fed Ex

Code	Qty	Description	Unit Price	Total
GC-006	3	Van	$9,899.95	$29,699.85
GC-111	2	Guernsey Cow	270.00	540.00
GC-122	1	Mountain Bicycle	5,225.00	5,225.00
			Subtotal:	$35,464.85
			Tax:	2,748.53
			Shipping:	354.65
			Total:	$38,568.03

CHAPTER

15

Database Design with Multiple Tables

*f*ast TRACK

● **You can use table lookup**   803

in multitable databases to fill in data automatically during data entry.

● **Referential integrity ties records in related tables together**   804

and prevents orphan records. In the familiar customers and orders scenario, referential integrity prevents you from entering an order if the associated customer doesn't exist and from deleting a customer when outstanding orders exist for that customer. It also governs how Paradox handles updates to the key field of the customer table.

● **To define referential integrity**   806

choose *Referential Integrity* from the Table Properties list in the **Create Table** or **Restructure Table** dialog box.

PARADOX for Windows allows you to manage data stored in separate, related tables. Determining when and how to divide data into separate, related tables is an important element of *database design*.

Sometimes it's obvious when data needs to be stored in separate tables. For instance, it makes little sense for a business to store all of its customer information and all of its inventory information in a single table. However, other situations are less obvious, and knowing exactly how to separate information into multiple tables can be tricky.

In this chapter, we'll look at basic multitable design concepts. The examples you'll find should serve as food for thought when deciding how best to store information for your own needs. We'll discuss the clues that can help you determine when two or more tables might be better than one. Finally, we'll explain how to make the most of referential integrity, a feature of Paradox for Windows that preserves the ties between related tables.

Types of Relationships between Tables

Three types of relationships can exist between tables: the *one-to-many* relationship, the *many-to-many* relationship, and the *one-to-one* relationship. The most common of these is the one-to-many relationship.

The One-to-Many Relationship

The one-to-many relationship describes a situation in which for every *one* record in a table, there may be *many* records of related information in another table. The classic example of a one-to-many relationship involves the task of managing customers and the orders they place. Because any *one* customer might place *many* orders over the course of time, you have a natural one-to-many situation.

Figure 15.1 shows one way you could divide information about customers and orders into two tables. The Cust No field acts as the *common field* (also called the *key field*) that relates information from one table to another. We can easily tell which customer a particular order belongs to by locating the customer number in the Orders table, then locating the same customer number in the CustList table.

FIGURE 15.1

Example of a one-to-many relationship between tables. The common field, Cust No, appears in both tables and indicates which customer placed each order.

Customer Table (one record per customer)

Cust No	Last Name	First Name	Address	etc...
1001	Smith	Andy	123 A St.	
1002	Miller	Martha	234 B St.	
1003	Jones	Jane	11 Oak Ave.	

Orders Table (one record per order)

Cust No	Prod Code	Qty	Unit Price	Date	etc...
1001	GC-006	3	$9,899.95	12/1/92	
1001	GC-111	2	$270.00	12/1/92	
1001	GC-122	1	$5,225.00	12/1/92	
1002	GC-111	4	$270.00	12/1/92	
1002	GC-006	3	$9,899.95	12/1/92	
1002	GC-112	2	$171.00	12/1/92	
1003	GC-122	2	$119.95	12/2/92	
1003	GC-987	3	$171.00	12/2/92	

When defining the common field that links two tables, you must keep these important points in mind:

- The common field must have the same field type in both tables.
- If the common field is alphanumeric, it must be the same size in both tables.

Figure 15.2 shows the underlying structure of the CustList and Orders tables shown in Figure 15.1. The common field, Cust No, is the Number field type in both tables.

In the CustList table shown in Figure 15.2, Cust No is marked as a primary key (★). Making Cust No the primary key in the CustList table will prevent us from assigning two different customers the same customer number, and will also speed things along down the road. (Chapter 4 explains how to define and use primary keys.)

We did not make Cust No a primary key in the Orders table because we wanted to ensure that customers could order as many items as they want. Had we made Cust No a primary key in the Orders table, we would have been able to enter only one order for each customer.

FIGURE 15.2

Structures of the sample CustList and Orders tables shown in Figure 15.1

Structure of the Customer Table

Field Name	Type	Size	Key
Cust No	Number		*
Last Name	Alpha	20	
First Name	Alpha	15	
Address	Alpha	35	
City	Alpha	20	
State	Alpha	2	
Zip Code	Alpha	10	
etc...			

Structure of the Orders Table

Field Name	Type	Size	Key
Cust No	Number		
Prod Code	Alpha	8	
Qty	Number		
Unit Price	$(Currency)		
Date	Date		
etc...			

The relationship between products and orders provides another example of a one-to-many relationship, as illustrated in Figure 15.3. In this example, the Products table stores one record for each inventory item.

FIGURE 15.3

The Products table keeps track of items in the inventory. The Orders table keeps track of individual orders.

Products Table (one record per product)

Prod Code	Description	In Stock	Unit Price	etc...
GC-006	Van	100	$9,899.95	
GC-111	Guernsey Cow	50	$270.00	
GC-122	Mountain Bicycle	100	$5,225.00	

Orders Table (one record per order)

Cust No	Prod Code	Qty	Unit Price	Date	etc...
1001	GC-006	1	$9,899.95	12/1/92	
1001	GC-111	2	$270.00	12/1/92	
1001	GC-122	1	$5,225.00	12/1/92	
1002	GC-006	4	$9,899.95	12/1/92	
1002	GC-111	5	$270.00	12/1/92	
1002	GC-122	1	$5,225.00	12/1/92	
1003	GC-111	1	$270.00	12/2/92	
1003	GC-122	2	$5,225.00	12/2/92	

Once again, we're using a common field to relate the two tables. Each product in the Products table has a unique product code (Prod Code) assigned to it. That code is used in the Orders table to identify the products each customer has ordered. As Figure 15.4 illustrates, Prod Code is an alphanumeric field with a length of eight in both tables.

Paradox for Windows has automatic updating features you can use to ensure that the Products table is always up-to-date. For example, you can have Paradox subtract the quantities of items sold from the in-stock quantities in the Products table as orders are filled. This way, the Products table will always accurately reflect the quantity of each item in stock. Chapter 18 discusses automatic updating in detail.

FIGURE 15.4

Structures of the sample Products and Orders tables shown in Figure 15.3. Here, Prod Code is the key field and is the same field type and size in both tables.

Structure of the Products Table

Field Name	Type	Size	Key
Cust No	Alpha	8	*
Description	Alpha	30	
In Stock	Number		
Unit Price	$(Currency)		
etc...			

Structure of the Orders Table

Field Name	Type	Size	Key
Cust No	Number		
Prod Code	Alpha	8	
Qty	Number		
Unit Price	$(Currency)		
Date	Date		
etc...			

The Many-to-Many Relationship

The many-to-many relationship occurs when *many* records from one table might be related to *many* records in another table. Suppose you're designing a database for a school and need to schedule students and courses. In this situation, there is a many-to-many relationship between students and the courses in which they enroll: The school offers many courses, and any given course will have many students enrolled in it.

So how do you set up tables for this many-to-many relationship between students and courses? As illustrated in Figure 15.5, you create one table of students, one table of courses, and then use a third table to place students in courses.

Notice how concise the tables are. The Students table contains information about students only. The Courses table contains information about courses only. (Both the Students and Courses tables could store much more information—they're summarized to fit on the page.) The third table, Schedule, links students to courses in a simple, direct manner.

FIGURE 15.5

The many-to-many design is used to keep track of which students are enrolled in which courses in a school.

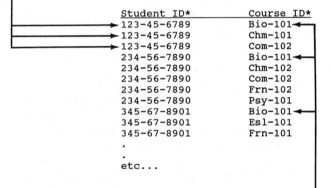

Students Table

Student ID*	Last Name	First Name	Address	etc...
123-45-6789	Adams	Andy	123 A St.	
234-56-7890	Baker	Bobby	234 B St.	
345-67-8901	Carlson	Carla	11 Oak Lane	
987-65-3421	Miller	Marie	227 Ocean Way	

.
.
etc...

Schedule Table

Student ID*	Course ID*
123-45-6789	Bio-101
123-45-6789	Chm-101
123-45-6789	Com-102
234-56-7890	Bio-101
234-56-7890	Chm-102
234-56-7890	Com-102
234-56-7890	Frn-102
234-56-7890	Psy-101
345-67-8901	Bio-101
345-67-8901	Esl-101
345-67-8901	Frn-101

.
.
etc...

Courses Table

Course ID*	Course Name	etc...
Bio-101	Intro to Biology	
Bio-102	Intermediate Biology	
Chm-101	Intro to Chemistry	
Com-101	Intro to Computers	
Com-102	Database Design	
Esl-101	English as a Second Language	
Frn-101	First Year French	
Frn-102	Second Year French	
Psy-101	Intro to Psychology	

.

If you look closely at Figure 15.5, you'll discover that the many-to-many relationship actually consists of several one-to-many relationships between tables. There's a one-to-many relationship between the Students and Schedule tables and a one-to-many relationship between the Courses and Schedule tables. The Schedule table creates the many-to-many relationship between Students and Courses. In fact, a many-to-many relationship is *always* a pair of one-to-many relationships between two tables, with a third table creating the many-to-many link.

NOTE There is also a many-to-many relationship between the CustList and Products tables described earlier. The Orders table acts as the linking table.

In Figure 15.5, we've placed an asterisk next to field names that are keyed in the underlying table structures. *Student ID* is keyed in the Students table to ensure that each *student* has a unique Student ID. *Course ID* is keyed in the Courses table to ensure that each *course* has a unique ID. Together, Student ID and Course ID form the primary key in the Schedule table. This prevents students from being enrolled in the same course more than once and will speed things up when working with the data.

NOTE When two or more fields in a table define the primary key, only records that have identical entries in all the keyed fields are considered duplicates. This type of key is called a *composite key*.

Of course, even with data spread across three tables, you can combine the information into data-entry forms, printed reports, and queries (see Chapters 16 and 17). With the Students, Schedule, and Courses tables, for instance, you can print student schedules and class roll sheets.

The One-to-One Relationship

In the one-to-one relationship, for every *one* record in a table, there's exactly *one* corresponding record in another table. Figure 15.6 provides an example of a one-to-one relationship: For every record in the Employee table, there is exactly one corresponding record in the EmpInfo table.

A one-to-one relationship like this usually indicates a flawed database design. After all, if an exact one-to-one relationship exists between every record in two different tables, why not just put all the information into one table? In the rare cases listed below, the one-to-one design might make sense.

- If you need more than 255 fields or 4000 bytes (Paradox for Windows' limit) to define a single record, you can split the fields into two tables. You still must use a common field (like Employee ID in Figure 15.6) to link records from one table to the other.

FIGURE 15.6

A one-to-one relationship exists between records in the Employee and EmpInfo tables.

Employee Table

Employee ID	Last Name	First Name	Department
10001	Smith	Wally	Accounting
10002	Jones	Mary	Sales
10003	Lopez	Frank	Sales
10004	Lim	Phon	Accounting
10005	d'Elgin	Tersha	Production

etc...

EmpInfo Table

Employee ID	Salary	Deductions
10001	$32,500	2
10002	$37,500	1
10003	$62,500	3
10004	$45,500	4
10005	$31,300	1

etc...

• If you need to limit access to some (but not all) fields, a one-to-one design can be useful. For instance, you could provide full access to all fields in the Employee table, but password protect the EmpInfo table, which contains salary information. However, a better solution is to place all fields in the Employee table, then assign auxiliary passwords with appropriate field rights to each field you want to protect. Chapter 14 explains how to assign passwords to tables and fields.

Categorizing Information

In general, it is *not* a good idea to use multiple tables to categorize information. Imagine, for example, that you want to manage personnel information for a company with several different departments. Your first inclination might be to create one table for people in the accounting department, then create a second table for people in the marketing department, and so on. This might be handy when you want to work with personnel data for people in a given department only, but it's going to be a pain when you need data for all employees or for employees from several departments.

You'd be much better off creating one table, perhaps named *Employee*, to store data for all employees in the company. Include a Department field to describe the department in which the employee works. When you need to retrieve records for people in a single department, a query, form, or report can easily extract those records.

NOTE   Queries are discussed in Chapters 8 and 16. Chapter 17 explains how to design multitable forms and reports.

Maintaining Historical Information

There are times when it makes sense to store categorized data in different tables. For example, an order processing application might require two tables with identical structures to store orders. You could use one table (*NewOrds*) for new, unfulfilled orders. A second table (*OldOrds*) could contain old, fulfilled orders.

When an order is fulfilled, you could move its record from the NewOrds table to the OldOrds table. Doing so would keep the NewOrds table down to a small and manageable size. OldOrds would act as a *history table*, keeping track of old fulfilled orders. If you needed to check on a problem in an old order, you would be able to find it in the OldOrds table. We'll look at examples that use history tables in Chapter 18.

Clues That Indicate When Multiple Tables Might Be Better

Understanding the relationships that can exist between tables will give you a head start on designing databases.

In many cases, your data will seem to fall naturally into separate, related tables. At other times, it won't be obvious when two or more tables would be better than one.

Suppose your starting point for designing a database is a printed form, like the order form shown in Figure 15.7. You've already learned why it's a good idea to put information about customers in one table and information about customer orders in another. However, you may not realize that you'll probably want to break up the order information into separate tables as well. In the sections that follow, we'll analyze the order form in Figure 15.7, looking for ways to store order information more efficiently. We'll also identify problems you might encounter when using tables that are poorly designed. In particular, we'll discuss how you can use repeating groups of fields and redundant data as clues that two or more tables might be better than one.

FIGURE 15.7

A sample printed order form filled in by a customer

Bill To Customer #: *1002*

Ship To: *Joe Adams*

5434 Oceanic Way

Silver Spring, MD 20910

Gift Corner
Order Form

Order Date	Payment	Ship Via
12/1/92	☐ Check Enclosed ☐ Bill Me Later ☒ PO # _110-5A_ ☐ Master Card _____ ☐ VISA _____	☒ US Mail ☐ UPS ☐ Fed Ex

Code	Qty	Description	Unit Price	Total
GC-006	3	Van	$9,899.95	$29,699.85
GC-111	2	Guernsey Cow	270.00	540.00
GC-122	1	Mountain Bicycle	5,225.00	5,225.00
			Subtotal:	$35,464.85
			Tax:	2,748.53
			Shipping:	354.65
			Total:	$38,568.03

Eliminating Repeating Groups of Fields

When using the sample form as the basis for a table design, your first inclination might be to store fields for the order as a whole (Cust No, Order Date, Ship Via, and so forth), then use repeating groups of fields to store the order details, as shown in Figure 15.8. Notice how the Prod Code, Qty, and Unit Price fields are repeated in the table design, using #1, #2, and so forth to identify each field group uniquely.

FIGURE 15.8

This table contains repetitive groups of fields to store information about orders.

```
Field Name

Cust No
Order Date
Ship Via
Payment
Customer's PO
Prod Code #1      ⎫
Qty #1            ⎬      First group
Unit Price #1     ⎭
Prod Code #2      ⎫
Qty #2            ⎬      Second group
Unit Price #2     ⎭
Prod Code #3      ⎫
Qty #3            ⎬      Third group
Unit Price #3     ⎭
Prod Code #4      ⎫
Qty #4            ⎬      Fourth group
Unit Price #4     ⎭
.
.
.
etc...
```

What's wrong with this design? For one thing, since a table can contain a maximum of 255 fields, the number of line items you can assign to each order is limited. A second problem arises when you want to analyze, perform calculations on, print, or sort information about orders. You're sure to find these tasks quite difficult with the orders spread across several fields in this manner.

Repetitive groups of fields like those in Figure 5.8 indicate that you're probably better off splitting the data into two tables. Use one set of field names in a group as the field names for a separate table. Then create a common field to link the two tables. You'll see an example in a moment.

Removing Redundant Data

Another clue to problems in an existing table design are fields that store the same information repeatedly. For instance, suppose you try to use the design shown in Figure 15.9 to store information about orders.

FIGURE 15.9

Another attempt to combine information about orders and customers in a single table

Field Name
Cust No
Prod Code
Qty
Unit Price
Order Date
Ship Via
Payment
Customer's PO

Imagine how this table will look when you start filling it with data. If a particular order requires five line items, the Order Date, Ship Via, Payment, and Customer's PO data will be repeated in each record, as shown in Figure 15.10.

FIGURE 15.10

Storing information about Orders in the single table design shown in Figure 15.9 leads to redundant data.

Cust No	Prod Code	Qty	Unit Price	Order Date	Ship Via	Payment	Customer's PO
1001	GC-006	1	$9,899.95	12/1/92	USMail	Invoice	
1001	GC-111	2	$270.00	12/1/92	USMail	Invoice	
1001	GC-122	1	$5,225.00	12/1/92	USMail	Invoice	
1009	GC-006	1	$9,899.95	12/2/92	UPS	PO	1234
1009	GC-093	1	$119.95	12/2/92	UPS	PO	1234
1009	GC-987	1	$3,665.00	12/2/92	UPS	PO	1234
1009	GC-164	1	$3,333.00	12/2/92	UPS	PO	1234
1009	GC-122	1	$5,225.00	12/2/92	UPS	PO	1234

Why does this present problems? For one thing, you'll get tired of retyping the same Order Date, Ship Via, Payment, and Customer's PO number for every single item a customer orders. For another, if you need to change the payment method or some other information in the order, you must be sure to make the same change in each relevant record.

The cure for both the repeating fields problem and the redundant data problem is simply to use two tables to store information about orders, as follows:

1. Place the data for the order as a whole—Cust No, Order Date, Ship Via, Payment, Customer's PO, and so on—in one table, named *Orders*.

2. Create a second table with fields for the individual line items— Prod Code, Qty, and Unit Price—and name the table *LineItem*. (We also suggest adding one more field, Extended Price, to store the results of multiplying the quantity by the unit price for each line item.)

NOTE   In Chapter 16 you'll learn how to create queries that perform calculations and store the results in a field.

3. Finally, create a common field (Order No) that links the Orders table to the LineItem table, and define this field as the primary key for the Orders table. To prevent duplicate line items for any given order, you can make the Order No and Prod Code fields the primary key for the LineItem table.

Figure 15.11 displays the structures of these two tables. Figure 15.12 shows how the two tables might look after adding some data to each one.

FIGURE 15.11

Structures of the
Orders and LineItem
tables

Structure of the Orders Table

Field Name	Type	Size	Key
Order No	Number		*
Cust No	Number		
Date Sold	Date		
Ship Via	Alpha	10	
Payment	Alpha	10	
Sold By	Alpha	3	
etc...			

Structure of the LineItem Table

Field Name	Type	Size	Key
Order No	Number		*
Prod Code	Alpha	8	*
Qty	Number		
Unit Price	Currency		
Extended Price	Currency		

FIGURE 15.12

The Orders and
LineItem tables with
some sample data
added. The arrows
show how the Order
No field links the two
tables.

Orders Table (one record per order)

Order No	Cust No	Date Sold	Ship Via	Payment	Sold By	etc...
2000	1002	12/1/92	USMail	Invoice	ACS	
2001	1001	12/1/92	UPS	PO	EAO	
2002	1007	12/1/92	FedEx	Check	KAO	

LineItem Table (many records per order)

Order No	Prod Code	Qty	Unit Price	Extended Price
2000	GC-006	3	$9,899.95	$29,699.85
2000	GC-111	2	$270.00	$540.00
2000	GC-122	1	$5,225.00	$5,225.00
2001	GC-111	4	$270.00	$1,080.00
2002	GC-006	3	$9,899.95	$29,699.85
2002	GC-112	2	$171.00	$342.00

The Bigger Picture

The final design for a database might include several tables, with numerous one-to-many relationships among them. Figure 15.13 shows the structures of all the tables in a sample database, with lines indicating the one-to-many relationships between the tables. (A *1* appears next to the table on the "one" side of the relationship, and an *M* appears next to the table on the "many" side of the relationship.)

FIGURE 15.13

A "clean" database design with five related tables of information

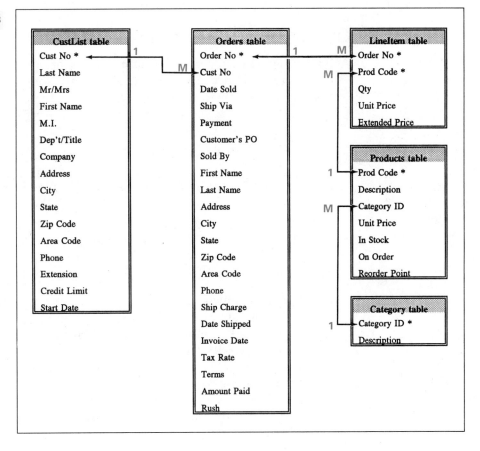

Note that the First Name, Last Name, Address, City, State, Zip Code, Area Code, and Phone fields in the Orders table refer to the customer's *shipping* address and phone. Those same fields in the CustList table refer to the customer's *billing* address and phone. We've used the same field names in the CustList and Orders tables so that we can take advantage of table lookups during data entry. Chapter 5 explains how to define and use table lookup.

Though we've included only the field names, Figure 15.13 should give you a good idea of how to break up the information for a business into several tables, without using repetitive groups of fields or storing redundant data.

Achieving Database Nirvana

The design sketched out in Figure 15.13 represents a kind of "database design nirvana" because every field in every table describes information that's relevant only to its own table.

> **NOTE**   The design term for "database design nirvana" is *normalization*.

We intentionally omitted most totals from the order form in Figure 15.7, since Paradox can calculate that information on-the-fly. The product description in the order form is already stored in the Products table, so there's no need to add a field for that information to the LineItem table.

For every table in your design, you still need to determine the field type, length (for alphanumeric fields), and any validity checks, as we did with the sample CustList table in Chapter 4. Here are some additional points to consider when designing related tables:

- When defining fields that link two or more tables (for example, Cust No, Order No, and Prod Code in Figure 15.13), give the fields the same field type and, if they're alphanumeric, the same length in all tables.

- If you plan to use table lookups to fill in fields automatically during data entry, corresponding fields must have the same name in both the lookup table and the table for which the lookup is defined.

- When a one-to-many relationship exists between two tables, identify the common field on the "one" side of the relationship as the primary key for that table. Doing so will speed operations, prevent duplicate entries in that field, and allow you to define referential integrity between the table on the "one" side and the table on the "many" side (as discussed later). Figure 15.13 identifies ideal primary key fields with an asterisk (*) next to appropriate field names.

It's important to remember that although you may be splitting your data into many separate tables, you can always pull it back together when creating queries, forms, and reports. Figure 15.14 shows a custom form built

FIGURE 15.14

A custom order-entry form, displaying information from the Orders, LineItem, and Products tables.

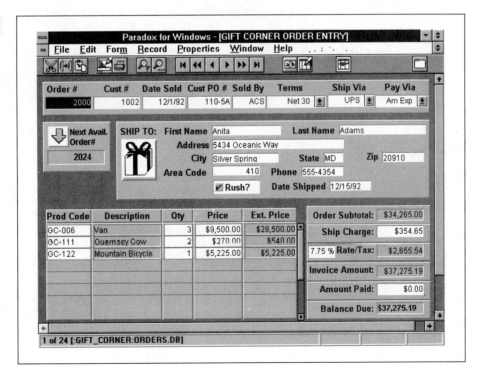

from the Orders, LineItem, and Products tables shown in Figure 15.13. The information on this form describes a customer's order completely. Figure 15.15 illustrates an invoice for this order. The "Bill To" address and phone on the invoice are taken from the CustList table. The next few chapters will explain how to mix and match data from multiple tables in your queries, forms, and reports.

FIGURE 15.15

An invoice for the order shown in Figure 15.14. The "Bill To" information is taken from the CustList table.

GIFT CORNER

8891 Gaudy Ave * West Fantasee, CA 92222
1-800-555-GIFT

Invoice Date: 12/21/92

INVOICE

Order #	Cust #	Date Sold	Cust PO #	Sold By	Terms	Pay Via
2000	1002	12/1/92	110-5A	ACS	Net 30	PO

BILL TO:	Anita Adams 5434 Oceanic Way Silver Spring, MD 20910 (410) 555-4354	SHIP TO:	Anita Adams 5434 Oceanic Way Silver Spring, MD 20910 (410) 555-4354	Ship Via	UPS
				Ship Date	12/15/92

Code	Description	Qty	Price	Extended Price
GC-006	Van	3	$9,899.95	$29,699.8
GC-111	Guernsey Cow	2	$270.00	$540.00
GC-122	Mountain Bicycle	1	$5,225.00	$5,225.00

Thanks for your order!
Don't forget our everyday guarantee: If you're not completely delighted with your purchase, simply return it and we'll cheerfully refund your money.

Order Subtotal:	$35,464.85
Tax:	$2,748.53
Ship Charge:	$354.65
Invoice Amount:	$38,568.03
Amount Paid:	$0.00
Balance Due:	**$38,568.03**

Keep in mind that regardless of whether your tables have one-to-one or one-to-many relationships, you can use the basic techniques discussed in Chapter 4 to create them. In many cases, you'll want to define secondary indexes for your tables, as discussed in Chapter 7.

Using Table Lookups

Table lookups can speed up data entry and improve accuracy in multi-table forms by filling in fields with corresponding data from another table. Recall from Chapter 5 that the table lookup feature provides the following capabilities:

- Allows you to require that values entered into a field exist in the first field of another table.

- Locates acceptable values for a field in another table.

- Lets you copy values from fields with *matching names* in the lookup table to the table you're editing.

NOTE   In the order entry form shown in Figure 15.14, table lookup automatically fills in the Ship To information (First Name, Last Name, Address, City, State, Zip Code, Area Code, and Phone) after a valid customer number is entered. We can modify the Ship To information if we wish.

You can define table lookups when creating your tables or just before designing a multitable data entry form. Remember that the first field of the lookup table must be the primary key for the lookup table, and any fields to be copied automatically must have matching names in both tables.

Using Referential Integrity

Like table lookup, referential integrity ensures that information entered into one table already exists in another table. However, referential integrity goes beyond table lookup because it also prevents the ties between data in separate tables from being broken.

Consider again the CustList and Orders example. When entering an order, you want to be absolutely sure that the customer number associated with the order also exists in the CustList table. Otherwise you might be unable to bill that customer later. Similarly, you wouldn't want Paradox to allow you to delete a customer record from the CustList table while an order for that customer is still outstanding. By defining referential integrity between the key field of the CustList table (Cust No) and the Cust No field of the Orders table, you can enforce the desired relationships.

> **N O T E**   You can establish referential integrity with a single-field key or a composite key.

In the CustList and Orders example, CustList is the *parent table* and Orders is the *child table*. Notice that the parent table is on the "one" side of a one-to-many relationship, while the child table is on the "many" side of the relationship. The key field of the parent table in a referential integrity relationship is called the *foreign key* because it is foreign to (outside of) the child table.

Choosing an Update Method

Imagine what would happen if you were to change the customer number in the CustList table. If referential integrity didn't exist between CustList and Orders, this change to CustList would create an "orphaned" order, since the Cust No field in Orders would no longer refer to the original customer. However, if referential integrity *did* exist between the CustList table and the Orders table, Paradox could treat this change to the parent table in one of two ways, depending on how you define the update method.

One method is to *prohibit* the update, so that you cannot change the key field in the parent table (CustList) if any orders are still associated with that field in the child table (Orders). This method is the more restrictive because you must delete that customer's records in the Orders table before changing the key field values in the CustList table.

The second method is to *cascade* the update, so that any change made to the key field in the parent table automatically flows down or "cascades" to the associated records in the child table. Thus, whenever you change the Cust No field value in CustList, Paradox will change the corresponding values in the Cust No field of the Orders table. Cascaded updates (the default method) keep data consistent between tables and provide flexibility during data entry.

Restrictions on Referential Integrity

Paradox for Windows imposes the following restrictions on referential integrity:

- The field used to tie the two tables together must be a primary key field in the parent table (for example, Cust No is the primary key for the CustList table).

- The child table must also have a primary key. However, the child table's key field need not be the same field you're using to tie the child and parent tables together.

- You can establish referential integrity only between like fields that contain matching values. The field *names* don't have to be the same, but the field *types* must be identical (and they must be the same length if you're using alphanumeric fields).

- You can establish referential integrity only between two tables in the same directory.

- You cannot define referential integrity between memo, formatted memo, graphic, binary, or OLE fields.

- Referential integrity is available between Paradox tables only.

If your tables do not conform to these restrictions, you may need to restructure them before defining referential integrity.

WARNING
If your tables already contain data, don't dive into the restructure operation without fully understanding the effects of doing so. Chapter 14 explains table restructuring in detail.

In the sample database shown in Figure 15.13, we've defined the referential integrity relationships listed below.

THIS FIELD	TIES CHILD TABLE	TO PARENT TABLE
Cust No	Orders	CustList
Order No	LineItem	Orders
Prod Code	LineItem	Products

Defining Referential Integrity between Tables

When you're ready to define referential integrity, close the child table for which you're defining the relationship (if it exists and is open) and close any tables that are (or will be) tied through referential integrity. If you forget to close tables, you may receive a "Table is Busy" message when you try to save your changes. Now proceed as follows:

1. Go to the **Create Table** or **Restructure Table** dialog box for the *child* table (for example, Orders is the child table for CustList).

N O T E   If you're *creating* a new child table, define all of its fields and specify the primary key before continuing with Step 2.

2. Choose *Referential Integrity* from the Table Properties list.

3. Click the Define button to open the **Referential Integrity** dialog box shown in Figure 15.16. The Fields list on the left displays all eligible fields from the child table. The Table list on the right displays all tables in the working directory.

4. In the Fields list, click the field you want to tie to the parent table, then click the → button above the list (or double-click the field name). The field you selected will appear under the Child Fields heading in the dialog box. If you choose the wrong field, click the ← button below the Fields list, then select another field.

FIGURE 15.16

The Referential Integrity dialog box

Referential Integrity

Fields: →

Order No [N]
Cust No [N]
Date Sold [D]
Ship Via [A10]
Payment [A10]
Customer's PO [A10]
Sold By [A3]
First Name [A15]
Last Name [A20]
Address [A35]
City [A20]
State [A2]
Zip Code [A10]
Area Code [N]
Phone [A8]

Child Fields   Parent's Key   ←   Table:

[None]   [None]   CATEGORY.DB
CUSTLIST.DB
LINEITEM.DB
ORDERS.DB
PRODUCTS.DB
RESTTEMP.DB

←

Update Rule:
◆ Cascade   ▷ Prohibit
☐ Strict Referential Integrity

✓ OK   ✗ Cancel   ? Help

5. In the Table list, click the name of the parent table, then click the → button above the list (or double-click the table name). The parent's key field or fields will appear under the *Parent's Key* heading in the dialog box. (If you choose the wrong table, click the ← button above the Tables list, then select another table.)

6. Choose the Update Rule you want. Your options are Cascade for cascaded updates (the default setting) or Prohibit to prevent updates to the parent table's key field if corresponding records exist in the child table.

7. If you do not want to enforce strict referential integrity when *previous* versions of Paradox access this table, click Strict Referential Integrity to remove the check mark from that option. Leave the option checked if you want to prevent previous versions of Paradox from opening this table.

NOTE

Unlike Paradox for Windows, earlier versions of Paradox did not completely enforce referential integrity. When Strict Referential Integrity is checked, earlier versions of Paradox will interpret the referential integrity definition as a password, which effectively prevents anyone from opening the table and adding data that could break the tie between parent and child tables.

8. Choose OK to name and save the referential integrity, as described below.

9. Choose Save or Save As to save the table structure.

Saving the Referential Integrity Definition

When you choose OK in Step 8, you'll see the **Save Referential Integrity As** dialog box shown below.

Type the name you want to give the referential integrity relationship (for example, *OrdersToCustList*), then choose OK. Referential integrity names can be up to 31 printable characters and require no file extension. The name you assign will appear in the list area below the Define button in the Create Table or Restructure Table dialog box. Paradox saves referential integrity definitions in a file with the table's name and the .val extension.

When you save the referential integrity rule, Paradox creates a secondary index on the child field(s) if one doesn't exist already. The index will have the name of the child field if you're using a single-field key to tie the tables together, or the name you gave the referential integrity if the tables are tied by a multifield key. You'll see the index name when you choose *Secondary Indexes* from the Table Properties list in the Create Table or Restructure Table dialog box.

If you define referential integrity on a table that contains data already, Paradox will place child records that have no parent record into the temporary Keyviol table in your private directory. Considering the Orders and LineItem tables, any existing LineItem records without a corresponding record in the Orders table would be moved to Keyviol when you defined referential integrity between the tables. To restore the moved records to the LineItem table, first enter all the missing parent records into the Orders table, and then choose File ➤ Utilities ➤ Add to add the child records from the Keyviol table to the LineItem table (see Chapter 14 for information on using Add).

NOTE If you delete the referential integrity, Paradox will not delete the secondary index automatically. If you wish, you can use the Restructure Table dialog box to delete the secondary index (see Chapter 7).

Changing or Erasing Referential Integrity

You can change or erase referential integrity via the Create Table or Restructure Table dialog box. To begin, choose *Referential Integrity* from the Table Properties list, then click the referential integrity relationship you want to change or erase. The Modify and Erase buttons will appear. Now perform either of the steps listed below.

- To change the selected referential integrity relationship, click the Modify button and complete the Referential Integrity dialog box as explained earlier.

- To erase the referential integrity relationship, click the Erase button.

WARNING To avoid "Table is Busy" messages, be sure to close the related tables before changing or removing referential integrity.

Entering Data When Referential Integrity Is in Effect

When entering data into a child table field that is tied to a parent table, you can either type the appropriate value, or you can request "Move Help." Keep in mind that the value you enter must be present in the parent table; otherwise, Paradox will reject the entry.

To request Move Help, choose Record ➤ Move Help or press Ctrl+Shif +spacebar. Figure 15.17 shows the Move Help dialog box for the Cust No field of the Orders table.

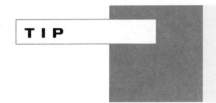

> **TIP**
>
> Move Help and Table Lookup Help are quite similar. Recall from Chapter 5 that you can request Table Lookup help by choosing Record ➤ Lookup Help or Ctrl+spacebar.

FIGURE 15.17

This dialog box appears after pressing Ctrl+Shift+spacebar in the Cust No field in the Orders table.

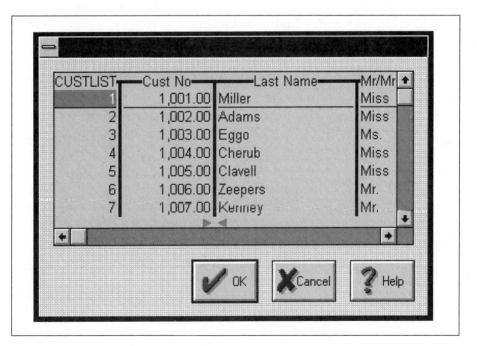

If you want to locate a specific record in the Move Help dialog box, press Ctrl+Z. You'll see the **Locate Value** dialog box. Select the field you want to search, choose a search method (if you wish), type the value you want to find, then choose OK. To find another occurrence of the same field value, press Ctrl+A. After locating the record you want, choose OK in the Move Help dialog box, then type in the appropriate value for the field. Unlike Table Lookup Help, Move Help does not automatically fill in values.

For added convenience during data entry, referential integrity can be used with table lookup. For example, we structured the Orders table to have a referential integrity relationship with CustList. We also assigned CustList as the lookup table for the Cust No field in Orders and chose the *All Corresponding Fields* and *Help and Fill* table lookup options. This combination of referential integrity and table lookup ensures the proper relationships between CustList and Orders records and supplies Ship To data automatically whenever we enter a valid customer number into the Orders table.

Here are some points to remember when working with tables that have referential integrity relationships:

- You cannot delete or rename the parent table if any records exist in the child table.

- You cannot delete a record from the parent table if the child table contains associated records. For example, you cannot delete a customer from CustList if an order for that customer exists in the Orders table. Such attempts are refused with the message "Master has detail records. Cannot delete or modify."

- If you've selected the Prohibit update rule, you cannot change the key field of the parent table if any associated records exist in the child table. Again, the message "Master has detail records. Cannot delete or modify" will appear when you try to move the cursor to another record. (You must choose Edit ➤ Undo or type in the previous key field value to clear the message.)

- You cannot insert a record into the child table unless a corresponding record exists in the parent table. For instance, you cannot insert a record into the LineItem table unless the Orders table already includes a record with the same value for the Order No field.

Similar rules are enforced when you use queries to change key fields or to delete or insert records in parent and child tables. If your queries would result in a violation of the referential integrity relationship, Paradox will refuse to make the requested changes. Instead, it will place a copy of the records that would violate the referential integrity relationship into temporary "Error" tables in your private directory. The Error table created depends on the type of query you perform, as listed below:

- A CHANGETO query will create an *ErrorChg* table (see Chapters 8, 16, and 18).

- A DELETE query will create an *ErrorDel* table (see Chapters 8 and 18).

- An INSERT query will create an *ErrorIns* table (see Chapter 18).

You can view or print the Error tables using the same techniques you would use for the Answer table (just be sure to do so before exiting Paradox, since these tables are only temporary). Then make any necessary changes to your parent or child table, or to your query criteria, and run the query again.

Copying Tables when Referential Integrity Is in Effect

It's a good idea to decide the name, location, and structure of your parent and child tables *before* you link them through referential integrity. As mentioned, you cannot rename or delete the parent table involved in a referential integrity relationship. You can, however, copy the tables to the same directory or to another directory. If you do so, follow the rules listed below:

- If you're copying tables in the *same* directory, use the Paradox Copy utility (File ➤ Utilities ➤ Copy), not the DOS Copy command or the Windows File Manager. The Paradox Copy command preserves the referential integrity relationship for the copy of the *child* table (since two child tables can refer to the same parent tables), but deletes it from the copy of the *parent* table (since a single field of a child table cannot refer to more than one parent table).

- If you're copying tables to *different* directories, you can use the Paradox Copy utility, the DOS Copy command, or the Windows File Manager, depending on whether you want to preserve referential integrity.

    The Paradox Copy utility *does not* preserve referential integrity across directories. You can use Restructure to rebuild the relationships after copying.

    The DOS Copy command or Windows File Manager *does* preserve the referential integrity relationships. If you use DOS Copy or the File Manager, be sure to include *all files* for *all tables* in the relationship.

- When distributing an application or moving it onto a network, use DOS Copy or the Windows File Manager to copy all the files and tables. Again, be sure to include all files for all tables in the referential integrity relationship.

NOTE

The files involved in a referential integrity relationship have the following extensions: *.db, .px, .tv, .mb, .x??, .y??,* and *.val*. You can specify the file names and extensions individually, or you can use a wildcard to copy all the related files at once. For example, typing the DOS command *copy orders.* c:\pdoxwin\newdir\orders.** would copy all the files for the Orders table from the current directory to the directory named *c:\pdoxwin\newdir.*

This chapter has covered the fundamentals of designing databases that contain multiple related tables. We discussed one-to-many, many-to-many, and one-to-one relationships, focused on ways to eliminate redundant data and repetitive fields, and explained how to define fields that tie separate tables together. We also covered referential integrity, which enforces strict ties between related tables and prevents orphan records.

In the next chapter, we'll take a look at advanced query and calculation techniques that are especially useful for managing related tables.

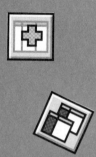

Query : <Untitled>

ORDERS.DB	Order No	Cust No	Date Sold	Ship Via	Payment	Cust
☑	☑ EG01	☐ EG03	☐	☐	☐	☐

LINEITEM.DB	Order No	Prod Code	Qty	Unit Price	Extended Pr	
☐	☐ EG01	☑ EG02	☑	☐	☐	

PRODUCTS.DB	Prod Code	Description	Category ID	Unit Price	In Stock	On
☐	☐ EG02	☑	☐	☐	☐	☐

CUSTLIST.DB	Cust No	Last Name	Mr/Mrs	First Name	M.I.	Depa
☐	☐ EG03	☑	☐	☑	☐	☐

CHAPTER

16

Advanced Queries and Calculations

f a s t

TRACK

NOW that you've learned some database design concepts, let's look at techniques for accessing data stored in multiple tables. In this chapter, we'll focus on using queries to combine data from multiple tables. We'll also discuss techniques for performing calculations with queries.

NOTE   As you read this chapter, keep in mind that forms and reports can also perform mathematical calculations. We'll get to those topics in Chapter 17.

Sample Tables

The examples in this chapter will use the Products, Category, Orders, LineItem, and CustList tables presented near the end of Chapter 15 (see Figure 15.13). Our database, though simplified for illustration purposes, represents a design that a retail or mail order business with both cash and charge orders might use.

Of course, there are many ways of doing business. Unlike socks and bathrobes, there is no one-size-fits-all database design that's suitable for every business. However, our sample database does stick to the basic design principle of avoiding repetitive groups of fields and redundant data.

The Products Table

The Products table stores information about each product sold by the company. Figure 16.1 shows the structure for this table, along with a brief description of each field. The bottom half of Figure 16.1 shows sample data for the first few fields of this table.

The Category Table

The Category table provides a description for each category of product sold. The structure of this table and a description of each field appear in Figure 16.2. The bottom half of the figure shows some sample data.

The Orders Table

The overall information about each order, including the customer's Ship To address and phone number, is stored in the Orders table. Since each order must have a unique identifying number, the Order No field is keyed. Details of individual items on the order are stored in the LineItem table, as you'll see in a moment.

FIGURE 16.1

Top: Structure of the sample Products table with brief descriptions of each field. Bottom: Sample data in the Products table. Each product has a unique identifying code.

Field Name	Type	Description
Prod Code	N *	Uniquely identifies each product
Description	A 30	Describes the product
Category ID	N	Identifies the product's category
Unit Price	$	Our cost for one item of this product
In Stock	N	Quantity currently in stock
On Order	N	Quantity currently on order
Reorder Point	N	Reorder point

Prod Code	Description	Category ID	Unit Price
GC-006	Van	114	$9,500.00
GC-086	Yacht - 180 ft	102	$900,000.00
GC-093	Camera and Case	110	$100.95
GC-105	Buckingham Palace Tour	113	$13,500.00
GC-111	Guernsey Cow	107	$225.00
GC-112	Never-Die Bulb	105	$150.00
GC-122	Mountain Bicycle	111	$5,000.00
GC-125	Bowling Ball and Pins	111	$325.00

FIGURE 16.2

Top: Structure of the sample Category table with descriptions of each field. Bottom: Sample data in the Category table. Each category has a unique Category ID.

Field Name	Type	Description
Category ID	N *	Uniquely identifies each category
Category Name	A 30	Describes the category

Category ID	Category Name
101	Airplane
102	Boat
103	Computer Equipment
104	House
105	Housewares
106	Livestock - Ancient
107	Livestock - Domestic
108	Livestock - Wild
109	Novelty
110	Photo Equipment

The structure and field descriptions for the Orders table appear at the top of Figure 16.3 (we've omitted the Ship To fields to conserve space). The bottom of Figure 16.3 shows sample data for a few fields of the table.

One question that might arise is "What do you do to a record after an order is fulfilled?" You could just delete the record, but then you would have no history of the transaction. To avoid this, we use the Date Shipped

FIGURE 16.3

Top: Structure of the sample Orders table, with brief descriptions of all fields except Ship To name, address, and phone. Bottom: Sample data in the Orders table.

Field Name	Type	Description
Order No	N *	Uniquely identifies each order
Cust No	N	Who placed the order
Date Sold	D	Date of sale
Ship Via	A10	Shipping method (e.g., FedEx)
Payment	A10	Payment method (e.g., Invoice)
Customer's PO	A10	Purchase order number
Shipping Charge	$	Shipping charge
Date Shipped	D	Shipping date (blank if unfulfilled)
Invoice Date	D	Date of invoice (blank until invoiced)
Tax Rate	N	Tax rate (e.g., 0.0775)
Terms	A10	Payment terms (e.g., Net 30)
Amount Paid	$	Amount paid on the order
Rush	A3	Rush the order? (Yes or No)

(Ship To name, address, and phone fields are not shown)

Order No	Cust No	Date Sold	Ship Via	Payment	Sold By
2000	1002	12/1/92	UPS	Invoice	ACS
2001	1001	10/22/92	UPS	Check	ACS
2002	1007	10/22/92	UPS	Check	EAO
2003	1002	10/22/92	Emery	Invoice	EAO
2004	1003	10/22/92	UPS	MC	EAO
2005	1007	10/22/92	FedEx	Check	EAO

field. While the order is outstanding, this field is blank; but as soon as the order is fulfilled, we place the date into the field. That way, we can use this field to track *outstanding* orders (Date Shipped is blank) and *fulfilled* orders (Date Shipped is not blank).

The Payment field of the Orders table indicates the customer's payment method. When this field has a value of "Invoice," we'll need to send the customer an invoice. Whenever we enter an order, the Invoice Date field will be blank to indicate that the customer hasn't been invoiced yet. When we ship the order and send an invoice, we'll fill in the invoice date. To determine which orders require invoicing, we would simply look for records with a Payment of "Invoice" and a blank Invoice Date.

NOTE   For simplicity, we'll use the Order Number as the invoice number.

The LineItem Table

The LineItem table tracks detail items for each order. We use the Order No field to link each detail record with its associated order in the Orders table. The Prod Code field links each item in an order to a particular product. The structure of the LineItem table is shown at the top of Figure 16.4; sample data appears at the bottom of the figure.

FIGURE 16.4

Top: Structure of the sample LineItem table, with brief descriptions of each field. Bottom: Sample data in the LineItem table.

Field Name	Type	Description
Order No	N *	Identifies customer order number
Prod Code	A8 *	Identifies product ordered
Qty	N	Quantity ordered
Unit Price	$	Selling price of one item of this product
Extended Price	$	Calculated by a query as Qty * Unit Price

Order No	Prod Code	Qty	Unit Price	Extended Price
2000	GC-006	3	$9,899.95	$29,699.85
2000	GC-111	2	$270.00	$540.00
2000	GC-122	1	$5,225.00	$5,225.00
2001	GC-111	-4	$270.00	($1,080.00)
2001	GC-129	4	$430.00	$1,720.00
2002	GC-006	3	$9,899.95	$29,699.85
2002	GC-112	-2	$171.00	($342.00)

A negative value in the Qty field represents a returned item. Placing a returned item in the LineItem table as a "negative" sale provides a record of the transaction, and also keeps the In Stock quantities in the Products table accurate during automatic updating. This will be discussed in Chapter 18.

Now, a database purist might argue that invoice transactions (those with an "Invoice" payment method), direct sales (those without an "Invoice" payment method), and adjustments (negative sales) should be stored in separate tables. Indeed, you *could* create separate tables for each type of transaction; however, there are certain conveniences to storing all these transactions in one table. First, it's easier to work with one big table of sales and adjustments rather than juggling different "types" of sales in separate tables. Second, automatic updating is easier when all the transactions are stored in one table.

The CustList Table

The CustList table, which keeps track of customers, is the same table we've been using throughout this book. Cust No is keyed in the CustList table to ensure unique customer identifiers, and it is used in the Orders table to link orders to the customers who placed them.

Now let's look at ways to combine data from all these tables to get information we need.

Combining Data from Multiple Tables

Queries are the basic tool required to *join* (combine) information from multiple related tables. All the query techniques that we covered in Chapter 8 apply here. However, when querying multiple tables, you need to consider two additional points:

- You must fill out a separate query table for each table.

- You must provide example elements that tell Paradox which field is the common field that links information from one table to information in another.

Understanding Example Elements

An example element in a query table plays the same role that a variable, or "placeholder," plays in math. The example element holds a value that's likely to change. For instance, we can make the general statement

X * Y = Extended Price

where X stands for any Quantity, * means "times" (multiplied by), and Y stands for Unit Price. Regardless of the number you substitute for X (the quantity), and the number you substitute for Y (the unit price), it remains true that X times Y results in the Extended Price.

When used to link multiple tables, the example element plays the additional role of "looking up" data in one table based on the contents of the example element in another table. While performing a query of the LineItem table, for example, Paradox might encounter a transaction involving product GC-006. If the Prod Code fields of the LineItem and Products tables are linked in a query, Paradox "knows" to get related information about product GC-006 in the LineItem table by looking up GC-006 in the Prod Code field of the Products table. You'll see some examples in a moment, but first let's discuss the "rules" for entering example elements into query tables.

Entering Example Elements in a Query Table

To enter example elements into a query table, proceed as follows:

1. Position the cursor where you want to type the example element in the query table.

2. Press the F5 key.

3. Type the example element, which can be any combination of letters and numbers, but cannot contain blank spaces or be a reserved word. *X, Y, hello, QUESTION1*, and ***PRODUCT*** are all valid example elements.

4. After typing the example element, move the cursor to any other column.

When using example elements, keep the following ground rules in mind:

* You cannot use example elements in memo, formatted memo, graphic, OLE, or binary fields.

* Unlike query (search) criteria and other elements used in query tables, example elements always appear in reverse video or in some color that makes them stand out.

* You can link up to 24 tables using example elements.

Adding and Removing Tables in the Query Window

 When you're ready to place another table in the Query window, click the Add Tables button in the SpeedBar (shown at left), or choose Query ➤ Add Table from the menus. When the **Select File** dialog box appears, click on the name of the table you want to add and choose OK. Paradox will add the new table to the bottom of the Query window.

To add several tables to the Query window at once, click the name of the *first* table you want to add, then Ctrl+click the remaining tables and choose OK. The selected tables will appear below any existing query tables in the window, in alphabetical order by table name.

 If you wish to remove a table from the Query window, click the Remove Table button in the SpeedBar (shown at left), or choose Query ➤ Remove Table. When the **Remove Table** dialog box appears, click on the name of the table you want to remove (or use Ctrl+ click to select several tables) and choose OK.

T I P

To add or delete names of several adjacent tables in the Select File or Remove Table dialog box, click the first table name, Shift+click the remaining names, then choose OK.

Using Example Elements to Link Tables

Suppose you want to list products from the Products table, but you also want to include the category name with each product. Since the category name is stored in the Category table, not the Products table, you'll need to combine data from the two tables.

To begin the query, choose File ➤ New ➤ Query. In the **Select File** dialog box, click the *PRODUCTS.DB* table name, then choose OK to open the Query window.

Now check the Prod Code, Description, and Category ID fields in the Products table by clicking on the empty check box in each field.

To display data from the related Category table, you must also place an example element in the Category ID field of the Products query table. This example element will act as the placeholder for the current Category ID when Paradox performs the query. Remember to press F5 before typing the example element.

In the example below, we used the abbreviation *CatID* as the example element. Keep in mind that the example element is just a placeholder which has no meaning of its own; you could have used *x* or *abc* or *HOWDY* or *category* or *row1* as the example element instead of *CatID*.

Now you're ready to add the Category table to the Query window. Click the Add Tables button in the SpeedBar or choose Query ➤ Add Table, select *CATEGORY.DB* from the list, and choose OK. Next you must place the same ***CatID*** example element in the Category ID field of the Category query table to define the link between the tables. Press F5, then type the example element. You must use the same example element in both the Products and the Category query tables so that Paradox will know to match those field values when processing the query.

Now you can check the Category fields you want to see in the resulting Answer table. We'll assume that you want to see the Category Name field. When you click the Run Query button in the SpeedBar or press F8 to perform the query, the resulting Answer table will include all records from the Products table, together with the associated category names from the Category table, as shown in Figure 16.5.

Because ***CatID*** is an example element and is identical in the two query tables, Paradox "knows" that you want matching information in these two fields when you perform the query. For instance, if the current record in the Products table contains 114 in the Category ID field, Paradox must find a record in the Category table that also contains 114 in the Category ID field when performing the query.

NOTE   We've resized and moved columns in many query tables and Answer tables in this chapter so you can view their contents more easily. We've also changed the number formats in many Answer table examples.

Notice that we checked the Category ID field in the query table for the Products table, but not in the query table for the Category table. This is because there's no need to see the Category ID twice in the resulting Answer table.

If you wish to check the common field in both tables, there's no harm in doing so. In Figure 16.6, for instance, we checked the Category ID field in both query tables. In the resulting Answer table, the field titled *Category ID* is the Category ID from the Products table. The field titled *Category ID_1* is the Category ID from the Category table. Even though we don't

FIGURE 16.5

Query tables for the Products and Category tables. The example element, **CatID**, in the Category ID field of both tables defines the common field that links the tables. Check marks indicate fields to display. The resulting Answer table appears below the Query window.

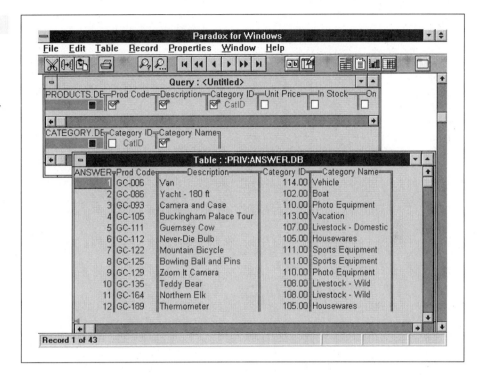

need to see the Category ID twice in the Answer table, the Answer table in Figure 16.6 demonstrates that Paradox did indeed find the Category ID in the Products table that matches the Category ID in the Category table. (The codes are identical in each record of the Answer table.)

Using the SpeedBar to Place Example Elements

As explained earlier in this chapter, you can link tables together manually by pressing the F5 key and typing the example element. However, Paradox for Windows provides a more efficient method of linking two or more tables. This method utilizes *automatic example elements*. To place automatic example elements in the common fields of two tables, follow the steps below.

FIGURE 16.6

In this example, we checked the Category ID field in both the Products and Category tables. Notice that the Category ID appears twice in the Answer table, proving that Paradox has displayed records from the two tables with matching Category ID codes.

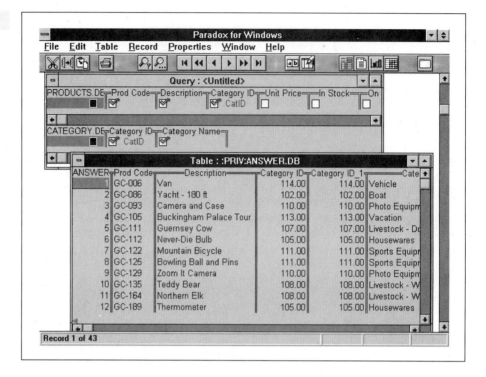

1. Click the Join Tables button in the SpeedBar (shown at left). The letters *EG* appear to the lower-right of the mouse pointer when you move the pointer to a field in the query table.

2. Click in the field where you want to place the first example element (for instance, the Category ID field of the Products query table). *EG01*, highlighted or in a different color, appears in that field.

3. Now click in the common field of the query table you want to link. The same highlighted example element appears in this field, as shown in Figure 16.7.

When using automatic example elements, keep the following points in mind:

- The fields of the tables being linked must be the same type, and they must contain corresponding data in order for the join to work.

FIGURE 16.7

The Products and
Category tables
joined by automatic
example elements

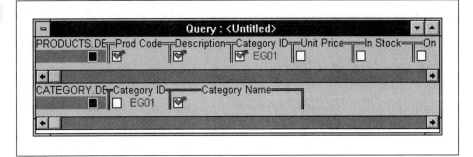

- The first automatic example element is **EG01**, the next is **EG02,**
  the next is **EG03**, and so on.
- To cancel the join, simply click the Join Tables button again. If
  you've already placed an automatic example element in one of the
  query tables, you can delete it as you would delete any text in a
  query.

Copying Example Elements

You can use copy and paste techniques to copy query elements from one
query table field to another. Not only does this guarantee accurately typed
examples, it can also save you time. Simply select the example element you
want to copy, then click the Copy To Clipboard button in the SpeedBar or
press Ctrl+Ins. Next, click in the query table and field where you want to
paste the example element, and click the Paste From Clipboard button or
prss Shift+Ins.

Combining Data from More than Two Tables

You can use the techniques presented in this chapter to query any number
of tables. For example, Figure 16.8 links four tables in a single query. The query

tables involved contribute the following example elements and checked fields:

Orders   *EG01* (in the Order No field) and *EG03* (in the Cust No field) are example elements linking the Orders table to the LineItem and CustList tables, respectively. The Order No field is checked for display.

LineItem   *EG01* (in the Order No field) links the LineItem and Orders table; *EG02* (in the Prod Code field) links the LineItem table to the Products table. The Prod Code and Qty fields are checked for display.

Products   The *EG02* example element (in the Prod Code field) links the Products table to the LineItem table. The Description field is checked for display.

CustList   Example element *EG03* (in the Cust No field) links the CustList table to the Orders table. Last Name and First Name are checked for display.

FIGURE 16.8

Sample query that takes data from four different tables. Example elements in each query table link the common fields among the tables.

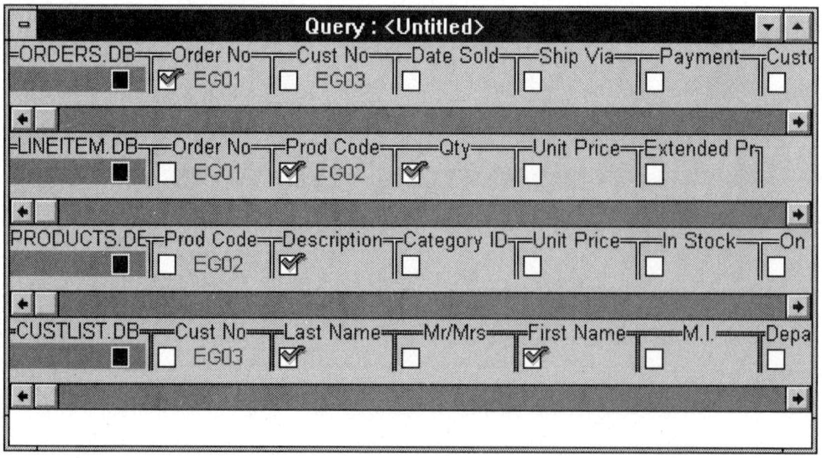

When you perform the query, the Answer table shown in Figure 16.9 will result. The table includes the order number, product code, quantity ordered, product description, and the name of the customer who placed each order.

N O T E

In Chapter 17 you'll learn how to print invoices from multiple tables.

When you have multiple query tables on the screen, the left-to-right and top-to-bottom order of checked fields in the query tables determines the initial order of fields in the Answer table, as well as the sort order.

Of course, you can arrange the columns in Table View by dragging the columns or pressing Ctrl+R. You can also modify the order of fields in the Answer table or define a sort order for the Answer tables as disussed in Chapter 8. In addition, if you'll be printing the contents of the Answer table or displaying it as a form, you can rearrange the fields any way you wish. You don't need to worry about the appearance of the Answer table while you're creating query tables.

FIGURE 16.9

Results of the query shown in Figure 16.8. Fields that were checked in the query tables are displayed in the Answer table.

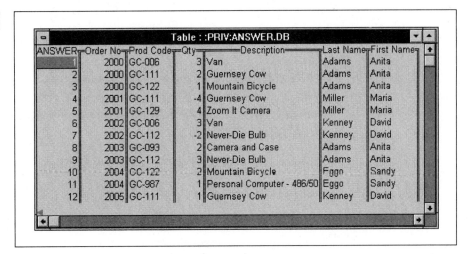

T I P   See Chapter 6 if you need a reminder about how to move columns and customize the appearance of text and numbers in Table View.

Using Query Criteria with Multiple Tables

You can add query criteria to any table in a multitable query, including operators such as <, >, LIKE, .., and all the others discussed in Chapter 8. A few important points are listed below.

- Do not press F5 before typing a query criterion (unlike example elements, query criteria should not be highlighted).

- If you want to include a query criterion in a field that contains an example element, follow the example element with a comma (and a space if you wish), then type the query criterion for that field.

Suppose you wanted to display only orders placed by Anita Adams. You could create the query shown in Figure 16.10 so that the CustList query table displays only records that contain Adams in the Last Name field and Anita in the First Name field. Because *Anita* and *Adams* are query criteria and not example elements, we did not press F5 before typing the names; therefore, they are not highlighted. The resulting Answer table lists records for Anita Adams only.

Figure 16.11 shows a slightly more complicated example. Here, the query isolates the transactions for invoice number 2001. This is practically the same as the query shown in Figure 16.8, but the query criterion 2001 in the Order No field of the Orders table restricts the Answer table to records that contain 2001 in the Order No field. Notice how a comma and a space precede each query criterion, and the query criteria are not highlighted (this distinguishes them from example elements).

The results of the query shown in Figure 16.11 appear below.

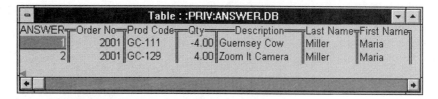

ANSWER	Order No	Prod Code	Qty	Description	Last Name	First Name
1	2001	GC-111	-4.00	Guernsey Cow	Miller	Maria
2	2001	GC-129	4.00	Zoom It Camera	Miller	Maria

AND and OR Queries with Multiple Tables

AND and OR queries with multiple tables are similar to AND and OR queries with a single table. For an AND query, place the query criteria on the same line. As with a single table, you can add as many selection criteria as you want.

FIGURE 16.10

A query that displays orders placed by Anita Adams

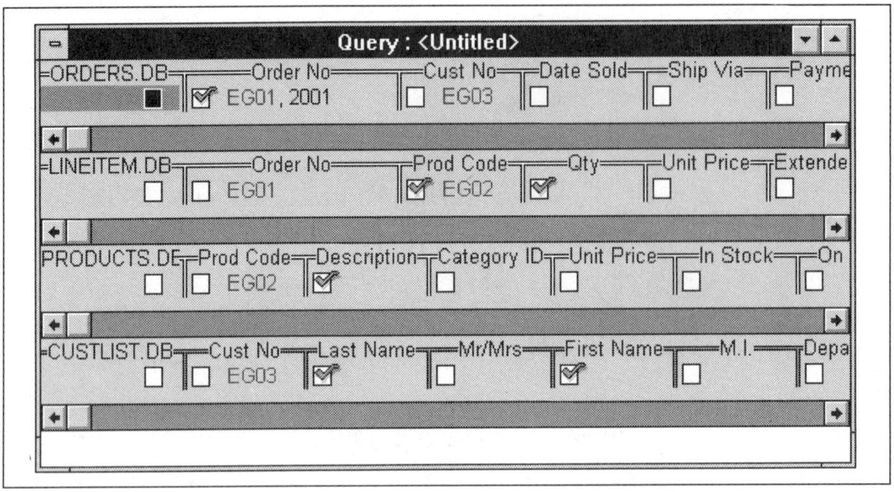

FIGURE 16.11

A multitable query that limits the Answer table to records that have the number 2001 in the Order No field

Even if you use different fields on two or more query tables, the relationship among the queries is still treated as an AND question. Suppose you want to know how much photo equipment salesperson ACS has sold (the Category ID for photo equipment is *110*). First, you would set up a query on the Orders table and put **ACS** in the Sold By field to isolate orders for that salesperson.

To limit the display of transactions to sales of photo equipment, add the LineItem and Products tables to the Query window. Next use the Join Tables button in the SpeedBar to link the Order No fields of the Orders and LineItem tables, then use the Join Tables button once more to link the Prod Code fields of the LineItem and Products tables. Check the fields you want to view, and type the query criterion **110** in the Category ID field of the Products query table, as shown in Figure 16.12.

Because both *ACS* and *110* are on the first row of their respective query tables, Paradox will interpret the query as requesting records that have ACS in the Sold By field of the Orders table *and* 110 in the Category ID field of the Products table. As Figure 16.12 demonstrates, the Answer table contains exactly those records.

NOTE

To use the *Category Name* in the query criterion instead of the Category ID, add the Category table to the Query window shown in Figure 16.12, link the Category ID fields of the Products and Category tables, erase *110* from the Category ID field in the Products table, and type *Photo Equipment* into the Category Name field of the Category table. Then run the query.

FIGURE 16.12

A multitable query that asks for transactions involving salesperson ACS **and** products in Category ID 110 (photo equipment). Example element **EG01** links the Orders and LineItem tables, and **EG02** links the ProdCode field of the LineItem and Products tables.

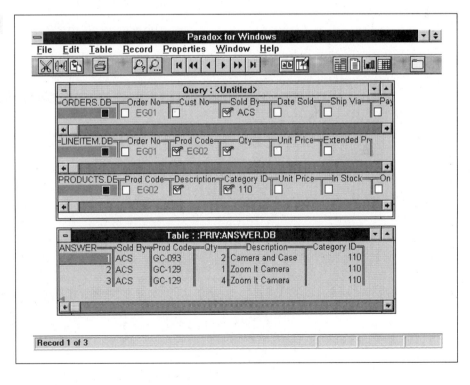

OR queries that involve a single field can be handled with the OR operator. The query in Figure 16.13 displays records for salesperson ACS that have either 103 (computer equipment) *or* 110 (photo equipment) in the Category ID field of the Products table.

If you want to ask OR questions with two separate tables, you need to "stack" them on separate lines in the query tables. To create a new query line, move the highlight to an existing query line and press ↓. (If you need to delete a query line, move the highlight to the line and press Ctrl+Del.)

When working with OR questions on separate tables, keep in mind these points:

- Each "question" (row) in each query table should have its own linking example element. For instance, if two questions are involved, you'll need two pairs of matching example elements.

- The same fields should be checked in each row of a query table.

FIGURE 16.13

A multitable query that asks for transactions involving salesperson ACS *and* products in either the computer equipment category (Category ID 103) *or* the photo equipment category (Category ID 110) of the Products table

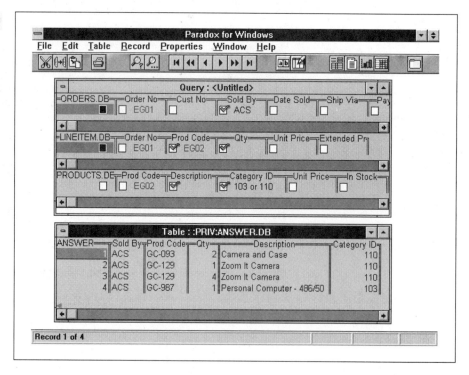

This may sound complicated, but an example should clear things up. Suppose we want to list all products sold by ACS (regardless of the category) or any products sold in Category ID 110 (regardless of the salesperson). The query and Answer tables shown in Figure 16.14 illustrate the stacking technique required to extract the information we want. Each query table contains two rows (one for each OR query criterion), and the check marks in the two rows of each query table correspond. The example elements are as follows: ***Ord1*** links the first row of the Orders and LineItem query tables; ***Ord2*** links the second row of Orders and LineItem; ***Prod1*** links the first row of the LineItem and Products query tables; ***Prod2*** links the second row of LineItem and Products.

FIGURE 16.14

A query that asks for records with *ACS* in the Sold By field (regardless of category) *or* with *110* in the Category ID field (regardless of salesperson).

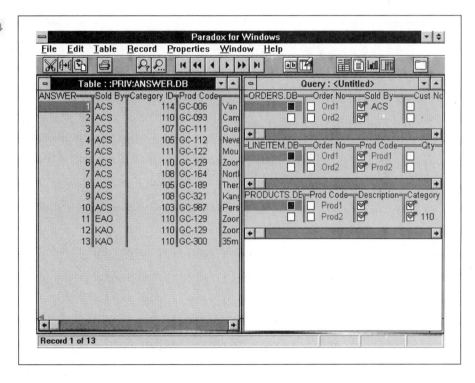

TIP To show the query and Answer tables side-by-side, as in Figure 16.14, choose Window ➤ Tile from the Query window menus.

Because *ACS* is on the first row of the Orders query table and *110* is on the second row of the Products query table, the two are treated as two separate questions. Consequently, the Answer table contains records with *ACS* in the Sold By field (regardless of category) *and* records with *110* in the Category ID field (regardless of salesperson).

Displaying Non-Matching Records

When you create a query that links two or more tables, Paradox usually displays only those records with matching values in the tables. This point is illustrated in Figure 16.15, where we've used the example element **EG01** to link the Cust No fields of the CustList and Orders tables. The Last Name, First Name, Order No, and Date Sold fields are checked for display, and the Answer table shown displays the results of the query.

Notice in Figure 16.15 that records for customers who did not place orders are excluded from the Answer table. Why? Because when Paradox is performing the query, the **EG01** example element requires matching values in the CustList and Orders tables; if the values don't match, the records are left out.

Suppose you want to list *all* customers, regardless of whether they've placed orders; and suppose you want to see the order number and date if a customer did place an order.

To display that information, you must perform an *outer join* using the *inclusion operator* (!). When entering the query, type the inclusion operator immediately following the example element, without any blank space between the example element and the operator.

FIGURE 16.15

This Answer table includes customer name, order number, and date sold. Because the *EG01* example element requires matching Cust No fields in the CustList and Orders table, the Answer table omits customers who haven't placed orders.

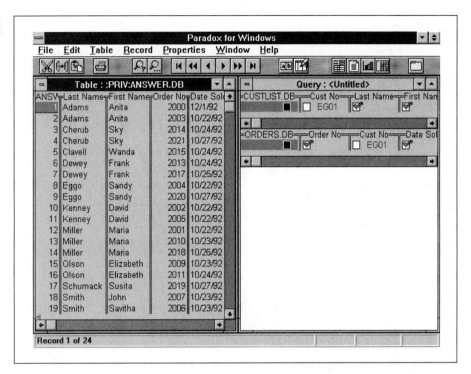

TIP

Because the inclusion operator includes records that have no matching records in a linked table, it can help you discover mistakes made while typing data into common fields.

In Figure 16.16, we placed the inclusion operator (!) after the *EG01* example element in the CustList table. In essence, we're telling Paradox to list every record from the CustList table, whether or not there's a corresponding order for that customer in the Orders table. The resulting Answer table includes *all* the records from the CustList table, with blank order information for customers who have not placed orders.

In summary, the basic technique for joining data from multiple related tables into a single table is to link the common fields through identical example elements. As with single-table queries, you can check the fields

FIGURE 16.16

The inclusion operator (!) tells Paradox to display all the records from the CustList table, even if there are no matching records in the Orders table.

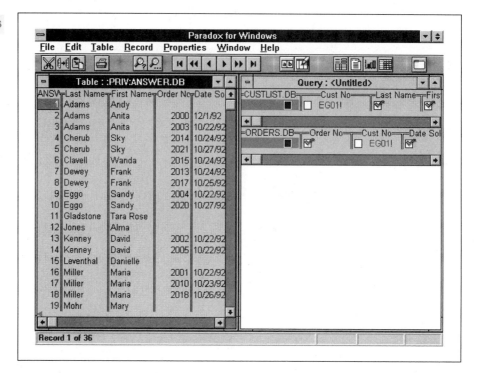

you want to view in the Answer table, and you can enter query criteria to specify which records to include in the Answer table.

Let's now turn our attention to an entirely different use of queries—performing mathematical calculations. This capability is useful for both single-table and multitable queries.

Using Queries to Perform Calculations

To perform calculations in queries, you type in an *expression* using any combination of the arithmetic operators listed in Table 16.1.

TABLE 16.1: Arithmetic Operators Used when Typing Calculation Expressions in Queries

OPERATOR	FUNCTION
+	Addition
-	Subtraction
*	Multiplication
/	Division
( )	Grouping

NOTE You can also use reports and forms to perform calculations, as described in the next chapter.

All Paradox for Windows calculations observe the standard mathematical *order of precedence*. That is, multiplication and division are performed before addition and subtraction.

To understand how order of precedence affects calculations, consider a simple expression such as **10+5*2**. Because multiplication is performed before addition, the result of this expression is *20*: five times two, plus ten.

If you want to override the standard order of precedence, you can use parentheses. Any portion of an expression that is enclosed in parentheses will always be calculated first. Thus, the result of the expression **(10+5)*2** is *30*, because Paradox first adds ten and five, then multiplies the result by two.

In Chapter 8 we explained how to use arithmetic operators in queries to locate records that fall within a specified range of dates. By subtracting a certain number of days from the **TODAY** operator, you can isolate records that fall within a range of dates in relation to the current date. For instance, the query below isolates records from the Orders table in which Date Sold is more than 90 days ago.

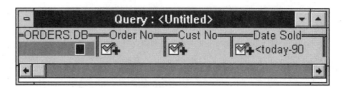

Using CALC to Display Calculation Results

The *TODAY-90* calculation shown above does not present the results of the calculation in the Answer table. To *display* the results of a calculation, you must precede the calculation with the keyword **CALC**. CALC displays the result of the expression in a new field in the Answer table. Unless you use the **AS** operator to name the field (as explained in a moment), the field takes the calculation expression as its name.

You can use *example elements* with calculations to display the results of calculations that involve two or more fields, to add a constant to a field, and to project "what-if" situations. Recall that the LineItem table has a Qty field and a Unit Price field. If we want to calculate the extended price for each detail line, we must multiply the quantity by the unit price in each record. Figure 16.17 shows the query we need, along with the resulting Answer table. Note that *QTY* and *PRICE* are example elements entered with the F5 key. After typing the *PRICE* example element, a comma, and a blank space in the Unit Price field, we entered an expression telling Paradox to multiply the quantity by the price (again pressing F5 to enter *QTY* and *PRICE* in the expression).

TIP

We've used check plus in this query, rather than check, to ensure that records with identical quantities and prices will be included in the Answer table, and not discarded as duplicates.

When we perform the query, Paradox puts the value in the current record's Qty field into the *QTY* example element, then puts the value in the current record's Unit Price field into the *PRICE* example element.

Next it performs the calculation **QTY** times **PRICE**. The result is a new field that displays the extended price of each transaction, as the Answer table in Figure 16.17 shows.

How Paradox Calculates Blank Fields

Normally, if any field that's used in a calculation is blank, the result of the calculation will also be blank. For instance, if either the Qty field or the Unit Price field (or both) were empty in one of the records in Figure 16.17, the result would be blank. If you would prefer that Paradox treat blank fields as the number zero, choose File ➤ System Settings ➤ Blank As Zero, as discussed in Chapter 13.

FIGURE 16.17

The extended price calculated using example elements and CALC

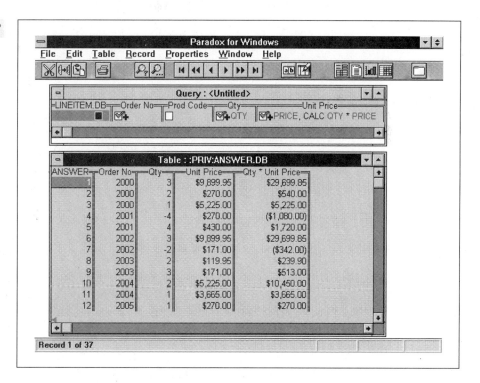

Renaming Calculated Fields

Notice in Figure 16.17 that the last column in the Answer table is named *Qty * Unit Price*. Paradox automatically uses the names of fields involved in the calculation to name the new field in the Answer table. If you'd rather assign a different name to the calculated field, you can use the AS operator. Renaming a calculated field can be useful when you intend to perform another query on the Answer table, or use the Answer table to create a report format.

The query in Figure 16.18 shows how to use the AS operator in a query table. Using the LineItem table again, we assigned the example element *X* to the Qty field, and the example element *Y* to the Unit Price field. The *Y* example element is then followed by a comma, a space, and the expression

CALC *X* * *Y* AS Extended

where *X* and *Y* are example elements. That expression is followed by another comma, a space, and the following expression:

CALC *X* * *Y* * 1.0775 AS Total

TIP

To use multiple CALC expressions in a field of the query table, separate the expressions with commas, as we did in Figure 16.18.

In the Answer table, the result of the first calculation is shown in the field named *Extended*. The result of the second expression, which adds 7.75% sales tax to the quantity times the unit price, appears in the field named *Total*.

You can place CALC in any field of the query table—even one that is not used directly in the calculation. Because the calculated field is *always* included in the result of a query, it need not be checked.

FIGURE 16.18

In the Answer table, the extended price (Qty times Unit Price) appears in the column named **Extended.** The extended price with 7.75% sales tax added appears in the field named **Total.**

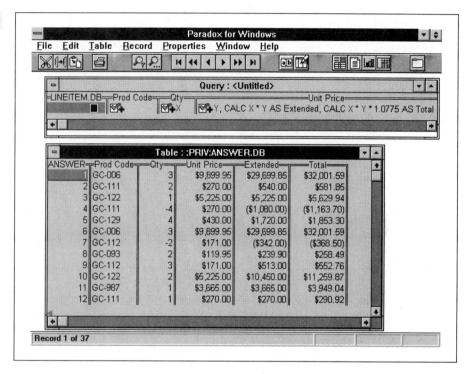

Calculations Using Fields from Multiple Tables

Paradox for Windows lets you use a field from another table in a calculation. Figure 16.19 shows a query in which the example element **EG01** links the LineItem and Products tables on the common Prod Code field. The example element **QTY** acts as the placeholder for the Qty field in the LineItem table; the example element **COST** is the placeholder for the Unit Price field of the Products table. The expression CALC **COST** * **QTY** AS Cost of Goods calculates the total cost of goods sold.

FIGURE 16.19

A query that uses
two tables to perform
a calculation

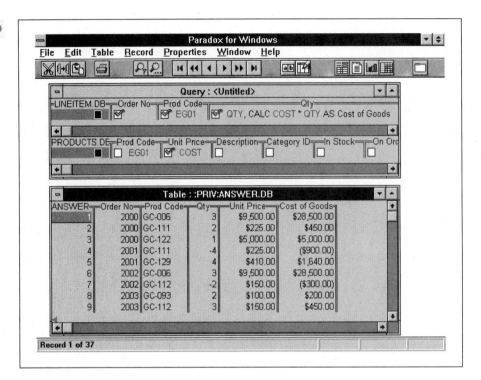

FIGURE 16.19

A query that uses two tables to perform a calculation

NOTE

In the Products table, Unit Price represents our cost for the item; in the LineItem table, Unit Price represents the item's selling price.

Once you've used example elements to link the common fields of two tables, performing a calculation is basically the same as performing calculations in a single table. So, even though the *COST* value comes from the Products table, we can still use that example element in a CALC expression in a query for the LineItem table.

Using Calculations to Change Values in Tables

In Chapter 8 you learned how to change the value in a field globally using a simple CHANGETO query. You can also use example elements and arithmetic operators with the **CHANGETO** operator. For instance, we can update the Extended Price field in every record of LineItem using the query below.

As in Figure 16.17, the *QTY* and *PRICE* example elements are used in the Qty field, Unit Price field, and in the calculation. This time, however, we used CHANGETO to update the LineItem table, instead of using CALC to display a result. As with any CHANGETO query, copies of original records that were changed during the query appear in the temporary Changed table. The actual changes take place in the original table—in this case Line Item .

NOTE

You cannot use CALC or checked fields with CHANGE-TO. Remember, CALC and the check marks are used to display calculation results, whereas CHANGETO updates records globally. You cannot combine these actions in the same Query window.

Now suppose you wanted to increase the selling price of all photo equipment in the LineItem table by 15 percent. In the example below, the *PRICE* example element holds the unit price for each record. CHANGETO *PRICE* * 1.15 multiplies the current price by 1.15 (increasing the unit price by 15 percent).

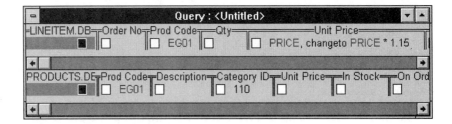

Because the Category ID field contains the value 110, only records in that category will be affected by the query. (Omitting the query criterion in the Category ID field would cause the query to increase the unit price of *every* record in the table by 15 percent). After updating the unit price for photo equipment, you could run the first CHANGETO query shown in this section to recalculate the extended price for each record.

You might be tempted to perform the price increase and extended price calculations in the same Query window, as shown below. However, this will *not* work properly.

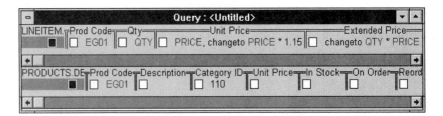

The reason this won't work is that Paradox always looks at the *original* records when performing calculations. In this example, the Unit Price field will be updated properly; however, the Extended Price field will be *incorrect* because Paradox hasn't "seen" the increased unit price values at the time it performs the extended price calculation. To solve the problem, run the query to increase the unit price first, then run the extended price calculation query. Alternatively, you can type **CHANGETO QTY ***
***PRICE *** 1.15 in the Extended Price field of the query table, instead of using the incorrect CHANGETO calculation shown above. This calculation works correctly because the original unit price is increased by the same amount—15 percent—in both the Unit Price and Extended Price calculations.

Performing Summary Calculations in Queries

You can perform statistical and summary calculations on table data using the *summary operators* listed in Table 16.2. As with the arithmetic operators, these can be used either with or without CALC in a query.

TABLE 16.2: Summary Operators Used in Query Forms

SUMMARY OPERATOR	CALCULATES	FIELD TYPES	DEFAULT GROUPING
SUM	Total of values	N, $, S	All
AVERAGE	Average of values	N, $, S, D	All
MAX	Highest value	A, N, $, S, D	Unique
MIN	Lowest value	A, N, $, S, D	Unique
COUNT	Number of values	A, N, $, S, D	Unique

Not all the summary operators can be used with all field types. The **SUM** operator works with numeric data types only, as these are the only ones that it makes sense to sum. The **AVERAGE** operator can also handle the date field type, since Paradox can determine an average date from a range of dates. The **MAX**, **MIN**, and **COUNT** operators work with alphanumeric data, since Paradox can find the "smallest" ("aardvark") and "largest" ("zzyxx") text values, and can count the number of particular text values ("how many Smiths are there?")

NOTE You cannot use summary operators with memo, formatted memo, OLE, graphic, or binary fields.

The default grouping for a summary operator determines whether it normally includes all values in a field, including duplicates, or whether it weeds out the duplicates. You can override the default grouping of a summary operator using the **ALL** or **UNIQUE** keywords in the query table, or by using check marks, as described later in this chapter.

To understand how the default grouping might affect the outcome of a summary calculation, suppose you have a table with an Invoice Date field that contains 30 records. Of the 30 records, 28 contain the date 10/1/93, 1 contains the date 10/15/93, and 1 contains 10/31/93.

If you used CALC AVERAGE in a query table to calculate the "average" date in all those records, the result would be 10/2/93, since the preponderance of 10/1/93 dates would skew the average toward the earlier date. However, if you used CALC AVERAGE UNIQUE, Paradox would treat all the 10/1/93 dates as one unique value. The resulting average date would be 10/15/93.

On the other side of the coin, the CALC COUNT operator defaults to a UNIQUE grouping, rather than an ALL grouping. Suppose you have a large table containing thousands of names and addresses. If you were to use CALC COUNT in the State field of that table, the result would be no greater than 51, since there would be at most 51 unique "states" in the table (50 states, plus the District of Columbia). However, if you used CALC COUNT ALL in that field, the result would be in the thousands, since every record, including those with duplicate state entries, would be counted.

In the sections that follow, we'll take a look at some practical examples using CALC queries.

Summarizing All Records

Summarizing a field for all the records of a table is one of the most common applications of summary operators. When you want to include all the records in a table in summary calculations, don't check any fields in the query table.

Recall that the sample CustList table includes a Credit Limit field. Suppose you want to know how much total credit you're extending to all customers, along with the average, highest, and lowest credit limits. The query and Answer table shown in Figure 16.20 answer those questions.

In Figure 16.20, each CALC expression results in a new field in the Answer table. Each new field name starts with the name of a summary operator followed by "of" and the *Credit Limit* field name (*Sum of Credit Limit*, *Average of Credit Limit*, and so forth). Although the query table contains no checked fields, the summary calculations appear because CALC always displays its result in the Answer table.

FIGURE 16.20

The sum, average, lowest, and highest credit limits in the CustList table

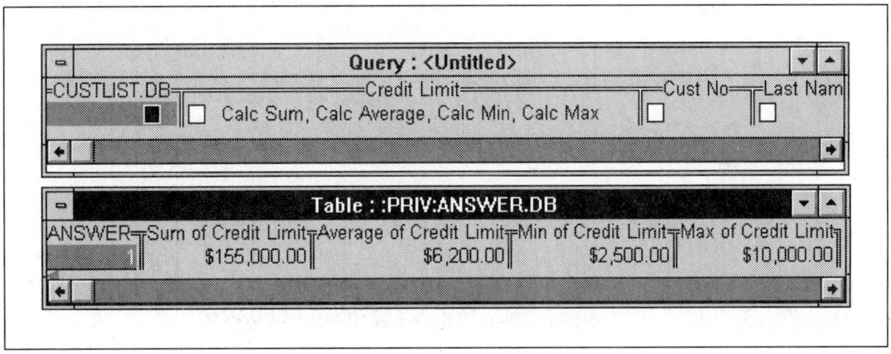

Performing Calculations on Groups of Records

When check marks are used with summary operators, they have a different effect from the effect they have in other types of queries. With summary operators, not only does a check mark display the checked field in the Answer table, it also groups identical values in the checked field (or fields) so that summary calculations are performed on each group separately.

The query table in Figure 16.21 illustrates this point. The check mark in the Prod Code field of the LineItem query table bases calculations on groups of like products. CALC SUM in the Qty field totals the values in the Qty field for each product. The resulting Answer table displays the total number of units sold for each product.

Checking multiple fields in a CALC query breaks down the resulting calculations even further. In Figure 16.22, for example, both the Prod Code field in the LineItem query table and the Sold By field in the Orders query table are checked. CALC SUM is again placed in the Qty field. The end result is the quantity of each item sold by each salesperson.

FIGURE 16.21

The sum of the Qty field for each product code

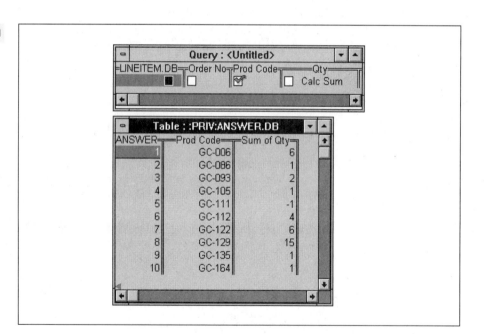

Frequency Distributions

The CALC COUNT ALL operator combined with a checked field (or fields) provides a quick way to determine frequency distribution. In the

FIGURE 16.22

Quantity of each
product sold by each
salesperson

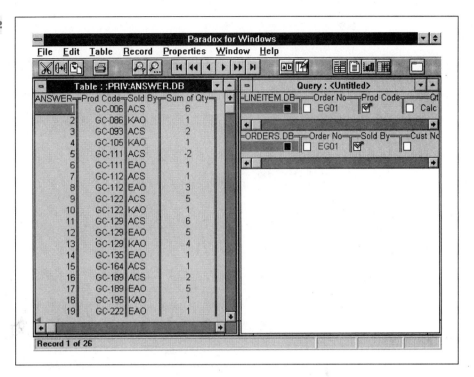

query shown in Figure 16.23, the State field of the CustList query table is checked for display and grouping. The expression CALC COUNT ALL counts the number of records containing each state. ALL is required in this example so that records with the same state will be counted. (If we omitted ALL, Paradox would not count duplicates, and the COUNT of the State field in the Answer table would contain the number 1 for each group with at least one record in it.)

Selecting Records Based on Summary Information

You can also use summary operators to select records based on a comparison to a summary calculation. To use the summary operators in

FIGURE 16.23

Frequency distribution
of states represented
in the CustList table

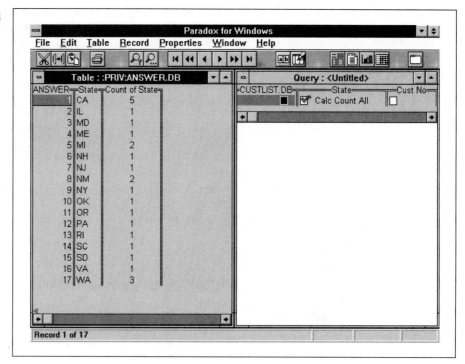

this manner, follow these guidelines:

- Omit the keyword CALC, and use the summary operator in a relational expression—that is, an expression that uses <, >, =, <=, or >=.

- Check the fields that define the groups you want to compare against the summary calculation.

Suppose you want to know which products in the LineItem table have a value of 5 or greater in the Qty field. The query shown in Figure 16.24 provides that information.

FIGURE 16.24

This query answers the question "Which products have we sold 5 or more units of?"

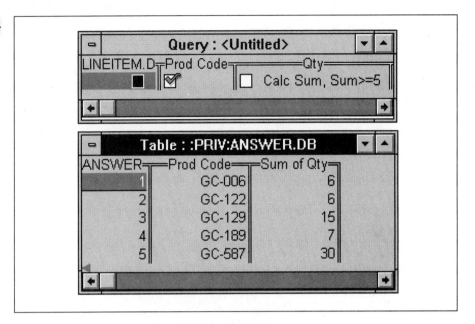

To understand this query better, you need to break it into its constituent parts:

- The check mark in the Prod Code field indicates that you want to perform a calculation on, and view the contents of, values in the Prod Code field.

- CALC SUM in the Qty field indicates that you want to sum and display the units sold for each product. You can omit this expression if you don't wish to display the sum.

- SUM >= 5 selects only records for which total units sold is greater than or equal to 5. The Answer table includes only those records.

To find out which states in the CustList table have only one customer, we performed the query shown in Figure 16.25. In this query, the check mark in the State field groups the records by state and displays the contents of the State field. The expression COUNT ALL = 1 counts the number of customers in each state, and displays only records in which the count (including duplicate states) is exactly 1. Here we omitted the CALC COUNT

FIGURE 16.25

A query that isolates states in the CustList table represented by only one customer

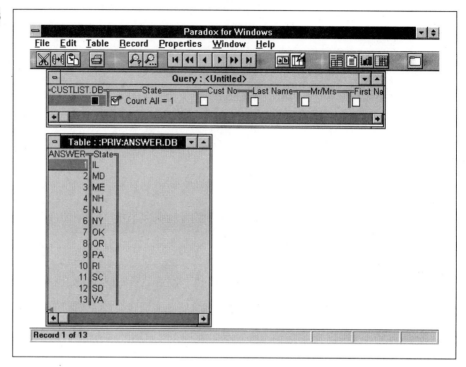

expression, so no field appears for the count. Nonetheless, the Answer table displays states represented by only one customer.

Complex Calculations with Multiple Tables

To help you understand how with some ingenuity (and patience) you can use calculations to answer questions that require several steps, we'll calculate the total amount owed for each customer's order.

TIP   If you intend to perform a sequence of queries on a regular basis (daily, weekly, monthly, and so on) or use them in a form or report, you should save each query. Chapter 8 explains how to save and reuse queries.

The first step is to calculate and update the Extended Price field in the LineItem table, using the query shown below.

After running the query, we saved it with the name *ExtPrice* so that we could reuse it later. (Figure 16.17 showed the results of calculating the extended price of records in the LineItem table.)

Next, you'll need to create a temporary table that holds the subtotal of the Extended Price for each order in the LineItem table, as shown in Figure 16.26. When creating the query, we checked the Order No field to group the calculation by order number and used CALC SUM in the Extended Price field to calculate the total extended price for all line items in each group. We also used the Answer Table Properties button in the SpeedBar to rename the Answer table to *c:\pdoxwin\giftco\subtotal.db*, and saved the query with the name *SubTotal* (see Chapter 8). Then we ran the query, which produced the Subtotal table shown in Figure 16.26.

As shown in Figure 16.27, the final query (which we named *OrdTotal*) calculates the total amount owed for each order and displays checked and calculated fields in a table named *OrdTotal*. Notice that the **OrdNo** example element links the Orders and SubTotal query tables, and the **CustNo** example element links Orders and CustList. In the Orders query table, we entered example elements ***ship*** (for shipping charges), ***tax*** (for the tax rate—0.0775 in all cases), and ***paid*** (for amount paid). Then we placed the **SubTotal** example element in the SubTotal field of the SubTotal query table. The final calculation appears below:

CALC **Subtotal** + (**Subtotal** * **Tax**) + **Ship** - **Paid** AS Total

This calculation starts with the subtotal stored in the SubTotal field, adds the tax amount (subtotal times the tax rate), adds the shipping charge, then subtracts the amount the customer has already paid and displays the result in a field named *Total*.

TIP

You can rerun the ExtPrice, SubTotal, and OrdTotal queries (in that order) whenever you want to view the latest order totals.

FIGURE 16.26

The Subtotal query calculates the total extended price for each order in the LineItem table and saves the result in a table named **Subtotal**.

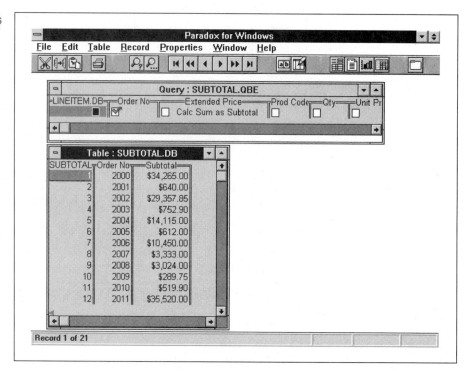

SUBTOTAL	Order No	Subtotal
1	2000	$34,265.00
2	2001	$640.00
3	2002	$29,357.85
4	2003	$752.90
5	2004	$14,115.00
6	2005	$612.00
7	2006	$10,450.00
8	2007	$3,333.00
9	2008	$3,024.00
10	2009	$289.75
11	2010	$519.90
12	2011	$35,520.00

Record 1 of 21

FIGURE 16.27

The OrdTotal query calculates the total order amount as SubTotal + Tax + Shipping Charge - Amount Paid.

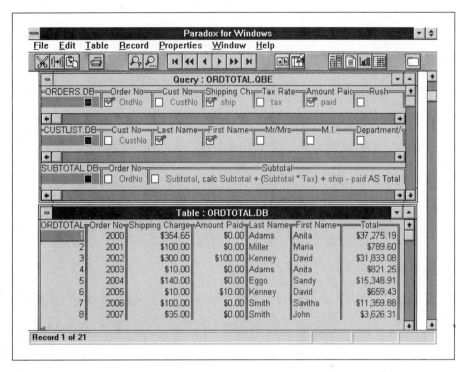

Asking about Sets of Records

SET queries ask questions about categories or sets of records, rather than about individual records. In essence, a SET query lets you answer questions that might otherwise require two or more queries.

Suppose you want to track the quantity of each product purchased by your customers at the end of the year, and then ask further questions about those purchases. To begin, create the query shown in Figure 16.28 and use the Answer Table Properties button in the SpeedBar to rename

FIGURE 16.28

The query and a
portion of the resulting
YearEnd table created
by combining fields
from the LineItem and
Orders tables

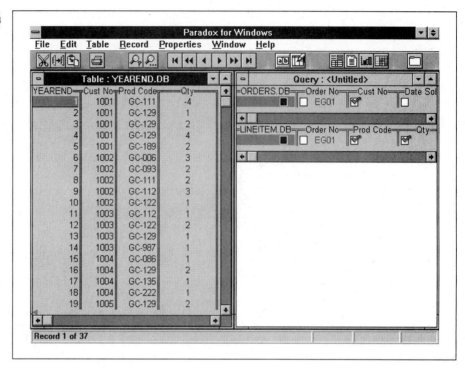

the Answer table to *YearEnd* (in your working directory). The figure illustrates the query and a portion of the YearEnd table that appears when
you run the query.

After creating the YearEnd table, you can use SET queries with the set
operators **ONLY, NO, EVERY,** and **EXACTLY** to ask questions about
which customers did (and which did not) buy products in various
categories. These operators are summarized in Table 16.3.

Figure 16.29 illustrates various set relationships, using shapes rather than
products. The group of shapes on the left could be called *TestShapes*. We'll
call this the *comparison set*. The group on the right in each example is a set
of shapes we're comparing to TestShapes.

TABLE 16.3: Set Comparison Operators and Sample Questions

SET OPERATOR	DISPLAYS	SAMPLE QUESTION
ONLY	Records that have only values of the defined set	Which customers have bought only computer equipment (Category ID 103)?
NO	Records that do not match any values in the defined set	Which customers did not buy any computer equipment?
EVERY	Records that match every value in the set	Which customers bought every product in the photo equipment category (Category ID 110)?
EXACTLY	Records that have exactly the same values as the defined set; no more or less (a combination of **ONLY** and **EVERY**)	Which customers bought every product in the photo equipment category, but no products in any other category?

Creating a SET Query

When formulating a SET query, you will follow these general steps (we'll get more specific in a moment):

- Include one or more lines that define the comparison set. These lines will include the **SET** reserved word in the leftmost column and an *example element* to group the set. Many comparison sets also include a *selection criterion* to restrict the set to specific values or ranges. (If you omit the selection criterion, the comparison set will be the entire table.)

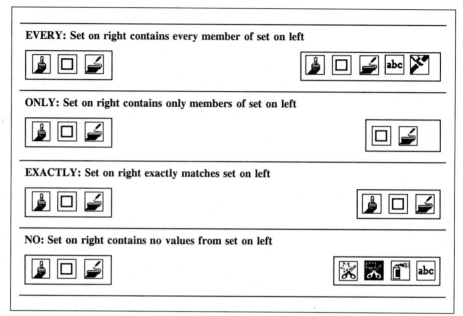

TIP

Defining a set of records is similar to selecting records to include in the Answer table, except that you use example elements instead of check marks.

- Include one or more lines that define the second set of records that you want to compare. These lines will include an appropriate *set operator* (EVERY, ONLY, EXACTLY, or NO) and a *check mark* or **GROUPBY** operator to group the records. Checked fields will appear in the Answer table. (GROUPBY fields are discussed later in this chapter.)

- If you wish, include one or more lines that display related information. These lines will contain linking *example elements* and *check marks*.

To illustrate the concepts presented above, we'll create a SET query that asks the question "Which customers bought items in the photo equipment category only (Category ID 110)?" The final query and its results appear in Figure 16.30.

FIGURE 16.30

This sample SET query displays customers who have purchased products in the photo equipment category only (Category ID 110).

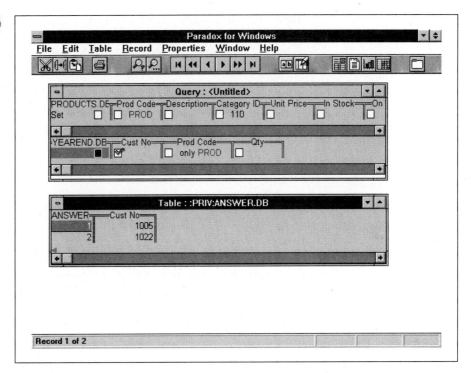

Defining the Comparison Set

Your first step is to define the comparison set, as follows:

1. Open the query table(s) for tables containing the records that will define the set. For example, open a new Query window and select *Products* as the table containing the set.

2. If you wish, enter *selection criteria* that further limit the records to include in the set. If the records are in more than one table, add the tables to the query windows and use example elements to link the tables. To select records in the photo equipment category, we would type **110** into the Category ID field of the Products table.

3. Enter the SET reserved word in the leftmost field of all query lines that define the set. To enter the reserved word, click in the leftmost field of the query table and type **S**. The word "Set" will appear below the table name.

4. Place an example element where you would normally use check marks to select and group fields. Since we want to compare groups of products, we would place the example element ***PROD*** into the Prod Code field of the Products query table.

The comparison set for our sample SET query appears below.

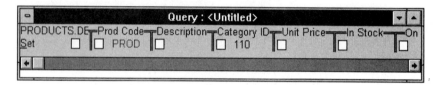

Defining the Second Set of Records

Once you've defined the comparison set, you can define the set of records to compare it against, as follows:

1. In the Query window defined so far, add the query table for the set of records to be compared. Continuing with our example, we would add the YearEnd table to the Query window.

2. Type a set operator into the common field that links this new query table to the table or tables containing the comparison set. For example, type **Only** into the Prod Code field of the YearEnd query table.

3. Follow the set operator with a space and the same example element used in the comparison table (***PROD*** in this example).

4. Check the field that will group the records in this set and that will also appear in the Answer table (Cust No in this example).

N O T E   The GROUPBY operator, discussed in the next section, provides an alternative to checking fields.

Because our query is seeking customer numbers only, we don't need any additional tables or linking elements; therefore, we can go ahead and run the query now. Figure 16.30 shows the completed query and Answer table. In the figure, the **PROD** example element links the two sets, and ONLY is the set operator restricting the retrieved records to Category ID 110. The check mark in the Cust No column defines that field as the one to display in the Answer table, and also groups the second set of records. That is, the check mark in the Cust No field says "group together all the records with the same Cust No, then compare that group to the set of records in Products that contain the Category ID of 110."

The resulting Answer table lists customers who bought only photo equipment. (These customers may have bought only one type of photo equipment, or several different types of photo equipment.)

If you want to view customers who didn't buy any photo equipment at all, change the ONLY operator to NO and perform the query again. To view customers who bought every type of photo equipment (and possibly products from other categories), use the EVERY operator. Finally, use the EXACTLY operator to see which customers have purchased exactly the products that make up the photo equipment category. The Answer table will include customers who bought every type of photo equipment, and no other product.

N O T E   You've probably discovered that SET queries aren't easy to put together. Remember that performing several queries in sequence will ultimately achieve the same result as a SET query.

Using the GROUPBY Operator

Check marks in SET queries with two or more tables specify which field or fields you want to see in the Answer table and define the group of records for the second set. If you want to group records by a field, without displaying that field, you can use the **GROUPBY** operator, rather than a check mark, in the query table. Then you can use an example element next to the GROUPBY operator to look up data from that field in another table. (The GROUPBY operator can only be used in SET queries.)

 To place the GROUPBY operator in a query table, choose the GROUPBY check mark (shown at left) from the check box menu for the field, or press Shift+F6 in the field until the GROUPBY operator appears.

In Figure 16.31, we've used the GROUPBY operator to display the *cities and states* in which only photo equipment was sold, rather than the customer number of people who bought photo equipment only.

Compare the query in Figure 16.31 to the query in Figure 16.30, and observe the following differences:

- Instead of using a check mark in the Cust No field to define that field for both grouping and display, the field contains the GROUPBY operator. Cust No is still the group being compared to the photo equipment set, but it will not appear in the Answer table.

- We've added a third table, CustList, to provide the city and state information we want.

- The *EG01* example elements in the Cust No fields link the Year-End and CustList query tables.

- The City and State fields are checked in the CustList table so they will be displayed in the Answer table.

Comparing Records to Summary Values

In the preceding examples, you saw how SET queries can compare records in one table to a set of records in another table. You can also use

FIGURE 16.31

The GROUPBY operator lets you use one field for grouping in a SET query and other fields to display results in the Answer table.

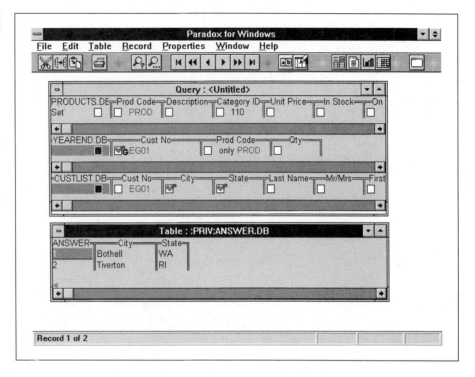

SET queries to compare records in a table to a summary calculation within that table, such as an average or a sum. You can use any of the summary operators (AVERAGE, COUNT, MAX, MIN) to perform such an analysis.

Figure 16.32 shows an example using the CustList table. The first line of the query includes **Set** in the leftmost column and the example **limit** element in the Credit Limit field. Because there are no search criteria in the top line of the query, the set includes all records in the table.

The check marks in the Last Name, First Name, and Credit Limit fields of the second query line mark the fields we want to see in the Answer table. The second line also includes the query criterion **> Average** *limit* to restrict the Answer table records to those in which credit limits are greater than the average credit limit.

Note that if we had used **> Min** *limit* in place of **> Average** *limit*, the Answer table would display records containing values that are greater

FIGURE 16.32

A SET query that finds individuals with higher than average credit limits in the sample CustList table

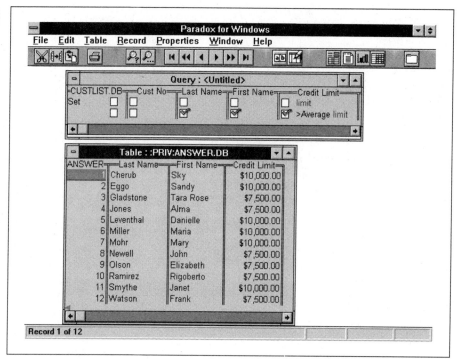

than the *smallest* credit limit. Using the criterion **Max** *limit* would display records containing the *highest* credit limits.

Calculating Percentages

Despite its powerful calculation capabilities, Paradox for Windows does not provide a simple method for calculating percentages. However, there are some ways around this problem.

Suppose you want to ask "How much does each product in my YearEnd table contribute to total sales?" One easy way to answer this question is to create a pie chart, which can calculate percentages automatically. To begin, open a new query for the YearEnd table, check the Prod Code field, type **Calc Sum** into the Qty field, and run the query. A sample query and the resulting Answer table appear in Figure 16.33.

Now click the Quick Graph button in the SpeedBar. When the **Define Graph** dialog box appears, click the drop-down arrow next to the Answer table name and select *Prod Code* for the X-Axis. Next click the Y-Value option in the dialog box, open the Answer table drop-down list again, and select *Sum of Qty*. Click OK. Now click the Design button in the Speed-Bar, inspect (right-click) the graph, and choose Graph Type ➤ 2D Pie. Finally, click the View Data button in the SpeedBar to view the graph. (See Chapter 12 for additional information on creating graphs and pie charts.)

FIGURE 16.33

The Answer table shows the total units sold for each product in the YearEnd table.

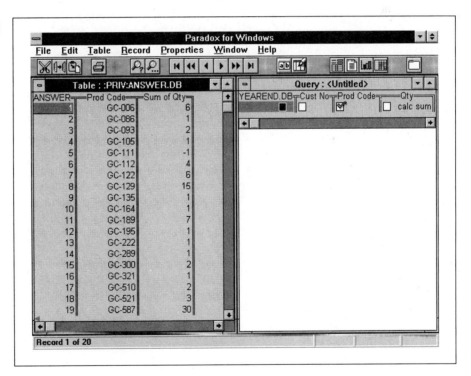

The pie chart will be quite cluttered if your company sells many different products. If you prefer to show the percentages in a form or report, proceed as follows:

1. First, you need to know the grand total of units sold. To get this information, close the Answer table and pie chart Form windows, if they're still open. Then, open a new Query window for the YearEnd table, type **Calc Sum** into the Qty field (don't add any check marks), and run the query to get the grand total.

2. Jot down the number that appears in the Answer table, then close the Answer table window. Let's assume the number is **85**.

3. Now, modify the YearEnd query table shown in Figure 16.33 to get a subtotal of units sold for each product. Just check the Prod Code field and perform the query to get the desired results.

4. Close the Answer table and create a new query, specifying *Answer* as the table to query.

5. Place check marks in the Prod Code and Sum of Qty fields.

6. In the Sum of Qty field, type the ***units*** example element, a comma, a space, and the CALC expression shown in Figure 16.34. The expression "CALC ***units*** / 85 as Percent" divides the value in the Sum of Qty field by 85 (the grand total determined earlier) and will place the result in a field named *Percent*.

7. Use the Answer Table Properties button to rename the Answer table (we used the name *c:\pdoxwin\giftco\percent*).

When you perform the query, the resulting Percent table will display the information you want. To display the numbers as percents, inspect the Percent column and choose Number Format ➤ Percent. Figure 16.34 shows the final result.

FIGURE 16.34

Each product's
contribution to total
units sold is displayed
in the rightmost
column.

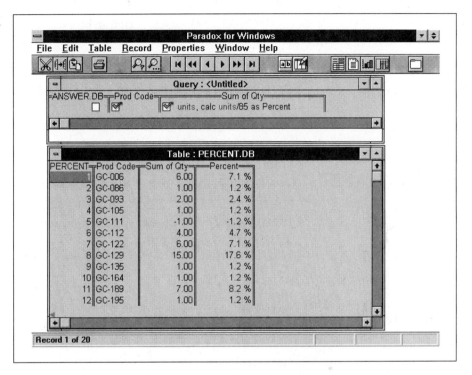

Changing the Query Window Options

You can display query tables in the Query window in a tiled or cascaded arrangement. To show the query tables in a cascaded arrangement, choose Properties ➤ Cascade Tables from the Query window menus. To return to the tiled arrangement shown throughout this book, choose Properties ➤ Tile Tables.

You can also tell Paradox what to do if data changes while you're running a query in a multiuser (network) environment. To begin, choose

Properties ➤ Restart Options. A dialog box will appear with the following options:

Restart Query on Changes   Starts the query over if data changes while the query is running. This is the fastest option when you know that no one will be changing data in the tables you're querying.

Lock All Tables to Prevent Changes   Locks all other users out of tables that are needed while the query is running. (This option is the least polite to other users.) If Paradox cannot lock a table, the query stops. If a lock fails, you must start the query again.

Ignore Source Changes   Runs the query even if someone changes the data while it's running. This option, which is the fastest, is useful for "rough" queries where accuracy is not the top concern.

N O T E   The Properties ➤ Restart Options in the Query window are similar to the Report ➤ Restart Options available from the Report Design window menus (see Chapter 11).

To save the current query Restart Options and your choice of tiled or cascaded query tables, choose Properties ➤ Query Options ➤ Save As Default. To restore the previous options as the default, choose Properties ➤ Query Options ➤ Restore Default.

In this chapter you've learned how to create complex queries that join data from multiple tables into a single table and perform math calculations. In the next chapter, we'll show you techniques for creating forms and reports that combine data from multiple tables and perform calculations.

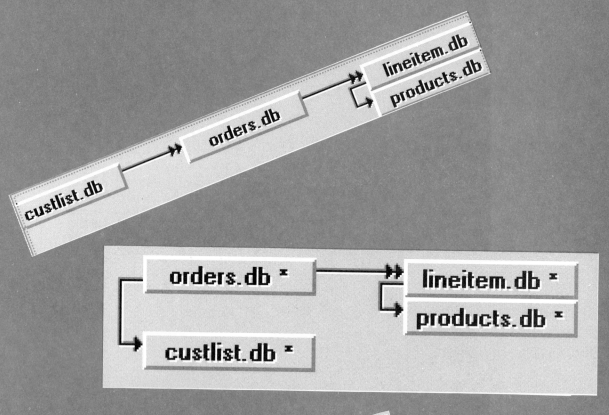

CHAPTER

17

Advanced Form and Report Techniques

f a s t **TRACK**

● **To define a summary field that calculates values**　　**880**

based on a group of records or all the records in a table, inspect the field in the Design window, select Define Field, then click the list header (...) or press ↵. Select the field name from the table's drop-down list in the **Define Field Object** dialog box, select a summary operator from the Summary drop-down list, and choose OK.

● **To hide the details in a report**　　**888**

remove field objects from the record band and place summary and calculated fields in the report's group bands, page band, or report band.

● **To define a calculated field in a form or report**　　**889**

inspect the field in the Design window, select Define Field, then click the list header (...) or press ↵. Click the Calculated option in the **Define Field Object** dialog box and type your calculation into the text box below the option.

● **Calculations can include**　　**890**

arithmetic operators, parentheses, ObjectPAL functions, field names, field object names, the + operator (for combining text strings), logical operators, comparison operators, and numeric constants.

● **When typing field names into a calculation**　　**891**

enter the names in the form *[TABLENAME.fieldname]*, as in *[LINEITEM.Extended Price]* * *1.0775*. When typing field object names, enter the field object name only (without brackets or a period), as in *Qty1* * *1.0775*.

You can perform calculations on summary fields   897

but you cannot perform summaries on calculations or calculated fields. In some situations, this restriction may require you to store the results of calculations directly in a table.

To copy field names into your calculation   901

position the insertion point in the Calculated text box, select the field from the table's drop-down list, and select a summary operator from the Summary drop-down list (if you wish). Click the Copy Field button.

To define a multitable document   902

identify the tables you want to use in the **Data Model** dialog box and define the relationship (if any) between the tables.

To draw a link between two tables in the Data Model dialog box   908

drag the mouse from the master table in the data model area to the detail table. If the **Define Link** dialog box appears, select the master table field to link and the detail index, then choose OK.

IN this chapter you'll learn how to create sophisticated design documents that perform calculations on your data and allow you to display, edit, and print data from multiple tables. The techniques in this chapter may not make your documents prettier, but they'll surely make them "smarter" and more useful.

Before attempting the advanced techniques presented here, you should know how to design forms and reports (Chapters 9 through 11), understand multitable database design (Chapter 15), and be familiar with using queries to perform calculations and link multiple tables (Chapter 16). You may also wish to review the structure and purpose of the CustList, Orders, LineItem, and Products tables presented at the end of Chapter 15 and the beginning of Chapter 16, since we'll use them in examples throughout this chapter.

NOTE   We'll frequently use the term "design documents" in place of "forms and reports" when discussing procedures that apply equally to form and report design.

Calculating Data in Design Documents

You can place summary and calculated fields anywhere in a design document to perform a variety of useful calculations on your data. In many cases, a few strategically placed calculations and the multitable techniques discussed later in this chapter can save you the trouble of designing complex queries that store temporary tables on your computer's disk.

Before diving into the topic of calculations, you should understand that summary and calculated fields can *display* or *print* data only; they *never* store data in your tables and they *cannot* be edited. For that job, you must use a query or an ObjectPAL method. For example, you can use a calculated field to multiply quantity ordered by unit price in order to display or print the extended price of a line item in an order. However, you cannot store the result of that calculation in the Extended Price field of a table without using a CHANGETO query or an ObjectPAL method.

N O T E   In Chapter 19 you'll find out how to use ObjectPAL to update fields with calculation results.

To place a summary or calculated field in a design document, follow these steps:

1. Open a form or report in the Form Design window or Report Design window.

2. If you want to create a new summary or calculated field, use the Field tool in the SpeedBar (see Chapter 9). Alternatively, you can select an existing field and redefine it as a summary or calculated field.

3. Right-click (inspect) the field, and choose Define Field from the property menu.

4. Click the menu header (…) or press ↵.

If you're designing a report, you'll see the **Define Field Object** dialog box shown in Figure 17.1. If you're designing a form, the Normal, Unique, and Cumulative options in the Summary panel will be absent. From this point, the remaining steps depend on whether you want to define a *summary field* or a *calculated field*, as discussed in the sections that follow.

FIGURE 17.1

The Define Field
Object dialog box for
a report. The Normal,
Unique, and
Cumulative options do
not appear when
you're defining a field
object in a form.

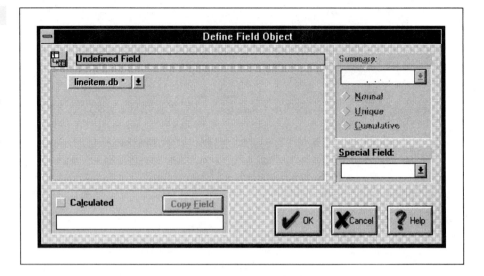

Defining Summary Fields

Summary fields perform statistical calculations on a set of records in a
table. If you've read Chapter 16, you already know about summary
operators used with queries. The operators used with summary fields
are basically the same. You can use them to sum (total), count, or
average the values in a field; find the minimum or maximum value in
a field; or find the standard deviation or variance of values in a field.
Table 17.1 lists the summary operators available in design documents.
Notice that the FIRST, LAST, and PREV operators are available in
reports only.

To define a summary field, open the Define Field Object dialog box as
described above, then follow these steps:

1. Click the drop-down arrow next to the table that contains the
   field you want to summarize, then select the field. (If you plan to
   use the COUNT operator, selecting the table's primary key field
   will give you the most accurate count.)

2. Click the Summary drop-down list and select a summary
   operator. The summary statement will appear in the box below
   the Define Field Object title bar, as shown in Figure 17.2.

3. If you're designing a report, you can select the Normal, Unique, or Cumulative summary option, as discussed below (Normal is the default choice). These options appear below the drop-down list of summary operators.

4. When you're finished, choose OK to return to the Design window.

When you return to the Design window, the field's label and name will change automatically, reflecting the summary operator you selected. Figure 17.3 illustrates the label (*Sum(Extended Price):*) and the field object name (*Extended_Price1*) that Paradox supplied after we selected *Extended Price* in Step 1 and the SUM operator in Step 2 above. As Figure 17.3 shows, the name of the field object will appear in the status bar when you select the field and in the header of the property menu when you inspect the field. (Field object names can be used in calculated fields, as you'll learn later.)

FIGURE 17.2

The Design Field Object dialog box after choosing a summary operator and a field to summarize

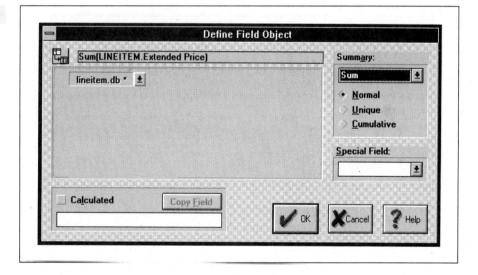

TABLE 17.1: Summary Operators Used in Forms and Reports

SUMMARY OPERATOR	CALCULATES
SUM	Total of non-empty values in the set
AVERAGE	Average of non-empty values in the set
MAX	Highest value in the set
MIN	Lowest value in the set
COUNT	Number of non-empty values in the set
VAR	Statistical variance of values in the set
STD	Standard deviation of values in the set
FIRST	(In reports only) First value in the set
LAST	(In reports only) Last value in the set
PREV	(In reports only) Previous value in the set

FIGURE 17.3

After you choose a field and a summary operator, Paradox assigns a label and field object name automatically.

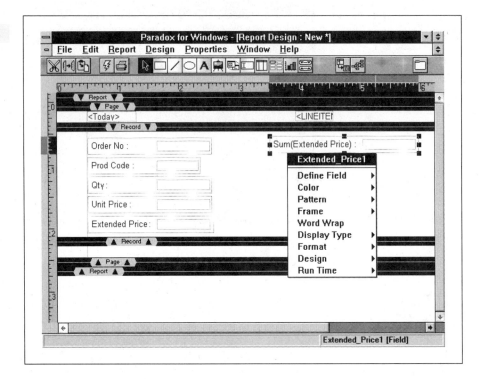

Figure 17.4 presents the last page of a report for the LineItem table discussed in Chapters 15 and 16. This report is grouped by product code (Prod Code) and illustrates three levels of summary (we used the Normal summary

GURE 17.4

eport is grouped
·oduct code (Prod
·) and shows
·ary totals at the
· level, page
and overall
·t level.

Sunday, November 01, 1992   *Summary of Product Sales (by Product)*

GC-112	Qty	Unit Price	Extended Price
	2	$171.00	$342.00
	1	$171.00	$171.00
	4		$684.00

GC-111	Qty	Unit Price	Extended Price
	2	$270.00	$540.00
	-4	$270.00	-$1,080.00
	1	$270.00	$270.00
	-1		-$270.00

◄── Scope is entire group band

GC-105	Qty	Unit Price	Extended Price
	1	$14,003.00	$14,003.00
	1		$14,003.00

GC-093	Qty	Unit Price	Extended Price
	2	$119.95	$239.90
	2		$239.90

GC-086	Qty	Unit Price	Extended Price
	1	$911,179.00	$911,179.00
	1		$911,179.00

GC-006	Qty	Unit Price	Extended Price
	3	$9,500.00	$28,500.00
	3	$9,899.95	$29,699.85
	6		$58,199.85

Summaries	*Qty*	*Unit Price*	*Extended Price*
Sum	85		$1,068,734.40
Minimum	-4	$0.50	-$1,080.00
Maximum	30	$911,179.00	$911,179.00
Average	2	$27,469.01	$28,884.71
Count	37		

Scope is entire report

Page: 3	Qty	12	Total	$983,864.75

◄── ˙Scope is entire page

After defining the summary field, you can click the Vie
press F8 to see the results of the summary operatio
change the field you're summarizing or the summary
return to the Design window, open the Define Field (
and repeat the steps above.

Normal, Unique, and Cumulative Summaries

The Normal, Unique, and Cumulative summary optic
the Define Field Object dialog box for reports only. The
how Paradox will perform the summary:

> **Normal** Normal summaries consider all non-e
> cluding duplicates, in the set of records being sur
> the default selection.

> **Unique** Unique summaries consider unique n
> ues only, ignoring duplicates. For example, you c
> COUNT summary operator with UNIQUE to a
> tion "In how many California zip codes do we h
> Note that selecting UNIQUE with a SUM or A\
> *not* yield accurate results, since duplicate values

> **Cumulative** Cumulative summaries return a r
> the operation they are performing. In a cumulativ
> the summary field is set to zero initially, then it ke
> from the start of the report through the end of the
> ulative summary is often used in the page footer t
> running total from the beginning of the report to
> current page.

Understanding Scope in Summary Fields

The location of a summary field in a form or report d
set or *scope* of records used to calculate the result.
report, the type of summary you select (normal, un
also governs the scope. We could describe all the tech
but since the concept is really quite intuitive, let's di
look at an illustrative example instead.

F

This
by ɼ
Coc
sum
grou
leve
repc

method). The first level shows the quantity, unit price, and extended price for each group of products sold. The next level is the page footer, which totals the quantity and extended price for all products on the page. Finally, the "Summaries" section at the end of the report provides an overall summary of the total quantity and extended price for all records; the minimum, maximum, and average quantity, unit price, and extended price for all records; and the count of the individual line items for the entire report.

Figure 17.5 shows the Report Design window for the report in Figure 17.4. Notice how the bands in the design correspond to the levels of summary information in the printed report. Summary fields in the *group band* total the quantity, unit price, and extended price of each product group. In the *page band*, the summary fields total the quantity and extended price for each page. And in the *report band*, summaries provide the total, minimum, maximum, average, and count for all records in the report.

FIGURE 17.5

The Report Design window for the report shown in Figure 17.4

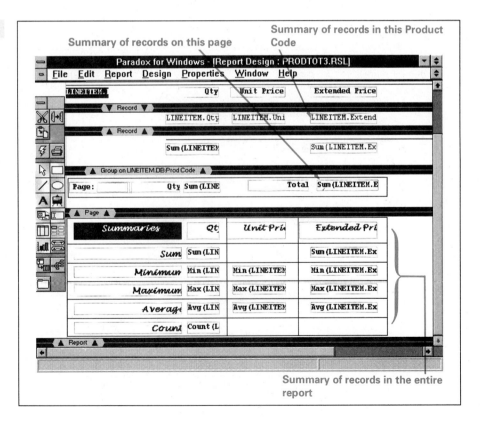

Hiding the Details in a Report

In some situations you might want to see *only* the summary data in a report, without all the details that contribute to the totals. The quickest way to hide details is simply to remove objects from the record band.

We used this technique in the sample report shown in Figure 17.6 and the corresponding Report Design window in Figure 17.7. To begin, we opened the report design shown in Figure 17.5 and saved it under a new name so that we could use the existing design as the basis for a new one. Next we deleted the Qty and Extended Price field objects from the record band and moved the Unit Price field object from the record band to the group band, between the two summary fields. (Remember, the unit price is the same for all items with the same product code.) Finally, we closed the record band, removed the horizontal line above the summary fields in the group band, and adjusted the spacing a bit. That's all there was to it!

FIGURE 17.6

A summary report that omits details of each product sold

Sunday, November 01, 1992		Summary of Product Sales (by Product)	
GC-112	Qty	Unit Price	Extended Price
	4	$171.00	$684.00
GC-111	Qty	Unit Price	Extended Price
	-1	$270.00	-$270.00
GC-105	Qty	Unit Price	Extended Price
	1	$14,003.00	$14,003.00
GC-093	Qty	Unit Price	Extended Price
	2	$119.95	$239.90
GC-086	Qty	Unit Price	Extended Price
	1	$911,179.00	$911,179.00
GC-006	Qty	Unit Price	Extended Price
	6	$9,899.95	$58,199.85

Summaries	Qty	Unit Price	Extended Price
Sum	85		$1,068,734.40
Minimum	-4	$0.50	-$1,080.00
Maximum	30	$911,179.00	$911,179.00
Average	2	$27,469.01	$28,884.71
Count	37		

FIGURE 17.7

The Report Design
for the report in Fig-
ure 17.6

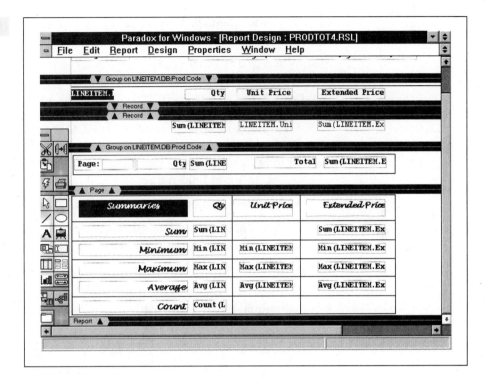

Defining Calculated Fields

In Chapter 16 you learned how to use queries to perform calculations on data in tables. The techniques for specifying calculations in design documents are similar in many ways. However, instead of using example elements to act as place holders in the calculation (as you do with queries), you use *field names* or *field object names* to represent values stored in table fields.

To define a calculated field, start from the Define Field Object dialog box and follow the steps below.

1. Click the Calculated option in the dialog box (a check mark will appear).

2. Type the calculation in the text box below the Calculated check box. (You'll see some examples in a moment.)

3. When you're finished, choose OK to return to the Design window.

You can use any of the following elements in a calculation:

- Field names, typed in the format **[TABLENAME.fieldname]**. For example, *[LINEITEM.Qty]* refers to the Qty field in the Line-Item table. It's best to use the Copy Field button, described below, to fill in field names.

- Field object names, such as *Tax*, *#EditRegion5*, and *Qty1*.

- Arithmetic operators: + (addition), – (subtraction), * (multiplication), / (division), and parentheses ( ) for grouping.

- Logical operators AND, OR, and NOT.

- Comparison operators < (less than), > (greater than), <> (not equal to), = (equal to), >= (greater than or equal to), and <= (less than or equal to).

- Numeric constants (for example, 1.5).

- Alphanumeric strings enclosed in quotes (for example, *"Hi there"*).

- Most ObjectPAL mathematical, statistical, string manipulation, and date / time methods. For example, the ObjectPAL function *today( )-30* calculates the date 30 days prior to the current date. The *ObjectPAL Reference Manual* and on-line help that come with Paradox for Windows document the functions available.

- Summary functions. For instance, *Sum([LINEITEM.Unit Price]) * Tax1* is a legal calculation.

NOTE   The same scope rules illustrated earlier for summary fields apply to calculated fields. See "Understanding Scope in Summary Fields," earlier in this chapter.

Using Field Names in Calculations

When used in a calculation, field names must appear in the format

[TABLENAME.fieldname]

in which *TABLENAME* is the name of a table in the data model, and *fieldname* is the name of a field in that table.

Although you can enter field names by typing them into the Calculated text box, the easiest and most accurate way to enter a field name is as follows:

1. Make sure the Calculated option is checked in the Define Field Object dialog box.

2. Position the insertion point in the Calculated text box, at the spot where you want the field name to appear in your calculation.

3. Click the drop-down arrow next to the table name and select the field you want.

4. If you wish to perform a summary calculation on this field, click the Summary drop-down list and select the summary operator.

5. Click the Copy Field button.

The field you chose will appear in the text box, in the proper format, and the expression that you copied will be selected. If you wish, you can edit the expression further using standard Windows editing techniques. When you return to the Design window, the word *[formula]* will usually appear in the field.

NOTE   Later in this chapter, we'll discuss some shortcuts for copying calculations and calculated fields.

In Figure 17.8, we selected the Qty field from the LineItem table's drop-down list, clicked the Copy Field button, pressed the End key, and typed an asterisk (*). We then selected the Unit Price field from the LineItem table's drop-down list and clicked Copy Field once more. The result? A calculation that multiplies the value in the Qty field by the value in the Unit Price field of the current record in the LineItem table.

FIGURE 17.8

A calculation entered into the Calculated text box

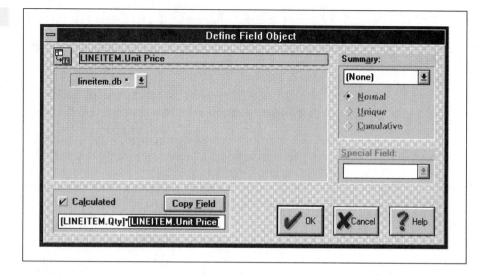

Using Field Object Names in Calculations

When you use a *field name* in an expression, you're telling Paradox to perform the calculation on the actual values in the table. You can also use *field object names* to display table values or calculation results. Calculations will often (but not always) display the same results whether you use a field name or a field object name. Rather than worrying about the exceptions, just keep this rule of thumb in mind: Use *field names* when performing calculations on actual table values, and use *field object names* when performing calculations on other calculated fields. (In a moment, you'll see an example that uses both field names and field object names to calculate percentages.)

NOTE

Remember that field names refer to actual fields in your table. Field object names refer to objects that exist only in the design document, not in your table.

To use a field object name in a calculation, type the *object name*, without dots or brackets, into the Calculated text box. For example, to multiply a field named *Qty1* by 10, you would type **Qty1 ★ 10**. You can use field names and field object names in the same calculation.

Remember that field object names appear on the status line when you select a field object in the Design window, and at the top of the property menu when you inspect an object. This makes it easy to find out the name of a field object.

Field object names are sometimes cryptic and difficult to type (objects may have names like *#EditRegion1*, for example). Fortunately, you can change field object names quite easily. To do so, inspect the field object in the Design window, press ↵ or click the header of the property menu, type a new name for the object, and choose OK.

TIP

It's a good idea to change the default names of field objects that you intend to use in other calculations. However, you must be sure that *all* object names in a given design document are unique.

Combining Alphanumeric Strings

You can use the + operator to combine alphanumeric strings. Suppose you wish to eliminate unsightly gaps between first and last names in the CustList table by separating the names with a single space, as shown below:

Maria Miller

To achieve this result, create a new field in your design document, then go to the Define Field Object dialog box and click the Calculated option. In the Calculated text box, enter the calculation shown below (use the Copy Fields button to help).

[CUSTLIST.First Name] + " " + [CUSTLIST.Last Name]

Notice how the + operators connect each part of the calculation. This calculation says, "Display the customer's first name, add a blank space, then display the customer's last name." Remember to type blank spaces and other text (alphanumeric strings) within double quotation marks. You'll see some examples using the + operator later in this chapter.

NOTE Two double-quotation marks placed together, as in " ", represent an empty or blank string. However, two double-quotation marks placed around a space, as in " ", represent a single space (this string is *not* blank).

Calculating Percentages

Recall from Chapter 16 that calulating percentages required several queries and some manual tallying. Such calculations are much simpler when performed in design documents. Figure 17.9 shows a sample report for the LineItem table that summarizes sales by product code and displays each product's contribution to total sales as a percentage. The corresponding Report Design window appears in Figure 17.10.

To create the percentage report, we started with a blank design based on the LineItem table. We added a group band (based on the Prod Code field) and placed titles, column headings, and a horizontal line in the page band. We placed two undefined fields in the group band and one in the report band, then selected and inspected all the fields and chose Display Type – Unlabeled from the property menu. NExt we added a horizontal line and the "Grand Total" text object to the report band. We then resized the bands to squeeze out unwanted white space. Finally, we inspected and defined the fields in the group and report bands. The letters in Figure 17.10 correspond to the field definitions listed below.

A   Displays the Prod Code field of the LineItem table.

B and D   Display extended price summaries. Both fields were defined as *Sum(LINEITEM.Extended Price)* by selecting *Extended Price* from the table's drop-down list and selecting the SUM operator from the Summary drop-down list.

The summary field in the Prod Code group band (labeled "B" in Figure 17.10) calculates the total extended price for each product. The summary field in the report band (labeled "D" in the figure) calculates the total extended price for *all* products; that is, it calculates the *grand total*. We changed this field's name to *Grand*, for use in the percentage calculation (labeled "C" in the figure).

FIGURE 17.9

This report
summarizes sales by
product code and
shows the contribution
of each product to
total sales as a
percentage.

Sales Breakdown by Product Code

Product Code	Sales	% of Total Sales
GC-006	$58,199.85	5.45 %
GC-086	$911,179.00	85.26 %
GC-093	$239.90	.02 %
GC-105	$14,003.00	1.31 %
GC-111	($270.00)	-.03 %
GC-112	$684.00	.06 %
GC-122	$31,350.00	2.93 %
GC-129	$6,450.00	.6 %
GC-135	$119.00	.01 %
GC-164	$3,333.00	.31 %
GC-189	$314.65	.03 %
GC-195	$35,000.00	3.27 %
GC-222	$150.00	.01 %
GC-289	$65.00	.01 %
GC-300	$520.00	.05 %
GC-321	$2,594.00	.24 %
GC-510	$1,000.00	.09 %
GC-521	$123.00	.01 %
GC-587	$15.00	.00 %
GC-987	$3,665.00	.34 %
Grand Total:	**$1,068,734.40**	

C Performs the percentage calculation. We defined this calculated field *after* defining and naming the *Grand* field. The formula is as follows:

Sum([LINEITEM.Extended Price])/Grand

FIGURE 17.10

The Report Design window for the report in Figure 17.9. The labels in the figure mark the important fields in the report.

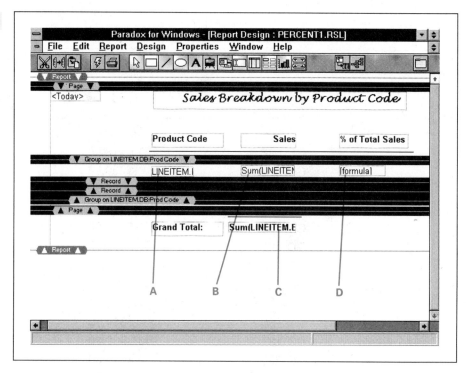

This calculation divides the total extended price in the group band by the *Grand* calculated field. In other words, we're dividing the total sales for all the products in a given product code by the total sales for all products.

WARNING

You must define and name a calculated field before you can use it in another calculation. If you try to use an undefined field name, or you type an erroneous calculation, Paradox will display an error message when you try to return to the Design window. You must either correct the calculation or choose Cancel in the Define Field Object dialog box.

After returning from the Define Field Object dialog box to the Design window, we inspected the percentage calculation field and defined a custom number format to display the results. The custom format is based on the standard Percent format, but displays two places to the right of the decimal point instead of just one. (See Chapter 6 for information on defining custom number formats.)

Working with Summary Operators and Calculated Fields

Notice that the percentage calculation in the previous example quite happily performed a calculation on a summary field. So you see that calculations can be very flexible. However, Paradox imposes one important restriction: *You cannot perform summary operations on a calculation or a calculated field.* For example, the following calculation on a summary field is perfectly *valid*:

    Sum([LINEITEM.Extended Price])

However, because you cannot perform a summary on a calculation, the following statement is *not valid*:

    Sum([LINEITEM.Qty] * [LINEITEM.Unit Price])

Therefore, although it's rarely necessary (or good practice) to store calculation results in your permanent tables, the restriction against performing summary operations on calculations or calculated fields sometimes forces you to make an exception to the "don't store calculation results in tables" rule.

The restriction above made itself painfully obvious when we designed the Orders and LineItem tables for our sample order entry database. Our goal was to avoid storing calculation results in the Orders and LineItem tables. To this end, we included fields in the LineItem table for the order number, unit price, and quantity of each item ordered, and fields in the Orders table for the shipping charges, amount paid, and tax rate of each order. However, we quickly realized that we couldn't calculate the total extended price or tax amount for an order without creating one extra field—Extended Price—in the LineItem table. This field stores the results of multiplying quantity ordered (Qty) by the unit price (Unit Price) for each item ordered.

Why do we need the Extended Price field? To determine the total amount and tax for an order, we must first calculate the extended price (quantity * unit price) for *all* line items on the order. We can't do *that* without the SUM operator. According to the restriction stated above, the formula *Sum([LINEITEM.Qty]* * *[LINEITEM.Unit Price])* is not allowed. Fortunately, *Sum([LINEITEM.Extended Price]* is perfectly acceptable. Therefore, our LineItem table needs the extra field to store the extended price calculation result for each line item. We can update this field through a query (see Chapter 16), an ObjectPAL method (see Chapter 19), or by typing it in (the least accurate method).

Once Extended Price is created and up to date, we can calculate the overall tax and amount due for each order. Later in this chapter you'll see a sample invoice and an order entry form that perform all the necessary calculations.

TIP   If you discover that an existing table requires additional fields to store calculation results, simply restructure the table (see Chapter 14). The new fields should be defined as Number or $ (currency).

Using the Function IIF to Make Decisions

You can use the ObjectPAL **IIF** function in a calculated field to create "smart" design documents that display one value if a condition is true, and another if a condition is false. The general form of the IIF statement is

    IIF(condition, true, false)

where *condition* is the condition you are testing, *true* is the value or field to display if the condition is true, and *false* is the value or field to display if the condition is false. Figure 17.11 shows an example of IIF in action, while Figure 17.12 shows the corresponding Form Design window.

FIGURE 17.11

A smart form that
displays one message
if a condition is true
and another message
if a condition is false

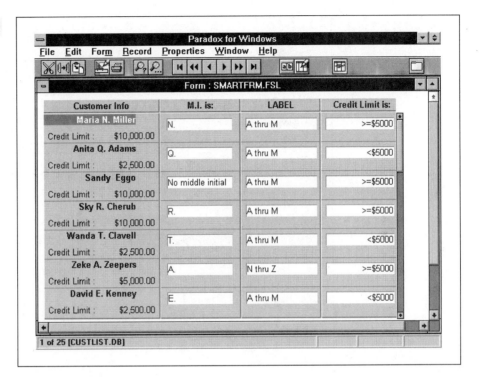

FIGURE 17.11

A smart form that
displays one message
if a condition is true
and another message
if a condition is false

NOTE   Like all keywords in a calculation, the IIF function can be typed in uppercase, lowercase, or a combination of upper- and lowercase letters.

In the sample form, the column labeled *Customer Info* displays some information about the customer. The customer name is a calculated field combining the first name, middle initial, and last name, with spaces in between, as shown below.

```
[CUSTLIST.First Name] + " " + [CUSTLIST.M.I.] + " " +
[CUSTLIST.Last Name]
```

FIGURE 17.12

The Form Design
window for the form
in Figure 17.11

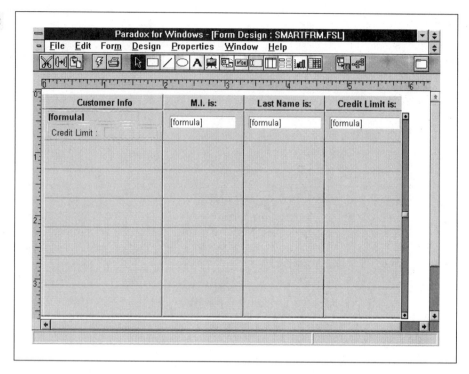

Calculated fields in the next three columns use the IIF statement to determine what to print. In the "M.I. is:" column, we use the IIF function shown below to display the words "No middle initial" if the middle initial is blank, or the middle initial if the customer has a middle initial (that is, if the middle initial is not blank):

iif([CUSTLIST.M.I.] = " ", "No middle initial", [CUSTLIST.M.I.])

The "Last Name is:" column displays the message "A thru M" if the last name is less than "N" or "N thru Z" otherwise, as follows:

iif([CUSTLIST.Last Name] < "N", "A thru M", "N thru Z")

Finally, the "Credit Limit is:" column displays ">=$5000" if the credit limit is greater than or equal to $5000 and "<$5000" otherwise. The IIF statement is as follows:

iif([CUSTLIST.Credit Limit] >= 5000, ">=$5000", "<$5000")

IIF can improve the appearance of mailing labels and other designs in which some fields might be blank. For example, to print the customer's name with proper spacing or punctuation even if there is no middle initial, try this calculation:

    [CUSTLIST.First Name] + " " + iif([CUSTLIST.M.I.] <> " ",
    [CUSTLIST.M.I.] + " "," ") + [CUSTLIST.Last Name]

The above calculation says, "Display the first name followed by a space. Then, if the middle initial is not blank (" "), display the middle initial followed by a space; otherwise display nothing. Finally, display the last name."

TIP   We also could have used the statement above to display the customer's name in the *Customer Info* column in Figure 17.11.

Tips for Typing Calculations

As you've seen, formulas in calculated fields can become quite long, and typing them properly may take a couple of tries. Here are some tips to help you along:

- We've broken some of the calculation statements shown above into several lines in order to fit them onto the pages of this book. However, you cannot do this when typing them into the Calculated text box. Instead, you must type the calculation on a single line until the statement is complete. You can use the Home, End, ←, and → keys if you need to move the insertion point through long calculation statements in the text box.

- Whenever you need to enter a field name into a calculation, position the insertion point where you want the field to appear in the Calculated text box, select the field from the table's drop-down list, select a summary operator from the Summary drop-down list (if you wish), then click the Copy Field button.

- You can copy and paste text in the Calculated text box just as you would any other Windows text: Select the text, press Ctrl+Ins to copy it, then position the insertion point where you want the copied text to appear and press Shift+Ins. This can save you some typing and improve your accuracy.

- If you want to use an existing calculated or summary field as the basis for another field in your design, select the field, then choose Design ➤ Duplicate from the menus. You can move the duplicated field wherever you want it, then inspect and change the calculation if necessary. This technique is a great way to create subtotals and grand totals for the same fields in group bands, page bands, and report bands.

WARNING

Be sure to use Design ➤ Duplicate, not copy and paste, when copying calculated or summary fields. Unlike copy and paste, Design ➤ Duplicate assigns unique names to each field duplicated. If you use copy and paste, you must then assign unique names to the copied fields.

Creating Multitable Design Documents

Multitable design documents let you view, edit, and print data from several tables simultaneously. This feature provides you with tremendous flexibility for data entry and display, and often eliminates the need to perform queries that generate temporary tables.

To define a multitable document, you simply identify the tables you want to use in the data model and define the relationship, if any, between the tables. (You'll see several examples of data models later in this chapter.) Multitable documents can contain *linked* tables, *non-linked* tables, or both.

Understanding Linked Multitable Documents

When tables are *linked*, they are joined by key fields. Figure 17.13, for example, shows an order-entry form in which the Orders table is linked to the LineItem table via the Order No key field, and the LineItem table is linked to the Products table via the Prod Code key field.

Notice that the form includes order header information (from the Orders table), each line item for the associated order (from the LineItem table), and a description of each product ordered (from the Products table). If we move the highlight to another order in this form (for example, by pressing PgDn when the highlight is in the field below Order #) or enter a new order, the line items and product descriptions will instantly change to reflect the detail information of the new order.

FIGURE 17.13

A sample order-entry form containing multiple linked tables. The Orders table is linked to LineItem and LineItem is linked to Products. Moving the highlight through the form displays information about specific orders and their associated line items.

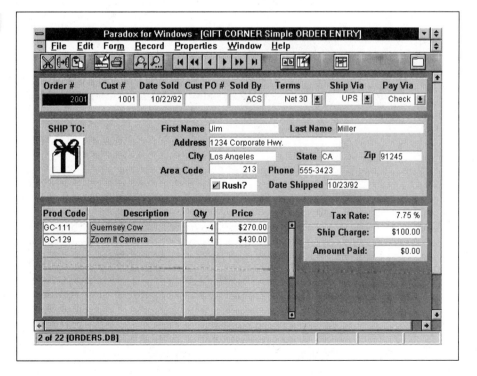

N O T E   In our discussion of multitable queries in Chapter 16, we used queries to join these tables. Linking tables in a design document is analogous to joining them in a query.

Keep in mind that you can use referential integrity, default values, and table lookups to make data entry in multiple related tables even more convenient. For instance, when we type a customer number into the appropriate field at the top of the form shown in Figure 17.13, default Ship To information from the CustList lookup table is filled in automatically. Likewise, typing a product code into the line item area of the form fills in the description and price data from the Products lookup table. Default values appear automatically for the Date Sold, Ship Via, Shipping Charge, Tax Rate, Terms, Amount Paid, and Rush fields whenever we enter a new order. Of course, we can override the defaults if we wish.

N O T E   Chapters 4, 5, and 15 discuss techniques for defining default values, lookup tables, and referential integrity in a table structure. Chapters 15 and 16 discuss the structure of our sample order-entry database.

Understanding Non-Linked Multitable Documents

Placing multiple *non-linked* tables on a form is handy when you want to keep a small table on the screen for reference during data entry or when you don't want to force the entry in one table to contain a value that's listed in the other table. Non-linked tables are also useful for graphing overall results in forms or reports (see Chapter 12).

Unlike fields in linked multitable documents, the fields in non-linked multitable documents are totally independent. Therefore, moving the highlight through one non-linked table has no effect on other non-linked tables. In Figure 17.14, for example, we've displayed the States table for

FIGURE 17.14

A form with several non-linked tables. The States table is completely independent of other tables on the form. The CustList table appears twice in this form to allow convenient scrolling to customer records.

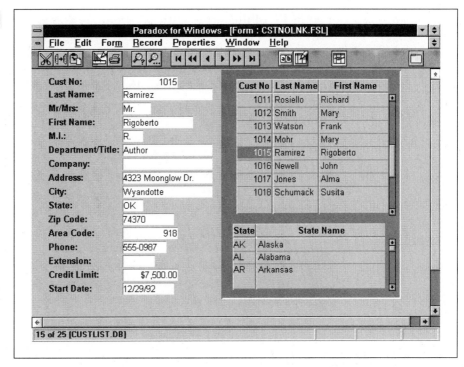

reference. This table is not linked to any tables on the form, so the user can scroll through it freely and change values without affecting other tables on the form.

NOTE

Things get a bit more complicated when tables are defined with referential integrity or table lookups. For example, if you've defined referential integrity between the CustList and States tables, changing a state abbreviation would change the corresponding abbreviation in the CustList table, whether or not the tables are linked in the form. See Chapter 15 for details on these topics.

Figure 17.14 illustrates a tricky technique you might like to try with your own forms. Notice that the CustList table appears twice, once in a single-record format and again in a tabular format. The CustList table at the right side of the form displays many records at once, so it's easy to locate a particular customer record simply by scrolling. Clicking on or scrolling to a customer record in the right-hand table displays that customer's fields on the left side of the form. Likewise, scrolling to a record in the left-hand table brings the corresponding record in the right-hand table into view. Furthermore, any changes made to the table on the right will be reflected immediately in the table on the left, and vice versa.

N O T E

Only one CustList table can appear in the form's data model; however, when we add a second instance of CustList to the form design (using the Table tool in the SpeedBar), the tables behave as though they were linked tables since they're actually the same table.

Adding Tables to the Data Model

All the tables you want to use in a multitable document must appear in the data model area of the **Data Model** dialog box, whether you link them or not.

 You can open the Data Model dialog box by creating a new form or report, or by clicking the Data Model button (shown at left) in the Speed-Bar of the Design window.

To add a table to the dialog box, simply double-click a table in the File Name list, or click the table name and then click the → button. Repeat this step until you've added all the tables you want.

When you finish adding tables, the dialog box will resemble Figure 17.15 (we used this data model for the form shown in Figure 17.14). If you don't need to link tables, you can choose OK to continue with your design. Otherwise, remain in the Data Model dialog box and link the tables, as explained a bit later.

FIGURE 17.15

The Data Model dialog box for a multitable document, before linking any tables

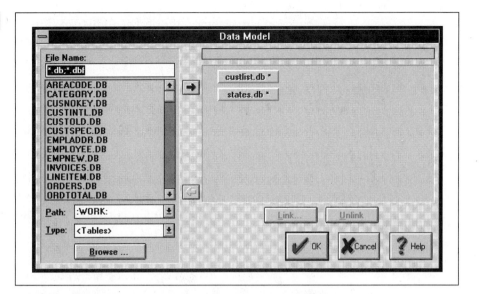

T I P

As an alternative to adding all the tables to the data model and then linking them, you may prefer to link each pair of tables as you add them. In multitable designs that include many tables, this technique reduces the need to scroll the data model to view all the tables you want to link.

Removing Tables from the Data Model

To remove a table from the data model, begin by selecting it in the data model area of the Data Model dialog box. (If the table you want to delete is linked, you must first click the Unlink button to unlink it.) Then click the ← button or press Alt+D. The table will disappear from the data model and return to the File Name list.

If your design includes objects that depend on the table you removed, Paradox will give you a chance to change your mind before pulling the plug. If you decide to go ahead and delete the table, Paradox will give you a chance to save a copy of the design. (This can come in handy if you discover that removing the table wasn't such a good idea after all.) The copy will appear minimized on the Desktop.

Rules for Creating Links

Before linking Paradox tables, you should understand the important points listed below.

- Linked tables *must* have a common field. Although the field names needn't be the same, the field type and size must match and the fields must contain corresponding data.

TIP

You can right-click a table name in the data model area for a reminder of the table's field names, types, and sizes. See Chapter 9 for details about options available when you inspect a table in the Data Model dialog box.

- The table you're linking *from* is called the *master table*. The table you're linking *to* is called the *detail table*.
- The detail table must be indexed on the field you want to use in the link. This index can either be the primary index or a secondary index. (See Chapters 4 and 7 for information on primary and secondary indexes, respectively.)
- Linked tables can have one-to-one, many-to-one, or one-to-many relationships (see Chapter 15).

Note that the rules for linking dBASE tables differ somewhat. Please see Appendix C for details.

Drawing a Link

After placing the tables you want to link into the data model area of the Data Model dialog box, you're ready to create the link. The following steps explain how to link two Paradox tables. (See Appendix C for information on linking dBASE tables.)

1. Click the master table in the data model area of the dialog box. The mouse pointer changes to a linking tool (shown at left) when you pass it over a table.

2. Click and drag the linking tool from the master table to the detail table, then release the mouse button.

If you haven't established referential integrity between the two tables (Chapter 15), Paradox will display the **Define Link** dialog box shown in Figure 17.16, and you can define the link as described below. If you *have* established referential integrity, Paradox will complete the link automatically and bypass the Define Link dialog box. (You can override the automatic link if you wish; see "Changing and Removing Links," below.)

FIGURE 17.16

The Define Link dialog box

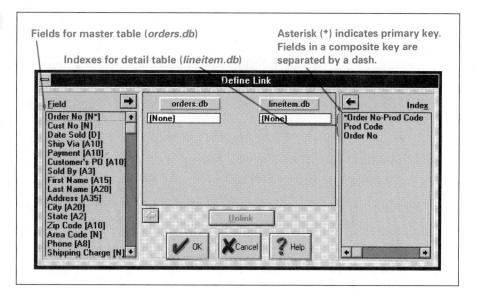

Defining the Link

If Paradox can determine which fields to use for the link, it will create the link automatically when it opens the Define Link dialog box. If you want to accept the automatic link, click OK. If you want to redefine the link, click the Unlink button.

To define the master table field you want to link, double-click the field in the Field list (see Figure 17.16), or click the field and then click the → button. If Paradox finds an index of the detail table that matches the name and type of the master table field you've chosen, it will complete the link for you automatically, as shown in Figure 17.17. (You can choose a different index, if you wish, as described next.)

NOTE

If you've chosen the wrong field from the master table, simply click the ← button that's closest to the Field list; the word *(None)* will appear under the master table name and you can select another master table field.

FIGURE 17.17

The Define Link dialog box after a link is completed.

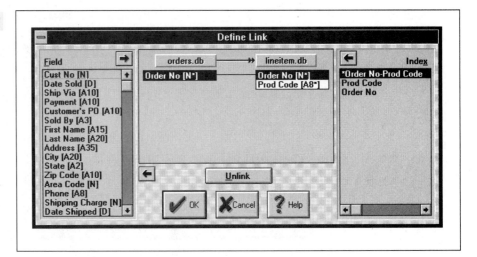

To link the selected master table field to an index field of the detail table, double-click the detail table's index name in the Inde<u>x</u> list (or click the index and then click the ← button above the list). After you define the master field and detail index, Paradox creates a link between the two tables and displays a diagram of the link below the title bar of the dialog box.

If you wish to change the link, you can double-click a different master field or detail index, or click the Unlink button and redefine the master field and detail index from scratch. When you're satisfied with the link, choose OK to return to the Data Model dialog box. The data model will reflect the type of link you created, as shown in Figure 17.18.

When viewing the data model and document design, keep the following points in mind:

- When two tables appear side by side, with a double-headed arrow between them, you've created a one-to-many link (for example, orders->>lineitem, as in Figure 17.17).

- When two tables are stacked, with an arrow joining them, you've created a one-to-one or a many-to-one relationship (for example, lineitem->products).

FIGURE 17.18

The Data Model dialog box after creating links between tables

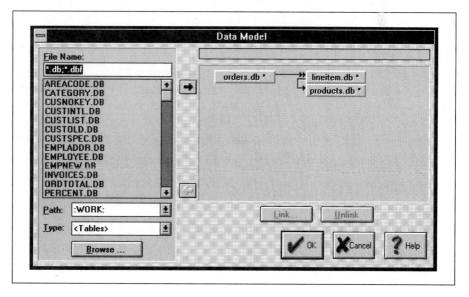

- The direction of the arrow indicates the direction of the link (master->detail or master->>detail).

- When tables are linked in a one-to-one relationship, Paradox combines their fields into one table object that includes the fields of all the tables.

- Field names in the design document always indicate the source table, and any data you enter through a multitable form is always stored in the proper source table.

You can continue to add and link tables in the Data Model dialog box for as long as the relationships make sense. In this way, you can build complex data models that combine data from many tables into a logically connected whole.

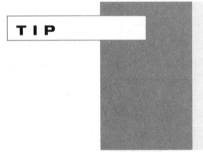

TIP

To review the links in the data model quickly, select a detail table in the data model area of the Data Model dialog box. (In Figure 17.18, the detail tables are LineItem and Products.) The area above the diagram will show the fields and indexes that link the master table to the selected detail table. You can use the arrow keys to move from table to table in the diagram.

Be aware that when you define a link, Paradox sets the Read-Only option for each linked table. When the Read-Only option is not checked (the more common situation), you can edit the table; when the option is checked, you *cannot* make changes. To change the setting, open the Data Model dialog box, inspect the table in the data model area, and select Read-Only. (This applies to forms only; you can never edit tables in report designs.)

Changing and Removing Links

You can easily change the way tables are linked in the Data Model dialog box. Simply right-click the link line (near the arrowhead), or select the detail table in the data model area, and click *Link* to return to the Define Link dialog box described above.

To remove an existing link in the Data Model dialog box, select the detail table in the data model area and click *Unlink*.

Choosing a Multitable Initial Layout

When you choose OK in the Data Model dialog box, Paradox will present the **Design Layout** dialog box if you're creating a new document, or return you to the Design window if you're modifying an existing document.

NOTE   To return to the Design Layout dialog box after you've reached the Design window, choose Design ➤ Design Layout. Be aware that after displaying an appropriate warning, Paradox will replace your existing layout with any new design layout you choose.

You learned how to use the Design Layout dialog box for single-table data models in Chapter 9. When you define a multitable data model involving one-to-many relationships, you have many more options to choose from, as illustrated in Figure 17.19. In this example, we used the Select Fields button to remove several Orders fields from the form design, allowing more room for the LineItem and Products table object. Note that if your data model includes one-to-one relationships *only*, the Design Layout dialog box will be the same as for single-table data models.

TIP   It's a good idea to use the Select Fields button *before* changing the Design Layout options so you can evaluate the effects of your choices more easily.

Initially, records from the master table are displayed one at a time, and appear in the single-record style. Records in the detail table are displayed in a table object. As mentioned earlier, Paradox will combine into a single

FIGURE 17.19

The Report Design window for the report in Figure 17.9. The labels in the figure mark the important fields in the report.

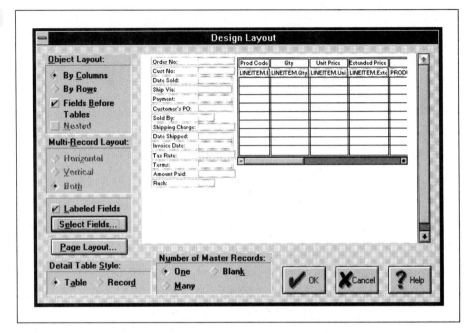

table frame fields of tables having a one-to-one relationship. In Figure 17.19, Paradox combined the LineItem and Products fields into a single table; the first field of the Products table is just barely visible at the right edge of the table frame. You can use the horizontal scroll bar in the table frame to view additional fields.

The basic steps for working with a multitable layout are as follows:

1. Use the Select Fields button to choose the fields you want Paradox to display in the design. The techniques for using the Select Fields dialog box are the same as those discussed in Chapter 9, except that you have more tables from which to choose fields.

2. Choose an option from the Number of Master Records area. Your choices are

   One Displays one master record at a time.

   Many Displays many master records at a time. This option creates multi-record objects. (To define the number of records across and down and the spacing between them, inspect a multi-record object and choose Record Layout after you reach the Design window. See Chapter 9 for details.)

Blank   Displays no master or detail records.

3. Choose an option from the Detail Table Style area to display detail tables as a Table object or a Record object.

4. In the Object Layout area, select from the advanced options described in the next section.

Each time you select an option from the Design Layout dialog box, the sample design area below the title bar will change to reflect your current choices. You can experiment with the initial layout to your heart's content. After choosing the layout that's closest to your intended form or report design, choose OK to open the Design window.

WARNING

Each record in a report design must be structured to fit on a *single* page. Paradox cannot split a record across two or more pages.

Before making any changes in the Design window, you should click the View Data button in the SpeedBar to preview your design. If you aren't happy with your initial layout choices, you can return to the Design window by clicking the Design button in the Form or Report window. Then open the Design Layout dialog box again (choose Design ➤ Design Layout) and try some different options. Remember that once you reach the Design window, any changes made in the Design Layout dialog box will completely replace your existing design. Therefore, it's a good idea not to waste time tweaking a design until you're satisfied with its overall layout.

NOTE

When you return to the Design Layout dialog box, you'll see only fields that are currently in the design. You can add or remove fields using the Select Fields button.

Choosing Object Layout Options

The Object Layout area of the Design Layout dialog box offers some advanced options for controlling your multitable design layout.

You can choose to display design objects By Columns (up and down the page or screen) or By Rows (across the page or screen). In Figure 17.19, the objects are displayed by columns, which is the default layout.

When the Fields Before Tables option is selected (checked), all the fields of the master record appear before fields in the detail records. To display detail records before master records, click this option to remove the check mark.

If the Nested option is available, you can select (check) it to place detail record objects inside their corresponding master multi-record object. Deselect this option to place detail records adjacent to or below the master objects (placement depends on whether you've chosen *By Columns* or *By Rows*).

NOTE

The Nested option will be available if you've chosen Many from the Number of Master Records area in a one-to-many form design, or you're designing a one-to-many-to-many form. The option is not available for report designs.

Defining Fields in Multitable Documents

Defining fields in multitable design documents is basically the same as defining them in single-table documents: Simply inspect the field in the Design window and choose Define Field. The list that appears will include fields from the master and detail tables (preceded by the table name). If the field you want to select appears in the list, click it. If it doesn't appear, click the list header or press ↵ to open the Define Field Object dialog box.

Figure 17.20 presents the Define Field Object dialog box for an order entry form. Notice that the tables are shown with the appropriate links, and they have drop-down arrows next to them. From this point, you can use the techniques described in this chapter and in previous chapters to define regular, summary, special, and calculated fields.

FIGURE 17.20

The Define Field Object dialog box for a multitable document

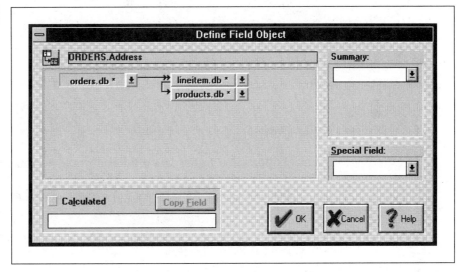

Understanding Scope in Multitable Documents

The various levels in the data model hierarchy and the relationships between master and detail tables affect the scope of summary and calculated fields in multitable documents. Rather than presenting a bunch of complicated rules to explain scope, we'll take a simpler approach and look at some practical examples that illustrate the concepts. First you'll see a handy order summary form that presents each customer's order at a glance. Next is a fancy order-entry form that performs a variety of calculations automatically. Finally, you'll see the invoice we promised earlier in this chapter.

A Summary of Orders for Each Customer

Let's begin with the data model shown below:

We can represent this data model using the following shorthand notation: *CustList->>Orders->>LineItem->Products*. This means that Cust-List is the master table in a one-to-many relationship with Orders; Orders is the master table in a one-to-many relationship with LineItem; and Line-Item is the master table in a many-to-one relationship with Products.

The relationships in this data model allow us to summarize values as follows:

- For each customer, we can show associated orders in the Orders table.

- For each order, we can summarize the associated detail records in the LineItem table.

- For each line item, we can show associated information from the Products table.

To understand the effects of this data model on summary field calculations, take a look at the order summary form in Figure 17.21. In this example, you can see all orders placed by customer number 1007, the line item details for the customer's first order (number 2002), and three tidbits of summary information. These are the definitions for the summary fields:

- The total amount paid by customer number 1007 on all orders is *Sum(ORDERS.Amount Paid)*.

- The number of orders placed by customer number 1007 is *Count(ORDERS.Order No)*.

- The total extended price for the first order (number 2002) is *Sum(LINEITEM.Extended Price)*.

FIGURE 17.21

An order summary form containing the data model CustList->> Orders->>Lineltem-> Products and three summary fields

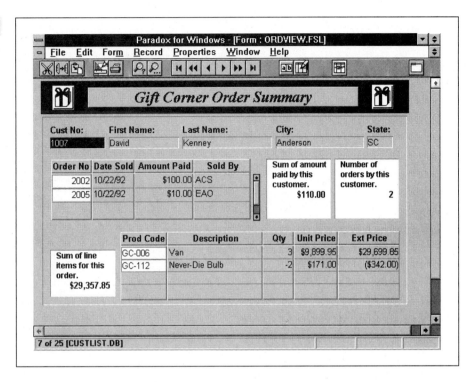

If you break out your trusty calculator, you can easily verify the results shown in the figure.

Paradox displays information for the *first* record at each level in the data hierarchy until you move to a different detail record.

Figure 17.22 shows the effect of moving the highlight to the second order (2005) for this customer (1007). As you can see, the line items have changed, and so has the sum of line items for the order. However, the amount paid by the customer and the number of orders placed remain the same, as expected.

FIGURE 17.22

The form shown in Figure 17.21, with the highlight moved to the second order for this customer

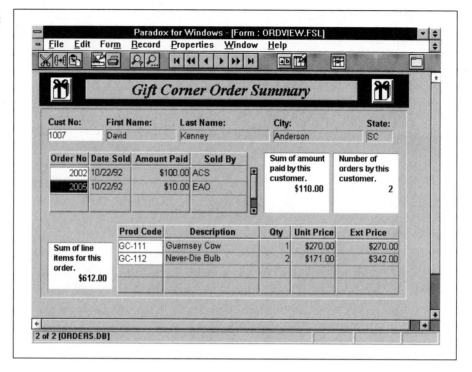

An Order-Entry Form

Figure 17.23 illustrates a fancier version of the order-entry form shown previously in Figure 17.13. This form features the data model relationships *Orders->>LineItem->Products* and performs several calculations, which are summarized below.

Next Avail. Order# A calculated field which is defined as *Max([ORDERS.Order No])+1*. This field displays the highest order number currently in the Orders table, plus 1. The user should type this number into the Order # field when entering a new order.

Order Subtotal A summary field which is defined as *Sum([LINEITEM.Extended Price])*. This field totals the extended prices for the current order.

Tax A calculated field which is defined as *Sum([LINEITEM.Extended Price]) * [ORDERS.Tax Rate]*. This totals the extended prices for the current order in the LineItem table and multiplies it by the tax rate stored in the Orders table. The tax rate appears just to the left of the calculated field.

Invoice Amount A calculated field which is defined as *Sum([LINEITEM.Extended Price]) + Sum([LINEITEM.Extended Price)] * [ORDERS.Tax Rate] + [ORDERS.Shipping Charge]*. This field adds the total extended price, the tax, and the shipping charge for the order.

Balance Due A calculated field which is defined as *Sum([LINEITEM.Extended Price]) + Sum([LINEITEM.Extended Price)] * [ORDERS.Tax Rate] + [ORDERS.Shipping Charge] – [ORDERS.Amount Paid]*. This gives us the final balance due for the order.

FIGURE 17.23

A fancier version of the order-entry form shown in Figure 17.13. This form shows the next available order number and calculates order subtotals and totals.

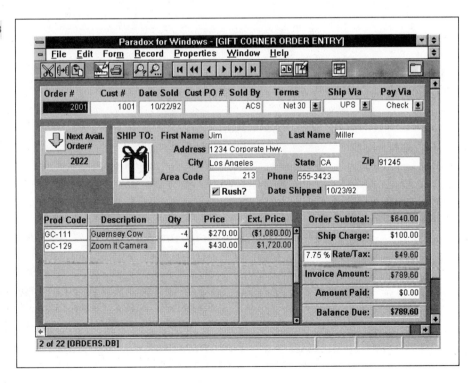

The accuracy of the calculations depends above all on having up-to-date amounts in the Extended Price field of the LineItem table. To update that field, we can use any of the following techniques:

- Calculate it manually and type it in—the least attractive option by far.
- Run a query and then return to the form. (We could add a button to the form, and attach an ObjectPAL method that runs the query whenever we click the button.)
- Attach ObjectPAL methods to the Qty and Price field objects. These methods calculate the extended price and update the Extended Price field of the LineItem table automatically, whenever the user changes a quantity or price in the order form. This is the best approach, and the one we took in this form.

We'll discuss ways to run queries and update fields using ObjectPAL in Chapter 19.

A Sample Invoice

The sample invoice report shown in Figure 17.24 uses the calculations discussed previously for the order-entry form. However, the data model is different, as shown below:

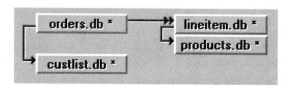

The invoice data model includes the CustList table (which wasn't needed in our order-entry form) and shows the Orders table at the top. Placing Orders on top by dragging the mouse from Orders to CustList in the Data Model dialog box creates a many-to-one relationship, ensuring one invoice per order. In this relationship, Orders is the master table and CustList is the detail table (after all, a single customer can place many orders).

The design for this invoice appears in Figure 17.25. Notice that the report is grouped first by the Cust No field of the Orders table, then by the Order

FIGURE 17.24

A sample invoice

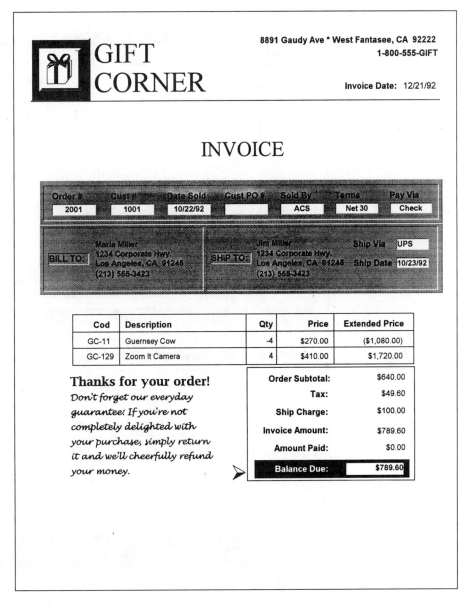

GIFT CORNER

8891 Gaudy Ave * West Fantasee, CA 92222
1-800-555-GIFT

Invoice Date: 12/21/92

INVOICE

Order #	Cust #	Date Sold	Cust PO #	Sold By	Terms	Pay Via
2001	1001	10/22/92		ACS	Net 30	Check

BILL TO: Maria Miller
1234 Corporate Hwy.
Los Angeles, CA 91245
(213) 555-3423

SHIP TO: Jim Miller
1234 Corporate Hwy.
Los Angeles, CA 91245
(213) 555-3423

Ship Via UPS
Ship Date 10/23/92

Cod	Description	Qty	Price	Extended Price
GC-11	Guernsey Cow	-4	$270.00	($1,080.00)
GC-129	Zoom It Camera	4	$410.00	$1,720.00

Thanks for your order!
Don't forget our everyday guarantee: If you're not completely delighted with your purchase, simply return it and we'll cheerfully refund your money.

Order Subtotal:	$640.00
Tax:	$49.60
Ship Charge:	$100.00
Invoice Amount:	$789.60
Amount Paid:	$0.00
Balance Due:	$789.60

No field. This keeps all invoices for each customer together. Because the subtotal, tax, invoice amount, and balance due calculations appear in the Order No band of the report, these amounts reflect totals for an individual order.

FIGURE 17.25

The design for the invoice report shown in Figure 17.24

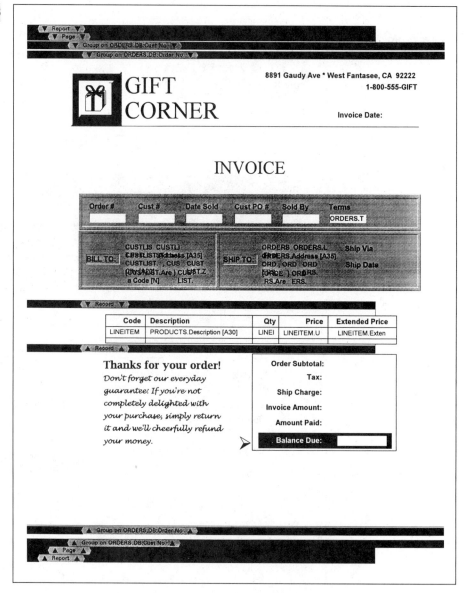

TIP

To print a report design like the one shown in Figure 17.25, return to the Report Design window and choose File ➤ Print ➤ Design. (Some field names in the printed design may appear garbled if Paradox doesn't have enough room to print them. However, the form or report should be just fine when you view or print it.)

Displaying and Editing Data in Multitable Forms

In Chapter 5 we discussed a variety of techniques for viewing and editing data in Form View. For the most part, the procedures are the same for multitable forms. However, you must remember that the hierarchy of the data model controls the movement of the highlight (cursor) from record to record within the fields and tables of a multitable form.

To understand how cursor movement works, flip back to Figure 17.22. Now imagine that the highlight is positioned in the field for product code GC-112, at the bottom of the LineItem table. In a single-table form, clicking the First Record button in the SpeedBar would move the highlight to the very first record in the LineItem table. In a multitable form, however, all cursor movement takes place within the hierarchy of the data model. Therefore, clicking the First Record button in the order summary form moves the highlight to the first record of the LineItem table *for the current customer and order* (that is, to the record for product code GC-111). Similarly, clicking the First Record button when the highlight is on order number 2005 of the Orders table moves the cursor to the first order *for the current customer* (to the record for order number 2002). Finally, clicking the First Record button when the highlight is on customer number 1007 of the CustList table moves it to the very first record in the CustList table (to the record for customer number 1001). In this example, CustList is at the top of the data model hierarchy, so moving the highlight through this portion of the form is the same as moving it through a single-table form for the CustList Table.

N O T E You can use the mouse, cursor movement keys (arrow keys, Tab, Shift+Tab, Home, End, Ctrl+Home, Ctrl+End, PgUp, and PgDn), and SpeedBar buttons to move the highlight through a form.

The most important points to remember about moving the highlight through multitable forms are summarized below.

- You can click the mouse in any field to move the highlight to that field (unless the Tab Stop property is turned off, as described in Chapter 10).

- The cursor positioning keys and SpeedBar buttons apply to the current level of the data hierarchy only.

- You can press the Super Tab (F4) key to move the highlight to the *next* table or multi-record region; press the Super Back Tab (F3) key to move the highlight to the *previous* table or multi-record region.

As you can see, multitable documents are an incredibly powerful and convenient tool. When updating tables through multitable forms, remember that your changes are always made to the proper table in the data model. Therefore, as long as your data model is set up correctly, you'll never need to open many table or form windows simultaneously in order to keep all your data in sync—a single form will do it all.

In this chapter, you learned how to perform summaries and calculations in design documents, and how to create multitable documents. In the next chapter, we'll introduce techniques that you can use to update tables automatically.

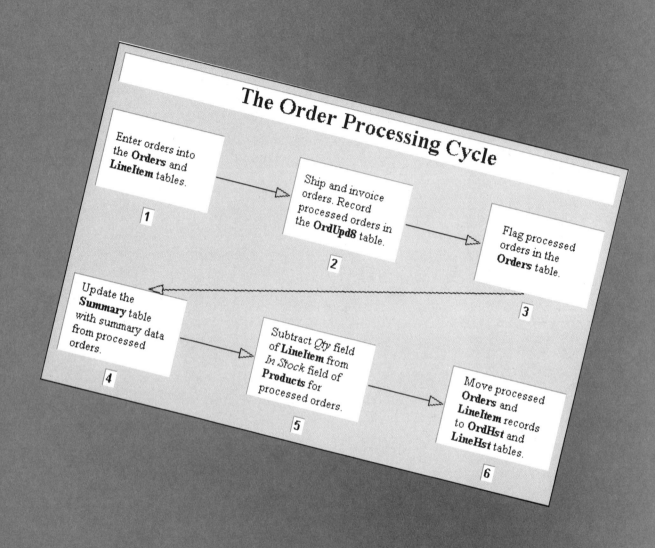

The Order Processing Cycle

Enter orders into the **Orders** and **LineItem** tables.

1

Ship and invoice orders. Record processed orders in the **OrdUpd8** table.

2

Flag processed orders in the **Orders** table.

3

Update the **Summary** table with summary data from processed orders.

4

Subtract *Qty* field of **LineItem** from *In Stock* field of **Products** for processed orders.

5

Move processed **Orders** and **LineItem** records to **OrdHst** and **LineHst** tables.

6

CHAPTER

18

Updating Tables
Automatically

f a s t

TRACK

● **An INSERT query provides an alternative method**   **941**

of inserting records from one or more source tables into a single target table.

● **To define an INSERT query**   **942**

add the source and target tables to the Query window. For each source table, specify selection criteria, if necessary. In the *target* table, move the highlight to the column under the table name and type the letter **I**. Place linking example elements in the source and target tables to indicate which fields in the source tables should update the target table. Then run the query as usual.

● **If you want to move posted records from their original table to a history table**   **949**

use File ➤ Utilities ➤ Add to add records to the history table, then use File ➤ Utilities ➤ Empty to empty the original table.

● **It is important to perform automatic update steps**   **952**

in the proper sequence. Using saved queries will help avoid unnecessary delays and improve the accuracy of your updates. However, to automate the steps fully, you'll need to learn ObjectPAL, the Paradox for Windows programming language, described in Chapter 19.

IN this chapter we'll look at techniques for updating information from one table based on information in another table. Here we'll pull together many techniques from previous chapters, including designing databases with multiple related tables (Chapter 15); querying single tables (Chapter 8); using CALC, CHANGETO, and example elements in queries to change data and perform calculations on multiple tables (Chapter 16); and using options from the File ➤ Utilities menus (Chapter 14). Please refer to these earlier chapters if you need additional reminders about how to use the features discussed in this chapter.

We'll also discuss the important topic of keeping track of which records have been used during an automatic updating procedure, and which have not. Since Paradox for Windows has no built-in means of determining whether a given record in a table has already been used or *posted* during an update, it's up to you to devise some scheme to prevent records from being posted more than once. We'll illustrate two commonly used techniques in this chapter: (1) marking or *flagging* posted records in their original table and (2) moving posted records from their original table to another table (often called a *history table*).

At this stage of the game, we'll present examples as "food for thought" which you can use in creating your own databases and applications. While we progress through the examples, you should keep in mind that we are only demonstrating examples, and that the ways in which you can mix and match data from multiple related tables are almost unlimited.

An Order Processing and Purchasing Example

Throughout this chapter, we'll use a simple order processing and purchasing system to illustrate our points. The system uses the Orders, Line-Item, Products, and Category tables presented in Chapter 15. Recall that we used referential integrity and table lookups to ensure consistent data in these related tables.

We'll also introduce several new tables, which are described below:

OrdUpd8   This table is used to record the date shipped and invoice date of each order we process. Its fields are Order No, Date · Shipped, and Invoice Date. We've defined a referential integrity relationship between OrdUpd8 and the Orders table to prevent entry of non-existent orders into OrdUpd8.

Summary   The Summary table consolidates each order for reporting and analysis only. The Summary fields are Order No, Cust No, Payment, Date Shipped, and Invoice Date.

Purchase   The Purchase table tracks the product code, quantity received, purchase price, and date received for items we've ordered to replenish our inventory. The Purchase table fields are Prod Code, Qty Recd, Purchase Price, and Date Recd. To facilitate data entry, we've defined Products as the lookup table for the Prod Code field of the Purchase table.

We'll also use three history tables to store posted records. *OrdHst* stores history data from the Orders table; *LineHst* stores history data from the LineItem table; and *PurHst* stores history data from the Purchase table. You'll see examples of all these tables later in this chapter.

An Overview of the Order Processing and Purchasing Cycles

Figure 18.1 provides an overview of the basic steps required to process customer orders for our products. The steps are summarized below and explained in more detail in the sections that follow.

1. First we enter each customer's order into the Orders and LineItem tables, perhaps using the multitable order-entry form presented in Chapter 17.

2. After shipping and invoicing a batch of customer orders, we record the Order No, Date Shipped, and Invoice Date (if any) of each shipped order in the OrdUpd8 table. (Recall from Chapter 16 that the Payment field of the Orders table indicates whether an invoice is necessary.)

3. Next we mark orders as "processed" by updating (flagging) the Date Shipped and Invoice Date fields of appropriate orders in the

FIGURE 18.1

The order processing cycle

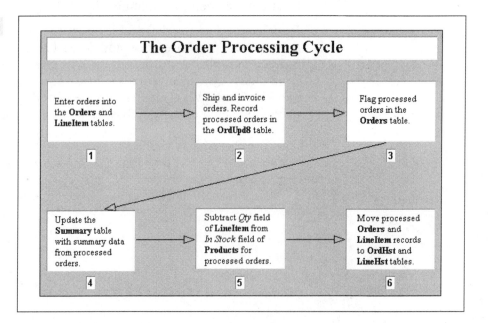

The Order Processing Cycle

1. Enter orders into the **Orders** and **LineItem** tables.

2. Ship and invoice orders. Record processed orders in the **OrdUpd8** table.

3. Flag processed orders in the **Orders** table.

4. Update the **Summary** table with summary data from processed orders.

5. Subtract *Qty* field of **LineItem** from *In Stock* field of **Products** for processed orders.

6. Move processed **Orders** and **LineItem** records to **OrdHst** and **LineHst** tables.

Orders table. Flagging these fields will prevent us from shipping the orders again or sending duplicate invoices.

4. We update the Summary table with selected fields from the Orders and OrdUpd8 tables. Although this table is not required for successful order processing, we've included it to illustrate how to copy records from one or more tables to a different table with an incompatible structure.

5. In this step, we update the current in-stock quantities for each product shipped.

6. Finally, we post the processed Orders and LineItem records to appropriate history files (OrdHst and LineHst, respectively), remove the processed records from the Orders and LineItem tables, and clear out the OrdUpd8 table.

Figure 18.2 presents the purchasing cycle, whereby we replenish inventory in our stockroom. The steps involved in this cycle are summarized below and further described later in this chapter.

FIGURE 18.2

The purchasing cycle

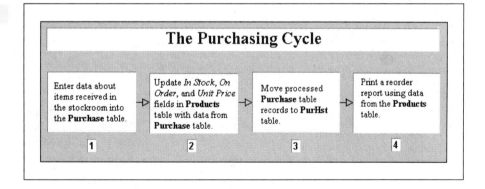

The Purchasing Cycle

1	2	3	4
Enter data about items received in the stockroom into the **Purchase** table.	Update *In Stock, On Order,* and *Unit Price* fields in **Products** table with data from **Purchase** table.	Move processed **Purchase** table records to **PurHst** table.	Print a reorder report using data from the **Products** table.

1. First we update the Purchase table with data about each item received into the stockroom.

2. Next we update the quantities and costs of inventory items in the Products table with data from the Purchase table.

3. In this step, we copy processed records from the Purchase table to the PurHst history table, then empty the Purchase table to prevent posted records from being reused.

4. Finally, we print a reorder report to find out which inventory items in the Products table need replenishing. (This step can be performed at any time.)

Now that you have an overview of the basic order processing and purchasing cycles, let's look at techniques for performing each step. Keep in mind that we're illustrating relatively simple approaches to some common business tasks. Full-blown order processing and purchasing applications are usually more complex than the ones presented here.

Copying Fields from One Table to Another

As mentioned earlier, after invoicing and shipping an order (Step 1 of Figure 18.1), we'll enter the order number, ship date, and invoice date of those orders into the OrdUpd8 table (Step 2 of Figure 18.1). A few sample records for the OrdUpd8 table appear below.

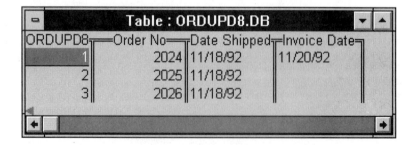

ORDUPD8	Order No	Date Shipped	Invoice Date
1	2024	11/18/92	11/20/92
2	2025	11/18/92	
3	2026	11/18/92	

Notice that all records in the OrdUpd8 table have entries in the Date Shipped field. However, the Invoice Date field has entries only for records in which the Payment field of the Orders table contains the value "Invoice."

> **N O T E**
>
> In this chapter you'll see the benefits of combining a concise transaction table like OrdUpd8 with multitable queries and a few well-chosen options from the File ➤ Utilities menus to update many master tables at once in a quick, efficient, and consistent manner.

Recall from Chapter 16 that we're using the Date Shipped and Invoice Date fields in the Orders table to determine whether an order has been fulfilled (shipped) and invoiced. These two fields are left blank initially to indicate that order processing is incomplete. After we fulfill and invoice an order, it is important to avoid shipping or invoicing it again; therefore, we need a way to mark, or *flag*, orders that have been processed (Step 3 of Figure 18.1).

The first step of the marking process is to enter the order number, ship date, and invoice date into the OrdUpd8 table, as described earlier. To complete the marking process, we use the simple *ShipInv* query shown in Figure 18.3.

FIGURE 18.3

The ShipInv query updates blank Date Shipped and Invoice Date fields in the Orders table with values from the OrdUpd8 table.

N O T E

We've moved fields, adjusted field widths, and changed default number formats of fields in Table windows and Query windows throughout this chapter so that you can see the queries and results more easily. We've also saved each query so we can reuse them as needed (the query name appears on the title bar of each Query window).

In the completed query, we've used the following example elements and query commands:

- *EG01* (entered via the Join Tables button) is the example element linking the common Order No field of the Orders and OrdUpd8 tables.

- *ShipDate* (entered by pressing the F5 key before typing the element name) is an example element representing the date we shipped the order.

- *InvDate* is an example element representing the date we invoiced the order.

- **BLANK, Changeto** *ShipDate* tells Paradox to plug in the Date Shipped value from the OrdUpd8 table if the Date Shipped field in the current Orders record is blank.

- **BLANK, Changeto** *InvDate* tells Paradox to plug in the Invoice Date value from the OrdUpd8 table if the Invoice Date field in the current Orders record is blank.

After you perform the query (by pressing F8 or clicking the Run Query button), the Changed table will appear. If you open the Orders table, you'll see that Paradox has indeed copied the appropriate data from Ord-Upd8 to Orders, as Figure 18.4 shows.

TIP

It's a good idea to close all windows (choose Window ➤ Close All) before performing the next query in a cycle. This precaution helps to avoid those exasperating "Table is Busy" messages that appear when Paradox cannot complete a query because a required table is opened on the Desktop.

FIGURE 18.4

After you perform the query in Figure 18.3, the Date Shipped and Invoice Date fields in the Orders table contain updated values from the OrdUpd8 table.

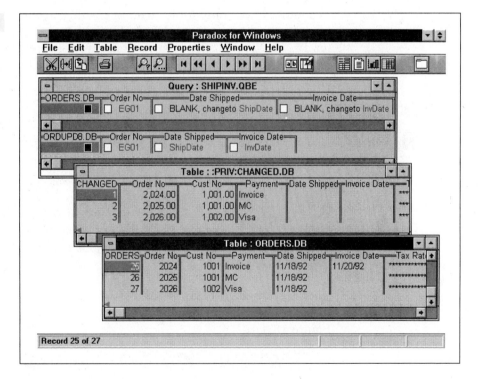

Copying "Incompatible" Records from One Table to Another

Sometimes you'll want to add records from one or more tables to another table. If you're copying just one table's records to another table and the two tables have compatible structures—that is, the field names and data types match—you can use File ➤ Utilities ➤ Add, as discussed in Chapter 14. However, if the records come from more than one table, or the structures of the tables are incompatible, it's best to use queries to accomplish your task.

NOTE   If you use File Utilities ➤ Add to copy records to a table that has an incompatible structure, some data may be lost. If data loss is likely, Paradox will display a Table Structure Mismatch Warning dialog box that is similar to the Restructure Warnings dialog box discussed in Chapter 14, and will give you a chance either to trim the data or back out of the operation.

Suppose you want to summarize data from several tables and add it to a more compact table, such as the Summary table shown below (Step 4 of Figure 18.1).

Paradox for Windows offers two methods that are especially useful for adding "incompatible" records from one table to another. The first method uses the Answer table as an intermediary. The second method uses example elements and the **Insert** reserved word to insert the records from the source tables into the target table.

The query shown in Figure 18.5 illustrates the first technique. The example element *EG01* joins the Orders and OrdUpd8 tables by their common Order No field, and the check marks select the fields we want to display. Running the query creates an Answer table with the same structure as the Summary table. Once the query has been performed, we could use File ➤ Utilities ➤ Add to add records from the Answer table to the Summary table. When the **Add** dialog box appears, we would select *:PRIV:ANSWER.DB* as the source table and *SUMMARY.DB* as the target table, then click the OK button.

FIGURE 18.5

A query that generates an Answer table with the same structure as the Summary table

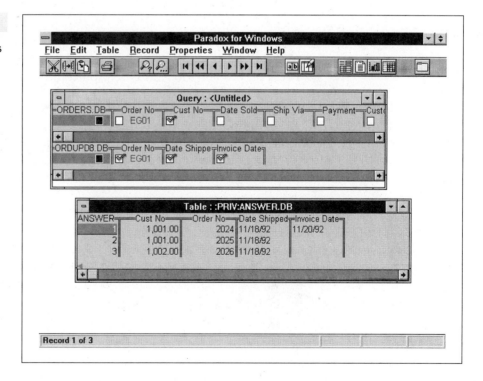

The Insert reserved word provides an alternative method of inserting records from one or more source tables into a single target table. You can also use Insert queries to insert records from dBASE tables into Paradox tables, and from Paradox tables into dBASE tables. The steps for creating an Insert query are as follows:

1. Create a new query (File ➤ New ➤ Query) and add the source table (or tables) and target table to the Query window. (See Chapter 16.)

2. For each source table, specify selection criteria, if necessary.

3. In the *target* table, move the highlight to the leftmost column (under the table name) and type the letter **I**; or click under the table name and choose *Insert* from the list that appears.

4. Link the source and target tables using example elements. Example elements indicate which fields in the source tables should be used to update the target table. If you omit an example element from a field in the target table, that field will not receive any values from the source table.

5. Press F8 or click the Run Query button to run the query.

After you run the query, the appropriate records from the source tables will be inserted into the target table and a temporary table named *Inserted* will appear. The Inserted table will include only the records inserted into the target table and will be overwritten every time you submit an Insert query.

NOTE

If necessary, you can use the Inserted table along with the Delete reserved word to undo an insertion. Be aware that if the Insert query inserted records that were already present in the target table, the Delete query will remove the *original* records from the target table as well as the duplicates.

Figure 18.6 shows an Insert query named *Summary* and the Inserted table that appears after you run the query. In this figure, the example element **Order** links the Orders and OrdUpd8 tables and limits the summarized orders to shipped and invoiced orders only. The example elements **Order**, **Cust**, **Payment**, **ShipDate**, and **InvDate** tell Paradox where to insert values from OrdUpd8 into the Summary table.

WARNING

If you're following along at your own computer, be aware that using *both* the Answer table method and the Insert query method discussed above will result in duplicate records in your Summary table. You can use a Delete query to delete the duplicate records, or open the Summary table, press F9, move the highlight to each duplicate record, and press Ctrl+Del.

FIGURE 18.6

The Summary query uses the Insert reserved word to insert records from the Orders and OrdUpd8 tables into the Summary table.

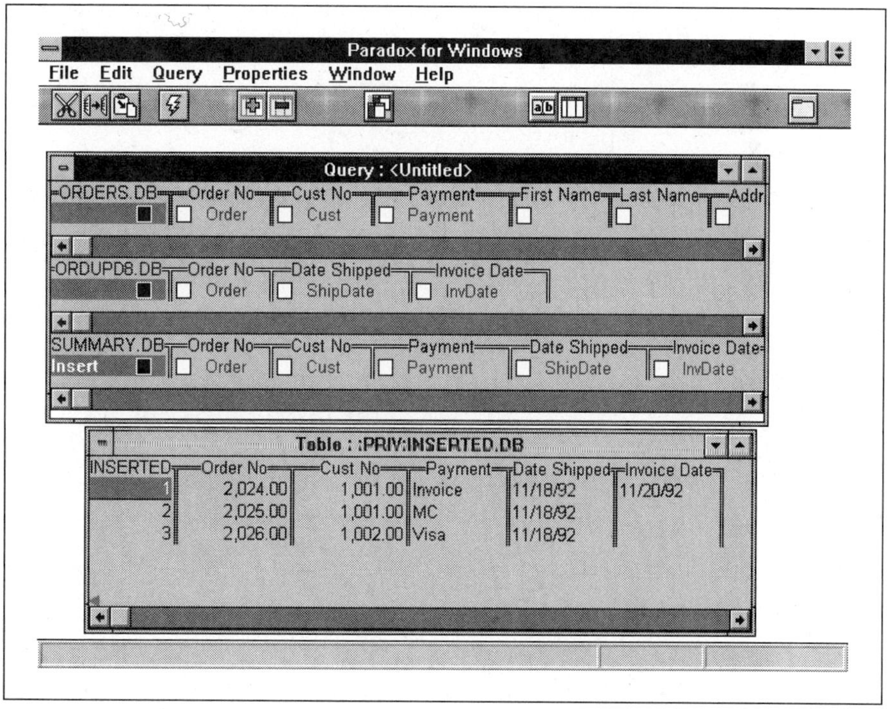

Changing Values in One Table Based on Another Table

Perhaps the most common use of automatic updating is to change the contents of one table based on the contents of another table. For instance, in our order processing example, we want to subtract the Qty values for shipped orders in the LineItem table from In Stock quantities in the Products table so that our In Stock quantities will be accurate and up to date (Step 5 in Figure 18.1). Performing this step manually would be a real pain; however, it's quite easy if we use the automatic updating procedures described below.

Subtracting Quantities Sold from In-Stock Quantities

In order to subtract quantities sold from in-stock quantities, we need to perform two steps:

1. Calculate the total quantity of each type of product shipped. That is, for each shipped product in the LineItem table, we must calculate the total value of the Qty field. Again, we'll use the OrdUpd8 table to indicate which items have been shipped and need processing.

2. Subtract the total quantity (Qty) of each item shipped from the In Stock quantity field of the Products table.

To make it easy to test and verify the updating procedure, we'll place some "dummy" values in the Products table. In Figure 18.7, for example, we've set the In Stock quantity to 100, the On Order quantity to 10, and the Reorder Point to 200 for products GC-093, GC-111, and GC-112. (We'll use the On Order and Reorder Point fields later when we discuss the purchasing cycle.)

FIGURE 18.7

The Products table with
some dummy values
entered for products
GC-093, GC-111,
and GC-112

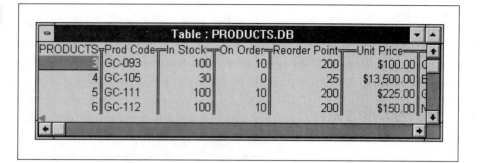

Now let's suppose that the LineItem table includes the fields and values
listed below for order numbers 2024, 2025, and 2026.

PROD CODE	ORDER NO	QTY
GC-093	2024	1
GC-093	2025	2
GC-111	2024	2
GC-111	2025	1
GC-112	2025	2
GC-112	2026	2

The query named *CalcSum* in Figure 18.8 shows the first step required
to update the In Stock quantities in the Products table: calculating the
total quantity sold for each product shipped. Notice that including the
OrdUpd8 query table in the Query window limits the calculation to
shipped orders only. The example elements **EG01** and **EG02** link the
common fields in the OrdUpd8, Products, and LineItem query tables.
The Sold field of the resulting Answer table shows the total quantity sold
for each product shipped.

The second step of the updating procedure is to subtract the quantities
in the Sold field of the Answer table from In Stock quantities in the Products table. To perform this update, we created and saved the *Upd8Prod*
query shown at the top of Figure 18.9. Here we've used the example
element **EG01** to link the Products and Answer table. The example element ***Current*** represents the current In Stock value in the Products

FIGURE 18.8

The CalcSum query shows the total quantity of each product sold in a field named **Sold** in the Answer table.

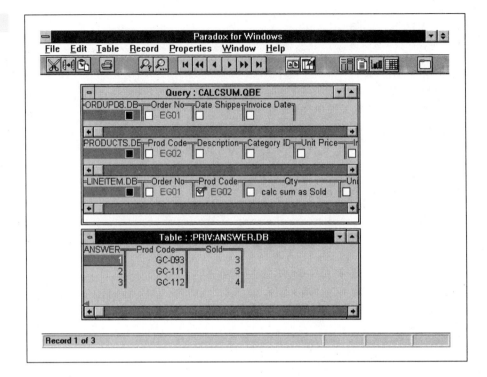

table, and the example element **QtySold** represents the value in the Sold field of the Answer table. The CHANGETO command in the query performs the desired calculation.

After we run the query, the changed records are copied to the Changed table as usual. If we open the Products table, we can see that Paradox has indeed subtracted the values in the Sold field from the In Stock quantities in the Products table, as shown at the bottom of Figure 18.9.

Using History Files

Now that we've completed the first five steps of the order processing cycle shown in Figure 18.1, we must find some way to ensure that each record

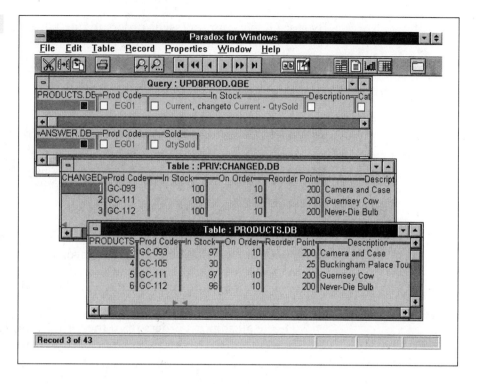

FIGURE 18.9

The Upd8Prod query subtracts the quantity of each product sold from the In Stock quantities. This example also shows the Changed table and a portion of the Products table.

in the LineItem table is used only once when subtracting quantities sold from In Stock quantities.

In the previous example, we accomplished this by flagging the Date Shipped and Invoice Date in each record of the Orders table with the dates from the OrdUpd8 table. We also designed the update queries so that only "unflagged" records (those with blank Date Shipped and Invoice Date fields) were updated. Another way to ensure that records are never posted more than once is to move all posted records from the original table to a separate history table.

There are advantages and disadvantages to each approach. The advantage of flagging posted records is that all the records remain in one table. In some ways this makes overall management easier, but the drawback is that the table grows indefinitely, requires extra fields to indicate which records have been processed, and could become huge by the end of a year. Since very large tables can slow down general processing, you will certainly want to take into account the disadvantages of flagging records.

By storing live (unprocessed) orders in one table and moving posted orders to a history table, you can keep the table of live orders fairly small and speed up day-to-day processing a bit. You must decide which approach is best on a case-by-case basis when developing applications on your own.

TIP Since history tables usually have the same structure as the original tables, reports and forms can easily be adapted to display and report on historical data.

For the sixth and final step in our order processing cycle, we'll demonstrate the history table method, which involves the following steps:

* Copy all shipped orders from the Orders and LineItem tables to history tables.

* Delete all shipped orders from the Orders and LineItem tables to prevent those records from being used in future updates.

* Clear the OrdUpd8 table so that we won't process shipped and invoiced orders again.

First, you need to create history tables to store the posted records. Since these tables use the same structure as the original tables (Orders and LineItem in this example), you can quickly create an empty history table by following these steps:

1. Choose File ➤ New ➤ Table, then choose OK to begin defining a new Paradox for Windows table.

2. In the **Create Table** dialog box, click Borrow, click on the name of the table you want to borrow (*ORDERS.DB* in this example), and choose OK.

3. Click the Save As button, type the name of the new history table (**ORDHST.DB** in this example), and choose OK.

Now Orders and OrdHst have exactly the same structures; the only difference between the two tables is that the OrdHst table is new and completely empty. Repeat the three steps above to create a history table for the LineItem table. This time, specify the table name *LINEITEM.DB* in Step 2 and type the name **LINEHST.DB** in Step 3.

Moving Posted Orders to the History Tables

Now you're ready to copy all the records from the Orders table to the OrdHst table and from the LineItem table to the LineHst table. Once you've done that, you'll want to remove those records from the original tables so they won't be posted again in the future. The steps are listed below.

1. Clear the Desktop (choose <u>W</u>indow ➤ Close <u>A</u>ll) to prevent "Table is Busy" messages.

2. Run the query shown in Figure 18.10 to copy shipped records from the LineItem table to the Answer table (we named this query *PostLine*). The example element **EG01** in the query restricts the selected line items to shipped items only.

3. Choose <u>F</u>ile ➤ <u>U</u>tilities ➤ <u>A</u>dd, select *:PRIV:ANSWER.DB* as the source table and *LINEHST.DB* as the target table, click Appe<u>n</u>d in the Options area of the Add dialog box, and click the OK button.

4. Clear the Desktop again, then run the Delete query shown in Figure 18.11 to remove the posted records from the LineItem table (we've named this query *ClrLine*). Paradox stores the de-leted records in the temporary Deleted table.

WARNING If you've set up referential integrity between tables, as we've done between Orders (the parent table) and LineItem (the child table), you must post and remove records from the child table before posting and removing records from the parent table (see Chapter 15).

FIGURE 18.10

The PostLine query selects shipped records from the LineItem table and places them in the Answer table. You can then use File ➤ Utilities ➤ Add to add the Answer table records to the LineHst table.

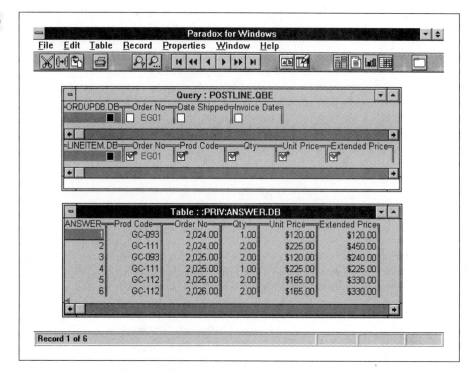

You can now repeat the four steps above to move shipped records from Orders to OrdHst. Briefly, these steps are as follows:

1. Clear the Desktop.

2. Run the query shown in Figure 18.12 to copy shipped orders to the Answer table (we've named the query *PostOrd*). Note that all fields are checked in the Orders table.

3. Choose File ➤ Utilities ➤ Add, select *:PRIV:ANSWER.DB* as the source table and *ORDHST.DB* as the target table, click Append in the Options area of the Add dialog box, and click OK.

4. Clear the Desktop, then run the query shown in Figure 18.13 to remove the posted records from the Orders table (this query is named *ClrOrd*).

FIGURE 18.11

The ClrLine query
removes the posted
records from the Line
Item table and prevents
records from being
posted more than once.

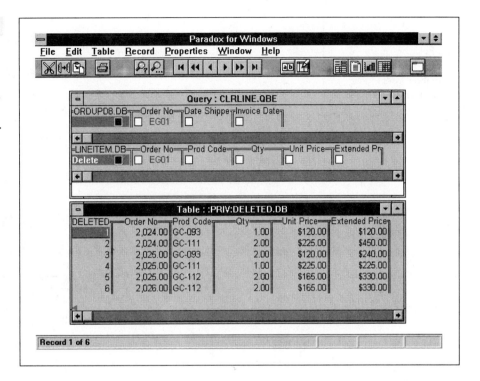

The final step is to clear out the OrdUpd8 transaction file. Choose File ➤ Utilities ➤ Empty, select *ORDUPD8.DB* as the table to empty, click the OK button, and choose Yes.

If you were to peruse the Orders, OrdHst, LineItem, LineHst, and Ord-Upd8 tables now, you would find that the OrdHst and LineHst tables contain the posted records that were in the Orders and LineItem tables, the Orders and LineItem tables no longer contain the posted records, and the OrdUpd8 table is empty.

Assuming you saved all the queries required to post records and remove posted records, you need only run those queries and choose the appropriate File ➤ Utilities options when you want to repeat the updates in the future.

FIGURE 18.12

The PostOrd query copies shipped records from the Orders table to the Answer table.

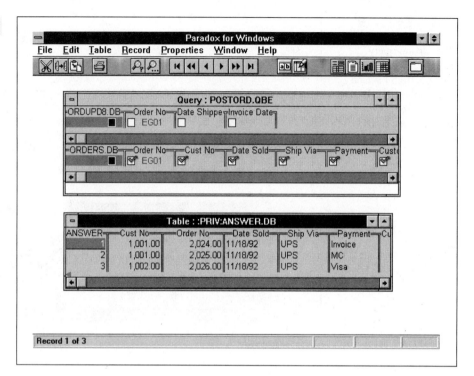

Automating Your Work

As you've seen, automatic updating procedures can involve quite a few steps, and it's very important to perform those steps in the proper sequence. Saved queries will certainly help avoid unnecessary delays and improve the accuracy of your updates. However, if you want to automate the steps fully, so that you can perform them with just the click of a button or a few selections from a menu, you'll need to learn ObjectPAL, the Paradox for Windows programming language. We'll introduce that topic in Chapter 19.

FIGURE 18.13

The ClrOrd query
removes the posted
records from the
Orders table.

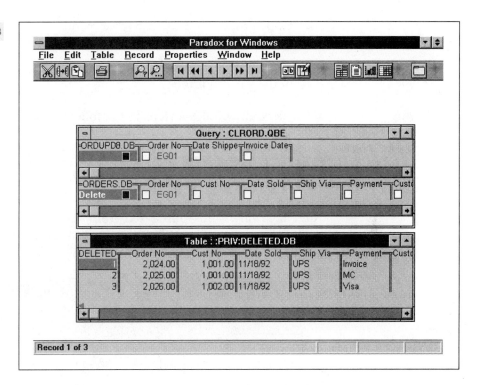

FIGURE 18.13

The ClrOrd query removes the posted records from the Orders table.

Completing the Purchasing Cycle

Now let's take a closer look at the purchasing cycle that updates the Products table with records in the Purchase table. Recall from Figure 18.2 that this cycle involves four main steps:

1. Enter received items into the Purchase table.

2. Update the In Stock, On Order, and Unit Price fields in the Products table with data from the Purchase table.

3. Copy processed Purchase table records to a history table named *PurHst*, and then empty the Purchase table.

4. Print a reorder report to determine which items need replenishing in the stockroom.

We'll elaborate on these steps in the following sections.

Entering Received Items into the Purchase Table

After receiving items purchased from vendors into the stockroom, we enter information about those items into the Purchase table, as shown below.

Table : PURCHASE.DB				
PURCHASE	Prod Code	Qty Recd	Purchase Price	Date Recd
1	GC-093	5	$115.00	11/19/92
2	GC-093	2	$120.00	11/23/92
3	GC-111	3	$225.00	11/19/92
4	GC-111	1	$225.00	11/20/92
5	GC-112	3	$150.00	11/20/92
6	GC-112	2	$165.00	11/23/92

Creating a History Table for Posted Purchases

You'll need a history table to store posted purchase transactions, so follow the steps you used to create the OrdHst and LineHst tables, as explained below.

1. Choose File ➤ New ➤ Table and choose OK.

2. In the **Create Table** dialog box, click Borrow, select *PURCHASE.DB*, and choose OK.

3. Click the Save As button, type **PURHST.DB**, and choose OK.

Let's assume that the Products, Purchase, and PurHst tables contain the data shown in Figure 18.14. Note that the PurHst table is currently empty and we've shown only the relevant records in the Products table.

TIP

It's always a good idea to use "dummy" data, as we're doing in this chapter, to develop and test updating procedures.

FIGURE 18.14

Sample data in the Products, Purchase, and (currently empty) PurHst tables

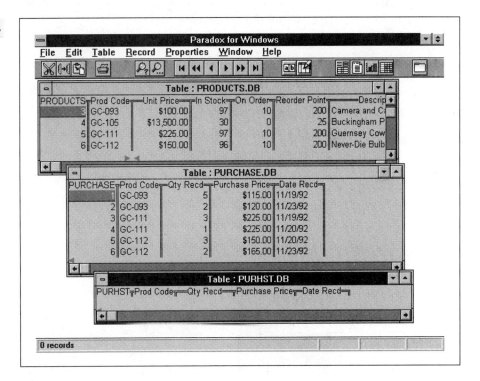

Adding Received Items to In-Stock Quantities

Now we're ready to update the master inventory in the Products table with quantities and prices from the Purchase table. We'll need to make the following adjustments:

• Add the quantities of products received to In Stock quantities in the Products table.

• Subtract the quantities of products received from the On Order quantities in the Products table.

• Change the Unit Price field in Products to the highest purchase price in the Purchase table.

• Copy all posted purchase transactions from the Purchase table to the PurHst table.

• Empty the Purchase table.

The procedure is essentially the same as updating Products from the LineItem table, but we've added some new twists to demonstrate additional updating techniques.

To begin, clear the Desktop (choose <u>W</u>indows ➤ Close <u>A</u>ll), then set up and run the query shown at the top of Figure 18.15 (we've named the query *CalcPurc*). Notice that the Prod Code field is checked, *Calc Sum* sums the Qty Recd in a new field named *Qty*, and *Calc Max* calculates the highest Purchase Price in a new field named *Cost*. The resulting Answer table appears at the bottom of the figure.

NOTE

The scheme for updating purchase prices for inventory in "real world" situations can become very complex, and many different techniques are used in business. However, to keep things simple in our examples, we've chosen to update the Unit Price field of the Products table with the maximum purchase price calculated for each corresponding product code in the Purchase table.

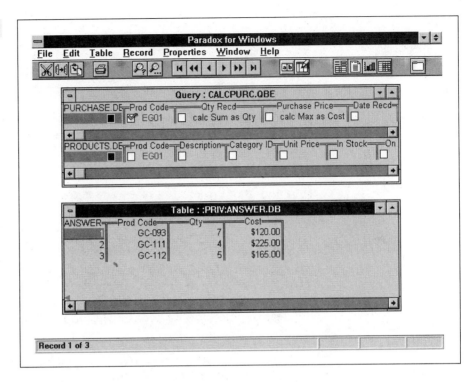

FIGURE 18.15

The CalcPurc query calculates the total quantity of each item received in the Purchase table and the highest purchase price of each product.

Now that you've calculated the total quantity received and the cost of each item, you can use the fields in the Answer table to update the Products table. Clear the Desktop and run the query shown in Figure 18.16 (we've named the query *Upd8Stoc*). Notice that the example element **EG01** links the Answer and Products tables. The other example elements in the Query window—**Cost**, **Qty**, **X**, and **Y**—are used to perform the calculations and updates to the Products table fields. After you run the query, the Changed table appears as usual.

NOTE

We rotated and narrowed the query table columns in Figure 18.16 to fit everything on the screen. Be sure to place the example elements and CHANGETO commands in the correct columns.

FIGURE 18.16

The Upd8Stoc query updates the Products Table with fields from the Answer Table.

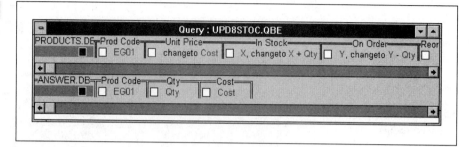

Moving Posted Purchases to the History Table

Now that you've updated the Products table, you must move all the updated records from the Purchase table to the PurHst table, so they won't be posted in future updates. Here are the steps:

1. Clear the Desktop by choosing Windows ➤ Close All.

2. Choose File ➤ Utilities ➤ Add, select *PURCHASE.DB* as the source table, select *PURHST.DB* as the target table, click Append in the Options area of the Add dialog box, and then click OK to add the records from the Purchase table to the PurHst table.

3. Choose File ➤ Utilities ➤ Empty, select *PURCHASE.DB*, click the OK button, and choose Yes to empty the Purchase table.

If you were to peruse the Products, PurHst, and Purchase tables now, you'd notice the following:

- The In Stock, On Order, and Unit Price fields in Products have been updated according to values in the original Purchase table.

- The PurHst table contains the posted records from the Purchase table.

- The Purchase table is empty.

Figure 18.17 shows a portion of each of these tables on the Desktop.

FIGURE 18.17

Portions of the
Products, PurHst, and
Purchase tables on
the Desktop after
performing the
update

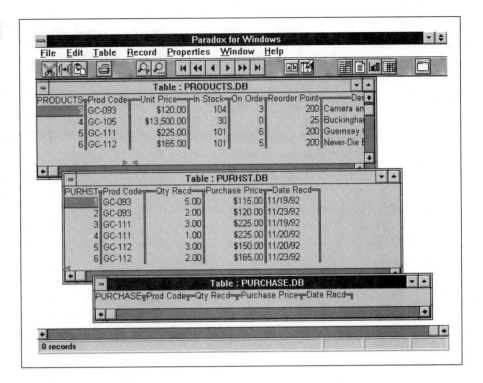

Printing a Reorder Report

After all this automatic updating, it might be nice to know which items
need to be reordered. A query that isolates records in which the in-stock
plus on-order quantities fall below the reorder point will do the trick. The
ReOrder example in Figure 18.18 illustrates this procedure. Notice that
InStock and **OnOrd** are example elements used in the calculations. After
running the query, you can use techniques discussed in Chapters 9 and
11 to design and print an attractive reorder report based on the Answer
table.

N O T E   The reorder query will produce an empty Answer table
if no products fall below the reorder point.

FIGURE 18.18

The ReOrder query selects records in which product quantities have fallen below the reorder point.

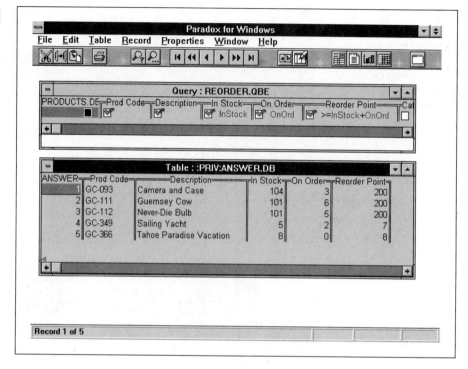

The purchasing cycle is now complete. As you begin to design and develop sophisticated database applications of your own, you'll find that you can use the techniques presented in this chapter to combine and update data among multiple related tables in any manner you wish. And after you've learned how to use ObjectPAL, you'll be able to reduce the whole procedure to a few simple mouse clicks or menu selections.

Correcting Updated Transactions

One problem always arises when you use automatic updating to change the contents of one table based on the contents of another table: If you discover an error in one of the transactions *after* the update, how do you fix it?

For instance, suppose you discover an error in the quantity ordered for a customer's order *after* performing the updates to the Products table and moving the original Orders and LineItem records to history files.

If you correct the problem in the OrdHst and LineHst tables directly, there's no way for Paradox to know that the correction should be reflected in the Products table. If you corrected the Products table manually as well, that would be OK. However, there would be no "audit trail" indicating that the changes were made to any tables.

The best way to correct an error after updating records is to add an *adjustment transaction* to the original tables. For instance, in Figure 18.19 we used a multitable form to make an adjustment transaction showing the return of two Never-Die Bulbs (at $165.00 a pop they shouldn't be faulty, but apparently a few duds slipped through).

FIGURE 18.19

An adjustment transaction on a custom form. The -2 indicates that two items were returned, and the Terms and Pay Via fields briefly explain the negative Qty value.

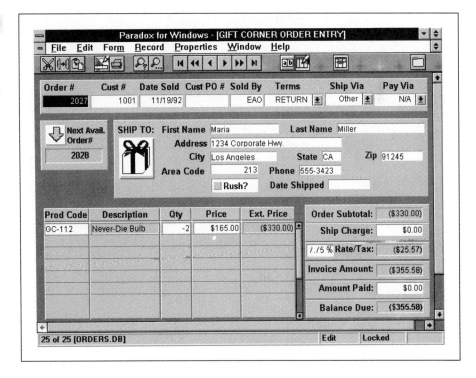

During automatic updating, this adjustment record will be processed just like any other. That is, its Qty field will be subtracted from the In Stock field of the Products table. However, given that Qty is a negative number, the net result will be to *add* the value of 2 to the In Stock quantity. Furthermore, the record will be copied to the OrdHst and LineItem tables, just like any other record, so there's a permanent history of the transaction on disk.

In this chapter, we've explored techniques for automatically updating tables and for keeping track of records that have been posted. In Chapter 19 we'll introduce you to ObjectPAL, the Paradox for Windows programming language, which enables you to automate your forms into full-fledged applications.

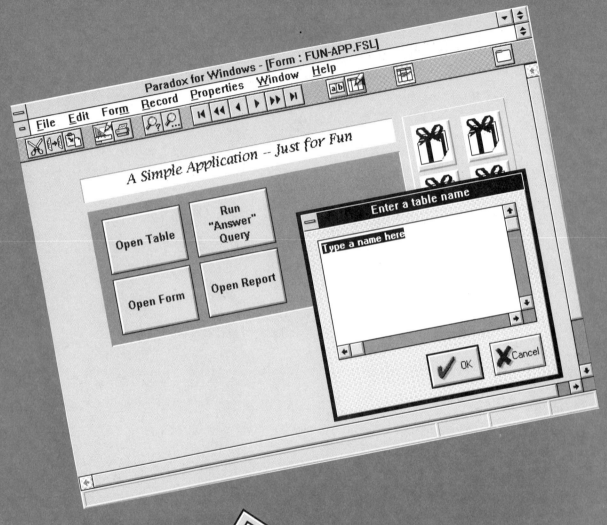

Paradox for Windows - [Form : FUN-APP.FSL]

File   Edit   Form   Record   Properties   Window   Help

A Simple Application -- Just for Fun

| Open Table | Run "Answer" Query |
| Open Form | Open Report |

Enter a table name

Type a name here

OK   Cancel

CHAPTER

19

Automating Your Work with ObjectPAL

f a s t **TRACK**

Help window) or click on any underlined Help topic. You can also copy sample code from the Example section of any Help window into the method you're entering.

To copy sample code from a Help window into your method   **981**

choose Edit ➤ Copy from the ObjectPAL Help menus. Use your mouse to select the block of code you want, click the Copy button, and then close the Help window. Switch to the ObjectPAL Editor window, place the insertion point where you want the sample code to appear, and press Shift+Ins. Revise the pasted code as necessary.

To begin testing a method   **983**

click the View Data button in the SpeedBar of the Form Design window or press F8. The remaining steps depend on the type of object you attached the method to and the event that triggers the method. In general, you can test the method by performing whatever action triggers it. For example, to test a method attached to a button, click the button.

This chapter describes a "starter set"   **990**

of ObjectPAL statements. To work with tables, forms, and queries, use the *Open*, *SetTitle*, *Maximize*, *Edit*, *Wait*, and *Close* statements. To run a saved query, use the *ExecuteQBEFile* statement. To display messages to users, use the *MsgInfo* and *MsgQuestion* statements. To get user input, use the *View* statement. To exit Paradox for Windows, use the *Exit* statement.

OBJECTPAL is a full-featured, visual programming language that you can use to automate your work and build sophisticated Paradox for Windows applications. The language provides hundreds of tools for automating *anything* that can be done in Paradox for Windows—and more.

Not surprisingly, a comprehensive explanation of ObjectPAL would require a hefty book at least as large as the one you're reading now and an equally hefty wheelbarrow to cart it around in. So instead of presenting an exhaustive (and exhausting) catalog of ObjectPAL features and syntax rules, we'll focus on the highlights of the language and take you through some practical examples that automate tasks discussed in previous chapters of this book. Once you've studied these examples, you should feel comfortable using *Learning ObjectPAL*, the *ObjectPAL Developer's Guide*, and the *ObjectPAL Reference* that come with Paradox for Windows to help you learn more about ObjectPAL programming.

N O T E

Learning ObjectPAL presents some tutorial examples to introduce the fundamentals of ObjectPAL programming. The *ObjectPAL Developer's Guide* covers the fundamental concepts of ObjectPAL programming and provides many examples. In the *ObjectPAL Reference*, you'll find two volumes of detailed reference material about each built-in method and each language statement available in ObjectPAL.

You certainly don't have to be a programming guru to reap the benefits of ObjectPAL or to understand the material presented in this chapter.

However, we do assume that you are familiar with basic programming concepts and that you know how to design custom forms using the techniques presented in Chapters 9 and 10 of this book.

Understanding ObjectPAL Terminology

Before jumping into our examples, we must first introduce some essential ObjectPAL terminology, including the terms *object*, *event*, *method*, and *application*.

What Is an Object?

As you learned in Chapter 1, just about anything you can create in Paradox for Windows is an *object*. For example, buttons, fields, graphics, tables, queries, forms, and reports are all objects.

Every Paradox object consists of *properties* (such as color, position, font, and frame style) and *methods* (code that defines how the object behaves). The specific properties and methods available depend on the type of the object. For example, the properties and methods available for buttons are different from those available for table frames. (Please see Chapters 9 through 11 and Appendix D for more information on properties.)

What Is an Event?

An *event* is an action that affects an object. Anything you do in Paradox for Windows can generate an event. Common types of events include

* Pressing a key or clicking the mouse.
* Opening or closing a form, report, or table.

- Changing a value in a field.
- Adding a record to a table.
- Clicking a button.
- Choosing an option from a menu.

What Is a Method?

A *method* is a snippet of ObjectPAL code that defines how an *object* responds to an *event*. Methods are activated (or *triggered*) when specific events occur. For example, the following method maximizes a window on the Desktop when the user arrives in a form:

```
method arrive(var eventInfo MoveEvent)
    maximize()
endmethod
```

Later in this chapter we'll explain each component of a method. For now, however, we just want to give you an idea of what a simple method looks like.

N O T E

A method in ObjectPAL is similar to a subroutine in a traditional programming language. When a subroutine finishes executing, control normally returns to the calling program. Likewise, when a method finishes executing, control normally returns to the form.

Methods are typically attached to objects in forms (see Chapters 9 and 10), but they can also be stored in stand-alone files called *scripts* and in collections of ObjectPAL code called *libraries*. In this chapter, we'll concentrate on methods attached to objects in forms.

What Is an Application?

An *application* is a system that automates database management tasks. Often, applications perform useful business functions, such as processing accounts receivable, fulfilling customer orders, and checking purchases into the stockroom. Most ObjectPAL applications are built from customized forms that contain buttons to which ObjectPAL methods are attached. The examples in this chapter include an automated order-entry form and a form that automates the order-processing and purchasing cycles discussed in Chapter 18. You'll find other sample applications in the directory *\pdoxwin\examples*, which is created automatically when you install Paradox for Windows. These samples are documented in the *ObjectPAL Developer's Guide*.

Objects Are "Smart" Things

When you were learning to design forms, you probably discovered that objects "know" about the objects inside them. What's more, you probably noticed that the same types of objects always have the same properties and methods available to them—they even tend to look alike and behave similarly. Thus, a form "knows" about the tables and fields in its data model, and all buttons in a form have the same general appearance and give basically the same response when you click them. For these reasons, we say that Paradox objects are "smart."

How ObjectPAL Differs from Traditional Programming Languages

If you've ever developed an application in a traditional programming language, such as BASIC, FORTRAN, Pascal, or C, you know that the process can be time consuming and frustrating, since you must write and debug program code for *every* action performed by the application.

When you use Paradox for Windows, however, a large part of your programming is done *automatically* (and correctly!) whenever you place objects on a form and set properties for those objects (see Chapters 9 and 10). Why? Because the standard behavior of each object on the form is defined automatically. ObjectPAL is needed only if you want to automate a series of steps, change the built-in behavior of an object, or exercise greater control over what the user sees and does. For example, you could use ObjectPAL to prompt for the name of a table or form to open; to automate the many steps required to update inventory and history files; or to calculate an Extended Price field automatically.

To speed the development process further and reduce the amount of programming you must do, ObjectPAL features many built-in methods. It also includes an extensive online Help system with lots of sample code that you can paste in and revise as needed.

Before setting out to develop a substantial application with ObjectPAL, you should understand basic programming techniques, and you should be comfortable using most of the Paradox features discussed in this book. If that sounds like a tall order, keep in mind that you may *never* need to write an iota of ObjectPAL code. Although ObjectPAL is a tremendously valuable tool for automating and simplifying your work, the standard Paradox for Windows features and some custom forms and reports may provide all the power you need.

Our advice is to begin by creating short and simple ObjectPAL methods like the ones presented in this chapter. Then, study the sample applications in the *c:\pdoxwin\examples* directory. As you gain experience, you can experiment with increasingly sophisticated ObjectPAL features and develop fancier applications.

Attaching a Method to an Object

Typically, you'll attach ObjectPAL methods to a button, a field, a page of a form, or to the form itself. To begin attaching a method, inspect (right-click) the object in the Form Design window and choose Methods, or select the object and press Ctrl+spacebar. Figure 19.1 shows the **Methods** dialog box, which appears when you inspect a button and choose Methods. In the figure, we've selected the *pushButton* method. This method is triggered when the user pushes (clicks) the button to which the method is attached.

FIGURE 19.1

The Methods dialog box appears after you inspect an object in the Form Design window and choose Methods.

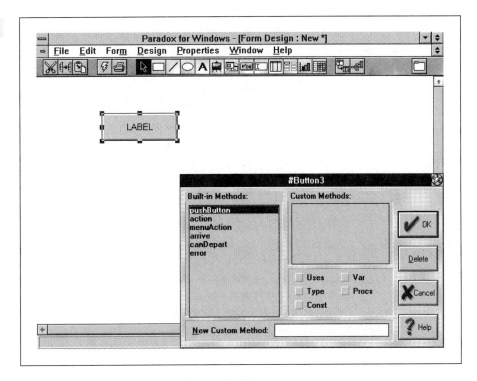

The most important areas of the Methods dialog box are explained below.

- The title bar displays the name of the object to which you're attaching the method.

- The left side of the dialog box presents a list of built-in methods provided by ObjectPAL. The name of the method reflects the type of event that triggers it. We'll focus on these built-in methods in this chapter. (You can also design custom methods, which will appear in the Custom Methods list of the dialog box.)

- The OK button accepts your selections and opens one or more ObjectPAL Editor windows.

- The Delete button allows you to delete a previously attached method.

- The Cancel button cancels your selections and returns you to the Form Design window.

- The Help button displays help information about the Methods dialog box and provides an entry into the ObjectPAL online help system described later in this chapter.

- The snap button allows you to keep the Methods dialog box on the screen as you select objects in the Form Design window or Object Tree. Each time you select an object, the Methods dialog box will change to reflect the methods available for that object.

The built-in methods displayed in the dialog box depend on the object you've inspected and the settings you've chosen in the Desktop ➤ Properties dialog box. The default Desktop ➤ Properties setting is Beginner, which provides a "starter set" of methods. If you choose Desktop ➤ Properties ➤ Advanced, more built-in methods will be available. When you're first learning ObjectPAL, it's best to stick with the default setting of Beginner to avoid confusion. You can change the Desktop ➤ Properties settings from any Paradox for Windows menu (see Chapter 3). Table 19.1 briefly describes the "beginner-level" built-in methods available.

TABLE 19.1: Some "Beginner-Level" Built-in Methods

METHOD	WHEN CALLED
action★	Called when an action takes place (e.g., the cursor is moved to another field in a table) or when a method wants some action performed (e.g., switch to Edit mode).
arrive★	Called after moving to (arriving at) an object such as a form, form page, field, table frame, or multi-record object.
canDepart	Called when trying to move off a field or record.
changeValue★	Called when a new value is about to be stored. (Available for fields only.)
error	Called when an error occurs. Objects (except the form itself) pass errors to their containers.

TABLE 19.1: Some "Beginner-Level" Built-in Methods (continued)

METHOD	WHEN CALLED
menuAction	Called when the user chooses an item from a menu or clicks a SpeedBar button that executes a menu action.
mouseClick	Called when the left mouse button is clicked on the object.
*pushButton**	Called when a user clicks on a button. (Available for buttons and fields defined as list boxes only.)

* Illustrated in this chapter

To select a method from the Built-in Methods list, click it and choose OK, or simply double-click the method. To select several adjacent methods, hold down the Shift key while clicking the method names, then choose OK. To select several non-adjacent methods, hold down the Ctrl key while clicking the method names, and choose OK.

An ObjectPAL Editor window will open for each method you selected. Figure 19.2 shows the ObjectPAL Editor window that appears after selecting the *pushbutton* method from the Methods dialog box. Paradox generates the *method* and *endmethod* statements automatically to define the method name and its parameters and to end the method you selected. These statements are required and you shouldn't need to change them.

The *method* statement specifies the method name (for example, *pushbutton*), and defines the information being passed to the method within parentheses. Every built-in method has the following information passed to it: the word *var* (which introduces a parameter), the parameter *eventInfo* (which provides information about the event that triggered the method), and the parameter's data type (e.g., *Event, MoveEvent*). The data type will depend on the method you selected and determines which methods you can use with *eventInfo* to get and/or store information about the event.

FIGURE 19.2

The ObjectPAL Editor window after selecting the pushButton method from the Methods dialog box

WARNING

For the simple tasks discussed in this chapter, you needn't concern yourself with the parameters in the *method* statement. Just be sure that you leave the *method* and *endmethod* statements unchanged when editing a built-in method.

The status bar indicates the current position of the insertion point (it's in column 1 of line 2 in the example). You should enter the program code after the *method* statement and before the *endmethod* statement (that is, between the method and endmethod statements).

NOTE ObjectPAL is not case-sensitive. Therefore, statements and variable names can be typed in uppercase, lowercase, or a mixture of upper- and lowercase letters.

The ObjectPAL Editor menu bar includes the File, Edit, Properties, Window, and Help menus common to all Paradox windows, plus the Language and Debug menus, which are unique to the ObjectPAL Editor window. Several ObjectPAL Editor menu options are discussed in this chapter. For additional information on the menu options, highlight the option you're interested in and press F1, or refer to the *ObjectPAL Developer's Guide*.

The general steps for writing and testing a method are listed below and explained in more detail in the sections that follow.

1. Enter the ObjectPAL code for the method into the ObjectPAL Editor window.

2. Check the syntax of the method and make any necessary corrections.

3. Save the method.

4. Test the method.

5. Change or delete the method if necessary.

Entering ObjectPAL Code

After opening the ObjectPAL Editor window, the simplest way to enter program code is to type it. For instance, you could type **maximize( )** on line 2 of the Editor window shown in Figure 19.2. (The maximize statement will cause the form to maximize when the button is clicked in Form View.) Later in this chapter, you'll see many more examples of program code entered in the ObjectPAL Editor window.

As in any Windows editor, you can use the ←, →, Home, and End keys or the mouse to position the insertion point for typing. You can also use the editing techniques summarized below.

- To select text, drag the mouse across the text or hold down the Shift key while pressing a cursor-positioning key such as ← or →. To select a word, double-click the word. To select an entire line, move the mouse pointer to the left edge of the line (the pointer will change from an I-beam to an arrow) and click.

- To delete text, use the Backspace or Delete key.

- To undo a change, choose Edit ➤ Undo or press Alt+Backspace.

TIP

You may wish to maximize the Editor window by double-clicking the title bar or clicking the Maximize button. This allows you to see more of the program code at once. You can also use options from the Window menu to rearrange windows on the screen and temporarily switch back to the Form Design window.

Saving Time when Entering ObjectPAL Code

Rather than typing ObjectPAL code in the ObjectPAL Editor window, you can use any of several shortcuts to enter program code. For example, to copy ObjectPAL code from another method, proceed as follows:

1. Open the ObjectPAL Editor window for the object where you want the new code to appear, as described earlier.

2. Switch to the Form Design window for the form that contains the ObjectPAL code you wish to copy, inspect the object you want to copy from, choose Methods, and double-click the name of the method you want to copy. (Methods that have code assigned to them will be marked with an asterisk (*) in the Methods dialog box.)

3. When the ObjectPAL Editor window appears, select the code you want to copy, press Ctrl+Ins, and close the Editor window (press Ctrl+F4).

4. Switch to the ObjectPAL Editor window for the method you're copying to. Now, position the insertion point where the new code should appear and press Shift+Ins.

You can also paste code from a saved text file (.*txt*) or query (.*qbe*). To do so, position the insertion point where you want the text or query to appear, then choose Edit ➤ Paste From File. In the **Paste From File** dialog box (shown below), type the complete file or query name or use the Browse button to locate the file or query (see Chapter 14). Choose OK.

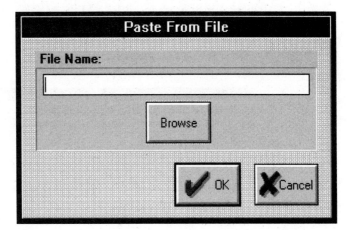

NOTE   To copy code from your method to a text file, select the code you want to copy, choose Edit ➤ Copy To File, then type a file name and extension. (It's a good idea to give the file a .*txt* extension.)

One of the handiest shortcuts—copying examples from the ObjectPAL online help system—is covered in the next section.

Using the ObjectPAL Help System

ObjectPAL's online help system provides the quickest, most efficient way to get up-to-speed with the language. In addition to providing detailed information about each language feature, ObjectPAL's online help also includes hundreds of program samples that you can paste into your own methods and then revise as needed.

To use the ObjectPAL online Help, open the Form Design or ObjectPAL Editor window, then choose Help ➤ ObjectPAL. You'll see the Contents page shown in Figure 19.3.

FIGURE 19.3

The ObjectPAL Contents page

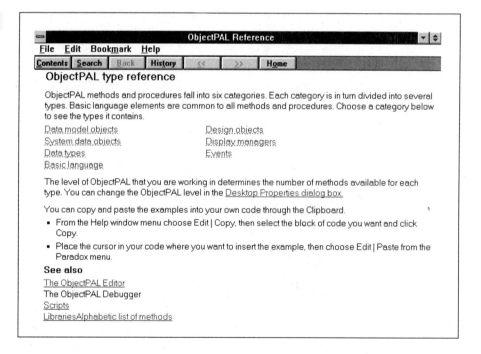

You can also reach the Contents page by clicking the Help button in the Methods dialog box and then clicking the Contents button.

From the ObjectPAL Contents page, you can click on any underlined topic to get more information about essential features of the language. If you want to search for help on a particular method or procedure, click the Search button in any Help window, or click on the *Alphabetic List of Methods* topic in the Contents page. To return from any ObjectPAL Help screen to the ObjectPAL Contents page, click the Contents button. (To return to the standard Paradox for Windows Contents page, click the Home button instead.) Other buttons and features in the ObjectPAL Help system are the same as those used in the standard Paradox for Windows Help system discussed in Chapter 3.

Figure 19.4 illustrates a sample Help topic describing the ObjectPAL statement used to maximize a Form object. To display this topic, we clicked *Alphabetic List of Methods* in the ObjectPAL Contents page, then we clicked the *Maximize* topic in the next list that appeared. Finally, we clicked *Form* in the last list that appeared.

Like the Maximize topic shown in Figure 19.4, most ObjectPAL Help topics are divided into several sections, including an "Example" section that contains sample code and a "See Also" section listing related topics that you can click on for more information. (The "See Also" section follows the "Example" section and is not shown in Figure 19.4.)

To copy sample code from the Example section of a Help topic into your ObjectPAL method, follow these steps:

1. Choose Edit ➤ Copy from the ObjectPAL Help menus. A **Copy** dialog box containing the Help text will open.

2. Use your mouse to select the block of code you want, click the Copy button, and close the Help window.

3. Switch to the ObjectPAL Editor window and place the insertion point where you want the sample code to appear.

4. To paste the code from the Clipboard, press Shift+Ins, click the Paste From Clipboard button in the SpeedBar, or choose Edit ➤ Paste.

5. Revise the pasted code as necessary.

FIGURE 19.4

The Maximize
Help topic

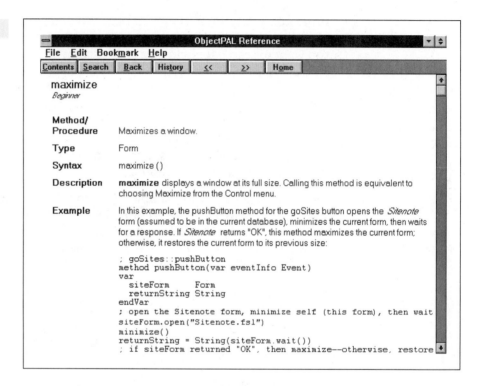

```
; goSites::pushButton
method pushButton(var eventInfo Event)
var
    siteForm      Form
    returnString String
endVar
; open the Sitenote form, minimize self (this form), then wait
siteForm.open("Sitenote.fsl")
minimize()
returnString = String(siteForm.wait())
; if siteForm returned "OK", then maximize--otherwise, restore
```

Checking the Syntax

After you're finished typing the code for your method, you should check the syntax to be certain that you haven't violated any rules of the ObjectPAL language. To check the syntax, click the Check Syntax button (shown at left), or choose Language ➤ Check Syntax. If all the syntax is correct, the status bar will display the message "No syntax errors." However, if ObjectPAL finds a syntax error, it positions the insertion point near the error in the ObjectPAL Editor window and displays an error message in the status bar. You should then correct the error.

> **WARNING** Even if your method is free of syntax errors, it may contain other types of errors (called *runtime* or *logic* errors). These won't be evident until you test the method.

Saving the Method

 After checking the syntax and correcting any syntax errors, you're ready to save the method and exit the ObjectPAL Editor window. To do so, click the Save Source And Exit The Editor button in the SpeedBar (shown at left), choose File ➤ Save, or simply close the window and choose Yes when asked if you want to save the code. Your method will be saved with the object to which it is attached, and you'll be returned to the Form Design window.

Testing the Method

After checking the syntax and saving the method, you should test it in Form View. That is, click the View Data button in the SpeedBar of the Form Design window or press F8. If the form wasn't compiled previously (that is, you didn't check the syntax first), Paradox will compile it and report any errors that occur. You must correct all syntax errors before you can use the form.

After opening the form in Form View, the actual steps for testing the method depend on the type of object you attached the method to and the event that triggers the method. In general, you can test the method by performing whatever action triggers it.

Suppose you attached the *arrive* built-in method containing the maximize statement shown below to the *page* of a form. (You may recall from "What Is an Object," above, that this method maximizes a window on the Desktop.)

```
method arrive(var eventInfo MoveEvent)
    maximize()
endmethod
```

To test this method, simply open the form (in Form View) and the form will be maximized automatically.

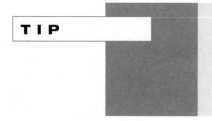

TIP To attach a method to the page of a form, click on an empty area of the page in the Form Design window and press Ctrl+spacebar. To attach a method to the form itself, press Esc until no objects are selected, then press Ctrl+spacebar.

By contrast, if you attached the *pushButton* built-in method shown below to a *button*, the form would be maximized only when you click the button in the Form window.

```
method pushButton(var eventInfo Event)
    maximize()
endmethod
```

Changing and Deleting a Method

After you define and save a method for an object, the method name will be marked with an asterisk (*) in the Methods dialog box. Changing a method is a lot like creating it in the first place. Simply return to the Methods dialog box for the object and double-click the method you want to change. The ObjectPAL Editor window will appear and you can edit the code, check its syntax, and save it as described above.

To delete a method that's attached to an object, click on the method you want to delete in the Methods dialog box, click Delete, and choose Yes when asked to verify the deletion.

Note that deleting a *built-in* method erases the ObjectPAL code you entered for that method and removes the asterisk next to the method name in the Built-In Methods list; however, it does not remove the method name from the list. By contrast, deleting a custom method from the Custom Methods list removes both the ObjectPAL code and the method name.

TIP

The Object Tree provides a bird's eye view of all objects in the Form Design window. Objects that have methods attached to them will be underlined. To open the Object Tree, press Esc until no objects are selected, then click the Object Tree button in the SpeedBar (see Chapter 9). You can then open the Methods dialog box by inspecting an object in the Object Tree and choosing Methods, or by clicking on the object and pressing Ctrl+spacebar.

Now that you've seen the basic steps for attaching, editing, saving, changing, and deleting methods, let's look at some practical examples. Keep in mind that our goal here is to give you a feel for the ObjectPAL language—not to transform you instantly into an ObjectPAL expert. After trying out the examples presented in this chapter, you'll probably be ready to develop some simple applications on your own. At the very least, you'll appreciate how ObjectPAL can be used to streamline your day-to-day work with Paradox for Windows, and you'll feel comfortable using ObjectPAL's online help and the language reference manuals that come with Paradox for Windows.

Adding ObjectPAL Methods to an Order-Entry Form

In Chapter 17 we presented an order-entry form that updated the Extended Price field automatically whenever we changed the Qty or Unit Price field for a line item in an order. That form appears in Figure 19.5.

To have Paradox maximize the form automatically whenever it's opened, first open the form in the Form Design window, then right-click the page, choose Methods, and double-click *arrive*. When the ObjectPAL Editor window appears, type **maximize( )** on line 2, check the syntax, and save the method.

FIGURE 19.5

A sample order-entry form that updates the Extended Price field automatically

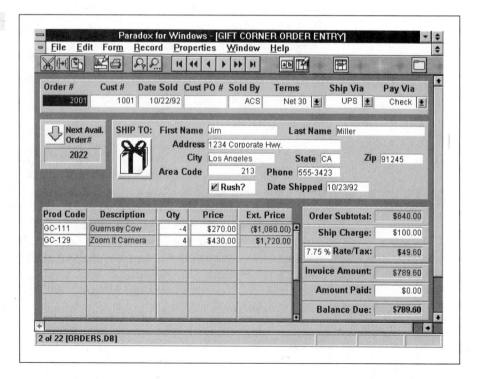

Next, attach the calculation method to the Qty field as follows:

1. Inspect the field, choose Methods, and double-click *changeValue* in the Methods dialog box. (The *changeValue* method will be triggered whenever you change the value in the field.)

2. When the ObjectPAL Editor window appears, type in the code shown between the *method* and *endmethod* statements below, check the syntax, and save the method. (An explanation of the code is given below.)

```
method changeValue(var eventInfo ValueEvent)
    action(DataPostRecord)          ; post current record
    Extended_Price = Qty * Unit_Price
endmethod
```

Repeat the two steps above for the Unit Price field.

NOTE   The semicolon in the example above introduces a comment, which is ignored by the compiler. We'll discuss comments later in this chapter.

To test the methods, click the View Data button in the SpeedBar of the Form Design window, change a value in the Qty field of the order form, and move the highlight to another field. (Moving the highlight lets Paradox know that you've finished changing the field, and activates the *changeValue* method.) The Extended Price field will be updated automatically. Repeat the test by changing a value in the Unit Price field and moving the highlight out of the field.

The statements in the *changeValue* method work as follows:

• The *action(DataPostRecord)* statement posts the current record so that the next calculation uses the most up-to-date values.

• The *Extended_Price = Qty * Unit_Price* calculation multiplies the value in the Qty field of the LineItem table by the Unit_Price field of the LineItem table and stores the result in the Extended_Price field of the LineItem table.

Note that in this example we're working with the Qty, Unit_Price, and Extended_Price field *objects* and the LineItem table *object*, not with the actual fields of the LineItem table. Although the field names were defined in the LineItem table as "Unit Price" and "Extended Price" (with a blank space between words), blanks and other punctuation are replaced by an underscore character (_) when objects are placed in the Form Design window.

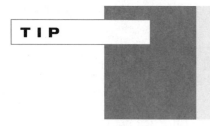

TIP The object *name* always appears in the status bar of the Form Design window when you click on the object. You can change the name of an object if you wish. Chapter 17 describes the differences between object names and objects and explains how to rename design objects.

Understanding Dot Notation

In the *changeValue* method shown above, we could have written the code a bit differently, like this:

```
method changeValue(var eventInfo ValueEvent)
    LineItem.action(DataPostRecord)    ; post current record
    LineItem.Extended_Price = LineItem.Qty * LineItem.Unit_Price
endmethod
```

The dot (.) notation is used throughout ObjectPAL to separate elements such as object names, variables, methods, and properties in a statement. For example, the first statement above means "In the LineItem table, post the current record." The second statement means "Multiply the LineItem table's Qty field by the LineItem table's Unit Price field and store the result in the LineItem table's Extended Price field."

NOTE Dot notation is also used in calculated fields and summary fields of forms and reports (see Chapter 17).

Earlier in this chapter, we explained that objects are "smart" things that know about the objects inside them. For example, the data model of the multitable order form in Figure 19.5 specifies three tables: Orders, Line-Item, and Products. Because the form "knows" about tables in its data model, we can omit the table name and dot when referring to fields in those tables in an ObjectPAL statement. However, if we were to attach another table that wasn't part of this form, we would need to tell ObjectPAL exactly which table we were referring to. (You'll find out how to attach tables later in this chapter.)

NOTE   The *data model* is a diagram of table relationships in the form. (See Chapter 9 and 17.)

Dot notation is also used to specify the hierarchy of objects. Suppose we designed a form in which a text object named "myText" is contained within a box object named "theBox." The statement *theBox.myText.text = "Hello there!"* would store *Hello there!* in the text object within the box. The *ObjectPAL Developer's Guide* discusses dot notation in more detail.

Using Comments, Blank Lines, and White Space

You may have noticed the semicolon (;) followed by text in the sample methods above. The semicolon introduces program comments in Object-PAL. You should make liberal use of comments to describe what's happening in a method and to make your programs more understandable. Contrary to popular folklore, comments *do not* slow down program execution.

Any text following a semicolon is considered to be a comment and is therefore ignored by ObjectPAL. If you begin a line with a semicolon, the whole line is treated as a comment. Note, however, that a semicolon within quotation marks is *not* treated as a comment. For example, the semicolon and following text are all part of the string assigned to *myText* in the statement *myText = "Brrrr; it's cold outside!"*.

If you want to create comments that occupy multiple lines, place a semicolon in front of each line of the comment. Alternatively, you can comment large blocks of text by placing a left brace ({) before the first comment line of the block and a right brace (}) after the last comment line of the block. The braces and all text between them will be treated as comments.

You can also use blank lines, blank spaces, and tabs to make your programs more readable. These elements are ignored, unless they appear in a quoted string. For example, the statement

```
msgInfo("Two Lines","This text
spans two lines.")
```

displays the dialog box shown below.

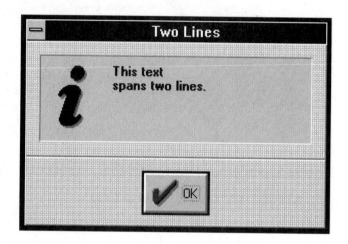

Creating an Application to Open Tables, Forms, Queries, and Reports

Now let's take a look at a complete (though simple) application. Figure 19.6 illustrates a form that lets us open tables, forms, and reports, or run queries simply by clicking a button. In the figure you can see what happened after we clicked the *Open Table* button.

FIGURE 19.6

A simple application after clicking the Open Table button. (After clicking the button, we moved the "Enter a table name" dialog box so that you could see all the buttons on the form.)

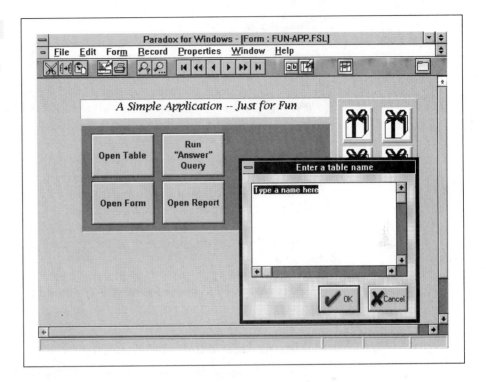

Here's how the application works:

1. When opened, the Form window maximizes automatically.

2. When we click one of the buttons, a dialog box requests the name of a table, form, query, or report (as appropriate). We then type the name of the desired object into the dialog box (with or without the file extension) and choose OK.

   • If the method fails to find the requested object, it displays an error message dialog box.

   • If the method finds the table, form, or report we requested, it opens the object on the Desktop. If the method finds the query we requested, it runs the query and opens the Answer table on the Desktop. All objects are maximized when opened.

TIP

You can use aliases when entering table, form, query, or report names into the dialog box. For example, to open a report named *areacode* that's stored in a directory with the alias name of *:Gift_Corner:*, simply click the Open Report button, type *:Gift_Corner:areacode* into the dialog box that appears, and choose OK.

3. To return to the application form shown in Figure 19.6, we simply close the Table, Form, or Report window by pressing Ctrl+F4 or double-clicking the Control-menu box.

The ObjectPAL techniques used to create the "action" in this form are listed below.

1. First we attached an *arrive* method containing a *maximize( )* statement to the page of the form. This method maximizes the form whenever it is opened.

2. Next we created four buttons and edited the button labels.

3. Finally, we attached a *pushButton* method to each button. The code for each *pushButton* method is presented in the following sections.

TIP

To center a button label, inspect the button and choose Center Label. Chapters 9 and 10 explain how to create buttons and edit text objects such as button labels.

Defining the Open Table Button

The *pushButton* method shown in Figure 19.7 is considerably more complex than the methods you've seen so far. Let's break it down statement by statement.

FIGURE 19.7

The *pushButton* method for opening a table

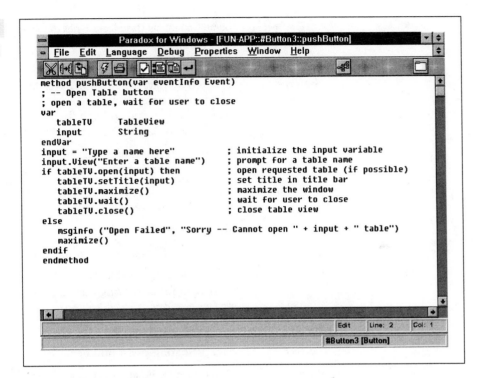

```
method pushButton(var eventInfo Event)
; -- Open Table button
; open a table, wait for user to close
var
    tableTV      TableView
    input        String
endVar
input = "Type a name here"        ; initialize the input variable
input.View("Enter a table name")  ; prompt for a table name
if tableTV.open(input) then       ; open requested table (if possible)
    tableTV.setTitle(input)       ; set title in title bar
    tableTV.maximize()            ; maximize the window
    tableTV.wait()                ; wait for user to close
    tableTV.close()               ; close table view
else
    msginfo ("Open Failed", "Sorry -- Cannot open " + input + " table")
    maximize()
endif
endmethod
```

Defining Variables

A variable is like a pigeonhole in which you can temporarily store an item of information. Before storing a value in a variable, you should declare the variable and define its data type using the *Var...EndVar* statement (see Figure 19.7). Although you are not required to declare variables explicitly, doing so allows the compiler to catch typing mistakes and inconsistent usage, speeds up program execution, and makes your program more readable.

Table 19.2 lists some commonly used ObjectPAL data types. For details about all ObjectPAL data types, please refer to the *ObjectPAL Developer's Guide*. Or, choose Help ➤ ObjectPAL and click one of the following object categories: *Data Types, Data Model Objects, System Data Objects, Design Objects, Display Managers,* or *Events.* Then, click the data type you're interested in.

TABLE 19.2:   Some Commonly Used Data Types in ObjectPAL

DATA TYPE	DESCRIPTION
AnyType	A catch-all data type that behaves like a string when assigned a string value, like a number when assigned a number value, and so forth. It cannot be used to store complex objects such as a *TCursor* (see below).
Currency	Stores currency values ranging from $3.4 \star 10^{-4930}$ to $1.1 \star 10^{4930}$, scaled to six decimal places.
Date	Stores date values ranging from January 1, 100 to December 31, 9999.
Form	Refers to the file containing a form.
Graphic	Allows you to manipulate graphic objects.
Logical	Stores the logical value *True* or *False*. Logical variables are useful for answering questions about other objects and operations.
Memo	Stores memo data.
Number	Stores floating-point numbers.
Report	Refers to the file containing a report.
String	Stores up to 32,000 characters. A quoted string can contain up to 255 characters.
Table	Refers to the file containing a table.
TableView	Refers to the data in a Table View window.
TCursor	Points to the data in a table. *TCursor* variables allow you to manipulate data at the table level, record level, and field level without having to display the table.
Time	Stores time data.
UIObject	Includes all the objects you can place on a form. Only UIObjects have built-in methods, have code attached to them, and can respond to events.

Getting User Input

You can use the *View* statement to display a prompt in a dialog box and store the user's response in a variable, as shown below:

```
input = "Type a name here"
input.View("Enter a table name")
```

The first statement above sets the value of the *input* variable to "Type a name here". The *View* statement displays the value of *input* in a dialog box with the title "Enter a table name." Any text typed into the dialog box will replace the current value of the *input* variable.

Making Decisions

IF statements are used to make decisions in an ObjectPAL method. They work just like the IF statements found in most other programming languages. For instance, the *If...Then...Else...EndIf* statement shown in Figure 19.7 behaves as follows:

1. The *Open* statement following the IF keyword tries to open the table specified by the *input* variable.

2. If the Open statement succeeds, the If condition is "True" and the four statements above the ELSE keyword are executed. First the *SetTitle* statement places the value of the *input* variable in the title bar of the Table View window (that is, whatever the user typed into the dialog box appears in the title bar). Next, the *Maximize* statement maximizes the Table View window, the *Wait* statement waits for the user to close the Table View window by double-clicking the Control-menu box or pressing Ctrl+F4, and the *Close* statement closes the Table View window. Notice that the *Open*, *SetTitle*, *Maximize*, *Wait*, and *Close* statements all use the Table-View variable named *tableTV* to access the Table View object.

3. If the Open statement fails (because the table doesn't exist, for instance), the two statements following the ELSE keyword display an error message (via *MsgInfo*) and maximize the Form window (via *Maximize*).

T I P

As an alternative to using a variable name in the Open statement, you can place the name of the object you want to open between double quotation marks, as in *tableTV.open("OrdUpd8.db")*.

Displaying a Message

ObjectPAL offers several ways to display messages to the user. For example, the *MsgInfo* statement in Figure 19.7 displays a dialog box containing an "i" icon, a title bar, a message, and an OK button. The first argument displays a message in the title bar, and the second argument displays a message in the dialog box itself. For example, if we had typed **ork** into the dialog box shown in Figure 19.6, we'd see this dialog box:

Notice that we used the plus (+) string operator in the MsgInfo statement to connect (concatenate) the text strings shown in the error message box. (See Chapter 17 for more information on using this operator.)

Defining the Open Form Button

The method for the *Open Form* button appears in Figure 19.8. Notice that this method is almost the same as the *Open Table* method shown in Figure 19.7. In this example, we changed the name and data type of the variable used to access the form and altered the prompts and comments. Thus, the variable name is *formV* and its data type is *Form*.

Instead of typing all the statements, we simply pasted text from the Open Table button's ObjectPAL Editor window into the Editor window for the Open Form button. Then we modified the statements as needed. To speed up editing, we used Edit ➤ Replace to make changes globally (see Chapter 5 for information on using Search and Replace).

FIGURE 19.8

The method for the Open Form button is almost the same as the method for the Open Table button.

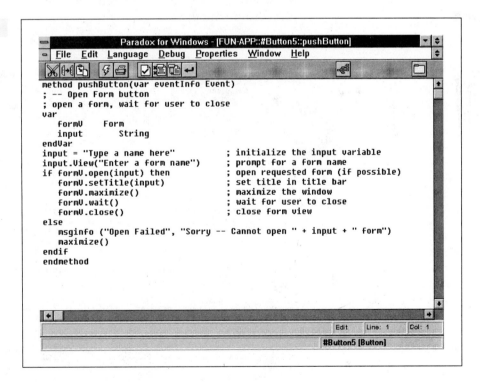

```
method pushButton(var eventInfo Event)
; -- Open Form button
; open a form, wait for user to close
var
    formV      Form
    input          String
endVar
input = "Type a name here"              ; initialize the input variable
input.View("Enter a form name")         ; prompt for a form name
if formV.open(input) then               ; open requested form (if possible)
    formV.setTitle(input)               ; set title in title bar
    formV.maximize()                    ; maximize the window
    formV.wait()                        ; wait for user to close
    formV.close()                       ; close form view
else
    msginfo ("Open Failed", "Sorry -- Cannot open " + input + " form")
    maximize()
endif
endmethod
```

Defining the Run "Answer" Query Button

Figure 19.9 shows the method for the *Run "Answer" Query* button. This button runs a query and then displays the Answer table on the Desktop. If the query cannot be opened (perhaps because it doesn't exist), or the Answer table cannot be opened (perhaps because the query generates a Changed, Deleted, or Inserted table instead of an Answer table), an appropriate message will appear.

Notice the differences between this method and the one shown in Figure 19.8:

- The prompts and comments specify "query" instead of "form."

- We replaced the *Open* statement with an *ExecuteQBEFile* statement. The *ExecuteQBEFile* statement allows you to run any saved query from a method.

FIGURE 19.9

The method for the Run "Answer" Query button

```
method pushButton(var eventInfo Event)
; -- Run "Answer" Query button
; run a query that generates an Answer table, open Answer, wait for close
var
    tableTV        TableView
    input          String
endVar
input = "Type a name here"              ; initialize the input variable
input.View("Enter a query name")        ; prompt for a query name
if executeQBEFile (input) then          ; run requested query (if possible)
    if tableTV.open(":priv:answer.db") then   ; open requested table (if possi
        tableTV.maximize()              ; maximize the window
        tableTV.wait()                  ; wait for user to close
        tableTV.close()                 ; close table view
    else
        msginfo ("No Answer Table!", "Sorry -- cannot open the Answer table")
        maximize()
    endif
else
    msginfo ("Query Failed", "Sorry -- Cannot open " + input + " query")
    maximize()
endif
endmethod
```

- We placed an *If...Then...Else...EndIf* statement inside the outer *If...Then...Else...EndIf* statement. The statements in the new IF statement display the Answer table if the table exists; otherwise, they display an error message.

- We used the alias name *:priv:* to refer to the private directory where the Answer table is stored. (As mentioned in Chapter 14, you can make applications more portable by using aliases instead of hard-coding full path names. For example, if your application uses the alias name *:Gift_Corner:*, you could use the statement *tableTV.open(":Gift_Corner:custlist.db")* to open the CustList table. As long as all users have a *:Gift_Corner:* alias defined, the application will have no trouble finding the CustList table—regardless of the actual path name referenced by the alias.)

NOTE   If you do supply full path names when referencing files in your ObjectPAL methods, you must place two back-slash characters between each level of the path name. For example, you would specify the path to the CustList table as *c:\\pdoxwin\\giftco\\CustList.db*.

In the examples shown in this chapter, we're assuming that tables, queries, forms, and reports are located in the user's current working directory (so we need only specify the file name) or the user's private directory. You can use the *SetDir* statement if you wish to change the user's working directory through ObjectPAL.

Defining the Open Report Button

The method for the *Open Report* button appears in Figure 19.10. As you can see, this method resembles the methods attached to the Open Table and Open Form buttons described previously. Here, however, we've changed the variable name to *RptName*, changed the data type to *Report*, removed the *SetTitle* and *Close* statements, and modified the prompts and comments.

FIGURE 19.10

The method for the
Open Report button

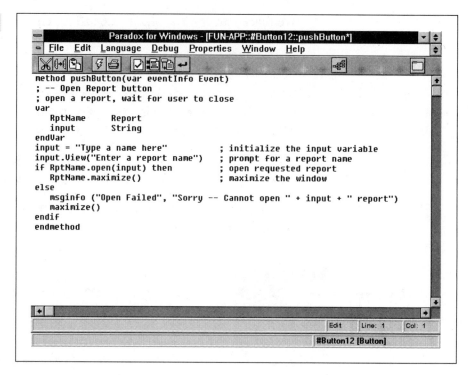

```
method pushButton(var eventInfo Event)
; -- Open Report button
; open a report, wait for user to close
var
    RptName      Report
    input        String
endVar
input = "Type a name here"          ; initialize the input variable
input.View("Enter a report name")   ; prompt for a report name
if RptName.open(input) then         ; open requested report
    RptName.maximize()              ; maximize the window
else
    msginfo ("Open Failed", "Sorry -- Cannot open " + input + " report")
    maximize()
endif
endmethod
```

Automating the Order Processing and Purchasing Cycle

In Chapter 18 you learned how to perform automatic updates via multi-table queries, history tables, and the Add and Empty options on the File ➤ Utilities menus. As you know, automatic updating can require many steps, each of which must be completed in sequence to ensure that tables are updated correctly. Performing these steps manually can be error-prone and time consuming. Fortunately, you can use ObjectPAL to streamline the entire process, making the job as easy as clicking a few buttons.

Figure 19.11 shows a form named *Cycles* that reduces the order processing and purchasing cycles presented in Chapter 18 to a few mouse clicks. To complete the Order Processing cycle, the user simply clicks the buttons on the left side of the form in sequence from 1 to 6. To complete the Purchasing cycle, the user clicks buttons 1, 2, 3, and 4 on the right side of the form.

FIGURE 19.11

A sample application for the Order Processing and Purchasing cycles presented in Chapter 18. To use the form, simply click the buttons in the sequence indicated on the button labels.

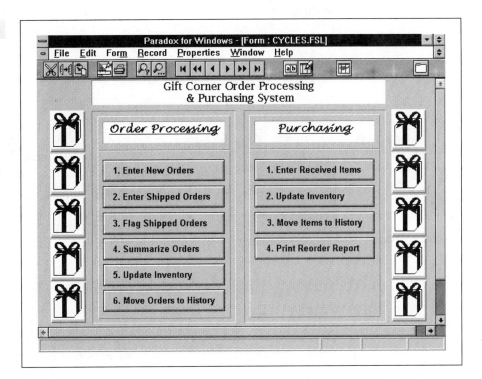

In a "real" application, we might prefer to combine the third, fourth, fifth, and sixth buttons on the Order Processing side of the form into a single button that performs all these related steps automatically. Likewise, we might wish to combine the second and third buttons on the Purchasing side of the form into a single button. However, to make it easier for you to understand the ObjectPAL methods used in our application, we've broken the steps into separate buttons that correspond to the Order Processing and Purchasing cycles illustrated in Figures 18.1 and 18.2 of the previous chapter.

To begin implementing the application, choose File ➤ New ➤ Form and click OK twice. This creates a blank form with no tables defined in the data model. Next, use the Button tool to create ten buttons with the labels shown in Figure 19.11, and then add text objects, graphic objects, and boxes to make the form more attractive (see Chapters 9 and 10).

With the basic design complete, the only remaining steps are to attach appropriate ObjectPAL methods to each button. As the following sections will show, these methods use ObjectPAL techniques you've seen already. They also employ previously saved queries, forms, and reports as building blocks for an integrated, easy-to-use application.

NOTE All buttons in the sample *Cycles* application in Figure 19.11 use the *pushButton* method, which is triggered when the user clicks the button to which the method is attached. To keep things simple, our examples do not perform extensive error-checking and they do not handle multiuser record-locking.

Defining the Order-Processing Buttons

First we'll take a look at the ObjectPAL method for each button in the Order Processing side of the sample application shown in Figure 19.11.

Entering New Orders

As its label implies, the *1. Enter New Orders* button allows users to enter new orders into the database. Figure 19.12 presents the ObjectPAL method for this button. The IF statement first tries to open the OrdEntry form discussed earlier under "Adding ObjectPAL Methods to an Order-Entry Form." If the Open statement succeeds, ObjectPAL places all

FIGURE 19.12

The ObjectPAL method for the order processing button named "1. Enter New Orders"

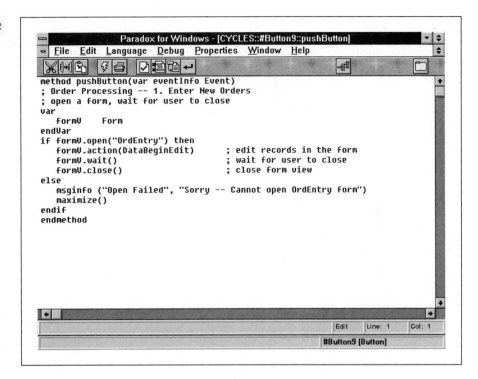

```
method pushButton(var eventInfo Event)
; Order Processing -- 1. Enter New Orders
; open a form, wait for user to close
var
    formV      Form
endVar
if formV.open("OrdEntry") then
    formV.action(DataBeginEdit)        ; edit records in the form
    formV.wait()                       ; wait for user to close
    formV.close()                      ; close form view
else
    msginfo ("Open Failed", "Sorry -- Cannot open OrdEntry form")
    maximize()
endif
endmethod
```

tables on the form into Edit mode via the *action(DataBeginEdit)* state-ment, waits until the user is finished using the form, and then closes the form. If the Open statement fails, an appropriate message appears and the application form is maximized. By now, the *Open*, *Wait*, and *Close* state-ments should be familiar to you. However, one statement—*FormV.action (DataBeginEdit)*—is new. This *action* statement places the active Form View window into Edit mode, just as if the user had pressed the F9 key.

Entering Shipped Orders

The button named *2. Enter Shipped Orders* allows users to record shipped and invoiced orders. Figure 19.13 presents the ObjectPAL method for this button. Notice that this code uses the well-known statements *Open*, *Maximize*, *Action*, *Wait*, *Close*, and *MsgInfo*.

FIGURE 19.13

The ObjectPAL method for the buttoon named "2. Enter Shipped Orders"

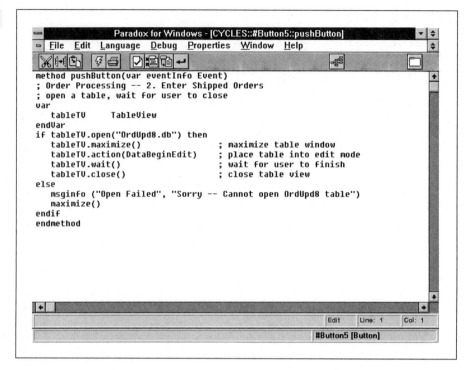

```
  Paradox for Windows - [CYCLES::#Button5::pushButton]
  File   Edit   Language   Debug   Properties   Window   Help

method pushButton(var eventInfo Event)
; Order Processing -- 2. Enter Shipped Orders
; open a table, wait for user to close
var
    tableTV      TableView
endVar
if tableTV.open("OrdUpd8.db") then
    tableTV.maximize()              ; maximize table window
    tableTV.action(DataBeginEdit)   ; place table into edit mode
    tableTV.wait()                  ; wait for user to finish
    tableTV.close()                 ; close table view
else
    msginfo ("Open Failed", "Sorry -- Cannot open OrdUpd8 table")
    maximize()
endif
endmethod
```

```
                                         Edit    Line: 1    Col: 1
                                         #Button5 [Button]
```

Flagging Shipped Orders

The method for the next button, *3. Flag Shipped Orders*, is illustrated in Figure 19.14. This code includes some new commands, as well as our old standbys. First, it executes the saved query named *ShipInv* (see Figure 18.3 in Chapter 18). Recall that this query updates blank Date Shipped and Invoice Date fields in the Orders table with corresponding fields from the OrdUpd8 table.

The statement

```
userChoice = msgQuestion("View Changed?",
    "Do you wish to view the Changed table?")
```

FIGURE 19.14

The ObjectPAL method
for the button named
"3. Flag Shipped
Orders"

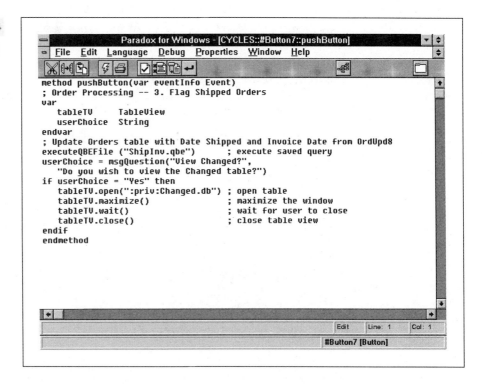

```
method pushButton(var eventInfo Event)
; Order Processing -- 3. Flag Shipped Orders
var
    tableTV     TableView
    userChoice  String
endvar
; Update Orders table with Date Shipped and Invoice Date from OrdUpd8
executeQBEFile ("ShipInv.qbe")           ; execute saved query
userChoice = msgQuestion("View Changed?",
    "Do you wish to view the Changed table?")
if userChoice = "Yes" then
    tableTV.open(":priv:Changed.db")  ; open table
    tableTV.maximize()                ; maximize the window
    tableTV.wait()                    ; wait for user to close
    tableTV.close()                   ; close table view
endif
endmethod
```

displays a dialog box and waits for the user to click the Yes or No button.
Notice how the arguments in the MsgQuestion statement correspond to
text in the title bar and dialog box shown below.

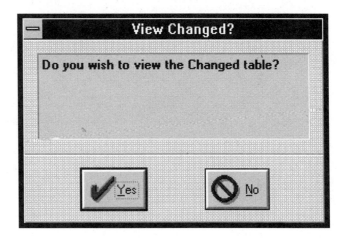

If the user clicks the Yes button in the dialog box, the value "Yes" is stored in the string variable named *UserChoice* and the Changed table in the user's private directory (*:priv:Changed.db*) appears maximized on the Desktop. If the user clicks No, the value "No" is stored in *UserChoice* and the method ends without displaying the Changed table.

Summarizing Shipped Orders

Figure 19.15 shows the method for the button *4. Summarize Orders*, which updates a summary table of shipped and invoiced orders. This method executes the saved query named *Summary* (see Figure 18.6 in Chapter 18) and allows the user to view the Summary table.

FIGURE 19.15

The ObjectPAL method for the button named "4. Summarize Orders"

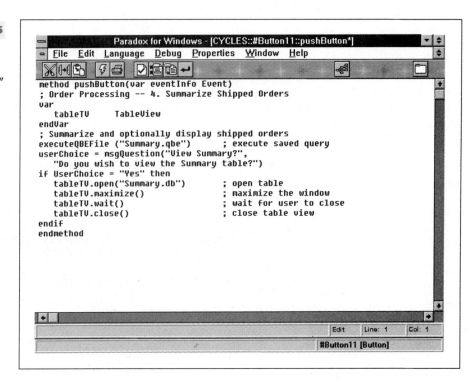

```
method pushButton(var eventInfo Event)
; Order Processing -- 4. Summarize Shipped Orders
var
    tableTV        TableView
endVar
; Summarize and optionally display shipped orders
executeQBEFile ("Summary.qbe")        ; execute saved query
userChoice = msgQuestion("View Summary?",
    "Do you wish to view the Summary table?")
if UserChoice = "Yes" then
    tableTV.open("Summary.db")        ; open table
    tableTV.maximize()                ; maximize the window
    tableTV.wait()                    ; wait for user to close
    tableTV.close()                   ; close table view
endif
endmethod
```

Updating the Inventory with Quantity Shipped

Figure 19.16 illustrates the method attached to button 5 of the Order Processing cycle. Here we're executing two queries in a row—*CalcSum* and *Upd8Prod* (see Figures 18.8 and 18.9 in Chapter 18). The first query calculates the sum of the quantity sold for each product shipped. The second query subtracts the calculated quantity from the In Stock quantity for each associated item in the Products table.

NOTE

Notice how similar the method in Figure 19.16 (button 5) is to the method in Figure 19.15 (button 4). Again, we used the copy and paste techniques discussed earlier in this chapter to save time and avoid typing mistakes.

FIGURE 19.16

The ObjectPAL method for the Order Processing button named "5. Update Inventory"

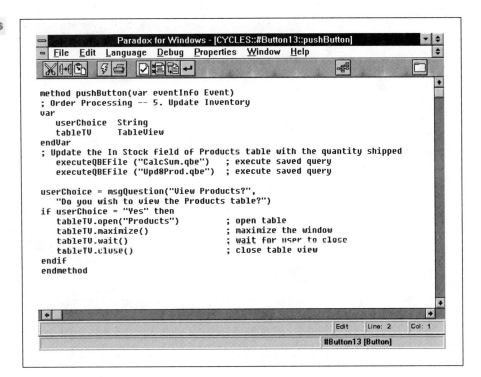

```
method pushButton(var eventInfo Event)
; Order Processing -- 5. Update Inventory
var
    userChoice  String
    tableTV     TableView
endVar
; Update the In Stock field of Products table with the quantity shipped
    executeQBEFile ("CalcSum.qbe")   ; execute saved query
    executeQBEFile ("Upd8Prod.qbe")  ; execute saved query

userChoice = msgQuestion("View Products?",
    "Do you wish to view the Products table?")
if userChoice = "Yes" then
    tableTV.open("Products")         ; open table
    tableTV.maximize()               ; maximize the window
    tableTV.wait()                   ; wait for user to close
    tableTV.close()                  ; close table view
endif
endmethod
```

Moving the Shipped Orders to History

When the user clicks the button 6. *Move Orders to History*, processed orders are moved to the history tables named *OrdHst* and *LineHst*. The method for this button appears in Figure 19.17.

The first section of this code is introduced by the comment "; Post line items" and continues through the statement that executes the ClrLine query. In this section we execute the saved query named *PostLine* (see Figure 18.10), which creates an Answer table containing shipped records from the LineItem table. The statements

```
ansTbl.attach(":priv:Answer.db")
ansTbl.add("LineHst.db")
```

associate the table variable named *ansTbl* with the Answer table in the private directory, and then add the Answer table records to the LineHst

FIGURE 19.17

The ObjectPAL method for the button named "6. Move Orders to History"

```
                     Paradox for Windows - [CYCLES::#Button15::pushButton*]

 File   Edit   Language   Debug   Properties   Window   Help

method pushButton(var eventInfo Event)
; Order Processing -- 6. Move Orders to History
var
    ansTbl    Table
    updTbl    Table
endVar
; Post line items
    executeQBEFile("PostLine.qbe")        ; post the line items to history
    ansTbl.attach(":priv:Answer.db")      ; attach Answer in private directory
    ansTbl.add("LineHst.db")              ; add records from Answer
    executeQBEFile("ClrLine.qbe")         ; clear records
; Post orders
    executeQBEFile("PostOrd.qbe")         ; post the order to history
    ansTbl.attach(":priv:Answer.db")      ; attach Answer in private directory
    ansTbl.add("OrdHst.db")               ; add records from Answer
    executeQBEFile("ClrOrd.qbe")          ; clear records
; Empty OrdUpd8
    updTbl.attach("OrdUpd8.db")           ; attach OrdUpd8 table
    updTbl.empty()                        ; empty OrdUpd8
msgInfo ("Done!", "Done moving orders and line items to history.")
endmethod

                                      Edit      Line: 1      Col: 1
                                              #Button15 [Button]
```

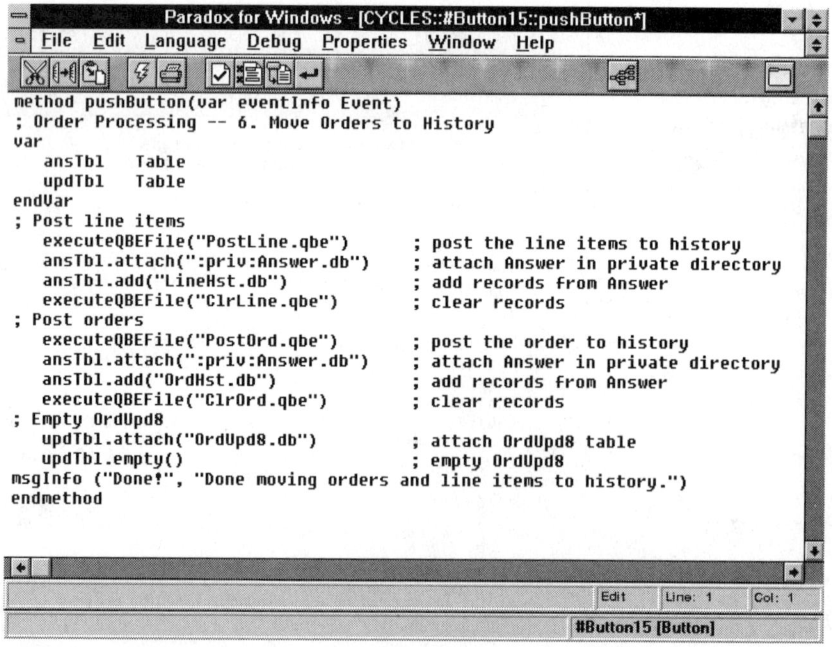

table. These statements are equivalent to choosing File ➤ Utilities ➤ Add from the menus and specifying Answer as the source table and LineHst as the target table. (The *attach* statement is similar to Open, but it does not display the table on-screen.) The last statement in this section executes the ClrLine query (see Figure 18.11), which clears the posted records from the LineItem table.

The second section of the code starts with the "; Post Orders" comment and ends with the command to execute the ClrOrd query. This section posts the shipped records from the Orders table to the OrdHst table, and then clears them from the Orders table. You'll find examples of the PostOrd and ClrOrd queries in Figures 18.12 and 18.13 of Chapter 18.

The last section of code (beginning with "; Empty OrdUpd8") attaches the OrdUpd8 table and then empties it. This is equivalent to choosing File ➤ Utilities ➤ Empty and specifying OrdUpd8 as the table to empty.

Defining the Purchasing Buttons

Now let's turn our attention to the four buttons in the Purchasing cycle. As you'll see, many of the ObjectPAL methods for the purchasing buttons are similar to those attached to the order-processing buttons.

Entering Received Items

When purchased items arrive in the stockroom, we can record them by clicking the *1. Enter Received Items* button in the Cycles application form and entering data into the Prod Code, Qty Recd, Purchase Price, and Date Recd fields of the Purchase table that appears. As Figure 19.18 shows, the code attached to this button features the familiar *Open*, *Maximize*, *Action*, *Wait*, *Close*, and *MsgInfo* statements.

Updating the Inventory with Quantity Received

The next step is to update inventory quantities and unit prices in the Products table with data from the Purchases table. Figure 19.19 shows the method attached to the button *2. Update Inventory*, which

FIGURE 19.18

The ObjectPAL method for the button named "1. Enter Received Items"

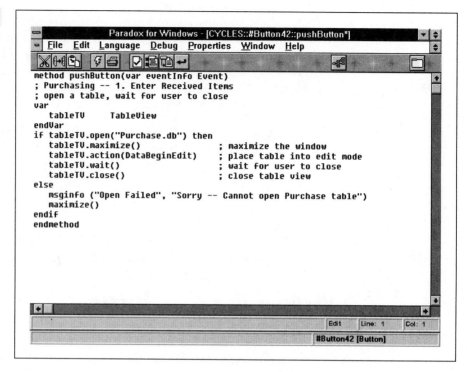

```
method pushButton(var eventInfo Event)
; Purchasing -- 1. Enter Received Items
; open a table, wait for user to close
var
    tableTV      TableView
endVar
if tableTV.open("Purchase.db") then
    tableTV.maximize()                  ; maximize the window
    tableTV.action(DataBeginEdit)       ; place table into edit mode
    tableTV.wait()                      ; wait for user to close
    tableTV.close()                     ; close table view
else
    msginfo ("Open Failed", "Sorry -- Cannot open Purchase table")
    maximize()
endif
endmethod
```

accomplishes this task. Notice how similar this method is to the method for the fifth button on the Order Processing side (see Figure 19.16). The main difference is that the Purchasing button for updating inventory executes the *CalcPurc* and *Upd8Stoc* queries (see Figures 18.15 and 18.16) instead of the *CalcSum* and *Upd8Prod* queries used by the corresponding Order Processing button.

Moving Received Items to History

The method for the button *3. Move Items to History* appears in Figure 19.20. Here we simply attach the Purchase table, add its records to the PurHst table, and empty the Purchase table.

Printing a Reorder Report

The *4. Print Reorder Report* button in the Purchasing cycle can be used at any time to display (and print) a reorder report. Its method, which

FIGURE 19.19

The ObjectPAL method for the Purchasing button named "2. Update Inventory"

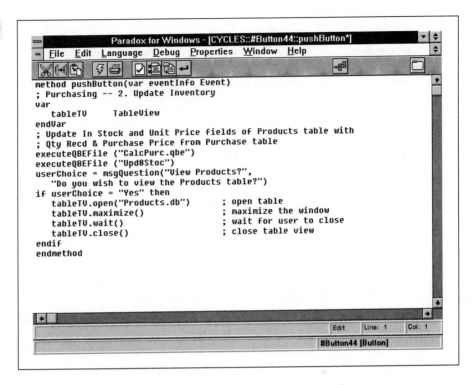

```
method pushButton(var eventInfo Event)
; Purchasing -- 2. Update Inventory
var
      tableTV      TableView
endVar
; Update In Stock and Unit Price fields of Products table with
; Qty Recd & Purchase Price from Purchase table
executeQBEFile ("CalcPurc.qbe")
executeQBEFile ("Upd8Stoc")
userChoice = msgQuestion("View Products?",
      "Do you wish to view the Products table?")
if userChoice = "Yes" then
      tableTV.open("Products.db")        ; open table
      tableTV.maximize()                 ; maximize the window
      tableTV.wait()                     ; wait for user to close
      tableTV.close()                    ; close table view
endif
endmethod
```

appears in Figure 19.21, executes the ReOrder query (see Figure 18.18) and opens the custom ReOrder report shown in Figure 19.22. Clicking the Print button in the SpeedBar will print the reorder report displayed on the screen.

Using Scripts

As you know, Paradox for Windows applications are typically developed by attaching ObjectPAL methods to objects in custom forms. You can also run applications from stand-alone files called *scripts*. Like methods attached to objects, scripts contain ObjectPAL program code; however, scripts run on the Paradox for Windows Desktop and are completely independent of any form.

FIGURE 19.20

The ObjectPAL method for the Purchasing button named "3. Move Items to History"

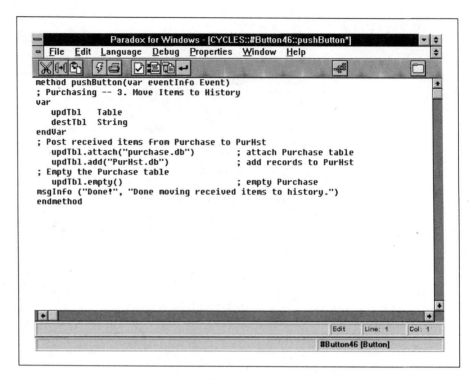

```
method pushButton(var eventInfo Event)
; Purchasing -- 3. Move Items to History
var
    updTbl    Table
    destTbl   String
endVar
; Post received items from Purchase to PurHst
    updTbl.attach("purchase.db")         ; attach Purchase table
    updTbl.add("PurHst.db")              ; add records to PurHst
; Empty the Purchase table
    updTbl.empty()                       ; empty Purchase
msgInfo ("Done!", "Done moving received items to history.")
endmethod
```

NOTE

Paradox for DOS also allows you to create scripts, applications, forms, reports, and queries. Unfortunately, those Paradox for DOS files *cannot* be used with Paradox for Windows. You can, however, view and update Paradox for DOS *tables* from Paradox for Windows (see Appendix C).

Scripts provide advanced capabilities that may not interest first-time ObjectPAL users, but might be helpful later in your ObjectPAL programming life. For example, scripts can be used to call other scripts; open and work with tables, forms, and reports; run queries; and use methods attached to other objects.

FIGURE 19.21

The ObjectPAL method for the Purchasing button named "4. Print Reorder Report"

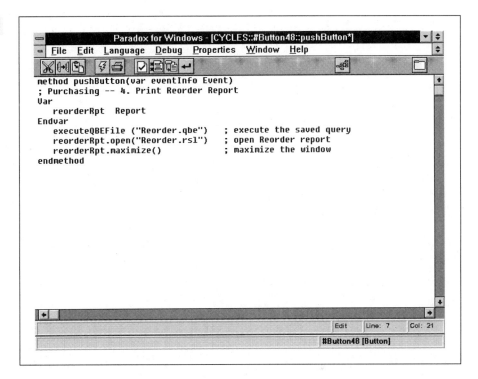

```
method pushButton(var eventInfo Event)
; Purchasing -- 4. Print Reorder Report
Var
    reorderRpt  Report
Endvar
    executeQBEFile ("Reorder.qbe")    ; execute the saved query
    reorderRpt.open("Reorder.rsl")    ; open Reorder report
    reorderRpt.maximize()             ; maximize the window
endmethod
```

Creating a Script

To create a script, choose File ➤ New ➤ Script. When the ObjectPAL Editor window appears, type the program code and check the syntax as described earlier. To save the script, choose File ➤ Save, specify a file name (no extension), and choose OK. Paradox will add the extension .ssl automatically.

Running a Script

To run the script from Paradox for Windows, choose File ➤ Open ➤ Script and double-click the script name in the **Open Document** dialog box that appears. Alternatively, you can place a script's icon in the Folder window and run the script by double-clicking the icon (see Chapter 14).

FIGURE 19.22

A simple report listing items that are due for reordering

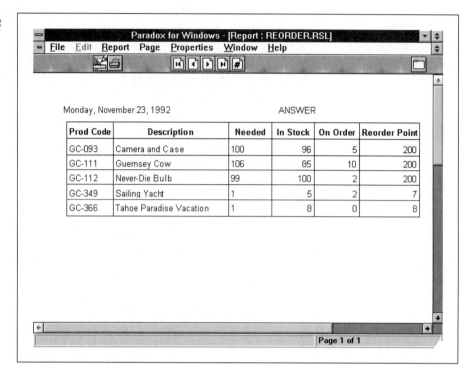

You can also run a script from a command line. To start Paradox for Windows and run a script from the Program Manager, choose File ➤ Run from the Program Manager, type *c:\pdoxwin\pdoxwin* and a space, then type the complete path name of the script. Press ⏎. For example, the command line

> *c:\pdoxwin\pdoxwin c:\pdoxwin\autoupd8\startup.ssl*

will start Paradox for Windows and immediately run the script named *startup*. (The same command line will also work when typed at the DOS command prompt or when entered into your *autoexec.bat* file.)

To start the script whenever you double-click the Paradox for Windows icon, choose File ➤ Properties from the Program Manager menu, add the blank space and complete path of the script to the end of the command in the Command Line text box, and choose OK.

Appendix A provides additional information about using command line options.

To understand just how useful a script can be, suppose you created a script like the one shown below and saved it with the name *startup*:

```
method run(var eventInfo Event)
var
    formV    Form
endVar
; open the Cycles form in the current directory.
formV.open("Cycles")
endmethod
```

When you use a command line to start Paradox and run this script, the *cycles.fsl* form shown in Figure 19.11 will open immediately. Because the *Startup* script opens the form as soon as Paradox starts up, anyone can perform essential business tasks simply by clicking a few buttons with the mouse. Users needn't know anything about tables, forms, reports, or other Paradox for Windows objects.

To make the application even easier to use, you could add a "Quit Paradox" button to the *Cycles* form, so that clicking the button would exit Paradox for Windows completely. To define the button, open the Form Design window for the *Cycles* form, use the Button tool in the SpeedBar to create a new button, and change its label to **QUIT PARADOX**. Inspect the button, choose Methods, and double-click the *pushButton* built-in method. Finally, type **exit( )** on line 2 of the ObjectPAL Editor window, double-click the window's Control-menu box, choose Yes, and then save the form.

Changing a Script

To change an existing script, choose File ➤ Open ➤ Script, select the name of the script you want to change, click Design in the Open Document dialog box, then click OK; or inspect the script's icon in the Folder window and choose Design.

In this chapter we have introduced ObjectPAL, the rich and powerful programming language supplied with Paradox for Windows. We hope the examples provided here will inspire you to begin creating applications of your own that can be run with pushbutton ease. Keep in mind that ObjectPAL offers an extensive online help system as well as several manuals to assist you in learning the language.

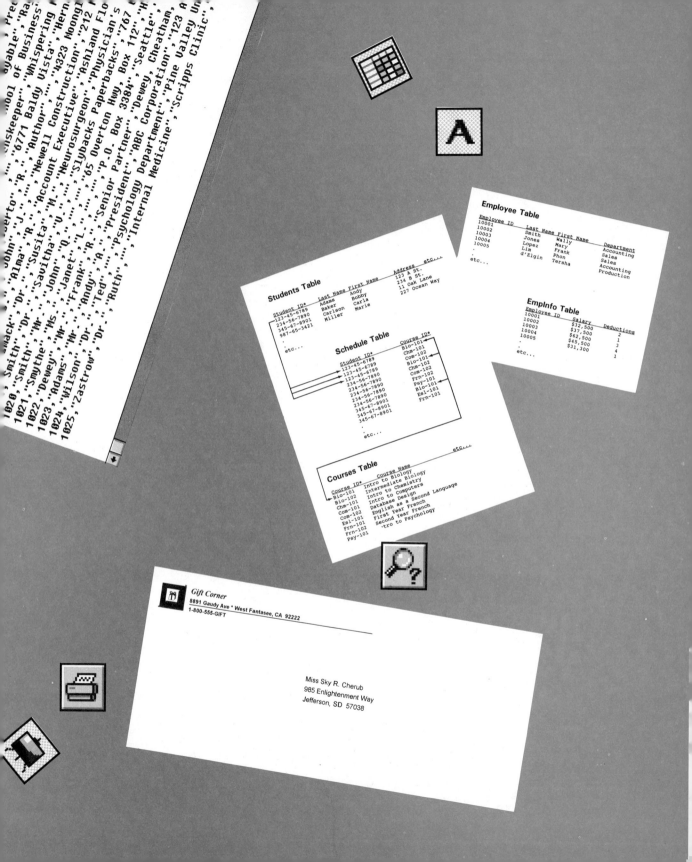

APPENDICES

Paradox for Windows Installation

Your Name:

Company Name:

Serial Number:

Install From: `B:\`

Install To: `C:\PDOXWIN`

ODAPI Directory: `C:\WINDOWS\SYSTEM`

✔ Install Paradox for Windows

✔ Install ODAPI Files

✔ Create Windows Group

✔ Install Sample Tables

✔ Install Sample Application

✔ Install ObjectPAL Examples

Subdirectories...

Current options require 14868kb, space available: 39652kb

Install

Exit

Reset Defaults

? Help

APPENDIX

Installing Paradox for Windows

BEFORE you can use Paradox for Windows, it must be installed on your computer. You need to install Paradox for Windows only once, not each time you use it. This appendix explains how to install Paradox for Windows on a single-user machine.

Hardware and Software Requirements

Before you install Paradox for Windows, please make sure your hardware and software meet the following minimum requirements:

- An IBM or compatible PC with 80286 or higher processor.
- A hard disk with at least 20MB of free space.
- 4MB of memory (RAM), preferably more.
- EGA or VGA display (preferably VGA). CGA is not supported.
- A mouse or similar pointing device.
- DOS Version 3.1 or later.
- Windows Version 3.1 or later, running in Standard or 386 Enhanced mode. Real mode is not supported.

Installing Paradox for Windows for the First Time

To install Paradox for Windows on a single-user computer, follow these steps:

1. Start your computer and get to the Windows Program Manager.

2. Place *Paradox for Windows Installation Disk 1* into the floppy drive and close the drive door.

3. From the Program Manager menu choose File ➤ Run.

4. If you inserted the installation disk into your A drive, type **a:\install** and click OK. If you inserted the disk into drive B, type **b:\install** and click OK.

5. After a few moments you will see the **Paradox for Windows Installation** dialog box shown in Figure A.1. Complete the dialog box as follows:

   • In the Your Name text box, type your full name and press Tab.

   • In the Company Name text box, type the name of your company and press Tab.

   • In the Serial Number text box, type the serial number that's printed on your Paradox for Windows Installation Disk.

   • Verify that the information you entered is correct, and then click the Install button to begin installing the files.

You shouldn't need to change the default settings in the dialog box, though you can do so if necessary. Note that the Install Paradox for Windows option and Install ODAPI Files option must be checked the first time you install Paradox. See the section "Installing Specific Files" for information on changing default settings.

NOTE You can cancel the Install program at any time by clicking the Exit or Cancel buttons that appear on your screen. For help with any option in a dialog box, click the Help button, and then click the option you're interested in.

6. As the installation progresses, you'll be prompted to replace the disk that's currently in drive A or B with the disk indicated in the instructions. Replace the disk, and then click OK to proceed. (If you accidentally insert the wrong disk, you'll be prompted to insert the correct disk; replace the disk and click OK to continue.)

FIGURE A.1

The Paradox for Windows Installation dialog box

Paradox for Windows Installation

Your Name:

Company Name:

Serial Number:

Install From: `B:\`

Install To: `C:\PDOXWIN`

ODAPI Directory: `C:\WINDOWS\SYSTEM`

☑ Install Paradox for Windows   ☑ Install Sample Tables

☑ Install ODAPI Files   ☑ Install Sample Application

☑ Create Windows Group   ☑ Install ObjectPAL Examples

Subdirectories...

Current options require 14868kb, space available: 39652kb

Install   Exit   Reset Defaults   Help

7. When copying is complete, the **README** file will appear in a window. Read this important late-breaking news file, and then close the window.

8. A message will remind you to load the DOS **SHARE** command before running Windows. SHARE must be active if you plan to access Paradox for Windows files from multiple applications concurrently, run more than one instance of Paradox at a time, or run Paradox in certain network configurations. Click OK to continue.

When installation is complete, the Install program will return to Windows, and the Paradox for Windows group will contain icons for Paradox for Windows and several related utilities (see Chapter 13).

Adjusting CONFIG.SYS and AUTOEXEC.BAT

Before running Paradox for Windows, you may need to change some settings in your *config.sys* and *autoexec.bat* files. In particular, you should

- Change your *config.sys* file settings to at least FILES=60 and BUFFERS=40. (The BUFFERS setting can be reduced to 10 if you use SMARTDRV.)

- Change your *autoexec.bat* file PATH statement to include the Paradox for Windows installation directory (usually *c:\pdoxwin*).

- Change your *autoexec.bat* file to activate SHARE automatically by placing the command **c:\dos\share f:4096 /l:400** on the line *above* any command that starts Windows or any Windows application (or at the end of the file, if you're not starting Windows from *autoexec.bat*).

NOTE

The /F parameter allocates file space (in bytes) for the DOS storage area used to record file sharing information. The /L parameter sets the number of files that can be locked simultaneously. You may need to increase the recommended /F and /L settings if you see error messages such as "Could not open" or "File doesn't exist" when you're sure that Paradox should be able to open or find the files you're trying to access.

After adjusting *config.sys* and *autoexec.bat*, remove any floppy disks from the drives, reboot the computer (press Ctrl+Alt+Del), and then start Windows as usual.

Starting Paradox for Windows

You can start Paradox for Windows by double-clicking its icon in the Paradox for Windows program group of Windows' Program Manager (see Chapters 2 and 3). You can also start Paradox from a command line, as described later in this appendix.

Installing Specific Files

Paradox for Windows comes with several sample applications which must be installed on your computer before you can use them. Normally, these components are installed automatically when you install Paradox for Windows for the first time. If you chose not to install these optional files during general installation, you can do so at any time by following these steps:

1. Repeat Steps 1 through 4 of the first-time installation procedure described earlier.

2. In the Paradox for Windows Installation dialog box, remove the check marks next to Install <u>P</u>aradox for Windows, Install <u>O</u>DAPI Files, Create <u>W</u>indows Group, and any sample files you've installed already. All options in the dialog box are checked initially and each one is described below.

3. If you wish to specify non-default subdirectories for the sample files, click the <u>S</u>ubdirectories button, make any required changes, and then click OK. (The default directories for sample files are listed below.)

T I P   To return to the default settings, click the Reset Defaults button in Step 2 or Step 3.

4. Click the Install button and continue with Steps 6 through 8 of the first-time installation procedure.

You can determine which files will be installed on your hard disk by checking any of the following options in the Paradox for Windows Installation dialog box:

Install Paradox for Windows   Installs the Paradox for Windows program. This option must be checked the first time you install Paradox for Windows. (The default Paradox for Windows directory is *c:\pdoxwin.*)

Install ODAPI Files   Installs the ODAPI (Open Database Architecture Programming Interface) files that provide concurrent access to other applications which use the ODAPI engine (see Chapter 13). This option must be checked the first time you install Paradox for Windows. (The default ODAPI directory is *c:\windows\system.*)

Create Windows Group   Creates a Paradox for Windows Group and places the Paradox for Windows icons in it.

Install Sample Tables   Installs some sample Paradox for Windows tables. (The default directory for the tables is *c:\pdoxwin\sample.*)

Install ObjectPAL Examples   Installs some sample ObjectPAL applications. (The default directory for these applications is *c:\pdoxwin\examples.*)

Install Sample Application   Installs the sample "Marine Adventures & Sunken Treasures" application discussed in the Paradox for Windows *Getting Started* manual. (The default directory for the application is *c:\pdoxwin\diveplan.*)

Running Paradox for Windows from the Command Line

As an alternative to starting Paradox for Windows by double-clicking its icon, you can run the program from a command line. The command line can include options that override certain default settings for the current session only.

Command-line options always begin with a space, and always must appear to the right of the command used to start Paradox for Windows. You can type command lines in uppercase, lowercase, or any combination of the two. For example, the command line shown below starts Paradox with an initial working directory of *c:\pdoxwin\giftco.*

    pdoxwin -w c:\pdoxwin\giftco

You can combine command-line options, as shown by the next example, which sets the initial working directory as above and immediately runs the script named *startup.ssl* in that directory.

    pdoxwin -w c:\pdoxwin\giftco startup.ssl

If your DOS path does not contain the Paradox for Windows system directory (normally *c:\pdoxwin*), you must include the directory name when specifying the command used to start Paradox. For example, typing **c:\pdoxwin\pdoxwin -c** would start Paradox with a clear Desktop.

Table A.1 describes the Paradox for Windows command line options available.

OPTION	DESCRIPTION
-c	Starts Paradox for Windows with an empty Desktop.
-d *filename*	Specifies an alternate *pdoxwork.ini* file. If you include a full directory path (e.g., *c:\pdoxwin\giftco\mywork.ini*), Paradox will use that file for *every* working directory you switch to.
-i *filename*	Specifies an alternate *pdoxwin.ini* file.
-m	Loads Paradox for Windows as a minimized application. (Alternatively, you can load Paradox as a minimized application by holding down Shift while double-clicking the Paradox for Windows icon.)
-n	Prevents Paradox from saving private and working directory settings in the *win.ini* file.
-o *filename*	Specifies an alternate *odapi.cfg* file.
-p *directory*	Specifies an alternate private directory.
-q	Starts Paradox for Windows without displaying the title screen.
-w *directory*	Specifies an initial working directory.
startfile	Opens a document and performs its default action.

filename is the name of the file to use; the name must include the file extension.
directory is the name of the directory to use.
startfile is the name of a Paradox form, report, table, query, or script to use; the name must include the file extension.

You can type command lines at the DOS prompt or in the Command Line text box that appears when you choose File ➤ Run from the Windows Program Manager menus. To run the command line automatically when you start your computer, enter it into your *autoexec.bat* file. If you

want the command line to run whenever you double-click the Paradox for Windows icon, enter it into the Command Line text box that appears when you choose File ➤ Properties from the Program Manager menus.

WARNING

When starting a second instance of Paradox for Windows, use both the -n command-line parameter and the -p *directory* parameter. When specifying the private directory, be sure to supply a name that is different from the private directory used by any other instance of Paradox.

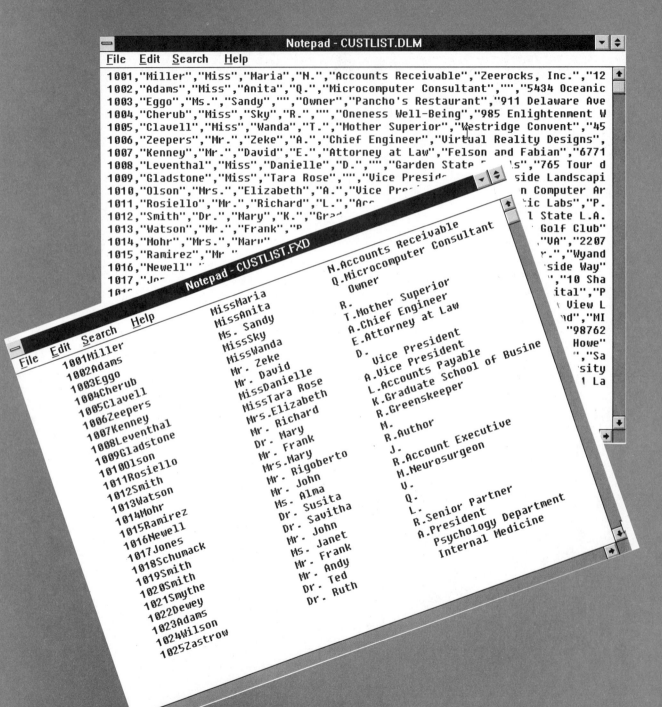

APPENDIX

B

Sharing Data with Other Applications

PARADOX for Windows provides many tools that allow you to transfer data to and from several application file formats, including delimited text, fixed length text, Quattro Pro, Quattro, Lotus 1-2-3, Excel, and dBASE.

Once you've successfully transferred data to a different application, you can use that data just as if you had created it in that application. For example, if you import an Excel spreadsheet to a Paradox for Windows table, you can use the new Paradox table just as if you had created it and added the data in Paradox. Likewise, if you export a Paradox for Windows table to an Excel spreadsheet, you'll be able to use the spreadsheet in Excel as if you created it from scratch in Excel.

NOTE

Quattro Pro for Windows can read Paradox for Windows tables directly, so you can usually bypass the Export options if you want to view, query, or edit a Paradox table in Quattro Pro for Windows.

After transferring the data, you may need to "tweak" it to compensate for assumptions Paradox might have made when importing or exporting it. For instance, after importing a text or spreadsheet file to a table, you may need to use Restructure to reorganize the table fields or change field names, field types, or field sizes. After exporting a table to a spreadsheet, you may need to use the spreadsheet application to widen or narrow a column.

TIP Before exporting data from Paradox, use queries to isolate specific data, select certain fields, or perform summary calculations.

Keep in mind that Paradox always converts data through copies of files. In all cases, your original files are left unchanged, while converted data is copied to a new file with a name you provide.

In this appendix, we'll begin by discussing general steps for transferring data; then we'll explain how to transfer data between Paradox and specific applications or file formats.

Exporting Paradox Tables to Other Formats

The basic steps for exporting Paradox tables to other application file formats are listed below.

1. Choose File ➤ Utilities ➤ Export, or inspect a table icon in the Browser dialog box or Folder window and choose Export. The **Table Export** dialog box shown in Figure B.1 appears.

2. Select the name of the table you want to export. If you performed a query that selected specific records or fields to export, specify Answer (or the table you chose in the Properties ➤ Answer Table ➤ Options command) as the table to export.

3. Click the file format you want to create in the Export File Type list.

4. Click OK.

5. The next dialog box depends on the file format you selected in Step 3. Complete the dialog box as explained in the sections below, then choose OK to begin exporting the table.

FIGURE B.1

The Table Export
dialog box

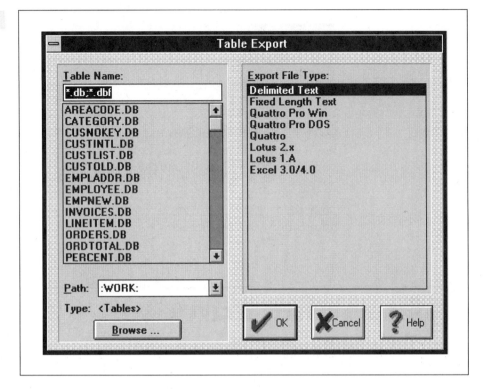

If the file you're exporting to already exists, you'll have
the opportunity to cancel the operation or replace the
existing file.

Importing Data into Paradox Tables

You can follow the steps below to import data from other file formats into
a Paradox table.

1. Choose File ➤ Utilities ➤ Import. Alternatively, you can inspect
   the icon of the file you want to import in the Folder window, then

choose <u>I</u>mport (for a spreadsheet), <u>D</u>elimited Text Import (for a de-limited text file), or <u>F</u>ixed Length Import (for a fixed length text file).

- If you chose <u>F</u>ile ➤ <u>U</u>tilities ➤ Import, the **File Import** dialog box shown in Figure B.2 will appear. Paradox initially suggests a file type of *<Delimited Text>* and displays the names of all files in the working directory that have a *.txt* extension. Continue with Step 2.
- If you inspected an icon in a folder, skip to Step 4.

FIGURE B.2

The File Import dialog box appears when you choose File ➤ Utilities ➤ Import.

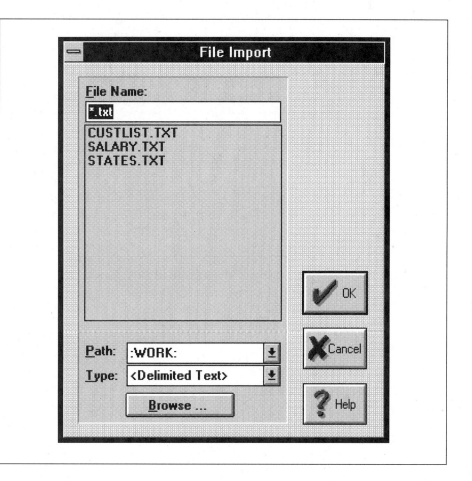

2. To import files in a format other than delimited text, click the Type drop-down arrow and select a file type.

3. Select the file you want to import, then click OK.

4. The next dialog box depends on the type of file you're importing. Complete the dialog box as explained below, then choose OK to begin importing the table.

N O T E   If the table you're importing to already exists, you'll have the option to cancel the operation or replace the existing table.

Using File Names, Directories, and File Name Extensions

When importing or exporting data on a computer with several directories, be sure to include the directory name if it's different from your current working directory (or use the Path drop-down list or Browse button to fill in the directory). For example, to import a Lotus 1-2-3 spreadsheet named *Sales* from the directory named *Lotus* on drive c:, enter the name of the file to import as *c:\lotus\sales*. You can also use an alias in place of a directory name. If you omit the drive and directory name, Paradox will look for files in your private directory or in the directory that contains the file you inspected in the Folder window or Browser.

If you omit the file name extension when entering a file name, Paradox will assign one automatically based on the file type you specified. Table B.1 lists each file type supported by Paradox and the file name extensions that Paradox expects when importing data or assigns automatically when exporting data.

NOTE Paradox reserves the name *import.db* in your private directory for import operations, and the name *export.db* in your private directory for export operations. Therefore, you should never use these names for permanent tables.

TABLE B.1: Data File Descriptions, File Types, and File Name Extensions Supported when Transferring Data to and from Paradox

DATA FILE DESCRIPTION	FILE TYPE	FILE NAME EXTENSION
Delimited text files	<Delimited Text>	.txt
Excel versions 3 and 4 spreadsheet files	<Excel>	.xls
Fixed length text files	<Fixed Length Text>	.txt
Lotus 1-2-3 version 2 and higher spreadsheet files	<Lotus 2.x>	.wk1
Lotus 1-2-3 version 1.A spreadsheet files	<Lotus 1.A>	.wks
Quattro spreadsheet files	<Quattro>	.wkq
Quattro Pro for Windows spreadsheet files	<Quattro Pro Win>	.wb1
Quattro Pro for DOS spreadsheet files	<Quattro Pro DOS>	.wq1

Exporting Data to a Spreadsheet

After you select a table to export and a spreadsheet format, you'll see the **Spreadsheet Export** dialog box shown in Figure B.3. You can edit the name of the table you're exporting in the Table Name text box and the name of the spreadsheet file you're creating in the New File Name text box. Normally, Paradox uses field names from the table to create the first row of labels in the spreadsheet. To omit the labels, click Make Row Headers From Field Names to deselect the option. Click OK to begin exporting the table to your spreadsheet.

After exporting the Paradox file to a spreadsheet format, you can start the spreadsheet program and open the new file as you would any other spreadsheet file. The exported file will have the name you assigned, plus the appropriate extension for the spreadsheet format you chose (see Table B.1). Data from the table will appear in the spreadsheet as follows:

- Table fields and records will appear in individual columns and rows.

- Each spreadsheet column will be as wide as the corresponding table field, up to the maximum allowed by the spreadsheet. If a table value is wider than the spreadsheet column display width, the full value will be converted, but will remain partially hidden.

FIGURE B.3

The Spreadsheet Export dialog box

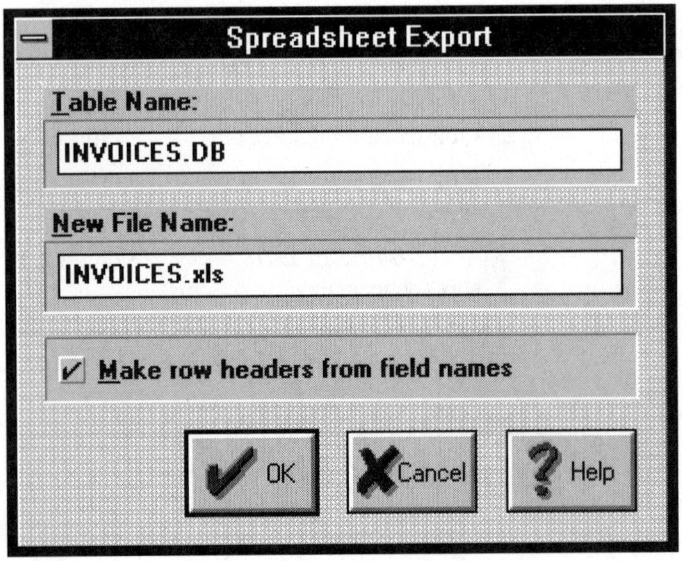

- Dates in the table that are beyond the range of dates allowed in the spreadsheet will have the value *ERROR*.

- Memo, formatted memo, binary, graphic, and OLE fields will be exported with their field names as column headings in the spreadsheet (if Make Row Headers From Field Names was checked), but data for those fields will be blank.

Importing Data from a Spreadsheet

Paradox tables store information in even columns (fields) and rows (records), whereas spreadsheets let you arrange text, numbers, and formulas in any manner you wish. However, Paradox cannot reliably import data that are randomly placed about a spreadsheet. Instead, it needs to import even columns (fields) and rows (records), where the top row contains the field names for the table.

If your spreadsheet contains labels or formulas outside of an even row-and-column orientation, or your spreadsheet uses headings, underlines, or other text enhancements, do not attempt to import these into a Paradox table. Instead, extract only the field names and values beneath them into a separate spreadsheet file, then use Paradox to import the extracted file only.

After you select a spreadsheet to import and a spreadsheet format, you'll see the **Spreadsheet Import** dialog box shown in Figure B.4. You can make any of the changes described below.

- To change the name of the file you're importing, edit the name in the File Name text box.

- To change the name of the table you're creating, edit the name in the New Table Name text box. Do not specify an extension, since this is assigned automatically when you choose the table type.

- To change the type of table you're creating, click the Paradox or dBASE option. Paradox is the default choice.

- By default, Paradox imports the entire spreadsheet file. To specify a range of cells to import, fill in the From Cell and To Cell text

boxes. If the spreadsheet has named ranges, you can click the
Named Ranges drop-down arrow and choose the range that contains the values you want to import.

- Paradox normally uses the top row of the spreadsheet to assign
  field names for the table. If you deselect *Get Field Names From
  First Row*, Paradox will assign names as *Field001*, *Field002*,
  Field003, and so on instead. This is useful if the top row of the
  spreadsheet or range contains data instead of field names.

Click OK to import the spreadsheet.

When importing data from a spreadsheet, Paradox assigns field types to
the data automatically. It scans each spreadsheet column and chooses a

FIGURE B.4

The Spreadsheet
Import dialog box

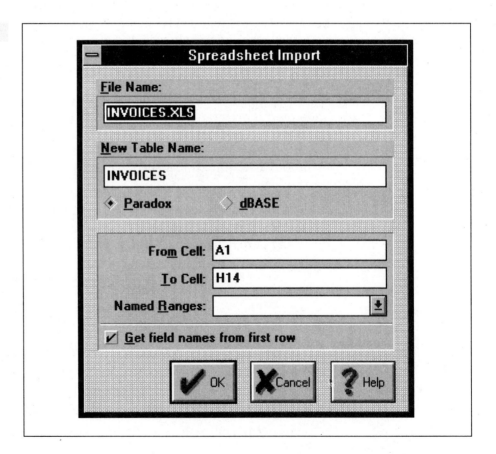

field type that can contain every value in the spreadsheet column. For example, if a column contains only numbers, Paradox will use Number. Any column that stores calculation results will be imported as values—Paradox will not import the formulas themselves.

Transferring Text Files

Paradox for Windows can export and import delimited text files and fixed length text.

In a *delimited text file*, fields are usually separated by commas, and each record is terminated by a carriage return–linefeed combination. Typically, character data is enclosed in double quotation marks ("). When you use the DOS TYPE command or the Windows Notepad accessory to view a delimited file, it typically resembles the example in Figure B.5.

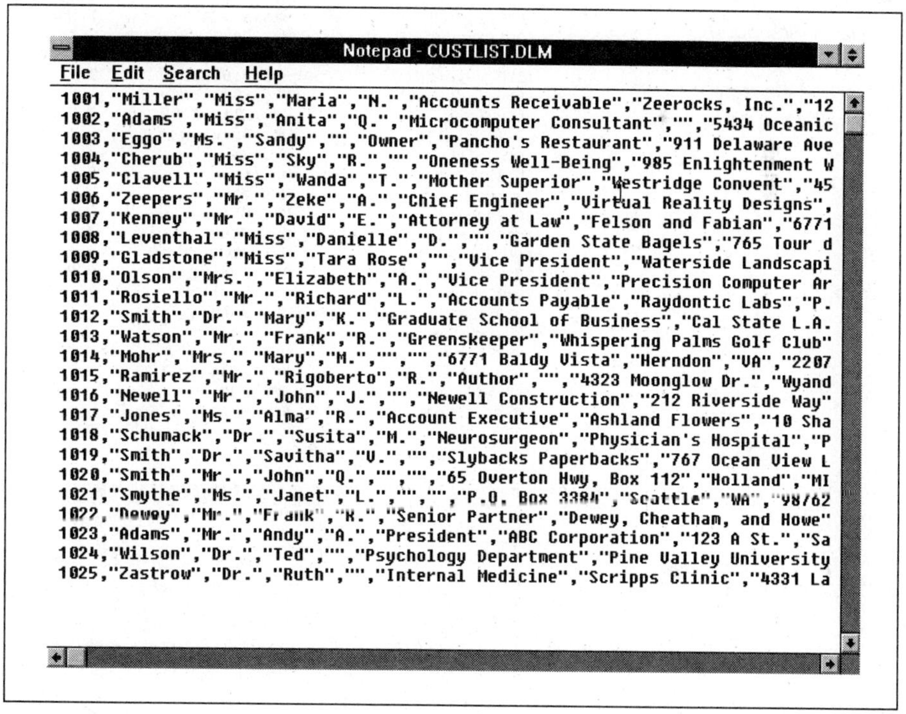

FIGURE B.5

The records of the CustList table exported to delimited text format and displayed in the Windows Notepad. (Some text has scrolled off the right edge of the screen.)

```
                              Notepad - CUSTLIST.DLM
 File  Edit  Search  Help
 1001,"Miller","Miss","Maria","N.","Accounts Receivable","Zeerocks, Inc.","12
 1002,"Adams","Miss","Anita","Q.","Microcomputer Consultant","","5434 Oceanic
 1003,"Eggo","Ms.","Sandy","","Owner","Pancho's Restaurant","911 Delaware Ave
 1004,"Cherub","Miss","Sky","R.","","Oneness Well-Being","985 Enlightenment W
 1005,"Clavell","Miss","Wanda","T.","Mother Superior","Westridge Convent","45
 1006,"Zeepers","Mr.","Zeke","A.","Chief Engineer","Virtual Reality Designs",
 1007,"Kenney","Mr.","David","E.","Attorney at Law","Felson and Fabian","6771
 1008,"Leventhal","Miss","Danielle","D.","","Garden State Bagels","765 Tour d
 1009,"Gladstone","Miss","Tara Rose","","Vice President","Waterside Landscapi
 1010,"Olson","Mrs.","Elizabeth","A.","Vice President","Precision Computer Ar
 1011,"Rosiello","Mr.","Richard","L.","Accounts Payable","Raydontic Labs","P.
 1012,"Smith","Dr.","Mary","K.","Graduate School of Business","Cal State L.A.
 1013,"Watson","Mr.","Frank","R.","Greenskeeper","Whispering Palms Golf Club"
 1014,"Mohr","Mrs.","Mary","M.","","","6771 Baldy Vista","Herndon","VA","2207
 1015,"Ramirez","Mr.","Rigoberto","R.","Author","","4323 Moonglow Dr.","Wyand
 1016,"Newell","Mr.","John","J.","","Newell Construction","212 Riverside Way"
 1017,"Jones","Ms.","Alma","R.","Account Executive","Ashland Flowers","10 Sha
 1018,"Schumack","Dr.","Susita","M.","Neurosurgeon","Physician's Hospital","P
 1019,"Smith","Dr.","Savitha","V.","","Slybacks Paperbacks","767 Ocean View L
 1020,"Smith","Mr.","John","Q.","","","65 Overton Hwy, Box 112","Holland","MI
 1021,"Smythe","Ms.","Janet","L.","","","P.O. Box 3384","Seattle","WA","98762
 1022,"Dewey","Mr.","Frank","K.","Senior Partner","Dewey, Cheatham, and Howe"
 1023,"Adams","Mr.","Andy","A.","President","ABC Corporation","123 A St.","Sa
 1024,"Wilson","Dr.","Ted","","Psychology Department","Pine Valley University
 1025,"Zastrow","Dr.","Ruth","","Internal Medicine","Scripps Clinic","4331 La
```

NOTE

Since many applications can use delimited text files, this format provides an excellent way to export Paradox data to word processing applications and other applications that cannot read Paradox or dBASE tables directly.

In a *fixed length text file*, each field has a specified starting position and length. Figure B.6 shows the same CustList table records exported to fixed length text format.

FIGURE B.6

The records of the CustList table exported to fixed length format and displayed in the Windows Notepad. (Some text has scrolled off the right edge of the screen.)

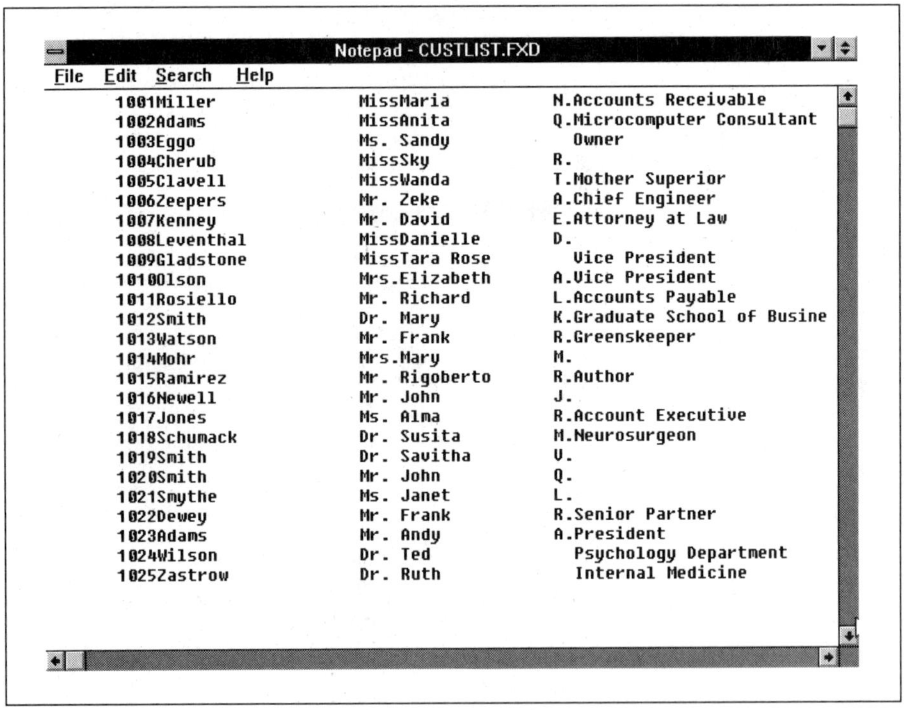

```
═                          Notepad - CUSTLIST.FXD                        ▼│▲
 File  Edit  Search  Help                                                    │▲
      1001Miller           MissMaria          N.Accounts Receivable          ▓
      1002Adams            MissAnita          Q.Microcomputer Consultant      ▓
      1003Eggo             Ms. Sandy             Owner                        ▓
      1004Cherub           MissSky            R.                              ▓
      1005Clavell          MissWanda          T.Mother Superior               ▓
      1006Zeepers          Mr. Zeke           A.Chief Engineer                ▓
      1007Kenney           Mr. David          E.Attorney at Law               ▓
      1008Leventhal        MissDanielle       D.                              ▓
      1009Gladstone        MissTara Rose         Vice President               ▓
      1010Olson            Mrs.Elizabeth      A.Vice President                ▓
      1011Rosiello         Mr. Richard        L.Accounts Payable              ▓
      1012Smith            Dr. Mary           K.Graduate School of Busine     ▓
      1013Watson           Mr. Frank          R.Greenskeeper                  ▓
      1014Mohr             Mrs.Mary           M.                              ▓
      1015Ramirez          Mr. Rigoberto      R.Author                        ▓
      1016Newell           Mr. John           J.                              ▓
      1017Jones            Ms. Alma           R.Account Executive             ▓
      1018Schumack         Dr. Susita         M.Neurosurgeon                  ▓
      1019Smith            Dr. Savitha        U.                              ▓
      1020Smith            Mr. John           Q.                              ▓
      1021Smythe           Ms. Janet          L.                              ▓
      1022Dewey            Mr. Frank          R.Senior Partner                ▓
      1023Adams            Mr. Andy           A.President                     ▓
      1024Wilson           Dr. Ted               Psychology Department        ▓
      1025Zastrow          Dr. Ruth              Internal Medicine            ▼
 ◀│                                                                       │▶
```

NOTE

Delimited and fixed length text files are also called ASCII files. ASCII is an acronym for American Standard Code for Information Interchange, a sequence of 128 standard characters. ASCII files provide a means of exchanging data between many applications.

Exporting Delimited Text Files

After selecting a table to export and specifying the delimited text file format, you'll see the **Delimited ASCII Export** dialog box shown in Figure B.7. You can edit the name of the table you're exporting in the Table Name text box, or the name of the delimited text file you're creating in the New File Name text box.

When creating the delimited text file, Paradox normally separates fields with commas and encloses non-numeric values in double quotation marks ("). Each record is separated by a carriage return and linefeed character. If you want to change the characters used to delimit fields and

FIGURE B.7

The Delimited ASCII Export dialog box

enclose non-numeric values, click the Options button to open the **Text Options** dialog box. (See Figure B.9 and the following sections for details on using this dialog box.) After making your selections, click OK to return to the Delimited ASCII Export dialog box.

When you're ready to export the table, choose OK in the Delimited ASCII Export dialog box.

TIP

Graphic, OLE, memo, and formatted memo fields cannot be stored as ASCII text. Therefore, you might want to exclude those fields with a query, then export the Answer table to a text file.

Importing Delimited Text Files

You can also import delimited text files into Paradox tables. When you select a file to import and choose the delimited text file format, you'll see the **Delimited ASCII Import** dialog box shown in Figure B.8. In this

FIGURE B.8

The Delimited ASCII Import dialog box

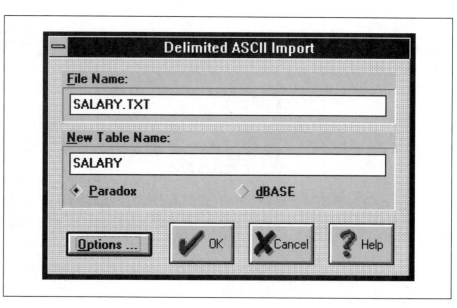

dialog box, you can change the names of the file to import and the table to create. You can also select a Paradox or dBASE table format by clicking the appropriate option.

If you click the Options button, the **Text Options** dialog box shown in Figure B.9 will appear. You can change the field separator, field delimiter, which fields are delimited, and the character set as described below. When you're finished, choose OK to return to the Delimited ASCII Import dialog box, then choose OK once more to begin importing the file.

The imported data will be stored in a new table with the field names *Field001*, *Field002*, *Field003*, and so on. Paradox scans the entire file to determine the number of fields and field types the file contains. Field types are determined on a "best guess" basis, and any delimited text longer than 255 characters is trimmed to 255 characters and stored in an alphanumeric field.

FIGURE B.9

The Text Options dialog box. After choosing the options you want, click OK to return to the previous dialog box.

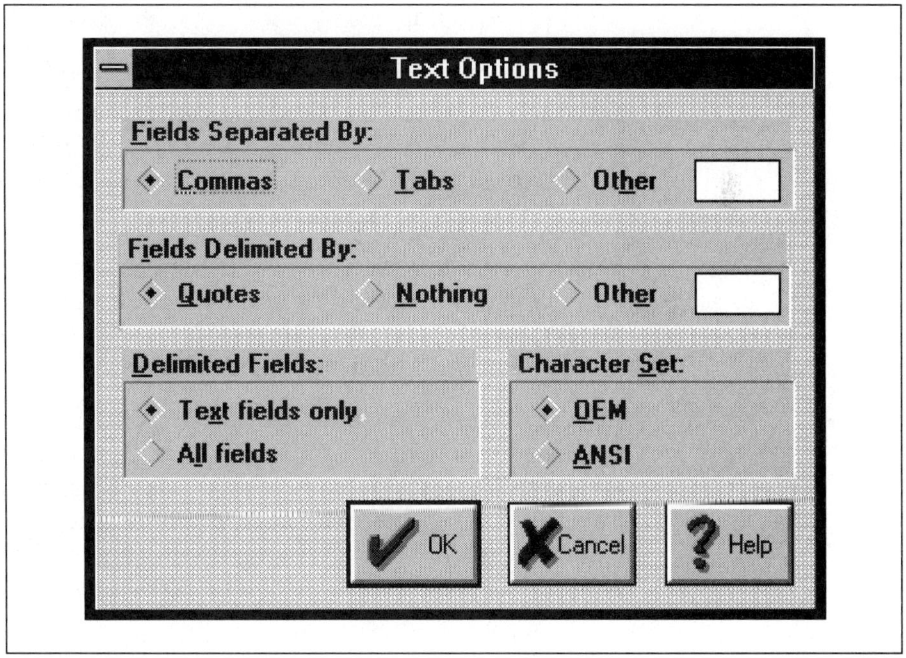

Text Options

Fields Separated By:
◆ Commas   ◇ Tabs   ◇ Other [   ]

Fields Delimited By:
◆ Quotes   ◇ Nothing   ◇ Other [   ]

Delimited Fields:
◆ Text fields only
◇ All fields

Character Set:
◆ OEM
◇ ANSI

✓ OK   ✗ Cancel   ? Help

Changing the Field Separator

By default, Paradox separates fields in a delimited text file with commas. To change this to a tab, select *Tabs* in the Fields Separated By area of the Text Options dialog box. To define your own delimiter character or characters, select *Other* in the Fields Separated By area, press →, then fill in the text box.

Changing the Field Delimiter Settings

The default character enclosing non-numeric (text) fields is the double quotation mark ("). If you don't want any characters to enclose text fields, select *Nothing* in the Fields Delimited By area of the Text Options dialog box. To define your own delimiter, select *Other*, press →, then fill in the text box.

Normally, Paradox places the field delimiter character around non-numeric text fields only. If you wish to place the delimiter around *all* fields, select *All Fields* in the Delimited Fields area of the text box.

Changing the Character Set

Although Paradox for Windows can recognize either of two character sets—OEM or ANSI—data in Paradox for Windows and dBASE tables is *always* stored in OEM characters. In contrast, Windows and Windows applications use ANSI characters.

Paradox handles the conversion between OEM and ANSI characters automatically when reading and writing data in tables. However, when exporting or importing text files, you must specify which set to use. If in doubt, stick with the default setting of OEM.

An *OEM* set (also called a code page) consists of 256 characters, numbered from 0 to 255. Characters 0-127 are the same for every code page. Characters 128-255 (called *extended characters*) differ for every code page. DOS 5.0 comes with several different code pages—English, Multilingual (Latin I), Slavic (Latin II), Portuguese, Canadian-French, and Nordic—although only one can be active at a time.

In contrast, only one set of *ANSI* characters exists. If you choose the ANSI option when importing, characters will be converted from ANSI to OEM. If you choose ANSI when exporting, characters will be converted from OEM to ANSI.

NOTE   Characters 32-126 are the same in the two sets; however, other characters are missing altogether, or are in different places in the character sets. Problems may arise during import or export because the two character sets are different.

Exporting Fixed Length Text Files

When you choose to export a table to a fixed length text file, the **Fixed Length ASCII Export** dialog box shown in Figure B.10 appears. The usual options are available for changing the name of the table you're exporting from and the file you're exporting to. You can also choose the OEM or ANSI character set options discussed above.

The Field Name, Start, and Length in the Export area are supplied automatically from the structure of the table you're exporting. You can change these settings if you want more control over the exported file, though you'll rarely need to do so. You can insert fields (press Ins), delete fields (press Ctrl+Del), edit field names, and modify the start position and length of any field.

If you'd like to save the export specification for later use, click the Save button, type a new file name, and choose OK.

If you want to use a previously saved specification, simply click the Load button, select a specification table from the list that appears, and choose OK. Again, you'll seldom need to change the default Export specifications.

When you're ready to begin exporting, click OK. Paradox will use the table structure you're exporting to control the location of each field in the exported records.

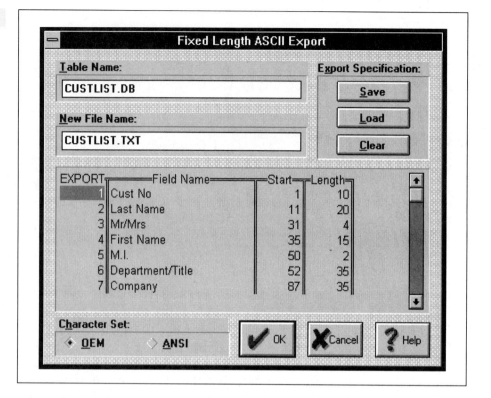

Importing Fixed Length
Text Files

The **Fixed Length ASCII Import** dialog box shown in Figure B.11 allows you to control how data is imported from a fixed length text file into your table. The usual options for changing the import file name and table names, the table type (Paradox or dBASE), and the character set (OEM or ANSI) are available.

When importing a fixed length text file, you must complete the Import field names, types, start, and length information in the dialog box. Your specifications must exactly match the arrangement of data in your text

FIGURE B.11

The Fixed Length
ASCII Import dialog
box

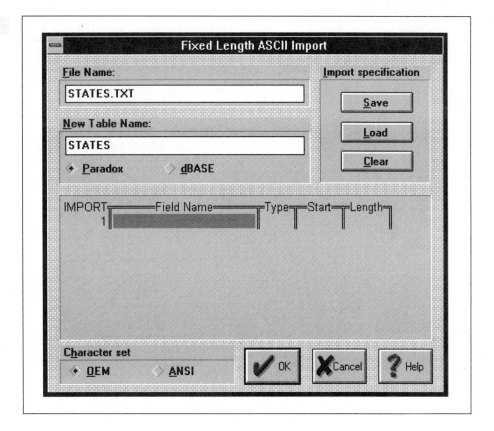

file. If the specification is incorrect, the imported data will make no sense. When editing the specification, you can insert rows (press Ins), delete rows (press Ctrl+Del), edit field names, and modify the start position and length of any field as needed.

If you wish to load a previously saved specification, click *Load*, select a specification table from the list, and choose OK.

As an aid to entering a correct specification, you can print part of your data file and mark the field name, starting position, and length for each field. For example, in Figure B.12, we marked some sample import data for the States lookup table discussed in Chapter 5.

FIGURE B.12

We've marked the field name, start position, and length for each field of a data file suitable for importing into the States table.

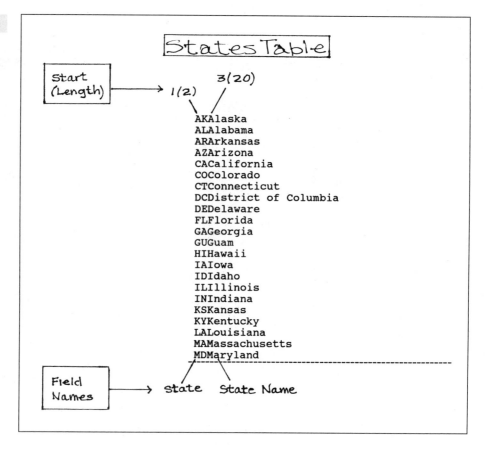

If you wish to clear the existing specifications and start over, click the Clear button. As when exporting files, you can save a specification by clicking the Save button, typing a new file name for your specification, and choosing OK.

When you're sure the Import specifications match the data you're importing, click OK. Paradox will use the structure you've defined in the dialog box to control the location of each field in the new table.

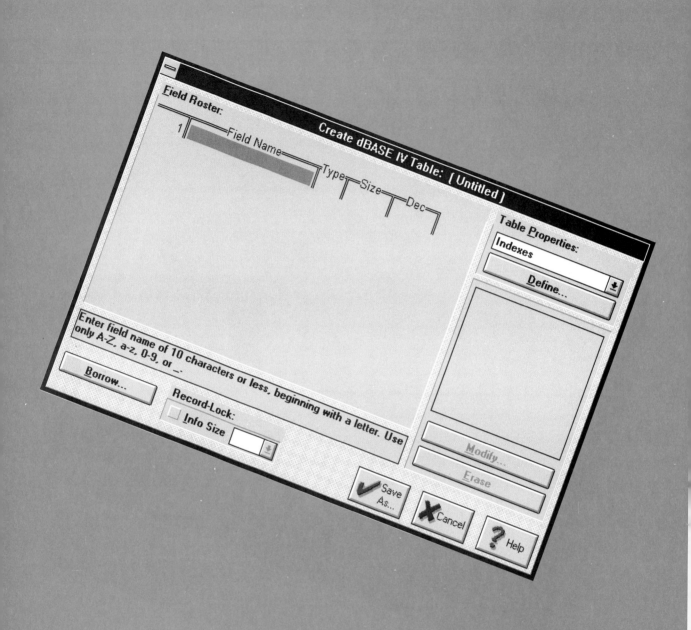

APPENDIX

Using Non-Paradox for
Windows Tables

I F you are currently using dBASE tables, or you're upgrading from an earlier version of Paradox, you can use Paradox for Windows to open, create, and modify your tables. You can also convert these tables to Paradox for Windows format. This Appendix explains how.

Using dBASE Tables

dBASE III+ and dBASE IV tables are entirely compatible with Paradox for Windows, although there are some differences between the dBASE and Paradox formats. For instance, dBASE offers a logical field that isn't available in Paradox for Windows. We'll describe special procedures for using dBASE tables in the following sections.

Creating dBASE III+ and dBASE IV Tables

The general techniques for creating dBASE tables are the same as those used to create Paradox for Windows tables (see Chapter 4). However, some of the details differ slightly. To begin creating a dBASE table in Paradox for Windows, proceed as follows:

1. Choose File ➤ New ➤ Table.
2. Click the drop-down arrow in the **Table Type** dialog box.
3. Choose *dBASE III+* or *dBASE IV* from the list.
4. Choose OK to open the **Create Table** dialog box.

5. Fill in the dialog box as described below.

6. Click Save As, specify a name for the table, and choose OK.

NOTE To restructure a dBASE table, choose File ➤ Utilities ➤ Restructure, specify the table name, choose OK, and then continue with Step 5 above. (See Chapter 14.)

The **Create dBASE IV Table** dialog box for dBASE IV tables is shown in Figure C.1. The **Create dBASE III+ Table** dialog box for dBASE III+ tables is slightly different.

NOTE Validity checks, referential integrity, and table lookup are not available for dBASE tables. The Table Properties drop-down list includes an Indexes option only.

Borrowing a Table Structure

If the Field Roster is empty, you can base your new dBASE table structure on an existing dBASE table. To borrow an existing table's structure, click the Borrow button in the Create Table dialog box. Select the table you want to borrow from. If you also want to use the borrowed table's maintained (*.mdx*) index definitions, check Indexes. Choose OK to return to the Create Table dialog box.

Defining dBASE Fields

When entering dBASE field names in the Field Roster of the dialog box, you must follow these rules:

• Names can have up to ten characters, including letters, digits, and underscores.

• The first character must be a letter.

FIGURE C.1

The Create dBASE IV
Table dialog box

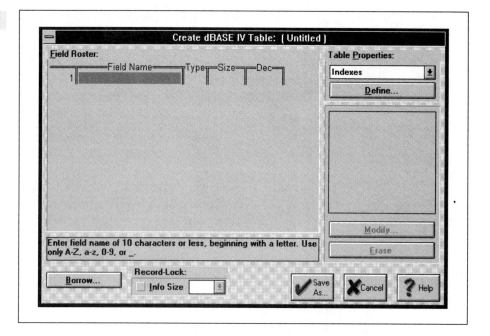

- No punctuation marks, spaces, or other special characters are allowed.

- Field names must be unique.

After entering a valid field name, define the field type. If the field type allows it, specify the field size and the number of digits to the right of the decimal point (*Dec*). (To display a list of valid field types in the dialog box, move the highlight to the Type column and press the spacebar.) Valid dBASE field types, sizes, and decimal point settings appear in Table C.1.

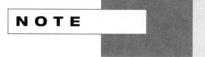

N O T E

The number of decimal places for a *float number* field must be no more than the field size minus two.

TABLE C.1: dBASE III+ and dBASE IV Field Types and Sizes

FIELD TYPE	SYMBOL	FIELD SIZE	DECIMAL POINT
Character	C	1-254	
Float Number	F	1-20	0-18 (must be <= Field Size-2)
Number	N	1-20	0-18 (must be <= Field Size-2)
Date	D		
Logic	L		
Memo	M		

NOTE: Memo field formats (M) differ between dBASE III+ and dBASE IV tables. The Float Number (F) format is available for dBASE IV tables only.

Defining dBASE IV Record Locks

When creating a dBASE IV table that will be used on a network, you may wish to check the Info Size option. When Info Size is checked, Paradox will add to the table a hidden field that shows when a record was locked and which user placed the lock. (Record Lock is not available for dBASE III+ tables.)

The amount of information displayed when you try to access a locked field depends on the *Info Size* you specify. The default size of 16 characters tells whether the record has been changed, shows the time and date of the lock, and displays the first eight characters of the name of the user who placed the lock. You can specify an Info Size of 8 to 24 characters.

Defining an Index for a dBASE Table

Unlike Paradox tables, dBASE tables do not have key fields. However, you can define one or more indexes for a dBASE table. Indexes can be based on a single field or on an expression (composite field).

To define an index, click the Define button in the Create Table or Restructure Table dialog box (see Figure C.1). You'll see the **Define Index** dialog box shown in Figure C.2.

To create a *single-field index*, select the field you want to index in the Field List, and then check (select) or uncheck (deselect) one or more of the options listed below:

Unique   Select this option to create an index with only one instance of each value. Duplicate values can exist in the table, but will be ignored. Deselect this option to allow the index to contain duplicate values.

Maintained   Select this option to have Paradox update the index whenever the table changes. Deselect this option if you want the index to be updated only when you link tables or run a query. Maintained indexes are also called "production indexes." This option is available for dBASE IV tables only.

Descending   Select this option to sort index values in descending order (*Z* to *A*). Deselect the option to sort index values in ascending order (*A* to *Z*).

WARNING   Maintained indexes are the recommended index type. Non-maintained indexes are much less desirable because of their many limitations. For example, operations such as adding, subtracting, and emptying tables will invalidate the non-maintained index. Moreover, you must use <u>T</u>able ➤ <u>O</u>rder/Range (Chapter 8) to open a non-maintained index each time you update or sort the table.

To create an *expression* or *composite* index, click the Expression Index button. The button will be replaced by an Index Field button. Next, enter the expression in the Expression Index text box. For example, the expression *Last_Name+First_Name* would create a composite index on the Last_Name and First_Name fields of a dBASE table.

FIGURE C.2

The Define Index dialog box lets you define single-field and expression indexes for a dBASE table.

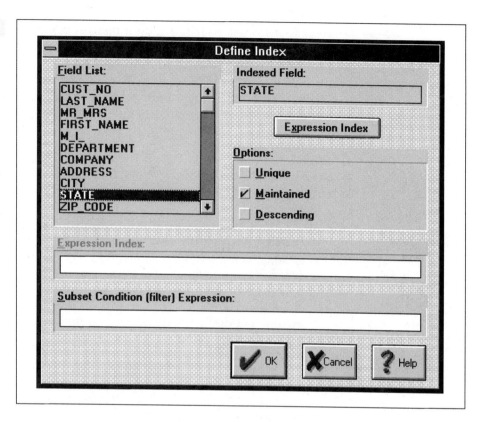

TIP   If you change your mind and want to go back to defining a single-field index, simply click the Index Field button that replaced the Expression Index button in the dialog box.

When entering the expression, you can either type the field names, or you can enter them automatically by placing the cursor in the Expression Index text box and clicking the field name in the Field List. The field name you clicked will appear in the text box at the cursor position. All fields in an expression index must be of the same type. (Please see your dBASE manual for more information on expression indexes.)

You can also base your index on a *subset condition* or filter that evaluates to true or false. Records that meet the condition are included in the index. For example, the subset condition *STATE=NY* would create an index for customers who live in New York. To create a subset condition, click in the Subset Condition (Filter) Expression text box and enter the condition. You may create a subset condition in either a single-field index or an expression index.

To save the index, click OK in the Define Index dialog box. When the **Save Index As** dialog box appears, fill in the text boxes described below, and then choose OK to return to the Create Table or Restructure Table dialog box.

Index File Name   This text box is available only when you're saving a *non-maintained* index. If you're creating a single-field index, Paradox will use the field name as the index file name. If you're creating an expression index, you must specify the index file name (*without* the extension) in the text box. The non-maintained index file is assigned an *.ndx* extension automatically.

Index Tag Name   This text box is available only when you're saving a *maintained* index. Enter the name for the index tag (again, do not type a file extension). The file used to store all maintained indexes for a table will have the same name as the table and the extension *.mdx*.

Defining dBASE Logic Field Formats

When typing data into a dBASE logic field, you can enter a single character to indicate whether a value is true or false. The *Logical Format* determines the character used to specify the true or false value and the value that's filled in when you move the highlight to another field in the table or form. For example, if the current Logical Format is True/False, typing **T** or **t** into the field would fill in the value *True*; typing **F** or **f** would fill in the value *False*.

To select a format for a logic field, inspect the field in the Table View window or Form Design window, select Logical Format, and select one of the formats from the list (for instance, True/False, Yes/No, or Male/Female).

To customize the logic field format, inspect the field, select Logical Format, and click the menu header (...) or press ↵. The **Select Logical Format** dialog box shown in Figure C.3 will appear. Complete the dialog box using the techniques discussed in Chapter 6.

N O T E

Like Paradox tables, dBASE tables can be customized and can have default properties defined. dBASE table properties are stored in a *.tvf* file with the same name as the table. (See Chapters 6 and 13.)

FIGURE C.3

The Select Logical Format dialog box lets you specify the values that will appear in a logical field.

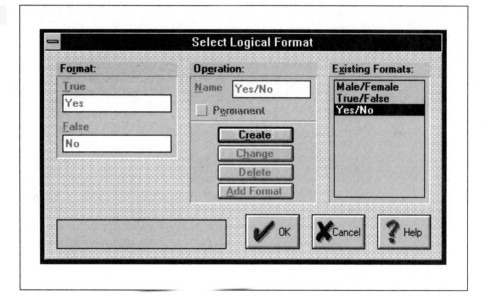

Restructuring a dBASE Table

You can use the File ➤ Utilities ➤ Restructure or Table ➤ Restructure options discussed in Chapter 14 to restructure a dBASE table. Keep in mind that changing the field type may mean trimming the data, or may result in records that cannot be converted at all. You'll be asked to confirm any data loss, and any records that cannot be converted will be stored in the temporary *Problems* table in your private directory. Table C.2 shows the effects of converting from one data type to another. See Chapter 14 for additional information.

TIP

If you add production indexes (*.mdx*), memo fields, or float fields to a dBASE III+ table, Paradox will convert it to a dBASE IV table automatically.

TABLE C.2: dBASE III+ and dBASE IV Field Types and Sizes

	TO C	TO F	TO N	TO D	TO L	TO M
From C	Yes	P	P	P	Yes	Yes
From F	Yes	Yes	Yes	No	Yes	No
From N	Yes	Yes	Yes	No	Yes	No
From D	Yes	No	No	Yes	No	No
From L	Yes	Yes	Yes	No	Yes	No
From M	Yes	No	No	No	No	Yes

NOTE: *Yes* means Paradox allows the conversion but may trim data.
No means the conversion is not allowed.
P means the conversion is allowed, but a *Problems* table will usually result.

Transferring Data between Paradox and dBASE

To convert a Paradox table to a dBASE table, or vice versa, use the File ➤ Utilities ➤ Copy options discussed in Chapter 14. When the **Copy** dialog box appears, click the source file you want to copy from. Then click in the <u>D</u>estination File text box and type the file name and extension for the new table. To convert a dBASE table to a Paradox table, specify a *.db* extension for the destination file. To convert a Paradox table to a dBASE table, specify a *.dbf* extension for the destination file.

Paradox will change the field types automatically to accommodate the new format. Table C.3 summarizes the effects of copying from a Paradox table to a dBASE table. Table C.4 summarizes the effects of copying from a dBASE table to a Paradox table.

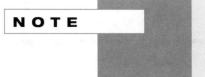

NOTE A dBASE III+ table type is created if the copy yields no production index (*.mdx* file) and no float fields or memo fields. A dBASE IV table type is created if any of these are produced by the copy.

TABLE C.3: Effects of Copying from a Paradox Table to a dBASE Table

FROM PARADOX TYPE	TO DBASE TYPE	SIDE EFFECTS
Alphanumeric	Character	
Number	Number	Size=20, Dec=4
Currency	Number	Size=20, Dec=4
Short Number	Number	Size=5, Dec=0
Date	Date	
Memo	Memo	
Formatted Memo	Memo	Data is lost
Graphic	Memo	Data is lost
OLE	Memo	Data is lost
Binary	Memo	Data is lost

TABLE C.4: Effects of Copying from a dBASE Table to a Paradox Table

FROM dBASE TYPE	TO PARADOX TYPE	SIDE EFFECTS
Character	Alphanumeric	
Float Number	Number	Removes size
Number	Number	Removes size
Logical	Alphanumeric	Size=1; keeps first character
Date	Date	
Memo	Memo	Size=10

Viewing Deleted dBASE Records

When you delete a record from a dBASE table, that record is simply *marked* for deletion; it isn't actually removed from your computer's hard disk.

To view records that have been marked for deletion, choose Table ➤ Show Deleted or Form ➤ Show Deleted. In Table View, deleted records are indicated by a deletion marker. In Form View, the status bar will display "(Record Deleted)." To hide the deleted records from view, choose the Show Deleted option from the Table or Form menu again.

To delete marked records from the computer's hard disk permanently, restructure the table (File ➤ Utilities ➤ Restructure), check the Pack Table option in the **Table Restructure** dialog box, and click Save.

Viewing dBASE Records with a Different Sort Order

To view a dBASE table with a different sort order, or to view a range of records, choose Table ➤ Order/Range or Form ➤ Order/Range when the table is opened in Table View or Form View. When the **Order/Range** dialog box appears, select an index tag from the Index List. To add another non-maintained index file (*.ndx*) or a production index file (*.mdx*) to the Index List, type the file name and extension in the Select dBASE Index File text box and press ↵. After selecting the index to use, you can complete the dialog box (Chapter 7) and choose OK.

Creating Multitable Design Documents with dBASE Tables

The steps and rules for creating multitable forms and reports with dBASE tables are similar to those described in Chapter 17 under "Creating Multitable Design Documents." As for Paradox documents, you start from the **Data Model** dialog box. Add the tables to the data model and use your mouse to draw the link from the master table to the detail table.

When the **Define Link** dialog box appears, select the master table field you want to link from the Field list. Then select the index for the detail table from the Index list. Choose OK to complete the link and return to the Data Model dialog box.

Figure C.4 shows the Define Link dialog box for linking *states.dbf* (a master table with a maintained index on the State field) to *custlist.dbf* (a detail table with maintained indexes on the Cust_No and State fields).

As an alternative to defining a field from the Field list, you can click the Master Expression option and type a valid dBASE expression. For instance, the expression *UPPER(State)* would convert the alphanumeric State field values to uppercase. Please refer to your dBASE manual for a list of valid master expressions.

Keep in mind that you can link dBASE tables only on maintained indexes (*.mdx* files). Furthermore, it's best to use a *unique* index for your master table. The fields being linked in the Define Link dialog box must be the same type, unless you use an expression index in the link.

FIGURE C.4

The States and CustList dBASE tables are linked by the State field and State index respectively.

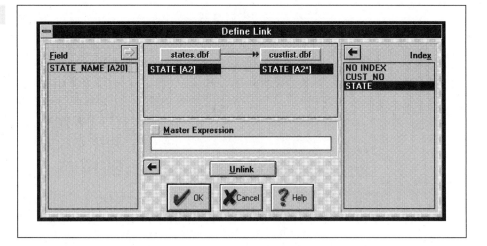

N O T E

When linking dBASE tables, you can link from a field to an expression index or single-field index, or from a master expression to an expression index or single-field index.

Using Tables from Other Versions of Paradox

Paradox for Windows recognizes two types of Paradox table files: level 1 and level 2. Files created in Paradox 3.5 or earlier are level 1 files; files created in Paradox 4.0 for DOS or Paradox for Windows are level 2 files.

NOTE Paradox for Windows does not recognize queries, reports, forms, scripts, or applications created in other versions of Paradox.

Updating Tables in Different Versions of Paradox

When updating and displaying tables in previous versions of Paradox, keep the following points in mind:

- Paradox for Windows can display and update tables created by *any* previous version of Paradox.

- Paradox 4.0 can display and update tables created by Paradox for Windows, provided all the field types are supported by Paradox 4.0. Paradox 4.0 cannot display or update formatted memo, graphic, OLE, and binary fields.

- Paradox 3.5 or earlier cannot display or update tables created by Paradox for Windows, unless the table was specifically created as a Paradox 3.5 table.

Restructuring Tables

When you use Paradox for Windows to restructure a level 1 table, it remains a level 1 table unless you add a memo, formatted memo, graphic, OLE, or binary field, define referential integrity, or define a secondary index or case-insensitive index. In those cases, the level 1 table is converted to a level 2 table. (See Chapters 4, 7, 14, and 15.)

You can use Paradox 4.0 to restructure a Paradox for Windows table, unless referential integrity has been defined. The restructured table will be saved as a level 2 table if you add a memo field or you choose FileFormat ➤ Standard in the Paradox 4.0 Restructure window.

Paradox 3.5 and earlier versions can restructure level 1 tables only.

Ensuring Data Integrity and Validity

Paradox for Windows is the only version of Paradox that fully supports referential integrity. If you use a Paradox for Windows table with another version of Paradox, you may violate the defined referential integrity (see Chapter 15).

Paradox 4.0 recognizes and enforces all the passwords and validity checks that are available in Paradox for Windows (see Chapters 4 and 14).

Paradox 3.5 does not support validity checks.

Using Indexes

If you create a composite secondary index for a Paradox for Windows table, Paradox 4.0 will be able to maintain the index but will not be able to use it to search for field values.

Both Paradox for Windows and Paradox 4.0 support case-insensitive indexing, in which uppercase and lowercase characters are considered the same. Paradox 3.5, however, does not allow case-insensitive indexing.

Accessing Tables Concurrently

Paradox for Windows and Paradox 4.0 for DOS use the same locking mechanism when sharing files on a network. Paradox 3.5 and earlier versions of Paradox, however, use a different locking mechanism. Practically speaking, this means that Paradox for Windows and Paradox 4.0 for DOS can access tables and directories concurrently. However, Paradox for Windows cannot access tables and directories that are currently in use by Paradox 3.5 or earlier versions.

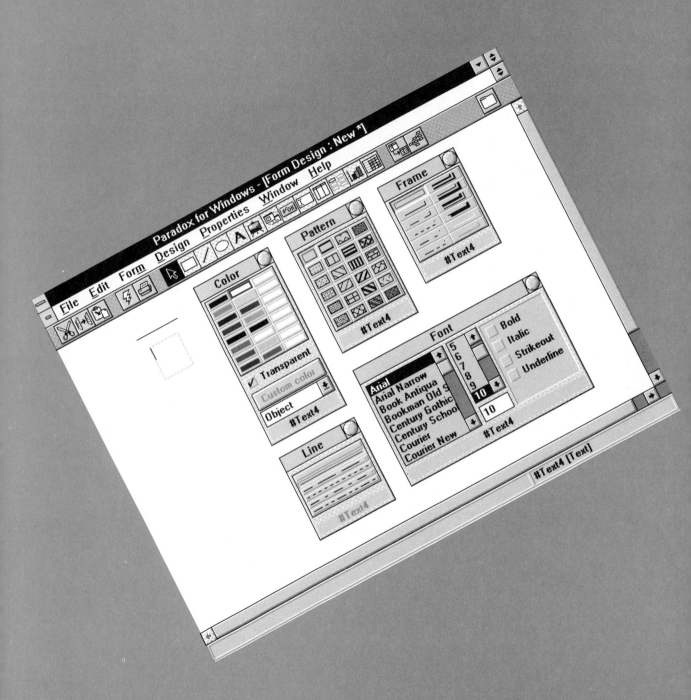

APPENDIX

D

Summary of Design Object Properties

YOU can change properties of any object in the Form Design or Report Design windows simply by inspecting the objects and selecting options from the property menus that appear. This appendix briefly describes design object properties and the objects to which they apply. For additional details on the topics listed below, please refer to the chapters indicated:

- Creating design documents, creating objects, selecting objects, and changing object properties (Chapter 9).

- Creating forms and changing properties of objects in form designs (Chapter 10).

- Creating reports and mail merge documents and changing properties of objects in report designs (Chapter 11).

- Creating graphs and crosstabs and changing their properties (Chapter 12).

- Attaching ObjectPAL methods to buttons and other objects in form designs (Chapter 19).

Design Object Properties

Table D.1 describes object properties for each design object. The Speed-Bar buttons in the table indicate which objects have each property.

Some design properties apply only to objects in forms, while others apply only to objects in reports. For example, buttons and crosstab properties apply to forms only, while report band properties apply to report designs only.

TABLE D.1: Summary of Design Object Properties

PROPERTY	DESCRIPTION	OBJECTS
Add A Category	Add a field (category) in the row area of a crosstab.	
Add A Summary	Add a field to display a calculation result at the intersection of each row and column in a crosstab.	
Alignment	Align text at the left, right, or center of the object border.	
Button Type	Display the button as a Check box, Push button, or Radio button.	
Center Label	Center the label text on the button.	
Color	Change the color of an object.	
Conditional	Print a group header object at the beginning of each page and/or each group. (Inspect an object in the group band.)	
Data Type	Change data type of a graph design to tabular, 1D, or 2D summary.	

SUMMARY OF DESIGN OBJECT PROPERTIES

TABLE D.1: Summary of Design Object Properties (continued)

PROPERTY	DESCRIPTION	OBJECTS
Define Crosstab	Define table data and other features of a crosstab.	
Define Field	Define field data for a field object.	
Define Graph	Define a complex graph.	
Define Graphic	Define the image for a graphic object.	
Define Group	Define the grouping for a 2D Summary graph or for a report band.	
Define OLE	Define an OLE value for an OLE object.	
Define Record	Define table data to display in the record area of a table or multi-record object.	
Define Table	Define the table to display in a table frame.	
Define X-Value	Define a field for a graph's X-axis.	
Define (New) Y-Value	Define a field for a graph's Y-axis.	
Delete When Empty	Delete this record from the report if its fields are empty.	
Design Sizing ➤ Fixed Size	Prevent the text object from changing size to fit entered text.	

TABLE D.1: Summary of Design Object Properties (continued)

PROPERTY	DESCRIPTION	OBJECTS
Design Sizing ➤ Fit Text	Expand or contract the text object to fit entered text.	
Design Sizing ➤ Grow Only	Expand, but do not contract, the text object to fit entered text.	
Design ➤ Contain Objects	Allow the object to contain and control objects within its borders.	
Design ➤ Pin Horizontal	Pin object so that it maintains its horizontal position within the design.	All
Design ➤ Pin Vertical	Pin object so that it maintains its vertical position within the design.	All
Design ➤ Size to Fit	Expand or contract the object to fit the data it contains.	
Detach Header	Move the table header containing field names away from the body of table data.	

SUMMARY OF DESIGN OBJECT PROPERTIES

TABLE D.1: Summary of Design Object Properties (continued)

PROPERTY	DESCRIPTION	OBJECTS
Display Type	Display field values as a Check Box, Drop-Down Edit List, or Radio Button.	
Display Type ➤ Labeled	Display the field value with a label.	
Display Type ➤ Unlabeled	Display the field value without a label.	
Explode	Explode a slice in a pie graph.	
Font	Change the typeface, size, style, or color of text.	
Format ➤ Date Format	Change the date field display format.	
Format ➤ Logical Format	Change the dBASE logical field display format.	
Format ➤ Number Format	Change the number field display format.	
Format ➤ Time Format	Change the time field display format.	
Format ➤ Timestamp Format	Change the time/date field display format.	
Frame	Change the frame style, color, or thickness of the object.	

TABLE D.1: Summary of Design Object Properties (continued)

PROPERTY	DESCRIPTION	OBJECTS
Graph Type	Define the display type for graphed data (e.g., 2D Pie, 2D Bar, 3D Area).	
Grid	Change the line color and style of grid lines; display a divider between multiple records.	
Headings	Print a group heading at top of the page and/or group.	
Horizontal Scroll Bar	Display a scroll bar below the object.	
Label	Define the format of labels used in a graph.	
Legend Pos	Define the position of a graph's legend.	
Line	Change the line thickness, color, or style for the object.	
Line Ends	Display an arrow at one or both ends of a line.	
Line Spacing	Set the spacing between lines of text.	
Line Style	Set the line style to solid, dashed, dotted, or combination from palette.	

TABLE D.1: Summary of Design Object Properties (continued)

PROPERTY	DESCRIPTION	OBJECTS
Line Type	Change the line to straight or curved.	
Magnification	Increase or decrease the size of an object within its container.	
Max Groups	Set the maximum number of group-by values in a 2D summary graph.	
Max X-Values	Set the maximum number of x-axis values in a graph.	
Methods	Attach ObjectPAL methods to an object (form design only).	All
Min X-Values	Set the minimum number of x-axis values in a graph.	
Options	Set parameters for graph axes, grid, labels, legend, and titles. (See Chapter 12.)	
Pattern	Change the fill pattern or fill color of an object.	
Raster Operation	Define how source graphic pixels combine with destination pixels.	

TABLE D.1: Summary of Design Object Properties (continued)

PROPERTY	DESCRIPTION	OBJECTS
Record Layout	Specify the number of records across and down, and the spacing between records in multi-record object.	
Remove This Y-Value	Remove the selected Y-value from a graph.	
Repeat Header	Print a report header at the top of each page.	
Run Time ➤ Breakable	Allow an object to divide at page breaks.	
Run Time ➤ Complete Display	Display the entire memo or formatted memo field.	
Run Time ➤ Field Squeeze	Adjust text to remove spaces around embedded fields.	
Run Time ➤ Fit Height	Grow or shrink the object vertically to fit contained objects.	
Run Time ➤ Fit Width	Grow or shrink the object horizontally to fit contained objects.	
Run Time ➤ Invisible	Do not display the object when the report is run.	

TABLE D.1: Summary of Design Object Properties (continued)

PROPERTY	DESCRIPTION	OBJECTS
Run Time ➤ Line Squeeze	Delete blank text lines.	A
Run Time ➤ No Echo	Do not display data entered into this field object.	I
Run Time ➤ Orphan/Widow	Adjust text to prevent orphans and widows.	A
Run Time ➤ Pin Horizontal	Pin object to maintain its horizontal position on the page at runtime.	All
Run Time ➤ Pin Vertical	Pin object to maintain its vertical position on the page at runtime.	All
Run Time ➤ Read Only	Do not allow user to change data in this field.	I
Run Time ➤ Show All Columns	Expand the table frame to fit all table columns.	⊞
Run Time ➤ Show All Records	Expand the object vertically (and horizontally for multi-record objects) to show all records.	⊞ ▤
Run Time ➤ Shrinkable	Shrink the object to fit on the page if the object contains no printable data and would otherwise move to the next page.	▢ ◯ ▤

TABLE D.1: Summary of Design Object Properties (continued)

PROPERTY	DESCRIPTION	OBJECTS
Run Time ➤ Tab Stop	Allow user to press *Tab* on a form to move to this object.	
Run Time ➤ Visible	Display the object in the form.	All
Search Text	Search and replace text values.	
Sort Order	Define ascending or descending sort order for a report group.	
Style	Define the button style (Windows or Borland) for a radio button or check box.	
Subtitle	Define the text or font of a graph's subtitle.	
Thickness	Define the thickness of a line or frame.	
Ticks	Define the font or number format of a graph's tick marks.	
Title	Define the text or font of a graph's title.	
Type Override	Define a different display type for a selected series in a graph.	

TABLE D.1: Summary of Design Object Properties (continued)

PROPERTY	DESCRIPTION	OBJECTS
Vertical Scroll Bar	Display a vertical scroll bar at the right side of an object.	
Word Wrap	Automatically begin a new line when text reaches the right border of the object.	

In addition to design properties, objects can have *Run Time* properties, which govern their behavior when you "run" a form or report. To see the effects of Run Time properties, click the View Data button in the Speed-Bar of the Design window or press F8. Different sets of Run Time properties apply to forms and reports.

Many property settings are "toggles" that are either on (checked) or off (unchecked). The descriptions in Table D.1 assume the toggle settings are on.

Using the Palettes

As discussed in Chapter 9, Paradox displays "visual" properties—Color, Line Style, Font, and Frame—on palettes instead of menus. To select an option from a palette, simply click on the option or appearance of your choice.

By default the palettes are temporary and disappear when you make a selection. However, if you want to leave the palette on the screen, just click the snap at the top. This creates a *floating palette* that you can move about on the Desktop by dragging its title bar. The floating palette remains on the Desktop until you click the snap button again. Figure D.1 shows all the floating palettes on the Paradox for Windows Desktop.

NOTE   The Thickness property for a line or frame always appears in a temporary palette.

Here's a brief description of each floating palette:

- The *Color* palette allows you to change the color of an object, line, pattern, frame, grid, or font.

- The *Frame* palette lets you change the appearance of the border around an object. To create three-dimensional frames, select either

FIGURE D.1

Floating palettes remain on the Desktop until you click the snap button.

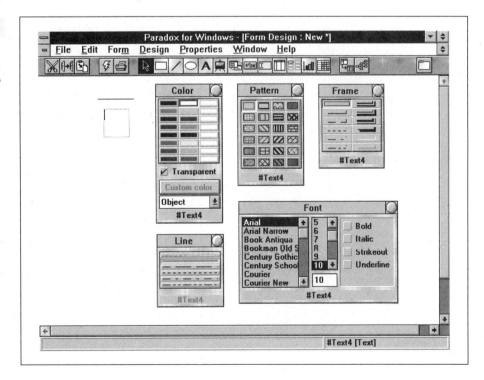

of the last two frame styles on the palette. (See Chapter 9 and Chapter 10.)

- The *Pattern* palette allows you to change the fill pattern for an object. To change the color of the fill pattern, choose Pattern ➤ Color from the property menu.

- The *Line* palette allows you to choose a line style (solid, dashed, etc.) To display this palette, inspect a line and choose Line Style.

Selecting Transparent and Opaque Colors

Nearly all design objects have Color properties that you can change by inspecting the objects and choosing Color from the property menu. When the Color palette appears, you can click on any of 16 predefined colors, or you can create and select any of nine custom colors.

The color you assign can be transparent, translucent, or opaque. If the color is transparent or translucent, objects behind it will show through; if the color is opaque, the opaque object will obscure objects behind it.

To make an object completely transparent—that is, completely clear and colorless—select the "color" at the bottom-right corner of the *temporary* color palette. To assign an opaque color, select any color from the temporary palette.

The floating Color palette includes a Transparent check box (see Figure D.1). If you check Transparent, the object's color will be *translucent*; that is, it will appear in a color that allows objects behind it to show through. If you deselect the Transparent option, the object in front will obscure anything behind it.

NOTE The drop-down list in the floating Color palette allows you to color an object, line, pattern, frame, grid, or font. (See Chapter 6.)

Creating Custom Colors

To create a custom color, follow the steps below.

1. Open the floating Color palette and highlight one of the white color samples in the right-hand column. You may create up to nine custom colors in one palette. (To reach the ninth color, click in the right-most column of the floating Color palette and press the → key.)

2. Click the Custom Color button to display the **Custom Color** dialog box shown in Figure D.2.

FIGURE D.2

The Custom Color dialog box allows you to define custom colors for design objects.

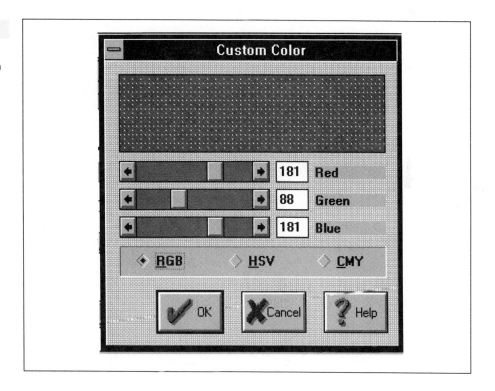

3. Select one of the following methods to mix the custom color; any method can be used to create any color.

   RGB   Defines the color as a mixture of red, green, and blue.

   HSV   Defines the color in terms of hue, saturation, and value (brightness).

   CMY   Defines the color as a mixture of cyan, magenta, and yellow.

4. Drag the scroll bars and click the scroll arrows, or type values into the text boxes, to create the color mix you want. A sample of the color will appear above the scroll bars.

5. When the color is to your liking, choose OK to save it on the palette.

You can assign the custom color to any object in a design simply by clicking on the color in the temporary or floating Color palette. Custom colors remain on the palette in future Paradox sessions. To change a custom color, highlight the color you want to change in the floating Color palette and repeat Steps 2 through 5 above. Changes to the custom color affect the selected objects only; unselected objects will retain their original custom colors.

Table Locks

Table Name:

`*.db;*.dbf`

CONTACTS.DB
CUSTOMER.DB
LINEITEM.DB
ORDERS.DB
STOCK.DB
VENDORS.DB
:PRIV:CUSTLIST.DB
:PRIV:LOCKS.DB
:PRIV:STATES.DB

Locks:

- ● **No Lock**
- ○ **Open Lock**
- ○ **Read Lock**
- ○ **Write Lock**
- ○ **Exclusive Lock**

Path: :WORK:

Type: <Tables>

Browse...

✔ OK

✘ Cancel

? Help

APPENDIX

Using Paradox
for Windows on a
Network

WHEN you use Paradox for Windows in a multiuser (network) environment, Paradox offers some additional features and behaves somewhat differently from the way it's described in the chapters of this book. This appendix addresses those features and differences. Here we'll explain how to view user names, lock tables and records, and set the retry period and screen refresh rate on a network. We'll also discuss some data security issues and explain how the File ➤ Utilities options behave in a multiuser environment.

N O T E

Installing Paradox for Windows on a network is considerably more complicated than performing the single-user installation (discussed in Appendix A). It should be undertaken only by a network administrator or supervisor who has full (or "parental") rights to all directories on the network and a thorough understanding of network concepts. Please refer to Chapter 15 of the *Getting Started* manual that comes with Paradox for complete instructions on installing and configuring Paradox for Windows on a network.

Viewing User Names

In a *multiuser* environment, each user has a "name" that uniquely identifies him or her to Paradox. Unlike many other multiuser databases, Paradox for Windows does not require a separate list of user names and passwords. For instance, if you log in to your Novell NetWare network as *SUSAN*, Paradox for Windows will identify you simply as *SUSAN*.

To view your user name, choose File ➤ Multiuser ➤ User Name. After viewing the dialog box that appears, click OK.

To view the names of other network users who are also running Paradox for Windows at the moment, choose File ➤ Multiuser ➤ Who. When you're finished viewing the list, click OK.

Securing Your Data from Unauthorized Access

In a multiuser environment, it is important to protect your data from unauthorized access and to control which users can access tables and fields. In Paradox for Windows, you control access to data by assigning passwords and security privileges separately for each table.

Each secure table can have a *master password* that provides full control over the table and its security. Tables can also have one or more *auxiliary passwords*, which provide an additional level of security for the table and its fields. For example, a user who enters the password **BASEBALL** may be able to insert or delete records from a Customer table. However, a user who enters the password **FOOTBALL** may only be able to read data from the Customer table, or may only be able to update certain fields.

Chapter 14 explains how to assign and use master and auxiliary passwords via the Restructure and Passwords options on the File ➤ Utilities menu.

Locking Tables and Records

In a multiuser environment, many users may need to read or update data at the same time. The database management system must prevent several people from changing data at the same time (this can corrupt the data), while still allowing multiple users to view the data or work with data in other parts of the database.

Paradox uses a system of locks to control who can do what, and when they can do it. In essence, the locking mechanism acts as a traffic cop, placing *locks* on data when a person needs to perform a certain function and then releasing the locks when the work is done.

Paradox for Windows' automatic locking schemes are usually adequate for any user's needs, so you shouldn't need to take any special action. For example, Paradox will *always* lock a record automatically when a user is updating it, and will release the lock automatically when the highlight is moved to another record. Similarly, it will place a special lock called an *Open* lock on a table when anyone opens the table, or when any form, report, query, or other document that uses the table's data is opened.

WARNING   Paradox for Windows does not set locks when it is running under Windows for Workgroups and accessing data from another local hard drive. This may cause data corruption.

If necessary, you can lock tables and records explicitly by choosing options from the Paradox Desktop menus or by writing ObjectPal programs. In this appendix, we'll discuss methods for locking tables and records from the Desktop. For information on locking records through Object-PAL programs, please refer to the *ObjectPAL Developer's Guide* that comes with Paradox for Windows.

Before setting locks, you should understand the implications thoroughly. In particular, be aware that you must explicitly remove any locks that you set from the Desktop. If you forget to remove the Desktop locks, other users may be unable to view or update the data. Also, be certain that you exit Paradox for Windows and the network properly to avoid leaving tables and records locked accidentally.

W A R N I N G   Never exit by simply turning off your computer. Doing so without properly exiting Paradox can corrupt your data and prevent other users from using Paradox on the network.

Locking a Table from the Desktop

To set an explicit lock on a table, proceed as follows:

1. Choose File ➤ Multiuser ➤ Set Locks. You'll see the **Table Locks** dialog box, as shown in Figure E.1.

2. Select the table for which you wish to set locks.

3. Select the type of lock you want from the Locks area. Each type of lock is described below. To remove all locks that you've placed on the table, select *No Lock*.

4. Choose OK.

In Step 3, above, you can select one of the following locks:

No Lock   Unlocks all locks that you've placed on the table. Note that this has no effect on locks set by *other* users. All users must explicitly remove their own table locks.

The Table Locks dialog box allows you to lock a table.

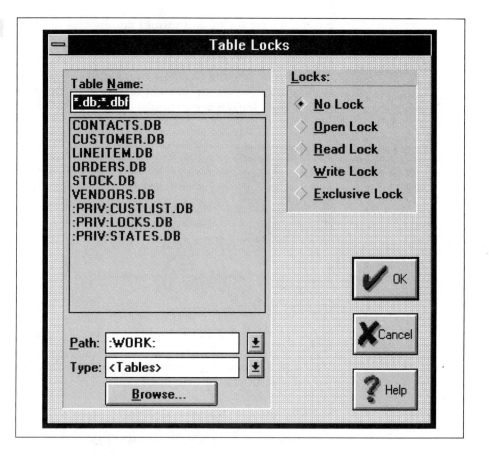

Open Lock Prevents other users from putting an Exclusive lock on the table. However, another user can still put a Write lock on the table even if you've placed an Open lock on it. An Open lock has the same effect as opening the table, but does not actually open it.

Read Lock Allows you to read (view) and write to (edit) the selected table. Other users can view the data in the table if they have sufficient rights, but they cannot write to the table unless they place a Write lock on the same table. If another user does place a Write lock on the table, you'll be unable to write to the table until the Write lock is removed. A table can have more than one Read lock on it at a time.

Write Lock   Allows you to read and write to the table. Other users can read from the table, but they cannot write to it. A table can have only one Write lock on it at a time.

Exclusive Lock   Gives you read and write access to the table. However, others cannot use the table in any way, nor can they create a table with the same name until you release the lock. This lock is the most restrictive and should be used only when absolutely necessary.

Keep in mind that Paradox places an Open lock on a table when anyone opens the table, or when any form, report, query, or other document that uses the table's data is opened. Users (including yourself) must remove Open locks by closing windows that contain the table's data before Paradox or any other user can place an Exclusive lock on it.

Table E.1 summarizes the effects of placing different types of table locks from the Desktop.

TABLE E.1:   Effects of Locking Tables from the Desktop

LOCK LEVEL	YOUR RIGHTS	OTHER USERS' RIGHTS	LOCKS OTHER USERS CAN PLACE
No Lock	None	All	All*
Open Lock	Read, Write (if no one else has a Read lock)	Read, Write	All except Exclusive if no record lock is in place. Otherwise, only Open.
Read Lock	Read, Write (if no one else has a Read lock)	Read	Open, Read
Write Lock	Read, Write	Read	Open
Exclusive Lock	All	None	None

* *No Lock* removes Desktop-level locks only; it has no effect on record locks or Open locks. You cannot obtain an Exclusive lock if the table is locked from the Desktop, through record locks, or through Open locks.

To view the current locks on a table, choose File ➤ Multiuser ➤ Display Locks, select the table you're interested in, and choose OK. The information appears in a temporary Paradox table named *Locks*, and includes the type of locks placed and the name of the user who placed each lock. This feature is not available for dBASE tables.

Locking a Record from the Desktop

Although Paradox tries to lock a record automatically when you begin to change it, you may occasionally wish to lock a record manually. For example, if you are talking with a customer who is about to provide some information about an address change, you can lock the record so that no one else can jump in and change that customer's data.

To lock a record, open the table or form, switch to Edit mode (press F9 or click the Edit Data button in the SpeedBar), move to the record you want to lock, and then choose Record ➤ Lock or press F5.

To unlock a record, move the highlight to another record, choose Record ➤ Unlock, or press Shift+F5.

NOTE
Unlocking a record commits the changes to the table. Chapter 5 provides more information about entering and editing data.

Setting the Network Retry Period

You can set the interval (in seconds) at which Paradox will try again to open a table if you are locked out. To do so, choose File ➤ Multiuser ➤

Set Retry, type an interval (in seconds) into the **Network Retry Period** dialog box that appears, and choose OK.

Setting the Network Refresh Rate

The Network Refresh Rate determines how often Paradox updates your current view of data. Since others may be updating tables that are of interest to you, you probably will want Paradox to display the latest data on your screen. To set the Network Refresh Rate, choose File ➤ System Settings ➤ Auto Refresh, type the refresh interval (in seconds) into the **Network Refresh Rate** dialog box that appears, and choose OK.

Using File Utilities in a Multiuser Environment

Many options on the File ➤ Utilities menus deal with tables that other network users might be reading or updating at the same time you're accessing them. Therefore, it's worth taking a look at how you, and other network users, might be affected when working with the file utilities in a multiuser environment. Please refer to Chapter 14 for general instructions on using the File ➤ Utilities options.

N O T E   In Windows, you or other users can have several views of the same data open at once. Thus, Paradox may consider a duplicate view on your own Desktop to be another "user," and you may be prevented from performing a file utility operation. For best results, close all views of your table before using File ➤ Utilities options.

Adding Records from One Table to Another Table

When you use File ➤ Utilities ➤ Add to add records from one table to another table, Paradox locks the target table. No other users can change data in the source table or place any locks on the target table until the operation is complete. If locks exist on either table before you begin, you must wait until they are cleared.

Copying Tables

When you use File ➤ Utilities ➤ Copy to copy a table, Paradox locks both the source and the target tables. No other users can change the data in the source table until you are finished with the copy. If anyone else has locked the source table before you begin, you'll have to wait until the locks are cleared.

Deleting Tables

When you delete a table via File ➤ Utilities ➤ Delete, no one can change the data in the table while it's being deleted. If other users are working with the table in any way, you cannot delete it until they are done and they remove all the locks.

Emptying Tables

When you empty a table using File ➤ Utilities ➤ Empty, Paradox locks the table, and no one can change data in the table while it's being emptied.

A *Paradox* table can be emptied while another user has a lock, although none of the disk space is recovered until the lock is released. In contrast, a *dBASE* table cannot be emptied at all if other users are working with the table in any way.

Renaming Tables

When you rename a table via File ➤ Utilities ➤ Rename, no one can change the table's contents until the rename is complete. You cannot rename a table while anyone is using it in any way.

Restructuring Tables

No one can access any table that you're restructuring via the File ➤ Utilities ➤ Restructure option until the restructure is complete. Likewise, if others are using the table in any way, you can't restructure the table until they have closed it.

Subtracting from Tables

When you use File ➤ Utilities ➤ Subtract to remove records from one table that exist in another table, Paradox locks both tables. No other user can work with either table until the operation is complete. By the same token, if anyone has either table open, you cannot perform the Subtract operation.

INDEX

Note to the Reader: Page numbers in boldface refer to primary discussions of a topic. Page numbers in italic refer to figures or tabular material.

Symbols & Numbers

$ (currency) fields, 112
  asterisks displayed in, 238
  data entry in, 173
$ (dollar sign), 173
* (asterisk)
  as wildcard in file filters, 722–723
  for key in table structure, 126
  for methods, 984
  in numeric or currency fields, 238, 255
➤ symbol, 79
+ (plus) string operator, 893–894, 996
; (semicolon), for ObjectPAL comments, 987, **989–990**
.. search operator, 185, 339, **341–344**
  in queries of OLE fields, 362
  queries involving, 702
... (list header), 461
{} (curly braces), to force entry of specific character, 138
! (inclusion operator), 840–841
" (quotation marks), for literal characters in queries, 357–358

? (question mark) wildcard character, in file filters, 722–723
@ (at sign) wildcard character, 185, 340
1-D summary graph data type, **626–631**
2-D summary graph data type, **626–631**
3-D Windows effect, for forms, 53

A

About Paradox for Windows dialog box, 687
action method, 974, 987, 1003
Add Band button (SpeedBar), *411, 414*, 555
Add dialog box, 739
Add Field button (Define Secondary Index dialog box), 309
Add Folder Item button (SpeedBar), 730
Add Tables button (SpeedBar), 826, 828
adjustment transaction, 961
Advanced Pattern Match, for locating records, **186–187**
Alias Manager dialog box, *90*

Help Yourself with
Another Quality Sybex Book

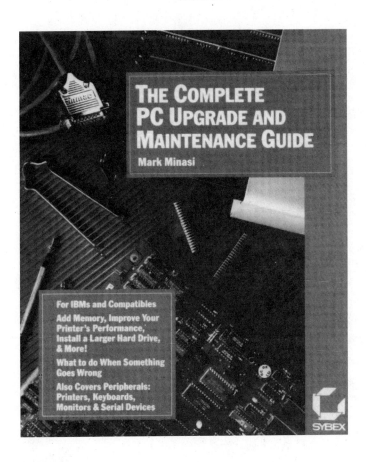

The Complete
PC Upgrade and
Maintenance Guide
Mark Minasi

Diagnose and repair 99% of your PC problems, and configure and install any expansion board yourself. No other book has this breadth, covering circuit boards, memory, hard drives, floppy drives, printers, modems, keyboards, video, and more, for dozens of PC compatibles. Based on the author's popular world-wide seminars.

610pp; 7 1/2" x 9"
ISBN: 0-89588-840-8

Available
at Better
Bookstores
Everywhere

Sybex Inc.
2021 Challenger Drive
Alameda, CA 94501
Telephone (800) 227-2346
Fax (510) 523-2373

Sybex. Help Yourself.

Help Yourself with
Another Quality Sybex Book

Windows 3.1
Instant Reference
Marshall L. Moseley

Enjoy fast access to concise information on every Windows 3.1 mouse and keyboard command, including the accessory programs and Help facilities. Perfect for any Windows 3.1 user who needs an occasional on-the-job reminder.

262pp; 4 3/4" x 8"
ISBN: 0-89588-844-0

Available
at Better
Bookstores
Everywhere

Sybex Inc.
2021 Challenger Drive
Alameda, CA 94501
Telephone (800) 227-2346
Fax (510) 523-2373

Sybex. Help Yourself.

Help Yourself with Another Quality Sybex Book

Mastering Windows 3.1
Robert Cowart

The complete guide to installing, using, and making the most of Windows on IBM PCs and compatibles now in an up-to-date new edition. Part I provides detailed, hands-on coverage of major Windows features that are essential for day-to-day use. Part II offers complete tutorials on the accessory programs. Part III explores a selection of advanced topics.

600pp; 7 1/2" x 9"
ISBN: 0-89588-842-4

Available
at Better
Bookstores
Everywhere

Sybex Inc.
2021 Challenger Drive
Alameda, CA 94501
Telephone (800) 227-2346
Fax (510) 523-2373

Sybex. Help Yourself.

Help Yourself with
Another Quality Sybex Book

Windows Magic Tricks
Judd Robbins

This book/disk combination brings you over 60 engaging, amusing, mesmerizing, and useful Windows programs, gleaned from dozens of shareware and freeware sources. Install the programs, then flip through the book to learn how to get the most fun out of each one.

200pp; 7 1/2" x 9"
ISBN: 0-7821-1119-X

Available
at Better
Bookstores
Everywhere

Sybex Inc.
2021 Challenger Drive
Alameda, CA 94501
Telephone (800) 227-2346
Fax (510) 523-2373

Sybex. Help Yourself.

Help Yourself with
Another Quality Sybex Book

Up & Running with
Windows 3.1
Joerg Schieb

A concise introduction to Windows 3.1, built on 20 steps that each take just 15 minutes to an hour to complete. Learn to install Windows 3.1, navigate the user interface, launch applications, use the File Manager, use the accessory programs, and more.

149pp; 5 7/8" x 8 1/4"
ISBN: 0-89588-843-2

Available
at Better
Bookstores
Everywhere

Sybex Inc.
2021 Challenger Drive
Alameda, CA 94501
Telephone (800) 227-2346
Fax (510) 523-2373

Sybex. Help Yourself.

Help Yourself with
Another Quality Sybex Book

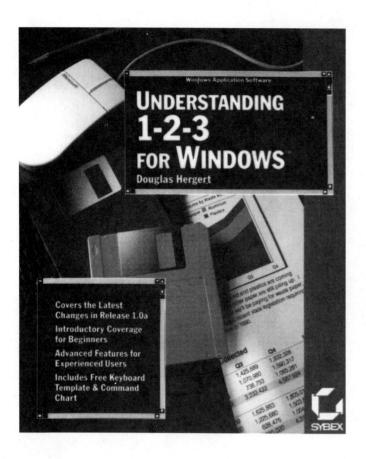

Understanding
1-2-3 for Windows
Douglas Hergert

This all-new guide to 1-2-3 is written especially for the new Windows version. There are self-contained chapters for beginning, intermediate, and advanced users, with business-oriented coverage of such topics as the Windows environment, worksheet development, charting, functions, database management, macro programming, and data sharing.

606pp; 7 1/2" x 9"
ISBN: 0-89588-845-9

Available
at Better
Bookstores
Everywhere

Sybex Inc.
2021 Challenger Drive
Alameda, CA 94501
Telephone (800) 227-2346
Fax (510) 523-2373

Sybex. Help Yourself.

Help Yourself with
Another Quality Sybex Book

Understanding
Harvard Graphics
for Windows

Rebecca Bridges Altman/Rick Altman

Here is the complete hands-on guide
to creating high-quality graphics,
charts, presentations, and slide
shows, using the new Windows version of Harvard Graphics. Engaging
tutorials and colorful examples show
how to create virtually any kind of
chart. Includes an introduction for
beginners, plenty of tips, many advanced topics, and a diskette of free
clip art.

496pp; 7 1/2" x 9"
ISBN: 0-7821-1009-6

Available
at Better
Bookstores
Everywhere

Sybex Inc.
2021 Challenger Drive
Alameda, CA 94501
Telephone (800) 227-2346
Fax (510) 523-2373

Sybex. Help Yourself.

Help Yourself with
Another Quality Sybex Book

Mastering
WordPerfect 5.1
for Windows
Alan Simpson

The complete guide to learning, using, and making the most of Word-Perfect for Windows, from first-time basics to advanced professional word processing. Readers explore every software feature, build practical examples, and learn dozens of special techniques for macros, data management, graphics, desktop publishing, and much more.

1130pp; 7 1/2" x 9"
ISBN: 0-89588-806-8

Available
at Better
Bookstores
Everywhere

Sybex Inc.
2021 Challenger Drive
Alameda, CA 94501
Telephone (800) 227-2346
Fax (510) 523-2373

SYBEX

Sybex. Help Yourself.

Help Yourself with
Another Quality Sybex Book

The ABCs of Microsoft Word for Windows,
Version 2.0
Second Edition
Alan R. Neibauer

Our popular introduction to word processing with Word for Windows is now in a new edition, featuring the latest software release. These quick and easy tutorials cover all the essentials: typing, editing, and printing; varying typefaces; laying out pages; printing form letters; using graphics; and even viewing and working on more than one document at a time.

417pp; 7 1/2" x 9"
ISBN: 0-7821-1052-5

Available
at Better
Bookstores
Everywhere

Sybex Inc.
2021 Challenger Drive
Alameda, CA 94501
Telephone (800) 227-2346
SYBEX Fax (510) 523-2373

Sybex. Help Yourself.

Help Yourself with
Another Quality Sybex Book

Mastering Microsoft Word for Windows,
Version 2.0

Second Edition
Michael J. Young

Here is an up-to-date new edition of our complete guide to Word for Windows, featuring the latest software release. It offers a tutorial for newcomers, and hands-on coverage of intermediate to advanced topicswith desktop publishing skills emphasized. Special topics include: tables and columns, fonts, graphics, Styles and Templates, macros, and multiple windows.

596pp; 7 1/2" x 9"
ISBN: 0-7821-1012-6

Available
at Better
Bookstores
Everywhere

Sybex Inc.
2021 Challenger Drive
Alameda, CA 94501
Telephone (800) 227-2346
Fax (510) 523-2373

Sybex. Help Yourself.

Help Yourself with
Another Quality Sybex Book

Mastering Excel 4 for Windows
Second Edition
Carl Townsend

This comprehensive tutorial and reference offers up-to-date coverage of the new Excel spreadsheet for Windows, with an emphasis on business applications. There's hands-on treatment of everything from worksheet basics to database management, presentation graphics, inventory control, financial calculations, trend analysis, and macro programming.

775pp; 7 1/2" x 9"
ISBN: 0-7821-1088-6

Available
at Better
Bookstores
Everywhere

Sybex Inc.
2021 Challenger Drive
Alameda, CA 94501
Telephone (800) 227-2346
Fax (510) 523-2373

SYBEX

Sybex. Help Yourself.

Help Yourself with
Another Quality Sybex Book

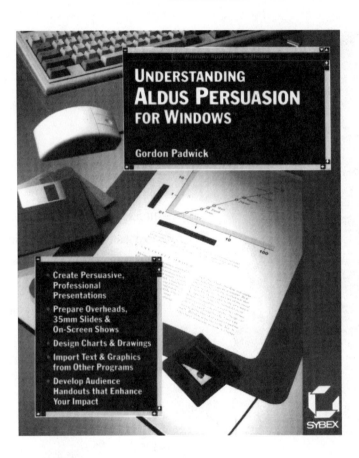

Understanding
Aldus Persuasion
for Windows
Gordon Padwick

Here is a complete hands-on guide
to creating presentation graphics
using the new Windows version of
Aldus Persuasion. Tutorials show exactly how to produce all kinds of
charts and graphs, slides and
transparencies, speaker notes and
handouts. More than this, the book
teaches an effective approach to
planning and delivering graphic
presentations with impact.

400pp; 7 1/2" x 9"
ISBN: 0-7821-1014-2

Available
at Better
Bookstores
Everywhere

Sybex Inc.
2021 Challenger Drive
Alameda, CA 94501
Telephone (800) 227-2346
Fax (510) 523-2373

SYBEX

Sybex. Help Yourself.

Help Yourself with
Another Quality Sybex Book

Up & Running with DOS 5
Alan Simpson

In only 20 time-conscious steps, you'll begin to take advantage of the powerful features of DOS 5.0. Access extended and expanded memory, so you can use more applications; use EDIT for faster screen-by-screen revisions; create batch files, for more efficient system operation; streamline macro functions with DOSKEY; and much more. A Sybex best seller.

153pp; 5 7/8" x 8 1/4"
ISBN: 0-89588-774-6

Available
at Better
Bookstores
Everywhere

Sybex Inc.
2021 Challenger Drive
Alameda, CA 94501
Telephone (800) 227-2346
Fax (510) 523-2373

SYBEX

Sybex. Help Yourself.

Help Yourself with
Another Quality Sybex Book

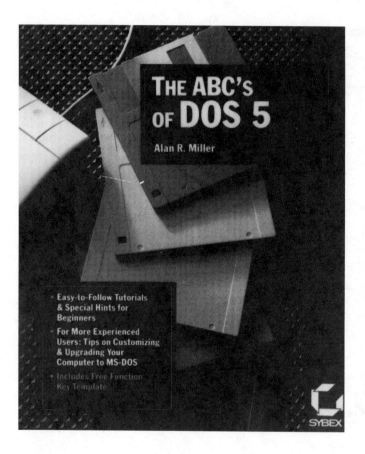

The ABC's of DOS 5
Alan Miller

Here's the quickest way to gain skill and confidence in using DOS 5. You'll tour the graphical interface; master the essentials of disks, directories, and files; and learn to back up your work and recover from common mistakes. Includes dozens of practical tips.

227pp; 7 1/2" x 9"
ISBN: 0-89588-770-3

Available
at Better
Bookstores
Everywhere

Sybex Inc.
2021 Challenger Drive
Alameda, CA 94501
Telephone (800) 227-2346
Fax (510) 523-2373

Sybex. Help Yourself.

Help Yourself with Another Quality Sybex Book

Mastering Harvard Graphics 3 for DOS

Glenn H. Larsen
with Kristopher A. Larsen

This highly praised hands-on guide uses engaging tutorials and colorful examples to show exactly how to create effective charts, graphs, presentations and slide shows. Readers create virtually every kind of chart, including many not covered in Harvard's manual. Includes an introduction for beginners, plus many advanced topics. Disk included—a $40 value!

534pp; 7 1/2" x 9"
ISBN: 0-89588-870-X

Available at Better Bookstores Everywhere

Sybex Inc.
2021 Challenger Drive
Alameda, CA 94501
Telephone (800) 227-2346
Fax (510) 523-2373

SYBEX

Sybex. Help Yourself.

Help Yourself with
Another Quality Sybex Book

Programmer's Introduction to Turbo Pascal for Windows
Scott D. Palmer

A comprehensive tutorial on Windows programming with Turbo Pascal for Windows. The text assumes some familiarity with Pascal, but provides an in-depth introduction to object-oriented programming, and an overview of Windows application design. Readers quickly learn to build simple Windows programs, then progress to more advanced programming techniques.

499pp; 7 1/2" x 9"
ISBN: 0-7821-1022-3

Available
at Better
Bookstores
Everywhere

Sybex Inc.
2021 Challenger Drive
Alameda, CA 94501
Telephone (800) 227-2346
Fax (510) 523-2373

Sybex. Help Yourself.

Help Yourself with
Another Quality Sybex Book

Programmer's Introduction to Visual Basic

Kenyon Brown

Visual Basic will make Windows programming accessible to millions of casual programmers, and this book will make Visual Basic accessible to those same millions. It's for newcomers and experienced programmers seeking a clear look at this exciting new graphical BASIC. Learn all about programming with Forms, Controls, Properties, Events, and Methods.

488pp; 7 1/2" x 9"
ISBN: 0-7821-1015-0

Available
at Better
Bookstores
Everywhere

Sybex Inc.
2021 Challenger Drive
Alameda, CA 94501
Telephone (800) 227-2346
Fax (510) 523-2373

Sybex. Help Yourself.

Help Yourself with Another Quality Sybex Book

Understanding Presentation Graphics
Michael Talman

A must for anyone using a computer to produce business graphics, reports, and presentations, whether on a Macintosh or a PC, and regardless of software used. It's an in-depth guide to effective communication, with guidelines for planning and organization; graphic design do's and don't's; ways to use color to best advantage; and proven techniques for conveying a clear message.

382pp; 7 1/2" x 9"
ISBN: 0-7821-1023-1

Available
at Better
Bookstores
Everywhere

Sybex Inc.
2021 Challenger Drive
Alameda, CA 94501
Telephone (800) 227-2346
Fax (510) 523-2373

Sybex. Help Yourself.

Help Yourself with Another Quality Sybex Book

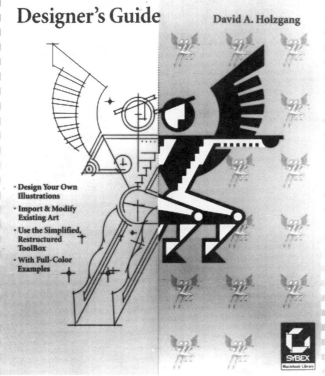

The Adobe Illustrator 3.2 Designer's Guide
David Holzgang

A thorough introduction to Adobe's sophisticated computer-aided graphics package—with an emphasis on making the most of today's state-of-the-art technology. Covers everything from basic drawing and text techniques, to advanced options for transforming graphics, working with scanned images, and more.

358pp; 71/2" x 9"
ISBN: 0-7821-1002-9

Available
at Better
Bookstores
Everywhere

Sybex Inc.
2021 Challenger Drive
Alameda, CA 94501
Telephone (800) 227-2346
Fax (510) 523-2373

Sybex. Help Yourself.

SYBEX

FREE BROCHURE!

Complete this form today, and we'll send you a full-color brochure of Sybex bestsellers.

Please supply the name of the Sybex book purchased.

_____

How would you rate it?

_____ Excellent   _____ Very Good   _____ Average   _____ Poor

Why did you select this particular book?

_____ Recommended to me by a friend

_____ Recommended to me by store personnel

_____ Saw an advertisement in _____

_____ Author's reputation

_____ Saw in Sybex catalog

_____ Required textbook

_____ Sybex reputation

_____ Read book review in _____

_____ In-store display

_____ Other _____

Where did you buy it?

_____ Bookstore

_____ Computer Store or Software Store

_____ Catalog (name: _____)

_____ Direct from Sybex

_____ Other: _____

Did you buy this book with your personal funds?

_____ Yes   _____ No

About how many computer books do you buy each year?

_____ 1-3   _____ 3-5   _____ 5-7   _____ 7-9   _____ 10+

About how many Sybex books do you own?

_____ 1-3   _____ 3-5   _____ 5-7   _____ 7-9   _____ 10+

Please indicate your level of experience with the software covered in this book:

_____ Beginner   _____ Intermediate   _____ Advanced

Which types of software packages do you use regularly?

_____ Accounting	_____ Databases	_____ Networks
_____ Amiga	_____ Desktop Publishing	_____ Operating Systems
_____ Apple/Mac	_____ File Utilities	_____ Spreadsheets
_____ CAD	_____ Money Management	_____ Word Processing
_____ Communications	_____ Languages	_____ Other _____
		(please specify)

Which of the following best describes your job title?

_____ Administrative/Secretarial   _____ President/CEO

_____ Director   _____ Manager/Supervisor

_____ Engineer/Technician   _____ Other _____

                                             (please specify)

Comments on the weaknesses/strengths of this book: _____

_____

_____

_____

_____

Name _____

Street _____

City/State/Zip _____

Phone _____

PLEASE FOLD, SEAL, AND MAIL TO SYBEX

-- --

SYBEX, INC.
Department M
2021 CHALLENGER DR.
ALAMEDA, CALIFORNIA USA
94501

SYBEX

SEAL

Alan Simpson's Mastering Paradox 4.0 for Windows
Optional Companion Disk

If you want to use some of the sample tables, custom forms, report forms, and ObjectPAL applications presented in this book without keying them in yourself, you can send for an optional companion disk containing all the files (excluding the files that already came with your Paradox 4.0 package). You can use these files to speed your learning (less typing!), or as modifiable applications that you can refine to better suit your needs. You must already have access to Paradox 4.0 for Windows to use these files.

To purchase the optional companion disk, please complete the order form below and return it with a check, international money order, or purchase order for $25.00 U.S. currency (plus sales tax for California residents) to the address shown on the coupon. Or, use your VISA or Master-Card.

If you prefer, you can return the coupon without making a purchase to receive free periodic newsletters and updates about Alan Simpson's latest books.

Alan Simpson Computing
P.O. Box 945
Cardiff-by-the-Sea, CA 92007
Phone (619) 943-7715   FAX (619) 943-7750

☐ Please send the companion disk for Mastering Paradox 4.0 for Windows
☐ No disk thanks, but please send free newsletters from Alan Simpson Computing

Name_____

Company _____

Address _____

City, State, Zip _____

Country_____   P.O. Number (if applicable)_____

Phone ( )_____   (required for Credit Card orders)

Check one:
☐ Payment enclosed ($25.00 + sales tax for CA residents) made payable to
    Alan Simpson Computing
☐ Bill my VISA / MasterCard   ☐ No charge (newsletters only)

Card Number_____   Exp. Date_____

Check one disk size:
☐ 5¼-inch disk   ☐ 3½-inch disk

SYBEX is not affiliated with Alan Simpson Computing and assumes no responsibility for any defect in the disk or files.

Designing and Using Custom Forms

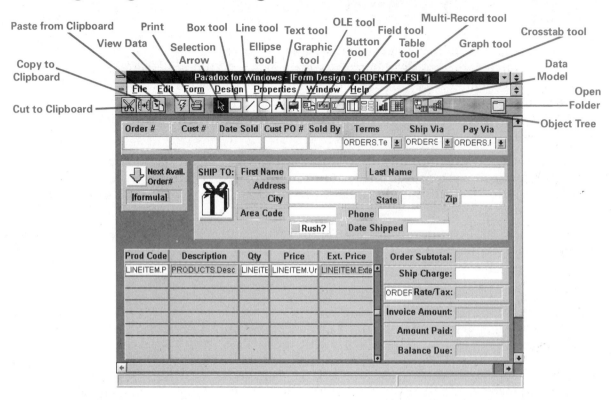

Paste from Clipboard · View Data · Copy to Clipboard · Cut to Clipboard · Print · Selection Arrow · Box tool · Ellipse tool · Line tool · Graphic tool · Text tool · Button tool · OLE tool · Field tool · Table tool · Multi-Record tool · Graph tool · Crosstab tool · Data Model · Open Folder · Object Tree

To Do This...	See Chapter[*]
Enter and edit data in a Quick Form or custom form	2, 5, 17
Design custom forms	2, 9, 10, 17
Choose tables to include	2, 9, 17
Select and sort data in a form	9
Choose an initial design layout	9
Save and open custom forms	2, 9
Create and copy objects	2, 9, 10
Select objects and change their properties	2, 9
Change properties of design tools in the SpeedBar	9
Change the appearance of the Form Design window and Form window	9, 10
Design multipage forms	10
Summarize data with graphs or crosstabs	12
Print a form or form design	10
Perform calculations on fields	17
Make decisions about which data to display	17
Combine data from multiple tables	17
Build "smart" forms to automate your work	19

[*] Note: Many techniques for designing forms and reports are identical.